"A top research psychologist provides a comprehensive analysis of why people misbehave. The discussion ranges from minor acts of incivility to major scandals in government and industry. The reader of this book will come away with an understanding of why people misbehave and what can be done to discourage it."

Paul Spector, University of South Florida, USA

"So why do people so often act badly—immorally, uncivilly, or just unrelentingly selfishly? Explanations often drift, inevitably, to the people themselves, citing their psychological drives, personality traits, character deficiencies, and the like ('bad apples'). These analyses, however, provide only part of the picture, for they overlook the interpersonal processes that cause people to turn from the good to the bad ('bad barrels'). Kevin Murphy, in his book *How Groups Encourage Misbehavior*, thoroughly reviews these processes, in an analysis that is both sweeping in vision but comprehensive in scope. Drawing deeply on studies of the group and organizational processes, including social influence, socialization, identity, and contagion, Professor Murphy explains the many ways people falter—including wartime atrocities of military squads, corporate decision makers, and overly committed members of extremist groups. The book is a one-stop shop for all you need to know about the social side of misbehavior."

Donelson R. Forsyth, The University of Richmond, The Jepson School of Leadership Studies, USA

HOW GROUPS ENCOURAGE MISBEHAVIOR

How Groups Encourage Misbehavior explores the psychological and social processes by which groups develop a tolerance for and even encourage misbehavior. Drawing from decades of research on social, cognitive, and organizational psychology, as well as a deep well of historical research, this book shows how commitment to groups, organizations, and movements can turn moral individuals into amoral agents.

Pulling together what have been traditionally distinct areas of study, *How Groups Encourage Misbehavior* provides a detailed and unified account of how good organizations go bad and how groups of all types can push otherwise honest and upright individuals to behave in ways that violate laws and social norms. This text describes how social norms, rationalization, the characteristics of formal and informal groups, attachment to groups and organizations, and the structure of organizational life can all contribute to misbehavior. Each chapter includes one or more sidebar discussions of relevant and interesting examples to illustrate the ways groups and organizations encourage and support misbehavior. The final two chapters discuss how many of these same attributes and processes can be used to encourage positive behaviors and foster recovery from dysfunctional and corrupt cultures and modes of behavior.

A valuable text for a broad range of psychology courses, *How Groups Encourage Misbehavior* will especially appeal to practitioners, scholars, and students interested in ethics in organizations and the intersection between social psychology and organizational behavior.

Kevin R. Murphy is Professor Emeritus at the University of Limerick. He is the author of over 190 articles and book chapters and author or editor of 11 books in areas ranging from psychometrics and statistical analysis to individual differences, performance assessment, and honesty in the workplace.

Series in Applied Psychology

Jeanette N. Cleveland
Colorado State University
Donald Truxillo
Portland State University
Edwin A. Fleishman
Founding Series Editor (1987–2010)
Kevin R. Murphy
Emeritus Series Editor (2010–2018)

Bridging both academic and applied interests, the Applied Psychology Series offers publications that emphasize state-of-the-art research and its application to important issues of human behavior in a variety of societal settings. To date, more than 50 books in various fields of applied psychology have been published in this series.

Aging and Work in the 21st Century
Edited by Kenneth S. Schultz and Gary A. Adams

Employee Retention and Turnover
Peter W. Hom, David G. Allen and Rodger W. Griffeth

Diversity Resistance in Organizations 2e
Kecia M. Thomas

Positive Psychological Science 2e
Stewart I. Donaldson, Mihaly Csikszentmihalyi and Jeanne Nakamura

Historical Perspectives in Industrial and Organizational Psychology 2e
Edited by Laura Koppes Bryan

How Groups Encourage Misbehavior
Kevin R. Murphy

For more information about this series, please visit: www.routledge.com/Applied-Psychology-Series/book-series/SAP

HOW GROUPS ENCOURAGE MISBEHAVIOR

Kevin R. Murphy

NEW YORK AND LONDON

First published 2021
by Routledge
52 Vanderbilt Avenue, New York, NY 10017

and by Routledge
2 Park Square, Milton Park, Abingdon, Oxon, OX14 4RN

Routledge is an imprint of the Taylor & Francis Group, an informa business

Library of Congress Cataloging-in-Publication Data
Names: Murphy, Kevin R., 1952– author.
Title: How groups encourage misbehavior / Kevin R. Murphy.
Description: New York, NY : Routledge, 2021. | Includes bibliographical references and index.
Identifiers: LCCN 2020054090 (print) | LCCN 2020054091 (ebook) | ISBN 9780367340278 (hardback) | ISBN 9780367340292 (paperback) | ISBN 9780429323515 (ebook)
Subjects: LCSH: Social groups—Psychological aspects. | Social psychology. | Social norms.
Classification: LCC HM716 .M85 2021 (print) | LCC HM716 (ebook) | DDC 305—dc23
LC record available at https://lccn.loc.gov/2020054090
LC ebook record available at https://lccn.loc.gov/2020054091

ISBN: 978-0-367-34027-8 (hbk)
ISBN: 978-0-367-34029-2 (pbk)
ISBN: 978-0-429-32351-5 (ebk)

Typeset in Bembo
by Apex CoVantage, LLC

BRIEF CONTENTS

PART II
The Workplace as a Focal Point for Understanding Misbehavior **171**

PART III
Positive Behavior in Organizations **321**

CONTENTS

PART II
The Workplace as a Focal Point for Understanding Misbehavior 171

SERIES FOREWORD

Bad behavior has been part of the human experience for as long as there have been human beings. We are all aware of examples of bad behavior in politics, government, sports, and business. Bad behavior manifests in myriad ways—bribery, deception, theft, cheating, and aggression, to name a few. And bad behavior results in the suffering of a range of victims, including coworkers, consumers, the public, and society at large.

While we know that bad behavior is part of the human condition, the specific causes of it are debated, complex, and often unclear. This is largely because bad behavior has been studied across so many disciplines (e.g., psychology, sociology, economics) and contexts (e.g., government, work organizations). Unfortunately, a broad, systemic view of what causes bad behavior has been lacking.

The goal of the present volume, *How Groups Encourage Misbehavior*, is to address this gap and explain the different causes of bad behavior across contexts in order to understand and prevent it. Kevin R. Murphy uses the current science to explain when and why bad behaviors emerge in different contexts, that is, the triggers of bad behavior. An eminent scholar of the behavior sciences, Professor Murphy integrates the research from a range of literatures, including social psychology, cognitive psychology, sociology, and the organizational sciences to understand the conditions under which people are most likely to engage in bad behaviors. Notably, his focus is not solely on individuals—that is, the specific types of people who will engage in bad behavior—but which contextual factors such as organizational culture lead (often good) individuals to behave badly. Murphy also provides rich, vivid examples of how bad behavior plays out across these contexts, using as examples a mixture of historical and current events.

The book is divided into three parts. Part I (Chapters 1–7) considers the psychology of bad behavior and why people might engage in it. It includes how issues such as group processes, social relationships, cognitive processes, and people's relationships with their groups can lead to misbehavior. Part II (Chapters 8–12) uses organizations as specific contexts for illustrating how bad behavior may develop. It focuses on how organizational processes (e.g., culture, treatment of members) and "bad" organizations can engender bad behaviors in their members. Here Murphy emphasizes that it is the individual, their environment and interaction of the two that will lead to bad behaviors. Finally, Part III (Chapters 13 and 14) shows the flip side of these issues—why people may exhibit positive, prosocial behaviors and how individuals, organizations, and society can support this good behavior.

The goal of the Applied Psychology Series is to use scientific research, theory, and findings to help solve real problems in society and in organizations. Professor Murphy has done so masterfully through this ambitious volume that reconciles one of the most fundamental problems in society—people behaving badly—and integrates a sprawling, multidisciplinary literature. He has amply fulfilled the primary goal of this series. He advances our understanding of when and why people behave badly, in what ways, and in which contexts—and how best to address it. We hope you enjoy reading it as much as we did.

Jeanette Cleveland
Donald Truxillo

PREFACE

I have a long-standing interest in understanding misbehavior. This is part a result of having grown up in Albany, New York, which at the time had one of the last remaining Democratic political machines in the U.S. This meant that small-scale corruption was simply a fact of life; just about everything was done based on knowing someone who knew someone else who could pull a few strings. As corruption goes, it was often fairly genial, nickel and dime business, but if you were a bar owner who did not want to carry the brand of beer favored by local politicians, or some poor homeowner who wanted to get a pothole fixed but was known to vote Republican, it could get ugly.

I am an organizational psychologist, and a significant portion of this book deals with misbehavior in organizations. I think, however, there is value in taking a larger perspective. Work organizations have several features (e.g., profit motives, formal lines of authority) that make particular forms of misbehavior particularly likely, but most people are part of many formal and informal groups, and these groups turn out to be a significant factor in driving misbehavior.

The theme of this book is that there are many social factors, ranging from group norms to structural features of organizations that encourage or tolerate misbehavior. To be sure, personal factors (e.g., personality, financial need) are an important factor in understanding misbehavior. Behaviors that violate widely held norms and that have the potential to harm individuals or institutions are often the result of individual choices, but these choices often play out in social settings, and it is important to understand the social forces that influence these behaviors.

This book is divided into three sections. The first (Chapters 1–7) examines the psychology of misbehavior. It draws from social, organizational, and cognitive psychology to help explain why people engage in behavior that violates widely accepted rules, norms, and laws. The second section (Chapters 8–12) examines the workplace as a focal point for understanding misbehavior. It outlines principles and findings that are relevant to many types of organizations, but the underlying research and theory has often been developed in the context of the world of work. The final section of this book (Chapters 13–14) examines positive behavior in organizations, showing how many of the concepts used to understand misbehavior apply just as well when examining positive behaviors.

Each chapter includes one or more sidebar discussions that present extensions or examples of concepts discussed in the chapter (e.g., Describing Situations: The Five "Ws", Chapter 1; A Day in the Life of a Telephone Psychic, Chapter 8), applications of these concepts (e.g., Want to Prevent Theft? Make It Boring, Chapter 11), or discussions of items from the news that relate to key concepts in this book (e.g., The Penn State Scandal, Chapter 9). I hope you will find the concepts and the examples presented in the text and in these sidebar discussions useful for understanding why people sometimes behave in ways that break rules, laws, and norms and that the analyses presented here will help you understand the crucial role of groups and organizations in promoting and tolerating misbehavior.

I have included discussions of several historical events (e.g., Rape of Nanjing) and organizational scandals (collapse of Enron) that I believe exemplify particular concepts of principles discussed in the text. Several chapters examine the Volkswagen diesel emissions scandal, which involved a concerted effort, spanning many years and several continents, to cheat on emissions tests, making their diesel-engine cars appear to perform well and get great mileage without polluting. I probably spend more time on this scandal than any other, in part because it illustrated the perils of over-identification with organization, but the emphasis is at least partly personal. I was about to order one of Volkswagen's "clean diesel" cars just before the scandal broke, and this incident contributed substantially to my interest in understanding misbehavior in groups and organizations.

Finally, I want to acknowledge many colleagues and researchers who provided help, suggestions, and insights that played a major role in shaping this book. Early in the process of writing this book, I reached out to researchers in many of the fields I hoped to cover for reprints, suggestions for topics to cover and literature to review, including Maureen Ambrose, Blake Ashforth, Julian Barling, Bob Baron, Yehuda Baruch, Art Brief, Judith Collins, Jason Colquitt, Samantha Conroy, Lillia Cortina, Michelle Duffy, Louise Fitzgerald, Michael Frone, Michelle Gelfand, Francesca Gino, Dennis Gioa, Teresa Glomb, Ricky Griffin, Dave Harrison, Bob Hogan, Barrie Litzky, Vicky Magley, Mark Martinko, Janet Near, Anne O'Leary-Kelly, Sandra Robinson, Paul Sackett, Ben Schneider, Dan Skarlicki, Paul Spector, Bennet Tepper, Linda Treviño, Tom Tyler, Yoav Vardi, Gary Weaver, Ely Weitz. The generosity and help of so many scholars in shaping and improving this book is a reminder that the term "scientific community" is an apt description, and that whatever success this book achieves in helping readers understand misbehavior is due in large part to the work of a large community of scholars in many different fields. This book is the culmination of several years of thinking and reading about the way groups and organizations sometimes bring out the worst in their members, and I hope you enjoy reading it as much as I enjoyed writing it.

PART I

The Psychology of Misbehavior

1

MISBEHAVIOR: THE ROLE OF PERSONS AND SITUATIONS

July 1863, New York City

It was the second day of the newly instituted draft in New York City, and angry crowds gathered in front of the office of the Provost Marshal. The Civil War was deeply unpopular in New York, especially among the immigrants who had flooded the city. They bitterly resented the war, in part because they were competing with Blacks for jobs, a competition that would become even more desperate if freed slaves were added to the mix. The fact that immigrants were subject to the draft, but Blacks were not (Black soldiers were only grudgingly accepted into the Union Army and were not drafted for service), only added fuel to the fire.

Tempers flared, and soon paving stones were coming through the windows. What started as a draft riot quickly morphed into a full-scale race riot. Over the next three days, raging mobs hunted down and killed over 100 Black men, women, and children, lynching many and burning others alive. Black-owned homes and businesses were destroyed, with over $20 million (in current dollars) in damage. In one of the worst outrages during this riot, the Colored Orphan Asylum on 5th Avenue was burned to the ground. Over 4,000 Union troops had to be pulled out of the Battle of Gettysburg to quell the riot.

What turned a protest against the draft into a three-day orgy of violence directed against Black men, women, and children in New York? Why did men (and sometimes women), who in their day-to-day lives in New York would never have assaulted Black citizens or attacked their homes and businesses, turn into a howling mob that has to be put down by the army? One answer is that several social forces can unleash the worst in people. The theme of this book is that there are several aspects of groups and organizations that can encourage, magnify, and sustain patterns of behavior that are harmful; that violate rules, norms, and laws;

and that tear at the very social fabric groups, social movements, and organizations supposedly create and protect.

Sometimes, misbehavior is a simple reflection of an individual's depravity, incapacity, or unwillingness to behave appropriately. Indeed, some of the most serious forms of misbehavior are committed by individuals acting alone (e.g., serial killers almost always work alone). Even when an individual is acting in the presence of others, their behavior might still be driven by individual beliefs, attitudes, preferences, and personality traits. However, when we look into the causes of a wide range of different behaviors that harm others or break rules and norms, social forces often loom large as explanations. For example, some of the most destructive forms of misbehavior, such as war crimes, mob violence, and the like, are almost always done in and by groups. Several less extreme forms of misbehavior are often a direct product of social-psychological forces, ranging from stereotypes to misperceptions of others' intentions and behaviors to the formation and communication of group norms that lead people to act in ways that harm others and that undermine social institutions.

What Do We Mean by Misbehavior?

This book focuses on the social-psychological forces that contribute to, support, or lead people to tolerate misbehavior. It is important, therefore, to define "misbehavior". First, this book is concerned with behavior—that is, things individuals do. So, having subversive thoughts and beliefs or unusual opinions and preferences is not a form of misbehavior, although in some cases acting on those or trying to influence others to adopt these same beliefs might constitute misbehavior. Second, misbehavior involves violating broadly accepted laws, norms, and societal values. The term "broadly accepted" is important here; there may be laws or social norms that are highly specialized or localized, in the sense that behaviors that violate them would not normally be met with disapproval or seen as wrong. For example, it is a federal crime (Federal Table of Misdemeanours 18:§46) to transport water hyacinths. There are places where this plant can be invasive or can clog waterways, and a case can be made for this federal law, but few of us would think of a person transporting this plant (especially a person unaware of its potential ecological harm in particular circumstances) as a criminal act. Third, misbehavior has the potential to be destructive or harmful, sometimes harming others directly and sometimes creating harm by undermining social institutions. Misbehavior runs the gamut from simple incivility and low-level bullying to gang violence and war crimes.

Of the three characteristics already cited, the fact that misbehavior violates widely accepted laws, rules, and norms is most important and, in many ways, most paradoxical. One of the primary functions of society and the various units of society (e.g., families, social groups, organizations, legal structures) is to *define* rules, norms, and expectations—that is, to lay out definitions of what is acceptable and what is expected. Misbehavior breaks these rules and laws and violates these norms, and yet misbehavior is often the direct result of social and normative processes. The key to understanding this apparent paradox is to understand that social influences almost always involve information. That is, one of the key functions of social groups is to help their members understand what is and what should be. Social groups influence an individual's behavior by providing information that reduces uncertainty (what is; see, for example, Hogg, 2007) and by providing information about what behaviors are and are not acceptable (what should be). This information often leads people to believe that their behaviors (including misbehaviors) are acceptable and consistent with norms and expectations.

One of the recurring themes that emerge from interviews of individuals who have been caught engaging in misbehavior is that they rarely believe they were doing something wrong. Rather, misbehavior is very often the product of a set of social and cognitive processes that lead people to believe that behaviors that appear to violate laws, rules, and norms are acceptable or even laudable. For example, interviews with war criminals often reveal that they did not think they were doing anything wrong, but rather that they were serving some higher cause that justified their actions (Bohr, Meyer, & Wiegrefe, 2014). Similarly, interviews with members of organized crime syndicates often emphasize themes such as family, brotherhood, and loyalty and show how criminal acts are often recast as part of the process of upholding these values (Rostami, Mondani, Liljeros, & Endling, 2018). In the same vein, people who engage in sexual harassment, bullying, or workplace incivility rarely think of themselves in negative terms. One of the central challenges of this book is to develop an understanding of how social groups, organizations, movements, and the like influence the perceptions and beliefs of individuals to allow and encourage them to engage in behaviors that violate widely accepted laws, rules, and norms.

Persons and Situations as Causes of Misbehavior

Most behaviors are a product of a combination of attributes of the person (e.g., abilities, personality traits, beliefs, perceptions) and the aspects of the situation that make particular behaviors more or less likely (Mischel, 1999; Weiss & Adler, 1984). For example, situations sometimes give people strong cues about how they should act and the range of acceptable behaviors (Meyer & Dalal, 2009; Meyer, Dalal, & Hermida, 2010). When a traffic light is red, people usually stop. At a funeral, people rarely play practical jokes or sing comic songs. At other times, situations may only weakly signal what behaviors are desired or expected. For example, people are often confused about precisely what they should do when a traffic light is yellow. Situations might make particular behaviors possible or impossible; you might want to bake a cake, but if there is no sugar in the house, you might not be able to. Situations might present easy opportunities to engage in behaviors that you would ordinarily avoid; if you have ever been in a bakery while on a diet, you will understand how strongly environmental cues can tempt you to break the diet. Numerous theories of motivation and behavior start with the assumption that to understand people's behavior, it is useful to consider both persons and situations as possible causes or influences (Ekehammar, 1974).

Like most other behaviors, misbehavior is influenced by both the characteristics of the person and the characteristics of the situation (Furnham & Taylor, 2004; Lefkowitz, 2009; Treviño, 1986). In this book, I will focus most strongly on one form of situational effects—that is, the effects of social influences on misbehavior. This is not to deny that other non-social aspects of the situation might encourage misbehavior. For example, if your boss were to tell you, "Could you put this large bag of rubies in the safe? I have not had time to count them, and I don't have a clear idea of how many I have", the temptation to help yourself to a few rubies might be so strong as to entice you to steal. However, social influences do create a special set of problems in studying misbehavior, because they often act in a way that will convince you that behaviors that would usually be met with disapproval are instead acceptable and perhaps even desirable.

Before launching into a detailed examination of the way groups and organizations influence misbehavior, it is useful to briefly review how several characteristics and attributes to persons contribute to misbehavior.

Person-Based Explanations for Misbehavior

Person-based explanations for misbehavior have been widely studied and debated. For example, many studies of misbehavior in the workplace (e.g., employee theft, violation of workplace rules or norms) have paid particular attention to workers' personality traits, attitudes, and beliefs. Misbehavior in the workplace is often explained in terms of constructs such as employee reliability (Hogan & Hogan, 1989), theft proneness (Ash, 1991), socialization (Collins & Bagozzi, 1999; Gough, 1960), conscientiousness and integrity (Hogan & Ones, 1997; Hough, Eaton, Dunnette, Kamp, & McCloy, 1990; Murphy, 1993). This research often has had direct practical application. For example, paper-and-pencil tests designed to measure conscientiousness and integrity have shown considerable success in reducing employee theft, disciplinary actions, substance abuse, and other types of misbehavior in the workplace (Jones, 1980; Jones, Slora, & Boye, 1990; Kobbs & Arvey, 1993; Ones, Viswesvaran, & Schmidt, 1993; Sackett, Burris, & Callahan, 1989; Werner, Jones, & Steffy, 1989). Four individual difference constructs (conscientiousness, thrill-seeking, psychopathy, envy and emotions) have been widely used to predict and explain misbehavior.

Conscientiousness

The personality trait conscientiousness is one of five constructs that are widely used to describe normal personality. The Five-Factor model suggests that personality can be described in terms of five key attributes—conscientiousness, agreeableness, emotional stability (often described in terms of the low end of the stability scale, neuroticism), extraversion, and openness to experience. Conscientiousness itself is sometimes described as a personality trait characterized by being careful and diligent. Individuals who score low on measures of conscientiousness are at higher risk for a wide range of misbehaviors (Murphy, 1993).

Analyses of measures of conscientiousness suggest that this personality attribute reflects six separate but related groups of behaviors—competence, order, dutifulness, achievement striving, self-discipline, and deliberation. People who are high on conscientiousness are likely to follow rules and carefully carry out their assigned duties and roles (Hogan & Hogan, 1989; Hogan & Ones, 1997; Ones et al., 1993). It is no surprise, therefore, that conscientious people are likely to be evaluated as good performers in a wide variety of jobs (Barrick & Mount, 1991). Indeed, conscientiousness is one of the few individual difference variables that is correlated with performance in virtually all jobs; general cognitive ability is one of the others (Schmidt & Hunter, 1988).

Furnham (2017) notes that while conscientiousness is usually a positive attribute, there is also a dark side to conscientiousness. Highly conscientious people can also be rigid, perfectionistic, and resistant to change. They can be rule-bound and unimaginative, which might be useful in a career bureaucrat, but is unlikely to lead to success as a leader or in situations where creativity is called for. Conscientious individuals might also have a harder time than others in adjusting to unemployment or losses of job responsibilities (Boyce, Wood, & Brown, 2010). Conscientious individuals are most likely to be successful in settings where the rules are clearly defined and where diligence translates fairly directly into success, but they may have a more difficult time in ambiguous situations that require creative responses.

Thrill-Seeking

Thrill-seeking, a personality trait that is a subset of the broader trait of sensation-seeking, has been linked with a variety of forms of misbehavior (Murphy & Luther, 1997). Sensation-seeking is a trait that is expressed in terms of a constant search for experiences and feelings that are varied, novel, complex, and intense (Zuckerman, 2009). Individuals high on sensation-seeking are often willing to take a variety of risks (physical, social, legal, etc.) to obtain these experiences. Thrill-seeking is a specific form of sensation-seeking that focuses on excitement and that often involves taking larger than normal risks.

The psychologist Frank Farley developed a theory that examines the "Big T" personality—that is, individuals who are strongly focused on living an exciting, interesting, and thrilling life (Morehouse, Farley, & Youngquist, 1990; Munsey, 2006). Individuals with "Big T" personalities are more willing than others to take risks and to try novel experiences, and as a result, may thrive as entrepreneurs and inventors. On the other hand, this personality can have a dark side. Individuals who are on the negative end of the "Big T" spectrum may be drawn to crime, violence, or terrorism.

There are two aspects of thrill-seeking, and sensation-seeking more broadly, that are particularly relevant to misbehavior. First, some people seek and experience excitement by breaking rules and norms. Thus, the very fact that a particular act is forbidden, or at least frowned upon, may make it attractive to individuals who score high on measures of sensation-seeking or thrill-seeking. Second, these individuals are more willing than most to take a wide range of risks. Sometimes, this is manifest in activities that are scary to some people and thrilling to others (e.g., parachute jumping, extreme roller coasters). Other times, this might be manifest in a higher willingness to bend the rules or to act in ways that are usually socially unacceptable. Thus, people who score high on thrill-seeking or sensation-seeking may be drawn to misbehavior not because they are attracted to the behavior itself (i.e., they may get no particular joy out of hurting others), but rather to the thrill of doing something that is forbidden.

Psychopathy

Psychopathy is a personality disorder characterized by persistent antisocial behavior, impaired empathy and remorse, and bold, disinhibited, and egotistical traits. Psychopathy is not a single disorder, but rather represents a set of related disorders that make individuals particularly likely to engage in misbehaviors (Skeem, Polaschek, Patrick, & Lilienfeld, 2011). The term "psychopath" often brings to mind images of manipulative executives, con artists, serial killers, or chronic offenders, and psychopathy is often (incorrectly) linked with violence, psychosis, or antisocial personality disorders. Current theories of psychopathy present a less spectacular, but also a more complex picture. Psychopaths appear to show three key patterns of behavior: (1) disinhibition—impulsiveness and difficulty in planning or controlling behavior, (2) boldness—the ability to remain calm and focused in threatening situations, showing high self-assurance and a high level of tolerance for unfamiliarity and danger, and (3) meanness—low empathy, disdain for personal relationships, callousness in the way one treats others. While many people might exhibit some of these traits, the combination of traits and behaviors that represent psychopathy is relatively rare; approximately 1% of the population are classed as psychopaths (Werner, Few, & Bucholz, 2015).

Psychologists have identified the "Dark Triad" (Paulhus & Williams, 2002), a set of three personality characteristics—narcissism (the tendency to seek admiration and praise), Machiavellianism (manipulativeness), and psychopathy—that make some people particularly successful in manipulating others and that contribute to misbehavior. Several books and articles have suggested that psychopathic behavior is surprisingly common among executives (Babiak & Hare, 2007;

Lipman, 2013). As noted earlier, in the general population, about one person in 100 is diagnosed with this disorder (Hare, 1991, 1994), but among executives, the incidence of this disorder *might* be considerably higher (Babiak, 1995; Boddy, 2010; Smith, Watts, & Lilienfeld, 2014). As I will note later, there have been important challenges to the belief that psychopathic tendencies are high among executives.

There is evidence that "Dark Triad" traits are indeed linked to career advancement (Boddy, 2010), and this has contributed to the belief that many executives are psychopaths. One explanation for the seeming prevalence of psychopathology, narcissism, and Machiavellianism in the ranks of executives is that these are the very traits that make them successful, at least in the short term. Individuals who score high on the Dark Triad are often charming, highly confident, ruthless, highly motivated to succeed, willing to take extreme risks, adept at sizing up the weaknesses of their opponents, and completely willing to do what is necessary to succeed. These same individuals are often drawn to power and skilled at skirting social norms and rules to attain it. All of these character flaws help managers and junior executives climb the ladder to the top of organizations. Some types of organizations seem especially attractive to psychopaths—particularly organizations in the financial industry, but rates of psychopathology are also relatively high in government and defense organizations and health care (Boddy, 2010).

A recent meta-analytic review has challenged some of the conventional thinking about the prevalence of psychopathy among corporate executives (Landay, Harms, & Credé, 2019). This study examined findings from 92 independent samples contain data on people's psychopathic tendencies, whether they became leaders and how their performance as leaders was rated by themselves or others. Results showed that individuals with psychopathic tendencies were only slightly more likely to become leaders but were less likely to be seen as effective leaders. This was especially true when ratings of leader effectiveness were made by their followers. Subsequent analyses uncovered a critical gender difference within these results. Men with psychopathic tendencies were more likely to become leaders and were rated as more effective leaders. However, women who displayed psychopathic tendencies were less likely to be selected as leaders and were rated as less effective in leadership roles.

Taken together, the results do not completely support the idea that corporate leaders tend to have substantially higher levels of psychopathic tendencies. Although higher levels of psychopathic tendencies may provide a small advantage in attaining leadership positions, the researchers did not find consistent evidence suggesting that most, or even many, corporate leaders are psychopaths. Of greater potential concern is the gender difference, which occurred along stereotypical lines. Acting in a psychopathic manner seemed to provide an advantage for men, but a disadvantage for women.

Envy

Attitudes toward and perceptions of others can trigger misbehavior. This has been demonstrated, for example, in research on envy (Silver & Sabini, 1978). Envy is often defined as the desire to possess something or some attribute (e.g., musical talent) that another possesses. Envy is often accompanied by a sense of unfairness—that is, that you deserve the desired thing as much as or more than the person you envy. There is evidence that unethical behavior, including deception (Moran & Schweitzer 2008) and dishonesty (Gino & Pierce 2009a, 2009b, 2010), is sometimes motivated by envy. For example, Gino and Pierce (2009a) conducted multiple studies examining the effects of inequity (e.g., unequal rewards) as a trigger for feelings of envy, and they have shown that envy is related to subsequent unethical behavior. They have even demonstrated that the presence of material items (e.g., stacks of money in a room) may influence people's experience of envy and induce cheating behavior as a response.

There is also evidence of a link between envy and misbehavior for research on negotiation. When bargaining or negotiating, individuals who envy a counterpart are more likely to use deception (Moran & Schweitzer, 2008). This research suggests that envy promotes deception by increasing psychological benefits and decreasing the psychological costs of engaging in deceptive behavior.

Jealousy and envy are not always destructive; Vardi and Weitz (2016) discuss ways organizations use feelings of envy to motivate competition and high levels of performance. Nevertheless, jealousy and envy are potentially important causes of misbehavior because people most often cope with or adjust to feelings of jealousy and envy with hostility and anger. Individuals who cope with jealousy or envy in this way are more likely to misbehave.

Emotions and Mood

Hackney and Perrewé (2018) have argued that events in the environment, such as the experience of being unfairly evaluated or rewarded or observing others being rewarded for what appears to be misbehaviors, might not lead *directly* to a person's decision to misbehave. Rather, the effects of these experiences might be mediated by the way individuals perceive and react to these events. In particular, their model cites emotional reactions as one of the key determinants of whether or not particular events or experiences will trigger misbehavior. Paradoxically, individuals who are in a positive mood at the time they experience events that might trigger misbehaviors may be *more* likely to react badly to these events, in part because they ruin the positive mood.

Events that elicit strong emotional reactions can be especially important causes of misbehaviors. In several subsequent chapters, I will discuss topics such as mob violence; one of the mechanisms that appear to transform a crowd of people who are not misbehaving into a lynch mob is emotional arousal and contagion of emotions. However, even when emotional reactions are confined to a single individual, there is a clear link between negative emotions and aggression (Scheff & Retzinger, 1991).

There is considerable debate over the relationships between emotions and behavior, in particular over whether emotions directly cause behaviors (e.g., you run away from a situation because you are scared) or whether emotions are the product of actions (e.g., you perceive a situation as dangerous and scary because you were startled and ran away). Both positions have considerable support (Baumeister, Vohs, De Wall, & Zhang, 2007; Schwarz & Clore, 2007), and both are likely to be at least partly true. However, the most complete explanation for links between emotions and behaviors of all sorts (including misbehavior) probably involves links between cognition and emotion (Schwarz & Clore, 2007). Emotion, especially strong emotion, influences the way you interpret and make sense of situations. For example, strong negative emotions are likely to increase the likelihood that you will interpret a negative event (e.g., someone spills their drink on you) as intentional and harmful (Baumeister et al., 2007). Emotions can even be a source of feedback. The fact that you experience emotions such as shame or remorse might lead you to interpret your behavior negatively, whereas positive emotions might lead to a more positive assessment of your behaviors.

Situational Explanations for Misbehavior

In contrast to person-based explanations, situational explanations stress the importance of the environment in which behavior occurs as a cause for misbehavior. There are many ways to define situational variables, and different researchers have focused on different types of situations as a basis for understanding behavior. For example, in their review of research on performance appraisal and performance management systems in organizations, Murphy, Cleveland, and Hanscom (2018) examine the roles of the broad cultural, legal, economic, technological, and physical contexts within which organizations operate, and show how different contexts encourage the development of different methods for evaluating people's job performance. In addition to these distal contexts, Murphy et al. (2018) discuss several more proximal contextual variables (i.e., environmental variables that more immediately influence the behaviors of employees and organizations), such as organizational climate, culture, and strategy; characteristics of the workgroup; and relationships between supervisors and subordinates.

In this book, I focus on characteristics of situations that are more narrowly defined than the broad contexts (e.g., the legal and economic context within which organizations operate) that are the focus of many of the theories developed and reviewed by Murphy et al. (2018). In particular, I will focus on social situations, where your behavior is or might be affected by the attitudes, preferences, beliefs, encouragement or discouragement of others, or by your perceptions of those attitudes, preferences, etc. However, it is useful to discuss first how "situations" are defined in social psychological research and to describe some of the critical features of situations.

Rauthmann, Sherman, and their colleagues have suggested three principles for defining what we mean by "situation" (Rauthmann & Sherman, 2018; Rauthmann, Sherman, & Funder, 2015). First, they suggest that the psychological experience of situations matters. Their "processing principle" states that situations are not completely separate from or external to persons, but rather that the way individuals perceive, experience, and understand the situation is an important determinant of the effects of situations on behavior. Second, situations are grounded in reality. That is, even though the psychological experience of situations is important, situations are not simply figments of the imaginations of individuals, but rather reflect external realities. There may be broad consensus about some aspects of a situation, and there may be aspects of a situation that are perceived in idiosyncratic ways by individual perceivers, but situations exist in some way independent of the person. Finally, the circularity principle states that situations that are defined solely in terms of perceptions would create circular definitions, in which a distinction between persons and situations could no longer be cleanly made.

Situations influence behavior in many ways, but two particular pathways for linking situations with behavior seem most important. First, situations (particularly social situations) often provide information about the types of behaviors that are expected, approved of, or discouraged. Second, situations place constraints on (and sometimes provide opportunities to engage in) particular behaviors. Suppose, for example, that you are a manager and you want to provide merit raises for your best performers. If the organization does not have a sufficient budget to support those raises, your ability to motivate and reward employees by linking pay with performance will be constrained.

BOX 1.1 DESCRIBING SITUATIONS: THE FIVE "WS"

The building blocks of the types of situations that influence behavior are often described in terms of (1) persons, relationships, and social interactions, (2) objects, (3) events/activities, (4) locations, and (5) time (Mehl & Robbins, 2012; Pervin, 1978). The five "W" questions that journalists are trained to ask when composing a story—Who, What, Where, When, and Why—represent an excellent framework for describing these situations. For example, Rauthmann et al. (2015) use the example of a "party" (Where?) with friends (Who?) who are dancing (What?) to illustrate this approach. Of the five questions, "why" might be the most important, because it distinguishes two of the general classes of social situations discussed in this book–that is, informal social situations, where there may be no clearly defined "why", and formally structured, purpose-driven situations (e.g., going to work, participating in a political meeting) where there are formal structures and goals and a range of systems for controlling the behaviors of individuals (e.g., defined work roles, rewards and sanctions). Situations where "why" is well defined often create a wider range of mechanisms and opportunities to control and direct behavior, and these situations will be examined in detail in the chapters that follow.

Situations Provide Information

The first way situations influence behavior is that they provide information about the types of behavior that are possible, preferred, tolerated, discouraged, or punished. The amount and the specificity of this information vary tremendously, depending on the type of situation involved. For example, a situation in which other people are displaying anger and making threatening gestures might prompt a "fight or flight" reaction, even if it is not clear that people are angry with or acting aggressively toward you. A situation in which other people are laughing and appear to be having a good time may prompt you to interpret the situation positively. For decades, television comedies used laugh tracks, based in part on the theory that laughter is contagious. The laugh track suggests that other people find a particular joke funny, increasing the likelihood that you will as well.

Some situations, particularly social situations (i.e., those that involve other people) provide a clear "script" that describes the actions, events, and responses that are expected and normal in a particular type of situation (Schank & Abelson, 1977). For example, suppose you are going to a restaurant. There is a whole set and sequence of behaviors and events you expect to encounter, starting with being seated, having orders taken by the wait staff, having meals delivered, asking for a check, and paying it. Your knowledge of and experience with situations like this one tell you what to expect and how to act, and if you go to a restaurant where these expectations are violated (e.g., nobody greets you and it is unclear where you should sit, orders are taken but not delivered), you will be frustrated and annoyed. Similarly, if you do not engage in the expected behaviors (e.g., you refuse to pay your check), this can lead to difficulties.

Situations can be described in terms of their strength—that is, the extent to which they influence and direct behavior. The central idea here is that, sometimes, situations provide clear and strong cues about what behaviors are expected and accepted, but in other cases, they might have only a small effect on behavior. For example, there are widely shared beliefs about the types of behaviors that are appropriate and expected at a funeral, and individuals who flirt with the opposite sex or who engage in silly behavior at a funeral will be met with strong disapproval. A funeral is an example of a strong situation. Weak situations, on the other hand, provide only limited information about the behaviors that are expected or tolerated and have only a weak influence on behavior. For example, a traffic light turning yellow creates a relatively weak situation. A yellow light does tell you that it will be necessary to stop soon, but it is not always clear how soon, and many people simply ignore yellow lights.

"Situational strength" represents a very important construct for understanding how situations can be assessed and how they influence behavior (Hattrup & Jackson, 1996; Hough & Oswald, 2008; Meyer, Dalal, & Hermida, 2010; Snyder & Ickes, 1985). Models of situational strength start with the proposition that situational or contextual variables provide both implicit and explicit cues about the behaviors that are desired or preferred (Meyer & Dalal, 2009; Meyer, Dalal, & Hermida, 2010). The central concern of these theories is to determine whether the influence of situational or contextual variables is likely to be strong or weak. In strong situations, situational cues provide clear direction about how people or organizations should behave, whereas, in weaker situations, the cues, situations, or context provided are indirect and have potentially small effects on behavior and actions.

The strength of a particular situation depends substantially on the clarity and consistency of the cues that the situation provides and on the extent to which contexts or situations constrain the behavior of individuals or organizations (Meyer et al., 2010). Several authors (e.g., Judge & Zapata, 2015; Meyer et al., 2010) note that contexts can be defined at multiple levels and that the strength of the contextual effects may vary considerably across levels. In general, however, the extent to which the context provides clear and consistent cues about what behaviors or actions are or are not acceptable and/or creates direct or indirect constraints on the behaviors or actions that can be undertaken will determine the strength of the context effects.

Gelfand et al. (2011) have applied concepts drawn from theories of situational strength to classify cultures in terms of their tightness, based on the strength of their social norms and tolerance of deviant behavior. They propose that tight cultures have a higher degree of situational constraint, which serves to restrict the range of behaviors deemed appropriate across everyday situations, whereas loose cultures have a much weaker situational structure, affording a wider range of permissible behavior across everyday situations.

Situational Opportunities and Constraints

Situations can present either opportunities or constraints. For example, in the workplace, you might lack the information, tools, equipment, material, and supplies needed to complete tasks, or may lack the budgetary support or the help from others needed to complete your work tasks (Peters & O'Connor, 1980; Peters, O'Connor, & Eulberg, 1985). On the other hand, situational factors can enhance people's ability to perform their jobs well (Cardy, Dobbins, & Carson, 1995). Workers who have an abundance of resources, help from others, limited time pressures, and the like probably perform better than other workers whose ability and effort are similar but whose situations are less bountiful.

The effects of situational opportunities or constraints are probably clearest in the workplace, where there is a definite set of tasks to accomplish and goals to meet, but the effects of situational constraints are by no means limited to the workplace. For example, you might plan a romantic evening with your significant other, but when you get to the restaurant, you find it is hot and noisy and that the service is slow and uneven. You might hope for a nice day with your children at the zoo and find that there is a special promotion going on that gives you access to new exhibits, fun rides, and special experiences that transform the day into one you and your children will remember for years to come. Aspects of the situation that either help you or prevent you from meeting your goals and expectations can influence your behavior, attitudes, and mood.

Situations can and do constrain people from engaging in many behaviors. The very presence of others might sometimes stop some people from violating rules and norms, although as I will show in several subsequent chapters, the presence of others can *encourage* misbehavior. Surveillance and law enforcement can constrain many serious types of misbehavior. There are even situational constraints that parallel those sometimes encountered in the workplace. You might decide to steal a car but find that you do not have the right sort of tools for jimmying the window and bypassing the key.

Socialization

Socialization is a developmental process by which individuals acquire the values, standards of behavior, attitudes, and skills required to function effectively in society. This same developmental process (together with genetic influences that predispose individuals to certain types of behavior; Bouchard, 1994) forms our personality. For example, individuals who are strongly socialized to adopt and accept the values, rules, and standards that society expects are likely to show higher levels of conscientiousness than individuals who are less well socialized.

Socialization can be thought of as a continuum. Some people are so thoroughly socialized that they accept every norm and every value of the society they live in; individuals who are highly socialized are unlikely to misbehave unless they come to believe that misbehavior is what their social system wants them to do. As I noted earlier, criminals and individuals engaged in war crimes and atrocities rarely think they are doing something bad or wrong. Rather, they are likely to be convinced that their destructive behavior is helping to advance some important societal goal and is something that will be met with approval rather than sanctions. At the other end of the scale is the state of normlessness. In the 1890s, the French sociologist Durkheim introduced the term "anomie" to describe the lack of normal ethical or social standards. In Durkheim's original work, anomie was thought to represent a condition of society—that is, the idea that during times of change or uncertainty, society does not provide individuals with sufficient guidance about what behaviors are expected or valued. We can also use the term normlessness to refer to individuals who, for any of several reasons, fail to learn or to accept the norms, values, and standards of the society they live in. As I noted earlier, some psychopaths might be aware of societal norms and values (e.g., it is wrong to steal or to harm others), but they may not accept these standards. Higher levels of normlessness are likely to increase the risk of misbehavior.

Individuals who live in communities where the normal rules and standards are not accepted are more likely to misbehave. For example, Dietz, Robinson, Folger, Baron, and Schulz (2003) provided evidence that organizational members located in a violent community may learn abusive behavior through observational learning, symbolic modeling, and imitation of the violence in the community and may be more likely than others to transfer this learning to the workplace. On the other hand, individuals who are raised in communities that value conformity and rule adherence may grow up to be more conscientious and less likely to break the law or the rules.

The term "socialization" is usually used to describe the process by which people learn and adopt the norms, standards, and values of society, but it can also be used to describe the process by which people learn and adopt the norms of the groups they belong to. For example, there is a robust research literature dealing with the process of organizational socialization (Chao, O'Leary-Kelly, Wolf, Klein, & Gardner, 1994), by which people learn the expectations and performance standards as well the goals and history of the organization that employs them. If the norms and standards of the organization are unhealthy, promoting or tolerating abusive behavior, bullying, dishonesty, or other forms of misbehavior, individuals who become well socialized to their organization may become more and more likely to misbehave (Mulvey & Padilla, 2010). It is probably important to understand both how well a person is socialized to his or her environment *and* what norms and standards these environments promote. That is, knowing that a person is well socialized may not be enough in predicting misbehavior; you might also need to know what sort of environment that person has socialized into (Collins & Schmidt, 1993).

The Social Context of Behavior

This book focuses on the effects of one class of situations—social situations—on behavior. That is, I will focus on how a variety of social influences support, sustain, or allow misbehavior. It is useful, then, to define what constitutes a social situation. Efforts to come up with a clear and concise definition of a social situation can be traced back to at least the 1940s. Psychologists tended to focus on the environment within which behaviors occur, asking questions such as whether other people are present or whether the activities a person engages in involve interacting with others (Smith, 1945). Sociologists tended to draw broader definitions that included people, cultural expectations and traits, and dynamic processes such as social control or social interaction (Carr, 1945).

In this book, I define a social situation as one in which the behavior of an individual (the actor) is open to social influence because of any of the following:

1. Others are present, believed by the actor to be present or believed by the actor to be informed about the actor's behavior
2. Socially defined norms, expectations, and values are relevant to the behavior in question
3. The judgments of others might be applied to the behavior in question
4. Others provide information about the situation or appropriate responses to the situation

Consider the social situation that will be the focus of Chapters 8–12, the workplace. This situation gets more attention than others in this book for several reasons. First, people at work usually have well-defined roles, often specified in a job description, and are usually working toward several personal, workgroup, and organizational goals. Second, the workplace provides a potential venue for an extremely wide range of misbehaviors, ranging from sustained incivility and bullying to employee theft and white-collar crime. As a result, the workplace becomes a sort of laboratory for studying and understanding the influence of these factors on misbehavior. For now, though, let's think about how the definition of a social situation applies to the workplace. First, with limited exceptions, we tend to work in situations where other people are either present or are likely to be informed about our behavior. These other people might include coworkers, subordinates, supervisors, customers, or clients, and their perceptions, beliefs, and actions can influence our behavior. Second, there are well-defined norms, expectations, and values about how people should behave at work. Some of these are part of the organization's charter and the individual's job description, but there are often informal norms that are quite important. For example, some workplaces are casual and relaxed while others dictate in some detail the types of dress and behavior that is expected. Third, the judgments of others are important. Your supervisor or manager is probably responsible for evaluating your job performance, and his or her judgments can directly influence the sorts of raises or promotions you get (Murphy et al., 2018). Finally, the input and opinions of others in the workplace help to shape your understanding of what is happening and what is to be expected at work.

There are a few components of the definition of a social situation offered here that will show up as recurring themes in the chapters that follow, including (1) information, (2) norms, expectations, and values, and (3) the judgments of others.

In the section that follows I describe the ways these components of social situations influence the behavior of individuals.

How Social Situations Influence Behavior

Like all situations, social situations sometimes provide constraints upon or opportunities to engage in particular behaviors. However, the two main pathways through which social situations influence behavior are through the information these situations provide and the rewards and sanctions these situations impose on different behaviors.

Social Groups Both Provide and Control Information

First, social situations provide information. The groups you and others you are linked with (e.g., members of the same group, friends, significant others), identify with, and interact with help to define: (1) what *is*, and (2) what *should be*. That is, groups provide information that can help reduce ambiguity about what is happening, what it means, and what you might expect in the future. This information is not always correct (groups might share incorrect ideas and perceptions), but most individuals find ambiguity upsetting, and groups that help you resolve or reduce ambiguity are very important to individuals (Holmes, 2015). The groups and individuals you interact with often provide a significant amount of information that helps to define your perceptions of events, activities, and the context within which they occur. In several subsequent chapters, I will discuss ways in which groups not only provide information but also take steps to control the perceptions, beliefs, and attitudes of their members.

Groups and the individuals you interact with also provide critically important information about what *should be*. That is, they convey norms, standards, and expectations that define what actions and what outcomes are valued, preferred, seen as problematic, or forbidden. First, societies tend to define general patterns of behavior that are preferred and valued. For example, the cultures of different nations differ substantially in terms of power distance—that is, the belief that hierarchy is important and valuable and that people who are at higher levels in the power structure should be free to make decisions that affect people at lower levels (Hofstede, 2001; Hofstede, Hofstede, & Minkov, 2010). Japan and several countries in the Arab world tend to be high on power distance whereas the U.S., U.K., or Netherlands tend to be low on power distance. Units within society (courts, schools, religion, the family) tend to provide more detailed instructions about what behaviors are viewed as good and valuable and what behaviors violate norms, laws, and rules. These norms, standards, and expectations help to define what individuals view as right or wrong, as permitted or forbidden and as helpful or harmful.

One of the important determinants of misbehavior is the tendencies for different groups within the same society to follow and advocate somewhat different norms, values, and expectations. Sometimes, these differences are obvious and extreme; organized crime families develop very different norms, standards, and expectations than church groups. Often, the norms that different groups embrace differ in more subtle ways, making some behaviors that are usually not viewed as acceptable by society as a whole (e.g., cheating on taxes) viewed as normal or as the "way things *really* work" among some groups within society. Indeed, one of the major themes that will be developed in the chapters that follow is that there are often differences in the norms that appear to apply in society at large (e.g., it is wrong to cheat on your taxes) and the norms that are believed to "really" apply in their group or their segment of society.

Social Groups Provide Sanctions and Rewards

Social groups provide rewards for behaviors that conform to their norms, preferences, and expectations and sanctions for behavior that violate these norms, preferences, and expectations. Sometimes, the rewards and sanctions are explicit and concrete; in the workplace, employees who perform well receive raises and promotions and employees who violate important rules and policies face dismissal. More frequently, however, rewards and sanctions do not come in the form of money or tangible financial rewards but rather in terms of approval and support. Nevertheless, the approval and regard of others is an immensely powerful motivator, and social groups have highly effective mechanisms for influencing the behavior and even the perceptions of their members by granting or withholding approval and support. Social groups can also punish members or people who aspire to become members by shunning or ostracizing individuals who the group does not approve of. Excluding others from a group is such a strong form of punishment and social control that it is often a key component of bullying (Williams & Nida, 2015). The ability of social groups to distribute rewards and sanctions is an important determinant of that group's ability to inspire and enforce conformity with the preferences, norms, and standards of the group.

Why Do Groups Pull Toward the Bad?

Social groups, ranging from informal friendship groups to formal organizations, are often a force for good. The news is full of stories about corporate greed and fraud (e.g., Enron, Volkswagen), but corporations often devote meaningful time, energy, and resources to the social good (Bradley, Brief, & Smith-Crowe, 2008). Many corporations appear to sincerely embrace the idea of corporate social responsibility (Cochran & Wood, 1984; Griffin & Mahon, 1997; Margolis & Walsh, 2003; Wood, 1991) and work hard to make this a better world.

Nevertheless, social groups are often a critically important force in pulling people in the direction of bad behavior, and this is something that requires explanation.

Social groups are the primary means by which the norms and standards of society are transmitted and enforced. How, then, do you explain the idea that social groups are also an important means by which deviant norms and standards that embrace breaking rules and laws are also transmitted and enforced? In general, the explanation for groups sometimes adopting and enforcing norms that are antisocial, in the sense that they run counter to norms in the broader society, is similar to the explanation for many other behaviors—that is, there are both personal and situational factors that likely have an effect. For example, groups that believe they compete with other groups for desired resources (e.g., native populations vs. immigrants) are likely to develop unrealistically negative perceptions of the groups they are competing with (King & Wheelock, 2007). Intergroup conflict or competition, or even the belief that this conflict might emerge, increases the likelihood of developing negative attitudes toward and carrying out negative behaviors toward members of the competing group.

The nature and content of group norms often reflect the personalities, preferences, and attitudes of early group members, and norms established early in the life cycle of a group can continue to influence the behavior of the group well after the early members have moved on from a group (Feldman, 1984). For example, suppose early group members harbor prejudices toward members of certain groups (e.g., racial or ethnic minorities, LGBT individuals). That group is likely to develop norms that encourage, or at least tolerate negative beliefs about and actions toward those individuals. If the founders of a group and its early members harbor strongly antisocial beliefs and attitudes (e.g., a criminal gang), the norms that develop in that group are likely to run strongly counter to the norms of the broader society from which this group is drawn.

Summary

Behavior is a function of attributes of the person (e.g., personality traits) and characteristics of the situation in which behavior occurs. This book is concerned with situational factors, particularly social ones. Groups, organizations, and institutions influence the behavior of individuals by several means, but two are of paramount importance. First, groups provide, control, and help you make sense of information. They help to define both your perception of what *is* (i.e., what is happening, what does it mean) and what *should be* (i.e., what is valued, what is good?). Second, they provide a range of rewards and sanctions that influence behavior. These two themes will be illustrated in examples throughout the remainder of this book. Groups, organizations, and institutions can be, and often are, forces for the good, but they can also create conditions that increase the likelihood that misbehavior (i.e., behavior that violated widely held beliefs and norms that describe what behaviors are good vs. bad and that have the potential to cause harm) will occur.

References

Ash, P. (1991). *The Construct of Employee Theft-Proneness.* Park Ridge, IL: SRA/London House.

Babiak, P. (1995). When psychopaths go to work: A case study of an industrial psychopath. *Applied Psychology: An International Review, 44*, 171–188.

Babiak, P. & Hare, R.D. (2007). *Snakes in Suits: When Psychopaths go to Work.* New York: Harper Business.

Barrick, M.R. & Mount, M.K. (1991). The Big Five personality dimensions and job performance: A meta-analysis. *Personnel Psychology, 44*, 1–26.

Baumeister, R.F., Vohs, K.D., De Wall, C.N. & Zhang, L. (2007). How emotion shapes behavior: Feedback, anticipation, and reflection, rather than direct causation. *Personality and Social Psychology Review, 11*, 167–203.

Boddy, C.P. (2010). Corporate Psychopaths and organizational type. *Journal of Public Affairs, 10*, 300–312.

Bohr, F., Meyer, C. & Wiegrefe, K. (2014). Interview with an Auschwitz Guard. *Spiegel Online*, August 28, www.spiegel.de/international/germany/spiegel-interview-with-a-91-year-old-former-auschwitz-guard-a-988127.html

Bouchard, T.J. (1994). Genes, environment and personality. *Science, 264*, 1700–1701.

Boyce, C.J., Wood, A.M. & Brown, G.D.A. (2010). The dark side of conscientiousness: Conscientious people experience greater drops in life satisfaction following unemployment. *Journal of Research in Personality, 44*, 535–539.

Bradley, J.C., Brief, A.P. & Smith-Crowe, K. (2008). The good corporation. In D.B. Smith (Ed.), *The People Make the Place: Exploring Dynamic Linkages Between Individuals and Organizations* (pp. 175–223). Mahwah, NJ: Lawrence Erlbaum Associates.

Cardy, R.L., Dobbins, G.H. & Carson, K.P. (1995). TQM and HRM: Improving performance appraisal research, theory and practice. *Canadian Journal of Administrative Sciences, 12*, 106–115.

Carr, L.J. (1945). Situational sociology. *American Journal of Sociology, 51*, 136–141.

Chao, G.T., O'Leary-Kelly, A.M., Wolf, S., Klein, H.J. & Gardner, P.D. (1994). Organizational socialization: Its contents and consequences. *Journal of Applied Psychology, 79*, 730–743.

Cochran, P.L. & Wood, R.A. (1984). Corporate social responsibility and financial performance. *Academy of Management Journal, 27*, 42–56.

Collins, J.M. & Bagozzi, R.P. (1999). Testing the equivalence of the socialization factor structure for criminals and noncriminals. *Journal of Personality Assessment, 72*, 68–73.

Collins, J.M. & Schmidt, F.L. (1993). Personality, integrity, and white-collar crime. *Personnel Psychology, 46*, 295–311.

Dietz, J., Robinson, S.L., Folger, R., Baron, R.A. & Schulz, M. (2003). The impact of community violence and an organization's procedural justice climate on workplace aggression. *Academy of Management Journal, 46*(3), 317–326.

Ekehammar, B. (1974). Interactionism in personality from a historical perspective. *Psychological Bulletin, 81*, 1026–1048.

Feldman, D.C. (1984). The development and enforcement of group norms. *The Academy of Management Review, 9*, 47–53.

Furnham, A. (2017). The dark side of conscientiousness. *Psychology, 8*, 1879–1893.

Furnham, A. & Taylor, J. (2004). *The Dark Side of Behaviour at Work.* Basingstoke: Palgrave.

Gelfand, M.J. et al. (2011). Differences between tight and loose cultures: A 33 nation study. *Science, 32*, 1100–1104.

Gino, F. & Pierce, L. (2009a). The abundance effect: Unethical behavior in the presence of wealth. *Organizational Behavior and Human Decision Processes, 109*, 142–155.

Gino, F. & Pierce, L. (2009b). Dishonesty in the name of equity. *Psychological Science, 20*, 1153–1160.

Gino, F. & Pierce, L. (2010). Lying to level the playing field: Why people may dishonestly help or hurt others to create equity. *Journal of Business Ethics, 95*, 89–103.

Gough, H.G. (1960). Theory and measurement of socialization. *Journal of Consulting Psychology, 24*, 23–30.

Griffin, J.J. & Mahon, J.F. (1997). The corporate social performance and corporate financial performance debate: Twenty-five years of incompatible research. *Business and Society, 36*, 5–31.

Hackney, K.J. & Perrewé, P.L. (2018). A review of abusive behaviors at work: The development of a process model for studying abuse. *Organizational Psychology Review, 8*, 70–92.

Hare, R.D. (1991). *The Hare Psychopathy Checklist-Revised* (PCL-R). Toronto: Multi-Health Systems.

Hare, R.D. (1994). Roles and relationships. In R.D. Hare, H.H. Blumberg, M.F. Davies and M.V. Kent (Eds.), *Small Group Research: A Handbook* (pp. 141–154). Norwood, NJ: Ablex.

Hattrup, K. & Jackson, S.E. (1996). Learning about individual differences by taking situations seriously. In K.R. Murphy (Ed.), *Individual Differences and Behavior in Organizations* (pp. 507–547). San Francisco: Jossey-Bass.

Hofstede, G. (2001). *Culture's Consequences: Comparing Values, Behaviors, Institutions and Organizations Across Nations*. Thousand Oaks, CA: Sage.

Hofstede, G., Hofstede, G.J. & Minkov, M. (2010). *Cultures and Organizations: Software of the Mind*. Revised and Expanded 3rd Ed. New York: McGraw-Hill.

Hogan, J. & Hogan, R. (1989). How to measure employee reliability. *Journal of Applied Psychology, 74*, 273–279.

Hogan, J. & Ones, D.S. (1997). Conscientiousness and integrity at work. In R. Hogan, J.A. Johnson, & S.R. Briggs (Eds.), *Handbook of Personality Psychology* (pp. 849–870). New York: Academic Press.

Hogg, M.A. (2007). Uncertainty-identity theory. In M.P. Zanna (Ed.), *Advances in Experimental Social Psychology* (Vol. 39, pp. 69–126). San Diego, CA: Academic Press.

Holmes, J. (2015). *Nonsense: The Power of not Knowing*. New York: Crown

Hough, L.M., Eaton, N.K., Dunnette, M.D., Kamp, J.D. & McCloy, R.A. (1990). Criterion-related validities of personality constructs and the effect of response distortion on those validities [Monograph]. *Journal of Applied Psychology, 75*, 581–595.

Hough, L.M. & Oswald, F.O. (2008). Personality testing and I-O psychology: Asking questions, offering answers, discussing unknowns, and providing direction. *Industrial and Organizational Psychology, 1*, 272–290.

Jones, J.W. (1980). Attitudinal correlates of employees' deviance: Theft, alcohol use, and nonprescribed drug use. *Psychological Reports, 47*, 71–77.

Jones, J.W., Slora, K.B. & Boye, M.W. (1990). Theft reduction through personnel selection: A control group design in the supermarket industry. *Journal of Business and Psychology, 5*, 275–279.

Judge, T.A. & Zapata, C.P. (2015). The person-situation debate revisited: Effect of situation strength and trait activation on the validity of the big five personality traits in predicting job performance. *Academy of Management Journal, 58*, 1149–1179.

King, R.D. & Wheelock, D. (2007). Group threat and social control: Race, perceptions of minorities and the desire to punish. *Social Forces, 85*, 1255–1280.

Kobbs, S.W. & Arvey, R.D. (1993). Distinguishing deviant and non-deviant nurses using the Personnel Reaction Blank. *Journal of Business and Psychology, 8*, 255–264.

Landay, K., Harms, P.D. & Credé, M. (2019). Shall we serve the dark lords? A meta-analytic review of psychopathy and leadership. *Journal of Applied Psychology, 104*, 183–196.

Lefkowitz, J. (2009). Individual and organizational antecedents of misconduct in organizations: What do we [believe that we] know, and on what bases do we [believe that we] know it? In C. Cooper & R. Burke (Eds.), *Research Companion to Crime and Corruption in Organizations* (pp. 60–91). Cheltenham, UK. Northampton, MA: Edward Elgar.

Lipman, V. (2013). The disturbing link between psychopathy and leadership. *Forbes*, April 25, www.forbes.com/sites/victorlipman/2013/04/25/the-disturbing-link-between-psychopathy-and-leadership/#2621bdd54104

Margolis, J.D. & Walsh, J.P. (2003). Misery loves companies: Rethinking social incentives by business. *Administrative Science Quarterly, 48*, 268–305.

Mehl, M.R. & Robbins, M.L. (2012). Naturalistic observation sampling: The Electronically Activated Recorder (EAR). In Mehl, M.R. & Conner, T.S. (Eds.), *Handbook of Research Methods for Studying Daily Life* (pp. 124–143). New York, NY: Guilford Press.

Meyer, R.D. & Dalal, R.S. (2009). Situational strength as a means of conceptualizing context. *Industrial and Organizational Psychology, 2*, 99–102.

Meyer, R.D., Dalal, R.S. & Hermida, R. (2010). A review and synthesis of situational strength in the organizational sciences. *Journal of Management, 36*, 121–140.

Mischel, W. (1999). Implications of person-situation interaction: Getting over the field's borderline personality disorder. *European Journal of Personality, 13*, 455–461.

Moran, S. & Schweitzer, M.E. (2008). When better is worse: Envy and the use of deception. *Negotiation and Conflict Management Research, 1*, 3–29.

Morehouse, R.E., Farley, Fl. & Youngquist, J.V. (1990). Type T personality and the Jungian classification system. *Journal of Personality Assessment, 54*, 231–235.

Mulvey, P.W. & Padilla, A. (2010). The environment of destructive leadership. In B. Schyns & T. Hansbrough (Eds.), *When Leadership Goes Wrong: Destructive Leadership, Mistakes, and Ethical Failures* (pp. 49–71). Greenwich, CT: Information Age.

Munsey, C. (2006). Frisky, but risky. *Monitor on Psychology, 37*(7), 40.

Murphy, K.R. (1993). *Honesty in the workplace*. Monterey, CA: Brooks/Cole.

Murphy, K.R, Cleveland, J.N. & Hanscom, M.E. (2018). *Performance Appraisal and Management: Why Does It Fail and How Can It Ce Fixed?* Thousand Oaks, CA: Sage.

Murphy, K.R. & Luther, N. (1997). Assessing honesty, integrity, and deception. In N. Anderson and P. Herriot (Eds.), *International Handbook of Selection and Assessment* (pp. 369–388). Chichester, UK: Wiley & Sons.

Ones, D.S., Viswesvaran, C. & Schmidt, F.L. (1993). Comprehensive meta-analysis of integrity test validities: Finding and implications for personnel selection and theories of job performance. *Journal of Applied Psychology, 78*, 679–703.

Paulhus, D.L. & Williams, K.M. (2002). The Dark Triad of personality: Narcissism, Machiavellianism, and psychopathy. *Journal of Research in Personality, 36*, 556–563.

Pervin, L.A. (1978). Definitions, measurements, and classifications of stimuli, situations, and environments. *Human Ecology, 6*, 71–105.

Peters, L.H. & O'Connor, E.J. (1980). Situational constraints and work outcomes: The influences of a frequently overlooked construct. *Academy of Management Review, 5*, 391–397.

Peters, L.H., O'Connor, E.J. & Eulberg, J.R. (1985). Situational constraints: Sources. consequences, and future considerations. In K. Rowland & G. Ferris (Eds.), *Research in personnel and human resource management* (Vol. 3). Greenwich, CT: JAI Press.

Rauthmann, J.F. & Sherman, R.A. (2018). The description of situations: Towards replicable domains of psychological situation characteristics. *Journal of Personality and Social Psychology, 114*, 482–488.

Rauthmann, J.F., Sherman, R.A. & Funder, D.C. (2015). Principles of situation research: Towards a better understanding of psychological situations. *European Journal of Personality, 29*, 363–381.

Rostami, A., Mondani, H, Liljeros, F. & Endling, C. (2018). Criminal organizing applying the theory of partial organization to four cases of organized crime. *Trends in Organized Crime, 21*, 315–342.

Sackett, P.R., Burris, L.R. & Callahan, C. (1989). Integrity testing for personnel selection: An update. *Personnel Psychology, 42*, 491–529.

Schank, R. & Abelson, R.P. (1977). *Scripts, Plans, Goals and Understanding: An Inquiry into Human Knowledge Structures*. Mahwah, N.J.: Erlbaum.

Scheff, T.J. & Retzinger, S.M. (1991). *Emotions and Violence: Shame and Rage in Destructive Conflicts*. Ann Arbor, MI: University of Michigan Press.

Schmidt, F.L. & Hunter, J.E. (1988). The validity and utility of selection methods in personnel psychology: Practical and theoretical implications of 85 years of research findings. *Psychological Bulletin, 124*, 262–274.

Schwarz, N. & Clore, G.L. (2007). Feelings and phenomenal experiences. In E.T. Higgins & A. Kruglanski (Eds.), *Social Psychology: Handbook of Basic Principles* (2nd Ed., pp. 385–407). New York: Guilford.

Silver, M. & Sabini, J.P. (1978). The perception of envy. *Social Psychology, 41*(2), 105–111.

Skeem, J.L., Polaschek, D.L.L., Patrick, C.J. & Lilienfeld, S.O. (2011). Psychopathic personality: Bridging the gap between scientific evidence and public policy. *Psychological Science in the public interest, 12*, 95–162.

Smith, M. (1945). Social situation, social behavior, social group. *Psychological Review, 52*, 224–229.

Smith, S.F., Watts, A.L. & Lilienfeld, S.O. (2014). On the trail of the elusive successful psychopath. *Psychologist, 27*, 506–510.

Snyder, M. & Ickes, W. 1985. Personality and social behavior. In G. Lindzey & E. Aronson (Eds.), *Handbook of Social Psychology* (3rd Ed., pp. 883–948). New York: Random House.

Treviño, L.K. (1986). Ethical decision making in organizations: A person-situation interactionist model. *Academy of Management Review, 11*, 601–617.

Vardi, Y. & Weitz, E. (2016). *Misbehavior in Organizations: A Dynamic Approach*. New York: Routledge.

Weiss, H.M. & Adler, S. (1984). Personality and organizational behavior. *Research in Organizational Behavior, 6*, 1–50.

Werner, K.B., Few, L.R. & Bucholz, K.K. (2015). Epidemiology, comorbidity, and behavioral genetics of Antisocial Personality Disorder and Psychopathy. *Psychiatric Annals, 45*, 195–199.

Werner, S.H., Jones, J.W. & Steffy, B.D. (1989). The relationship between intelligence, honesty, and theft admissions. *Educational and Psychological Measurement, 49*, 921–927.

Williams, K.D. & Nida, S.A. (2015). Ostracism: Consequences and coping. *Current Directions in Psychological Science, 20*(2), 71–75.

Wood, D.J. (1991). Social issues in management: Research and theory in corporate social responsibility. *Journal of Management, 17,* 383–406.

Zuckerman, M. (2009). Sensation seeking. In M. Leary & R. Hoyle (Eds.), *Handbook of Individual Differences in Social behavior* (pp. 455–465). New York: The Guildford Press.

2

MISBEHAVIOR IN GROUPS AND SOCIAL SITUATIONS

Social groups, organizations, movements, and the like often act as forces for good. For example, groups ranging from the British and Foreign Anti-Slavery Society (1838–1956), the Maryknoll Fathers and Brothers, and the International Red Cross and Red Crescent Society to Doctors Without Borders (Médecins Sans Frontières) devote time and effort, and their members often undergo hardships and undertake significant risks, to further socially important goals. However, even groups whose main mission is laudable will sometimes engage in harmful and destructive behavior. For example, during the 1850s and 1860s, some abolitionist groups distributed "Beecher's Bibles"—that is, Sharps carbines and rifles. The name "Beecher's Bibles" was inspired by the comments and activities of the abolitionist Henry Ward Beecher, of the New England Emigrant Aid Society, who considered these guns as having more moral power against slavery than a hundred bibles. It is claimed that these guns were sometimes shipped to Kansas and Nebraska in boxes labeled "books" or "bibles" (Kansas Historical Society, 2004); Beecher's Bibles contributed to the violence in the turbulent period leading up to the Civil War.

The central goal of this book is to show how social groups can cause, encourage, and reward harmful behavior that violates the norms, rules, and laws that are broadly accepted in society. In this chapter, I will use a series of case studies to illustrate many of the psychological and social processes that are involved when groups are causes or contributing factors in misbehavior; Chapters 3–12 will examine these processes in more detail. Before moving on to the case studies and the lessons that might be learned from each one, I will first describe in more detail the range of behaviors that fall under the general heading of misbehavior and the distinct roots of different varieties of misbehavior.

A Taxonomy of Misbehavior

In Chapter 1, I defined misbehavior as behaviors (as opposed to thoughts or opinions) that violate broadly accepted laws, norms, and societal values and that have the potential to be harmful or destructive. Thus, misbehavior is not simply something that goes against a social norm or expectation. For example, wearing different clothing than is expected in a particular setting is not necessarily misbehavior. Some offices have very strict and precise dress codes, even if these are unwritten, and a junior banking executive who shows up in a blue suit when the office norm is black pinstripe is not engaging in misbehavior. He or she may be making a bad choice, and might even end up being sanctioned for not fitting in, but the behavior is not in itself harmful or dangerous. However, suppose an important client is coming in today and this junior banker comes in dressed in a garish, ill-fitting, and oddly colored suit that would look out of place even for a shady used car salesman. This choice might harm the relationship between the bank and the client, causing the client to question his or her choice of a bank, and this potential for harm might shift this behavior from the realm of poor choices to the realm of misbehavior.

There have been several attempts to describe and categorize misbehavior. Many studies deal with misbehavior in particular contexts, such as wrongdoing in medical practice (Dubois, Yates, & Vasher, 2012) or in scientific research (Banks, Rogelberg, Woznyj, Landis, & Rupp, 2016; Neuroskeptic, 2012). In particular, there has been a substantial literature dealing with the different categories of misbehavior in work organizations (e.g., Hollinger & Clark, 1983, Robinson & Bennett, 1995, 1997; Vardi & Weitz, 2016), some of it highly specific to work settings (e.g., employee theft) and others relevant across a much wider range of settings (e.g., bullying).

Robinson and Bennett (1995) suggested two dimensions that are useful for classifying and describing misbehaviors across a wide range of contexts—that is, the target of the misbehavior and the seriousness of the behavior, especially the potential to cause harm. First, misbehaviors can be self-targeted; individuals might drink or abuse a variety of legal or illegal substances that harm their physical and mental health and that may interfere with their ability to interact positively with others (e.g., friends, family, coworkers). Misbehaviors might be targeted to other individuals (e.g., bullying), groups (e.g., systematic sexual harassment), or larger organizations (e.g., workplace theft). Second, behaviors might cause, or have the potential to cause, relatively small amounts of harm (e.g., occasional incivility) or might be fatal in their consequences (e.g., lynching). It is important to note that relatively mild misbehaviors might nevertheless have substantial consequences over time, especially if they are repeated on a frequent basis. Repeated minor insults and slights in the workplace (sometimes referred to as microaggressions) can lead to substantial decreases in productivity (Smoker & Walecha, 2011) and increases in stress, sleep disturbances and anxiety (Demsky,

Fritz, Hammer, & Black, 2019). Table 2.1 lists examples of misbehaviors that fall within all of the cells of this taxonomy.

First, some behaviors are self-injurious. They include behaviors that deviate in a small way from social norms (e.g., eating a notably unhealthy diet), and while these small deviations might not cause much harm at the time they occur, a long-term pattern of carrying out these behaviors might lead to meaningful harm. This group of self-injurious behaviors also includes behaviors that could carry meaningful short-term harm (substance abuse) as well as the potential for more substantial harm if these behaviors recur over time. Finally, some behaviors are likely to cause immediate and serious self-harm, up to and including suicide and attempted suicide. All of these behaviors meet the definition of misbehavior offered here in the sense that they violate widely held social norms and have at least the potential to be dangerous or harmful.

Next, misbehaviors might be directed to an individual or toward specific individuals. These might range from mild departures from widely accepted norms (e.g., incivility) that are likely to cause less harm if they occur in isolation but might be quite harmful, in that they represent a chronic pattern of behavior. Small misbehaviors that might escalate into more serious misbehaviors include social aggression (behavior intended to harm another's social standing, friendships, or status) and bullying. The most serious examples of misbehavior directed at an individual or groups might include violence or assault.

Misbehaviors might be directed to specific groups. These might start with avoidance or disparagement of members of a group (e.g., groups based on sex, gender, race, or ethnicity), but can become more serious if they take the form of discriminatory treatment (e.g., refusal to hire women). Finally, misbehaviors directed at groups can escalate to include aggression and attacks on group members, and even to systematic attempts to rid society of that group through mass expulsions or genocide.

TABLE 2.1 A Taxonomy of Misbehavior

		Seriousness	
	Milder	Serious	Very Serious
Directed at			
Self	Chronic unhealthy behaviors	Substance abuse	Self-harm, suicide
Another Individual	Incivility	Social aggression, bullying	Assault
A Group	Avoidance disparagement	Discrimination	Aggression toward a group, genocide
An Organization	Disengagement	Goldbricking, cyber loafing	Employee theft, workplace violence

Finally, misbehaviors might be directed toward larger and more diverse social units, such as organizations. Mild forms of this category of misbehavior might include disengagement—that is, continuing as a member of an organization but only in the form of going through the motions, and without any real input or participation. Systemic violations of group norms might take many forms; there is, for example, a substantial research literature dealing with goldbricking—that is, purposefully doing less work than you are capable of, or than you are expected and required to do (Mars, 1994; Roy, 1952). Originally, research on goldbricking was largely concerned with purposefully slow work on the factory floor, but the concern has shifted to a different form of goldbricking that occurs in information-intensive work—that is, cyber loafing, or using your computer as a tool for wasting time at work (e.g., Lim, 2002). Misbehavior directed at organizations might take a more severe form, such as systematic employee theft or violence directed at coworkers.

As Table 2.1 suggests, the term "misbehavior" might apply to a wide variety of behaviors that differ in their targets and their seriousness. These behaviors might also differ in terms of their precise causes. For example, factors that lead to a violent assault on members of a social group are likely to be somewhat different from the factors that lead people to sometimes be a bit rude to members of these same groups. Nevertheless, there is a core set of social and psychological processes that contribute to a wide range of misbehaviors. In the next section, I will use a series of case studies to illustrate several of these processes; Chapters 3–12 will discuss them in more detail.

Case Studies Illustrating Social and Psychological Processes That Promote Misbehavior

There is a range of social and psychological processes that can lead to misbehavior, and these can be illustrated by discussing a series of famous cases of misbehavior that range from behaviors caused by the mere presence of other individuals (e.g., diffusion of responsibility) to behaviors that are legitimized and sustained by a warped set of norms and beliefs that make it possible for otherwise moral and upstanding individuals to participate in mass murder and crimes against humanity.

Kitty Genovese—Diffusion of Responsibility

The brutal rape and murder of Kitty Genovese shocked the nation and helped to launch a program of research aimed at understanding the behavior of bystanders. In the early morning of March 13, 1964, Winston Moseley killed Kitty Genovese in the Kew Gardens district of New York City. The murder was prolonged and gruesome; Mosley first stabbed Kitty Genovese in the back with a hunting knife, and although severely injured, Kitty was able to crawl back into her building. Ten minutes later, Mosley returned and searched for Kitty, finding her in a hallway of her building, and he proceeded to rape her, rob her, and stab her again. Kitty Genovese died en route to the hospital.

What made this murder especially shocking was the story published two weeks after the murder in the *New York Times* claiming that

> for more than half an hour 38 respectable, law-abiding citizens in Queens watched a killer stalk and stab a woman in three separate attacks. . . . Not one person telephoned the police during the assault; one witness called after the woman was dead.
>
> (*Gansberg, 1964*)

It was claimed that an unnamed neighbor saw at least part of the attack but decided not to call the police, claiming "I did not want to get involved". The Kitty Genovese story became for many a symbol of the cruelty and apathy that characterized life in the big cities of America.

BOX 2.1 WERE THERE REALLY 38 WITNESSES?

Much of what people know, or think they know about the Kitty Genovese case is either exaggerated or simply wrong. In particular, there was no evidence that 38 witnesses had watched the murder; only three or four witnesses had seen Genovese and Moseley together for a short time, and not during the fatal stabbing. Also, there is some evidence of attempts to intervene, including phone calls to the police, as well as shouts of alarm that caused Moseley to withdraw (Rosenthal, 1999). Why, then, did the story that 38 witnesses did nothing to intervene take hold?

First, the report of 37 (later 38) uncaring witnesses was part of a front-page story published in the *New York Times*, a prestigious newspaper that even then had a strong reputation for investigative reporting and for getting stories right. More compelling, however, was the way this story fit so well with underlying stereotypes about New York City. I was 11 years old at the time and lived in Albany, about three hours north of New York City, and the prevailing image of the city at that time was that it was dangerous, cruel, and uncaring. This story hit all three of these bases, and it helped to reinforce already-existing beliefs about that city. The "uncaring" stereotype was particularly strong at the time, and the Kitty Genovese story was a perfect illustration of the apathy of New Yorkers toward their fellow citizens. Because this stereotype was both widely shared and strongly held in many parts of the country (and indeed, in many parts of New York State), the story was easy to believe and therefore became yet another piece of evidence of how depraved this city seemed to be.

The Kitty Genovese case helped to launch numerous studies on the way witnesses and bystanders react to emergencies. One of the key ideas emerging from many of these studies was the "diffusion of responsibility" (Latané & Darley, 1970). When a group of people all witness an emergency or an event that seems like it requires a response (e.g., an older person who trips and falls on the sidewalk), individuals are often unsure of who should respond, or of whether someone else has already responded (perhaps an ambulance is already on its way). Individual bystanders are particularly unlikely to respond when the group is large or when they do not know or do not have any connection with the victim. Each individual might realize that *something* should be done and that *someone* should respond, but he or she might not be certain *who* should respond or *what* the response should be. Bystanders who see others not responding are particularly unlikely to take responsibility themselves.

Failure to intervene in the Kitty Genovese attack might not be seen as misbehavior; Mosley attacked with a hunting knife, and active intervention might have been dangerous to the individual attempting to intervene without necessarily being helpful to Kitty Genovese. Failure to call the police, on the other hand, does represent a type of misbehavior, at least by omission. Society usually encourages its members to look out for the welfare of others, and each of the witnesses who did not call the police probably felt at some point that he or she *should* call the police. However, the very fact that the initial attack occurred in a place where there might be many witnesses probably increased the uncertainty of each witness about what he or she should do.

The diffusion of responsibility is a phenomenon that can occur in all types of groups (e.g., a group of friends, a workgroup). Diffusion is especially likely to occur in nominal groups, such as the group of people who all see the older individual take a fall. In these nominal groups, individual roles are not well defined; there is no leader and there is no specific individual who is supposed to take care of specific sorts of issues and problems. As a result, members of these nominal groups often do not know what they are supposed to do and assume that there must be somebody else who is responsible for responding to this situation.

The Volkswagen Scandal—The Downsides of Employee Loyalty and Identification

In the mid-2000s, Volkswagen embarked on a bold plan to become the world's largest auto manufacturer, and a key part of that plan was to dramatically increase its sales in the United States. An important part of their strategy was to do something that no other auto manufacturer had successfully done—that is, to develop diesel automobiles that performed well, were fuel-efficient and that did not pollute. Their engineers quickly realized that it was not possible to accomplish all three goals, and in 2006, the company settled on the only feasible strategy—they cheated. Volkswagen decided to install a "cheat device" that could detect when an emissions test was being performed so that pollution controls (which hurt both mileage and performance) could be switched on, and then switched back off when the cars hit the road. The result was a generation of diesel automobiles that performed well and had good mileage, but that did not meet pollution regulations. If not for the efforts of a research team from West Virginia University, their cheating might not have been exposed (Ewing, 2017).

Volkswagen created a very successful marketing campaign built around the theme of "clean diesel", but the whole house of cards collapsed by 2015, when Volkswagen was forced to confess its violations to the U.S. Environmental Protection Agency. Volkswagen and its allied companies have paid billions in fines and several executives have gone to jail (Ewing, 2017; Tabuchi & Ewing, 2016).

Like many other organizational scandals (see, for example, Danner, 2004), there was initially an attempt to blame the Volkswagen scandal on a few rogue engineers ("bad apples"). That attempt soon fell apart; the Volkswagen scandal spanned many years and several continents, and it enmeshed (or exposed) several other automakers. This was a wide-ranging, long-lived conspiracy that involved large numbers of employees, managers, and executives.

Several factors contributed to the Volkswagen scandal, but one important one was the strong sense of identification and loyalty common among many employees (Strauss, 2017). Volkswagen was seen as a prestigious company—one of the mainstays of the German economy—and its employees often identified strongly with the organization. Identification with an organization often has real and tangible benefits (Lee, Park, & Koo, 2015), but there is also a dark side to identifying with an organization (Conroy, Henle, Shore, & Stelman, 2017). People who strongly identify with an organization are more likely to go along with corrupt schemes of this type in the belief that they serve the greater good—that is, the welfare of the organization.

Racism in European Football—Social Contagion

Football (what Americans call soccer) is the most popular sport in the world, particularly in South American and Europe, home of many of the traditional powerhouse clubs in the sport. Football matches in Europe are well attended and spirited but are often blighted by large-scale displays of blatant racism. In one recent incident, Raheem Stirling, the leader of the English team and one of the outstanding players in that country, was subjected to such a torrent of racial abuse by fans in Sofia, Bulgaria, that play had to be halted twice, and the crowd had to be warned that further abuse would lead to the cancellation of the match (Smith, 2019). So-called fans made Nazi salutes and yelled monkey chants.

Racism and racist chants by soccer fans have been blamed in part on the rise of right-wing nationalism in Europe (Santora & Schaverein, 2019). While this might be a contributing factor, racist abuse of Black and South Asian players is widespread, even in areas where right-wing extremism is a relatively weak force.

Several laws have been passed in an attempt to control this behavior (The Football [Disorder] Act 2000 was passed by the Parliament of the United Kingdom),[1] and the organizations that govern this sport, such as the Union of European Football Associations (UEFA), have made concerted efforts to combat racism in their sport.[2] Nevertheless, the problem of vicious racism continues to haunt this sport.

How does social contagion relate to racism in football matches? It is clear that some of the racist behavior that occurs in European football stadiums is premeditated; fans who throw bananas on the field while directing monkey chants toward Black players did not bring bananas to the stadium as a snack. However, the extent of this racist behavior (sometimes, entire sections of a stadium participate in racist chants, songs, and taunts) is probably a result of the spread of bad behavior from a small group who intended to engage in racist taunts from the time they entered the stadium to others who had not come to the match with this intention. That is, some fans come prepared to shout racist slogans and abuse players, and their example spreads so that large sections of the stadium might also show the same behaviors.

Social or behavioral contagion occurs when the behavior of one person or a group of persons is copied by others. Sporting events create conditions that make contagion more likely and that enable the spread of behaviors that would normally be met with strong social disapproval. First, these stadiums are crowded; density is one of the factors known to promote social contagion (Freedman, Birsky, & Cavoukian, 1980). Second, fans are often intensely excited, either because the game itself is exciting or (as in the case of the Bulgarian episode) the home team is losing badly. This intensity of emotion, especially when coupled with aggression, is a factor that facilitates social contagion (Bandura, Ross, & Ross, 1961). Finally, sporting events create strong social pressures to conform; fans who root for the visiting team are often criticized and shunned, especially in sections of the stadium that are dominated by fans of the home team. The pressure to conform is known to increase the likelihood of social contagion (Wheeler, 1966).

The social contagion of behaviors is closely related to emotional contagion, the spread of emotional states from one person to another (Hatfield, Cacioppo, & Rapson, 1993). Sporting events can evoke strong emotions, and individuals who exhibit strong emotional reactions often lead others to feel those same emotions. There is evidence that observing others exhibiting a particular emotion (e.g., smiling, to indicate pleasure) leads to behavioral mimicry (i.e., smiling), which in turn leads to experiencing the same emotion as the original sender. Behavioral and emotional contagion can lead to many positive outcomes (e.g., greater feelings of group solidarity; Kelly & Barsade, 2001). However, these same processes often appear to be at work in settings where horrific violence or abuse occurs, such as a lynch mob. In certain situations, bad behavior and negative emotions can be highly contagious and, unfortunately, sporting events often create conditions that are ripe for the contagion of misbehavior.

Price Waterhouse v. Hopkins—Sex Stereotypes at Work

Ann Hopkins was a highly successful manager at Price Waterhouse (now PricewaterhouseCoopers), one of the largest professional services firms in the world. In 1982, she was the only woman out of 88 candidates for partnership, and her credentials were arguably better than the great majority of her male competitors. By her admission, she could be brash, aggressive, and even vulgar (Barnes, 2018), but was highly successful in bringing major contracts to Price Waterhouse and should have been a strong candidate. She was turned down twice for partnership and was told by her superior that she needed to dress, act, and talk more femininely and that she needed a course in charm school. Her behavior was similar to, and often a good deal more effective than that of her male colleagues, but because she did not conform to the senior partners' stereotype of a female executive, she was not promoted.

Ann Hopkins filed a lawsuit charging employment discrimination, and her case eventually made its way to the U.S. Supreme Court. The court, in *Price Waterhouse v. Hopkins*, 490 U.S. 228, ruled that Ann Hopkins was discriminated against by Price Waterhouse and it established clear criteria for demonstrating (and for defending oneself against charges of) sex discrimination in employment. In essence, the court ruled that holding men and women to different standards when evaluating their performance and effectiveness in the same job is unlawful discrimination. In this particular case, rewarding men for being aggressive and brash while punishing women for the same behaviors represents a violation of the woman's civil rights.

The term "stereotype" refers, in its simplest form, to beliefs about a group that are applied uncritically to all members of that group. For example, you might believe that Scandinavians are highly concerned with social equality. If you find out that your neighbor has recently immigrated from Norway, you might assume that this neighbor will, therefore, be highly concerned with social equality. Stereotypes are not necessarily negative (as in this example), and they do not always cause harm. However, the tendency to ascribe the characteristics of a group or the characteristics you believe are characteristic of a group uncritically to all members of that group (e.g., Joe is of Italian heritage, and all Italians are. . .) can create many problems. First, they are likely to lead to unwarranted assumptions about the behavior of individuals. Groups are rarely so homogeneous *all* of their members will behave in the same way, and even if the beliefs you have about a particular group are true (e.g., the Dutch and Swedish are, on average, taller than members of most other European nations), these assumptions are unlikely to fit all group members. Second, people can be treated badly because of assumptions about how they behave and how they *should* behave. In Ann Hopkins' case, her behavior did not fit the prevailing stereotype of female partners, and she was penalized for not acting the way her bosses assumed female managers and executives should act. She was able to prevail in her discrimination suit because she was able to prove that she was penalized for acting in ways that bought promotions and rewards to her male colleagues.

Stereotypes are not always negative, but negative stereotypes do appear to be part of the explanation for discrimination against women, older people, people with disabilities and members of racial, ethnic, and religious minorities. In the U.S., federal civil rights laws have been passed to help protect members of these groups from discrimination in employment, education, housing, and access to public services, but it is not clear whether these laws have been successful in reducing discrimination, and it has been argued that they may remain powerless to change the attitudes, beliefs, and assumptions that help to fuel discrimination (King, Avery, & Sackett, 2013).

#MeToo Movement—Objectivization and Social Support

Sexual harassment and sexual assault are depressingly common in our society. Over 45% of women experience sexual harassment of one form or another at work (e.g., Pina, Gannon, & Saunders, 2009). This harassment often unfolds over time, starting with subtle nonverbal behaviors and escalating into verbal and physical behaviors that create a hostile work environment (Fitzgerald, Drasgow, Hulin, Gelfand, & Magley, 1997). Sexual assaults are more frequent than is often assumed; more than one-third of men, for example, report committing a sexual assault toward a woman (e.g., Abbey, McAuslan, Zawacki, Clinton, & Buck, 2004; De Gue & Di Lillo, 2004). These assaults often involve partners, friends, and relatives rather than strangers. Similarly, rape is more frequent in the context of existing relationships (e.g., between acquaintances, casual dating partners, those in committed relationships) than between strangers, and it usually occurs in private rather than public spaces (Koss, Gidycz, & Wisniewski, 1987).

Several psychological processes contribute to sexual harassment and sexual assault. Sexual harassment in the workplace, for example, is better understood as a manifestation of power and dominance in the workplace than as a desire for sexual gratification (Cleveland & Kerst, 1993). Sexual harassment can even be used by male subordinates against female managers and supervisors as a way of undercutting their formal power (McLaughlin, Uggen, & Blackstone, 2012). Sexual assault, on the other hand, can be conceptualized as a form of objectification in which "a woman's body is treated as a mere instrument or thing by her perpetrator" (Fredrickson & Roberts, 1997, p. 186). Objectification is part of a broader process of dehumanization in which a person is treated like an object or a thing, and it is a key concept for understanding many of the unsavory aspects of sexual relationships between men and women; the term "sex object" captures this aspect of dysfunctional ways women (and sometimes men) are often perceived in society. Attitudes and beliefs that allow or even encourage people to treat another person as an object are particularly dangerous because objects do not have rights and individuals have no obligation to treat objects with justice or compassion.

There is another face of debates over sexual harassment that exemplifies the positive power of social support. In 2017, the Hollywood producer Harvey Weinstein was credibly accused of sexually harassing and assaulting numerous women. On October 15, 2017, actress Alyssa Milano wrote: "If you've been sexually harassed or assaulted write 'me too' as a reply to this tweet", and reposted the following phrase suggested by a friend: "If all the women who have been sexually harassed or assaulted wrote 'Me too.' as a status, we might give people a sense of the magnitude of the problem" as a way of drawing attention to the frequency of sexual harassment and assault. Within 24 hours, this phrase was retweeted more than 500,000 times. After this tweet, Alyssa Milano became aware of an earlier Me Too movement founded in 2006 by Tarana Burke to help women of color who had been the victims of sexual violence, and she credited this movement with helping to awaken men and women to the frequency and severity of sexual exploitation and violence in our society.

The #MeToo movement illustrates the power of information sharing and social support. The first few women who posted messages describing their own experiences of sexual harassment were taking a substantial risk, especially in cases where the perpetrator was a powerful and influential figure (before 2017, Harvey Weinstein was one of the most powerful, and one of the most successful producers in Hollywood). As the number of women coming forward with their descriptions of their experience of sexual harassment and assault grew, the power dynamics changed substantially. First, the #MeToo posts of the first several women made it progressively less threatening for other women to share their stories. Perhaps even more remarkably, the #MeToo movement shifted the center of gravity in the struggle against sexual harassment, to the point where credible accusations of mistreatment of women caused the downfall of many powerful men.

The Rape of Nanjing—Dehumanization

During the Second Sino-Japanese War (1937–1945), Nanjing served as the capital of China. The Japanese attacked Nanjing in 1937, expecting an easy victory. To their surprise, there were many casualties, and the city was not taken until nearly the end of that year. The occupation of Nanjing turned into a sustained bloodbath.

Starting in December of 1937, a six-week orgy of mass murder and rape committed by Japanese troops led to the death of over 200,000 civilians and unarmed combatants, together with the rape of at least 20,000 women (Chang, 1997). One-third of the city was destroyed by arson and theft was widespread. In one of the more notorious incidents, multiple newspapers reported a contest between two Japanese officers to see who could first kill 100 people using only a sword.[3]

The Japanese armies in China had often been operating under orders to kill all captives, in part a reflection of the Japanese belief that surrender was an act of cowardice and a violation of all military codes. As a result, in Nanjing and elsewhere, Japanese soldiers tended to look upon the captured enemy with contempt. They shot the great majority of their captives, and after the military captives were dealt with, the Japanese army turned on the civilian population of Nanjing. At least initially, attacks on civilians were carried out on the orders of senior officers, but as the days passed, the violence appears to have become so widespread that it was now beyond the immediate control of these officers.[4]

The Rape of Nanjing appears to have followed a pattern that is common to several forms of mass violence, ranging from lynch mobs to the Holocaust—that is, escalation (i.e., progressing to more and more serious forms of violence and abuse) and dehumanization (i.e., treating the victims of abuse as less than human). Thus, the scale and ferocity of violence grew over time, and violence that was initially focused on military prisoners spilled over to the treatment of civilians. There is an extensive literature dealing with escalation of violence in families and domestic relationships (Chalk & King, 1988), and in these contexts, escalation of violence is often a process that unfolds over a significant period. This slow escalation is especially problematic because the victims of violence often acclimate to each new escalation, accepting violent behavior as normal. In wartime conditions, escalation can be much quicker, and this appears to be the case in Nanjing.

The violence and depravity exhibited by Japanese troops in Nanjing illustrate the risks that the process of dehumanization can create (Harris & Fiske, 2006; Haslam, 2006). Dehumanization refers to a set of processes by which individuals or members of some group are denied their status as humans and are treated as subhuman. Dehumanization is thought to be one of the components of extreme racism; in a previous case, I discussed how Black soccer players are sometimes treated as monkeys by racist fans. It sometimes involves associating extremely negative attributes with some group (e.g., as in the way Nazis used negative stereotypes of Jews to argue that they were enemies of humanity and not worthy of humane treatment); the belief that some group exhibits several very negative characteristics makes it easier to deny that group's humanity (Bar-Tal, 2000). There is a large research literature dealing with dehumanization, and Bar-Tal (2000) has proposed two main variants: (1) animalistic dehumanization—in which uniquely human characteristics such as civility, moral sensitivity, rationality, and logic are denied to individuals or groups, and (2) mechanistic dehumanization—in which individuals or groups are viewed as soulless machines, displaying inertness, passivity, and rigidity. Studies of the Rape of Nanjing do not provide enough information to determine which of these types of dehumanization were present, but the more general historical record suggests that Japanese soldiers viewed captured soldiers and civilians alike as animals rather than fully human. Earlier, I noted the strong norm in the Japanese armed services to treat surrender as a disgraceful exhibition of cowardice and to treat captured soldiers with contempt. These same attitudes likely applied to civilians.

Regardless of the type of dehumanization shows in Nanjing, there is little doubt that the perpetrators of this violence had few qualms about their behavior.

In the numerous diaries and reports emerging from the Rape of Nanjing, there are few reports of senior officers, noncommissioned officers, or regular soldiers objecting to or trying to stop the violence, although there is evidence that the general in command of the Japanese expeditionary force did later express regret for the murders and rapes (Chang, 1997).

White Fragility—Denial

Di Angelo and Dyson (2018) popularized the term "White fragility" to describe resistance to open discussion of racism, and indeed, denial that systematic racism exists. Very few people are unaware of racial disparities in income, wealth, housing, etc., but a significant portion of the population (primarily, but not exclusively White people) deny that systematic racism exists, arguing that any differences in outcomes are due to the bad choices or lack of effort on the part of members of disadvantaged groups. In part, this may be a reflection of different beliefs about what "racism" means.

As I will note in several subsequent chapters (e.g., Chapters 4, 8, 11), the nature of racism in America has changed over time, and some people believe that because it is no longer socially acceptable to openly make racial insults, and because many forms of racial discrimination are forbidden by law, racism is a thing of the past. There has been controversy over changes in the definition of racism in the Merriam-Webster dictionary;[5] the revised definition of racism includes reference to the systematic oppression of racial minorities that results from a combination of prejudice and social and institutional power.

Nelson, Adams, and Salter (2013) examine the *Marley hypothesis* that suggests that denial of racism is sometimes the result of a lack of knowledge about past racism. Efforts to examine and talk about role of racism in American history (e.g., the *New York Times* 1619 Project) have been controversial; backlash to these efforts have led to a proposal to create a "1776 Commission" with the avowed goal of promoting a more traditional presentation of American history with fewer references of racism.[6]

The denial of racism is not unique to the U.S.; there is evidence from around the world that members of dominant groups consistently perceive less racism than members of racial and ethnic groups who are the targets of racism (Durrheim, Mtose, & Brown, 2011). Several psychological processes are involved in minority-majority differences in perceptions of racism and racial oppression, but the most fundamental is the desire to maintain a positive self-image, a dynamic that also appears central to understanding why so many seemingly moral individuals willingly participated in the Holocaust.

The Workers of the Holocaust—Motivated Reasoning

During World War II, the Germans carried out an organized and sustained campaign of genocide that killed approximately 6 million Jews, as well as large numbers of Roma (then called Gypsies), homosexuals, and other groups deemed inferior in the ideology of Nazi Germany. Many of the individuals who organized and helped carry out this campaign of atrocities were true believers in the Nazi cause or were sufficiently committed to the Nazi regime to justify, in their own minds, their continuing loyalty in the face of increasingly horrific incidents. However, as historians and others who documented this period have pointed out, the work of genocide involved a large number of people who were not part of the Nazi party, the Gestapo or the SS, but whose daily jobs were an integral part of the Nazi death machine. These ranged from train drivers to construction workers, manufacturers, doctors, barbers, and members of many other trades and professions. Why did these people cooperate with the ongoing slaughter?

After the war, it was believed that many Germans knew little or nothing about the roundup and slaughter of Jews and others, or that they worked under coercion, with the real possibility of prison or execution if they disobeyed orders to participate in the Holocaust. The true picture is more complicated and more troubling. There is abundant evidence, summarized in Goldhagen's (1996) book *Hitler's Willing Executioners*, that ordinary Germans knew about and willingly participated in the Holocaust (see also Hilberg, 1961). Some of his conclusions, especially his belief that deeply rooted anti-Semitism led Germans to accept and believe in the goal of eliminating the Jews, are controversial, but the evidence he presents that people worked without coercion and that individuals who refused to participate did not suffer drastic consequences is substantial.

Claude Lanzman's epic documentary *Shoah* featured extensive interviews with survivors of the death camps, camp guards, bystanders, and individuals working in the many trades that supported the operation of these camps. His interviews with Henryk Gawkowsk, an assistant train driver who helped transported prisoners to Treblinka, and with a barber at this same camp are especially illuminating because they deal with the day-to-day work of running these camps. Both were working under differing levels of coercion (especially the barber, who was an inmate) and both talked about their fear and the horrible things they saw, but both also talked about the day-to-day work itself and the ways they separated themselves from the horrible events happening around them. One strategy for shielding themselves from the horrors all around them was to engage in motivated reasoning, distorting their perceptions of what was happening to make it easier to accept their participation in this horrible process.

Motivated reasoning is a cognitive process by which people seek information that conforms with the opinions, beliefs, and preferences (Epley & Gilovich, 2016). For example, Henryk Gawkowsk claimed that the reason he continued to work on the train bringing victims to Treblinka was that he would be shot if he refused. This may have been a sincere belief, but another possibility is that there was little real likelihood of being shot or imprisoned (as Goldhagen, 1996 argues), and that Gawkowsk was actively trying to convince himself that he acted out of necessity. Another facet of motivated reasoning is the tendency to avoid or distort information that runs counter to these opinions, beliefs, and preferences. Many of the persons interviewed in *Shoah* noted that they tried to focus on the mundane details of their work (e.g., is the train running well today) rather than thinking about what their work was contributing to.

As I will argue in several subsequent chapters, people are strongly motivated to preserve a positive self-image and to think of themselves as generally good people. A large number of people whose work made the Holocaust possible probably shared this desire to maintain a positive self-image, and it was therefore often important for them not to think too carefully about what they were doing and what effects it would have. Many people were able to minimize their feeling for responsibility for their part in the genocide by motivated reasoning.

A Framework for Understanding How Groups Encourage Misbehavior: Social Influence and Social Cognition

The case studies in the preceding section highlight several processes that can lead individuals to behave in ways that violate widely held norms and have the potential for harm (i.e., misbehavior). These range from ignoring others who are in danger or in need of help (diffusion of responsibility) to participating in fraud and white-collar crime out of loyalty to an organization, to discriminatory treatment of others on the basis of sex-role stereotypes or negative beliefs about members of racial and ethnic groups. They include sexual harassment and assault, but also include demonstrations of how social support can help to energize effective responses to the perpetrators of these behaviors. In extreme cases (e.g., the Rape of Nanjing, the Holocaust), processes such as dehumanization and motivated reasoning can lead people to participate in horrific crimes against humanity.

In the last section of this chapter, I will describe a general framework that can be used to organize the social and psychological processes that help lead individuals to commit and to participate in a range of misbehaviors, running the gamut from incivility to genocide. In general, there are two ways groups affect the behaviors of individuals. First, groups, organizations, and institutions directly influence behavior by offering rewards and sanctions for particular behaviors, by inspiring or modeling these behaviors, and by changing people's perceptions and understanding of the situations they are in. This is a process of social influence. Second, groups, organizations, and institutions indirectly influence behavior by influencing the way people think about particular behaviors. For example, the norms that are communicated by a group may lead its members (or people who aspire to become members) to believe that behaviors that are normally viewed negatively by society (e.g., cheating on your taxes) are, in this case, tolerated or even approved of. This is a process involving social cognition. Both social influence and social cognition represent important pathways for groups to influence the misbehavior of their members.

Social Influence

Groups, organizations, and institutions frequently intervene to influence the behavior of their members or of people with whom they interact. Kelman (1958) developed an influential model of social influence that recognized three ways individuals might respond to this influence and modify their behavior to conform with the preferences, requirements, or instructions of a group: (1) compliance—when individuals accept influence and carry out the behavior suggested or requested by a group to gain rewards (or, approval) and avoid punishments (or, disapproval), (2) identification—when individuals carry out the behavior suggested or requested by a group to create or maintain a desired and beneficial relationship to another person or a group, and (3) internalization—when individuals carry out the behavior suggested or requested by a group because it is congruent with their (adopted) value system. In essence, these represent: (1) doing what you are told, (2) *wanting* to do what the group wants, and (3) believing that what the group wants you to do was, in fact, your idea all along.

Attempts at social influence do not always succeed. Latané (1981) suggested that the likelihood of successful social influence depends upon three factors: (1) strength of links to the group—the importance of the influencing group to the individual, (2) immediacy to the group—physical (and temporal) proximity of the influencing group to the individual at the time of the influence attempt, and (3) number in the group—the number of people in the group. Of these three, strength appears to be the most important factor; people who identify strongly with a group who believes that this group, organization, or institution is important to them are most easily influenced by the group's preferences and requests. In Chapter 3, I will explore the processes and determinants of social influence in more detail.

Social Cognition

Social cognition refers to the processes by which individuals process social information, including the way this information is encoded, stored, retrieved, and applied in social situations. In this context, social information refers to information about other people or groups of people, and social situations involve interacting with (or anticipating interactions with) individuals, including virtual interactions—that is, interactions where you believe that others are present or are observing and evaluating your behavior. There is a broad and diverse literature dealing with social cognition, some of which draws from research on animal behavior and on the responses of human infants to particular stimuli and situations, and some of which is drawn from observation and experimental research on human cognition.

First, social cognition is shaped by what we learn and what we respond to. Humans use a wide range of methods to learn about their environments. At a most basic level, we appear to be hard-wired (i.e., we do not need to be taught this or to learn it) to recognize and respond to specific emotions and reactions exhibited by others. In particular, we immediately recognize and respond to cues from others indicating fear or disgust (Frith, 2008; Frith & Frith, 2012); these responses probably conveyed evolutionary advantages to our forebearers who often lived in environments where it was important to immediately identify danger. We use social referencing to learn from others what things, behaviors, etc. are viewed as good vs. bad. We learn from others' responses to stimuli and situations, often mirroring them in important ways (Chartrand & Bargh, 1999. Learning through observation and instruction helps us align our actions and goals with others (Frith, 2008).

Second, social cognition is shaped by the cognitive systems by which we process information about people and social events. We observe information, store it in short-term and long-term memory, retrieve it for use at some later point and integrate information to form judgments. All of these cognitive processes have a role in how we understand and think about social situations and in the behavioral choices we make when responding to these situations.

Social influence and social cognition are not always forces that pull us in the direction of misbehavior. On the contrary, both systems are critical for learning the norms and rules of society and for understanding what behaviors are valued, tolerated, or frowned upon. However, under a variety of circumstances, paralleling those in the case studies in this chapter and in the various situations that will be articulated in the chapters that follow, these two sets of processes can play a pivotal role in creating conditions where misbehavior is likely.

Summary

This book is concerned with misbehavior—that is, behaviors that violate widely accepted norms and that have the potential to be destructive or cause harm. The term "misbehavior" covers a wide range of possibilities, from incivility to genocide, but there are two broad strands that link different types of misbehaviors together, First, misbehavior might be self-directed (e.g., substance abuse), directed toward individuals (e.g., sexual harassment) or organizations and institutions (e.g., employee theft). Second, they vary in terms of the amount of harm they might involve; an isolated incident of incivility might cause relatively little harm, but the social and psychological processes documented in this book can lead people to participate willingly in murder, rape, arson, and the like. Seven case studies are presented that vividly illustrate various categories of misbehavior as well as some of the processes that contribute to misbehavior (e.g., diffusion of responsibility, dehumanization, motivated reasoning).

I describe the two main pathways by which the social and psychological processes that encourage or allow misbehavior most often operate—that is, social influence and social cognition. First, groups, organizations, and institutions use a range of rewards and sanctions to influence the behavior of their members and of individuals they interact with. Second, people learn to think about particular types of behavior differently, sometimes leading them to believe that behaviors that seem to violate widely held norms are expected and approved of. These two processes will be examined in Chapters 3 and 4; the ways these processes sometimes lead to misbehavior will be examined in several of the chapters that follow.

Notes

1. Information about related laws and their enforcement is regularly updated at www.cps.gov.uk/legal-guidance/football-related-offences-and-football-banning-orders
2. www.uefa.com/insideuefa/social-responsibility/respect/no-to-racism/
3. Some Japanese historians have argued that this story is not true, and indeed there has been a steady stream of Japanese historical research, as well as claims from numerous Japanese government officials, that seeks to downplay the massacre and rapes
4. The details of this massacre are still contested, and the concerted effort of some of the Japanese military and some Japanese historians has had the effect of obscuring both the actions of various Japanese units and the eventual outcomes of their attacks
5. www.bbc.com/news/world-us-canada-52993306
6. www.npr.org/2020/09/17/914127266/trump-announces-patriotic-education-commission-a-largely-political-move?t=1600433691128

References

Abbey, A., McAuslan, P., Zawacki, T., Clinton, A. & Buck, P.O. (2004). Attitudinal, experiential, and situational predictors of sexual assault perpetration. *Journal of Interpersonal Violence, 16*, 784–807.

Bandura, A., Ross, D. & Ross, S.A. (1961). Transmission of aggression through imitation of aggressive models. *Journal of Abnormal and Social Psychology, 63*, 575–582.

Banks, G.C., Rogelberg, S.G., Woznyj, H.M., Landis, R.S. & Rupp, D.E. (2016). Editorial: Evidence on questionable research practices: The good, the bad and the ugly. *Journal of Business and Psychology, 31*, 323–338.

Bar-Tal, D. (2000). *Shared Beliefs in Society: Social Psychological Analysis*. Thousand Oaks, CA: Sage.

Barnes, B. (2018, July 17). Ann Hopkins, who struck an early blow to the glass ceiling, dies at 74. *New York Times* www.nytimes.com/2018/07/17/obituaries/ann-hopkins-winner-of-a-workplace-bias-fight-dies-at-74.html

Chalk, R. & King, P.A. (1988). *Violence in Families: Assessing Prevention and Treatment Programs*. Washington: National Academy Press.

Chang, I. (1997). *The Rape of Nanking*. New York: Basic Books.

Chartrand, T.L. & Bargh, J.A. (1999). The chameleon effect: The perception—behavior link and social interaction. *Journal of Personality and Social Psychology, 76*, 893–910.

Cleveland, J.N. & Kerst, M.E. (1993). Sexual harassment and perceptions of power: An under-articulated relationship. *Journal of Vocational Behavior, 42*, 49–67.

Conroy, S., Henle, C., Shore, L. & Stelman, S. (2017). Where there is light, there is dark: A review of the detrimental outcomes of organizational identification. *Journal of Organizational Behavior, 38*, 184–203.

Danner, M. (2004, Oct. 7). Abu Gharaib: The hidden story. *The New York Review*, https://www.nybooks.com/articles/2004/10/07/abu-ghraib-the-hidden-story/

De Gue, S. & Di Lillo, D. (2004). Understanding perpetrators of nonphysical sexual coercion: Characteristics of those who cross the line. *Violence and Victims, 19*, 673–688.

Demsky, C.A., Fritz, C., Hammer, L.B. & Black, A.E. (2019). Workplace incivility and employee sleep: The role of rumination and recovery experiences. *Journal of Occupational Psychology, 24*, 228–240.

Di Angelo, R. & Dyson, M.E. (2018). *White Fragility: Why It Is so Hard for White People to Talk About Racism*. Boston: Beacon Press.

Dubois, J.M., Yates, E. & Vasher, M. (2012). The development of a taxonomy of wrongdoing in Medical practice and research. *American Journal of Preventative Medicine, 42*, 89–98.

Durrheim, K., Mtose, X. & Brown, L. (2011). *Race Trouble: Race, Identity and Inequality in Post-Apartheid South Africa*. Lanham, MD: Lexington Books.

Epley, N. & Gilovich, T. (2016). The mechanics of motivated reasoning. *Journal of Economic Perspectives, 30*(3), 133–140.

Ewing, J. (2017, March 16). Engineering a deception: What led to Volkswagen's diesel scandal. *New York Times*, www.nytimes.com/interactive/2017/business/volkswagen-diesel-emissions-timeline.html

Fitzgerald, L.F., Drasgow, F., Hulin, C.L., Gelfand, M.J. & Magley, V.J. (1997). Antecedents and consequences of sexual harassment in organizations: A test of an integrated model. *Journal of Applied Psychology, 82*, 578–589.

Fredrickson, B.L. & Roberts, T.A. (1997). Objectification theory: Toward understanding women's lived experiences and mental health risks. *Psychology of Women Quarterly, 21*, 173–206.

Freedman, J.L., Birsky, J. & Cavoukian, A. (1980). Environmental determinants of behavioral contagion: Density and number. *Basic and Applied Social Psychology, 1*, 155–161.

Frith, C.D. (2008). Social cognition. *Philosophical transactions of the Royal Society of London. Series B, Biological sciences, 363*(1499), 2033–2039.

Frith, C.D. & Frith, U. (2012). Mechanisms of social cognition. *Annual Review of Psychology 62*, 287–313.

Gansberg, M. (1964, March 27). 37 who saw murder didn't call the police. The *New York Times*, p. 1.

Goldhagen, D. (1996). *Hitler's Willing Executioners: Ordinary Germans and the Holocaust*. New York: Knauf.

Harris, L. & Fiske, S. (2006). Dehumanizing the lowest of the low: Neuroimaging responses to extreme out-groups. *Psychological Science, 17*, 847–853.

Haslam, N. (2006). Dehumanization: An integrative review. *Personality and Social Psychology Review, 10*, 252–264.

Hatfield, E., Cacioppo, J.T. & Rapson, R.L. (1993). Emotional contagion. *Current Directions in Psychological Science, 2*, 96–99.

Hilberg, R. (1961). *The Destruction of the European Jews*. New York: Martino Fine Books.

Hollinger, R.C. & Clark, J.P. (1983). *Theft by Employees*. Lexington, MA: Heath.

Kansas Historical Society. (2004). *Beecher Bibles*. https://www.kshs.org/kansapedia/beecher-bibles/11977

Kelly, J.R. & Barsade, S.G. (2001). Mood and emotions in small groups and work teams. *Organizational Behavior and Human Decision Processes, 86*, 99–130.

Kelman, H.C. (1958). Compliance, identification, and internalization: Three processes of attitude change. *Journal of Conflict Resolution, 2*, 51–60.

King, E.B., Avery, D.R. & Sackett, P. (2013). Editorial: Three perspectives of employment discrimination 50 years after the Civil Rights Act—A promise fulfilled? *Journal of Business and Psychology, 28*, 375–382.

Koss, M.P., Gidycz, C.A. & Wisniewski, N. (1987). The scope of rape: Incidence and prevalence of sexual aggression and victimization in a national sample of higher education students. *Journal of Consulting and Clinical Psychology, 55*, 162–170.

Latané, B. (1981). The psychology of social impact. *American Psychologist, 36*, 343–356.

Latané, B. & Darley, J.M. (1970). *The Unresponsive Bystander: Why Doesn't He Help?* New York, NY: Appleton-Century-Crofts.

Lee, E.S., Park, T.Y. & Koo, B. (2015). Identifying organizational identification as a basis for attitudes and behaviors: A meta-analytic review. *Psychological Bulletin, 141*, 1049–1080.

Lim, V.K.G. (2002). The IT way of loafing on the job: Cyber loafing, neutralizing and organizational justice. *Journal of Organizational Behavior, 23*, 675–694.

Mars, G. (1994). *Cheats at Work: An Anthropology of Workplace Crime* (Vol. 4). Brookfield, VT: Dartmouth.

McLaughlin, H., Uggen, C. & Blackstone, A. (2012). Sexual harassment, workplace authority, and the paradox of power. *American Sociological Review, 77*, 625–647.

Nelson, J.C., Adams, G. & Salter, P.S. (2013). The Marley Hypothesis: Denial of racism reflects ignorance of history. *Psychological Science, 24*, 213–218.

Neuroskeptic. (2012). The nine circles of scientific hell. *Perspectives on Psychological Science, 7*, 643–644.

Pina, A., Gannon, T.A. & Saunders, B. (2009). An overview of the literature on sexual harassment: Perpetrator, theory, and treatment issues. *Aggression and Violent Behavior, 14*, 126–138.

Robinson, S.L. & Bennett, R.J. (1995). A typology of deviant workplace behaviors: A multidimensional scaling study. *Academy of Management Journal, 38*, 555–572.

Robinson, S.L. & Bennett, R.J. (1997). Workplace deviance: Its definitions, its manifestations, and its causes. In R.J. Lewicki, R.J. Bies, & B.H. Sheppard (Eds.), *Research on Negotiations in Organizations* (vol. 6, pp. 3–28). Greenwich, CT: JAI Press Inc.

Rosenthal, A.R. (1999). *Thirty-eight Witnesses: The Kitty Genovese Case*. Berkeley, CA: University of California Press.

Roy, D. (1952). Quota restrictions and goldbricking in a machine shop. *American Journal of Sociology, 57*, 427–442.

Santora, M. & Schaverein, A. (2019, Oct. 15). Bulgarian soccer chief resigns after fans' racist abuse of England. *New York Times*, www.nytimes.com/2019/10/15/world/europe/bulgaria-england-racist-abuse.html

Smith, R. (2109, Oct. 16). On soccer. *New York Times*, www.nytimes.com/2019/10/16/sports/soccer-racism-england-bulgaria.html

Smoker, P. & Walecha, A. (2011). The impact of workplace incivility on the work environment, manager skill, and productivity. *Journal of Nursing Administration, 41*, 41–47.

Strauss, K. (2017, July 26). How Volkswagen rallied its employees after its emissions scandal (at least for now). *Forbes*, www.forbes.com/sites/karstenstrauss/2017/07/26/how-volkswagen-rallied-its-employees-after-its-emissions-scandal-at-least-for-now/#8df017181b00

Tabuchi, H. & Ewing, J. (2016, June 27). Volkswagen to pay 14.7 billion to settle diesel claims in U.S. *New York Times*, www.nytimes.com/2016/06/28/business/volkswagen-settlement-diesel-scandal.html?module=inline

Vardi, Y. & Weitz, E. (2016). *Misbehavior in Organizations: A Dynamic Approach*. New York: Routledge.

Wheeler, L. (1966). Toward a theory of behavioral contagion. *Psychological Review, 73*, 179–192.

3

SOCIAL PROCESSES THAT ENABLE OR SUPPORT MISBEHAVIOR

In this chapter and the one that follows, I discuss social and cognitive processes that enable and support misbehavior. In this chapter, I focus on social processes, starting with a discussion of norms, particularly social norms. In this context, norms refer to both beliefs about what other people do (descriptive norms) and beliefs about what other people approve of (injunctive norms; Frone, 2009, 2012). I explore the role of social groups in developing and communicating norms, and I go on to describe social identity. In particular, I explore the way social identity influences self-perception and self-image, which in turn act as powerful motivators of behavior.

Next, I discuss roles. In both formal and informal groups, individuals often have well-defined roles. In organizations, people have particular jobs (e.g., manager, supervisor). In informal groups, individuals often have stable and well-defined roles. Some people are informal leaders, other people are "foot soldiers", others are the "go-to" person when it comes to specific activities the group engages in (e.g., choosing restaurants, hosting parties). Norms, social identity, self-images, and roles can all lead people to engage in a wide range of misbehaviors.

From the outset, it is important to understand that the distinction between social and cognitive processes is not hard and fast; many social processes affect the way people think about their behavior. A distinction can be made, however, and it is that social processes involve other people. They might involve the direct action of others or they might involve perceptions of or beliefs about what other people expect or prefer, but all of the processes described here involve other people, sometimes individuals and sometimes groups.

Social Norms

The simplest definition of a norm is that it is what is typical or standard—that is, it is the normal thing. Social norms are simply norms that apply to behavior in social settings. They are sometimes described as unwritten rules that govern our behavior in these settings (Gavac, Murrar, & Brauer, 2017). Social norms are: (1) shared by group members, (2) relevant to both behaviors and beliefs, (3) a statement of what *is* and what *should be*, and (4) relevant to all group members.[1] Norms can be descriptive, in the sense that they tell you what people usually do in a particular situation, but they are more often thought of as telling us what we should or should not us do.

Descriptive vs. Injunctive Norms

The distinction between descriptive norms and injunctive norms (Cialdini, Kallgren, & Reno, 1991; Lapinski & Rimal, 2005; Trockel, Williams, & Reis, 2003) is a useful one. Descriptive norms refer to what people usually do, but they do not necessarily carry a value judgment. Injunctive norms, in contrast, tell people what they should or should not do. For example, in an office where most employees are in their 30s, you might find that most men will wear khakis and a polo shirt on casual dress days. Suppose you come to work wearing khakis and a short-sleeve button-down shirt. This outfit might be slightly different from the norm, but if your outfit is not met with much notice, much less with disapproval, we would think of "khakis and a polo shirt" as a descriptive norm.

Violating a descriptive norm might mean that you are doing something unusual, whereas violating an injunctive norm means you are doing something wrong. Injunctive norms can be prescriptive (telling you what you should do) or proscriptive (telling you what you should not do). Prescriptive and proscriptive norms are a key part of the process of social control (Wilson, Lizzio, Zauner, & Gallois, 2001), especially if norms are intense and/or tight. Trockel, Williams, and Reis (2003) note that injunctive norms—due in part to their punitive associations—are more predictive of choices between prosocial and antisocial behaviors than descriptive norms. Lapinski and Rimal (2005) suggest that injunctive and descriptive norms can be differentiated by the amount of potential social sanctions associated with a norm. If violating a norm results in some type of social penalty, the norm can be classified as injunctive. If violation bears little to no social cost, a norm is more descriptive.

Norms influence behavior, but they do not necessarily control behavior directly. As noted earlier (and as described in the following Return Potential Model), norms vary in their strength (i.e., how strongly they convey messages about what behaviors are preferred or forbidden) and their effectiveness. For example, some groups have very clear norms that are pervasive, clearly defined, and, most important, imposed on most members of that group; Gelfand et al. (2011) refer to this as normative tightness. The idea that some groups have tighter norms that more closely control the behavior of their members is hardly a new one; Gelfand, Harrington, and Jackson (2017) note that the ancient historian Herodotus commented on the differences between the Persians, who were very flexible in their norms and very willing to adapt ideas and customs from different countries and the Egyptians, who followed a rigid system of norms governing everything from personal hygiene to relationships between rulers and their subjects.

Gelfand and her colleagues (Gelfand et al., 2011, 2017) developed rigorous theories of cultural tightness-looseness and have studied the degree of normative tightness in over 30 nations. They have extended this work to examine variations on normative tightness within countries. For example, they have examined state-level differences in normative tightness within the United States. They have not only shown that some states tend to have tighter norms than others, but they have also documented some of the correlates (and likely consequences) of tight vs. loose normative control. They note,

> Tight states had greater social organization (e.g., lower mobility, less divorce) and greater self-control (e.g., less drug and alcohol abuse), but they also had more discrimination (e.g., higher rates of Equal Employment Opportunity Commission claims and fewer women and minority-owned businesses), and lower creativity (e.g., fewer utility patents and artists per capita) compared to loose states.
>
> *(Gelfand et al., 2017, pp. 803–804)*

BOX 3.1 DESCRIBING NORMS—THE RETURN POTENTIAL MODEL

Norms have their strongest effects when they are widely accepted and when they deal with important issues (i.e., something members of a group or society care deeply about). Jackson's (1965) Return Potential Model (RPM) is useful for assessing both the intensity and the degree of consensus of a norm. The model examines the range and intensity of reactions to a specific behavior or course of action (e.g., aggressive behavior); this model is illustrated in Figure 3.1.

The Return Potential Model plots social approval of a course of behavior in a reference group (i.e., a social group you identify with or believe are important) against the intensity of that behavior. Suppose, for example, that Figure 3.1 refers to approval for being physically aggressive in a basketball game. The graph suggests that the reference group disapproves of passivity, shows approval of a range of aggressive behaviors (e.g., blocking out for rebounds), but shows disapproval if the aggression gets too intense (e.g., throwing punches). There is often a point of peak acceptability on RPM graphs, and this represents the behavior that is most strongly approved of by the group, and therefore, often the behavior you are most likely to

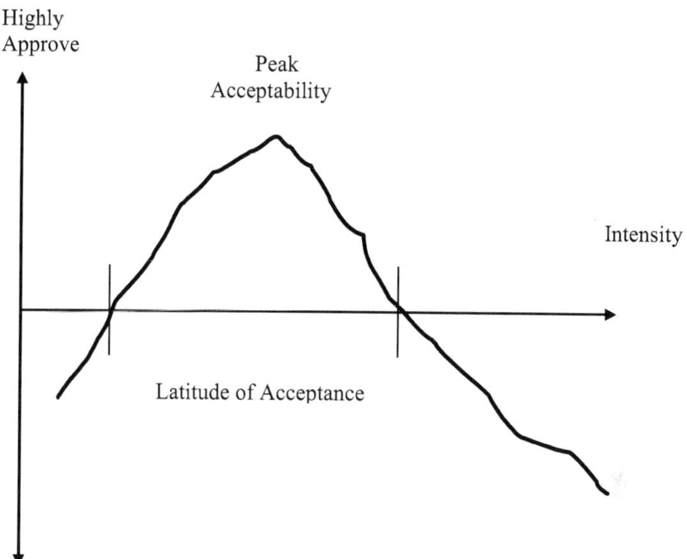

FIGURE 3.1 The Return Potential Model

engage in. There is also a range of behaviors that are seen as acceptable to the group (latitude of acceptance). Finally, the graph is asymmetric. That is, there is strong disapproval for highly aggressive behavior. More passive behavior does meet with some disapproval, but the norms are stronger for violations that involve being over-aggressive than for violations that involve insufficient aggressiveness. This model is illustrated in Figure 3.1.

The two features of Figure 3.1 are useful for describing and diagnosing norms. First, there are some behaviors where the peak of the graph is not very high—that is, behaviors where the reference group does not have strong feelings one way or another. The height of the peak, and perhaps more important, the difference between the peak of an RPM graph and its low point is a sign of the intensity of the norm. Second, the width of the latitude of acceptance is an indication of the tightness of the norm. Sometimes, there might be a very narrow range of behaviors that are approved of, but for other behaviors, the range of acceptable choices might be fairly wide.

Jackson's (1965) Return Potential Model has been used to analyze norms and their effects on behavior in contexts ranging from voting (Glynn, Huge, & Lunney, 2009) to recycling (Nolan, 2015). It has proved to be both a good descriptive tool (the RPM graph conveys a lot of information about the intensity and tightness of norms) and a useful tool for making predictions about the effects of norms on behavior.

The tightness of normative control not only differs between groups, it also often differs within groups. That is, it has long been known that social norms are not necessarily equally relevant to all group members; high-status members of a group sometimes have more flexibility in violating norms (Wahrman, 1970). However, norm violation can be a risky course of action; high-status individuals (e.g., group leaders) are usually not sanctioned for fairly small or unimportant violations of norms, but when the norm and the associated behavior are important to the group, high-status individuals are often expected to set a good example, and violations of important norms can threaten the standing of even the highest-status group member.

Norms About What?

Groups rarely have norms to deal with all behaviors; many behaviors fall outside of the range of normative regulation. Feldman (1984) suggested several principles for determining what behaviors will or will not be regulated by norms. First, norms are almost certain to be developed and enforced if they deal with behaviors that are important to the survival of the group. For example, a workgroup might develop a strong norm that salaries will not be discussed because inequities in pay could lead to stresses within the group that would break the group apart. Second, norms are likely to develop if they help group members understand what behaviors are expected from them. These norms help to reduce uncertainties and to make life simpler and more predictable for group members. Third, norms are likely to develop if they help group members avoid conflict or embarrassing situations. Sometimes, for example, friends and family develop a norm that they will not discuss politics because they want to avoid the conflict these discussions often lead to. Finally, and most important, norms are likely to develop if they express the central values of a group or if they relate to the things that are distinctive about the group. For example, many organizations have strict dress codes, even if these are informally rather than formally set and enforced. In 2014, President Obama wore a tan suit while holding a live news conference dealing with the Syrian civil war. This suit was so far from the norm of dark or pinstripe suits presidents are expected to wear that it led to intense criticism in the press and even in Congress (Coscarelli, 2014).

Whose Norms?

Earlier in this chapter, I noted that norms are shared by group members. This formulation leads to the question of *which* group or groups define norms, and there is no simple answer. At a most general level, the society you live in defines norms. For example, Hofstede and his colleagues have devoted the last 40 years to the study of national cultures (Hofstede, 1980, 2001; Hofstede, Hofstede, & Minkov, 2010; Hofstede, Neuijen, Ohayv, & Sanders, 1990). They have argued that national differences in work-related values and preferences can be understood in terms of a small number of dimensions: (1) power distance—beliefs about social inequality, or the degree of separation between people at different levels in organizations or groups; (2) individualism-collectivism—an orientation toward individuals vs. groups; (3) masculinity-femininity—a preference for achievement and assertiveness vs. cooperation and caring; (4) uncertainty avoidance—a tolerance for vs. avoidance of ambiguity and lack of control; (5) long-term vs. short-term normative orientation—a focus on immediate vs. more distant outcomes; and (6) indulgence vs. restraint—an orientation toward free expression and satisfaction of desires vs. suppression of these desires. Their studies show, for example, that power distance tends to be relatively high in Latin American and Asian countries, and relatively low in many European countries, the U.K., and the U.S.A. These cultural values could be thought of as injunctive norms. In Latin American and Asian countries, people are taught that they should defer to powerful figures, and individuals who fail to follow this cultural preference are treated with disapproval. These are certainly not the only norms that are defined at a national level. In the U.S.A., many professional football players were criticized, and some lost their positions on their team, for refusing (in protest against the treatment of racial minorities) to stand for the national anthem. In many other countries, playing the national anthem at sporting events would seem strange, and refusing to stand during that anthem would hardly be noticed.

In studying the effects of norms on behavior, the concept of "reference group" is an important one. In social psychology, reference groups are often defined as groups a person belongs to, aspires to belong to, or admires—that is, the group or groups a person cares about. One of the key features of identifying with a particular reference group is that it colors one's perceptions of the world. For example, people who identify with a particular group tend to evaluate individuals from their groups more favorably than individuals from other groups (Avery, Hernandez, & Hebl, 2004; Goldberg, 2005). Humans are especially motivated to understand and to follow the norms of these reference groups. This motivation is so strong and so consistent that one of the most effective strategies for changing behavior is to change perceptions of relevant social norms (Tankard & Paluck, 2016).

At any point in time, there might be many different reference groups whose norms might affect an individual's behavior. First, there are the broad norms of society—for example, "thou shalt not steal". Next, there might be norms of broad demographic groups, most notably sex role norms. Most societies have norms that describe what behaviors are expected of men and women and what behaviors will meet with approval or disapproval. For example, a young boy who plays with dolls might be a source of concern to his parents and this behavior may be met with stern disapproval. Similarly, a female manager who is aggressive, decisive, and ambitious might be viewed very negatively (e.g., unfeminine), whereas a male manager might be rewarded for precisely these behaviors (Heilman, 1983;

Heilman & Chen, 2005). Then, there might be norms of broad occupational groups you belong to (e.g., a lawyer who helps clients set up shell companies to hide income might not think there is anything wrong with his or her activity, while at the same time endorsing the principle of "thou shalt not steal"). Every individual belongs to multiple groups (e.g., coworkers, friends, bowling league, family), and the norms of these groups might strongly influence that person's behavior, especially groups that are seen as particularly important to that individual. Finally, people might aspire to belong to particular groups. Someone highly motivated to achieve financial success might take on and imitate what he or she believes to be the norms of the rich or those who are at least comfortably well off.

The existence of multiple reference groups helps to explain the apparent paradox in research on normative influence—that is, that groups often influence individuals to engage in behaviors (e.g., sexual harassment, theft, race discrimination) that run counter to the norms of the broader society. Many behaviors are not approved of by society in general (e.g., cheating on your taxes) but are viewed as normal and acceptable in specific subgroups of society (e.g., your business colleagues). One of the striking findings from research on individuals who engage in a wide range of misbehaviors is that they rarely think that what they are doing is wrong. Even if the general social norm is that it is wrong to steal, if important members of your reference believe that what you are doing is not *really* stealing, or that it is justified (e.g., it is okay to steal from your employer, because the employer is cheating you by not paying all the hours you work), you will not only be more likely to steal but will also do it with a clean conscience. One key to understanding misbehavior is to understand the norms of the particular group or groups an individual most closely identifies with (Kim & Hunter, 1993; Wilder, 1990).

How Norms Develop and Spread

There are many ways norms develop. First, explicit statements by group members, especially high-status group members, can create a norm. Feldman (1984) gives the example of a supervisor who tells his or her workgroup that it is not okay to drink during the lunch hour and potentially comes back to work under the influence of alcohol. Second, important events in a group's history can create a norm. For example, a group of friends might try some new activity (e.g., skydiving) and have a terrible time. This might lead to norms that push group members to avoid doing new things. Finally, norms might carry over from previous experiences. A new lawyer who was taught in college that the client's interests do *not* always come first (e.g., lawyers are not supposed to help clients carry out a criminal enterprise) may carry this attitude into his or her new law firm and may even influence the beliefs and norms of other lawyers in the firm.

Group norms develop over time, arising mainly from a wide range of shared experiences (Feldman, 1984). Group members form their ideas about what is socially normative in a social context or within a community by observing others' behavior. They learn about the norms of their reference groups over time, updating their impressions as they interact with their group or learn about their group through other sources. Suppose you observe members of your reference group showing up to work 10–15 minutes late each day. You are likely to develop the belief that this behavior is normal—that is, that the *real* starting time is 9:15, not 9:00. If you see that other group members get sanctioned for showing up on time (e.g., being told that they make their coworkers look bad), you are likely to form the impression that there is both a descriptive norm that people show up late and an injunctive norm that says you *should* show up late.

The situation described in the preceding paragraph is one that creates uncertainty and ambiguity. The formal rules of the company tell you that you should show up to work by 9:00, but the behavior of the workgroup suggests that there is a different norm in play. Most people find ambiguity and uncertainty uncomfortable, and this conflict between the formal rules of the organization and the informal rules of the workgroup can lead to stronger attachment to an identification with the workgroup. Identification with a group helps to reduce uncertainty; the group becomes a source of information about what is and what ought to be (Hogg & Abrams, 1988; Hogg & Mullins, 1999; Hogg & Terry, 2000).

Certain individuals, called social referents, are particularly influential over others' perceptions of norms (Rogers, 1959). For example, group leaders typically have a strong impact on the norms of a group, especially when the leader is perceived to be legitimate, fair, and prototypical of the group (Hogg, 2010). However, even in informal groups, where there is no designated leader, some group members are likely to have higher status than others (e.g., because they are attractive, or because they are more charismatic, or because they have access to valuable assets), and these high-status individuals often have an important role in setting the tone of a group.

Norms are preserved and communicated through a range of social processes. First, there is socialization—that is, the process by which people learn how they should behave in a range of situations. Next, and more important is internalization—that is, acceptance of the norm in a way that we no longer need to consciously refer to the norm to determine whether particular behaviors are expected and viewed as right. Once a person internalizes a norm, it is no longer necessary for the reference group to enforce the norm. Finally, norms can become institutionalized, by becoming embedded in social institutions (e.g., law enforcement, religion, schools). Formal and informal institutions create social identities (Scott, 1995) that help define who people are and what they are expected to do (Misangy & Weaver, 2008). The term "social norms" is sometimes used to describe these institutionalized norms (Paluck & Shepherd, 2012); once they become institutionalized, social norms can morph into policies, laws, and even commandments.

Destructive Norms

Subgroups within a society often develop norms that are sufficiently different from the norms of general society that they lead to misbehaviors that are destructive of the social order. Researchers have identified two pathways to the development and maintenance of patterns of destructive or harmful behaviors that violate laws, widely held norms, or broadly accepted rules (Kemper, 1966). "Parallel deviance" arises when individuals follow the norms and model the behaviors of individuals who break laws or violate general societal norms (i.e., "When in Rome . . ."). This process is especially strong when high-status or high-power individuals create norms that encourage socially deviant behavior. For example, Richard Nixon resigned in disgrace as President shortly before the House of Representatives was scheduled to vote on his impeachment. He had encouraged his aides to violate the law in an attempt to cover up the Watergate burglary, and several of them went along willingly. Many of these aides ended up in prison, and while some later showed remorse, they mainly appeared to believe that what they were doing while they broke these laws was acceptable because it was done in support of their President.

A second process that leads to the development of deviant norms is referred to as "reciprocal deviance" (Kemper, 1966). Reciprocal deviance results from weakened bonds between individuals and society due to perceived mistreatment. In this situation, the individual repays the mistreatment in kind with deviance (i.e., "An eye for an eye . . ."). For example, society usually encourages norms like "play by the rules" and "follow the law". Groups who believe they have been disenfranchised or treated unfairly may develop norms that encourage their members to be skeptical of the rules, the law, and those in charge of enforcing rules and laws (e.g., police). For example, there is evidence that members of racial minority communities are often hesitant to call the police, especially in situations where there have been previous incidents of racial bias in policing (Gabar & Stern, 2018). In the U.S., it is so common for Black parents to feel the need to prepare their children for potentially fatal interactions with police officers that the term "The Talk" has entered into our lexicon (Lopez, 2016).

Norms have a very strong effect on behavior, and norms that support or allow misbehavior can greatly increase its incidence. Groups define moral norms, which tell group members what behaviors are right and wrong (Ellemers, 2017), and as a result, peers represent a potentially powerful influence on (un)ethical behavior (Bandura 1986, Kohlberg 1969, Robinson & O'Leary-Kelly 1998). Peers help to establish a standard for ethical behavior through their actions or inaction (Moore & Gino, 2013), and a common group identity leads to a process of moral contagion, in which moral beliefs of group members, especially high-status members tend to spread to others (Gino, Ayal, & Ariely, 2009). For example, in many workplaces, there are clear norms about whether and when it is acceptable to call in sick or take the day off. If the group norm tells people that it is normal and acceptable to take a four day weekend or take the day off when the fishing is especially good, individuals will tend to conform to group norms about absence (Gellatly, 1995; Geurts, Buunk, & Schaufeli, 1994; Harrison & Schaffer, 1994; Mathieu & Kohler, 1990). Workgroup norms can lead to consequences more serious than absenteeism; deviant workgroup norms can encourage workers to steal from their employers and customers or to sabotage their work (Altheide, Adler, Adler, & Altheide, 1978; Greenberg, 1997; Greenberg & Scott, 1996; Hollinger & Clark, 1983).

We tend to think about crime in terms of violent felonies—murder, rape, assault, but the vast majority of crimes are both nonviolent and committed by otherwise honest, upstanding citizens (Gabor, 1994). A substantial portion of law-breaking involves fraud, violation of legal restrictions (e.g., driving while intoxicated), software and internet piracy, tax evasion, and the people who engage in these activities tend to believe that they are not doing anything wrong. Gabor (1994) explains this discrepancy by citing a distinction between *ideal* norms and *operational* norms—the way things *really* work. I believe that a better explanation is given by the fact that there are often important differences between the norms of society in general (ideal norms) and the norms of the particular reference groups whose influence is strongest (operational norms), and that when important reference groups establish a descriptive norm that a particular class of misbehaviors is, in fact, common or normal, people are more likely to go along with that norm. When important reference groups establish an injunctive norm that a particular class of misbehaviors is not only normal, but it is approved of by the group, the likelihood of following this destructive norm might increase substantially. For example, suppose your friends and family convey a strong message that law enforcement cannot be trusted and that the right thing is to talk to the neighborhood crime boss rather than to the police if someone steals your property. The societal norm may be to trust and rely on the police, but if important reference groups encourage you to take another path, you may be very reluctant to cooperate with the police or other law enforcement agencies.

Social Identity

Why are norms important? Why do we care about the opinions, beliefs, and preferences of reference groups? One answer is that social groups are a key part of our identity; we do not think about ourselves simply as individuals, but rather as a member of many different groups, some of which are a very important part of the way we see and understand ourselves. Social identify (Tajfel, 1974; Tajfel & Turner, 1979, 1986) and self-categorization theories (Turner, 1987, 1999) both emphasize the role of the group in forming and determining a person's identity, and both theories say that group norms are most powerful when that particular group represents an important part of the way a person represents or thinks of him- or herself.

Tajfel (1978) defined social identity as "that part of an individual's self-concept which derives from his knowledge of his membership of a social group (or groups) together with the value and emotional significance attached to that membership" (p. 63). Social Identity Theory argues that group members tend to use their group to maintain or enhance a positive social identity and self-esteem, and as a consequence are motivated to conform with norms that provide them with an in-group identity (i.e., identity as a member of the reference group), rather than an out-group one (Rubin & Hewstone, 1998).

Social identity and self-categorization theories suggest that we understand ourselves a part of one or more groups and that our self-evaluations (i.e., the extent to which we feel positively or negatively about ourselves) depend in large part on our relationship to and evaluations of these groups. That is, a person who has positive feelings about a group and identifies strongly with that group is likely to have a positive image of him- or herself. Different theories, however, make different predictions about comparisons you might make between yourself and a high-status or high-performing group member. Social Identity Theory suggests thinking about high-status members of your group will lead to increased levels of in-group identity, on the theory that you will admire and aspire to imitate high-status group members. Self-Evaluation Maintenance Theory (SEM; Tesser, 1988) suggests the opposite—that is, that upward in-group comparisons can be threatening, reducing identification with the group. Schmitt, Branscombe, Silva, Garcia, & Spears (2006) attempted to resolve these differing predictions using Self-Categorization Theory, arguing that SEM applies to contexts that make salient one's identity, and SIT applies to contexts that make collective identity salient. In other words, these theories suggest that the way a person categorizes him- or herself can be context-dependent.

Studies of social identity have yielded important insights for understanding misbehavior. For example, there is strong evidence that group norms have a strong effect on dishonest behavior in organizations (Kish-Gephart, Harrison, & Treviño, 2010). Individuals are more willing to cross moral boundaries if it will help them fit in (Leavitt & Sluss, 2015) or benefit their career/advance in the organization (Strelan & Beckmann, 2006). Similarly, studies of why people join terrorist groups show that members are often people who are in some sort of transition and are lacking a strong group identity—immigrants, people who have lost jobs, students—that these groups give them. Youth gangs are often successful in much the same way—that is, recruiting people who do not have other good prospects or strong group attachments. In both cases, acceptance by the group appears to be more important to many people than abiding by formal rules and regulations.

How the Presence and Example of Others Affects Behavior

Groups that are important to an individual influence his or her behavior, in large part by defining what is normal and what behaviors are approved of. However, this is not the only route to group influence. The mere presence of others, regardless of whether they are members of a group you identify with or aspire to join, can have a substantial effect on an individual's behavior. The literature on social forces that can influence behavior is extensive; in the sections that follow, I discuss research on four social processes that can, under the right circumstances, increase the likelihood that an individual will behave in ways that are destructive or harmful and that run counter to broadly accepted social norms: (1) social influence, (2) social diffusion and contagion, (3) diffusion of responsibility and bystander effects, and (4) escalation. In Chapter 2, I discussed several noteworthy examples of misbehavior, ranging from the Kitty Genovese incident to the Volkswagen scandal to the Rape of Nanjing and noted that one or more of these processes appeared to explain important aspects of these events.

Social Influence

The opinions, preferences, and beliefs of other people can influence one's behavior, even if those other people are not members of important reference groups. Latané (1981) proposed a very general Social Impact Theory in which the impact of others' attempts to influence a person's behavior is a multiplicative function of the strength, immediacy, and number of social influence sources. Strength refers to the set of factors that might make a particular person influential, such as status, wealth, power, or belonging to the same group. Immediacy refers to the recency of influence attempts. This theory suggests that there are many ways social influence attempts can be successful. For example, one very powerful or high-status person might be enough to influence your behavior but influence attempts from people who have no special status might be successful if enough people are trying to exert this influence at about the same time.

Latané (1996) extended this theory to explain processes by which groups develop and change and how social influence processes influence this development. His Dynamic Social Impact Theory proposes several different processes that influence the development of groups and especially the interplay between minority and majority subgroups (e.g., subgroups who have different opinions or approaches) that influence the eventual choices groups make. These include: (1) consolidation—as group members interact over time, their attitudes, opinions, and beliefs become more uniform, (2) clustering—group members who are closest to or who have the most frequent interactions with others have the largest influence on beliefs, attitudes, and opinions, and (3) continuing diversity—subgroups can become homogeneous and shielded from the rest of the group, creating distinct minorities within a group. This theory not only sheds light on how social influence spreads over time but also on ways minority subgroups can resist social influence by clustering together and walling themselves off from frequent interaction with the rest of their group.

MacDonald, Nail, and Levy (2004; See also Nail and MacDonald (2007) developed a model of social influence that tries to predict how people will react to attempts at social influence. For example, suppose a group is giving you signals that you should falsify an expense report. In predicting what you will do, this model takes into account: (1) your pre-exposure position regarding the behavior, (2) whether the behavior is private or public, and (3) your post-exposure position. The model takes as a starting point the proposition that social influence is more likely to be successful if it involves influencing you to do something you might be likely to do in any case, or at least that you would not find objectionable. Second, it predicts that it is harder to change your behavior if, for example, you have already made a public commitment to do something else (e.g., file an honest expense report) or if the results of your behavior will be known to others.

BOX 3.2 TACTICS FOR INFLUENCING OTHERS

There is a large literature on different tactics that might be used to influence people's behavior. Pratkanis (2007) compiled an extensive list of these tactics. For example, in a group that is charged with making a decision, you can influence the decisions the group will make by:

- Limiting choices of options
- Valence framing—frame decision in terms of gains vs. losses. People are loss averse (Kahneman & Tversky, 1979), so focusing on risks rather than potential benefits can discourage people from choosing a particular option
- Creating decoys—create an inferior option nobody would choose. Getting people to focus on and agree to reject this decoy can help steer them toward an alternative you prefer
- Asking (mis)leading questions—ask questions that structure information and imply certain answers or solutions
- Forming coalitions and packing committees with your supporters
- Creating an impression of a fait accompli—create the sense that an outcome is inevitable
- Being a credible source—be an admired person, or associate with one
- Emphasizing your shared characteristics with other group members
- Taking advantage of the bandwagon effect—emphasize the broad social consensus for a position
- Using the pique technique—make a strange or unusual request to pique someone's interest (e.g., a panhandler might ask "can you spare 17 cents" rather than "can you spare a quarter")

This is just a sampling of the techniques Pratkanis (2007) discusses, but they give us insight into the wide range of methods one might employ to influence the behavior of others.

All of the theories discussed here deal with the same basic question—that is, whether and how influence will occur. Some of this research deals with conscious attempts on the part of one or more individuals to influence someone else (e.g., Pratkanis' [2007] review of social influence tactics) while others deal with spontaneous processes by which influence occurs (e.g., consolidation). Both spontaneous influence processes and conscious decisions on the part of some individual or group to influence a person's behavior can lead that person to behave in ways that conform to social norms, rules, and laws or in ways that are harmful or destructive and that violate general social norms. The theories described here provide a roadmap for how that influence is likely to be manifest and how it is likely to work.

Social Diffusion and Contagion

People are motivated to share information, even in cases where the information is false or not completely believed by the recipients (Karlova & Fisher, 2013). This process of diffusion of information has potentially important implications for understanding misbehavior. First, the objective truth of information is important, but the truth is not always the most important determinant of whether this information will spread. On the contrary, people are considerably more receptive to information if it fits with their preconceptions (Nickerson, 1998). I will discuss this process in more detail in Chapter 4, but one implication of this bias toward confirming prior opinions and beliefs is that information that fits with beliefs about what is normal and expected (i.e., descriptive norms) is more likely to be accepted and to spread from person to person. Of course, normative information is not always true, but to the extent it makes sense to individuals and fits with their preconceptions, it is likely to be accepted and to spread.

Researchers in several disciplines have been interested in the study of the diffusion of information in groups of people. For example, several studies have developed mathematical models of the spread of rumors (e.g., Isea & Mayo-García., 2015). Similarly, there have been studies of the diffusion of information in social networks and over social media (e.g., Louni & Subbalakshm, 2014). The mathematical models in these papers are often impressive, but these models rarely consider the psychological factors (e.g., prior knowledge, confirmation biases, consistency with norms) that make people more or less receptive to new information. This line of research would arguably advance more rapidly and yield more useful insights if the mathematical sophistication of the analytic and descriptive models developed in communications research and allied fields could be combined with the insights of psychologists on factors that make people more or less willing to pass on and to accept information.

People not only communicate information; they also communicate emotional states. Ideas like "crowd mind", the contagion of mood and loss of individuality were prominent in early theorizing about crowd behavior, particularly the behavior of mobs. Early ideas about "crowd mind" began to fall out of favor by the

1980s, in part because they were descriptive rather than explanatory (Hatfield, Cacioppo, & Rapson, 1994). That is, they described a phenomenon but do little to explain it.

Research on emotional contagion (i.e., the spread of emotional states from person to person has drawn on theories from a range of fields (e.g., Evolutionary Theory, cognitive psychology) to try and explain how one person's emotional state might influence the emotions experienced by others he or she comes into contact with. Hatfield, Cacioppo, and Rapson (1994) note that

> emotional contagion is also a multilevel phenomenon: The precipitating stimuli arise from one individual, act upon (i.e., be perceived and interpreted by) one or more other individuals, and yield corresponding or corresponding/complementary emotions in these individuals. Thus, an important consequence of emotional contagion is an attentional, emotional, and behavioral synchrony that has the same adaptive utility (and drawbacks) for social entities (dyads or groups) as has emotion for any individual.
>
> *(p. 160)*

Modern thinking on emotional contagion (Hatfield et al., 1994; Lynch, 1996) has suggested a specific physical to emotional pathway by which contagion is likely to occur. First, people tend to mimic other people's facial expressions, speech patterns, gestures, motor activity, and expressions of emotion (e.g., laughter, shouting). A key concept in this literature is referred to as primitive emotional contagion—that is, the tendency to mimic and synchronize facial expressions, vocalizations, postures, and movements with those of another person's and, consequently, to converge emotionally. This primitive emotional contagion is relatively automatic, unintentional, uncontrollable, and largely inaccessible to awareness. Individuals who mimic another person's expressions, postures, and movements are, in turn, likely to experience the emotions that are associated with those expressions, that speech, those gestures, or movement. That is, this mimicry of behavior tends to lead to common experiences of emotion. For example, viewing emotional facial expressions elicits facial expressions in the viewer, and the viewer's facial expressions, in turn, elicit changes in one's emotional state.

Emotional contagion is thought to be a key determinant of the behavior of mobs (Carrigan, 2008). One of the consistent themes in reports of the behavior of lynch mobs is the high level of emotional intensity of the crowd and the spread of that emotion from person to person. Indeed, you could argue that a high level of emotional intensity is almost a prerequisite for many types of mob violence; it is unlikely that individuals, acting alone in a state where they were able to calmly think through the justification and implications of their behavior, would break down the doors of jails, haul screaming victims to a tree, and hang them or burn them alive.

Emotions are contagious, but so are patterns of behavior. We learn how to behave by observing and imitating others (Bandura, 1977), and that imitation can sometimes lead to misbehavior. For example, one of the factors that can lead individuals to commit crimes, violate rules, or misbehave is contagious dishonesty or the tendency for people to be more likely to engage in dishonest behavior when they see others similar to them do the same (Gino & Galinsky, 2012; Innes & Mitra, 2012). Reference groups are often powerful forces in shaping the behavior of individuals, but even the mere presence of others who are not part of a meaningful reference group can lead to powerful processes in which behaviors are modeled and observed and in which information, emotion, and behaviors can spread from one person to another.

Diffusion of Responsibility and Bystander Effects

Some types of misbehavior are acts of omission rather than acts of commission. You might see a person carrying heavy packages fall on the sidewalk in front of you, and simply walk by without offering to help. You might witness a crime and fail to call the police, not wanting to get involved. There are several social and psychological processes that can lead to these results. I will discuss two of these processes in this section: (1) diffusion of responsibility and (2) bystander effects. These related effects occur when there is a group of people present, and it is not completely clear who is responsible.

In Chapter 2, I discussed the Kitty Genovese incident. Kitty was violently murdered, and the initial reports in the media suggested that there were many witnesses to this murder, none of whom intervened or called the police. This shocking murder was a stimulus for many studies of the "bystander effect"—that is, the tendency for individuals to fail to offer help to a victim when other people are present. This research has helped in identifying factors that can either contribute to or diminish the bystander effect. For example, bystander effects are typically stronger when the number of non-helping bystanders increases (Latané & Nida, 1981). Bystanders are more likely to help if the victim asks for help (especially if the victim asks a specific individual to help as opposed to calling more generally for help) and if the situation is a severe emergency rather than a minor nuisance. Thus, bystanders are more likely to respond if you are seriously hurt than if you drop a book or a package.

There have been numerous studies of the bystander effect, and meta-analyses of these studies confirm the strength and generality of the effect, as well as some of the factors that moderate bystander effects (e.g., emergencies, the degree of danger involved in responding; Latané & Nida, 1981; Fischer et al., 2011). There have been numerous applications of this research, including studies of responses (or failure to respond) to war crimes and genocide. Two sets of studies focused on factors that reduce external bystanders' willingness to support interventions and aid to victims of genocide. One of these factors is the tendency to blame victims for their fate. A series of studies conducted among British students demonstrated that people were more likely to donate money to aid victims of the 2004 tsunami in Asia than to aid victims of the genocide in Darfur because victims of the genocide were blamed more for their plight than were victims of the natural disaster (Zagefka, Noor, Brown, de Moura, & Hopthrow, 2011). Another series of studies demonstrated a "collapse of compassion" in the face of the enormous suffering caused by genocide (Cameron & Payne, 2011; Slovic, 2007).

Latané and Darley (1968) note that the first step in responding in a bystander situation is simply noticing that there is a problem or emergency that might require a response (see also Darley & Latané, 1968). Individuals who notice a potential problem must also recognize it as such. One of the critiques of early coverage of the Kitty Genovese murder was that many of the so-called witnesses may not have actually seen or heard anything or may not have interpreted what they saw or heard as an emergency requiring response (Manning, Levine, & Collins, 2007). On the other hand, people's reports of what they saw or heard are not always reliable, and it is possible that some people who failed to respond came to believe or convinced themselves that they had not *really* seen or heard anything. I will explore this type of motivated thinking in Chapter 4.

Individuals who recognize that there is a situation where some help or some active response is required may still fail to act if it is unclear *who* should help. They may, for example, believe that they are not competent to help (e.g., they do not have the medical knowledge to respond effectively to someone who is injured). More commonly, each member of a group of bystanders might recognize that *someone* should help, but also be uncertain whether *they* should help. The process of the diffusion of responsibility across members of a group is a general process that is not limited to bystander events (Treviño, Den Nieuwenboer, & Kish-Gaphart, 2014).

Bystander effects are usually thought of as occurring in nominal groups—that is, groups of people who happen to be gathered together at some place and point in time, but who do not have a common identify or purpose, but diffusion of responsibility occurs in many types of groups, and its effects are arguably stronger in groups that have a definite structure and clearly defined roles and responsibilities for members (Treviño et al. 2014). This is particularly true in groups where responsibility for decisions resides in (or can appear to reside in) formal leaders. The term "displacement of responsibility" refers to the process of attributing responsibility for one's actions to authority figures who may have tacitly condoned or explicitly directed behavior (Treviño et al., 2014). A recurring theme in research on diffusion and displacement of responsibility is that group members come to believe that the response a situation requires is not their responsibility. They may believe that there is someone in the group who is responsible for responding, or there might be real ambiguity about who should respond. In subsequent chapters that deal with misbehavior in formal groups and organizations,

I will explore several structural features of groups that can lead to diffusion or displacement of responsibility.

Escalation of Conflict

Conflicts between individuals have a nasty way of morphing into conflicts between groups. Conflicts can even create groups, by being the foundation for dividing a mass of people into groups with conflicting goals (Eckert & Willems, 2003). There are many different models of the processes by which conflicts emerge, become more serious, and get settled (e.g., Glasl, 1999; Lund, 1996), but they share many common elements. In particular, the process of conflict escalation, which expands the scope and intensity of conflicts is central to most models of interpersonal or intergroup conflict, and a key aspect of escalation is the tendency for individuals involved in a conflict to seek allies and supporters, moving from conflicts between individuals to conflicts between groups.

Several of the social processes discussed in this chapter can lead to the escalation of conflict between groups—that is, a process by which initially small conflicts can become more intense and serious over time. Conflict often escalates through a series of feedback loops. First, conflict between groups tends to enhance the solidarity of the groups (Coser, 1956). This starts a chain of events elaborated in Collins' (2004) model of human interactions in the face of conflict. According to this model:

- Conflict motivates people to interact, and these face-to-face interactions provide a means of communicating emotions and signals of group identification
- Attention to the conflict focuses group members' attention on the actions of their rivals and the actions of their group
- Anger and fear of rivals heightens emotions within each group
- These first three processes heighten perceptions of group solidarity and the willingness of group members to sacrifice their interests to the interests of the group
- These processes also create sharper boundaries between groups, in particular, a good (own group) vs. evil (rival group) boundary. Beliefs about the rival's actions become increasingly extreme (in warfare, it is common to believe that opponents are committing atrocities), which increases group polarization
- These same processes produce high levels of emotional energy and confidence in the victory of your group

The Collins (2004) model shares an important feature with many other models of conflict escalation—that is, a mix of cognitive and emotional processes. Conflict channels people's attention and perception to focus on the actions of their group and those of the competitor group. This heightened attention makes these actions more salient, but this by itself is probably not sufficient to trigger meaningful conflict. Rather, conflict escalates as emotions are engaged. Earlier, I discussed processes of emotional contagion and noted that they can lead to ugly extremes of behavior (e.g., the formation of lynch mobs). Even when emotions are not directly or indirectly communicated to other group members, a conflict can elicit emotions, which can, in turn, make the conflict more intense.

Collins (2011) notes that conflicts do not last forever and charts the processes by which conflicts de-escalate. He notes that group members may start to avoid within-group interactions as a result of conflict (or as a result of the resolution of conflicts, as in the case of one side defeating another in a war), and that high levels of emotional activation are likely at some point to lead to burnout, reducing the emotional intensity of the conflict.

Summary

Many social processes can contribute to misbehavior. Of these, norms are probably the most important. Groups develop both descriptive norms (i.e., expectations of what is typical or normal) and injunctive norms (i.e., beliefs about what people should or should not do), and these norms have a powerful impact on behavior. In particular, misbehavior is highly likely if the norms of important groups (reference groups) run counter to the norms of society in general. The fact that most people belong to many groups, whose norms might differ, is critical for understanding the social origins of many classes of misbehavior. Individuals who engage in patterns of behavior that are harmful or destructive and that violate the norms of society in general often believe that they are in fact doing the right thing because their behaviors conform to the norms of the particular groups they belong to or identify with.

The norms of the various groups you belong to are important precisely because group membership is an important component of a person's identity. People have a strong motivation to maintain a positive self-image, and one part of that effort is to follow the norms of the reference groups you most closely identify with; if the group says that a particular behavior is good, carrying out that behavior can contribute to a positive self-image.

The preferences, beliefs, and norms of important reference groups are a critical factor in determining whether individuals will engage in particular classes of misbehavior, but they are not the only factor. Other people can influence your behavior even if they are not part of a group you belong to or aspire to belong to. For example, you are subject to a barrage of social influence attempts (e.g., television commercials, political campaigns, community outreach) daily, and this can include negative or destructive influence. Both information and emotional states can spread from person to person, and this contagion can transform individuals who would otherwise be peaceful and law-abiding into a howling, violent mob. The presence of others might diminish your sense of responsibility to respond to persons in need or may lead to ambiguity about who should undertake what responses. Finally, the presence of others will sometimes lead to conflicts, and conflict often leads to a cycle of escalation in which conflict spreads to others and intensifies. Understanding the processes that lead to conflict escalation and de-escalation can be critical to preventing conflicts from getting out of hand.

Note

1. However, they are not always equally relevant to all group members. High-status group members often have more latitude in terms of obeying or violating norms

References

Altheide, D.L., Adler, P.A., Alder, P. & Altheide, D.A. (1978). The social meanings of employee theft. In J.M. Johnson & J.D. Douglas (Eds.), *Crime at the Top: Deviance in Business and the Professions*. Philadelphia: J.B. Lippincott.

Avery, D.R., Hernandez, M. & Hebl, M.R. (2004). Who's watching the race? Racial salience in recruitment advertising. *Journal of Applied Social Psychology, 34*, 146–161.

Bandura, A. (1977). *Social Learning Theory*. Englewood Cliffs, NJ: Prentice-Hall.

Bandura, A. (1986). *Social Foundations of Thought and Action: A Social Cognitive Theory*. Englewood Cliffs, NJ: Prentice-Hall.

Cameron, C. & Payne, B. (2011). Escaping affect: How motivated emotion regulation creates insensitivity to mass suffering. *Journal of Personality and Social Psychology, 100*, 1–15.

Carrigan, W.D. (2008). *Lynching Reconsidered: New Perspectives in the Study of Mob Violence*. New York: Routledge.

Cialdini, R.B., Kallgren, C.A. & Reno, R.R. (1991). A focus theory of normative conduct. *Advances in Experimental Social Psychology, 24*, 201–234.

Collins, R. (2004). *Interaction Ritual Chains*. Princeton, NJ: Princeton University Press.

Collins, R. (2011). C-escalation and D-escalation: A theory of the time dynamics of conflict. *American Sociological Review*, 77, 1–20.

Coscarelli, J. (2014). Eternally outraged congressman not trying to be 'trivial,' but doesn't think Obama's tan suit was appropriate. *New York Magazine*, http://nymag.com/intelligencer/2014/08/peter-king-outraged-over-obamas-tan-suit.html

Coser, L. (1956). *The Functions of Social Conflict*. Glencoe, IL: Free Press.

Darley, J.M. & Latané, B. (1968). Bystander intervention in emergencies: Diffusion of responsibility. *Journal of Personality and Social Psychology, 8*, 377–383.

Eckert, R. & Willems, H. (2003). Escalation and de-escalation of social conflicts: The road to violence. InW. Heitmeyer and J. Hagan (eds) *International Handbook of Violence Research*. Springer, Dordrecht.

Ellemers, N. (2017). *Morality and the Regulation of Social Behavior: Groups as Moral Anchors*. New York: Routledge.

Feldman, D.C. (1984). The development and enforcement of group norms. *Academy of Management Review, 9*, 47–53.

Fischer, P., Greitemeyer, T., Kastenmuller, A., Krueger, J.I., Vogrincic, C., Frey, D. et al. (2011). The bystander effect: A meta-analytic review on bystander intervention in dangerous and non-dangerous emergencies. *Psychological Bulletin, 137*, 517–537.

Frone, M.R. (2009). Does a permissive workplace substance use climate affect employees who do not use alcohol and drugs at work? A U.S. national study. *Psychology of Addictive Behaviors, 23*, 386–390.

Frone, M.R. (2012). Workplace substance use climate: Prevalence and distribution in the U.S. workforce. *Journal of Substance Use, 17*, 72–83.

Gabar, H. & Stern, M.J. (2018, May 10). The privilege of 911. *Slate*, https://slate.com/news-and-politics/2018/05/in-america-calling-911-is-still-a-privilege-of-being-white.html

Gavac, S., Murrar, S. & Brauer, M. (2017). Group perception and social norms. In R. Summers (Ed.), *Social Psychology: How Other People Influence Our Thoughts and Actions* (pp. 333–361). Santa Barbara, CA: ABC-CLIO.

Gellatly, I.R. (1995). Individual and group determinants of employee absenteeism: Test of a causal model. *Journal of Organizational Behavior, 16*, 469–485.

Gelfand, M.J. et al. (2011). Differences between tight and loose cultures: A 33 nation study. *Science, 32*, 1100–1104.

Gelfand, M.J., Harrington, J.R. & Jackson, J.C. (2017). The strength of social norms across social groups. *Perspectives of Psychological Science, 12*, 800–809.

Glasl, F. (1999). *Confronting Conflict. A First-Aid Kit for Handling Conflict*. Gloucestershire, U.K.: Hawthorn Press.

Glynn, C.G., Huge, M.E. & Lunney, C.A. (2009). Influence of perceived social norms on college students' intention to vote. *Political Communication, 26*, 48–64,

Geurts, S.A., Buunk, B.P. & Schaufeli, W.B. (1994). Health complaints, social comparisons, and absenteeism. *Work and Stress, 8*, 220–234.

Gino, F., Ayal, S. & Ariely, D. (2009). Contagion and differentiation in unethical behavior: The effect of one bad apple on the barrel. *Psychological Science, 20*, 393–398.

Gino, F. & Galinsky, A.D. (2012). Vicarious dishonesty: When psychological closeness creates distance from one's moral compass. *Organizational Behavior and Human Decision Processes, 119*, 15–26.

Goldberg, C.B. (2005). Relational demography and similarity-attraction in interview assessments and subsequent offer decisions: Are we missing something? *Group and Organization Management, 30*, 597–624.

Greenberg, J. (1997). The STEAL motive: Managing the social determinants of employee theft. In R. Giacalone & J. Greenberg (Eds.), *Antisocial Behavior in Organizations* (pp. 85–108). Thousand Oaks, CA: Sage.

Greenberg, J. & Scott, K.S. (1996). Why do workers bite the hands that feed them? Employee theft as a social exchange process. In B.M. Staw & L.L. Cummings (Eds.), *Research in Organizational Behavior* (Vol. 18, pp. 111–156). Greenwich, CT, and London: JAI Press.

Harrison, D.A. & Shaffer, M.A. (1994). Comparative examinations of self-reports and perceived absenteeism norms: Wading through Lake Wobegon. *Journal of Applied Psychology, 79*, 240–251.

Hatfield, E., Cacioppo, J.T. & Rapson, R.L. (1994). *Emotional Contagion*. Paris: University of Cambridge Press.

Heilman, M.E. (1983). Sex bias in work settings: The lack of fit model. *Research in Organizational Behavior, 5*, 269–298.

Heilman, M.E. & Chen, J.J. (2005). Same behavior, different consequences: Reactions to men's and women's altruistic citizenship behavior. *Journal of Applied Psychology, 90*, 431–441.

Hofstede, G. (1980). *Culture's Consequences: International Differences in Work-Related Values*. Beverly Hills, CA: Sage.

Hofstede, G. (2001). *Culture's Consequences: Comparing Values, Behaviors, Institutions and Organizations Across Nations*. Thousand Oaks, CA: Sage.

Hofstede, G., Hofstede, G.J. & Minkov, M. (2010). *Cultures and Organizations: Software of the Mind*. Revised and Expanded 3rd Ed. New York: McGraw-Hill.

Hofstede, G., Neuijen, B., Ohayv, D.D. & Sanders, G. (1990). Measuring organizational cultures, *Administrative Science Quarterly, 35*, 286–316.

Hogg, M.A. (2010). Influence and leadership. In S.T. Fiske, D.T. Gilbert, & G. Lindzey (Eds.), *Handbook of Social Psychology* (pp. 1166–1207). Hoboken, NJ: Wiley.

Hogg, M.A. & Abrams, D. (1988). *Social Identifications: A Social Psychology of Intergroup Relations and Group Processes*. London: Routledge.

Hogg, M.A. & Mullin, B.A. (1999). Joining groups to reduce uncertainty: Subjective uncertainty reduction and group identification. In D. Abram & M.A. Hogg (Eds.), *Social Identity and Social Cognition* (pp. 249–279). Oxford, UK: Blackwell.

Hogg, M.A. & Terry, D.J. (2000). Social identity and self-categorization processes in organizational contexts. *Academy of Management Review, 25*, 121–140.

Hollinger, R.C. & Clark, J.P. (1983). *Theft by Employees*. Lexington, MA: Heath.

Innes, R. & Mitra, A. (2012). Is dishonesty contagious? *Economic Inquiry, 51*, 722–734.

Isea, R. & Mayo-García, R. (2015). Mathematical analysis of the spreading of a rumor among different subgroups of spreaders. *Pure and Applied Mathematics Letters, 2015*, 50–54.

Jackson, J. (1965). Structural characteristics of norms. In L. Steiner & M. Fishbein (Eds.), *Current studies in social psychology* (pp. 301–309). New York: Holt, Rinehart & Winston.

Kahneman, D. & Tversky, A. (1979). Prospect theory: An analysis of decision under risk. *Econometrica, 47*, 263–291.

Karlova, N.A. & Fisher, K.E. (2013). A social diffusion model of misinformation and disinformation for understanding human information behavior. *Information Research, 18*(1), paper 573.

Kemper, T.D. (1966). Representative roles and the legitimation of deviance. *Social Problems, 13*, 288–298.

Kim, M.S., Hunter, J.E. (1993). Attitude-behavior relations: A meta-analysis of attitudinal relevance and topic. *Journal of Communication, 43*, 101–142.

Kish-Gephart, J.J., Harrison, D.A. & Treviño, L.K. (2010). Bad apples, bad cases, and bad barrels: Meta-analytic evidence about sources of unethical decisions at work. *Journal of Applied Psychology, 95*, 1–31.

Kohlberg, L. (1969). Stage and sequence: The cognitive developmental approach to socialization. In D.A. Goslin (Ed.), *Handbook of Socialization Theory and Research* (pp. 347–480). Chicago: Rand McNally.

Lapinski, M.K. & Rimal, R.N. (2005). An explication of social norms. *Communication Theory, 15*, 127–147.

Latané, B. (1981). The psychology of social impact. *American Psychologist, 36*, 343–356.

Latané, B. (1996). Dynamic social impact. In R. Hegselmann, U. Mueller and K.G. Mueller (Eds.), *Modelling and Simulation in the Social Sciences from the Philosophy of Science Point of View* (pp. 287–310). Dordecht, Germany: Springer.

Latané, B. & Darley, J.M. (1968). Group inhibition of bystander intervention in emergencies. *Journal of Personality and Social Psychology, 10*, 308–324.

Latané, B. & Nida, S. (1981). Ten years of research on group size and helping. *Psychological Bulletin, 89*, 307–324.

Leavitt, K. & Sluss, D.M. (2015). Lying for who we are: An identity-based model of workplace dishonesty. *Academy of Management Review, 40*, 587–610.

Lopez, G. (2016, Aug. 8). Black parents describe "The Talk" they give to their children about police. *Vox*, www.vox.com/2016/8/8/12401792/police-black-parents-the-talk

Louni, A. & Subbalakshm, K.P. (2014). Diffusion of information in social networks. In: M. Panda, S. Dehuri, & G.N. Wang (Eds.), *Social Networking. Intelligent Systems Reference Library* (Vol. 65, pp. 1–2r). Cham: Springer.

Lund, M.S. (1996). *Preventing Violent Conflicts: A Strategy for Preventive Diplomacy*. Washington, DC: United States Institute of Peace Press.

Lynch, A. (1996). *Thought Contagion: How Beliefs Spread Through Society*. New York: Basic Books.

MacDonald, G., Nail, P.R. & Levy, D.A. (2004). Expanding the scope of the Social Context Response Model. *Basic and Applied Social Psychology, 26*, 77–92.

Manning, R., Levine, M. & Collins, A. (2007). The Kitty Genovese murder and the social psychology of helping: The parable of the 38 witnesses. *American Psychologist, 62*, 555–562.

Mathieu, J.E. & Kohler, S.S. (1990). A cross-level examination of group absence influences on individual absence. *Journal of Applied Psychology, 75*, 217–220.

Misangy, V.F. & Weaver, G.R. (2008). Ending corruption: The interplay among institutional logics, resources, and institutional entrepreneurs. *Academy of Management Review, 33*, 73–770.

Moore, C. & Gino, F. (2013). Ethically adrift: How others pull our moral compass from true north and how we can fix it. *Research in Organizational Behavior*, 33, 53–77.

Nail, P.R. & MacDonald, G. (2007). On the development of the Social Response Context Model. In A.R. Pratkanis (Ed.), *The Science of Social Influence* (pp. 193–222). New York: Psychology Press.

Nickerson, R.S. (1998). Confirmation bias: A ubiquitous phenomenon in many guises. *Review of General Psychology, 2*, 175–220.

Nolan, J. (2015). Using Jackson's Return Potential Model to explore the normativeness of recycling. *Environment and Behavior, 47*, 835–855.

Paluck, E.L. & Shepherd, H. (2012). The salience of social referents: A field experiment on collective norms and harassment behavior in a school social network. *Journal of Personality and Social Psychology, 103*, 899–915.

Pratkanis, A.R. (2007). Social influence analysis: An index of tactics. In A.R. Pratkanis (Ed.), *The Science of Social Influence* (pp. 17–82). New York: Psychology Press.

Robinson, S.L. & O'Leary-Kelly, A.M. (1998). Monkey see, monkey do: The influence of workgroups on the antisocial behavior of employees. *Academy of Management Journal, 41*, 658–672.

Rogers, C. (1959). A theory of therapy, personality and interpersonal relationships as developed in the client-centered framework. In S. Koch (Ed.), *Psychology: A Study of a Science: Formulations of the Person and the Social Context* (Vol. 3, pp. 184–256). New York: McGraw Hill.

Rubin, M. & Hewstone, M. (1998). Social identity theory's self-esteem hypothesis: A review and some suggestions for clarification. *Personality and Social Psychology Review, 2*, 40–62.

Schmitt, M.T., Branscombe, N.J., Silva, P.J., Garcia, D.M. & Spears, M. (2006). Categorizing at the group-level in response to intra group social comparisons: A self-categorization theory integration of self-evaluation and social identity motives. *European Journal of Social Psychology, 36*, 297–314.

Scott, W.R. (1995). *Institutions and organizations*. Thousand Oaks, CA: Sage.

Slovic, P. (2007). "If I look at the mass I will never act": Psychic numbing and genocide. *Judgment and Decision Making, 2*, 79–95.

Strelan, P. & Beckmann, R. (2006). Why drug testing in elite sports does not work: Perceptual deterrence theory and the role of personal moral beliefs. *Journal of Applied Social Psychology, 36*, 2909–2934.

Tajfel, H. (1974). Social identity and intergroup behaviour. *Social Science Information, 13*, 65–93.

Tajfel, H. (1978). The achievement of inter-group differentiation. In H. Tajfel (Ed.), *Differentiation between Social Groups* (pp. 77–100). London: Academic Press.

Tajfel, H. (1982). *Social Identity and Intergroup Relations*. Cambridge, UK: Cambridge University Press.

Tajfel, H. & Turner, J.C. (1979). An integrative theory of intergroup conflict. In S. Worchel & W.G. Austin (Eds.), *The Social Psychology of Intergroup Relations* (pp. 33–37). Chicago: Nelson Hall.

Tajfel, H. & Turner, J. (1986). The social identity theory of intergroup behavior. In S. Worchel & W.G. Austin (Eds.), *The Psychology of Intergroup Relations* (pp. 7–24). Chicago, IL: Nelson-Hall.

Tankard, M.E. & Paluck, E.E. (2016). Norm perception as a vehicle for social change. *Social Issues and Policy Review, 10*, 181–211.

Tesser, A. (1988). Toward a self-evaluation maintenance model of social behavior. *Advances in Experimental Social Psychology, 21*, 181–227.

Treviño, L.K., Den Nieuwenboer, N.A. & Kish-Gaphart, J.J. (2014). (Un)ethical behavior in organizations. *Annual Review of Psychology, 65*, 635–660.

Trockel, M., Williams, S. & Reis, J. (2003). Considerations for more effective social norms based alcohol education on campus: An analysis of different theoretical conceptualizations in predicting drinking among fraternity men. *Journal of Studies on Alcohol, 64*, 550–559.

Turner, J.C. (1987). A self-categorization theory. In J.C. Turner, M.A. Hogg, P.J. Oakes, S.D. Reicher, & M.S. Wetherell (Eds.), *Rediscovering the Social Group: A Self-Categorization Theory* (pp. 43–67). Oxford: Blackwell.

Turner, J.C. (1999). Some current issues in research on social identity and self-categorization theories. In N. Ellemers, R. Spears, & B. Doosje (Eds.), *Social identity: Context, Commitment, Content* (pp. 6–34). Oxford, England: Blackwell.

Wahrman, R. (1970). Status, deviance and sanctions. *The Pacific Sociological Review, 13*, 229–240.

Wilder, D.A. (1990). Some determinants of persuasive power of in-groups and out-groups: Organization of information and attribution of independence. *Journal of Personality and Social Psychology, 59*, 1202–1213.

Wilson, K.L., Lizzio, A.J., Zauner, S. & Gallois, C. (2001). Social rules for managing attempted interpersonal domination in the workplace: Influence of status and gender. *Sex Roles, 44*, 129–154.

Zagefka, H., Noor, M., Brown, R., de Moura, G.R. & Hopthrow, T. (2011). Donating to disaster victims: Responses to natural and humanly caused events. *European Journal of Social Psychology, 41*, 353–363.

4

COGNITIVE PROCESSES THAT ENABLE OR SUPPORT MISBEHAVIOR

This chapter deals with cognitive processes, and more particularly, the processes that affect how people think about their behavior and the behavior of others. I will review research documenting a wide range of processes that lead people to distort or adjust their perceptions, memories, and conclusions about behavior in social settings in ways that allow them to misbehave without feeling discomfort or remorse. One way of understanding the links between the different cognitive processes that allow people to behave badly while still thinking of themselves as good people is to think about why people might be motivated to think about their behavior and misbehavior in this way.

Several factors motivate people's behavior, but two factors consistently emerge in reviews of research on cognitive processes that affect how people think about their own behavior and the behavior of others (see, for example, Elstak, Bhatt, Van Rielk, Pratt, & Berens, 2015; Hogg & Mullin, 1999; Reid & Hogg, 2005). First, people are strongly motivated to maintain a positive self-image (Tajfel, 1982; Tajfel & Turner, 1979). Many psychologists believe that the maintenance of self-esteem or self-worth is among the strongest and most persistent of human goals (Hales, 1985).

Second, uncertainty makes people uncomfortable, and people are strongly motivated to find ways of reducing uncertainty and ambiguity. Social groups are often highly important in providing information and in providing a context for making sense of information. As I noted in Chapter 3, groups help to define people's understanding of what is normal and typical, of what is going on in their social environment, and of what is acceptable and approved of. The more closely an individual identifies with the group, the more likely he or she is to act consistently with the group's beliefs, norms, and values, and generally to act in "group-typical" ways (Ashforth & Mael, 1989; Dutton & Dukerich, 1991;

Hogg & Abrams, 1988), and the less uncertainty he or she will feel about how to make sense of the environment and how to act.

In this chapter, I will discuss research on cognitive processes that lead people to think about their behavior in ways that absolve them of guilt or discomfort when they behave in ways that violate widely accepted norms. I will start, though, by discussing ways people resolve uncertainty by learning what they *should* do in different situations.

Social Learning

Throughout their lives, people learn what they should and should not do through a wide range of experiences and sources. Parents, schools, churches, and other institutions teach people what they are expected to do. Societies develop strong descriptive and prescriptive norms that: (1) allow people to make sense of the world (descriptive norms), and (2) tell them what they should do (prescriptive norms). One explanation for behavior that seems to run counter to widely accepted social norms (e.g., telling lies, hurting others) is that people often learn a complex set of norms that are not always consistent. For example, people might accept the broad social norm that we should not tell lies but might also adopt a set of norms that are particular to their social group, workplace, occupation, etc. that tell them that a certain behavior (e.g., taking a business tax deduction for a social lunch with a group of friends) is not *really* wrong, because everyone does it or it is not *really* lying. One explanation for behaviors that violate broad social norms is that people have learned other norms that allow, and sometimes even encourage them to behave in ways that are not approved of by society as a whole, but that are accepted by important reference groups.

Social Learning Theory describes how people's behavior is learned through observing and imitating the behaviors of others and seeing how these behaviors can be positively reinforced by rewards and negatively reinforced by punishments (Weiss, 1990). That is, people observe the behavior from others within their environment to obtain information about values, norms, expectations, and behavior outcomes (Glomb & Liao, 2003). These social norms guide people's behavior (Goldstein & Cialdini, 2007), and if these norms accept or encourage behavior that runs counter to general social norms, the likelihood that individuals will break with those general norms increases. As Goldstein and Cialdini (2007) note, "our personal conviction of what we consider moral behavior is shaped in part by the norms, conventions and practices of the social groups that are important to us" (p. 13).

According to Social Information Processing Theory, individuals develop attitudes about their surroundings that are in line with normative group behaviors and their typical consequences (Cialdini & Trost, 1998; Salancik & Pfeffer, 1978). As an example, employees who observe their managers or coworkers engaging in dishonest behaviors, such as taking home office supplies or getting reimbursed for personal expenses without notice or punishment from the company, will likely conclude that these behaviors are acceptable and may start to adopt these behaviors themselves. Both Social Learning Theory (Bandura, 1977) and Social Information Processing Theory (Salancik & Pfeffer, 1978) have been used by researchers to explain deviant and antisocial behaviors (Fine, Horowitz, Weigler, & Basis, 2010). Both theories suggest that if a situation permits behavior that violates general social norms, then one should expect to observe these violations (Shu, Gino, & Bazerman, 2011).

Social Comparison Theory suggests another process by which we might adopt the norms of a particular reference group. In particular, this theory suggests that we may adopt the norms of groups we aspire to join, for example by comparing oneself to and by imitating the behavior of superiors or people higher in status (Gerber, Wheeler, & Suls, 2018). Once again, if the norms if these groups run counter to the norms of general society, the likelihood of misbehavior increases.

Social Construction of Reality

Descriptive and injunctive norms tell us a great deal about what is going on and how it should be interpreted. More broadly, the beliefs, attitudes, and perceptions of members of important reference groups help to shape your perception of the world and your behavior (Ferguson & Bargh, 2004), even when these perceptions, attitudes, and beliefs do not deal with normative matters (i.e., what is normal, customary, or expected; what is good or bad, approved of or sanctioned). One way to interpret this body of research is to recognize that drawing on the perceptions and beliefs of others helps to reduce uncertainty.

Individuals who identify with different reference groups can have fundamentally different perceptions of and beliefs about reality. For example, there has been a growing trend of political polarization in the United States since at least the 1990s (Pew Research Center, 2015, 2016). One manifestation of this polarization is people who are strongly committed to particular political points of view of different news sources (e.g., Fox News vs. MSNBC) and develop consistently different beliefs about what is important, what is happening, and what forces are driving society (Mitchell, Gottfried, Kiley, & Matsa, 2014).

The importance of socially defined perceptions of reality has long been recognized. Almost a century ago, Thomas and Thomas (1928) developed what has come to be known as the Thomas Theorem—that is, if people define situations as real, they are real in their consequences. The effects of the perceptions, beliefs, and attitudes of others in defining your own perceptions are arguably strongest when: (1) important norms are involved, (2) the reference groups are important to you, and (3) these attitudes, beliefs, and perceptions are held by high-status members of these groups. The beliefs, attitudes, and perceptions of others not only shape our *perception* of reality, they can also shape reality itself. For example, suppose I mistakenly label you as hostile, based on the attitudes and beliefs of my coworkers. My behavior toward you might be more aggressive and defensive, and that in turn might make you more hostile. The beliefs we hold about people are often confirmed because we behave in ways that make their confirmation more likely, and this has clear implications for misbehavior. Snyder and Swan (1978) note, "Having once been tagged with a label that implies deviance, one's behavioral options may be constrained in a way that force one to become deviant" (p. 148). The belief that some people are trustworthy and that others should be carefully watched will change your behavior toward those persons, and it might bring about the very thing you first believed to be true, even if your initial beliefs were unfounded or incorrect.

Primary Socialization Theory

Primary Socialization Theory (Oetting, Deffenbacher, & Donnermeyer, 1998; Oetting & Donnermeyer, 1998) was developed to integrate research on personal characteristics and social influences in the etiology of adolescent deviance. This theory provides useful insights for explaining the way individuals learn norms that may conflict with one another (e.g., a general social norm that honesty is important and a group norm that everyone inflates their expense claims). The fundamental premise of Primary Socialization Theory is that many, if not all, social behaviors are learned, including deviance. This learning takes place through interactions within a network of socialization sources that define, monitor, and sanction behavior. Ultimately, it is the interactions between the individual and the primary socialization forces that dictate patterns of prosocial and deviant behavior. In other words, deviance does not simply result from an absence of prosocial forces; rather deviant behaviors are actively learned through repeated interactions with key socialization sources.

Primary socialization sources are the entities having the greatest social influence over attitudes, beliefs, values, and behavior (Oetting & Donnermeyer, 1998). Critical information about acceptable and unacceptable social behavior is channeled to the individual by these socialization agents, who monitor and shape behavior, as is illustrated in Figure 4.1. While there is a myriad of potential socialization forces present in any individual's development, primary socialization sources are distinctive by their direct influence on the individual. Primary socialization sources bond directly with the individual, directly communicate normative standards, and directly monitor and shape behavior through reward and sanction power. All additional (i.e., secondary) socialization effects are routed through the primary socialization process. That is, the effects of coworkers, acquaintances, media, and the like are not important unless they are consistent with or part of the socialization that comes to you from primary socialization sources.

Within the primary socialization process, two critical forces combine to shape individual behavior: the normative climate of the socialization source (i.e., what

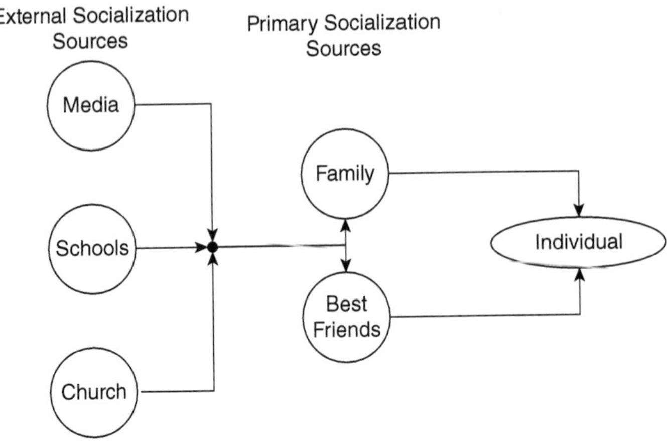

FIGURE 4.1 Primary Socialization Model

norms that socialization source strongly supports) and the strength of the bond linking the individual and the socialization source (i.e., the importance of that socialization source to the individual). In general, primary socialization sources follow societal conventions by encouraging and rewarding honest or prosocial behavior (Oetting & Donnermeyer, 1998). However, it is not unusual for primary socialization sources to encourage or espouse deviance. Primary Socialization Theory suggests that "differential exposure to prosocial and deviant messages . . . determines (the) learning of deviant attitudes and behaviors" (Oetting & Donnermeyer, 1998, p. 1010). For example, if a primary socialization source suggests that you are justified in stealing from your employer, you are more likely to steal. Similar to Sutherland's (1947, 1949) Differential Association Theory, Primary Socialization Theory suggests that deviance is more probable when the normative forces encouraging deviance outweigh the forces discouraging deviance. If several primary socialization sources tell you that stealing is justified, while a few others tell you it is not, you are more likely to conform to the majority opinion. However, mere exposure to deviant norms is not sufficient to influence individual behavior.

Primary Socialization Theory (Oetting & Donnermeyer, 1998) suggests that the strength and nature of the bonds between the individual and the socialization source modify the impact of norms on individual behavior. Strong bonds reflect a high level of identification with the socialization source and they also suggest that the socialization source is likely to have more reward and sanction power over individual behavior. For example, children who strongly identify with their parents are more likely to follow their norms and their advice. Therefore, strong bonds increase the likelihood of compliance with the specific normative proscriptions. It follows that strong bonds with prosocial or honest socialization sources help inoculate against deviant behavior, while strong bonds with deviant sources create a context ripe for deviance.

Primary Socialization Theory also suggests that personality exerts influence on deviance through the socialization process in one of two ways; personality prevents or disrupts bonds with prosocial/honest socialization sources or enhances bonds with deviant sources. For example, conscientiousness is the personality characteristics most reliably related to workplace deviance (Murphy, 1993); individual differences in conscientiousness are likely to affect bonding with socialization sources. For example, employees who are low on conscientiousness tend to avoid extra work, have problems with authority, and fail to conform to rules and standards (see Hogan & Ones, 1997; Murphy & Luther, 1997; and Ones, Viswesvaran & Schmidt, 1993, for reviews), and all of these types of behaviors tend to disrupt or prevent bonding with prosocial socialization sources. Furthermore, poor or erratic work performance (resulting from low conscientiousness or integrity) is likely to create conflicts with management and coworkers, thereby weakening bonds at both the organization and workgroup levels (Levinson, 1965; Robinson & Morrison, 1995).

Personality may also enhance bonds with deviant socialization sources (Oetting et al., 1998). Individuals tend to bond more readily with others having similar interests, attitudes, and abilities (Oetting & Donnermeyer, 1998; Tesser, Campbell, & Smith, 1984). In the area of deviance, it has been suggested that individuals predisposed to deviance will seek out similar others (Merriam, 1977; Sutherland, 1947; Tucker, 1989), thereby creating a climate or culture of deviance. Also, people tend to self-select into work situations that are compatible with their preferences, personalities, and attitudes and select out of situations which conflict with those preferences, etc. (Schneider, 1987, 2008; Schneider, Goldstein, & Smith, 1995). This suggests that individuals who are low on integrity or conscientiousness are likely to seek out similar others or gravitate toward work situations corresponding to their own views.

Moral Identify and Self-Regulation

The socialization processes that teach us what is right and wrong help to form what is referred to as a "moral identity". People who place a strong emphasis on being a moral person and following the rules and norms of society are described as having a strong moral identity (Hardy & Carlo, 2011). Moral identity is rooted in Social Identity Theory (Ashforth & Mael 1989) as well as in the self-regulatory assumptions of Social Cognitive Theory (Bandura 1986). Aquino and Reed (2002) describe moral identity as "a self-conception organized around a set of moral traits" (p. 1424).

Moral identity is often closely tied to the concept of self-regulation or self-control, in the sense that individuals with a strong moral identity are assumed to be better equipped to control their behavior and avoid misbehaving. Research linking self-regulation with misbehavior suggests that self-control, or self-regulation, is a finite resource (Baumeister & Heatherton, 1996; Muraven, Tice, & Baumeister, 1998) that is easily used up. That is, when exercised, self-regulatory resources become depleted, and subsequent self-control becomes much more difficult. Indeed, when people self-regulate their behavior (e.g., by not buying a tempting product they do not need), they consume self-regulatory resources and have few such resources available for a subsequent task. Compared with people who have not recently had to self-regulate their behavior, people who have done so are more likely to overeat, procrastinate, or shop impulsively (e.g., Baumeister, Bratslavsky, Muraven, & Tice, 1998; Vohs, 2006; Vohs, Baumeister, & Ciarocco, 2005; Vohs & Faber, 2007; Vohs & Heatherton, 2000). Gino, Schweitzer, Mead, and Ariel (2011) suggest that when a person's self-control is depleted the likelihood of unethical behavior increases. From this perspective, a strong moral identity might be thought of as a larger pool of resources for self-control, which makes it less likely that failures of self-control (e.g., misbehavior) will occur.

Primary Socialization Theory suggests that research on moral identities glosses over a critical point. As I have noted in earlier chapters, people who break rules or norms (e.g., employees who steal from the workplace) rarely think they have done something wrong (Murphy, 1993; O'Bannon, Goldinger, & Appleby, 1989). Moral Identity Theory emphasizes individuals' inability to resist doing wrong, but Primary Socialization Theory suggests that many people who misbehave have been socialized by their most important reference groups to believe that what they are doing is perfectly acceptable. Thus, a person with a very strong moral identity might engage in a wide range of misbehavior without depleting self-control capabilities, simply because he or she sees nothing wrong with the behavior in question. That is, some unethical behaviors are likely to occur without people knowing consciously that they are doing something wrong or immoral (Bazerman & Tenbrunsel, 2011; Chugh, Bazerman, & Banaji, 2005; Gino, Moore, & Bazerman, 2009).

In all likelihood, there are three pathways to misbehavior. First, the norms of important reference groups might be different from the norms of society in general, leading people who identify with those groups to believe that behaviors that are not accepted by society are nevertheless acceptable to the groups they most closely identify with. I will examine the ways groups develop deviant norms (i.e., norms that permit or encourage behavior that is not accepted by society at large) in several of the chapters that follow. Second, some misbehavior is likely to be the result of a failure of self-regulation—that is, people understand that the behavior is wrong but are incapable of resisting the urge of pressures to engage in that behavior. Third, people may engage in behaviors that they would typically know or understand to be wrong but find ways to convince themselves that, in this case, the behavior is acceptable. This third explanation is taken up in the sections that follow.

Self-Protective Cognitions

The motivation to maintain a positive self-image explains a wide range of phenomena in social psychology (Allport, 1955; Jones, 1973; Rogers, 1962; Rosenberg, 1979). For example, this drive to maintain a positive self-image helps to explain the widespread and strong "above-average" effects in self-evaluation; on almost any desirable human trait, from kindness to trustworthiness to the ability to get along with others, the average person consistently rates him- or herself above average (Alicke & Govorun, 2005; Dunning, Meyerowitz, & Holzberg, 1989; Klar & Giladi, 1997). Social Identity theorists such as Schlenker (1982) and Tajfel (1982) have argued that people want to feel good about themselves and strive to maintain a positive self-image, even when doing so requires a degree of self-deception, pretense, or guile. Misbehavior creates a threat to people's positive self-concept (Shalvi, Gino, Barken, & Aval, 2015) and they typically respond to this threat in one of two ways: (1) by limiting their immoral behavior (Sachdeva, Iliev, & Medin, 2009), or (2) by changing the way they think about these behaviors. One of the main questions this chapter asks is how people who choose to misbehave manage the conflict between the norms and laws they claim to respect and their behaviors.

For example, people typically attach high value to honesty and strongly believe that they are moral (Gino, 2015; Greenwald 1980; Sanitioso, Kunda, & Fong, 1990), even when their behavior violates widely accepted norms, rules, or laws. A wide range of self-serving mechanisms allows people to retain a positive moral identity even when they are engaging in behaviors that would normally be viewed as immoral. For example, some people follow a strategy that includes moral disengagement and moral credentials—reasoning that "I am a moral person, so what I am doing must be moral" (Gino & Galinsky, 2012). Cohen (2001) documents a wide variety of mechanisms and framing devices, ranging from desensitization to willful ignorance that allows people to misbehave while at the same time maintaining a positive self-image.

Before examining the various strategies people follow to help them rebrand their misbehaviors in a positive light, it is useful to look at a very general process that pervades social cognition—that is, motivated reasoning. We like to think of ourselves as rational actors who collect information and use it to reach logical and well-supported conclusions, but in many cases, we appear to follow a very different model, starting with the conclusion we want to reach (e.g., the conclusion that, regardless of my behavior, I am a good and moral person) and fitting our search for information and our reasoning in a way that will allow us to reach that desired conclusion. Motivated reasoning is particularly relevant to understanding misbehavior because people are so strongly motivated to maintain a positive self-image. Misbehavior is a threat to this self-image, and people will often work hard to distort their perceptions, memories, and conclusions to reconcile their harmful and destructive behaviors with this primal need to think of themselves in positive terms.

Motivated Reasoning

One of the most robust findings in research on social cognition is that there are strong and predictable biases in the way people search for and interpret information (e.g., Koriat, Lichtenstein, & Fischhoff, 1980; Nickerson, 1998; Pitz, 1969; Ross, Lepper, & Hubbard, 1975). People search for and give weight to information that confirms their current perceptions and opinions and they distort their perceptions of information that do not quite fit their preconceptions to increase the fit (Baron & Jost, 2019; Ditto & Lopez, 1992; Krueger & Funder, 2004; Kunda, 1990). Also, people are motivated to believe and accept information that is consistent with attitudes and beliefs that predominate in their group. Particularly when a particular belief (e.g., climate change is a hoax) is seen as important to a group, individuals will seek out information consistent with this and reject inconsistent information. Several distinct processes appear to be involved in motivated reasoning.

First, people actively search for information that is consistent with their current beliefs or their desired conclusions, and they actively avoid information that might disconfirm their beliefs or desired conclusions. Even when people do not actively avoid information, psychological research demonstrates that they have an easier time recruiting the evidence supporting what they want to be true than the evidence supporting what they want to be false (Epley & Gilovich, 2016).

Second, when people encounter information that might disconfirm their beliefs or desired conclusions, they tend to selectively credit and discredit evidence in ways that will make it less threatening to those beliefs and conclusions (Sherman & Cohen 2002, 2006). Kahan (2017) notes that this pattern of identity-protective cognition helps to explain people's willingness to accept incorrect or misleading information. Misleading information that helps to maintain a positive self-image is much easier to accept.

Third, even when individuals have information that might lead them to change their minds or to revise their conclusions, individuals give greater weight to information that supports their existing beliefs or their preferred conclusions than to evidence that contradicts these beliefs and conclusions. This process of seeking out information that confirms existing beliefs or preferred conclusions, of discounting information that does not support their views and of giving more weight to confirming than to disconfirming information creates a biased process that can lead individuals who are exposed to the same information to reach very different conclusions.

Motivated reasoning has clear implications for studying unethical behavior. People are strongly motivated to maintain a positive self-image, and they are more than willing to cognitively distort information that runs counter to this image. People who engage in unethical or antisocial behaviors are likely to deploy a wide range of cognitive strategies to make these behaviors seem more palatable, and people who can successfully reconceptualize unethical behaviors as socially approved ones will be more likely to engage in these unethical behaviors (Bersoff, 1999).

BOX 4.1 *HOW TO RATIONALIZE BAD BEHAVIOR*

Sykes and Matza (1957) outlined several strategies people use to rationalize or to justify their bad behavior, including

- Denial of responsibility—it was not my fault, I did not mean to do it
- Denial of injury—nobody really got hurt, the harm was so small as to be unimportant
- Denial of the victim—they deserved it
- Condemn the condemners—everybody does this, society is corrupt
- Appeal to higher loyalties—whatever was done happened as part of an effort to achieve some worthwhile goal

This widely cited paper provides a useful starting point for understanding the different strategies for rationalization, but it has been criticized for being insufficiently comprehensive. Kaptein and van Helvoort (2019) developed a more elaborated model that is organized around four general strategies:

1. Distorting the facts
   a. Nuancing the facts—"Nobody really knows what happened"
   b. Denying the facts—"I did not see/know that"
   c. Inventing new facts—"He deserved it because of some bad thing he might have done"
2. Negotiating the norm
   a. Reducing norms to facts—"That is just your opinion. Nobody knows what to do here"
   b. Appealing to another norm—"I did this to serve a higher good"
3. Blaming circumstances
   a. Blaming limited options—"I did not have a choice"
   b. Blaming limited role—"It was not my responsibility"
   c. Blaming factors that limit choice—"I was just following orders"
4. Hiding behind oneself
   a. Hiding behind imperfect knowledge—"I just did not know"
   b. Hiding behind imperfect capabilities—"There was nothing I could do"
   c. Hiding behind imperfect intentions—"I did not mean to do this. I was really mad at the time"

Like Sykes and Matza (1957), this model is useful because it illustrates the range of strategies that are available to people who have done something that they know is wrong but who want to maintain that all-important positive self-image.

Moral Disengagement

According to Social Cognitive Theory, when self-regulatory capabilities are working properly, people should experience discomfort, and sometimes even distress when they engage in behavior that conflicts with their internalized moral standards. In theory, then, individuals who misbehave should feel shame, remorse, or at least discomfort, but they often find ways to morally disengage from their actions (Moore, Detert, Treviño, Baker, & Mayer, 2012). Moral Disengagement Theory examines how this self-regulatory process can fail because moral disengagement mechanisms disable the cognitive links between transgressive behavior and the perception of wrongdoing that should prevent it (Bandura, 1986, 1990a, 1990b, 1999).

Bandura (1999) proposed moral disengagement frees the individual from the self-sanctions and guilt that would normally accompany violation of one's ethical standards. He proposed three categories of moral disengagement mechanisms, each of which can manifest itself in multiple ways: (1) cognitive reconstruction of behavior (moral justification, euphemistic labeling, and advantageous comparison), (2) minimizing one's role in the harmful behavior (displacement of responsibility, diffusion of responsibility, and disregarding or distorting of the consequences), and (3) focus on the targets' unfavorable acts (dehumanization and attribution of blame) (Bandura, 1986). All three of these represent part of a broader process of neutralization, in which the moral content of an unethical action is masked or overlooked (Bandura 1999; Sykes & Matza, 1957).

Justification

Motivated reasoning can be thought of as a process of information processing that helps people reconcile information about their behavior with their preferred beliefs or conclusions. Other processes can be thought of as post-processing—that is, as a set of processes that occur after people have become aware of behaviors that conflict with their desire to maintain a positive self-image. Moral justification, euphemistic labeling, and advantageous comparison represent three mechanisms of moral disengagement that serve to cognitively restructure unethical acts so that they appear less harmful.

Moral justification cognitively reframes unethical acts as being in the service of a greater good. This is a process for rationalizing unethical behavior as being justified because it serves a more important purpose. Euphemistic labeling is the use of sanitized language to rename harmful actions to make them appear more benign. For example, the United States has long used the term "enhanced interrogation" to describe techniques for interrogating prisoners that are regarded by virtually all nations as torture. The use of sanitized language makes it much easier for people to act unethically. Advantageous comparison exploits the contrast between a behavior under consideration and an even more reprehensible behavior to make the former seem innocuous. This is a strategy for making what you do seem less problematic because other options are even worse.

The core idea of justification is that people actively search for reasons that will allow them to portray (both to themselves and others) their misbehaviors in a more positive light. Shalvi, Dana, Handgraaf, and De Dreu (2011) discuss the concept of "ethical maneuvering"—that is, the tendency for people to revise their ethical standards in response to their behavior. Research has suggested that people are subject to "bounded ethicality"; that is, their morality is constrained in systematic ways that favor self-serving perceptions. Behaviors that would normally be seen as inconsistent with commonly accepted ethical standards can be reinterpreted in a more favorable light (Banaji, Bazerman, & Chugh, 2003), and this reinterpretation can make it more likely that those unethical behaviors will recur.

Highly creative individuals appear to be particularly skilled in generating justifications for one's unethical behavior (Gino & Ariely, 2012). Monin and Miller (2001) show that bolstering people's moral self-regard can liberate them to act less ethically, perhaps because the conviction that they are moral people will make it more likely that they will come to label their behavior as moral, even when it runs counter to widely accepted norms. Similarly, Mazar and Zhong (2010) found that people were more likely to cheat and steal after purchasing environmentally friendly products as opposed to conventional products. Research has even shown that it is important for individuals to live up to their internal standards of right and wrong in the absence of external sanctioning agents (Cialdini, Finch, & De Nicholas, 1990; Hales, 1985; Reis, 1981). If an insult or potential insult to one's self-image cannot be avoided, then a whole series of ego-defensive processes are brought to bear.

Displacement of Responsibility

Haidt (2007) argues that moral thinking is complex and multidimensional and that behaviors that look to external observers to be immoral are not seen that way by perpetrators. One of the ways individuals avoid the blame (and self-blame) for behavior that violates social norms is to disown responsibility for their actions. People who have engaged in behavior that they know violated widely shared norms, rules, or laws often resort to the strategy of displacing responsibility, claiming that they had no choice or no other option but to behave in ways that would normally be considered as wrong. For example, virtually every defendant at the Nuremberg trials of Nazi war criminals claimed that they were merely following orders and that they had no choice in their actions. Some scholars maintain that the participants in the Holocaust were indeed deferring to authority figures (Bauman, 1989) while others maintain that the war conditions and the breakdown of authority during the prewar period allowed Germans to engage in behaviors that they wanted to carry out but had been prevented from doing under the older social order (Goldhagen, 1996).

A useful distinction can be drawn between diffusion of responsibility (which was discussed in Chapter 3) and displacement of responsibility. In a crowd that witnesses an emergency (e.g., a pedestrian is hit by a car), people might be unsure who should respond or whether they should respond and might have a reasonable fear that they will just get in the way. Displacement is a different phenomenon, in which people who have committed a violation of general social norms, rules, or laws, or who are about to do so (e.g., a squad of soldiers who have been ordered to burn down a church) come to believe that they are not responsible for their actions, or that they had no choice but to go along with someone else's orders.

In one of the most famous series of experiments in social psychology, Stanley Milgram studied obedience to authority; this work is summarized in Milgram (1974). He asked experimental subjects to act as a "teacher", who gave a "learner" (actually, an actor hired by the experimenters) what appeared to be a series of increasingly severe electrical shocks as they made errors in a simple learning task. The "teachers" were informed that they could withdraw from the study at any time but were given simple verbal prods to give the "learner" shocks ("Please continue", "You have no other choice, you must go on"). The point of the study was to determine whether, and under what conditions, people would obey authority and give what appeared to be increasingly painful shocks. The results shocked Milgram and his readers. In his first set of experiments, *all* subjects gave shocks that appeared to be very painful, and nearly two-thirds gave the maximum possible shock. Subsequent experiments showed that fairly small variations in the procedure could influence subjects' willingness to deliver shocks (e.g., shocks were more likely and more painful if there were signs of authority, such as the experimenter dressing in a lab coat or the experiment being run at a university), but on the whole, this work and many subsequent replications suggests that people are much more willing to defer to authority, even when the authority figures have little real power or influence.

Attribution of Blame

Finally, an individual who has violated social norms and has harmed someone or some institution can always find a way to blame the victim—that is, create a mental scenario in which the person or institution that is harmed deserves it. For example, employee theft is often rationalized by the belief that the organization is treating employees unfairly, and that theft is simply a way to even the score (Murphy, 1993). There is evidence that the experience of mistreatment can lead to retaliatory behaviors that would normally be seen as unacceptable, For example, Huang, Greenbaum, Bonner, and Wang (2019) describe how inconsiderate and rude treatment of staff by customers can initiate a process of growing hostility, devaluation of the customer, and retaliatory behavior. This negative cycle is especially worrisome for people who are prone to hostility.

Many individuals show a hostile attribution bias—that is, tendency to interpret others' behaviors as having hostile intent, even when the behavior is ambiguous or benign (Dodge, 2006; Nasby, Hayden, & DePaulo, 1980). Individuals who exhibit consistent and high levels of hostile attribution bias across development are much more likely to engage in aggressive behavior (e.g., hitting/fighting, reacting violently, verbal or relational aggression) toward others (De Castro, Veerman, Koops, Bosch, & Monshouwer, 2002; Dodge, 2006). This aggression does not trigger feelings of remorse or shame or the concern that it will be socially sanctioned because it is attributed to something the victim has done. In many ways, this type of blame-shifting is a mirror image of displacement of responsibility, in the sense that it ultimately places the responsibility of your own misbehavior on someone else, either the person who ordered or directed the behavior (displacement of responsibility) or the person who is the victim of your behavior (victim-blaming). Thus, the victim of a sexual assault might ultimately be blamed, in the eyes of the perpetrator and perhaps of the community as well, for inviting an attack by wearing suggestive clothing or having too much to drink at a party.

Thinking About Other People

The way we think about other people and the cognitive processes involved in thinking about them depend substantially on how much we know about them. Thus, when you think about your younger brother, you may be able to draw on extensive memories and information. When you think about others who you have had less contact with (e.g., neurosurgeons, Croatians), you may depend on very different types of information, in particular stereotypes.

Stereotypes

Stereotypes represent one of the most widely studied topics in social psychology. They represent a cognitive strategy for thinking about other people that can simultaneously help make sense of the world, by making our thinking consistent and efficient, and create a platform for justifying and motivating misbehavior. Most simply, a stereotype starts with information or beliefs about a category of people. For example, I might believe (probably correctly) that players in the NFL are typically bigger, stronger, heavier, and faster than most other people. In this sense, a belief becomes a form of knowledge that can, under the right circumstances, make the process of thinking about people more efficient. Thus, if you tell me that Walter is an NFL player, this will immediately bring to mind a mental image that might contain quite a bit of information, much of which might be accurate.

Stereotypes, however, go beyond simple beliefs or knowledge. The usual definition of a stereotype includes two elements: (1) they are likely to be applied uncritically to all members of a group, and (2) they may include "knowledge" that is ill-founded or incorrect. So, for example, the stereotype that the Irish are friendly and talkative might become generalized to the belief that *all* Irish, or people of Irish ancestry, are friendly and talkative. This generalization of attributes of the group as a whole of all of the members of a group is thought to be one of the hallmarks of stereotyping. Second, stereotypes often include broad generalizations that may or may not have much basis in reality. For example, Americans are often stereotyped as happy and outgoing, but numerous polls and studies place the U.S.A. much nearer the middle of the pack in terms of characteristics such as satisfaction with life, well-being, and willingness to interact with others. If I list several nationalities (e.g., Germans, Italians, Japanese) it is likely that you will be able to rattle off a list of adjectives that describe them, and while some of these might be at least partially correct (at least in terms of something like the average level of social deference shows by Italian vs. Japanese citizens), much of what we think we know about different groups in society might be rooted in myths or in social attitudes that have built up over time (Cuddy, Fiske, & Glick, 2008).

BOX 4.2 TWO DIMENSIONS OF STEREOTYPING: WARMTH AND COMPETENCE

We tend to think of stereotypes as negative views that give rise to prejudice, but many groups do not receive a one-dimensional, hostile type of prejudice. Rather, many social stereotypes include a mixture of positive and negative elements. For example, my heritage is partly Irish. The Irish are simultaneously stereotyped as friendly and outgoing and prone to laziness and drunkenness. Cuddy, Fiske, and Glick's (2008) stereotype content model (SCM) suggests that two fundamental dimensions of social perception, warmth and competence, determine many of the effects of social stereotypes. The stereotype of the Irish mentioned combines elements of warmth and incompetence.

The SCM proposes that the four combinations of high versus low warmth and competence judgments elicit four unique emotional responses: admiration, contempt, envy, and pity. Groups stereotyped as warm and competent (e.g., the reference groups you most closely identify with)—elicit admiration. Groups stereotyped as incompetent and cold (e.g., homeless people) elicit contempt. Groups stereotyped as competent but not warm (e.g., Asians) elicit envy. Groups stereotyped as warm but not competent (e.g., elderly people) elicit pity.

Two variables long identified as important in intergroup relations—that is, competition and status—predict warmth and competence judgments. People viewed as competitors are judged as lacking warmth whereas people viewed as noncompetitors are judged as warm; people viewed as high status are judged as competent, whereas people viewed as low status are judged as incompetent.

This model suggests that stereotypes have the greatest potential for harm when they depict a particular group as lacking in either warmth or competence, but stereotypes can be harmful and even dangerous when the individuals targeted are viewed as being high on one dimension. For example, the stereotypes of Jews that were a constant theme of Nazi propaganda often emphasized competence, portraying Jews as the masterminds of various financial calamities and as cunning enemies of the Reich. Cuddy (2018) has argued that groups that are seen as competent but cold can elicit envious prejudice and that this prejudice is one factor that accounts for anti-Semitism. This finding extends beyond anti-Semitism; a stereotype that portrays all members of a group as both competent and cold substantially increases the risk that members of that group will suffer ill-treatment (Fiske, Cuddy, Glick, & Xu, 2002).

Stereotypes can be a genuine help in making sense of the world when they are: (1) rooted in reality, and (2) not over-generalized. For example, stereotypes of men vs. women include many elements, some of which are reality-based. So, if I am trying to figure out how many people can safely ride in an elevator, the fact that women are typically lighter than men may make a difference in the answer I give, but the fact that *some* men are quite a bit lighter than *some* women should also factor into my judgment. Stereotypes become potentially problematic when they are over-applied (e.g., Joe "knows" that Italians are excitable, and therefore assumes that everyone with Italian heritage is excitable) and inflexible (e.g., since Joe already "knows" all about Italians, he will not change his mind about individuals who have Italian heritage but do not seem excitable).

Stereotypes are not always negative, but they can contribute to prejudice and discrimination. Stereotypes regarding some groups (e.g., Jews, Asians) can even combine forms of admiration or at least belief that these groups are superior at some things (Cuddy et al., 2008). Indeed, positive feelings toward other groups are sometimes present even when the overall treatment of the group is negative. The classic example was the paternalistic attitudes of slaveholders in the 1860s (Fox-Genovese. & Genovese, 2005), many of whom claimed to like individual slaves and to truly believe that their system was more benign than the alternatives (e.g., wage slavery in the North). The other classic illustration is gender stereotyping, where a man undertakes multiple actions that harm women in the absence of general hostility toward women as a group. For example, men might put women on a pedestal, and with what is sometimes described as "benevolent sexism" (Glick et al., 2004), restrict them from professions or situations that are not "feminine".

Stereotypes are particularly likely to lead to prejudice and discrimination when the contents of those stereotypes are negative and/or when groups are seen as competing. For example, stereotypes and biases toward African Americans are part and parcel of a long (and sadly continuing) history of racial prejudice and mistreatment. Dovidio, Gaertner, and Pearson (2016) note that overt prejudice has declined substantially in the U.S.A., but that it is often replaced by aversive racism. Aversive racists can sympathize with victims of past injustice, support principles of racial equality, and genuinely regard themselves as nonprejudiced, but at the same time possess conflicting, often nonconscious, negative feelings and beliefs about Blacks that are rooted in basic psychological processes. The negative feelings that aversive racists have toward Blacks typically do not reflect open antipathy but rather consist of more avoidant reactions of discomfort, anxiety, or fear.

Conditions Under Which We Are More Likely to Rely on Stereotypes

The process of categorizing people into groups automatically activates stereotypes and biases toward members of those groups, and it also tends to build closer identification with one's group (Gaertner & Dovidio, 2012). Stereotypes achieve much of their force from being shared by members of social groups (Haslam et al., 1988), and the stronger the group's belief in or attachment to this stereotype, the more likely it is that group members will employ this stereotype in thinking about others. Groups often tolerate, share, and perpetuate stereotypes, and people who believe it is socially acceptable, and perhaps even expected to express prejudice are more likely to do this (Crandall, Eshleman, & O'Brien, 2002). Group members are likely to adhere to social norms when expressing prejudice, evaluating scenarios of discrimination, and reacting to hostile statements and jokes, especially when the group is cohesive.

It is generally thought that to be a good group member, one must adopt the prejudices that the group holds and abstain from those prejudices that the group frowns upon. However, dissent from group prejudices can, in some circumstances, have a powerful effect. For example, Blanchard, Crandall, Brigham, and Vaughn (1994) found that a single group member expressing antiracist views could dramatically reduce the tolerance for racist acts. One potential explanation for this finding is that although the norms of the group might tolerate this type of prejudice, the norms of society are less tolerant. Likely, a dissenting opinion that is not supported by these general social norms would have less influence.

It was long held that increasing contact between groups would reduce prejudice, but the data do not support this hypothesis. What is more likely is that prejudice reduction occurs when people see themselves as members of the *same* group. There is evidence that inducing members of different social groups (e.g., Blacks and Whites) to view one another as members of a shared in-group (e.g., Americans) tends to improve their intergroup attitudes.

It is also likely that stereotypes have stronger effects when individuals have little contact with or first-hand knowledge about the group that is the target of the stereotype. For example, there is evidence that opposition to immigrants in the United States is strongest in those parts of the country where there are few immigrants (Brownstein, 2017). There is evidence (e.g., Landy, 2008) that people rely on stereotypes when all they know is group membership, but that individuating information can reduce or eliminate the effects of stereotypes.

Dehumanization

One of the dangers of stereotypical thinking is that it can lead people to treat members of stereotypes groups as less than human, or as objects. Dehumanization can have devastating consequences (Haslam & Loughnan, 2014). For example, during warfare, each side makes concerted efforts to convey and encourage an exaggerated view of the enemy's evil nature, communicated through propaganda depicting the enemy as monstrous or as allied with the devil (Herf, 2006; Keen, 1986). This type of propaganda can be a major catalyst for spiraling hostilities (White, 2004) and even war crimes (Volhardt & Campbell-Obaid, 2016). Early work on dehumanization emphasized its role in war, ethnopolitical conflict, and genocide (Kelman, 1976; Staub, 1989). The more recent empirical literature confirms that dehumanizing the enemy has real implications in these contexts. For example, Maoz and McCauley (2008) found that Israelis who dehumanized Palestinians to a greater extent were more likely to support harsh policies such as forced population transfers.

Staub (1989) proposes taking societal conditions as a starting point. Specifically, Staub suggests that "difficult life conditions" (e.g., a sudden economic crisis or conditions of war) frustrate basic human needs for security, control, a positive social identity, and meaning. If these frustrated needs are then satisfied in destructive ways (e.g., by attacking others who you believe are responsible for your distress) that can initiate a continuum of destruction whereby genocide and mass atrocities gradually develop and unfold, as opposed to suddenly erupting. For example, under economic or social stress, people often scapegoat minority groups who are blamed for societal problems and whose marginalization and ultimate removal from society is seen as a solution to the problems that society faces. In this process, destructive ideologies are often promulgated that glorify the in-group while derogating other groups in society (Newman, 2002). Similarly, Harff identified several factors that differentiated these cases from those that did not lead to genocide or politicide. In all but one of the studied cases, genocide occurred either during or in the aftermath of political upheaval (defined as "an abrupt change in the political community" and including "defeat in wars, revolutions, anti-colonial rebellions, separatist wars, coups, and regime transitions"; Harff, 2003, p. 62).

A major emphasis of dehumanization research has been the attribution of lesser humanness to particular ethnic groups. Subtle forms of dehumanization have been demonstrated in perceptions of numerous groups, including people from lower social class backgrounds, medical patients, and the mentally ill (Lammers & Stapel, 2011). Several theories of dehumanization have been proposed, including (1) infrahumanization—Leyens et al. (2001) proposed that people tend to perceive out-group members as less human than in-group members even in the absence of significant intergroup antagonism, (2) dual model—Haslam (2006) suggests that whereas humans are distinguished from animals on attributes involving cognitive capacity, civility, and refinement, we differ from inanimate objects because we demonstrate emotionality, vitality, and warmth. This "animalistic" form of dehumanization captures phenomena such as the most blatant genocidal labeling of people as vermin. In contrast, when individuals are denied human nature, they are seen as lacking warmth, emotion, and individuality, and likened to inanimate objects. This "mechanistic" form captures phenomena described by previous writers on dehumanization in the contexts of technology, medicine, and forms of objectification in which people are perceived as inert or instrumental, and (3) stereotype content model—Harris and Fiske (2006) defines dehumanization as the failure to spontaneously consider another person's mind, or to engage in social cognition when perceiving them. According to the stereotype content model, group stereotypes vary on the dimensions of warmth and competence. Admired groups (e.g., in-groups) are perceived as high on both dimensions, pitied groups (e.g., the elderly) are seen as warm but incompetent, envied groups (e.g., the rich) are seen as cold but competent, and groups that evoke disgust (e.g., the homeless) are unambivalently seen as low on both dimensions.

Kelman (1976) argued that when dehumanization occurs in the context of mass violence, it weakens the perpetrator's normal restraints on violent behavior. In essence, dehumanization disinhibits violence when conflict already exists. Bandura (1999) gave a more specific account of this process of disinhibition, suggesting that dehumanization disengages the perpetrator's moral self-sanctions: the internal restraints of guilt and related moral emotions that normally apply the brakes to aggressive conduct. Opotow (1990) presented an alternative account of why moral restraints are disengaged, focusing on the process of "moral exclusion", placing someone "outside the boundary in which moral values, rules, and considerations of fairness apply" (p. 1). Bar-Tal (1989) proposed yet another explanation, arguing that attaching a subhuman or demonic label to a hated out-group enables violence by supplying a legitimate justification of the in-group's aggression. As the moral exclusion of victim groups, as well as violence against them, progresses, new norms are established, and this violence is normalized in society. As violence becomes the norm, people can become habituated to violence and desensitized after an initial period of shock and physical discomfort (e.g., Carnagey, Anderson, & Bushman, 2007).

Disgust and contempt are strong, anger-tinged aversions whose targets are seen as impure, tainted, or revolting; for example, drug addicts, homeless people, and prostitutes (Harris & Fiske, 2006). A different kind of aversion, based on fear rather than anger and hatred, involves the perception of threat. Several researchers have shown that perceptions of threat also promote dehumanizing perceptions of the threatening person or group. Maoz and McCauley (2008), for example, demonstrated that Israeli participants who perceived Palestinians as more threatening were more likely to dehumanize them by seeing them as disgusting and contemptuous, and this dehumanizing perception was in turn associated with support for coercive policies such as population transfers, curfews, use of rubber bullets to break up demonstrations, and administrative detention.

Objectification

Objectification is a related process in which people are treated in ways that minimize their full humanity; this process is believed to be central to many forms of misogyny, sex discrimination, and sexual harassment. Objectification continues to be on almost daily display in the media and advertising, where women are often valued solely for their physical beauty. In these contexts, women are treated as sexual objects who have little function except to attract the attention of and provide sexual gratification to males. However, objectification goes beyond advertising and the media, and it can have disturbing consequences. For example, Viki and Abrams (2003) found that men holding harmful attitudes such as hostile sexist beliefs tended to deny women complex emotions (e.g., nostalgia, remorse, love). Men who hold these harmful beliefs deny women the emotional capacity necessary to be fully human.

Gervais (2016) argues that objectification leading to sexual violence is a complex process that involves a range of antecedents (e.g., hostile beliefs about women [Glick & Fiske, 1996], prior experiences with sexual violence [Patterson, 1982], previous objectification and sexual abuse experiences [De Gue & Di Lillo, 2004], alcohol use [Abbey, 2002], threats to social identity [Maass, Cadinu, Guarnieri, & Grasselli, 2003], power differentials [Gruenfeld, Inesi, Magee, & Galinsky, 2008], social and organizational norms [Pryor, Giedd, & Williams, 1995], cognitive biases in viewing women [Bernard, Gervais, Allen, Campomizzi, & Klein, 2012], and tendencies to visually assess women in sexual terms [Fredrickson & Roberts, 1997]). If women are seen as objects that exist for the enjoyment of men, it will become much easier for men to harass, demean, and assault them without feeling that they have misbehaved.

The objectification of women and girls is a worldwide phenomenon that is linked to rates of sexual violence, unhealthy body images, and harmful gender stereotypes (Swift & Gould, 2019). Like dehumanization, objectification increases the likelihood of mistreatment because there are not the same moral norms for the treatment of objects or subhuman entities as there are for humans. Thinking about women in terms that deny them full humanity dramatically lowers the bar for a wide range of behaviors that are harmful to their targets.

Acting Without Much Thinking: Automatic Processes That Contribute to Misbehavior

Kahneman (2011) suggested that there are two distinct systems of cognition: (1) System 1—which is fast, unconscious, stereotypic, and emotional and (2) System 2—which is slower, more deliberate, logical, and conscious. There is evidence that people react emotionally and automatically to ethically charged situations (e.g., with disgust or other emotions) and often form instant judgments of right and wrong without much thought, judgments that are later rationalized (Haidt, 2001, 2007). The fast system that is at the root of a wide range of misbehaviors relies extensively on existing knowledge structures, such as stereotypes. Two other knowledge structures are also potentially relevant to understanding misbehavior—that is, schemas and scripts.

A schema is a knowledge structure in memory that contains ideas and beliefs about some aspect of the world. For example, suppose I tell you that Joe has been working as an accountant for the last ten years. This will activate a wide range of things you "know" about accountants, some of which might be true (he probably works in an office, probably on a computer), others of which might not (he has low interpersonal skills). The website www.tvtropes.org catalogs hundreds of figures, themes, images, and plot elements that are widely used in all sorts of media (e.g., black hat = villain; pirate booty will always come in a wooden chest, buried in the ground or in a cave; all bombs have a red countdown device that will probably be stopped just before it reaches zero) that give readers or the audience an instant sense of what is going on and what is likely to happen next, and these represent one type of schema. People have schemas about social roles (e.g., how should a doctor act when you visit his or her office?), about groups of people (e.g., stereotypes), and situations. Once a schema is activated, people will make predictions and judgments based on that schema.

A special type of schema that applies to how people behave in situations is a script. A script is defined as a generic knowledge of the typical or expected patterns of action (Abelson, 1991). Scripts describe what people *do* in particular situations and what you should expect. For example, if you visit an art gallery, you have a reasonably clear set of expectations about how you and other people should behave (quiet, attentive to and appreciative of the art), and behavior that is far from your expectations (e.g., loud arguments) will be especially jarring. Scripts share several features in common with descriptive and prescriptive norms, in that they tell you what is normal to do and to expect, and also help you understand what is and is not appropriate. Scripts are different from norms in terms of their specificity. They often tell you not only what actions you might expect or encounter but also the specific sequence of events that should be expected.

Schema and scripts do not necessarily lead to misbehavior, but they can. In particular, schemas that lead you to think of individuals or groups in narrow and inflexible terms (i.e., stereotypes) have considerable potential for harm because they make it easier to attribute negative characteristics to the targets of those stereotypes and they make it harder for you to free yourself from the preconceptions these stereotypes imply. Similarly, scripts can lead to misbehavior if the pattern of behavior that is part of the script includes acts that are harmful or dangerous to some of the people who are part of the script. Imagine, for example, that your script for going to a restaurant includes what you think is playful banter with an attractive server. This could easily create an uncomfortable situation for the server that could constitute the sort of hostile work environment that can arise when people are discriminated against on the basis of their gender (EEOC, 2019).

Kahneman's (2011) System 1 is a potentially strong source of misbehavior precisely because it is fast, emotion-based, and unconscious. It is likely that many misbehaviors result from people acting impulsively, and that they might be less likely to behave badly if they were more deliberate and reflective. Emotion-based information processing can be particularly insidious when the emotional climate is agitated. In Chapter 3, I discussed how emotional contagion could in some circumstances turn a peaceful crowd into a howling lynch mob, and how normally honorable soldiers could find themselves participating in atrocities and genocide. One potential remedy to many instances of misbehavior may be to help people move away from automatic, emotion-based thinking and to encourage people to think critically about their behavior.

Summary

This chapter starts with a discussion about how we learn what types of behaviors and actions are normal and expected and what types are accepted and approved of or regarded negatively. One of the themes that pulls this literature together is that a great deal of social learning is directed toward a general goal—that is, reducing uncertainty about how we should behave in different situations. I then go on to examine cognitive processes that focus on a second goal that is important to most individuals—that is, maintaining a positive self-image. Individuals who behave in ways that violate broad social norms and that have the potential to harm others *should* feel like they have done something wrong and *should* feel guilt and remorse. I discuss a range of cognitive processes people use to rationalize, justify, reconceptualize, and mentally distort their behavior to help keep up this positive image.

A great deal of psychological research has examined the influences of stereotypes on people's thoughts and behaviors. Stereotyping can contribute to harmful and destructive behavior, particularly when the stereotype of a group portrays them as competent but cold. Under extreme conditions, stereotypes can lead to dehumanization—that is, treating members of particular groups as animals or objects who do not deserve humane treatment. However, conditions do not need to be extreme for stereotypic thinking to be harmful. For example, women and girls are routinely treated as sex objects, valued for their attractiveness and their capacity to please men. The objectification of women is practically the mainstay of advertising and is so routine in all types of media that it almost passes unnoticed, despite the substantial harm (e.g., increased sexual harassment and violence, unhealthy body images) that objectification does.

Finally, I briefly describe some important automatic processes that can lead individuals to behave in ways that violate social norms and that harm others. We like to think of ourselves as rational creatures, but a good deal of our behavior is guided by emotions, preconceptions, schema, and scripts that can lead us to behave in ways that are dangerous and destructive to the social order.

References

Abbey, A. (2002). Alcohol-related sexual assault: A common problem among college students. *Journal of Studies on Alcohol, 14*, 118–128.

Abelson, R.P. (1991). Psychological status of the script concept. *American Psychologist, 36*, 715–729.

Alicke, M.D. & Govorun, O. (2005). The better-than-average effect. In M. Alicke, D. Dunning, & J. Krueger (Eds.), *The Self in Social Judgment* (pp. 85–106). New York: Psychology Press.

Allport, G.W. (1955). *Becoming: Basic Considerations for a Psychology of Personality*. New Haven, CT: Yale University Press.

Aquino, K. & Reed, A., II. (2002). The self-importance of moral identity. *Journal of Personality and Social Psychology, 83*, 1423–1440.

Ashforth, B.E. & Mael, F. (1989). Social identity theory and the organization. *Academy of Management Review, 14*, 20–39.

Bandura, A. (1977). *Social Learning Theory*. Englewood Cliffs, NJ: Prentice-Hall.

Bandura, A. (1986). *Social Foundations of Thought and Action: A Social Cognitive Theory*. Englewood Cliffs, NJ: Prentice-Hall.

Bandura, A. (1990a). Mechanisms of moral disengagement. In W. Reich (Ed.), *Origins of Terrorism: Psychologies, Ideologies, States of Mind* (pp. 161–191). New York, NY: Cambridge University Press.

Bandura, A. (1990b). Selective activation and disengagement of moral control. *Journal of Social Issues 46*, 27–46.

Bandura, A. (1999). Moral disengagement in the perpetration of inhumanities. *Personality and Social Psychology Review, 3*, 193–209.

Banaji, M.R., Bazerman, M.H. & Chugh, D. (2003). How (un)ethical are you? *Harvard Business Review, 81*(12), 56–64.

Baron, J. & Jost, J.T. (2019). False equivalence: Are liberals and conservatives in the United States equally biased? *Perspectives on Psychological Science, 14*, 292–303.

Bar-Tal, D. (1989). Delegitimization: The extreme case of stereotyping. In D. Bar-Tal, C.F. Grauman, A. Kruglanski, & W. Stroebe (Eds.), *Stereotyping and Prejudice: Changing Conceptions* (pp. 169–182). New York: Springer.

Bauman, Z. (1989). *Modernity and the Holocaust.* Cambridge, UK: Polity.

Baumeister, R.F., Bratslavsky, E., Muraven, M. & Tice, D.M. (1998). Ego-depletion: Is the active self a limited resource? *Journal of Personality and Social Psychology, 74*, 1252–1265.

Baumeister, R.F. & Heatherton, T.F. (1996). Self-regulation failure: An overview. *Psychological Inquiry*, 7(3), 1–15.

Bazerman, M.H. & Tenbrunsel A.E. (2011). *Blind Spots: Why We Fail to Do What's Right and What to Do About It.* Princeton: Princeton University Press.

Bernard, P., Gervais, S.J., Allen, J., Campomizzi, S. & Klein, O. (2012). Integrating sexual objectification with object versus person recognition: The sexualized body-inversion hypothesis. *Psychological Science, 23*, 469–471.

Bersoff. (1999). Why good people sometimes do bad things: Motivated reasoning and unethical behavior. *Personality and Social Psychology Bulletin, 25*, 28–39.

Blanchard, F.A., Crandall, C.S., Brigham, J.C. & Vaughn, L.A. (1994). Condemning and condoning racism: A social context approach to interracial settings. *Journal of Applied Psychology, 79*, 993–997.

Brownstein, R. (2017, August 22). Places with the fewest immigrants push back hardest on immigration. *CNN*, www.cnn.com/2017/08/22/politics/immigration-trump-arizona/index.html

Carnagey, N.L., Anderson, C.A. & Bushman, B.J. (2007). The effect of video game violence on physiological desensitization to real-life violence. *Journal of Experimental Social Psychology, 43*, 489–496.

Chugh, D., Bazerman, M.H. & Banaji, M.R. (2005). Bounded ethicality as a psychological barrier to recognizing conflicts of interest. In D.A. Moore, D.M. Cain, G. Lowenstein, & M. Bazerman (Eds.), *Conflicts of Interest: Challenges and solutions in Business, Law, Medicine, and Public Policy* (pp. 74–95). New York: Cambridge University Press.

Cialdini, R.B., Finch, J.F. & De Nicholas, M.E. (1990). Strategic self-presentation: The indirect route. In M.J. Cody & M.L. McLaughlin (Eds.), *The Psychology of Tactical Communication* (pp. 194–206). Clevedon, UK: Multilingual Matters.

Cialdini, R.B. & Trost, M.R. (1998). Social influence: Social norms, conformity, and compliance. In D.T. Gilbert, S.T. Fiske, & G. Lindzey (Eds.), *The Handbook of Social Psychology* (pp. 151–192). New York: McGraw-Hill.

Cohen, S. (2001). *States of Denial: Knowing About Atrocities and Suffering.* Cambridge, UK: Polity.

Crandall, C.S., Eshleman, A. & O'Brien, L. (2002). Social norms and the expression and suppression of prejudice: The struggle for internalization. *Journal of Personality and Social Psychology, 82*(3), 359–378.

Cuddy, A. (2018, November 3). The psychology of antisemitism. *New York Times* www.nytimes.com/2018/11/03/opinion/sunday/psychology-anti-semitism.html

Cuddy, A., Fiske, S.T. & Glick, P. (2008). Warmth and competence as universal dimensions of social perception: The Stereotype Content Model and the BIAS Map. *Advances in Experimental Social Psychology, 40*, 62–149.

De Castro, B.O., Veerman, J.W., Koops, W., Bosch, J.D. & Monshouwer, H.J. (2002). Hostile attribution of intent and aggressive behavior: A meta-analysis. *Child Development*, 916–934.

De Gue, S. & Di Lillo, D. (2004). Understanding perpetrators of nonphysical sexual coercion: Characteristics of those who cross the line. *Violence and Victims, 19*, 673–688.

Ditto, P.H. & Lopez, D.F. (1992). Motivated skepticism: The use of differential decision criteria for preferred and nonpreferred conclusions. *Journal of Personality and Social Psychology, 63*, 568–584.

Dodge, K.A. (2006). Translational science in action: Hostile attributional style and the development of aggressive behavior problems. *Development and Psychopathology, 18*(03), 791–814.

Dovidio, J.F., Gaertner, S.L. & Pearson, A.R. (2016). Racism among the well intentioned. In A.G. Miller (Ed.), *The Social Psychology of Good and Evil* (pp. 95–118). New York: Guilford.

Dunning, D., Meyerowitz, J.A. & Holzberg, A.D. (1989). Ambiguity and self-evaluation: The role of idiosyncratic trait definitions in self-serving assessments of others. *Journal of Personality and Social Psychology, 57*, 1082–1090.

Dutton, J.E. & Dukerich, J.M. (1991). Keeping an eye on the mirror: Image and identity in organizational adaptation. *Academy of Management Journal, 34*, 517–554.

EEOC. (2019). *Harassment*. www.eeoc.gov/laws/types/harassment.cfm

Elstak, M.N., Bhatt, M., Van Riel, C., Pratt, M.G. & Berens, G.A. (2015). Organizational identification during a merger: The role of self-enhancement and uncertainty reduction motives during a major organizational change. *Journal of Management Studies, 52*, 32–62.

Epley, N. & Gilovich, T. (2016). The mechanics of motivated reasoning. *Journal of Economic Perspectives, 30*, 133–140.

Ferguson, M.J. & Bargh, J.A. (2004). How social perception can automatically influence behavior. *Trends in Cognitive Science, 8*, 33–39.

Fine, S., Horowitz, I., Weigler, H. & Basis, L. (2010). Is good character good enough? The effects of situational variables on the relationship between integrity and counterproductive work behaviors. *Human Resource Management Review, 20*, 73–84.

Fiske, S.T., Cuddy, A., Glick, P. & Xu, J. (2002). A model of (often mixed) stereotype content: Competence and warmth respectively follow from perceived status and competition. *Journal of Personality and Social Psychology, 82*, 878–902.

Fox-Genovese, E. & Genovese, E.D. (2005). *The mind of the master class*. New York: Cambridge University Press.

Fredrickson, B.L. & Roberts, T.A. (1997). Objectification theory: Toward understanding women's lived experiences and mental health risks. *Psychology of Women Quarterly, 21*, 173–206.

Gaertner, S.L. & Dovidio, J.F. (2012). Reducing intergroup bias: The common in group identity model. In P.A.M. Van Lange, A.W. Kruglanski, & E.T. Higgins (Eds.), *Handbook of Theories of Social Psychology* (Vol. 2, pp. 439–457). Thousand Oaks, CA: Sage.

Gerber, J.P., Wheeler, L. & Suls, J. (2018). A Social Comparison Theory meta-analysis 60+ years on. *Psychological Bulletin, 144*, 177–197.

Gervais, S.J. (2016). A social interaction approach to objectification: Implications for the social-psychological study of sexual violence. In A.G. Miller (Ed.), *The Social Psychology of Good and Evil* (pp. 224–248). New York: Guilford.

Gino, F. (2015). Understanding ordinary unethical behavior: Why people who value morality act. *Current Opinion in Behavioral Sciences, 3*, 107–111.

Gino, F. & Ariely, D. (2012). The dark side of creativity: Original thinkers can be more dishonest. *Journal of Personality and Social Psychology, 102*, 445–459.

Gino, F. & Galinsky, A.D. (2012). Vicarious dishonesty: When psychological closeness creates distance from one's moral compass. *Organizational Behavior and Human Decision Processes, 119*, 15–26.

Gino, F., Moore, D.A. & Bazerman, M.H. (2009). See no evil: Why we fail to notice unethical behavior. In R.M. Kramer, A.E. Tenbrunsel, & M.J. Bazerman (Eds.), *Social Decision Making: Social Dilemmas, Social Values, and Ethical Judgments* (pp. 241–263). New York: Psychology Press.

Gino, F., Schweitzer, M.E., Mead, N.L. & Ariely, D. (2011). Unable to resist temptation: How self-control depletion promotes unethical behavior. *Organizational Behavior and Human Decision Processes, 115*, 191–203.

Glick, P. & Fiske, S.T. (1996). The Ambivalent Sexism Inventory: Differentiating hostile and benevolent sexism. *Journal of Personality and Social Psychology, 70*, 491–512.

Glick, P., Lameiras, M., Fiske, S.T., Eckes, T., Masser, B., Volpato, C., Manganelli, A.M., Pek, J., Huang, L., Sakalli-Uğurlu, N., Castro, Y.R., Luiza, M., Pereira, D., Willemson, T.M., Brunner, A., Materna, I. & Wells, R. (2004). Bad but bold: Ambivalent attitudes toward men predict gender inequality in 16 nations. *Journal of Personality and Social Psychology, 86*, 713–728.

Glomb, T.M. & Liao, H. (2003). Interpersonal aggression in work groups: Social influence, reciprocal, and individual effects. *Academy of Management Journal, 46*, 486–496.

Goldhagen, D.J. (1996). *Hitler's Willing Executioners: Ordinary Germans and the Holocaust.* London: Little, Brown & Co.

Goldstein, N.J. & Cialdini, R.B. (2007). Using social norms as a lever of social influence. In A.R. Pratkanis (Ed.), *The Science of Social Influence* (pp. 167–191). New York: Psychology Press.

Greenwald, A.G. (1980). The totalitarian ego: Fabrication and revision of personal history. *American Psychologist, 35*, 603–618.

Gruenfeld, D.H., Inesi, M.E., Magee, J.C. & Galinsky, A.D. (2008). Power and the objectification of social targets. *Journal of Personality and Social Psychology, 95*, 111–127.

Haidt, J. (2001). The emotional dog and its rational tail: A social intuitionist approach to moral judgment. *Psychological Review, 108*, 814–834.

Haidt, J. (2007). The new synthesis for moral psychology. *Science, 316*, 998–1002.

Hales, S. (1985). The inadvertent rediscovery of self in social psychology. *Journal for the Theory of Social Behavior, 15*, 237–282.

Hardy, S.A. & Carlo, G. (2011). Moral identity: What is it, how does it develop, and is it linked to moral action? *Child Development Perspectives, 5*, 212–218.

Harff, B. (2003). No lessons learned from the Holocaust?: Assessing risks of genocide and political mass murder since 1955. *American Political Science Review, 1*, 57–73.

Harris, L. & Fiske, S. (2006). Dehumanizing the lowest of the low: Neuroimaging responses to extreme out-groups. *Psychological Science, 17*, 847–853.

Haslam, N. (2006). Dehumanization: An integrative review. *Personality and Social Psychology Review, 10*, 252–264.

Haslam, N. & Loughnan, S. (2014). Dehumanization and infrahumanization. *Annual Review of Psychology, 65*, 399–423.

Haslam, N, Turner, J.C., Oakes, P.J., Reynolds, K.J., Eggins, R.A., Nolan, M. & Tweedie, J. (1988). When do stereotypes become really consensual? Investigating the group-based dynamics of the consensualization process. *European Journal of Social Psychology, 28*, 755–776.

Herf, J. (2006). *The Jewish Enemy: Nazi Propaganda during World War II and the Holocaust.* Cambridge, MA: Harvard University Press.

Hogan, J. & Ones, D.S. (1997). Conscientiousness and integrity at work. In R. Hogan, J.A. Johnson, & S.R. Briggs (Eds.), *Handbook of Personality Psychology* (pp. 849–870). New York: Academic Press.

Hogg, M.A. & Abrams, D. (1988). *Social Identifications: A Social Psychology of Intergroup Relations and Group Processes.* London: Routledge.

Hogg, M.A. & Mullin, B.A. (1999). Joining groups to reduce uncertainty: Subjective uncertainty reduction and group identification. In D. Abrams and M.A. Hogg (Eds.), *Social Identity and Social Cognition* (pp. 249–279). Oxford: Blackwell.

Huang, Y., Greenbaum, R.L., Bonner, J.M. & Wang, C.S. (2019). Why sabotage customers who mistreat you? Activated hostility and subsequent devaluation of targets as moral disengagement mechanisms. *Journal of Applied Psychology, 104*, 495–510.

Jones, S.C. (1973). Self- and interpersonal evaluations: Esteem theories versus consistency theories. *Psychological Bulletin, 79*, 185–199.

Kahan, D.M. (2017). Misconceptions, misinformation, and the logic of identity-protective cognition. *Cultural Cognition Project Working Paper Series No. 164 and Yale Law School, Public Law Research Paper No. 605.*

Kahneman, D. (2011). *Thinking, Fast and Slow.* New York: Macmillan.

Kaptein, M. & van Helvoort, M. (2019). A Model of neutralization techniques. *Deviant Behavior, 40*, 1260–1285.

Keen, S. (1986). *Faces of the Enemy: Reflections of the Hostile Imagination.* San Francisco: Harper & Row.

Kelman, H.C. (1976). Violence without restraint: Reflections on the dehumanization of victims and victimizers. In G.M. Kren & L.H. Rappoport (Eds.), *Varieties of Psychohistory* (pp. 282–314). New York: Springer.

Klar, Y. & Giladi, E.E. (1997). No one in my group can be below the group's average: A robust positivity bias in favor of anonymous peers. *Journal of Personality and Social Psychology, 73*, 885–901.

Koriat, A., Lichtenstein, S. & Fischhoff, B. (1980). Reasons for confidence. *Journal of Experimental Psychology: Human Learning and Memory, 6*, 107–118.

Krueger, J.I. & Funder, D.C. (2004). Towards a balanced social psychology: Causes, consequences and cures for the problem-seeking approach to social behavior and cognition. *Behavioral and Brain Sciences, 27*, 313–327.

Kunda, Z. (1990). The case for motivated reasoning. *Psychological Review, 108*, 480–498.

Lammers, J. & Stapel, D. (2011). Power increases dehumanization. *Group Process and Intergroup Relations, 14*, 113–126.

Landy, F.J. (2008). Stereotypes, bias, and personnel decisions: Strange and stranger. *Industrial and Organizational Psychology: Perspectives on Science and Practice, 1*, 379–392.

Levinson, H. (1965). Reciprocation: The relationship between man and organization. *Administrative Science Quarterly, 9*, 370–390.

Leyens, J.-P., Rodriguez-Torres, R., Rodriguez-Perez, A., Gaunt, R., Paladino, M. et al. (2001). Psychological essentialism and the differential attribution of uniquely human emotions to ingroups and outgroups. *European Journal of Social Psychology, 81*, 395–411.

Maass, A., Cadinu, M., Guarnieri, G. & Grasselli, A. (2003). Sexual harassment under social identity threat: The computer harassment paradigm. *Journal of Personality and Social Psychology, 85*, 853–870.

Maoz, I. & McCauley, C. (2008). Threat, dehumanization, and support for retaliatory aggressive policies in asymmetric conflict. *Journal of Conflict Resolution, 52*, 93–116.

Mazar, N. & Zhong, C. (2010). Do green products make us better people? *Psychological Science, 21*, 494–498.

Merriam, D.H. (1977). Employee theft. *Criminal Justice Abstracts, 9*, 375–406.

Milgram, S.A. (1974). *Obedience to Authority: An Experimental View*. New York: Harper & Row.

Mitchell, A., Gottfried, J., Kiley, J. & Matsa, K.E. (2014, October 21). Political polarization and media habits. Pew Research Center.

Monin, B. & Miller, D.T. (2001). Moral credentials and the expression of prejudice. *Journal of Personality and Social Psychology, 81*, 33–43.

Moore, C., Detert, J.R., Treviño, L.K., Baker, V.L. & Mayer, D.M. (2012). Why employees do bad things: Moral disengagement and unethical organizational behavior. *Personnel Psychology, 65*, 1–48.

Muraven, M., Tice, D. M. & Baumeister, R. F. (1998). Self-control as a limited resource: Regulatory depletion patterns. *Journal of Personality and Social Psychology, 74*, 774–789.

Murphy, K.R. (1993). *Honesty in the workplace*. Monterey, CA: Brooks/Cole.

Murphy, K.R. & Luther, N. (1997). Assessing honesty, integrity, and deception. In N. Anderson & P. Herriot (Eds.), *International Handbook of Selection and Assessment* (pp. 369–388). Chichester, England: Wiley & Sons.

Nasby, W., Hayden, B. & DePaulo, B.M. (1980). Attributional bias among aggressive boys to interpret unambiguous social stimuli as displays of hostility. *Journal of Abnormal Psychology, 89*(3), 459–468.

Newman, L.S. (2002). What is a "social-psychological" account of perpetrator behavior?: The person versus the situation in Goldhagen's Hitler's Willing Executioners. In L.S. Newman & R. Erber (Eds.), *Understanding Genocide: The Social Psychology of the Holocaust* (pp. 43–67). New York: Oxford University Press.

Nickerson, R.S. (1998). Confirmation bias: A ubiquitous phenomenon in many guises. *Review of General Psychology, 2*, 175–220.

O'Bannon, R.M., Goldinger, L.A. & Appleby, J.D. (1989). *Honesty and integrity testing: A practical guide*. Atlanta: Applied Information Resources.

Oetting, E.R. & Donnermeyer, J.F. (1998). Primary socialization theory: The etiology of drug use and deviance. *Substance Use and Misuse, 33*, 995–1026.

Oetting, E.R., Deffenbacher, J.L. & Donnermeyer, J.F. (1998). Primary socialization theory: The role played by personal traits in the etiology of drug use and deviance. *Substance Use and Misuse, 33*, 1337–1366.

Ones, D.S., Viswesvaran, C. & Schmidt, F.L. (1993). Comprehensive meta-analysis of integrity test validities: Finding and implications for personnel selection and theories of job performance. *Journal of Applied Psychology, 78*, 679–703.

Opotow, S. (1990). Moral exclusion and injustice: An introduction. *Journal of Social Issues, 46*, 173–182.

Patterson, M.L. (1982). A sequential functional model of nonverbal exchange. *Psychological Review, 89*, 231–249.

Pew Research Center. (2015, April). *A Deep Dive into Party Affiliation*.

Pew Research Center. (2016, June). *Partisanship and Political Animosity in 2016*.

Pitz, G.F. (1969). An inertia effect (resistance to change) in the revision of opinion. *Canadian Journal of Psychology, 23*, 24–33.

Pryor, J.B., Giedd, J.L. & Williams, K.B. (1995). A social psychological model for predicting sexual harassment. *Journal of Social Issues, 51*, 69–84.

Reid, S.A. & Hogg, M.A. (2005). Uncertainty reduction, self-enhancement, and social identification. *Personality and Social Psychology Bulletin, 31*, 804–817.

Reis, H.J. (1981). Self-presentation and distributive justice. In J.T. Tedeschi (Ed.), *Impression management theory and social psychological research* (pp. 269–291). New York: Academic Press.

Robinson, S.L. & Morrison, E.W. (1995). Psychological contracts and OCB: The effect of unfulfilled obligations on civic virtue behavior. *Journal of Organizational Behavior, 16*, 289–298.

Rogers, E. (1962). *Diffusion of Innovations*. New York, NY: Free Press.

Rosenberg, M. (1979). *Conceiving the Self*. New York: Basic Books.

Ross, L., Lepper, M.R. & Hubbard, M. (1975). Perseverance in self-perception and social perception: Biased attributional processes in the debriefing paradigm. *Journal of Personality and Social Psychology, 32*, 880–892.

Sachdeva, S., Iliev, R. & Medin, D.L. (2009). Sinning saints and saintly sinners: The paradox of self-regulation. *Psychological Science, 20*, 523–528.

Salancik, G.J. & Pfeffer, J. (1978). A social information processing approach to job attitudes and task design. *Administrative Science Quarterly, 23*, 224–253.

Sanitioso, R., Kunda, Z. & Fong, J.T. (1990). Motivated recruitment of autobiographical memories. *Journal of Personality and Social Psychology, 59*, 229–241.

Schlenker, B.R. (1982). Translating actions into attitudes: An identity-analytic approach to the explanation of social conduct. In L. Berkowitz (Ed.), *Advances in Experimental Social Psychology* (Vol. 15, pp. 194–248). New York: Academic Press.

Schneider, B. (1987). The people make the place. *Personnel Psychology, 40*, 437–453.

Schneider, B. (2008). The people still make the place. In D.B. Smith (Ed.), *The People Make the Place: Dynamic Linkages Between Individuals and Organizations* (pp. 267–289). New York, NY: Taylor & Francis Group/Lawrence Erlbaum Associates.

Schneider, B., Goldstein, H.W. & Smith, D.B. (1995). The ASA framework: An update. *Personnel Psychology, 48*, 747–773.

Shalvi, S., Dana, J., Handgraaf, M.J.J. & De Dreu, C.K.W. (2011). Justified ethicality: Observing desired counterfactuals modifies ethical perceptions and behavior. *Organizational Behavior and Human Decision Processes, 115*, 181–190.

Shalvi, S., Gino, F., Barken, R. & Aval, S. (2015). Self-serving justifications: Doing wrong and feeling moral. *Psychological Science, 24*, 125–130.

Sherman, D.K. & Cohen, G.L. (2002). Accepting threatening information: Self-affirmation and the reduction of defensive biases. *Current Directions in Psychological Science, 11*, 119–123.

Sherman, D.K. & Cohen, G.L. (2006). The psychology of self-defense: Self-affirmation theory. *Advances in Experimental Social Psychology, 38*, 183–242.

Shu, L.L., Gino, F. & Bazerman, M.H. (2011). Dishonest deed, clear conscience: When cheating leads to moral disengagement and motivated forgetting. *Personality and Social Psychology Bulletin, 37*, 330–349.

Snyder, M. & Swan, W.B. (1978). Behavior confirmation in social interaction: From social perception to social reality. *Journal of Experimental Social Psychology, 14*, 148–162.

Staub, E. (1989). *The Roots of Evil: The Origins of Genocide and Other Group Violence*. New York: Cambridge University Press.

Sutherland, E. (1947). *Principles of criminology* (4th Ed.). Philadelphia: Lippencott.

Sutherland, E.H. (1949). *White Collar Crime*. New York: Dryden Press.

Swift, J. & Gould, H. (2019, January 31). *Not an Object: On Sexualization and Exploitation of Women and Girls*. www.unicefusa.org/stories/not-object-sexualization-and-exploitation-women-and-girls/30366

Sykes, G. & Matza, D. (1957). Techniques of neutralization. *American Sociological Review, 22*, 664–670.

Tajfel, H. (1982). *Social Identity and Intergroup Relations*. Cambridge, UK: Cambridge University Press.

Tajfel, H. & Turner, J.C. (1979). An integrative theory of intergroup conflict. In S. Worchel & W.G. Austin (Eds.), *The Social Psychology of Intergroup Relations* (pp. 33–37). Chicago: Nelson Hall.

Tesser, A., Campbell, J. & Smith, M. (1984). Friendship choice and performance: Self-evaluation maintenance in children. *Journal of Personality and Social Psychology, 46*, 561–574

Thomas, W.I. & Thomas, D.W. (1928). *The Child in America: Behavior Problems and Programs*. New York: Knopf.

Tucker, J.C. (1989). Employee theft as social control. *Deviant Behavior, 10*, 319–334.

Viki, G.T. & Abrams, D. (2003). Infra-humanization: Ambivalent sexism and the attribution of primary and secondary emotions to women. *Journal of Experimental Social Psychology, 39*, 492–499.

Vohs, K.D. (2006). Self-regulatory resources power the reflective system: Evidence from five domains. *Journal of Consumer Psychology, 16*, 217–223.

Vohs, K.D., Baumeister, R.F. & Ciarocco, N. (2005). Self-regulation and self-presentation: Regulatory resource depletion impairs management and effortful self-presentation depletes regulatory resources. *Journal of Personality and Social Psychology, 8*, 632–657.

Vohs, K.D. & Faber, R.J. (2007). Spent resources: Self-regulatory resource availability affects impulse buying. *Journal of Consumer Research, 33*, 537–547.

Vohs, K.D. & Heatherton, T.F. (2000). Self-regulatory failure: A resource-depletion approach. *Psychological Science, 11*, 249–254.

Volhardt, J.R. & Campbell-Obaid, M. (2016). The social psychology of genocide and mass atrocities. In A.G. Miller (Ed.), *The Social Psychology of Good and Evil* (pp. 159–184). New York: Guilford.

Weiss, H.M. (1990). Learning theory and industrial and organizational psychology. In M.D. Dunnette & L.M. Hough (Eds.), *Handbook of Industrial and Organizational Psychology* (2nd Ed., Vol. 1, pp. 171–221). Palo Alto, CA: Consulting Psychologists Press.

White, R.K. (2004). Misperception and war. Peace and Conflict. *Journal of Peace Psychology, 10*, 399–409.

5

INFORMAL GROUPS

The major focus of this book is on how groups and group processes contribute to misbehavior. I will look in detail at two different types of groups: (1) informal groups—in which there is little or no externally imposed structure to the group or its activities (examples include groups of friends, families, and neighborhoods, but also virtual groups and communities), and (2) formal groups—in which there are well-defined roles, rules, tasks, and goals, often externally imposed (e.g., in job descriptions, charters, organizational charts). Most of us are or have been part of one or more formal groups in the workplace, but formal groups also exist in other settings, such as the classroom (e.g., groups assigned to complete classroom projects). Both formal and informal groups share many key features and processes, but there are enough distinctions in how these groups work and how they influence the behavior of their members to justify treating them separately. This chapter deals with informal groups; formal groups are discussed in the chapter that follows.

Both formal and informal social groups share four fundamental characteristics: (1) group members interact with one another, (2) some group members have different rights and responsibilities and higher status than others, (3) groups pursue goals, which include externally set goals (e.g., increase productivity) and internally determined ones (e.g., keep the group together), and (4) there is a shared sense of social identity. One key difference between formal and informal groups is the extent and source of their structure. Formal groups have well-defined structures that define the lines of authority, tasks, rights, and responsibilities. For example, in work organizations, there are job descriptions, mission statements, organizational charts, and handbooks that specify what group members are expected to do and there are often formal processes (e.g., internships, training programs) that are designed to instruct new members about not only the requirements of their jobs but also the norms and culture of the organization. These structures often stay in place with little modification as members join or remove themselves from the organization. Informal groups are structured (i.e., different group members have different roles and responsibilities), but their structure develops as a result of the interactions among group members (Hare, 1993, 2003), and the structure and function of the group can be dramatically changed as new members join or as old members leave the group.

Both formal and informal groups have goals (Hare, 1993). In formal groups, these are often explicitly defined (e.g., maximize return to shareholders) and a good deal of attention is devoted to making sure that the behavior of individual group members helps to move the groups as a whole toward that goal (Aguinis, 2013). Informal groups also pursue a range of goals, but these are not always explicitly defined. They include forming and carrying out immediate plans for the group (e.g., organize a camping trip) and longer-term goals related to the survival of the group (e.g., recruit and retain members).

Informal groups tend to be small (Wicker, 1969), although some loosely structured groups (e.g., the hacker community) might be quite large. In many ways, the small size of face-to-face informal groups makes sense. As the number of group members increases arithmetically the number of different connections within a group expands geometrically. Within a six-person group, there are 15 possible pairings of group members; in a 12-person group, there are over 250. Formal groups manage this problem by imposing a structure that simplifies relationships among members, but in informal groups, there is no comparable external source of structure. Informal groups sometimes manage this by creating interaction structures where social interactions tend to focus on a small number of individuals (often the informal leaders of the group), but these structures can take time to develop, and it is sometimes difficult for large informal groups to manage their patterns of relationships.

Finally, formal and informal social groups are an important part of people's identities. As I have noted in previous chapters, social groups meet many important needs and perform several important functions for their members. Groups provide critically important information in the form of descriptive and injunctive norms that tell people what they can expect, how they should evaluate it, and what values they should draw upon to make these evaluative judgments (Feldman, 1984; Hare, 1982, Napier & Gershenfeld, 1999). Identification with a group helps to reinforce a positive self-image and it creates a sense of "us"—that is, a sense of belonging to something greater than oneself. In conflict situations, this can morph into a sense of "us vs. them" (Napier & Gershenfeld, 1999), and as I will note later in this chapter, the tendency to view competing groups in a negative light contributes substantially to many types of misbehavior.

Four Characteristics of Groups

As noted earlier, the four key characteristics of groups are: (1) interaction among members, (2) structure (e.g., hierarchy, roles), (3) goals, and (4) identification with the group. I explore research dealing with each of these characteristics next. In the section that follows, I examine how small groups sometimes promote or tolerate misbehaviors.

Group Members Interact

Group members communicate and interact with each other. There is a large body of research dealing with these interactions, which can be traced back over 75 years, and it suggests that the pattern and nature of these interactions depend on factors such as the size, structure, and purpose of the group. Bales (1950) suggested that there are two main types of interactions in a group—that is, relationship interactions and task interactions. Relationship interactions are actions performed by group members that relate to or influence the emotional and interpersonal bonds within the group. They can include both positive actions (social support, consideration) and negative actions (criticism, conflict). Task interactions represent actions performed by group members that are relevant to the group's projects, tasks, and goals. Relationship interactions are designed to maintain the group as a viable unit, whereas task interactions are geared to help the group accomplish important tasks. The relative frequency and criticality of these two classes of tasks are likely to vary as a function of the type of group they apply to. For example, family and friendship groups do have tasks that they are trying to accomplish (e.g., plan a trip), but it is the group itself rather than the tasks the group performs that is likely to be most important, and relationship behaviors are likely to be more frequent and more important in these groups. Task forces and work teams, on the other hand, exist mainly to accomplish particular tasks and to meet specific goals, and task interactions are likely to be more critical.

Research in the field of Social Network Analysis focuses on the pattern of interactions and ties between people—that is, who each group member communicates, interacts, and has relationship ties with. These ties can be complex and multifaceted. For example, virtually all workers have ties of one sort or another with many others in the workplace, ranging from ties based on friendship or shared activities to ties based on the role requirements of their jobs. Ties can be fleeting or long-lasting and can be weak or strong. Studies of interactions among group members date back to the 1930s, and research in this field progressed quickly. In the early stages of research on group behavior Simon (1950) developed a complex mathematical theory of interactions among group members that provided rigorous explanations for a wide range of group phenomena (e.g., the formation of cliques, competition among groups, enforcement of norms). One of the earliest findings in this line of research was that there were distinct patterns of communication in different types of groups. Figure 5.1 illustrates four distinct patterns of communication that might be encountered in a five-person group.

Social networks in informal groups are likely to be fairly simple, with ties that reflect common interests, preferences, experiences, bonds of affection, and shared identity. In contrast, formal organizations are likely to have social networks in which there are interpersonal ties, ties related to the processes by which work is performed and ties related to organizational levels. In a group that has a strong hierarchical structure, communications and interactions might take the form of a chain, in which communication flows strictly from the top down, with little or no breaks in the chain of command. Alternately, communications might flow in a circle, where each group member communicates freely with some other group members, and in which communication can eventually flow through the entire group. In a circle communication structure, each group member has a subset of other group members they interact with. A modified circle might include hierarchical patterns of communications (e.g., person A communicates with persons B and C, and always or almost always initiates and controls these communications).

The "Y" pattern shown in Figure 5.1 appears to be a common pattern of communication and interaction within groups. It has been recognized since the 1930s that some network positions were more central, while others were more peripheral (Roethlisberger & Dickson, 1939). People who occupy more central positions in a social network often have more influence on the behavior of the group (Brass & Burkhardt, 1993).

Finally, groups can have the free-flowing pattern of communication and interaction exemplified by the network structure, where everyone interacts and communicates with everyone else. As I noted earlier, this structure can become increasingly complex and unwieldy as groups become larger, and groups with

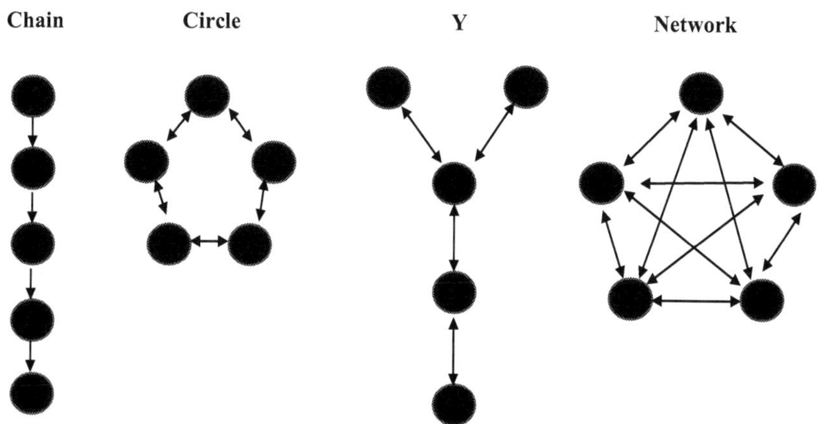

FIGURE 5.1 Patterns of Group Communication

a network structure are likely to become impossible to maintain once they are much larger than four to five people (Fay, Garrod & Carletta, 2000).

Figure 5.1 is a useful starting point, but it oversimplifies some critical determinants of patterns of interaction. In particular, it suggests two potential organizing principles for group interaction—that is, hierarchy and limited networks. That is, the "chain" and "Y" structures are based on hierarchy, or the notion that some group members have more influence than others. The circle structure is based on the notion that each group member interacts with a subset of other group members, but that eventually, all communications can flow to all group members. Another possibility is that groups might be divided into subgroups that do not interact frequently or comfortably, creating "fault lines" where interaction is less productive, and may even be a source of conflict. For example, Lau and Murnighan (1998, 2005) studied the effects of demographic divisions in groups and showed that conflicts often flared in circumstances where a group was divided into clear demographic subgroups (e.g., groups defined by race or ethnicity), particularly if the distinct groups need to communicate or cooperate to achieve the group's goal.

The complexity of maintaining a true network relationship among large numbers of individuals is one of the factors that tend to lead to the development of formal or informal group structures (both hierarchies and the formation of subgroups). Strong and stable hierarchies are probably more likely in formal groups, where they are often defined a priori (e.g., by contracts, role descriptions, reporting relationships), but in both formal and informal groups, some sort of structure will likely emerge over time.

BOX 5.1 IS THERE AN UPPER LIMIT ON THE NUMBER OF SOCIAL RELATIONSHIPS WE CAN MANAGE?

In an influential paper, Dunbar (1992) suggested that because of cognitive limits that are essentially hard-wired, people can maintain no more than 150 stable social relationships (i.e., relationships in which an individual knows who each person is and how each person relates to every other person). This Dunbar number was popularized by Malcolm Gladwell (2000), and it has been widely cited in anthropology, economics, and other social sciences. It is now common to see the claim that people are simply incapable of managing more than 150 or so relationships at any point in time. The idea that there is a firm upper limit to the number of social relationships that can be managed at one time has important implications. It suggests, for example, that as you gain friends and social connections, you might have to shed some of your old ones. However, there are good reasons to question the accuracy of Dunbar's number.

First, Dunbar based his estimate on data from primates, which showed a consistent relationship between group size and the size of the cerebral cortex. These figures were then extrapolated to humans and to hominids at various stages of evolution (for example, Neanderthals had a Dunbar number of 144). However, brain size is only moderately related to intelligence (Gray & Thompson, 2004; Koch, 2016); links between brain size and social skills in humans are poorly understood. As a result, inferences about social behavior based on brain size are potentially suspect. Second, there are many ways of estimating the size of social networks, and depending on precisely how social relationships are defined, very different upper bounds might make sense. More recent research (e.g., McCormick, Salgnick, & Zheng, 2010) suggests that the maximum number of social relationships a person can maintain might be as high as 600.

There are useful lessons to be learned from an analysis of the strengths and weaknesses of Dunbar's number. First, caution is warranted when making inferences about human behavior from gross physiological measures such as brain size. There are too many intervening variables to make these inferences reliably. Second, concepts such as Dunbar's number are appealing because they are simple and definite, hence the popular appeal of this concept. Social behavior is far from simple or definite, and we should be skeptical about claims on absolute upper or lower bounds of social behaviors. Dunbar's basic claim, that keeping track of many social relationships is more difficult than keeping track of only a few is certainly true, but there are likely to be at least some people who successfully juggle large social networks. Dunbar's number is a useful starting point for discussions about how to make sense of people's social capabilities, but we should think of it as a point of departure, not as a hard-wired limitation.

Status and Roles

Both formal and informal groups have a definite structure. This structure might be more precisely defined and more stable in formal groups and might be particularly open to change early in the lifespan of informal groups, but some form of structure is the norm. In particular, both formal and informal groups are characterized by status hierarchies (i.e., some group members have more power and influence than others) and roles (i.e., different members are responsible for or more likely to engage in different types of behaviors and tasks). Status hierarchies and roles are more loosely defined and dynamic in informal groups than in formal ones, where roles, responsibilities, power differentials, and the like might be assigned, formally negotiated, and preserved in contracts, agreements, charters, and organizational charts, but it is rare to find informal groups without well-understood status hierarchies and roles.

Status Hierarchies

Anderson and Kilduff (2009) define status in informal groups, noting that "status in face-to-face groups is defined as an individual's prominence, respect, and influence in the eyes of others" (p. 295). Other definitions of status emphasize the fact that some members have more influence and more access to group resources than others (Hogan, 1983). While there are varying definitions of status, there is broad agreement that groups almost always have one or more leaders and that they almost always have a set of members with less status and influence. Indeed, leadership is thought to be virtually universal in both human and nonhuman groups, and there is considerable evidence that leadership has a strong evolutionary basis (Brown, 1991; VanVugt, 2006).

There are two main individual characteristics that groups tend to value—that is, competence and a strong commitment to the group, and both of these are consistent predictors of status. Meta-analyses have empirically confirmed that individuals who possess superior abilities related to the group's tasks and who have strong social/leadership abilities achieve higher status (Lord, De Vader, & Alliger, 1986). Anderson and Kilduff (2009) argue that individuals actively pursue status by creating the impression that they are highly competent, by enhancing their apparent attachment to the group, and by developing more social connections. However, personality also matters. The personality trait dominance (i.e., a preference for possessing authority and the tendency to behave assertively) predicts who emerges as the leader in groups more consistently than any other individual-difference dimension examined, including intelligence (Lord et al., 1986).

Informal and leaderless groups often develop a status hierarchy quite early in the process of their formation and development, and it is not unusual for task leaders and social-emotional leaders to emerge. The former are in charge of whatever the group is trying to achieve, whereas the latter are concerned with group morale and cohesion, and they may or may not be the same persons (Hare, 1994). This process of emergent leadership in informal groups forms the basis for a widely used assessment tool, the Leaderless Group Discussion (Bass, 1954, Borteyrou, Lievens, Bruchon-Schweitzer, Congard, & Rascle, 2015).

The Leaderless Group Discussion is often used in evaluating candidates for managerial jobs and leadership positions. It involves assembling a small group (usually four–six) of strangers and giving them a topic or a problem to discuss. Pillay (2016) describes a Leaderless Group Discussion that used the prompt,

> An airplane crash-landed on a deserted island. Only six persons survived: a pregnant woman, an inventor, a doctor, an astronaut, an ecologist, and a

vagrant. Whom do you think should be given the only one-person hot-air balloon to leave the island?

In these discussions, leaders inevitably emerge, and the leadership of the group can change during the brief period of discussion (e.g., one individual might start the discussion and dominate at first, only to be replaced by another individual who emerges as a leader). Leadership that is exhibited in this assessment exercise is a useful predictor of effectiveness and performance in many jobs (Borteyrou et al., 2015).

Research on status hierarchies usually focuses on leaders, but there is much to be learned by studying followers (Uhl-Bien, Riggio, Lowe, & Carsten, 2014). Kelly (1992) argued that leadership is most likely to be effective in organizations that cultivate strong followership—that is, enthusiastic, intelligent, and self-reliant participation in pursuit of the group's goals. Followership research has shown that effective followers are far from passive and that accepting leadership is not the same thing as simply doing what you are told. Strong followership requires trust between leaders and followers and mutual commitment to the goals of the group.

Roles

Social roles are sets of behaviors that are expected and approved, together with a delineation of duties and privileges that come with holding and executing that role (Hare, 2003).

Roles define the cognitive schemas that tell people how to act and what to expect (DiMaggio, 1997), and they help to provide the structure that governs behavior in specific situations (Ashforth & Mael, 1989; Berger & Luckmann, 1966; Hogg & Terry, 2000; Misangy & Weaver, 2008). In addition to defining the behaviors that are expected in particular situations, social roles also define injunctive norms that specify which behaviors are viewed as good or bad in that situation (Berger & Luckmann, 1966). In informal groups, roles may evolve and may change as the membership of the group changes. In more formal settings (e.g., the workplace) roles might be defined with some precision (e.g., job descriptions), but even here, the precise content of a role might depend on characteristics of the person and of the situation (Hare, 2003).

In a groundbreaking work, Benne and Sheats (1948) identified three general categories of group roles that are present in both formal and informal groups: (1) task roles—groups often have to accomplish particular tasks (e.g., build a barn, plan a party), and different individuals tend to reliably take on particular roles and responsibilities when the group is trying to accomplish a task, (2) social-emotional-personal roles—some people are leaders, some are followers, and others are peacekeepers in groups; these personal roles help the group to survive and function smoothly, and (3) dysfunctional roles—group members often engage in behaviors that are harmful to the group, but potentially helpful to the individual (e.g., aggressors, self-seekers).

Over the years, numerous authors have built upon this foundation to add new categories (e.g., procedural roles) and to elucidate distinct roles group members might occupy (Hare, 1993, 2003). Table 5.1 lists several distinct roles group members might occupy. Some of the roles listed in Table 5.1 are self-explanatory, but several deserve comment.

First, in both formal and informal groups, certain individuals are likely to emerge who initiate and define the tasks the group will engage in (Initiator). These individuals are often recognized by group members as leaders, even if they do not occupy positions of authority in formal groups (e.g., supervisor). The person who initiates a task is not always the same as the person who organizes group members to accomplish the task (Coordinator), and sometimes different group members may help point the way toward solving problems or accomplishing tasks (Orienter) without necessarily doing the day-to-day work of getting tasks accomplished. Other roles are also important to helping a group accomplish important tasks. For example, many groups have one or more members who serve as the collective memory of the group, especially in terms of keeping track of how tasks get accomplished (Recorder).

There is often a useful distinction between group products (what they get done) and group processes (how they function), and there is a range of roles that are primarily concerned with managing and maintaining the processes by which groups function and survive (e.g., Harmonizers and Encouragers). Others work to manage the flow of information (Facilitator) and to maintain the balance in communication within a group (Gatekeeper). Finally, some group members fulfill the critical role of Followers, who do what the group wants and support the directions and the assignments of the group.

Several roles do more to disrupt than to support the functioning of a group. Aggressors attempt to dominate group communications and processes and to stir

TABLE 5.1 Functional Roles of Group Members

Task Roles	*Social-Emotional-Personal Roles*	*Dysfunctional Roles*
Initiator	Encourager	Aggressor
Information Seeker	Harmonizer	Blocker
Information Giver	Compromiser	Recognition-Seeker
Opinion Seeker	Gatekeeper	Self-Confessor
Opinion Giver	Observer/Communicator	Disruptor
Elaborator	Follower	Help-Seeker
Orienter	Facilitator	Special Interest Pleader
Evaluator		Joker
Energizer		
Procedural Technician		
Recorder		

conflict. Blockers are naysayers who consistently come up with reasons why something cannot be done. Self-Confessors try to divert the group to solve their interpersonal problems, whereas Jokers distract the group from its tasks by injecting often inappropriate humor into situations where it is not functional for the group.

In informal groups, roles are emergent and dynamic. That is, the organization of a group may vary over time (Hare, 2003). First, in a newly formed group, it may take several periods of conflict before an informal status hierarchy can be established. Second, people may join or drop out of a group, and this might cause roles to be redistributed. Third, different tasks or purposes may require different sets of activities and roles, and these can also change at different stages of activity. For example, different roles are needed when a new task is started (e.g., Initiator) than when the group is well along in the process and needs to be kept motivated and on track (Encourager, Facilitator).

In Chapter 6, I will explore the implications of formalizing roles. For example, in work organizations, job descriptions, handbooks, organizational charts, and the like spell out in some detail the expectations, rights, and responsibilities associated with different positions in the organization. This formalization, particularly the formalization of power hierarchies, increases the probability that group members will defer to their superiors and will be willing to undertake many types of dishonest or norm-defying actions because their superiors take or are believed to take responsibility for these acts.

Groups Have Goals

Formal groups are usually created to achieve specific objectives, such as completing projects or carrying out a set of processes in a larger system (e.g., assembling chassis in an automotive plant), and the goals of the group are necessarily linked to (but not necessarily limited to) those objectives. Earlier, I noted that Bales (1950) sorted group interactions into task and interpersonal categories, and that formal groups are likely to have goals related to both their core tasks and to maintain the viability of the group. However, in formal groups, the core tasks of the group usually take precedence, and once the objective of the group is accomplished, it is not unusual for the group to dissolve.

BOX 5.2 VIRTUAL GROUPS

We typically think of groups as being composed of individuals who have frequent face-to-face interactions, but the evolution of computer and communication technology has led to the development of virtual groups, whose members might never interact face to face, and in some cases might never interact directly at all. Barnett (2011) documented the development of technology-supported social networks, starting with slow, text-based messaging systems, followed by messaging and file-sharing systems developed for academic use (e.g., BITNET), and finally evolving into sophisticated online communities as well as platforms for sharing information, pictures, opinions, videos, and the like (e.g., Facebook).

Interactions in virtual groups are often very different from those in face-to-face groups. First, in some groups, there might be little direct interaction between group members, and when it comes, it might involve significant delays. For example, person A might post information and person B might respond after a significant delay. Person C might then comment on person B's response, and person A might never see or notice the response. Other groups might involve a high level of engagement among members, with immediate responses and online cooperation among members. Differences in the level of involvement of group members and the immediacy of interactions might influence the structure of the group. There might, for example, be a group moderator, but this person's role is sometimes solely administrative, and not necessarily a role that provided much power or influence. Nevertheless, even in virtual groups, it is common to see some members interacting very frequently, effectively dominating the virtual communication in this group. For example, I belong to a Facebook group titled "Old Guitar Pickers". There is a group of three–five individuals who post material virtually every day, and their posts account for a surprising proportion of the information and performances that are posted. Other people, like me, are mainly Followers and Communicators, rarely posting new material but occasionally commenting on other people's posts. Like other social groups, virtual groups can be an important part of a person's identity, and for some people (e.g., members of the hacker community, serious gamers), they may represent a primary source of identity.

Virtual interactions provided opportunities for worldwide interactions, but they also provide opportunities for a range of offensive behaviors, especially on platforms where people interact anonymously. Juvonen and Graham (2014) summarize research on cyberbullying—that is, electronically mediated bullying that involves texting via cell phone, emailing, or instant messaging, or posting messages on social networking sites and in chat rooms. Much like bullying in general, cyberbullying can be either direct (i.e., threats or nasty messages are sent to the target) or indirect (i.e., malicious comments, pictures, and private messages are spread much like rumors). Cyberbullying can have serious implications (it has been implicated in numerous suicides, especially among younger users), and the anonymity of virtual communications is an important risk factor for cyberbullying (Bartlett, Gentile, & Chew, 2016).

Virtual teams are becoming more common in the workplace, but there are reasons to question the wisdom of forming virtual teams. First, computer-mediated groups tended to be characterized by less interaction and exchange than face-to-face groups and tend to take longer in their work (Hollingshead & McGrath, 1995). They are also more likely to gravitate to extreme communications (e.g., flaming—that is, posting attacks, insults, and offensive language) and risky decisions (Kiesler & Sproul, 1992; Lea & Spears, 1991). A meta-analysis of 27 studies suggests that as a result, virtual teams are slower and less accurate than face-to-face teams (Baltes, Dickson, Sherman, Bauer, & La Ganke, 2002).

The COVID-19 pandemic has led to an increased reliance on virtual interactions, with computer-mediated media replacing classroom instruction and workplace meetings in many countries. It is too soon to determine how a change from face-to-face to virtual meetings affects the quality of instruction or the effectiveness of meetings, but some clear trends are emerging. First, workplace meetings tend to be shorter, but more frequent (Schwartz, 2020). Second, online instruction can be effective, but the move from live classrooms to virtual instruction is likely to exaggerate the effects of inequality on education. Poorer families often lack computers, high-quality internet access, and separate spaces for students to interact with and concentrate on classroom activities (North, 2020). It is not clear if or when we will go back to classrooms or to the office, much less to face-to-face meetings (Murphy, 2020), and it is likely that virtual meetings will be an important part of both education and work for the foreseeable future.

In contrast, informal groups exist primarily to meet the social and psychological needs of their members, and while these groups often have a range of tasks to accomplish, maintaining the social fabric of the group is likely to be a more critical goal than accomplishing particular tasks. First, the group will necessarily be concerned with retaining members, particularly members who identify with the norms and values of the group. They might actively recruit members, but they will also be concerned with setting boundaries (e.g., who is accepted as a member) and keeping the group from getting too large.

One of the mechanisms informal groups use to maintain the close relationships among group members of their group is to promulgate and enforce norms (Horne, 2001). As I have noted in previous chapters, descriptive norms help group members to develop consistent perceptions of what *is* happening in their groups, while injunctive norms help them develop consistent perceptions of what *should be* happening in their group. Group members are rewarded for complying with injunctive norms and sanctioned for disobeying them (Horne, 2001), and this process of sanction and reward helps to develop consistent patterns of behavior and expectations within the group. In highly cohesive groups, where a high value is placed on group membership, people are often willing to make personal sacrifices for the benefit of the group (Prapavessis & Carron, 1997), but even in less cohesive groups, the development of a stable and well-accepted set of norms is one of the things that holds a group together.

Although group-maintenance goals are likely to be paramount in informal groups, these groups also carry out all sorts of tasks, and the development of informal roles and well-understood norms help the group substantially to get things done. When a group of friends plans an outing, it is often well understood who will choose the destination, who will provide transportation, who will arrange accommodations, etc. When a family prepares dinner, there is often a well-rehearsed routine regarding the specifies of who will do the shopping, cooking, cleaning up, and the like.

Members Identify With Groups

Finally, groups are a crucial part of people's social identity, and they satisfy important psychological needs, most fundamentally the need to become connected with others (Baumeister & Leary, 1995). Most individuals are members of multiple informal groups (e.g., friends, neighbors, coworkers), and different groups may have very different norms, including norms that tolerate or even support misbehavior. Understanding why individuals identify more strongly with some groups than with others is, therefore, an important part of understanding how groups can influence their members to behave in ways that either support or violate general social norms.

Deaux (1996) suggests that the social identification process is complex and that it involves cognitive processes, emotional associations, and perceptions or beliefs about the interdependence between group members. Jackson (2002) and Cameron (2004) describe these three factors in terms of: (1) self-categorization—a cognitive component that refers to the centrality of the group in describing the individual's identity, (2) an emotional evaluation of the group (an affective component), and (3) perceptions of the strength of ties among group members, often reflected in terms of similarity and bonds with other group members. The direct causal links among these three aspects of social identification are not completely understood, but a case can be made that the centrality of a particular group to a person's social identity is driven largely by emotional evaluations of the group—that is, perceptions that the group is valuable and important. In Chapter 3, I discussed the concept of a reference group—that is, a group a person belongs to, aspires to belong to, or admires. These last two characteristics of reference groups (i.e., groups a person aspires to belong to or admires) may be particularly important in determining the strength of identification with particular groups.

Why do people aspire to become members of particular groups? In previous chapters, I have noted the centrality of two motivational factors for understanding the effects of groups on the behavior of their members: (1) maintaining a positive self-image, and (2) reducing ambiguity and uncertainty. Groups that help individuals feel better about themselves and that help them make sense of their world are particularly attractive. However, we cannot account for group formation and group identity solely in terms of which needs groups meet. Two simple features of social life often account for the formation of groups and group members' identification with the group—that is, proximity and similarity.

People who live or work in the same area are more likely to interact, and simple proximity often explains how and why groups get started. Similarity is an even more potent factor in creating groups. People with similar backgrounds, personalities, or interests find it easier to establish relationships, and similarity (or perceived similarity) is a strong factor in identification with a group.

BOX 5.3 FROM GROUP MINDS TO SHARED MENTAL MODELS

In 1865, Gustav Lebon published *Psychologie des Foules* (Psychology of Crowds), in which he introduced the concept of a "crowd mind". Subsequent writers, including Sigmund Freud, elaborated on the idea individuals in a crowd lose their sense of personal freedom and responsibility, and that the crowd functions like a primitive unitary organism, which follows emotion and a shared unconscious that impels them to behave in ways that they would never behave when acting alone. Over the next 100 years, many variations of the idea that people acting in groups share some form of group mind or collective consciousness have emerged (Tsoukalas, 2007). This concept has been particularly influential in the study of mob behavior.

Chaplin (1985) defines a mob as a crowd acting under strong emotional conditions that often lead to violent, destructive, or criminal acts. This emphasis on acting under emotion is shared across several theories and reviews (Forsyth, 1999; Milgram & Toch, 1969; Staub & Rosenthal, 1999). First, there is contagion, an idea can be traced back to Lebon's original work in the 1890s. Contagion theories suggest that behaviors and arousal levels that start with a few individuals spread through the mob (Goldstein, 2002). An alternative theory focuses on convergence, suggesting mobs are formed by people with similar needs and desires (Forsyth, 1983). Emergent Norm Theory (Horowitz, 2001; Turner & Killian, 1972) suggests groups might start with no intention to misbehave, but gatherings of people can be susceptible to rumors or to malevolent interpretations of events they experience which heighten arousal. Interstimulation and intensification can turn a crowd into a mob. Sociocultural theories (Staub, 1993) suggest that several factors can instigate mobs, ranging from the presence of many people under stressful circumstances (e.g., high temperatures) to the existence of grievances and precipitating events (e.g., assignation of Martin Luther King). All of these theories can be useful for understanding mob behavior, but the core idea that links many of them—that is, the mob mind—is deeply problematic.

We usually think of a mind as representing a product of the cognitive activities of an individual. Where does the mob mind reside? If the mob mind draws on a shared unconscious, it is fair to ask *whose* unconscious and how is it shared. It is one thing to say that a mob *behaves* like it has a single mind, but quite another to say that the mob *has* a mind.

The more modern concept of "shared mental models" has proved a much more useful one for understanding how groups or teams act as a unit (Mohammed & Dumville, 2001). As Mathieu, Heffner, Goodwin, Salas, and Cannon-Bowers (2000) note, teams and groups function more efficiently and effectively when there is a shared understanding of what the task requires, how group members should interact, how roles are defined, etc. Although the link is rarely drawn in the research literature on shared mental models, group norms regarding the behaviors that are expected, rewarded, and sanctioned in particular settings can help in establishing shared mental models in informal groups. For example, the analysis of the behavior of mobs is likely to make more progress when focusing on noncognitive determinants of behavior (e.g., the contagion of emotion) than in attempts to isolate and understand the mob's "mind".

Transactive memory represents a second useful construct for understanding what appear to be "group minds". Austin (2003) defines transactive memory as "a combination of the knowledge possessed by each individual and a collective awareness of who knows what" (p. 866). Groups and teams perform many tasks in which no single member has the knowledge or skills to complete the task. Knowing who has the requisite knowledge and skills to accomplish each part of a complex task is often critical to a group's ability to function effectively. Rather than representing the mind of a group, transactive memories can be thought of as a sort of library, complete with a catalog showing where each piece of information is stored.

How Informal Groups Contribute to Misbehavior

Informal groups influence the behavior of their members in many ways. First, the mere presence of other people can influence people's behavior. For example, Kent (1994b) described three distinct ways of how being with other people changes an individual's behavior. First, the presence of others can create social facilitation effects, which are the result of arousal that is a frequent result of the presence of others. In many settings, higher arousal translates into higher performance, but it can also lead to hasty decisions and impetuous behavior. Second, there are social inhibition effects, where the presence of others suppresses behaviors that would be likely to occur alone if people were acting alone. In previous chapters, I have discussed bystander effects, where the presence of others makes it less likely that individuals will intervene in emergencies. Finally, there are affiliation effects, which are the result of emotion-producing effects of the presence of others, especially in anxiety-producing situations. For many people, the presence of others can reduce uncertainty and anxiety, which in turn is likely to reduce inhibitions on a range of behaviors (some of which might be misbehaviors). However, for some people, the presence of others triggers fear of rejection, which could narrow their range of behavioral responses (Wirth & Schultheiss, 2006).

In Chapter 3, I discussed the diffusion and displacement of responsibility, and these two phenomena can lead directly to misbehavior. Of the two, diffusion of responsibility is more likely in informal groups, where it is often unclear who should respond to emergencies or to situations where help and intervention are called for. In groups, each member might believe that *someone* should act, but be uncertain *who* should take action. If group members observe others in their group hanging back and showing reluctance to act, the probability that nobody in the group will take action goes up. Although this diffusion of responsibility is typically cited in bystander incidents, where many people observe an emergency but none of them intervenes to help, it is not limited to emergencies (Treviño, Den Nieuwenboer, & Kish-Gaphart, 2014). Diffusion of responsibility can help to explain the lack of response to long-standing problems, ranging from world poverty to budget deficits.

A distinction is usually drawn between diffusion of responsibility and displacement of responsibility, with the latter being more common in groups with a formal authority structure. As I will illustrate in the following chapter, the fact that some person has a formal authority role in a group makes it considerably easier for individuals to act in ways that would normally run counter to their ethical and moral standards, displacing authority for decisions that lead to misbehavior to people in authority. People who believe they should follow orders or directions from someone in a position of authority are capable of a shocking range of misbehaviors; a common response from soldiers who have committed war crimes or from individuals who have been involved in carrying out genocide is that they were only following orders (Milgram, 1974; Staub, 1989).

Several group-level processes can lead to misbehaviors, notably the development of deviant norms, pressure to conform, and the negative stereotypes of out-groups. First, group norms are an important influence on the behavior of group members; groups reward members who abide by group norms and punish members who deviate from them. Once they are formed, these norms can be long-lived, and can even outlast the group members who originally established the norm (Jacobs & Campbell, 1961). Groups that create norms that tolerate or even encourage misbehavior can be a powerful force in encouraging misbehavior in individuals. Consider the influence of gangs and gang norms on the behavior of their members.

Youth gangs served as the focus of a substantial body of research through the 1990s, but gangs of this sort are not limited to young people. There is a long history of gangs and vigilante groups in the U.S., and these gangs have many characteristics in common (Goldstein, 2002). Gangs, vigilante groups, and other similar groups usually have relatively stable membership and identification, are perceived by themselves and others as a social unit, and most importantly, are involved in antisocial or illegal activity. These gangs perform valued functions for their members (support, sense of belongingness, mutual protection) but they can also have a corrosive effect by increasing criminality, violence, toleration for destructive behavior.

Gangs meet all of the definitions of a social group, albeit being groups whose activities defy the norms of the general society in which they are embedded. They are perhaps an extreme version of a broader phenomenon—that is, groups within a society whose norms tolerate or support some forms of misbehavior. This phenomenon is not limited to gangs or to career criminals. For example, more than half of all women report experiencing sexual harassment in the workplace (Ilies, Hauserman, Schwochau, & Stibal, 2003). These behaviors occur in large part because the norms of workgroups and the workplace allow them to occur. Similarly, the Brookings Institute suggests that one in every six dollars owed in federal taxes is not paid and that deliberate tax evasion is a significant part of this problem (Gale & Krupkin, 2019). Misbehavior on this scale occurs in part because many people believe there is nothing wrong with some level of tax evasion. Criminal gangs are different from other groups mainly in the range of illegal and antisocial activities that they accept as normal and worthwhile, but crime is not the exclusive provenance of gangs; corporate crime is widespread (Clarke, 1990; Clinard & Yeager, 1980) and a substantial proportion of crimes are committed by otherwise honest individuals who believe it is acceptable to cheat on taxes, plagiarize papers, falsify reports, steal music, etc. (Gabor, 1994).

Informal groups do not have to create antisocial norms to encourage misbehavior; many other group processes can indirectly encourage behavior that would normally be seen as violating important social norms. First, dissent within a group is uncomfortable, and groups work hard to enforce conformity, at least on matters that are important to the group (Kent, 1994a). This tendency is particularly strong when groups are cohesive, and/or the dissent creates a threat to the positive self-image of the group. Earlier, I noted the incidence of sexual harassment in the workplace. One of the explanations for the frequency of sexual harassment is that people feel pressure to conform to societal norms and to group norms that emphasize masculinity and devalue women (Seabrook, Ward, & Giaccardi, 2018). However, this drive toward conformity and suppression of dissent can contribute substantially to misbehavior even in the absence of antisocial norms. For example, individual group members might be willing to offer help or to intervene in situations where help seems to be called for (e.g., they observe someone who is not a part of the group being bullied), but if the group norm is to stay out of situations like this, they will probably choose not to intervene.

One factor that contributes to the cohesiveness of groups is the so-called "false consensus effect". People tend to overestimate the extent to which their opinions, beliefs, preferences, values, and habits are normal and typical of those of others (Marks & Miller, 1987). Selective sorting is likely to magnify this effect. People tend to associate with those whose attitudes are similar to their own (Berscheid & Walster, 1978) and to avoid associating with others whose attitudes are different (Rosenbaum, 1986), and as a result, they are likely to experience many situations in which nearly everyone they interact with shares a set of beliefs and attitudes. This is likely to reinforce the belief that everyone feels the same way.

Second, threats to the group will often trigger: (1) stronger attachment to the group, and (2) negative thoughts and stereotypes about competing groups (Riek, Mania, & Gaertner, 2006; Turner & Pratkanis, 1994). One of the principal explanations for racial and ethnic prejudice cites actual or perceived competition among groups as a starting point for the development of prejudiced beliefs and discriminatory action (Blumer, 1958; Bobo & Hutchings, 1996; Dovidio, Glick, & Rudman, 2005). Even where there are no pre-existing negative perceptions of a group, groups who pose a threat to the position or the self-image of an individual's important reference groups are likely to be perceived negatively, and these negative perceptions can lead to misbehaviors that range from incivility to genocide (see Chapter 2).

Finally, social learning occurs within formal and informal groups, and this can sometimes include acquiring patterns of behavior that violate broad social norms or laws. For example, Gino, Ayal, and Ariely (2009) showed that exposure to other people's unethical behavior can increase or decrease an individual's dishonesty. Gino and Galinsky (2012) argue that in situations where there is ambiguity about the appropriate way of behaving, we look to others and use their behavior to understand the prevailing norms. Others' behavior thus defines the social norm or provides the social proof that then leads us to behave similarly to those around us (e.g., Cialdini, 1993; Goldstein, Martin, & Cialdini, 2008).

These social learning effects are particularly strong when they occur within important reference groups. When people are exposed to an in-group member's unethical behavior, they align with the behavior and behave dishonestly themselves, on the assumption that an in-group member's behaviors provide information about what's appropriate in the given context (Gino, Ayal, & Ariely, 2009; Gino, Gu, & Zhong, 2009b). The frequency and intensity of interaction with other members of your reference group tend to make this influence stronger (Zey-Ferrell & Ferrell, 1982).

Ashforth and Anand (2003) argued that the capacity of isolated, polarized groups to normalize unusual behavior (see also Ashforth & Kreiner, 2002) means that groups can uphold improper behavior that their members, in isolation, could not. Several scholars have empirically demonstrated positive peer-effects on individual ethical behavior (Beams, Brown, & Killough, 2003; Izraeli, 1988; Jones & Kavanagh, 1996; Zey-Ferrell, Weaver, & Ferrell, 1979), and it is reasonable to expect similar effects for unethical behavior. Robinson and O'Leary-Kelly (1998) report similar patterns for antisocial behavior, showing that antisocial behavior of group members is related to an individual's choice to engage in antisocial behavior that is similar to that of coworkers.

Summary

Both formal and informal groups share many key features that can influence the behaviors of their members. Group members interact; they have varying levels of status, rights, and responsibilities; they pursue goals; and there is a shared sense of identity, and all four of these characteristics can affect the tendency of group members to misbehave. In informal groups, interaction patterns, roles, status, and goals may all be more loosely defined and dynamic than in informal that in formal groups, but these characteristics are important determinants of behavior in all types of groups.

Interactions patterns, status hierarchies, roles, and goals all define what types of behavior group members are expected to engage in and they all play a role in defining the range of behaviors that can be expected of individuals. Any of these group processes can contribute to misbehavior, particularly when the norms of important reference groups support or tolerate misbehavior. Gangs, for example, tolerate and even encourage criminal and antisocial behavior, but many groups that think of themselves as upstanding and law-abiding also tolerate many types of misbehavior. However, even in the absence of antisocial norms, group processes such as a drive to enforce conformity, the diffusion of responsibility, and stereotyping of out-groups can encourage misbehavior.

This chapter has focused on informal groups, where roles, status, goals, and the like are informally defined and potentially fluid. As you will see in the chapter that follows, any of the processes described in this chapter (e.g., pressure to conform, diffusion, and displacement of authority) that have the potential to encourage misbehavior are magnified when they occur in more tightly structured formal groups.

References

Aguinis, H. (2013). *Performance Management* (3rd Ed.). Upper Saddle River, NJ: Pearson/Prentice Hall.

Anderson, C. & Kilduff, G.J. (2009). The pursuit of status in social groups. *Current Directions in Psychological Science, 18*, 295–298.

Ashforth, B.E. & Anand, V. (2003). The normalization of corruption in organizations. In R.M. Kramer & B.M. Staw (Eds.), *Research in Organizational Behavior: An Annual Series of Analytical Essays and Critical Reviews* (Vol. 25, pp. 1–52). Oxford, England: Elsevier Science.

Ashforth, B.E. & Kreiner, G.E. (2002). Normalizing emotion in organizations: Making the extraordinary seem ordinary. *Human Resources Management Review, 12*, 215–235.

Ashforth, B.E. & Mael, F. (1989). Social identity theory and the organization. *Academy of Management Review, 14*, 20–39.

Austin, J.R. (2003). Transactive memory in organizational groups: The effects of content, consensus, specialization, and accuracy on group performance. *Journal of Applied Psychology, 88*, 866–878.

Bales, R.F. (1950). *Interaction Process Analysis: A Method for the Study of Small Groups*. Reading, MA: Addison-Wesley.

Baltes, B.B., Dickson, M.W., Sherman, M.P., Bauer, C.C. & La Ganke, J.S. (2002). Computer-Mediated communication and group decision making: A meta-analysis. *Organizational Behavior and Human Decision Process, 87*, 156–179.

Barnett, G.A. (2011). *Encyclopedia of Social Networks*. Thousand Oaks, CA: Sage.

Bartlett, C.P, Gentile, D.A. & Chew, C. (2016). Predicting cyber bullying from anonymity. *Psychology of Popular Media Culture, 5*, 171–180.

Bass, B.M. (1954). The leaderless group discussion. *Psychological Bulletin, 51*, 465–492.

Baumeister, R.F. & Leary, M.R. (1995). The need to belong: Desire for interpersonal attachments as a fundamental human motivation. *Psychological Bulletin, 117*, 497–529.

Beams, J.D., Brown, R.M. & Killough, L.N. (2003). An experiment testing the determinants of non-compliance with insider trading laws. *Journal of Business Ethics, 45*(4), 309–323.

Berscheid, E. & Walster, E.H. (1978). *Interpersonal Attraction*. Reading, MA: Addison-Wesley.

Benne, K.D. & Sheats, P. (1948). Functional roles of group members. *Journal of Social Issues, 4*, 41–49.

Berger, P.L. & Luckmann, T. (1966). *The Social Construction of Reality: A Treatise in the Sociology of Knowledge*. Garden City, NY: Doubleday.

Blumer, H. (1958). Race prejudice as a sense of group position. *Pacific Sociological Review, 1*, 3–7.

Bobo, L. & Hutchings, V.L. (1996). Perceptions of racial group competition: Extending Blumer's theory of group position to a multiracial social context. *American Sociological Review, 61*, 951–972.

Borteyrou, X., Lievens, F., Bruchon-Schweitzer, M., Congard, A. & Rascle, N. (2015). Incremental validity of leaderless group discussion ratings over and above general mental ability and personality in predicting promotion. *International Journal of Selection and Assessment, 23*, 373–381.

Brass, D.J. & Burkhardt, M.E. (1993). Potential power and power use: An investigation of structure and behavior. *Academy of Management Journal, 36*, 441–470.

Brown, D. (1991). *Human Universals*. Boston: McGraw-Hill.

Cameron, J. (2004). A three-factor model of social identity. *Self and Identity, 3*, 239–262.

Chaplin, J.P. (1985). *Dictionary of Psychology*. New York: Bantam.

Cialdini, R.B. (1993). *Influence: Science and Practice*. New York: Harper Collins.

Clarke, M. (1990). *Business Crime: Its Nature and Control*. Cambridge: Polity Press.

Clinard, M.B. & Yeager, P.C. (1980). *Corporate Crime*. New York: Macmillan.

Deaux, K. (1996). Social identification. In E. Higgins & A. Kruglanski (Eds.), *Social Psychology: Handbook of Basic Principles* (pp. 777–798). New York: Guilford.

DiMaggio, P.J. (1997). Culture and cognition. *Annual Review of Sociology, 23*, 263–287.

Dovidio, J.F., Glick, P. & Rudman, L.A. (2005). *On the Nature of Prejudice: Fifty Years After Allport*. Madden, MA: Blackwell.

Dunbar, R. (1992). Neocortex size as a constraint on group size in primates. *Journal of Human Evolution, 22*, 469–493.

Fay, N., Garrod, S. & Carletta, J. (2000). Group discussion as a dialogue or a serial monologue: The influence of group size. *Psychological Science, 11*, 481–486.

Feldman, D.C. (1984). The development and enforcement of group norms. *Academy of Management Review, 9*, 47–53.

Forsyth, D.R. (1983). *An Introduction to Group Dynamics*. Pacific Grove, CA: Brooks/Cole.

Forsyth, D.R. (1999). *Group Dynamics* (3rd Ed.). Belmont, CA: Brooks/Cole.

Gabor, T. (1994). *Everybody Does It: Crime by the Public*. Toronto, Ontario, Canada: University of Toronto Press.

Gale, W.G. & Krupkin, A. (2019, Apr. 9). *How Big Is the Problem of Tax Evasion*? www.brookings.edu/blog/up-front/2019/04/09/how-big-is-the-problem-of-tax-evasion/

Gino, F., Ayal, S., & Ariely, D. (2009). Contagion and differentiation in unethical behavior: The effect of one bad apple on the barrel. *Psychological Science, 20*, 393–398.

Gino, F. & Galinsky, A.D. (2012). Vicarious dishonesty: When psychological closeness creates distance from one's moral compass. *Organizational Behavior and Human Decision Processes, 119*, 15–26.

Gino, F., Gu, J. & Zhong, C.B. (2009b). Contagion or restitution? When bad apples can motivate ethical behavior. *Journal of Experimental Social Psychology, 45*, 1299–1302.

Gladwell, M. (2000). *The Tipping Point—How Little Things Make a Big Difference*. New York: Little, Brown and Company.

Goldstein, A.P. (2002). *The Psychology of Group Aggression*. New York: Wiley.

Goldstein, N.J., Martin, S.J. & Cialdini, R.B. (2008). *Yes! 50 Scientifically Proven Ways to be Persuasive*. New York: Free Press.

Gray, J.R. & Thompson, P.M. (2004). Neurobiology of intelligence: Science and ethics. *Nature Reviews Neuroscience, 5*, 471–482.

Hare, A.P. (1982). *Creativity in Small Groups*. Beverly Hills, CA: Sage.

Hare, A.P. (1993). Small groups in organizations. In R.T. Golembiewski (Ed.), *Handbook of Organizational Behavior* (pp. 61–89). New York: Marcel Dekker.

Hare, R.D. (1994). Roles and relationships. In R.D. Hare, H.H. Blumberg, M.F. Davies, & M.V. Kent (Eds.), *Small Group Research: A Handbook* (pp. 141–154). Norwood, NJ: Ablex.

Hare, A.P. (2003). Roles, relationships and groups in organizations: Some conclusions and Recommendations. *Small Group Research, 34*, 123–154.

Hogan, R. (1983). A socio analytic theory of personality. In M. Page (Ed.), *Nebraska Symposium on Motivation, 1982: Personality-Current Theory and Research* (pp. 163–179). New York: Guilford.

Hogg, M.A. & Terry, D.J. (2000). Social identity and self-categorization processes in organizational contexts. *Academy of Management Review, 25*, 121–140.

Hollingshead, A.B. & McGrath, J.E. (1995). Computer-assisted groups: A critical review of the empirical research. In R.A. Guzzo & E. Salas (Eds.), *Team Effectiveness and Decision Making in Organizations* (pp. 46–78). San Francisco: Jossey-Bass.

Horne, C. (2001). The enforcement of group norms: Group cohesion and meta-norms. *Social Psychology Quarterly, 64*, 253–266.

Horowitz, D.L. (2001). *The Deadly Ethnic Riot*. Berkeley, BA: University of California Press.

Ilies, R., Hauserman, N., Schwochau, S. & Stibal, J. (2003). Reported incidence rates of work-related sexual harassment in the United States: Using meta-analysis to explain reported rate disparities. *Personnel Psychology, 56*, 607–631.

Izraeli, D. (1988). Ethical beliefs and behavior among managers: A cross-cultural perspective. *Journal of Business Ethics, 7*, 263–271.

Jackson, J. (2002). Intergroup attitudes as a function of different dimensions of group identification and perceived intergroup conflict. *Self and Identity, 1*, 11–33.

Jacobs, R.C. & Campbell, D.T. (1961). The perpetuation of arbitrary tradition through several generations of a laboratory micro culture. *Journal of Abnormal and Social Psychology, 62*, 649–658.

Jones, G. & Kavanagh, M. (1996). An experimental examination of the effects of individual and situational factors on unethical behavioral intentions in the workplace. *Journal of Business Ethics, 15*, 511–523.

Juvonen, J. & Graham, S. (2014). Bullying in schools: The power of bullies and the plight of victims. *Annual Review of Psychology, 65*, 159–185.

Kelly, R.E. (1992). *The Power of Followership: How to Create Leaders People Want to Follow and Followers Who Lead Themselves*. New York: Doubleday.

Kent, M.V. (1994a). Conformity. In R.D. Hare, H.H. Blumberg, M.F. Davies, & M.V. Kent (Eds.), *Small Group Research: A Handbook* (pp. 107–137). Norwood, NJ: Ablex.

Kent, M.V. (1994b). Presence of others. In R.D. Hare, H.H. Blumberg, M.F. Davies, & M.V. Kent (Eds.), *Small Group Research: A Handbook* (pp. 81–106). Norwood, NJ: Ablex.

Kiesler, S. & Sproul, L. (1992). Group decision making and communication technology. *Organizational Behavior and Human Decision Processes, 52*, 96–123.

Koch, C. (2016). Does brain size matter? *Scientific American Mind, 27*(1), 22–25.

Lau, D.C. & Murnighan, J.K. (1998). Demographic diversity and fault lines: The compositional dynamics of organizational groups. *Academy of Management Review, 23*, 325–340.

Lau, D.C. & Murnighan, J.K. (2005). Interactions within groups and subgroups: The effects of demographic fault lines. *Academy of Management Journal, 48*, 645–659.

Lea, M. & Spears, R. (1991). Computer-mediated communication, de-individuation and group decision-making. *International Journal of Man-Machine Studies, 34*, 283–301.

Lord, R.G., De Vader, C.L. & Alliger, G.M. (1986). A meta-analysis of the relation between personality traits and leadership perceptions: An application of validity generalization procedures. *Journal of Applied Psychology, 71*, 402–410.

Marks, G. & Miller, N. (1987). Ten years of research on the false-consensus effect: An empirical and theoretical review. *Psychological Bulletin. 102*, 72–90.

Mathieu, J.E., Heffner, T.S., Goodwin, G.F., Salas, E. & Cannon-Bowers, J.A. (2000). The influence of shared mental models on team process and performance. *Journal of Applied Psychology, 85*, 273–283.

McCormick, T.H., Salgnick, M.J. & Zheng, T. (2010). How many people do you know?: Efficiently estimating personal network size. *Journal of the American Statistical Association, 105*, 59–70.

Milgram, S.A. 1974. *Obedience to Authority: An Experimental View*. New York: Harper & Row.

Milgram, S.A. & Toch, H. (1969). Collective behavior: Crowds and social movements. In G. Lindzey & A. Aaronson (Eds.), *The Handbook of Social Psychology* (Vol. 4, pp. 507–610). Reading, MA: Addison-Wesley.

Misangy, V.F. & Weaver, G.R. (2008). Ending corruption: The interplay among institutional logics, resources, and institutional entrepreneurs. *Academy of Management Review, 33*, 73–770.

Mohammed, S. & Dumville, B.C. (2001). Team mental models in a team knowledge framework: Expanding theory and measurement across disciplinary boundaries. *Journal of Organizational Behavior, 22*, 89–106.

Murphy, K.R. (2020, Oct. 12). How the end of the office might also mean the end of your boss. *RTE Brainstorm*, www.rte.ie/brainstorm/2020/1012/1170916-office-working-from-home-boss-manager-superviser/.

Napier, R.W. & Gershenfeld, M.K. (1999). *Groups: Theory and Experience* (6th Ed.). New York: Houghton Mifflin.

North, A. (2020, Apr. 9). The shift to online learning could worsen educational inequality. *Vox*, www.vox.com/2020/4/9/21200159/coronavirus-school-digital-low-income-students-covid-new-york

Pillay, S. (2016, Feb. 19). How leaderless groups end up with leaders. *Harvard Business Review—Leadership*, https://hbr.org/2016/02/how-leaderless-groups-end-up-with-leaders

Prapavessis, H. & Carron, A.V. (1997). Sacrifice, cohesion and conformity to norms in sports teams. *Group Dynamics: Theory, Research and Practice, 1*, 231–240.

Riek, B.M., Mania, E.W. & Gaertner, S.L. (2006). Intergroup threat and outgroup attitudes: A meta-analytic review. *Personality and Social Psychology Review, 10*, 336–353.

Robinson, S.L. & O'Leary-Kelly, A.M. (1998). Monkey see, monkey do: The influence of workgroups on the antisocial behavior of employees. *Academy of Management Journal, 41*, 658–672.

Roethlisberger, F.J. & Dickson, W.J. (1939). *Management and the Worker.* Cambridge, MA: Harvard University Press.

Rosenbaum, M.E. (1986). The repulsion hypothesis: On the nondevelopment of relationship. *Journal of Personality and Social Psychology, 51*, 1156–1166.

Schwartz, S.A. (2020, Aug. 7). Meetings are shorter but there are more of them in the pandemic. *CIODive* www.ciodive.com/news/virtual-meeting-work-hours-balance-pandemic/583061/

Seabrook, R.C., Ward, L.M. & Giaccardi, S. (2018). Why is fraternity membership associated with sexual assault? Exploring the roles of conformity to masculine norms, pressure to uphold masculinity, and objectification of women. *Psychology of Men & Masculinity, 19*, 3–13.

Simon, H.A. (1950). A formal theory of interaction within groups. *American Sociological Review, 17*, 202–211.

Staub, E. (1989). *The Roots of Evil: The Origins of Genocide and Other Group Violence.* New York: Cambridge University Press.

Staub, E. (1993). The mob. In *Report of the American Psychological Association.* Washington, DC: Author.

Staub, E. & Rosenthal, L.H. (1999). Mob violence: Cultural-societal sources, instigators, group processes and participants. In L.D. Eron, J.H. Gentry, & P. Schlegl (Eds.), *Reason to Hope: A Psychosocial Perspective on Violence and Youth* (p. 377–403). Washington, DC: American Psychological Association.

Tsoukalas, I. (2007). Exploring the micro foundations of group consciousness. *Culture and Psychology, 13*, 39–81.

Treviño, L.K., Den Nieuwenboer, N.A. & Kish-Gaphart, J.J. (2014). (Un)ethical behavior in organizations. *Annual Review of Psychology, 65*, 635–660.

Turner, J.C. & Killian, L.M. (1972). *Collective Behavior* (2nd Ed.). Englewood Cliffs, NJ: Erlbaum.

Turner, J.C. & Pratkanis, A.R. (1994). Social identity maintenance prescriptions for preventing groupthink: Reducing identity protection and enhancing intellectual conflict. *International Journal of Conflict Management, 5*, 254–270.

Uhl-Bien, M., Riggio, R.E., Lowe, K.B. & Carsten, M.K. (2014). Followership theory: A review and research agenda. *The Leadership Quarterly, 25*, 83–104.

VanVugt, M. (2006). Evolutionary origins of leadership and followership. *Personality and Social Psychology Review, 10*, 354–371.

Wicker, A.W. (1969). Size of church membership and members' support for church behavior settings. *Journal of Personality and Social Psychology, 13,* 278–288.

Wirth, M.M. & Schultheiss, O.C. (2006). Effects of affiliation arousal (hope of closeness) and affiliation stress (fear of rejection) on progesterone and cortisol. *Hormones and Behavior, 50*, 786–795.

Zey-Ferrell, M. & Ferrell, O.C. (1982). Role-set configuration and opportunity as predictors of unethical behavior in organizations. *Human Relations, 35*, 587–604.

Zey-Ferrell, M.K., Weaver, M. & Ferrell, O.C. 1979. Predicting unethical behavior among marketing practitioners. *Human Relations, 32*, 557–569.

6

FORMAL GROUPS, PARTIES, AND ASSOCIATIONS

Both formal and informal groups share four key characteristics: (1) group members interact, (2) group members have different rights, responsibilities, status, (3) groups pursue goals, and (4) the group has a shared sense of social identity. These two types of groups differ in terms of their purposes and their degree of structure. Informal groups (e.g., friendship groups) exist mainly to satisfy the needs of their members, whereas formal groups are usually created to satisfy external goals or objectives that are set for the group. Informal groups have loose and dynamic structures, whereas formal groups have structures that are clear, well defined, and that exist independently of the particular people who are included in the group at any point in time.

The traditional definition of a formal group is that they are created deliberately by persons in authority to fulfill specific objectives. These groups are usually characterized by a division of labor—that is, the assignment to duties, rights, and responsibilities to positions rather than specific persons and an explicitly defined power hierarchy. Formal groups often have documented policies and practices, and the policies, practices, roles, and status hierarchy of the group usually do not change as the membership of the group changes.

In this chapter, I will follow a slightly more expansive definition of a formal group. The previous definition works very well for groups such as task forces, laboratory teams, or workgroups, but there are other types of groups that have some degree of formal structure without having the same level of specification of roles, rights, responsibilities, and goals for their members. Consider, for example, a political party. This sort of group has a core set of members with carefully defined roles and reporting relationships (e.g., the professional staff of the party), but the vast majority of the membership consists of people who have some level of identification with the party, but who do not have day-to-day roles in the management of the party, its finances, or its affairs. Similarly, there are many interest groups and professional associations that have a similar structure—that is, a small core staff of professionals and a large membership of individuals with no formal role and varying levels of involvement and identification. Many professional associations and interest groups have a hybrid structure, with a professional staff, a group of officers, and committee members who have varying levels of power and varying levels of responsibility, together with a large membership in which there are few formal roles to carry out. Nevertheless, parties, interest groups, professional associations, and the like are important parts of many people's social identify and they can have important effects on the behavior of their members.

It is useful to distinguish between traditional formal groups, in which the group structure helps to guide the behavior of virtually all members (e.g., workgroups, task forces, professional sports teams) and formal groups with a hybrid structure, in which many members have unstructured and somewhat peripheral roles (e.g., the American Medical Association). The first section of this chapter deals with two of the prototypes of a formal group—that is, a task group or workgroup and a team. The section that follows deals with formal groups that have a hybrid structure, such as interest groups or associations.

Groups and Teams

Almost all of us who work have experience with formal groups. Workgroups are defined in terms of several factors. First, they are created to perform or accomplish specific tasks. Second, they see themselves and are seen as others as a distinct social entity (Guzzo & Dickson, 1996). Third, they work together in ways that might range from simple co-location (e.g., a group of pieceworkers who all carry out their tasks in the same part of a factory) to depending on each other to complete their tasks (i.e., interdependence). These groups have the same defining features as informal groups (i.e., they interact, pursue goals, have defined roles and responsibilities, are part of their members' social identity), but they differ from informal groups in two important ways. First, the goals they pursue are not their own. Task groups and workgroups might have a good deal of autonomy in setting day-to-day goals and in designing their work procedures (Kemp, Wall, Clegg, & Cordrey, 1983), but the ultimate goals they pursue benefit others (e.g., the organization that created the workgroup) rather than the members of the group. Members of a workgroup might benefit in terms of raises, bonuses, or promotions if they are successful in meeting the organization's goals, but the primary focus of a workgroup or task group is on meeting the goals of the organization rather than on meeting the goals of the members of the group.

Second, duties, responsibilities, roles, and power are usually assigned to positions rather than to individuals. That is, if a member leaves a workgroup, the usual strategy is to recruit and select a new member who can fulfill the duties and responsibilities that had been covered by the member who left. Unlike informal groups, duties, responsibilities, and roles are impersonal. That is, they exist independently of the person who happens to occupy the position at any point in time. They are also external and explicit, in the sense that they can be defined and recorded by the organization or the entity that created the group and could exist in their current form even if there is 100% turnover in group members.

The duties and responsibilities associated with each position in a team or workgroup are often preserved in the form of a contract or a job description. Table 6.1 presents sections of a job description used by a national railroad for the job of Carman. It lays out the principal duties and activities that make up the job, along with a variety of job requirements.

The formalization of roles and responsibilities in a task group or a workgroup has important implications for understanding the links between groups and misbehavior. When roles and responsibilities are tightly and explicitly defined, this greatly increases opportunities for one of the common social-cognitive mechanisms that are used to justify misbehavior—that is, the diffusion of responsibility. Contracts, job descriptions, organizational charts are often quite clear in what they say, but also in what they omit. For example, suppose you are an employee in a large organization who witnesses a colleague experiencing serious and repeated episodes of sexual harassment. As I noted in Chapter 5, sexual harassment is depressingly common (Ilies, Hauserman, Schwochau, & Stibal, 2003 present meta-analytic evidence that approximately 50% of all women will experience sexual harassment at work). One potential explanation for the failure of colleagues, managers, and others to effectively intervene is that protecting employees

TABLE 6.1 Job Description—Railroad Carman

- **Job Summary**
  - Paint and Repair Rail Cars
    - Must complete 2-year apprenticeship program
    - Propane and oxygen torch operation and knowledgeable of welding processes
    - Rail car repair, including trucks, underframe, body, doors, air brake, blasting and painting, and recordkeeping
    - Miscellaneous activities and responsibilities as assigned by manager.
- Physical Requirements—
  - Stoop/bend/kneel/crouch/crawl/balance/climb
  - Walk long distances over uneven terrain
  - Climbing on and off equipment
  - Moderately heavy to heavy industrial work
- Job Requirements—
  - Work safely to prevent on the job accidents and injuries
  - Must pass a post-offer medical examination, including drug and physical capabilities test
  - Wear protective equipment such as hard hat, hearing protection, or safety-toe boots
  - Work hours may include a nonstandard workweek

from sexual harassment is not part of the formal job description of many employees, but it *is* often part of the job description of someone in the organization (e.g., some senior Human Resource Management executive). People who witness sexual harassment in organizations may fail to do anything about it because: (1) it is not their role to deal with this problem, (2) it is someone else's role to respond to this, and (3) the person or persons in those roles will take care of things. Further, an employee who observes sexual harassment and who also sees the organization do nothing in response may infer that whatever he or she has seen must not be that bad, precisely because there are people in the organization tasked with monitoring and responding to harassment, and *they* have not done anything.

The formalization of roles not only specifies duties and responsibilities, but it also makes power relationships explicit. That is, in formal groups, different roles often involve different levels and even different types of power.

Power in Formal Groups

Roles in formal groups often involve well-defined lines of power and authority. For example, teachers in an elementary school have authority over their pupils. This authority is not absolute and may be carefully delineated by school policy and laws (e.g., corporal punishment in public schools is effectively banned through a combination of state laws and school board policies in 32 states), and it is sometimes successfully challenged by parents or by advocacy groups. However, within the confines of these policies, teachers often have significant power in the classroom and in enforcing school policies outside of the classroom. In work organizations, there is often a well-defined hierarchy, where top executives have power and authority that flows down to divisional, departmental, and workgroup levels through a series of executives, managers, and supervisors. In the military, there is a strict chain of command, but even here, power is not absolute. The U.S. Uniform Code of Military Justice requires military personnel to follow *lawful* orders; in *United States v. Keenan*, the U.S. Supreme Court upheld the murder conviction of Private Keenan for following an order to shoot an elderly Vietnamese citizen.

Power in a formal group is not simply limited to the ability to give people orders. In an influential study, French and Raven (1959) suggested that there were multiple bases of power. In their original work, they identified five distinct ways a person might obtain or exert power. Later, Raven (1992) added a sixth possibility. These six bases of power are shown in Table 6.2.

First, an individual might have power because he or she is in a position to punish those who do not comply with instructions, orders, or directives. Punishments do not have to involve force; an individual can exert coercive power by threatening to impose, or by imposing many different sanctions (e.g., demotion or firing, social ostracism). The legal power of the state and its agents (e.g., police forces) is based at least in part on coercive power, such as the power to

TABLE 6.2 French and Ravens' Six Bases of Power

Coercive Power	The power to punish or to threaten punishment to coerce compliance
Reward Power	The power to provide or authorize rewards, including virtually any outcome valued by the recipient, in exchange for compliance
Legitimate Power	Power that is accepted by the follower or followers as being inherent in a position or title
Referent Power	Power that is the result of the follower's loyalty, respect, admiration, affection, or connection with the person exerting power
Expert Power	Power based on specialized knowledge, skills, or competence that are relevant to the goals of the follower or followers
Informational Power	Power based on the possession of information that is needed or desired to accomplish the goals of the follower or followers

arrest, fine, and imprison individuals who violate the law. Reward power is to some extent the flip side of coercive power, where power is based on the ability to provide things of value (e.g., raises, recognition, social support) in exchange for compliance. These two bases of power are often interrelated. The power to grant rewards implies the power to withhold them, meaning that a manager who has the (reward) power to grant a raise is likely to also have the (coercive) power to block one. Similarly, the same judge who has the (coercive) power to impose a sentence may also have the (reward) power to dismiss a pending charge. The distinction between coercive and reward power is mainly one of emphasis on the carrot (reward) vs. the stick (punishment).

Legitimate power exists in situations where followers accept that particular positions convey power. The power of kings, for example, is based in part on the ability to both punish and reward one's subjects, but the institution of royalty invests very heavily in efforts to broadcast and reinforce the idea that power is the king's right and that kingship is sacred. Thus, kings are usually crowned in elaborate ceremonies that remind the realm of the king's divine sanction (e.g., the British monarch is crowned by the Archbishop of Canterbury and is anointed with holy oil during the coronation ceremony), and ceremonies are conducted regularly to remind the realm of the legitimacy of the king or queen. Similarly, states, police forces, and the other parts of the apparatus of lawgiving and law enforcement work hard to reinforce the belief that they have the right to exert power, and legitimate power is an important part of the power of states, independent of their power to reward or punish their subjects.

The collapse of legitimate power is often fatal to a state. There are, for example, numerous theories for the fall of the Roman Empire, but one of the key themes linking virtually every account of this decline is the crisis of legitimacy—that is, the decreasing acceptance of the right to rule of a consul or emperor as these offices were sold through bribery and corruption or seized through assassination and civil war.

Legitimate power is not restricted to political entities (e.g., kings, nobles, states). The power that goes with many formal positions, ranging from executives to kindergarten teachers, is effective because people accept the idea that these positions *should* be invested with particular powers. That is, legitimate power depends substantially on the consent of the governed. Legitimate power is arguably the most robust source of power precisely because it is impersonal—that is, legitimate power goes with the position and not necessarily the person. This linkage between the position and power provides considerable stability; when a monarch dies, his or her successor is immediately invested with power. In the same way, a soldier who is promoted from corporal to sergeant or a worker who is promoted to supervisor immediately receives power and continues to hold it as long as he or she holds that position.

Legitimate power, which is connected to particular positions (e.g., judge, mayor) stands in stark contrast to referent power, which depends on the relationship between leaders and followers. Leaders who are respected, admired or liked gain power as a result of their subordinates' positive views of the leader. However, popularity and positive reputations can be fleeting, and referent power can change substantially as attitudes toward a particular leader change. Even more to the point, referent power is entirely personal and entirely context-bound. That is, particular persons might hold referent power today because their followers respect them, but if followers change (e.g., some people leave, and others join a workgroup), referent power might be diminished. Similarly, referent power might diminish over time. There is an old French saying that translates as "no man is a hero to his valet". The underlying thought here is that admiration and respect are hard to sustain over a long period of intimate interaction, especially interaction with one's social superior. Over time, you are likely to see the person you admire in less favorable circumstances ("warts and all") and are likely to see at least some behaviors that do not inspire this high level of respect. Even people who are widely admired for their virtues (e.g., Gandhi, Dr. Martin Luther King) had their difficult sides and their dark days.

Expert power is the result of the perceived competence of the individual. Experts have knowledge, skills, and competencies that are sometimes very useful to the group, and this expertise can be a source of power and authority. This power can be long-lasting if the core tasks of the group stay the same and some sort of specialized knowledge or skill is required to accomplish these tasks, but it can be fleeting if the skills of the expert can be easily learned by the rest of the group or if the nature of the group task changes in ways that decrease the relevance of that expertise.

Finally, people can attain informational power if they have access to or control over specific information that is needed by a follower to complete a task.

A distinction is made here between knowledge and skills that are a source of task competence (expert power) and "knowing where the bodies are buried". There are often people in a group who know who to ask for a favor, or who know the combinations to the safes where critical plans are stored. The best administrative assistants are not necessarily those who are skilled in clerical tasks and in managing their manager's calendar; they are often the people who know who you should call when different sorts of problems need to be solved.

These six bases of power do not exhaust the set of possibilities. Charismatic power is related to several of the types of power enumerated by French and Raven, but there are important distinctions (Kudish, Poteet, Dobbins, Rush, & Russell, 1995). Charismatic leaders often demonstrate a combination of confidence, attractiveness, social skills, charm, likeability, competence, and these qualities help them to establish a strong emotional connection with their followers. Charismatic leaders often articulate bold visions and a strong sense of mission, but perhaps the factor that best distinguishes charismatic power from expert and/or referent power is the sense of magnetism that charismatic leaders show. Followers of charismatic leaders sometimes describe themselves as being spellbound and as having no option but to follow a truly charismatic leader. Unfortunately, some charismatic leaders are responsible for great harm, precisely because their followers are essentially carried away by the leader. For example, Adolph Hitler is often described as a charismatic leader (especially in the period 1930–1940; see, for example, Kershaw, 2000), and for at least a decade, he mesmerized a significant proportion of the German nation, eventually leading them, and much of the rest of Europe, to an awful doom.

Most of the forms of power described here might be observed in either formal or informal groups, but there are critical differences between the nature of and the use of power in these two groups. First, power in formal groups is more likely to be stable over time, particularly if it rests at least in part on legitimate power. Legitimate power can exist in some informal groups (e.g., families, where parental power is accepted by children, at least until their teenage years), but for the most part, a group in which specific positions are invested with power will, by definition, be a formal group. In contrast, in most informal groups, power is personal, and it rests on some combination of expertise, information, and the relationships among group members. Second, because formal groups often have well-defined tasks as their *raison d'être*, the more task-relevant forms of power (e.g., expert power) are likely to be a more consistent and important source of influence in formal rather than in informal groups.

The greater the power of the leader, the more likely followers are to displace responsibility for actions that harm others or violate social norms. Leaders who can tap multiple sources of power (e.g., legitimate plus expert) might be especially powerful in circumstances where these multiple sources are all relevant, but the power of leaders also depends on cultural factors. In Chapter 1, I described the cultural value that is often referred to as power distance (i.e., the belief that hierarchy should be respected and that people who are at higher levels in the power structure should be free to give binding orders and directives; Hofstede, Hofstede, & Minkov, 2010). In countries where power distance is high (e.g., Japan), deference to leaders is a central part of the country's culture, and by inference, diffusion of responsibility for unethical acts might be especially likely.

The Psychological Contract

Formal groups, especially workgroups and task forces, often have detailed documents that specify the duties, responsibilities, and rights of their members. In addition to their written contracts and job descriptions, individuals often form a *psychological* contract with their organization. In work organizations, this psychological contract represents a set of expectations (which are not always made explicit) about the mutual responsibilities of employees and organizations to one another (Guest & Conway, 2002; Robinson & Brown, 2004; Rousseau, 1989, 1995). One way of thinking about the distinction between formal and informal groups is that formal groups have both formalized (often written) statements that describe roles, duties, and responsibilities *and* psychological contracts that encompass widely shared expectations that are not made explicit, whereas informal groups often operate strictly based on unwritten rules.

The classic statement of a psychological contract in work organizations is "a fair day's work for a fair day's pay",[1] but the notion of the psychological contract between workgroup members and the group itself and the larger organization the group is a part of goes well beyond this simple formula. For example, in work organizations, employers expect that workers will go beyond the bare minimum requirements of their organization and will show commitment and a willingness to step up when needed. That is, there is often an implicit assumption that workers will also carry out what are often referred to as contextual performance behaviors (the term "organizational citizenship" and "contextual performance" often used interchangeably). These behaviors are not necessary to accomplish the specific tasks in an individual's job, but they are necessary for the smooth functioning of teams and organizations (Borman & Motowidlo, 1993; Brief & Motowidlo, 1986; Organ, 1988; Smith, Organ, & Near, 1983). Examples include helping others, cooperating and showing courtesy, self-development, initiative, persistence, and loyalty to the organization and compliance with its rules and policies.

Employees have many expectations about their organizations that can have important implications. For example, employees might expect that their organization will evaluate them fairly, protect them from harm (e.g., accidents, workplace harassment) and treat them with consideration and respect. Violations of these expectations can reduce job satisfaction, turnover intentions, organizational commitment, and job performance (Zhao, Wayne, Glibkowski, & Bravo, 2007).

Because they are not always made explicit, the expectations that constitute a psychological contract can be an invitation for trouble. Suppose, for example, that your contract and your job description says nothing about helping others or cooperating with coworkers. The fact that supervisors and managers expect you to do these things and evaluate you negatively if you do not demonstrate these behaviors (Borman, White, & Dorsey, 1995) creates significant potential for confusion and conflict. You might argue that some aspects of organizational citizenship are not *really* part of your job, and if they are, that should be made explicit in your contract and you should be paid for these additional duties. Your supervisor might argue that contracts never say "don't be a pain in the . . .", but that everyone understands that an employee who constantly complains, does not help others when help is needed, and badmouths the workgroup and the organization is a bad employee. Written contracts make roles and expectations explicit, but there are virtually always topics that are not covered by written contracts but that are important to employers and employees alike. These unwritten expectations can go completely unnoticed as long as everyone has consistent expectations, but they can become a source of dissatisfaction when they differ.

As I will explain in more detail in several subsequent chapters, violations of the psychological contract can be a powerful motivator for misbehavior. If people feel like they are being cheated, or at least not treated in the way they believe is appropriate, they are more likely to lash back at their supervisor, manager, or organization. For example, Greenberg (1990) studied a group of manufacturing plants that instituted a temporary 15% pay reduction and showed that this unplanned pay cut was associated with a significant increase in employee theft. He also showed that when an explanation was provided for the pay cut (it was linked to the loss of some production contracts), there was a markedly lower rate of employee theft.

BOX 6.1 IN PRAISE OF BUREAUCRACY

When you hear the term "bureaucracy" you probably conjure an image of a large, faceless mass of paper-pushers whose main job seems to be to make your life more difficult. It might surprise you to learn that bureaucracy was once seen as a solution rather than as a problem. This term was popularized by the German sociologist Max Weber, the first scientist to systematically study bureaucracy. He saw bureaucracy as the most efficient and rational method of organizing human activity and claimed that bureaucracy was also the most moral system of organization. His vision of bureaucracy included formal lines of authority, well-defined rules and regulations, a division of labor, career advancement based on qualifications, and a substantial degree of predictability.

We all know how frustrating it can be to deal with bureaucracies, so what led Weber to sing its praises? One way to understand the virtues of a bureaucracy is to think about how non-bureaucratic systems work. Without set rules, roles, reporting relationships, etc., decisions become increasingly unpredictable and arbitrary. Non-bureaucratic systems typically end up working based on connections and favoritism. Non-bureaucratic systems (the term "adhocracy" is sometimes used to describe the opposite of a bureaucratic system) are sometimes praised for their agility and adaptability (Toffler, 1970), but it is difficult to maintain *ad hoc* systems that will produce decisions seen by those involved as fair and consistent. Weber praised bureaucracies because they strove to make decisions that were rational and fair. This same reaction against decisions based on connections and favoritism was a major factor in the development of the U.S. Civil Service and related governmental bureaucracies.

The choice between bureaucracy and adhocracy (or about where on the continuum from bureaucracy to adhocracy) you want to locate your business or your government depends substantially on the tension between consistency and fairness and getting things done. At its worst, bureaucracy slows decisions and action to a crawl. It can, for example, take years to get the environmental permits needed for some major construction projects, and the temptation to find a way around the bureaucrats can be substantial. On the other hand, building without regard for environmental constraints might cause irreparable harm, and your feelings about bureaucracy might be very different if you are a member of the community who bears the brunt of ill-considered projects than if you are the head engineer anxious to get construction going. Bureaucracy can be frustrating, but it is sometimes the best of many imperfect ways of organizing activities.

Teams

There are many types of formal groups; teams are both important and special in terms of many of the features of formal groups that have the potential to contribute to misbehavior. There are two distinctions between teams and other types of groups. First, teams exhibit high levels of interdependence (Kozlowski & Ilgen, 2006). Team-based tasks are often structured in a way that the team's success and the success of any individual team member depend on other members also fulfilling their roles. Because of this interdependence, team performance is typically higher when the team is cohesive and when it communicates frequently (Barrick, Bradley, Kristof-Brown, & Colbert, 2007). In other types of groups, social loafing (i.e., the tendency of group members to exert less effort; see Karau and Williams [1993] for a meta-analytic review of social loafing research) can be a significant problem, but in a well-functioning team, members are likely to be aware that their failure to perform will hurt the team and other team members, and are less likely to perform poorly.

Second, teams are often characterized by relatively high levels of commitment to and identification with both the group and its tasks (Katzenbach & Smith, 1993). Members of sports teams (particularly teams at the top levels of their sports), for example, often show high levels of commitment and the willingness to make substantial sacrifices for the good of their team (Prapavessis & Carron, 1997). This type of commitment is especially likely if team members show high levels of mutual trust. For team members to trust in the team, they must feel that (1) the team is competent enough to accomplish their task, and (2) that the team will not harm the individual or his or her interests (Ilgen, Hollenbeck, Johnson, & Jundt, 2005). Research demonstrates that identifying with a team has powerful positive effects on individual team members' behavior, attitudes, and performance (Ashforth & Mael, 1989).

The use of teams is increasingly common in the workplace and it is not unusual for employees to be assigned to multiple work teams simultaneously. When there are multiple teams, an individual's attachment to any particular team will depend on the team's prestige and its cohesiveness, as well as on what the team is doing (Rapp & Mathieu, 2018). Research suggests that team cohesiveness is linked to team performance (Evans & Dion 1991; Guzzo & Shea 1992), but the direction of this relationship is not always clear. For example, cohesion may increase communication and the strength of identification with the team, and this translates into higher performance. However, it is also possible that effectiveness breeds cohesion, and that people identify more strongly with a team when it is successful than when it is falling behind.

Finally, Guzzo, Yost, Campbell, and Shea (1993) note that a group or team's collective belief that it can be effective (i.e., group potency) can be important. Groups and teams that are confident of their ability to accomplish particular tasks are likely to put more effort into those tasks and to persist if at first they do not seem to succeed. Teams that doubt their ability to tackle important tasks may be less willing to even try and more willing to give up at the first setback.

Team vs. Task Processes

When people collaborate on tasks, two types of activities are often required: (1) task processes, and (2) team processes. That is, many activities are required to carry out a task, such as planning, the gathering of necessary information and resources, and the execution of tasks. However, teams cannot simply focus on specific tasks; they must also invest time and resources in building and maintaining an effective and efficient team. The term "team processes" refers to the activities that are necessary for a team or group to function smoothly, and these are every bit as necessary as task processes. These activities are necessary for groups of all sorts (including informal groups), but the high levels of interdependency and cohesion often required in teams makes them especially relevant to team success.

In Chapter 5, I discussed social and emotional roles in groups. Many of these roles relate to building and maintaining an effective team rather than accomplishing specific team tasks. For example, roles and responsibilities within a team must be allocated and communicated. This might be a one-time activity in a team that performs the same task over and over. Consider, for example, a professional football team. Individuals are hired for very specific roles (e.g., punter, long snapper) and are coached on how to carry out these roles most effectively. These players do not need to renegotiate roles before each game (e.g., this time, I will punt and you can snap; next week we'll switch), but there may be a need for fine-tuning from time to time (e.g., decisions might be needed about what each team member should do if the opposing team shows a particular formation). The problem of assigning roles and responsibilities in a team becomes more complex if tasks change over time.

There is increasing emphasis on the importance of adapting effectively to instability and change in work organizations (National Research Council, 2012). Pulakos, Arad, Donovan, and Plamondon (2000) note that as jobs become more complex and as organizations and their environments become more unpredictable, effective job performance will involve adapting to new demands and new circumstances. In dynamic or unstable task environments, it might be necessary to frequently re-evaluate and renegotiate roles, duties, and responsibilities within a team.

Team processes are not limited to simply deciding who does what and who is responsible for various activities or outcomes. It is also important to monitor and maintain the processes used to distribute resources and rewards. Perceptions of fairness and equity are an important factor in the cohesion and effectiveness of a team, and when some members are seen as receiving special favors or sweetheart deals, this can substantially increase conflict and reduce the effectiveness of a team (Marescaux, De Winne, & Sels, 2019).

Because of their heightened level of interdependence, team members often find it both necessary and useful to provide support and coaching for their fellow team members. Earlier, I noted the importance of organizational citizenship (also referred to as contextual performance) in organizations. Helping and supporting others is a key component of being a good organizational citizen, and it is doubly important in teams.

Teams are increasingly common and important in work organizations, but it is hard to avoid the feeling that much of what is written about teams applies to only a small subset of this universe. Successful sports franchises, for example, show high levels of teamwork, commitment, identification, and the like. The same can probably be said for *some* work teams, but it is unlikely that most work teams exhibit the same level of commitment and identification. Work teams are most likely to resemble a cohesive sports franchise when they are: (1) involved in work that is important and that brings prestige, (2) successful, and when (3) members join the team voluntarily or are recruited through a competitive process. Many of the teams in organizations are probably more like workgroups, in that they do not show the level of interdependence, cohesiveness, and commitment that is so widely discussed in the business literature. However, regardless of the nature of the team, it is likely that substantial investments of time and energy on team processes will be necessary for the team to be successful in carrying out its core tasks.

Associations: Formal Groups With Hybrid Structures

Associations, political parties, and interest groups exist primarily to serve their members' interests, enhance their status, and restrict rivals (e.g., by sponsoring strict licensing laws that keep others from practicing your chosen profession). These groups have a hybrid structure, with a small core of full-time professionals and a large membership whose level of involvement varies considerably. For example, I belong to several professional societies, including the Society for Industrial and Organizational Psychology (SIOP). SIOP is an organization devoted to the science and practice of industrial and organizational psychology. It represents Division 14 of the American Psychological Association and is an organizational affiliate of the Association for Psychological Science. It has over 5,000 members and over 4,000 student affiliates. The majority of members attend SIOP conferences, often on an irregular basis, pay annual dues, and sometimes vote in elections for association officers. There is a very small professional staff and then a group of 100–200 or so members who consistently serve on SIOP committees and serve as elected or appointed officers of the association. Like many professional associations, this group lobbies for its members' interests and creates events (e.g., conferences) to bring members together and share research and practice ideas. This association is an important part of the professional and sometimes the personal identity of many of its members.

The distinguishing feature of this sort of group is that the involvement of members is so highly variable, with a small professional staff, a relatively small cadre of highly dedicated and involved members and a large number of individuals whose involvement is intermittent at best (e.g., a higher level of involvement and identification during annual conferences, minimal involvement during the rest of the year). This hybrid structure places a substantial burden on, and gives substantial influence to a small cadre of members who are strongly involved (e.g., by holding offices, serving on important committees), and who have an outsized role in setting the policies and priorities of the organization. Associations of different types serve different needs (Weeks, 2011), but what all of these associations have in common is their potential to become an important part of their members' identities.

Political Parties

The goal of political parties, most simply put, is to elect public officials. A distinction is often made between the party as an organization (e.g., national, state, and local committees), the party as a set of government officials who act in concert, and the party as an organization of voters who identify with the party (who may or may not register as members of that party and who may or may not vote).

Political parties in the U.S. are often linked to broader social, ethnic, and religious groups. For example, Black, Asian, and Hispanic Americans, as well as Jewish and religiously unaffiliated, are more strongly affiliated with the Democratic Party, whereas Mormons, White Evangelical Protestants, and White men without college degrees are more strongly affiliated with the Republican Party (Pew Research Center, 2015). Political parties can be an especially strong basis for identification at the local level, where they have greater opportunities to intervene to directly affect the immediate interests of their constituents (Robinson, 1973).

Like any other organization, if political parties become an important part of defining a person's identity, people will be increasingly motivated to act in ways that they believe are consistent with the interests and values of their party, and to view people affiliated with opposing parties in a negative light. There is clear evidence of growing political polarization in the U.S., leading to increasing animosity and conflict, even among family and friends (Pew Research Center, 2016). A recent survey suggests that nearly one out of five Republicans and Democrats agree with the statement that their political adversaries "lack the traits to be considered fully human—they behave like animals" (Kalmoe & Mason, 2019).

While there is evidence that political polarization has contributed to intergroup conflict, the causal direction of these effects can sometimes be ambiguous (Mason, 2016). For example, Mason and Wronski (2018) have argued that political alignments are substantially affected by membership and identity with racial, religious, and ideological groups, and these pre-existing differences might pull people into particular political parties. However, there is little doubt that political parties can lead to conflict, and often even to violence. In the U.S., political polarization has almost certainly fueled interpersonal conflict and disagreement (Pew Research Center, 2016), and has sometimes contributed to violent episodes (online political conspiracy theories contributed to a 2016 shooting at the Comet Ping Pong restaurant and pizzeria). Political divisions in other countries (e.g., India) have led to many deaths and scores of injuries.

Political parties often play a pivotal role in the ultimate example of misbehavior—war. For example, political divisions in Germany in the 1930s played a crucial role in the rise of the Nazi party. Even more important, political paralysis resulting from party conflict in France (Shirer, 1969) and in other allied countries made an effective response to Hitler's early aggressive moves (e.g., the remilitarization of the Rhineland, the massive rebuilding of the German army and air force, the *Anschluss* with Austria) impossible, and this arguably emboldened him to make further moves in Czechoslovakia and Poland that led to World War II (Shirer, 1960). However, the potential of political parties to contribute to war and international conflict is not their sole, or even their most important, contribution to misbehavior.

Political parties exist, in part, to motivate and mobilize their members, and they often do this by: (1) the emotional arousal of their members, and (2) dehumanizing and demonizing their opponents. As I noted in Chapter 2, emotional arousal is a key component of mob violence and can increase the likelihood of virtually any type of rule breaking. Strong attachment to political parties, combined with concerted efforts of those parties to whip up the excitement and motivation of their members can decrease members' willingness to restrain their behavior and to conform to rules and social norms. Second, political parties depend on and are fueled by opposition; parties that agree on essential policies and priorities find it difficult to generate enthusiasm and loyalty. Even where there are few major policy differences, political parties will often work hard to differentiate themselves from their competitors, and one nearly universal strategy is to cast the opposing party as being more untrustworthy, dishonest, corrupt, or evil. By generating and fueling ill will between members of parties that often advocate very similar policies, political parties arguably add to levels of conflict within society. More importantly, if these parties can convince you that your opponent is a malevolent and dangerous group, you will be much more likely to feel justified in treating members of opposing parties badly.

Political parties illustrate one of the key features that distinguish associations from other types of formal groups—the relevance and centrality of the group to its members is highly variable, both across group members and across time. For example, there are many registered Democrats and Republicans whose membership in their party has little day-to-day influence on their behavior, but who might become strongly involved in and dedicated to their respective parties as elections approach. This phenomenon is even more noticeable in countries where the election season is a short one. Unlike the U.S., where the process of electing a president stretches routinely over a year, and where campaigning for president sometimes starts years before an election, election season in most countries with a representative form of government is relatively short, and there can be long periods when most members of political parties barely think about, much less act on, their political affiliation. Unlike other important reference groups, associations might have only intermittent effects on the beliefs and behaviors of their members.

Associations and Movements

People sometimes join groups because the goals of the group are consistent with their values and interests. These can range from communities of interest (e.g., in earlier chapters, I mentioned that I am part of a Facebook group "Old Guitar Pickers" that posts songs and information that is of interest to long-time guitar enthusiasts) to social movements (e.g., the website https://metoomvnt.org provides opportunities to join the Me Too movement, along with links to resources, news, and events relevant to the movement) to professional associations (e.g., American Psychological Association, The Royal Society of Medicine) and fraternal associations (e.g., the Elks, Freemasons, the Shriners). These groups vary tremendously in their focus, size, and resources, but they all have several features in common.

First, these groups typically have a hybrid or tiered structure, with a small full-time staff, a relatively small cadre of highly involved members (who often serve on important committees or become officers of the group), and a large pool of members whose involvement is variable and intermittent. Second, members of these groups sometimes invest significant amounts of time and money to join and participate in the activities of these groups, and these investments are usually made without the expectation that members will benefit materially. Some professional associations do provide their members with concrete benefits (e.g., subscriptions to professional journals at reduced costs, professional credentials), but even in these groups, the costs of membership usually exceed the concrete benefits. Nevertheless, members often find it worthwhile to join these groups, and groups of this sort are often an important part of their members' social identity (Dunleavy, 1988; Fowler & Cam, 2007).

Third, interest groups, movements, and professional associations are a worldwide phenomenon, but these groups have been particularly important in the United States. In his great 1840 survey of democracy in the United States, Alexis de Tocqueville noted that

> In the United States, as soon as several inhabitants have taken an opinion or an idea they wish to promote in society, they seek each other out and unite together once they have made contact. From that moment, they are no longer isolated but have become a power seen from afar whose activities serve as an example and whose words are heeded.
>
> *(de Tocqueville, 2003, 599)*

There are over 90,000 trade and professional associations in the United States, ranging from the well known (e.g., American Bar Association, National Educational Association) to more obscure associations that are nevertheless important to their members (e.g., National Candle Association). Over our history, there have been hundreds of fraternal orders in the U.S., ranging from the familiar (e.g., the Lions, Benevolent and Protective Order of Elks, Ancient Order of Hibernians) to the more exotic and sometimes defunct (e.g., American Order of Druids, Chevaliers de Pythias). There are certainly important fraternal orders in many other countries (e.g., the Orange Order in Northern Ireland), and many fraternal orders are international in scope (e.g., Freemasons, B'nai Brith). Some fraternal organizations have strong mystical overtones (e.g., Ancient and Mystical Order Rosæ Crucis, or the Rosicrucians) or exist more strongly in legend than in reality (e.g., the Illuminati), but membership in one or more associations has been a common feature of American life since the time of de Tocqueville, and there is no sign that this love of joining is dying out of the American character.

Rowley and Moldoveanu (2003) noted that interest groups do not have to be formed around some existing ideas or ideologies, but they often are. For example, I spent most of my career as a professor in various departments of psychology, and we encouraged our graduating students to join the American Psychological Association, as well as specialized societies such as the Society for Industrial and Organizational Psychology to help develop and strengthen their identity as psychologists.

The more central a group is, the stronger the influence of the norms, standards, and values of this group will be in influencing your behavior. Because members of these groups vary so strongly in terms of the strength and consistency of their identification with the group, it might not be possible to learn a great deal about a person's behavior if you find out that they are a member of the Lions or the Elks, but if you also find out that this individual devotes a substantial amount of time and effort to the causes that are central to this group, you might be able to draw more and more accurate inferences about that person's values, norms, and behavior.

Of the three types of groups described in this section, movements and political parties have the strongest potential to arouse emotions and passion on the part of their members. It is unlikely that you will have a strong emotional involvement in a professional association. You might feel more strongly about this association the day annual dues need to be paid or on the rare occasions when the association does something that directly affects you, but these groups are not designed to get their members marching in the streets. Many movements and political parties have exactly this goal of mobilizing their members, and this can at times lead to civil disobedience (e.g., between 2011 and 2012, there were over 7,000 arrests of members of the Occupy Movement), rioting (e.g., 1992 riots in Los Angeles, the 2021 assault on the U.S. Capital), and violent assault (numerous authoritarian parties have paramilitary wings whose main job is to intimidate and disrupt the opposition). This mobilization of membership is often focused in the direction of positive social change (e.g., Mothers Against Drunk Driving) and movements directed toward human rights, but there are also numerous movements and groups with more sinister purposes (e.g., Ku Klux Klan, Proud Boys, Aryan Brotherhood). The potential for even the most benevolent movement to engage in lawbreaking or antisocial behavior is likely to be proportional to the extent to which members become emotionally engaged in the group and its goals. As discussions of mob behavior in several previous chapters suggest, emotional engagement can motivate many positive behaviors, but it can also lower the barriers against behaviors that have the potential to do substantial and lasting harm.

BOX 6.2 BLAND NAME/SINISTER PURPOSE

What do the American Freedom Party, Creativity Movement, Keystone United, and the National Alliance have in common? These may sound like fairly innocuous groups, but they are all listed as hate groups by the Southern Poverty Law Center. These groups are connected with ideologies such as White nationalism, White supremacy, and/or anti-Semitism. What do Citizens' Councils, the State Sovereignty Commission, and Councils of Conservative Citizens have in common? Again, the titles seem relatively innocuous, but the reality is a bit uglier. All of these groups were an important part of the resistance to racial integration and Black civil rights in the 1960s. In all of the cases cited here, group names were chosen that had the effect (and very likely the intention) of disguising the nature of the group's activities, making it easier for people to participate in, fund, and support these ideologies without appearing to do anything antisocial.

Many groups disguise the nature of their activities by choosing bland names that feature terms like Freedom, American, Sovereignty, and the like, but this strategy is not embraced by all hate groups or groups designed to perpetuate discrimination. The most visible and successful hate group, the Ku Klux Klan, very deliberately chose a different approach.

The original Klan was founded shortly after the end of the Civil War. After a period of violent activities designed to terrorize freed slaves and their supporters, the original Klan was suppressed through a series of federal laws. The Klan was reviewed in 1915, borrowing ideas and inspiration from the movie *Birth of a Nation*, and at one point claimed membership in the millions.[2] The Klan had significant political influence, especially in the South and Midwest, and in 1925, 25,000 Klan members marched in full regalia in Washington, D.C. The third iteration of the Klan originated in the 1950s and 1960s in reaction to the Civil Rights movement.

The organization of the Klan has varied somewhat over time, but a few elements have stayed very much the same since the 1860s. First, the Klan has often referred to itself as an "Invisible Empire", a term that implies that the Klan is ubiquitous and powerful. Second, there has always been an element of mysticism in the titles chosen for leaders and high officers (e.g., Wizard, Dragon); the second Klan created a whole series of mysterious titles for positions, activities, and meeting places, all starting with Kl (e.g., Kleagle, Klavern, Kludd), all of which helped to support the impression of a mysterious, important group. The name, the titles, and the "Kl" vocabulary all helped to create an aura of power and menace that was used to attract members and to project influence.

Studying the names and terminology connected with various groups can give several insights into the goals and strategies those groups pursue. Both of the strategies described here—that is, using an innocuous name to hide the nature of its activities vs. choosing names and titles to advertise particular aspects of the group or to create impressions about that group's potency—represent a conscious set of choices about how to build and maintain a group. Unfortunately, both strategies can claim numerous "successes"—if you call building a hate group an accomplishment.

How Formal Groups Contribute to Misbehavior

Like informal groups, formal groups create establish descriptive and injunctive norms that influence members' perceptions of what *is* and what *ought to* be. These groups have many of the same tools of social control as informal groups and have the power to bestow rewards to some members (e.g., recognition and honors, pay raises, promotions) and sanctions to others (e.g., expulsion from the group, loss of positions and responsibilities. The difference is that formal groups have a higher degree of stability and structure, and this can give their rewards and sanctions greater scope. For example, the American Psychological Association rewards members who have made outstanding contributions by recognizing them as Fellows and gives annual awards to individuals who have made significant contributions to the science and practice of psychology. They also publish *Ethical Principles of Psychologists and Codes of Conduct* (American Psychological Association, 2013), and every year they publish a list of psychologists who have been expelled from this association because of violations of those principles and codes. Similarly, workgroups have formal tools for evaluating the performance and effectiveness of their members (e.g., annual performance appraisals) and for rewarding good performers and sanctioning poor performers.

Both formal and informal groups are structured, in the sense that roles are delineated and power relationships are established. There are, however, substantial differences in the strength and stability of that structure, and these have important implications for misbehavior. First, roles in formal groups are assigned to positions rather than to individuals, and they are explicitly defined in such a way that group members have a much clearer sense of who is responsible for what and who holds the power and authority to make particular decisions than they would in an informal group. The existence of charters, organizational charts, job descriptions, handbooks, and the like gives roles in formal groups clarity and permanence, and this can have decisive effects on behavior. People who would normally avoid and even resist harming others might be entirely willing to be part of the process of polluting a river their community depends on, forcing underprivileged people out of their homes, destroying villages that might or might not shelter enemy soldiers, raping and killing civilians, etc. The existence of well-delineated roles and lines of authority makes it much easier for people to displace responsibility for their actions, follow orders, and behave without thinking about the consequence of their actions.

The most critical difference between formal and informal groups has to do with power. Formal groups have access to more types of power than informal groups. In particular, power is often legitimized in formal groups, and legitimate power carries the possibility of redefining norms and expectations in ways that expert, informational, or even referent power might not. In an extreme case, a king or a head of government might be able to define what is acceptable and what is not in a society. Similarly, executives in an organization or association might be able to set, or at least influence, injunctive norms. As I will outline in several of the chapters to follow, formal groups are often able to set up a parallel set of norms and expectations that differ from those of society in general, but that specify what members of their organizations are expected to do. The existence of a parallel set of norms and expectations that are antisocial in some important way turns out to be an essential feature of the types of sick and corrupt organizations described in Chapters 11 and 12.

The combination of explicitly defined roles and lines of authority allows formal groups to have significantly higher levels of influence on the behavior of their members than is typically seen in informal groups. Informal groups can be highly influential, but they rarely become the springboard for misbehavior on a scale comparable to formal groups, which might become the driving force in large-scale thefts and frauds, shocking levels of violence and destruction. The potential for formal groups to influence their members to misbehave is significantly enhanced when members have a high level of attachment and commitment to the group. I will take up the topic of attachments between individuals and groups in the chapter that follows.

Summary

Formal groups share several characteristics with informal groups (e.g., members interact, groups set norms, groups are part of members' social identity), but they add two critically important factors. First, they show a more well-defined and stable structure. In formal groups, duties, roles, and responsibilities are often assigned to positions (e.g., Treasurer) rather than to persons, and roles are often defined in detail in documents, charters, and the like. Second, power and authority are more clearly defined in formal groups, and these groups often have access to types of power (e.g., legitimate power) that are not available to most informal groups. There are, however, important variations in the structure of different types of formal groups that can have important implications for understanding how these groups might encourage or restrict misbehavior.

There are, for example, variations in the level of interdependence shown by different groups, with some groups representing little more than a set of people who are located together but who act independently. Teams, on the other hand, often show high levels of involvement, commitment, and interdependence, and these characteristics can increase the impact of team norms and values on the behavior of members.

Many associations exhibit a hybrid structure, with a small number of professional employees, a small cadre of highly dedicated members who are consistently involved in the activities of the group, and a large membership whose involvement in and attachment to the group is highly variable. Some groups, such as political parties and social movements, can successfully motivate and engage their members, while others (e.g., professional associations) may rarely have much impact of the bulk of their membership.

In many formal groups, a combination of well-defined roles, clear lines of power, and authority and norms that support the legitimacy of that authority greatly enhances the likelihood of certain categories of misbehavior, particularly if group members can be persuaded to go along with behaviors that seem to be required by the group or mandated by group leaders. Virtually every large-scale violation of laws and social norms (e.g., corporate frauds, wartime atrocities) involve many individuals who are simply following orders or acting in what they perceive to be the best interests of the group. In Chapters 8–12, I will explore misbehavior in work organizations, and these chapters will make clearer how various features of formal groups can become springboards for misbehavior.

Notes

1. In the former Soviet Union and in many nations that were part of the Warsaw Pact (the Soviet counterpart to NATO), the near-collapse of their economies and dysfunctional relationships between employees and organizations led to a more cynical version of this motto—i.e., "They pretend to pay us and we pretend to work"
2. These claims are disputed, and true membership figures are hard to obtain

References

American Psychological Association. (2013). *Ethical Principles of Psychologists and Codes of Conduct*. Washington, DC.

Ashforth, B.E. & Mael, F. (1989). Social identity theory and the organization. *Academy of Management Review*, *14*, 20–39.

Barrick, M., Bradley, B., Kristof-Brown, A. & Colbert, A. (2007). The moderating role of top management team interdependence: Implications for real teams and working groups. *Academy of Management Journal*, *50*, 544–557.

Borman, W.C. & Motowidlo, S.J. (1993). Expanding the criterion domain to include elements of contextual performance. In N. Schmitt & W.C. Borman (Eds.), *Personnel Selection in Organizations* (pp. 71–98). San Francisco: Jossey-Bass.

Borman, W.C., White, L.A. & Dorsey, D.W. (1995). Effects of ratee task performance and interpersonal factors on supervisor and peer performance ratings. *Journal of Applied Psychology*, *80*, 168–177.

Brief A.P. & Motowidlo, S.J. (1986). Prosocial organizational behaviors. *Academy of Management Review, 10*, 710–725.

de Tocqueville, A. (2003). *Democracy in America and Two Essays on America*. London: Penguin Books.

Dunleavy, P. (1988). Group identities and individual influence: Reconstructing the theory of interest groups. *British Journal of Political Science, 18*, 21–49.

Evans, C.R. & Dion, K.L. (1991). Group cohesion and performance: A meta-analysis. *Small Group Research, 22*, 175–186.

Fowler, J.H. & Cam, C.D. (2007). Beyond the self: Social identity, altruism, and political participation. *The Journal of Politics, 69*, 813–827.

French, J. & Raven, B.H. (1959). The bases of social power. In D. Cartwight (Ed.), *Studies in Social Power* (pp. 251–260). Ann Arbor: Institute for Social Research, University of Michigan.

Greenberg, J. (1990). Employee theft as a reaction to underpayment inequity: The hidden costs of pay cuts. *Journal of Applied Psychology, 75*, 561–568.

Guest, D.E. & Conway, N. (2002). Communicating the psychological contract: An employer perspective. *Human Resource Management Journal, 12*, 22–38.

Guzzo, R.A. & Dickson, M.W. (1996). Teams in organizations: Recent research on performance and effectiveness. *Annual Review of Psychology, 47*, 308–338.

Guzzo, R.A. & Shea, G.P. (1992). Group performance and intergroup relations in organizations. In M.D. Dunnette & L.M. Hough (Eds.), *Handbook of Industrial and Organizational Psychology* (2nd Ed., Vol. 3, pp. 269–313). Palo Alto, CA: Consulting Psychologist Press.

Guzzo, R.A., Yost, P.R., Campbell, R.J. & Shea, G.P. (1993). Potency in groups: Articulating a construct. *British Journal of Social Psychology, 32*, 87–106.

Hofstede, G., Hofstede, G.J. & Minkov, M. (2010). *Cultures and Organizations: Software of the Mind*. Revised and Expanded 3rd Ed. New York: McGraw-Hill.

Ilgen, D.R., Hollenbeck, J.R., Johnson, M. & Jundt, J. (2005). Teams in organizations: From Input-Process-Output models to IMOI models. *Annual Review of Psychology, 56*, 517–543.

Ilies, R., Hauserman, N., Schwochau, S. & Stibal, J. (2003). Reported incidence rates of work-related sexual harassment in the United States: Using meta-analysis to explain reported rate disparities. *Personnel Psychology, 56*, 607–631.

Kalmoe, N.P. & Mason, L. (2019). *Lethal mass partisanship: Prevalence, correlates and electoral contingencies*. NCAPSA American Politics Meeting, Washington, DC: April.

Karau, S.J. & Williams, K.D. (1993). Social loafing: A meta-analytic review and theoretical integration. *Journal of Personality and Social Psychology, 65*, 681–706.

Katzenbach, J.R. & Smith, D.K. (1993). The discipline of teams. *Harvard Business Review, 71*, 111–120.

Kemp, N.J., Wall, T.D., Clegg, C.W. & Cordrey, J.L. (1983). Autonomous work groups in a green field site: A comparative study. *Journal of Occupational Psychology, 56*, 271–288.

Kershaw, I. (2000). *Hitler: 1889–1936, Hubris*. New York: Norton.

Kozlowski, S.W.J. & Ilgen, D.R. (2006). Enhancing the effectiveness of work groups and teams. *Psychological Science in the Public Interest, 7*, 77–124.

Kudish, J.D., Poteet, M.L., Dobbins, G.H., Rush, M.C. & Russell, J.E.A. (1995). Expert power, referent power and charisma: Toward the resolution of a theoretical debate. *Journal of Business and Psychology, 10*, 177–195.

Marescaux, E., De Winne, S. & Sels, L. (2019). Idiosyncratic deals from a distributive justice perspective: Examining co-workers' voice behavior. *Journal of Business Ethics, 154*, 263–281.

Mason, L. (2016). A cross-cutting calm: How social sorting drives affective polarization. *Public Opinion Quarterly, 80*(S1), 351–377.

Mason, L. & Wronski, J. (2018). One tribe to bind them all: How social group attachments strengthen partisanship. *Advances in Political Psychology, 39*(S1), 257–277.

National Research Council. (2012). *Education for Life and Work: Developing Transferable Knowledge and Skills in the 21st Century*. Committee on Defining Deeper Learning and 21st Century Skills, J.W. Pellegrino & M.L. Hilton (Eds.). Washington, DC: The National Academies Press.

Organ, D.W. (1988). *Organizational Citizenship Behavior: The Good Soldier Syndrome*. Lexington, MA: Lexington, Books.

Pew Research Center. (2015, April). *A Deep Dive into Party Affiliation*.

Pew Research Center. (2016, June). *Partisanship and Political Animosity in 2016*.

Prapavessis, H. & Carron, A.V. (1997). Sacrifice, cohesion and conformity to norms in sports teams. *Group Dynamics: Theory, Research and Practice, 1*, 231–240.

Pulakos, E.D., Arad, S., Donovan, M.A. & Plamondon, K.E. (2000). Adaptability in the workplace: Development of a taxonomy of adaptive performance. *Journal of Applied Psychology, 85*, 612–624.

Rapp, T.L. & Mathieu, J.E. (2018). Team and individual influences on members' identification and performance per membership in multiple team membership arrangements. *Journal of Applied Psychology, 104*, 303–320.

Raven, B.H. (1992). A power interaction model on interpersonal influence: French and Raven thirty years later. *Journal of Social Behavior and Personality, 7*, 217–244.

Robinson, F.S. (1973). *Albany's O'Connell Machine: An American Political Relic*. Albany, NY: Washington Park Spirit.

Robinson, S.L. & Brown, G. (2004). Psychological contract breach and violation in organizations. In R.W. Griffin & A. O'Leary-Kelly (Eds.), *The Dark Side of Organizational Behavior* (pp. 309–337). San Francisco, CA: Wiley.

Rousseau, D.M. (1989). Psychological and implied contracts in organizations. *Employee Responsibilities and Rights Journal, 8*, 121–139.

Rousseau, D.M. (1995). *Psychological Contracts in Organizations: Understanding Written and Unwritten Agreements*. Newbery Park, CA: Sage.

Rowley, T.J. & Moldoveanu, M. (2003). When will stakeholder groups act? An interest- and identity-based model of stakeholder group mobilization. *Academy of Management Review, 28*, 204–219.

Shirer, W.L. (1960). *The Rise and Fall of the Third Reich: A History of Nazi Germany*. New York: Simon & Schuster.

Shirer, W.L. (1969). *The Collapse of the Third Republic: An Inquiry into the Fall of France in 1940*. New York: Simon & Schuster.

Smith C.A., Organ, D.W. & Near J.P. (1983). Organizational citizenship behavior: Its nature and antecedents. *Journal of Applied Psychology, 68*, 653–663.

Toffler, A. (1970). *Future Shock*. New York: Random House.

Weeks, L. (2011, May 25). Time for associations to trade in their past? *National Public Radio*, www.npr.org/2011/05/25/136646070/time-for-associations-to-trade-in-their-past

Zhao, H.A.O., Wayne, S.J., Glibkowski, B.C. & Bravo, J. (2007). The impact of psychological contract breach on work-related outcomes: A meta-analysis. *Personnel Psychology, 60*, 647–680.

7

RELATIONSHIPS BETWEEN INDIVIDUALS AND GROUPS

Attachment, Identity, and Commitment

This chapter deals with the relationships between people and groups. In general, the more important the group is to the individual, the more likely it is that the norms, values, and expectations of that group will affect the individual's behavior. However, there are many ways that people might relate to groups and simply describing this relationship along a continuum from weak to strong oversimplifies a complex set of relationships.

Why Are We Drawn to Groups?

Before exploring in detail *how* individuals are related to the various groups that might be relevant to them, it is useful to return to the question taken up in several preceding chapters of *why* people are drawn to groups. Many studies and theories try to explain the importance of social groups (both formal and informal groups) to individuals, and I believe the answer to the question of why people are drawn to groups can best be explained in terms of three fundamental motivations: (1) the need to belong, (2) the desire to maintain a positive self-image, and (3) the desire to reduce uncertainty and ambiguity. In Chapter 4, I discussed the role of groups in building and maintaining a positive self-image and reducing ambiguity. I will expand on these ideas in this chapter but first will take up a topic that has not been adequately examined in previous chapters—that is, the need to belong.

Need to Belong

Belongingness has been identified as a universal and fundamental human need that transcends cultures (Baumeister & Leary, 1995). There is strong empirical evidence that failure to satisfy the need to belong causes discomfort and distress.

In particular, numerous studies have shown that when individuals are accepted, welcomed, or included in groups that are important to them, this leads to positive emotions such as happiness, elation, calm, and satisfaction. Conversely, when individuals are rejected or excluded, they feel strong negative emotions such as anxiety, jealousy, depression, and grief (Baumeister & Leary, 1995; MacDonald & Leary, 2005). There is even evidence that the psychological pain caused by social rejection is sufficiently intense that it involves the same brain regions involved in the experience of physical pain (MacDonald & Leary, 2005).

Leary and Cox (2008) refer to belongingness as "a mainspring of social action" (p. 27) and claim that the first premise of virtually any theory of social or cultural behavior should be that humans have a strong drive to create and maintain interpersonal relationships. MacDonald (2007) suggests that self-esteem is a reflection of the relationships between individuals and groups, and that self-esteem can be best understood as a reflection of an individual's sense of her or his acceptability to important others.

Some researchers claim that belonging to a group is not enough and that what is important is status, or a person's relative standing in a group (Anderson, Hildreth, & Howland, 2015). This controversial argument about the centrality of status goes back at least to the 1940s; Maslow's (1943) theories of motivation especially gave prominence to status. While there is no doubt that status is valued, the theory that status rather than belongingness is the fundamental driver of social motivation implies that belonging to a group as a follower rather than as a leader should not meet fundamental needs, and it is far from clear whether this is true. One possible reconciliation of these two claims is that belongingness by itself is valued, and the adding status on top of belonging increases the value of membership in groups.

Maintaining a Positive Self-Image

Second, membership in groups contributes to self-esteem and positive self-images. Groups also provide a variety of means for maintaining and enhancing a sense of self-worth, especially when the groups are viewed positively (Crocker & Luhtanen, 1990). Membership in a group with a positive reputation helps to boost the self-image of all of its members. However, even when the reputation of the group is not its primary advantage, the very fact that you are accepted as a member of a group can enhance an individual's self-esteem. As I noted in Chapter 4, the motivation to maintain a positive self-image is one of the strongest and most persistent of human goals (Hales, 1985; Tajfel, 1982; Tajfel & Turner, 1979).

Uncertainty Reduction

Third, people are usually uncomfortable with uncertainty and ambiguity, and groups play a pivotal role in providing people with information about the world and about how they should behave (Hogg, 2000). That is, groups not only satisfy the need to belong, they also provide members with information, assistance, and social support. Groups help to answer questions about identity (who am I?) and about how they should behave (what is normal and what is expected). Individuals who share a sense of social connectedness often come to internalize the opinions, beliefs, goals, and motivations of their groups (Walton & Cohen, 2007).

Why Are Some People Not Drawn to Groups?

Thinking about why we need groups also gives insight into the subset of people who *don't* want or need to be affiliated with groups. In Chapter 1, I discussed narcissism and psychopathy. True psychopaths show a combination of self-assurance and disdain for interpersonal relationships which makes it difficult, and perhaps even pointless for them to affiliate with groups. These traits can contribute to startling levels of success in some endeavors, and there has been speculation that many managers and executives show psychopathic tendencies (Babiak & Hare, 2007; Boddy, 2010). Current evidence, however, suggests that the incidence of psychopathy among executives and the advantages this personality might bring to the climb for corporate success have been substantially overstated (Landay, Harms, & Credé, 2019). Regardless of whether they are likely to become corporate executives or con men, approximately 1% of the population are classified as psychopaths (Werner, Few, & Bucholz, 2015), and these individuals have neither the desire nor the ability to affiliate with groups.

Psychologists suggest that two other personality traits, narcissism (the tendency to seek admiration and praise) and Machiavellianism (manipulativeness) combine with psychopathy to create the Dark Triad (Muris, Merckelbach, Otgaar, & Meijer, 2017; Paulhus & Williams, 2002)—a cluster of personality characteristics that are thought to be a strong indicator of antisocial behavior. It is likely that individuals who are high on either narcissism or Machiavellianism will also have difficulty with, and perhaps little real interest, in forming meaningful bonds with groups. In contrast with true psychopaths, narcissists and Machiavellians might join many groups, but their connections and staying power might be minimal. To the extent that narcissists and Machiavellians are affiliated with groups at all, these affiliations are likely to be transactional. That is, narcissists and Machiavellians might be quite willing to join a group if there is something in it for them and to leave the group as soon as that advantage dissipates.

BOX 7.1 ADDICTION AND THE DARK TRIAD

The Dark Triad of personality traits is associated with many negative psychosocial outcomes (e.g., low levels of job satisfaction; Muris et al., 2017), including, perhaps paradoxically, addictive behaviors (Jauk & Dieterich, 2019). In particular, individuals who show elevated levels of either narcissism or psychopathy are more likely to have problems with alcohol and illicit drugs. In many ways, this is inconsistent with the stereotype often portrayed in the media of individuals who score high on the Dark Triad (e.g., Gordon Gecko, *Wall Street*; Frank Underwood, *House of Cards*; Vicomte de Valmont, *Dangerous Liaisons*; Snyder, Smith, Øverup, Paul, & Davis [2019], discuss media portrayals of these villains). These individuals are often portrayed in the media as sophisticated operators, master criminals, and manipulators who are always in control and always seeking an angle. The reality is a bit more complicated.

For example, despite their braggadocio, narcissistic individuals often experience low levels of self-esteem, and narcissists who fail to receive praise from others are more likely to turn to substance abuse to manage their emotional responses. Psychopathy, on the other hand, is linked with substance abuse through a very different set of mechanisms. Individuals who score high on measures of psychopathy often become involved in substance abuse because of their heightened levels of sensation-seeking (Chapter 1 discussed the links between sensation-seeking and misbehavior) and their reduced levels of inhibitory control.

The third leg of the Dark Triad, Machiavellianism, does not appear to be related to substance abuse. It is possible to be Machiavellian without also being narcissistic or psychopathic, and pure Machiavellians do not share some of the weaknesses that push Dark Triad individuals in the direction of substance abuse. Jauk and Dieterich (2019) suggest that narcissism and psychopathy can be placed on the *externalizing* spectrum of mental disorders (i.e., mental disorders that involve maladaptive behaviors), a spectrum that also includes substance abuse. This suggests that the increase in substance abuse seen in individuals who score high on narcissism or psychopathy might not be directly caused by their Dark Triad traits, but rather might be simple extensions of the patterns of dysfunctional behavior that characterize these disorders. That is, the same self-doubt and lack of control that makes people narcissistic and psychopathic might also push them in the direction of substance abuse.

Recent research has suggested the utility of studying what is arguably the antithesis of the Dark Triad—that is, the Light Triad (Kaufman, Yaden, Hyde, & Tsukayama, 2019). The Light Triad represents a loving and beneficent orientation toward others ("everyday saints") and it consists of three facets: (1) Kantianism (treating people as ends unto themselves), (2) humanism (valuing the dignity and worth of each individual), and (3) faith in humanity (believing in the fundamental goodness of humans). Individuals who receive high scores on measures of the Light Triad also show higher levels of life satisfaction, compassion, empathy, enthusiasm, and acceptance of others. There is not yet sufficient research to be certain that these traits also translate into closer and more meaningful relationships with social groups, but it is a very good bet that they do. The Dark Triad is epitomized by real and fictional characters such as Ted Bundy or Hannibal Lector. The Light Triad is epitomized by characters such as the Dali Lama or Atticus Finch.[1]

Inability to Become a Member of a Group

Finally, some people *want* to be members of groups but find it difficult to do so. Consider introverts. Human personality is often described in terms of five general traits: (1) conscientiousness, (2) extroversion, (3) agreeableness, (4) emotional stability and (5) openness to experience (Digman, 1990). All of these traits might have a bearing on your ability to form meaningful relationships with groups, but most of them relate to the likelihood that groups will want you as a member, not to the likelihood that you will find it difficult to become one. People who are undependable and disorganized (low conscientiousness) might not be sought or accepted as members of groups, particularly groups that are put together to accomplish specific tasks. People who are disagreeable or neurotic (low emotional stability) may find it difficult to find groups that will accept them. People who are rigid, close-minded, and uncurious (low openness to experience) may have a similarly difficult time finding groups that want them as members. Finally, and perhaps uniquely, highly introverted people (low extroversion) may find it difficult to seek out and join groups.

Introversion is often confused with shyness, but these two constructs are distinct. Introversion refers to a preference for being alone and is often associated with the idea that interacting with others can be exhausting and that being alone gives introverts a chance to recharge and relax. Shy people do demonstrate higher levels of introversion, but shyness is a more complex phenomenon than it first appears. Cheek and Krasnoperova (1999) suggest that there are four distinct types of shyness: (1) shy-secure—people who do not need much social interaction, (2) shy-withdrawn—people who are anxious about social interaction and fearful of rejection, (3) shy-dependent—people who want to be with others so much that they overcompensate, and (4) shy-conflicted—people who have a strong desire for social contact but high levels of anxiety about it. The Cheek-Buss Shyness scale (Cheek & Buss, 1981) and its successors provide useful measures of several facets of shyness, and research on this scale suggests that some types of shyness (e.g., shy-withdrawal, temperamental shyness) are correlated with difficulty in forming social relationships and with many physical and mental health problems (e.g., low self-esteem, withdrawal, eating disorders; Jones, Schulkin, & Schmidt, 2014; Schmidt & Fox, 1995).

Links Between Individuals and Groups

Every individual is a member of or is in some way affiliated with many groups (e.g., your family, workgroup, friends, bowling league, political party), and the strength and nature of the relationships between that person and each of those groups are likely to vary. Four different types of links between people and groups can be described: (1) membership, (2) attachment, (3) identity, and (4) commitment. An individual will likely exhibit different types of links to different social groups, and it is also likely that the links to specific groups might change over time (e.g., an individual might be a passive member of a group at one point in time and identify strongly with that same group at another point in time).

Membership

First, you can be a member of a group without establishing close linkages to the group and without being substantially influenced by the group. In Chapter 6, I discussed associations and interest groups, and these give a good example of this form of relationship between an individual and a group. A person who is a member of a group might not identify strongly with the group, or this identification might be periodic at best. For example, during times of relatively low political polarization, many people are members of a political party, but party membership might be only intermittently relevant or important to them (e.g., during political campaigns). Similarly, many people belong to professional or trade associations, but they rarely participate in the association's activities and rarely look to the association as a source of descriptive or injunctive norms.

There are likely to be graduations of membership, ranging from whole passive and uninvolved nominal membership (e.g., I am still formally a member of several professional associations, but I have never been to a meeting of some of them and probably would not still be a member if my dues were not already paid up) to a type of membership that is sometimes dormant and sometimes intense (e.g., a political party). The hallmark of the membership model is that a person is regarded as and regards themself as being linked to a group, but the links are either consistently weak (nominal membership) or weak much of the time, with occasional spikes of interest.

Most of us are members of many groups, and some of these groups do little to define our identity or our sense of how we should behave. That is, you can be a member of a group, but have relatively little involvement in or identification with the group. Even in groups that are important to the individual, there may be times when the group is more or less relevant to the individual's activities. Figure 7.1 illustrates two patterns of group membership that might represent weak links between people and groups.

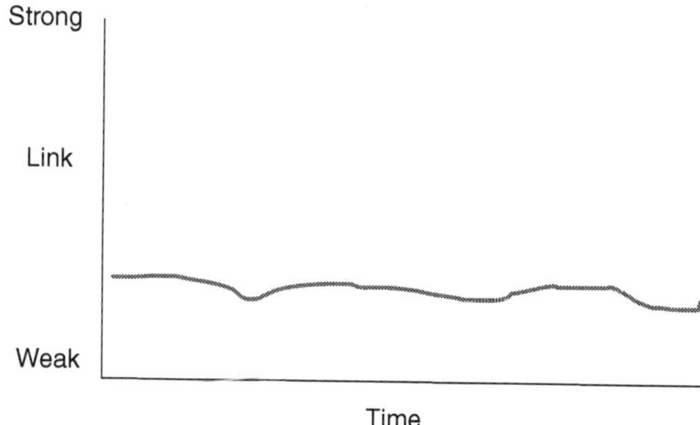

Periodically Strong, Generally Weak

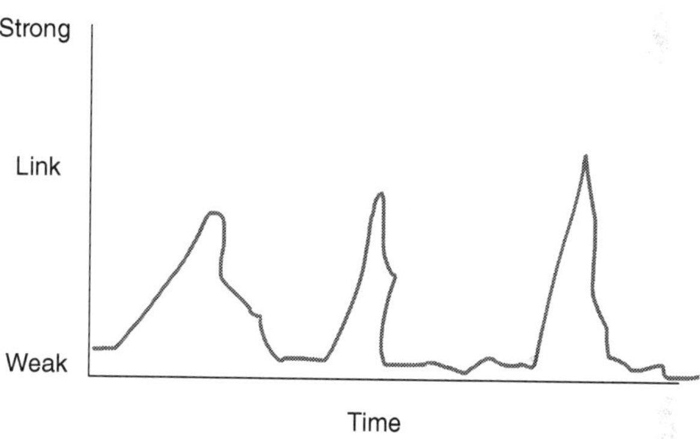

FIGURE 7.1 Two Patterns of Weak Person-Group Linkages

First, as the first panel in Figure 7.1 illustrates, an individual might have consistently weak linkages with one or more groups. Another possibility (illustrated in the second panel of Figure 7.1) is that an individual might have links that are sometimes strong and sometimes weak with a group. For example, an individual might have strong ties to family members, but family considerations, norms, and values might not be activated or considered in many social situations (e.g., the workplace), meaning that a group that is generally important to an individual might nevertheless have highly variable levels of influence on his or her behavior. Thus, your family might be a highly important reference group in some situations, whereas in others, the family might be one of several groups you are a member of, and it may not be as relevant to behavior. In some situations, your family might define your norms and behaviors, whereas, in others, you retain membership in the family, but it might not come into play in influencing the choices your make.

Attachment

One model of the link between an individual and a group is that of a nominal group member who has little involvement in or identification with the group. If we think about person-group links as being arranged on a continuum, the opposite pole from nominal group membership would probably be described as an attachment to a group. Attachment research and theory grew out of studies of parents (mostly mothers) and infants and was built around the belief that secure and healthy patterns of attachment create strong emotional bonds between the people. For example, parents can provide infants with a sense of security and protection that is vital to their physical and psychological development, but several environmental and individual conditions (e.g., poverty, mental illness) can disrupt this relationship, with the potential for lifelong negative effects (Turner, Beidel, & Costello, 1987).

Theories and concepts from the study of bonds between parents and children have been extended (not without controversy) to studies of the bonds between romantic partners and the bonds between individuals and groups (Hazan & Shaver, 1987; Smith, Murphy, & Coats, 1999; Sochos, 2015). For example, Sochos (2015) proposes that human beings need the protection and security offered by the social group in a similar way to the child needing the protection of the parent or caregiver. Like the bonds between parents and your children, there several different ways an individual can become attached to a group (Sochos, 2015). The most impactful and durable links are created when individuals attain a secure attachment to the group.

Individuals who show secure attachment view themselves as worthy and trust others to meet their needs. Other individuals show patterns of anxious attachment, in which links between individuals and groups are weaker and in which individuals feel insecure about whether they are accepted by the group. Still others show patterns of avoidant attachment, meaning that they resist the idea of becoming attached to a group and maintain as much distance as they can. The strength of attachment to groups depends in part on the individual's level of self-esteem. Individuals who have high self-esteem are typically less dependent on groups, and therefore less likely to become strongly attached (DeMarco & Newheiser, 2019).

Attachment theorists often claim that the attachment between parents and infants is qualitatively different from the attachments between romantic partners or between individuals and groups, but studies in these three domains exhibit many similarities. In particular, all three research literatures contrast secure attachment with anxious and ambivalent types, and similar terms are used in all three streams of research to describe these patterns of attachment in terms of two factors, trustworthiness and availability. Secure attachment is characterized by a high level of comfort with the relationship, ease in establishing and maintaining that relationship, and low fear of rejection. Anxious attachment is characterized by a desire for closeness that is tempered by fear of rejection by the relationship partner. In this attachment style, relationship partners are viewed as inconsistent and unpredictable, meaning that a relationship might look strong and secure today, but might lead to rejection in the future. Avoidant attachment involves the belief that others are untrustworthy and the fear of closeness and dependency.

Like membership, the strength and nature of attachment relationships are likely to vary across groups and also across time. That is, most individuals are likely to be attached to some groups and uninvolved in others, and their level of attachment to that subset of groups where there are potentially strong emotional bonds is likely to vary over time. Thus, individual experiences or stress in the environment (e.g., a change in life circumstances, a severe economic downturn) might make the group and the security and support that groups offer more or less relevant over time (Smith et al., 1999), and it is useful to keep in mind that measures of attachment might capture the average strength of individual-group relationships while missing variations in those relationships over time.[2]

In previous chapters, I have used the term "reference groups" to refer to groups that are important to an individual, particularly in terms of setting descriptive and injunctive norms. Attachment, especially secure attachment, represents a particularly strong link between individuals and groups, and it is reasonable to assume that any group to which you show a strong attachment will serve as a reference group. It is not clear whether the reverse assumption is justified. That is, some groups might be an important source of norms without necessarily having the same emotional relevance as groups you are strongly attached to. However, if a group provides you with a strong feeling of belongingness, security, and support, it is quite likely that that group will be an important source of normative information, and that the norms and expectations of that group will strongly affect your behavior.

Identification

As I have noted in several previous chapters, groups form an important part of people's identities. If someone asks you to describe yourself, it is a good bet that many of the terms you use will refer in one way or another to groups that are important to you (e.g., I am a father, a husband, a psychologist, a professor, etc.). Social Identity Theory (Tajfel, 1974, 1982; Tajfel & Turner, 1979, 1986) argues that self-concepts are formed primarily by the groups a person affiliates or identifies with and that this identification with groups helps to explain both intergroup behaviors (e.g., competition and conflict) and intragroup behaviors (e.g., power dynamics and roles within groups). Self-categorization Theory (Hogg & Terry, 2000; Turner, Hogg, Oakes, Reicher, & Wetherell, 1987; Turner & Oakes, 1986) explores the way that both personal identity (who am I?) and social identity (who are we?) can be shaped by groups that are seen as important and desirable by individuals.

One of the important principles of Self-categorization Theory is that individuals have multiple identities whose salience might vary over time and situations. The theory also posits that depersonalization and self-stereotyping, processes that tend to emphasize the group rather than individual attributes in defining self-concepts, can occur if the group is sufficiently important to the individual (Turner, 1985). Given the importance of positive self-image, many individuals are motivated to identify with groups that have relatively high levels of status, and high-status groups often place substantial barriers to entry. For example, many military organizations, police forces, sports teams, and fraternities practice some form or hazing or initiation, where new members are required to go through some sort of uncomfortable (sometimes, painful and dangerous) experience to qualify for membership in the group. You might think that this negative experience would make the group less inviting, but it has long been known that going through a difficult process to qualify for a group *increases* new members' liking for and identification with the group (Aronson & Mills, 1959).

There are some similarities between attachment to and identification with a group, but there are also important differences. First, attachment has a strong emotional component, in the sense that people can have very strong feelings about the groups (e.g., families) they are attached to (Bowlby, 1979). Identification does not necessarily require this sort of emotional bond; indeed, the topics of affect and emotion are not major components of Social Identity or Self-categorization Theory. Second, identification with a group implies some form of similarity, which allows people to think in terms such as "I am one of them" or "they are like me". Attachment might occur in groups where there is relatively little similarity between members (e.g., attachment between parents and young children). Finally, identification with a group is primarily a question of the place of that group in forming a self-concept. Strong identification implies that people will think of themselves in terms of "I am a. . . [group name]". In contrast, attachment has to do mainly with the strength of emotional bonds. A high level of secure attachment promotes feelings of security and well-being, whereas a high level of identification serves to erode barriers between individuals and groups.

Social Identity and Self-categorization theories suggest that the likelihood that you will identify with the group is linked back to the two functions of groups described earlier in this chapter. You are most likely to identify with a group if it helps you reduce uncertainty about the world (e.g., what is going on, how should I behave?) and/or it enhances your self-concept and feeling of worth.

Commitment

Research on workgroups, teams, and organizations has examined the nature, determinants, and effects of commitment to those groups (Mathieu & Zajac, 1990; Meyer & Allen, 1997; Riketta & Dick, 2005). Commitment is related to identification and attachment, but there are important distinctions between these states and commitment. Van Knippenberg and Sleebos (2006) note that there are several ways of defining the psychological relationship between individuals and groups or organizations. Individuals might, for example, define themselves largely in terms of the group, team, or organization they belong to (Ashforth & Mael, 1989; Mael & Ashforth, 1992). Van Knippenberg and Sleebos (2006) suggest that identification with groups, teams, and organizations is a cognitive/perceptual process in which the organization becomes a key part of an individual's self-concept. Individuals who do not organize their self-concept around the group or the organization may nevertheless become strongly committed to maintaining their relationship with a group. Unlike identification, in which the group or organization becomes a central part of how people define themselves, commitment is thought to be a reflection of an exchange relationship between people and groups (Van Knippenberg & Sleebos, 2006). That is, commitment to a group arises because of what the group does for you, and what you do for the group in exchange. For example, you might join a professional organization because it provides status and support, and in exchange for this, you might be willing to pay dues, serve on committees, and devote time and effort to the group's activity. However, if you see yourself putting in time, effort, and money, and getting little in return, you are likely to be less committed to the group and less willing to maintain your membership.

Meyer and Allen (1997) examined commitment to work organizations and suggested that there are at least three distinct forms of commitment: (1) affective commitment, (2) continuance commitment, and (3) normative commitment. First, people might form a close emotional attachment with the organization in the form of a strong desire to maintain a relationship with an organization. This is affective commitment. People who are affectively committed to their organizations often internalize the norms and goals of the organization, and their link with organizations is generally described as *wanting* to be a member of the organization. In contrast, some people *need* to stay with a work organization, even if they feel no particular attraction to or loyalty to that organization (continuance commitment). For example, you might be committed to staying with your current employer because your spouse has a good job and it is not possible to move, or because you do not think you will have similar opportunities elsewhere. Continuance commitment implies that you see the costs of leaving an organization as being higher than the benefits of going to another organization (Becker, 1960).

Finally, people might be committed to an organization because they believe they *should* be a loyal employee (normative commitment). Normative commitment is based on a feeling of obligation. For example, an organization might invest time and resources to train you, and you might believe that you, therefore, owe the organization something in return, making the prospect of leaving less attractive.

Meyer and Allen's (1997) model was built to help explain why some people stay with their employers and others leave, but the core concepts of this model apply to a wider array of groups. For example, you might join a bowling league and stay for years because you like and enjoy the experience, but you might also stay because there are no good alternatives available to you or because you don't think of yourself as a quitter. Regardless of the type of group, the strength and durability of bonds between an individual and the group might vary depending on whether they involve wanting to be a part of the group, feeling like you do not have good alternatives available to you or feeling like you should stay because that is the right thing to do or the thing people expect you to do.

Attachment to, identification with, and commitment to groups and organizations has long been thought to be beneficial to both employees and those groups. For example, there is considerable evidence that attachment to, identification with, and/or commitment to work organizations are all related to several positive organizational and individual-level outcomes (e.g., higher satisfaction, lower turnover; Ashforth & Mael, 1989; Conroy, Becker, & Menges, 2017; Lee, Park & Koo, 2015). Similarly, attachment, identification, and commitment to informal groups is related to several positive individual outcomes, including higher levels of life satisfaction and physical and mental health (Cohen, 2004; Glass, De Leon, Bassuk, & Berkman, 2006; Wakefield et al., 2017).

Outcomes of Strong Links Between Individuals and Groups

Membership, attachment, identification, and commitment represent four different types of links between people and groups. They are not mutually exclusive. Strong attachment, for example, also implies membership, identification, and commitment. Commitment, on the other hand, might be strictly transactional. For example, people might be committed to their employers because they cannot afford to move to a new town and start over. On the other hand, affective commitment might be hard to distinguish from attachment and identification. On the whole, the strength of the link between people and groups might be more important than the nature of that link. Strong links between people and groups have many potentially positive effects, including enhanced physical and mental health and higher levels of engagement. These links can also have negative outcomes (e.g., groupthink) and under the right circumstances can contribute to misbehavior.

Positive Mental and Physical Health

Strong and meaningful links to groups are good for you. Wakefield et al. (2017) reviewed research showing belonging to social groups and feeling that there are important similarities among members of social groups are linked to life satisfaction. They also showed that the more groups one identifies with, the higher the satisfaction. Perhaps most important, their results suggest that it is the identification and a sense of belonging rather than simple contact with groups that matters. Jetten et al. (2015) showed that strong links with groups contribute to self-esteem and that this effect is stronger when there are multiple important groups.

Sani, Madhok, Norbury, Dugard, and Wakefield (2015) note that identification with groups contributed to physical health and healthy behavior. For example, they showed physical exercise, weight loss, reduction in smoking and drinking, and adoption of healthier diets were all linked to feeling strong links to groups. They conclude that individuals who are strongly linked to groups find life more meaningful and feel a sense of responsibility to those groups that make it easier to initiate and sustain healthy behaviors. Jetten, Haslam, Haslam, and Dingle (2014) argue that "social groups are important psychological resources that have the capacity to protect health and well-being, but that they are only utilized effectively when individuals perceive they share identity with another individual or group" (p. 103). Social networks that include friends, family, and informal groups (e.g., clubs) have positive effects ranging from enhancing healthy behaviors (e.g., quitting smoking, getting exercise) to reduced levels of obesity and blood pressure (Holt-Lunstad, Smith, & Layton, 2010). Several studies have turned the question around to ask whether social isolation has negative health effects. There is substantial evidence that the failure to maintain meaningful contact with others has negative effects on physical and mental health (Cornwell & Waite, 2009; Grant, Hamer, & Steptoe, 2009; Hawkley, Preacher, & Cacioppo, 2010).

Jetten et al. (2014) suggest that we should treat shared identity the same way we treat other resources that might support a healthy life (e.g., financial support, health insurance). For example, they note that a common strategy for enhancing population health is to raise household income. Their results suggest that it is possible that similar effects might be obtained by helping to build sustainable social communities, and that this social strategy might end up being more cost-effective than traditional economic strategies.

BOX 7.2 GROUPS AND UNHEALTHY BEHAVIOR

Groups are a source of satisfaction, self-esteem, and enhanced physical and mental health, but they are also a key influence in initiating and continuing patterns of unhealthy behavior that can undo all of the good that attachment to groups does for us. For example, peer pressure is an important factor in teenage smoking (Liu, Zhao, Chen, Falk, & Albarracín, 2017). Peer influences are similarly important in drinking among young adults (Reifman & Watson, 2002). Teens and your adults are particularly susceptible to these social influences, but social groups have the potential to influence unhealthy behaviors across the life span.

Families and social groups influence our behavior throughout our lives, and while social ties are usually a positive factor in determining physical and mental health, social groups can also encourage unhealthy behaviors, particularly overeating and substance abuse (Umberson, Crosnoe, & Reczek, 2010). First, the norms of these groups might directly encourage unhealthy behaviors; you might find that whenever you get together with certain groups of friends or families you over-indulge, and you might be directly encouraged or even pressured to eat, drink, or smoke more. Second, social relationships can be a significant source of stress, which can have both direct and indirect health effects. Stress by itself can have serious effects on health, and people often cope with stress in ways that are themselves unhealthy (e.g., smoking, drinking).

Close relationships with others usually serve as a buffer against unhealthy behaviors; family members, spouses, and friends will often intervene to discourage behaviors such as overeating or substance abuse (Umberson et al., 2010). However, if the groups that are important to you view over-indulgence or substance abuse as normal, or as just part of having a good time, these norms and beliefs can be decisive in pushing people down a path that might severely undermine their health. One of the keys to understanding the circumstances under which group influence will either support or undermine healthy behavior is to understand both the descriptive and injunctive norms of key reference groups. For example, your family might believe that healthy eating is important, but they might also be in the habit of preparing huge meals and encouraging each other to eat more. Your friends might be sincerely interested in your health but might also encourage each other to drink more whenever you get together. Teens and young adults might be particularly vulnerable to peer influence, but it is important that families, friends, and social groups continue to influence us throughout our lives, and that these influences can be pivotal to initiating and continuing patterns of unhealthy behavior.

Engagement

Individuals benefit from forming strong links with groups, but groups benefit as well. For example, individuals who show strong emotional attachment to groups and commitment to their goals are more likely to be engaged in activities that benefit the group and that reinforce its importance to the individual.

The concept of employee engagement has been widely discussed in the business press and has been the focus of a growing body of research (Albrecht, 2010; Byrne, 2015; Christian, Garza, & Slaughter, 2011; Kahn, 1992; Macey, Schneider, Barbera, & Young, 2009). There is evidence that highly engaged employees perform better (Christian et al., 2011; Rich, Le Pine, & Crawford, 2010) and that engagement helps to buffer employees against work-related stress and burnout (Halbesleben, 2010). Nevertheless, there have been important criticisms of the concepts of engagement, starting with ongoing disagreement about precisely what employee engagement means, and how it relates to other concepts such as job satisfaction and organizational commitment (Byrne, 2015; Macey & Schneider, 2008; Wefald & Downey, 2009).

In the business press, engagement is often defined in terms of emotional commitment to the job, commitment to and internalization of the goals of the organization, and/or willingness to go beyond the strict definition of the job description and do what is necessary for the organization to succeed. It has even been defined as the opposite of disengagement (i.e., the state of being uninvolved and unmotivated; Macey & Schneider, 2008). In research on engagement, this concept is sometimes discussed in terms of traits (e.g., enduring positive views of life and work), sometimes in terms of states (e.g., feelings of energy and absorption), and sometimes in terms of behaviors (e.g., voluntary extra-role behaviors, organizational citizenship). The proliferation of definitions is one sign that researchers and business leaders have a hard time deciding precisely what it means to be an engaged employee.

Byrne (2015) reviewed and synthesized both popular descriptions of and research on employee engagement and suggests that this concept is best defined in terms of investing oneself, being authentic in the job, and delivering one's work performance with passion, persistence, and energy. Engaged employees internalize the goals of the organization, invest themselves strongly in accomplishing those goals, and achieve high levels of satisfaction from working to attain those goals.

Although research on engagement has concentrated on employees and their degree of investment in their jobs and roles, this concept has clear relevance for groups of all sorts. An individual who has internalized the goals and norms of his or her group and who shows a real passion for (and achieves satisfaction from) advancing the goals and fortunes of the group will prove a benefit to the group regardless of whether it is a workgroup, a sports league, or a gang. Highly engaged members are likely to exhibit all four forms of linkage between individuals and groups, by being active members who identify with, are emotionally attached to and committed to a group.

Engagement is related to the concept of "flow" (Csikszentmihalyi, 1997). Flow is sometimes described as a state of being completely absorbed in an activity, especially an activity which involves their creative abilities. People who are in this state of flow report altered perceptions of time (hours can sometimes seem like minutes, while at other times a few seconds spent in this state might feel like a much longer time span), a melting together of action and conscientiousness (e.g., being able to act instinctively and perform at a high level without consciously thinking through your actions), and feelings of effortlessness and control. Group members who are highly invested and highly involved in the activities of the group, and who can become absorbed in the group's activities are likely to contribute substantially to the group's continuing viability and success.

Groupthink

Close links between individuals and groups convey many advantages, but they can also cause problems. For example, cohesive groups, where many members are strongly committed to the group and its goals, have been known to make disastrously bad decisions, and it was once thought that excessive commitment to the group was at least partly to blame for this phenomenon.

Janis (1972, 1982) popularized what has become one of the most widely cited concepts from social psychology—that is, groupthink. He observed that cohesive decision-making groups seek consensus, especially when operating under pressure or threat, and suggested that their decision processes were characterized by high levels of group identification, overestimation of the group's ability and correctness, stereotyping of out-group members, selective information processing, and commitment to decisions. Case studies that Janis used to build this theory include Bay of Pigs, Pearl Harbor, and the escalation of the Vietnam War, and in all of these cases, Janis saw a tendency to shut out dissenting views, a focus on maintaining high levels of agreement, and an inability to effectively process information that did not match the group's consensus. Granström and Stiwne (1998)[3] suggest that there are two distinct versions of groupthink: (1) omnipotent (paranoid)—marked by feelings of invulnerability and by omnipotence being the prevailing mood, a distinct pattern of a belief that this group is superior to other groups, and (2) depressive—a group marked by a prevailing feeling of uselessness, incompetence, and fatigue. The feeling of having tried everything with no results, with no solutions to their problems, means that the members rely heavily on the leader or some outside force to save them. In both cases, groups might have a difficult time processing information efficiently and making effective decisions.

Despite its popularity, Janis' theory and predictions have come under considerable criticism. There is surprisingly little support for Groupthink Theory, and numerous replacements have been proposed (Aldag & Riggs Fuller, 1993; Riggs Fuller & Aldag, 1998; Turner & Pratkanis, 1994). As a piece of popular psychology, groupthink has been an unquestionable hit, but as a serious psychological theory of decision making, it has been less successful. Nevertheless, there is considerable value in thinking seriously about the way links between individuals and groups might affect the way the group functions, and groupthink research provides a useful starting point for asking questions about ways in which strong links can interfere with effective group functioning.

For example, Haslam et al. (2006) examined one aspect of the groupthink syndrome—the tendency for group members to remain committed to their decisions "through thick and thin". They argued that "one key determinant of continued commitment to group projects is the extent to which group members define themselves in terms of a shared social identity rather than as individuals" (p. 607). They found, for example, that as group projects began to falter, groups whose members have a strong sense of shared social identity tended to remain committed. Kruglanski, Pierro, Mannetti, and De Grada (2006) found that group-centrism (pressures to opinion uniformity, encouragement of autocratic leadership, in-group favoritism, rejection of deviates, resistance to change, conservatism, and the perpetuation of group norms) tends to increase as the need for closure and discomfort with ambiguity grow in a group. There is evidence that at least some aspects of Groupthink Theory do remain viable, and it is reasonable to conclude that when people are strongly connected to and committed to a group, they may adopt a narrow, group-centric perspective when solving problems and they may find it difficult to accept or deal effectively with information that runs counter to the biases and preferences of the group.

Dysfunctional Behavior

There is evidence that attachment to and identification with organizations can lead to dysfunctional behaviors. First, identification with and loyalty to a group changes the way you think about that group's actions and the actions of other groups. Loyalty to a group encourages group identification (Tajfel, 1982; Tajfel & Turner, 1979, 1986) and favorable social comparison of the in-group relative to out-groups (Tajfel, 1974), including denigration of and prejudice against other groups and out-group hostility (Turner & Oakes, 1986). This can even extend to an increased tendency to condone and engage in out-group (vs. in-group) violence (Cohen, Montoya, & Inski, 2006).

Martin, Kish-Gephart, and Detert (2014) suggested that because the self-image of highly identified employees is linked to the organization's image, they are likely to employ a range of cognitive tactics (e.g., moral disengagement, rationalization) to reinterpret harmful or unethical behaviors as ethical. Strong links to groups increase willingness to forgive bad behavior and violations of social norms by members of that group (Bernhard, Fehr, & Fischbacher, 2006). For example, people judge an unethical action less harshly when an in-group member, as compared to an out-group member, is responsible.

Dukerich, Kramer, and Parks (1998) note that employees can over-identify with their organization, making the organization such a central part of their identity that they lose their individuality and may be unwilling to express criticism or dissent if the organization behaves inappropriately. Over-identified individuals may be particularly likely to engage in unethical behaviors that appear to help their organization in the short run, particularly if the organization appears to be under threat, even if these behaviors are more harmful to the organization in the long run (Umphress, Bingham, & Mitchell, 2010). Virtually every review of large organizations caught engaging in serious misbehavior (e.g., Volkswagen engaged in an ongoing conspiracy to cheat on emissions tests; this scandal has been noted earlier and will be examined in detail in several later chapters) includes reports of employees going along with abusive or illegal behaviors in the sincere belief that these behaviors benefited the organization, and perhaps were vital to the organization's survival. Conroy, Henle, Shore, and Stelman's (2017) review confirms that organizational attachment/identification can lead to unethical behaviors, resistance to organizational change, lower performance, interpersonal conflict, negative emotions, and reduced well-being. They identify the pursuit of positive group distinctiveness and the associated in-group biases as especially important explanations for the potentially negative effects of organizational identification.

Loyalty is usually regarded as a valuable trait, but loyalty to a corrupt group can lead to unethical behavior (Hildreth, Gino, & Bazerman, 2016). People who are loyal to their group tend to discount, rationalize, or justify the unethical actions of other members of that group (Valdesolo & De Steno, 2007). Loyalty plays an important role in corruption because people discount or ignore their immoral actions when it benefits their groups. For example, in the military, police forces, street gangs, and organizations more broadly, loyalty can help foster cultures of crime by demanding members' silence to others' transgressions (Rothwell & Baldwin, 2007; Skolnick, 2002).

In the chapters that follow, I will examine the implications of commitment and loyalty toward groups and organizations for understanding misbehavior. One of the recurring themes in the research reviewed in these chapters is that strong links between individuals and groups can change the way people think about behaviors that violate general social norms, leading them to believe that misbehaviors ranging from incivility to war crimes are both acceptable and expected. Understanding the ways that group norms and the structure of groups (e.g., roles and status) influence the beliefs, perceptions, and motivations of their members is an important step toward making sense of misbehavior.

Summary

The strength and nature of the links between people and groups vary both between and within people. Some people are more strongly drawn to groups than others, and most people are members of many different formal and informal groups, but strongly linked to some and only nominally linked to others. Strong links can take many forms, three of which were discussed in this chapter. People might have emotional links to groups, especially groups that serve as sources of support and protection (attachment). People's sense of who they are is often determined at least in part by the social groups that are important to them (identity). People might be committed to remain as a member of a group for any number of different reasons, ranging from *wanting* to be a member to *having to remain* because of limited opportunities to move to other groups (commitment).

Strong links to groups usually have positive physical and mental health benefits, but groups can often be a critical factor in initiating and sustaining patterns of unhealthy behavior. It is no coincidence that behaviors such as smoking and drinking often start in teenage and young adult years; teens and young adults are particularly susceptible to peer pressure. However, your friends, family, and coworkers may end up encouraging unhealthy behaviors such as overeating and substance abuse, all in pursuit of having a good time together. Strong links to groups can also foster engagement in the group's pursuits—that is, a feeling of strong identification with the goals of the group and strong satisfaction with helping the group succeed. Engagement can be beneficial to both individuals and groups, but it can also be manifested in terms of workaholism and over-involvement in one important group, to the detriment of other groups that are also important in your life.

Strong links to groups can increase cohesion, but that cohesion can lead to some dysfunctional behaviors. Research on groupthink has a somewhat rocky history; groupthink is one of the most widely cited concepts from social psychology, but there is little genuine empirical support for many aspects of Groupthink Theory. Nevertheless, this research has contributed important insights, especially to the importance of keeping groups from developing a narrow focus on their preferred framing of events and preferred solutions and keeping an open mind to opposing points of view.

Loyalty to groups is beneficial in many ways, but like cohesion, it can have its downsides. Strong loyalty to groups can open the floodgates to many forces that contribute to misbehavior, ranging from over-identification with your group and disparagement of other groups to a willingness to overlook or excuse misbehavior by members of groups you are loyal to. Chapters 8–12 will examine ways in which becoming a member (especially a committed member) of formal organizations (e.g., employers, the military, the priesthood) can create pressures to misbehave and can lower the usual barriers to engaging in these behaviors.

Notes

1. At least the Atticus portrayed in *To Kill a Mockingbird*. In *Go Set a Watchman* (actually, the first draft of *Mockingbird*, but published decades later), Atticus Finch is not quite the noble giant portrayed in *To Kill a Mockingbird*, and shows more condescending views toward his Black neighbors
2. Similar arguments have been made regarding the measurement of job performance; Kane (1983, 1986) has proposed methods of evaluating the distribution of performance over time that might capture temporal changes in performance levels
3. See also Rosander, Stiwne, and Granström (1998)

References

Albrecht, S.L. (2010). Employee engagement: 10 key questions for research and practice. In S.L. Albrecht (Ed.), *Handbook of Employee Engagement: Perspectives, Issues, Research and Practice* (pp. 3–19). Northampton, MA: Edward Elgar.

Aldag, R. & Riggs Fuller, S. (1993). Beyond fiasco: A reappraisal of groupthink phenomena and a new model for group decision processes. *Psychological Bulletin, 113*, 533–552.

Anderson, C., Hildreth, J.A.D. & Howland, L. (2015). Is the desire for status a fundamental human motive? A review of the empirical literature. *Psychological Bulletin, 141*, 574–601.

Aronson, E. & Mills, J. (1959). The effect of severity of initiation on liking for a group. *Journal of Abnormal and Social Psychology. 59*, 177–181.

Ashforth, B.E. & Mael, F. (1989). Social identity theory and the organization. *Academy of Management Review, 14*, 20–39.

Babiak, P. & Hare, R.D. (2007). *Snakes in Suits: When Psychopaths Go to Work.* New York: Harper Business.

Baumeister, R.F. & Leary, M.R. (1995). The need to belong: Desire for interpersonal attachments as a fundamental human motivation. *Psychological Bulletin, 117*, 497–529.

Becker, H.S. (1960). Notes on the concept of commitment. *American Journal of Sociology, 66*, 32–40.

Bernhard, H., Fehr, E. & Fischbacher, U. (2006). Group affiliation and altruistic norm enforcement. *American Economic Review, 96*, 217–221.

Boddy, C.P. (2010). Corporate psychopaths and organizational type. *Journal of Public Affairs, 10*, 300–312.

Bowlby, J. (1979). *The Making and Breaking of Affectional Bonds.* London: Tavistock.

Byrne, Z.S. (2015). *Understanding Employee Engagement: Theory, Research Practice.* New York: Routledge.

Cheek, J.M. & Buss, A.H. (1981). Shyness and sociability. *Journal of Personality and Social Psychology, 41*, 330–339.

Cheek, J.M. & Krasnoperova, E.N. (1999). Varieties of shyness in adolescence and adulthood. In L.A. Schmidt & J. Schulkin (Eds.), *Extreme Fear, Shyness, and Social Phobia: Origins, Biological Mechanisms, and Clinical Outcomes* (pp. 224–250). New York: Oxford University Press.

Christian, M.S., Garza, A.S. & Slaughter, J.E. (2011). Work engagement: A quantitative review and test of its relations with task and contextual performance. *Personnel Psychology, 64*, 89–136.

Cohen, S. (2004). Social relationships and health. *American Psychologist, 59*, 676–684.

Cohen, T.R., Montoya, R.M. & Inski, C.A. (2006). Group morality and intergroup relations: Cross-cultural and experimental evidence. *Personality and Social Psychology Bulletin, 32*, 1559–1572.

Conroy, S., Becker, W., & Menges, J. (2017). The meaning of my feelings depends on who I am: Work-related identifications shape emotion effects in organizations. *Academy of Management Journal, 60*, 1071–1093.

Conroy, S., Henle, C., Shore, L. & Stelman, S. (2017). Where there is light, there is dark: A review of the detrimental outcomes of organizational identification. *Journal of Organizational Behavior, 38*, 184–203.

Cornwell, E.Y. & Waite, L.J. (2009). Social disconnectedness, perceived isolation, and health among older adults. *Journal of Health and Social Behavior, 50*, 31–48.

Crocker, J. & Luhtanen, R. (1990). Collective self-esteem and ingroup bias. *Journal of Personality and Social Psychology, 58*, 60–67.

Csikszentmihalyi, M. (1997). *Finding Flow: The Psychology of Engagement with Everyday Life.* New York, NY: Basic Books.

DeMarco, T.C. & Newheiser, A. (2019). Attachment to groups: Relationships with group esteem, self-esteem, and investment in in-groups. *European Journal of Social Psychology, 49*, 63–75.

Digman, J.M. (1990). Personality structure: Emergence of the five-factor model. *Annual Review of Psychology, 41*, 417–440.

Dukerich, J.M., Kramer, R. & Parks, J.M. (1998). The dark side of organizational identification. In D.A. Whetten & P. Godfrey (Eds.), *Identity in Organizations: Building Theory Through Conversations* (pp. 245–256). Newbury Park, CA: Sage.

Glass, T.A., De Leon, C.F., Bassuk, S.S. & Berkman, L.F. (2006). Social engagement and depressive symptoms in late life longitudinal findings. *Journal of Aging and Health, 18*, 604–628.

Granström, K. & Stiwne, D. (1998). A bipolar model of groupthink—an expansion of Janis' concept. *Journal of Small Group Research, 29*, 32–56.

Grant, N., Hamer, M. & Steptoe. A. (2009). Social isolation and stress-related cardiovascular, lipid and cortisol responses. *Annals of Behavioral Medicine, 37*, 29–37.

Hales, S. (1985). The inadvertent rediscovery of self in social psychology. *Journal for the Theory of Social Behavior, 15*, 237–282.

Hawkley, L.C., Preacher, K.J. & Cacioppo, J.T. (2010). Loneliness impairs daytime functioning but not sleep duration. *Health Psychology, 29*, 124–129.

Hazan, C. & Shaver, P. (1987). Romantic love conceptualized as an attachment process. *Journal of Personality and Social Psychology, 52*, 511–524.

Halbesleben, J.R.B. (2010). A meta-analysis of work engagement: Relationships with burnout, demands, resources, and consequences. In A.B. Bakker & M.P. Leiter (Ed.), *Work Engagement: A Handbook of Essential Theory and Research* (pp. 102–117). New York: Psychology Press.

Haslam, S.A., Ryan, M.K., Postmes, T., Spears, R., Jetten, J. & Webley, P. (2006). Sticking to our guns: Social identity as a basis for the maintenance of commitment to faltering organizational projects. *Journal of Organizational Behavior, 27*, 607–628.

Hildreth, J.A.D., Gino, F. & Bazerman M. (2016). Blind loyalty? When group loyalty makes us see evil or engage in it. *Organizational Behavior and Human Decision Processes, 132*, 16–36.

Hogg, M.A. (2000). Subjective uncertainty reduction through self-categorization: A motivational theory of social identity processes. *European Review of Social Psychology, 11*, 223–255.

Hogg, M.A. & Terry, D.J. (2000). Social identity and self-categorization processes in organizational contexts. *Academy of Management Review, 25*, 121–140.

Holt-Lunstad, J., Smith, T.B. & Layton, J.B. (2010). Social relationships and mortality risk: A meta-analytic review. *PLoS Med*, 7(7).

Janis, I.L. (1972). *Victims of Groupthink*. Boston: Houghton-Mifflin.

Janis, I.L. (1982). *Groupthink: Psychological Studies of Policy Decisions and Fiascos* (2nd Ed.). Boston: Houghton-Mifflin.

Jauk, E. & Dieterich, R. (2019). Addiction and the Dark Triad of personality. *Frontiers of Psychiatry, 10*, 662–683.

Jetten, J. et al. (2015). Having a lot of a good thing: Multiple important group memberships as a source of self-esteem. *PLoS One, 10*(5).

Jetten, J., Haslam, C., Haslam, S.A. & Dingle, G. (2014). How groups affect our health and well-being: The path from theory to policy. *Social Issues and Policy Review, 8*, 103–130.

Jones, K., Schulkin, J. & Schmidt, L.A. (2014). Shyness: Subtypes, psychosocial correlates, and treatment interventions. *Psychology, 5*, 244–254.

Kahn, W.A. (1992). To be fully there: Psychological presence at work. *Human Relations, 45*, 321–349.

Kane, J.S. (1983). Performance distribution assessment: A new breed of performance appraisal methodology. In H.J. Bernardin & R.W. Beatty (Eds.), *Performance Appraisal: Assessing Human Behavior at Work* (pp. 325–341). Boston: Kent.

Kane, J.S. (1986). Performance distribution assessment. In R. Berk (Ed.), *The State of Art in Performance Assessment*. Baltimore: John Hopkins University Press.

Kaufman, S.B., Yaden, D.B., Hyde, E. & Tsukayama, E. (2019). The light vs. dark triad of personality: Contrasting two very different profiles of human nature. *Frontiers in Psychology, 10*, Article 467, www.frontiersin.org/articles/10.3389/fpsyg.2019.00467/full

Kruglanski, A.W., Pierro, A., Mannetti, L. & De Grada, E. (2006). Groups as epistemic providers: Need for closure and the unfolding of group-centrism. *Psychological Review, 113*, 84–100.

Landay, K., Harms, P.D. & Credé, M. (2019). Shall we serve the dark lords? A meta-analytic review of psychopathy and leadership. *Journal of Applied Psychology, 104*, 183–196.

Leary, M.R. & Cox, C.B. (2008). Belongingness motivation: A mainspring of social action. In J. Shah & W. Gardner (Eds.), *Handbook of Motivation Science* (pp. 27–40). New York: Guilford Press.

Lee, E.S., Park, T.Y. & Koo, B. (2015). Identifying organizational identification as a basis for attitudes and behaviors: A meta-analytic review. *Psychological Bulletin, 141*, 1049–1080.

Liu, J., Zhao, S., Chen, X., Falk, E. & Albarracín, D. (2017). The influence of peer behavior as a function of social and cultural closeness: A meta-analysis of normative influence on adolescent smoking initiation and continuation. *Psychological Bulletin, 43*, 1082–1115.

MacDonald, G. (2007). Self-esteem: A human elaboration of prehuman belongingness motivation. In C. Sedikides & S.J. Spencer (Eds.), *The Self* (pp. 235–257). New York: Psychology Press.

MacDonald, G. & Leary, M.R. (2005). Why does social exclusion hurt? The relationship between social and physical pain. *Psychological Bulletin, 131*, 202–223.

Macey, W.H. & Schneider, B. (2008). The meaning of employee engagement. *Industrial and Organizational Psychology, 1*, 3–30.

Macey, W.H., Schneider, B., Barbera, K.M. & Young, S.A. (2009). *Employee Engagement: Tools for Analysis, Practice, and Competitive Advantage*. Chichester, UK: Blackwell.

Mael, F. & Ashforth, B.E. (1992). Alumni and their alma mater: A partial test of the reformulated model of organizational identification. *Journal of Organizational Behavior, 13*, 103–123.

Martin, S.R., Kish-Gephart, J.J. & Detert, J.R. (2014). Blind forces: Ethical infrastructures and moral disengagement in organizations. *Organizational Psychology Review, 4*, 295–325.

Maslow, A.H. (1943). A theory of human motivation. *Psychological Review, 50*, 370–396.

Mathieu, J.E. & Zajac, D.M. (1990). A review and meta-analysis of the antecedents, correlates, and consequences of organizational commitment. *Psychological Bulletin, 108*, 171–194.

Meyer, J.P. & Allen, N.J. (1997). *Commitment in the Workplace: Theory, Research, and Application*. Thousand Oaks, CA: Sage.

Muris, P., Merckelbach, H., Otgaar, H. & Meijer, E. (2017). The malevolent side of human nature: A meta-analysis and critical review of the literature on the Dark Triad (narcissism, Machiavellianism, and psychopathy). *Perspectives on Psychological Science, 12,* 183–204.

Paulhus, D.L. & Williams, K.M. (2002). The Dark Triad of personality: Narcissism, Machiavellianism, and psychopathy. *Journal of Research in Personality, 36,* 556–563.

Reifman, A. & Watson, K. (2002). Binge drinking during the first semester of college. *Journal of American College Health. 2003, 52,* 73–81.

Rich, B.L., Le Pine, J.A. & Crawford, E.R. (2010). Job engagement: Antecedents and effects on job performance. *Academy of Management Journal, 53,* 617–635.

Riggs Fuller, S. & Aldag, R. (1998). Organizational Tonypandy: Lessons from a quarter century of the groupthink phenomenon. *Organizational Behavior and Human Decision Processes, 73,* 163–184.

Riketta, M. & Van Dick, R. (2005). Foci of attachment in organizations: A meta-analytic comparison of the strength and correlates of workgroup versus organizational identification and commitment. *Journal of Vocational Behavior, 67,* 490–510.

Rosander, M., Stiwne, D. & Granström, K. (1998). Bipolar groupthink: Assessing groupthink tendencies in authentic work groups. *Scandinavian Journal of Psychology, 39,* 81–92.

Rothwell, G.R. & Baldwin, J.N. (2007). Ethical climate theory, whistle-blowing, and the code of silence in police agencies in the State of Georgia. *Journal of Business Ethics, 70,* 341–361.

Sani, F., Madhok, V., Norbury, M., Dugard, P. & Wakefield, J.R. (2015). Greater number of group identifications is associated with healthier behaviour: Evidence from a Scottish community sample. *British Journal of Health Psychology, 20,* 466–481.

Schmidt, L.A. & Fox, N.A. (1995). Individual differences in young adults' shyness and sociability: Personality and health correlates. *Personality and Individual Differences, 19,* 455–462.

Skolnick, J. (2002). Corruption and the blue code of silence. *Police Practice and Research, 3,* 7–19.

Smith, E., Murphy, J. & Coats, S. (1999). Attachment to groups: Theory and management. *Journal of Personality and Social Psychology,* 77, 94–110.

Snyder, G.K., Smith, C.V., Øverup, C.S., Paul, A.L. & Davis, T.M. (2019). Characters we love to hate: Perceptions of dark triad characters in media. *Psychology of Popular Media Culture, 8,* 420–428.

Sochos, A. (2015). Attachment—beyond interpersonal relationships. *The Psychologist, 28,* 986–991.

Tajfel, H. (1974). Social identity and intergroup behavior. *Social Science Information, 13,* 65–93.

Tajfel, H. (1982). *Social Identity and Intergroup Relations.* Cambridge, UK: Cambridge University Press.

Tajfel, H. & Turner, J.C. (1979). An integrative theory of intergroup conflict. In S. Worchel & W.G. Austin (Eds.), *The Social Psychology of Intergroup Relations* (pp. 33–37). Chicago: Nelson Hall.

Tajfel, H. & Turner, J. (1986). The social identity theory of intergroup behavior. In S. Worchel & W.G. Austin (Eds.), *The psychology of intergroup relations*: (pp. 7–24). Chicago, IL: Nelson-Hall.

Turner, J.C. (1985). Social categorization and the self-concept: A social cognitive theory of group behavior. *Advances in Group Processes: Theory and Research, 2,* 77–122.

Turner, S., Beidel, D.C. & Costello, A. (1987). Psychopathology in the offspring of anxiety disorders patients. *Journal of Consulting and Clinical Psychology, 55*, 229–235.

Turner, J.C., Hogg, M.A., Oakes, P.J., Reicher, S.D. & Wetherell, M.S. (1987). *Rediscovering the Social Group: A Self-Categorization Theory*. Oxford: Basil Blackwell.

Turner, J.C. & Oakes, P. (1986). The significance of the social identity concept for social psychology with reference to individualism, interactionism and social influence. *British Journal of Social Psychology, 25*, 237–252.

Turner, J.C. & Pratkanis, A.R. (1994). Social identity maintenance prescriptions for preventing groupthink: Reducing identity protection and enhancing intellectual conflict. *International Journal of Conflict Management, 5*, 254–270.

Umberson, D., Crosnoe, R. & Reczek, C. (2010). Social relationships and health behavior across life course. *Annual Review of Sociology, 36*, 139–157.

Umphress, E.E., Bingham, J.B. & Mitchell, M.S. (2010). Unethical behavior in the name of the company: The moderating effect of organizational identification and positive reciprocity beliefs on unethical pro-organizational behavior. *Journal of Applied Psychology, 95*, 769–780.

Valdesolo, P. & De Steno, D. (2007). Moral hypocrisy: Social groups and the flexibility of virtue. *Psychological Science, 18*(8), 689–690.

Van Knippenberg, D. & Sleebos, E. (2006). Organizational identification versus organizational commitment: Self-definition, social exchange, and job attitudes. *Journal of Organizational Behavior, 27*, 571–584.

Wakefield, J.R.H. et al. (2017). The relationship between group identification and satisfaction with life in a cross-cultural community sample. *Journal of Happiness Studies, 18*, 785–807.

Walton, G.M. & Cohen, G.L. (2007). A question of belonging: Race, social fit, and achievement. *Journal of Personality and Social Psychology, 92*, 82–96.

Wefald, A. & Downey, R. (2009). Job engagement in organizations: Fad, fashion, or folderol? *Journal of Organizational Behavior, 30*, 141–145.

Werner, K.B., Few, L.R. & Bucholz, K.K. (2015). Epidemiology, comorbidity, and behavioral genetics of Antisocial Personality Disorder and Psychopathy. *Psychiatric Annals, 45*, 195–199.

PART II

The Workplace as a Focal Point for Understanding Misbehavior

8

MISBEHAVIOR IN ORGANIZATIONS

In this chapter, I start the examination of misbehavior in organizations. I will focus on the workplace because this is the context where the bulk of the research has been carried out, but it is important not to lose track of a broader perspective. There are many types of formal and even informal organizations that are not traditional workplaces (e.g., the military, volunteer organizations, professional associations, gangs) where misbehavior is sometimes a significant problem. Likely similar processes to those observed in research on misbehavior in the workplace contribute to misbehavior in other types of organizations. Understanding how workplaces can sometimes tolerate and even encourage misbehavior helps us understand how similar processes can play out in many other types of formal and informal organizations.

A review of research on misbehavior in organizations leads to several sobering conclusions regarding the seriousness, scope, and incidence of fraud and crime in these settings, and perhaps even more depressing conclusions about behavior such as sexual harassment, bullying, or abusive supervision. Before discussing the incidence and scope of misbehavior in organizations, it is useful to ask *why* I focus so strongly on formal organizations. Organizations are, after all, the focus of more than half of the book. What is it about organizations that make them both the target and the source of misbehavior?

Why Organizations?

We spend much of our lives in organizations of one sort of another (e.g., schools, the workplace, church; Herzog, 2018) and formal organizations of all sorts and even semi-formal ones (e.g., gangs) have several features that increase the likelihood and seriousness of misbehavior. Five of these are listed in Table 8.1.

TABLE 8.1 Features of Organizations That Increase the Likelihood and Severity of Misbehavior

Defined roles and responsibilities
Power relationships
Superordinate goals
Compensation, reward and control systems
Structured interactions with others

Defined Roles and Responsibilities

First, formal organizations create well-defined roles and responsibilities for their members. Work organizations often formalize this set of roles and responsibilities by creating job descriptions that lay out in detail what each individual who holds that position is supposed to do and what he or she is responsible for. Some individuals may find ways to adjust their jobs to best fit their preferences and skills (Wang, Demerouti, & Bakker, 2017), but the process of developing detailed job descriptions gives both employers and employees a very good idea of what is expected of each member of the organization and what they are responsible for. Most crucially, job descriptions often also suggest what individual employees are *not* responsible for. Indeed, one implication of having well-defined roles in work organizations is that many members of organizations are likely to conclude that preventing or responding to misbehaviors (ranging from incivility to white-collar crime or workplace theft) is not their job and that there is someone else in the organization who is responsible for dealing with these behaviors. When roles, duties, and responsibilities are well defined, people might stop acting as autonomous individuals and start acting in a role, which can lead them to suspend their normal judgments about right and wrong and to go along with what their role requires.

In most circumstances, going along with what your formal role requires will not lead to misbehavior; very few job descriptions tell people that they should defraud customers or sexually harass their subordinates. However, behavior in role, as opposed to behaving as an autonomous individual, can lead to serious misbehavior, because acting in a role can release individuals from the restraints that might prevent them as individuals from acting badly. You might think it is wrong to throw a poor family out of their home, but in your role as a bank manager who sees that the mortgage has not been paid in months you might conclude that your job requires you to start eviction proceedings.

Power Relationships

Second, formal organizations often create well-defined power relationships, in which virtually every member of the organization reports to a superior and in which these superiors have the power to influence the distribution of rewards and sanctions (reward power and coercive power—French & Raven, 1959). Rewards and sanctions are one source of power, but it is not the only source. People who are in positions of authority in organizations might be seen as deserving of respect and deference (legitimate power) and they might have skills or information (expert and informational power) that make it likely that their subordinates will be influenced by their requests, orders, or preferences. The point is, there are many ways to attain and exercise power, and in formal organizations (particularly hierarchically structured ones), power relationships are an important part of defining where each member of the organization fits into the bigger picture.

Power relationships make it considerably easier for individuals to suspend their normal social judgments and to go along with what their superiors want them to do. As I noted in Chapter 2, many of the people who are involved in wartime atrocities are willing to do things that they might normally recognize as wrong because they are following orders. Even when they are not directly ordered to carry out attacks on civilians, wipe out villages, or butcher prisoners, many soldiers and functionaries claim (probably truthfully) that they are following the preferences, example, or implicit demands of their leaders (Chang, 1997; Shirer, 1960). "I was just following orders" can be a potent tool for rationalizing and accepting misbehavior of virtually any type.

Superordinate Goals

Third, members of organizations pursue a variety of individual goals (e.g., advancement, mastery of tasks and duties), but also work toward and are frequently emotionally invested in the pursuit of the goals of that organization. These higher-level or superordinate goals can have powerful effects on the behavior of organization members (Sherif, 1958). For example, members of organizations are sometimes willing to behave in ways that run sharply counter to societal norms and values because they believe these behaviors are necessary to ensure the survival or the welfare of their organization. There have been numerous cases of organizations that engage in large-scale cheating or the systematic abuse of workers and/or the public, and this type of cheating or abuse often requires the cooperation, or at least the passive consent of many executives, managers, and employees. Employees who identify with and are loyal to their organization are often willing to go along with frauds, crimes, and abuse because they believe that these behaviors help the organization and that they are necessary for the organization to survive. As an individual employee, you might be pressured to go along with behaviors that violate norms, but in many cases, no pressure is needed. Loyalty to and identification with an organization will lead many people to want that organization to survive and prosper, and they may be willing to do whatever they think is necessary to accomplish this goal.

Compensation, Reward, and Control Systems

Fourth, formal organizations often have well-developed systems for monitoring and controlling the behavior of their members. Most work organizations, for example, have formal systems for performance evaluation, and the results of these evaluations are often used to make decisions about salary, promotions, layoffs, and the like (Murphy, Cleveland, & Hanscom, 2018). Many organizations are moving beyond traditional performance appraisal systems to embrace formal performance management systems. These systems involve structured efforts to align the behavior of individual employees with the strategic goals of the organization, give them frequent feedback, and provide both rewards and sanctions designed to make sure that their behavior is contributing to the overall goals of the organization (Aguinis, 2013; Buckingham & Goodall, 2015). Other types of organizations might not conduct formal performance evaluations, but they can and do evaluate whether their members are abiding by important norms, and they use rewards and sanctions to enforce those norms (Feldman, 1984). These mechanisms for monitoring and controlling the behavior of members of formal and informal organizations are an important tool for enforcing the rules, regulations, and norms of the organization, and if these norms, rules, or regulations encourage or support misbehavior, members of these organizations will be pressured to go along with and participate in these misbehaviors.

Structured Interactions With Others

Finally, the interactions between group members are structured in formal organizations in ways that can have a substantial impact on misbehavior. Many of your interactions with other people in organizations are part of your role requirements (e.g., your job might require you to make frequent reports to management and to convey information to superiors) rather than representing voluntary interactions. Interactions that are required by your role do not necessarily require that you *like* the person you are interacting with or that you *want* to interact with this person, and this probably makes it much easier to treat that individual instrumentally and to limit your interaction to carrying out your required role. That is, you sell customers tickets at a window or attend a meeting in your organization because this is part of your job, and you might often interact with others strictly as their role requires rather than interacting with them as individuals. The potential lack of meaningful connections between individuals makes it easier to ignore or downplay their humanity and act without worrying about the consequences. Thus, an individual who is kind and generous to family and friends might be perfectly willing to make decisions about clients or customers that have devastating consequences for them (e.g., denying them health care, sending a hungry family away without food) without feeling that he or she has done anything wrong. Phrases like "I am just doing my job" provide the same rationalization for decisions that hurt others as "I was just following orders".

Finally, the very nature of the activities you engage in as a member of a formal organization may spur dishonesty. Consider the job of a banker. The culture of this industry features a high level of competitiveness and it uses incentive schemes that focus on enhancing short-term profits and a focus on money. Cohn, Fehr, and Marechal (2014) show that international bankers act honestly in an experiment, but when primed to focus on their identity as bankers, they are more likely to cheat. In other jobs, performance pressures can increase the incidence of cheating (Mitchell, Baer, Ambrose, Folger, & Palmer, 2018.)

Jobs sometimes require or encourage us to behave in ways that are harsh, inconsiderate, or dishonest. Indeed, there are entire industries that are built around selling dubious products or services (e.g., multilevel marketing schemes, astrology, and fortune-telling), and it may be hard to maintain high personal standards of behavior if your job is to sell snake oil to naïve customers.

BOX 8.1 A DAY IN THE LIFE OF A TELEPHONE PSYCHIC

Some jobs probably require you to be a bit looser with the truth than others. Used car salespeople often have a reputation for putting an unrealistic spin on their sales pitch, but they are at least selling a commodity that has some genuine value. Other jobs may require you to sell things that probably do not exist, or that have little value. In information technology, the term "vaporware" is often used to refer to software or products that are advertised but that do not exist, and many people make their living selling vaporware. There are whole industries that exist to peddle services whose value is dubious, at best. Consider the job of a telephone psychic (Noll, 2010; O'Regan, 2020).

A leading job search site describes the work in the following terms:

> Telephone psychics answer questions and predict the future of paying customers over phone lines. Over a million people call telephone psychics every year for advice on their futures, relationships, careers, personal decisions, friendships, curses, money, lost items, business decisions, and plenty of other topics.[1]

Some companies advertise services to help you build and expand your psychic network (e.g., MeetYourPsychic.com) and there is no shortage of psychic hotline sites willing you offer you an opportunity to sell your services.

Some of the people who work as telephone psychics might honestly believe that they have psychic abilities, and others who doubt their psychic abilities might believe that they nevertheless provide a valuable service to the people who call in. The entire industry, however, is built on the unlikely premise that the same people who settle for working for a few cents per minute to answer your calls can predict the future or see into others' hearts and minds. There is little evidence that they can.

An online article on the website Vice described the job:

> My first shift was on Valentine's Day, which was like learning how to Parkour[2] without first learning how to walk. The service would link to my personal phone with the caller from their 800 number, so I was able to work from home. That night my phone rang constantly with needy, single callers. The majority of these lonely hearts asked about people they hadn't even met yet from online dating sites. They were spending $3.50 a minute to obsess over someone they'd never even kissed. I was collecting $1.99 a minute to tell them what I saw in the cards, which was, by and large, bullsh*t.[3]

Little is known about the long-term effects of working in a job like this, where the services you offer are dubious at best and where the important thing is to keep your client on the line (these calls are almost invariably billed by the minute), but it is reasonable to believe that this line of work is likely to breed and reinforce some level of cynicism. It is also plausible that this line of work might influence your tendency to be honest in other settings, but we do not have sufficient evidence to determine whether there is spillover from the job to other parts of your life.

Putting It Together

Since the 2000 movie and 1997 book *The Perfect Storm*, this phrase has been bandied about whenever some combination of factors or events makes something worse, and it is probably time to retire this phrase. Nevertheless, "a perfect storm" is an apt description of the role of organizations in fostering and tolerating misbehavior. A combination of well-defined roles, authority structures, superordinate goals, and reward and control mechanisms is precisely what makes formal and semi-formal organizations a potential hotbed of misbehavior. None of these structures or mechanisms are designed to produce misbehavior, and in most instances, they do not. Defined roles, authority structures, reward and control systems, and the like are critical to the success and survival of organizations, and without them, it would be very difficult to envision modern society. Formal and semi-formal organizations continue to be a critical and productive part of society, and the structures and processes that define them continue to often be a force for good. However, when organizations are under threat or pressure or when norms develop within organizations that push people in an antisocial direction, the same structures that allow organizations to build and produce can also help them to become a significant source of misbehavior—that is, a perfect storm. Indeed, some of the most extreme types of misbehavior, such as war crimes and genocide would be virtually unthinkable without organizations, and many other types of misbehavior, such as corporate corruption, white-collar crime, and employee theft, occur almost by definition within organizations.

This chapter examines how and why organizations sometimes create or tolerate misbehavior. Before going into the *why* of misbehavior, it is useful to explore the *what*. That is, it is useful to understand the varieties of misbehaviors that occur in organizations and to have some idea of their incidence and severity.

Types, Incidence, and Severity of Misbehavior

Stories about misbehavior in formal organizations have been a staple of the business press and media for decades, with reports of numerous frauds, scandals, and white-collar crimes. The first, and in many ways most spectacular, of these modern corporate scandals involved the energy and commodity company Enron. Founded in 1985, Enron was long hailed as a corporate leader and was named America's Most Innovative Company by *Fortune* magazine six years running. Unfortunately, a substantial factor in their apparent success was the use of creative and often fraudulent accounting practices to make it seem that the company was successful (McClean & Elkind, 2013). Enron managed to keep huge debts off their balance sheet and to inflate their claimed profits, and for many years, this was a very successful approach. When Enron collapsed in 2001, the fraudulent nature of their activities became apparent and several executives went to prison. Enron shareholders lost over $70 billion.

That same year, WorldCom was the world's largest telecommunications company, and like Enron, it reported impressive profits. Like Enron, the profits were in large part the result of dishonest accounting, including inflated assets and underreported costs (Romero & Atlas, 2002). WorldCom's internal auditing department reported over $3 billion in fraud, and the company went bankrupt (re-emerging as MCI, a subsidiary of Verizon). The WorldCom CEO, Bernard Ebbers, was sentenced to 25 years in prison, and shareholders and employees lost substantially.

In the early 2000s, HealthSouth was the largest publicly traded health care organization in the U.S.A. A series of accounting frauds (e.g., at one point, HealthSouth appeared to inflate earnings by over $1 billion to meet stockholders' expectations) totaling over $4 billion were uncovered (Freudenheim, 2004). Several HealthSouth executives ended up in prison, and once again, investors lost staggering amounts of money. A few years later, AIG, a well-established multinational insurance group collapsed. Similar to Enron, WorldCom, and HealthSouth, accounting fraud (nearly $4 billion), bid-rigging, and stock price manipulation were all allegedly involved in AIG's collapse (Ehrbar, 2006).

In 2009, one of the most spectacular corporate frauds in American history was uncovered when Bernie Madoff pleaded guilty to several federal crimes and admitted to running one of the largest private Ponzi schemes in history.[4] He was sentenced to 150 years in prison for fleecing investors and was required to pay restitution of over $170 billion.

A corporate scandal in 2015 was smaller in scope but has potentially larger long-term implications than many of the scandals mentioned earlier. As I have noted in earlier chapters, Volkswagen represents one of the largest and most revealing corporate scandals in recent memory. Before 2015, Volkswagen was one of the world's most respected automobile manufacturers, with ambitions to become the largest producer of automobiles in the world. One barrier to this ambition was that their sales in the U.S. were embarrassingly small. As part of their campaign to ramp up sales in the United States, Volkswagen embarked on a "clean diesel" campaign that promised to do what no other manufacturer had successfully done before—that is, sell cars with diesel engines that had excellent mileage, good performance, and low emissions. Unfortunately, this turned out to be virtually impossible to do, and Volkswagen "solved" the problem by cheating. They created and executed a long-running multinational strategy designed to allow their cars to detect when they were in an emissions test and to turn on some pollution controls during the test[5] (Ewing, 2017; Tabuchi & Ewing, 2016). Once the test was over, the pollution controls that tended to decrease the performance and mileage of diesel engines in these cars would be turned back off, making the cars perform better but pollute more.

This scheme was exposed in 2015, and Volkswagen was eventually forced to pay over $14 billion in fines in the U.S. alone. Diesel automobiles are still very popular in Europe, where the high cost of fuel makes their efficiency and mileage very important. Until 2015, many of the drivers of these diesel-engine cars assumed that they were achieving high mileage and good performance without causing undue pollution, but it is now clear that diesel engines that used this cheat device (this strategy for cheating on emission tests was not limited to Volkswagen; several other European automakers have been implicated) have been polluting European air at a much higher rate than testing authorities assumed. The health costs associated with years of excess pollution in Europe from diesel cars are still being debated, and there is growing speculation that the level of pollution expelled by many diesel engines could spell the end of diesel engines in Europe (Hockenos, 2018). The Volkswagen scandal is an important contributor to this debate over whether the costs of diesel engines exceed their benefits.

Misbehavior Is Widespread

Dishonest business practices are not the sole province of large corporations. Scott (2013) estimates that over 40% total of the economy in sub-Saharan Africa and Latin/Central America is made up of informal, off-the-books trades[6] and that 15–20% or more of economic activity consists of informal, off-the-books activities in more developed areas of the world. This activity covers everything from small and informal firms and individual providers that do jobs under the table to organized prostitution and gambling. This off-the-books business often skirts laws and regulations, and has significant costs for society (e.g., lost tax revenue, shoddy or dangerous products and services). The extent and importance of this underground economy, even in developed nations, challenge the notion that behaviors such as cheating and fraud are the fault of a small number of greedy executives, and they suggest that a large number of people throughout the world are routinely involved in dishonest or criminal behavior.

The conclusion that cheating, fraud, and crime are widespread is supported by many reviews on criminal behavior. For example, Gabor (1994) documents the widespread involvement of regular citizens in criminal behavior. Sometimes this involves behaviors that people do not regard as dishonest, even though they might be forbidden by law (e.g., unauthorized downloads of songs), but Gabor (1994) notes the surprising frequency with which otherwise law-abiding individuals are involved in behaviors that they probably recognize as illegal, or at least dishonest (e.g., deceptive sales practices). Similarly, reviews of dishonesty, cheating and fraud in organizations (including virtually every one of the corporate frauds described in this section) suggest that dishonesty usually results from the actions of many people who cheat a little, not from the actions of a few people who cheat a lot (Gino, Ayal, & Ariely, 2009; Mazar, Amir, & Ariely, 2008).

These small transgressions of large numbers of people have a significant impact on our daily lives. For instance, otherwise honest workers commit occupational fraud (e.g., theft, dishonest claims for disability or sick pay) that costs the U.S. economy an estimated $994 billion annually (Association of Certified Fraud Examiners, 2008). An estimated $16 billion in losses to the U.S. retail industry are due to the fraudulent purchase, use, and return of worn clothing (Speights & Hilinski, 2005). Up to 50% of employees commit to at least some low-level theft in the workplace (e.g., $5–10). This proportion declines substantially as the amount stolen increases (Wimbush & Dalton, 1997), and there are legitimate debates over precisely what behaviors should be treated as theft as opposed to normal business practices. For example, suppose you sometimes take a few office supplies home and use them for purposes other than work. This might be considered small-scale theft, but it might also be considered a normal perquisite of your job (Murphy, 1993). Nevertheless, many small thefts can add up to significant losses, and in many industries, shrinkage (i.e., losses of inventory due to theft, mismanagement, accidents, etc.) is a significant cost of doing business (McCue, 2019).

Targets of Misbehavior

Corporations and large organizations are not only the perpetrators of fraud and theft, they are also often the victims. In previous sections of this chapter, I have described fraud and thefts carried out *by* organizations, but there is also theft and fraud targeted *at* the organization. For example, I noted earlier that employee theft can be a serious matter; the annual cost of employee theft is estimated to be at least $15 billion, and probably higher (Moraca & Hollinger, 2017; Treviño, Butterfield, & McCabe, 1998). Henle, Giacalone, and Jurkiewicz (2005) estimate that employee theft inflicts a total loss of $50 billion annually to the U.S. economy, once all of the ancillary costs (e.g., replacement costs, cost of investigating and prosecuting theft) are factored in. The annual cost of time theft alone (i.e., employees goofing off and wasting time at work) is estimated to be over $700 billion annually (Martin, Brock, Buckley, & Ketchen, 2010). Organizations lose a significant amount every year to theft and counterproductive behaviors such as time theft.

A great deal of attention is focused on theft and large-scale frauds, but there are also high levels of what Greenberg (2010) labels "insidious workplace behavior" in organizations that can have substantial and costly long-term effects. These behaviors represent acts that are: (1) often legal, (2) are subtle and low level rather than severe, (3) repeated over time, and (4) directed at individuals or organizations (Greenberg, 2010, p. 4). Notable examples include incivility, bullying, and harassment based on sex, race, or other demographic characteristics.

A 2017 survey reported that almost 20% of employees report being targets of bullying in the workplace, and an equal number reported witnessing bullying (WBI Workplace Bullying Survey, 2017). Workplace bullying has been documented as a significant predictor of anxiety and depression and as a contributor to lower levels of job satisfaction and higher levels of absenteeism (Hauge, Skogstad, & Einarsen, 2010). Similarly, a substantial percentage of employees report being harassed on the basis of sex, race, age, or other demographic factors. In the U.S., the Equal Employment Opportunity Commission has commissioned several reports on the incidence and severity of workplace harassment. Several of the major conclusions of their most recent report (Select Task Force on the Study of Harassment in the Workplace, 2016) are summarized in Table 8.2.

The data show that large numbers of employees are the targets of or witnesses of bullying and harassment in the workplace and that they suffer consequences that range from a less satisfying experience at work to substantial declines in physical and mental health. Even behaviors that might appear minor (e.g., incivility in the workplace) can and do have a substantial impact on the quality of life and the physical and mental health of a large number of employees when these behaviors are repeated and sustained (Lim et al., 2008).

TABLE 8.2 Major Conclusions of EEOC Taskforce Regarding Harassment in the Workplace

1. Workplace harassment is a persistent and widespread problem—the EEOC receives up to 90,000 charges per year, and up to one-third of these involve harassment
2. Harassment is often unreported—up to three-quarters of employees who experience harassment never talk with their supervisor, manager, or union representative about their harassment
3. Harassment comes in many forms—45% of harassment claims in the private sector and state or local government involve harassment on the basis of sex, 34% involve claims of harassment on the basis of race, and there are thousands of complaints each year dealing with harassment on the basis of disability, age, national origin, and religion
4. Sexual harassment is common. Depending on the samples and survey methods used, at least 25% and up to 75% of female employees report experiencing sexual harassment in the workplace
5. Sexual harassment has well-documented negative psychological, health, and work-related effects, and harassment on the basis of race, age, disability, etc. is likely to have similar negative consequences

This brief review leads to two important conclusions. First, misbehavior in organizations is widespread and it has serious consequences. These range from financial losses in the billions to serious threats to the physical and mental health of a large proportion of the workforce. Second, these misbehaviors are only rarely the results of a handful of bad individuals. Fraud, theft, harassment, and the like often involve large numbers of individuals, and they sometimes (as in the Volkswagen scandal) involve people acting in concert over long periods. The remainder of this chapter reviews research on the varieties of misbehavior in the workplace and lays out the basic frameworks currently used to explain why misbehaviors occur in the workplace. Chapters 9–12 explore these potential explanations in more detail.

Varieties of Misbehavior in Organizations

In Chapter 2, I introduced a taxonomy of misbehavior that described these behaviors in terms of two dimensions: (1) the target of the behavior—self, other individuals, organizations, and (2) the seriousness of the behavior—milder, serious, very serious. This taxonomy is useful as a classification device, but it does not necessarily identify actual behaviors. Research on misbehavior in organizations (primarily work organizations) has identified a large number of specific behavioral patterns, including incivility (Lim, Cortina, & Magley, 2008; Lim & Lee, 2011), cyber loafing (Lim, 2002), bullying (Juvonen & Graham, 2014), sexual harassment (Cortina & Berdahl, 2008; Fitzgerald, Drasgow, Hulin, Gelfand, & Magley, 1997), discrimination (King, Shapiro, Hebl, Singletary, &

Turner, 2006; Ragins & Cornwell, 2001), non-compliant behavior (i.e., refusal to abide by rules and regulation; Puffer, 1987), dishonesty (Anand, Ashforth, & Joshi, 2004), workplace deviance (Bennett & Robinson, 2000), counterproductive work behavior (Spector, Fox, Penney, Bruursema, Goh, & Kessler, 2006), antisocial behavior (Robinson & O'Leary-Kelly, 1998), the dark side of organizational behavior (Griffin & O'Leary-Kelly, 2004), workplace violence and aggression (Glomb & Liao 2003; O'Leary-Kelly, Griffin, & Glew, 1996), unethical behavior in organizations (Andreoli & Lefkowitz, 2009; Lefkowitz, 2017), and most generally, behavior that violates broad societal norms (Sagie, Stashevsky, & Koslowsky, 2003; Vardi & Weitz, 2016).

Numerous reviews of misbehavior in organizations (e.g., Hackney & Perrewé, 2018; Murphy, 1993; Vardi & Weitz, 2016; Vardi & Wiener, 1996) capture the surprising range of misbehaviors in these settings. The sheer variety of misbehaviors in organizations [Ackroyd and Thompson (1999, p. 2) go so far as to define misbehavior in the workplace as "anything you do at work you are not supposed to do"] makes it difficult to develop coherent theories of these behaviors, and as a result, much of the scholarship in this area has focused on particular subsets of misbehaviors. Two broad classes of behavior, counterproductive work behaviors and abusive behaviors in organizations, have been the focus of much of this research.

Deviance and Counterproductive Work Behaviors

There has been a long-standing interest in behaviors in the workplace that are contrary to the norms and rules of organizations and that tend to harm organizations or their members (Hollinger & Clark, 1982, 1983; Mars, 1973). Early research in this area focused on two variants of misbehavior in organizations: (1) property deviance—misappropriation or misuse of another's property—theft, embezzlement, sabotage, and (2) production deviance—willful restriction of performance or production, violating norms regarding quality and quantity of work, purposefully slow or sloppy work, taking excessive breaks, goofing off, or wasting time at work. Hollinger and Clark (1982, 1983) and their colleagues (e.g., Hollinger, 1986; Hollinger, Slora, & Terris, 1992) played a major role in defining these constructs and in exploring the potential causes of these two types of behavior. In particular, Hollinger and Clark (1983) emphasized the role of attitudes toward the organization and toward the job (e.g., perceptions that you are being treated unfairly, low levels of job satisfaction) as important drivers of production deviance. Other researchers have noted that theft and other forms of property deviance are sometimes undertaken to get back at organizations for perceived mistreatment, such as low pay, bad working conditions, or unfair supervision (Henry & Mars, 1978).

Property and production deviance are important categories of misbehavior in organizations, and research into these behaviors has provided significant insight into the social and psychological processes that lead to these forms of deviant behavior. Perhaps the most useful insight to emerge out of this research is that both property and production deviance are often a means employees and organization members use to respond to perceived mistreatment (Sims, 2009). For example, employees may lack the power to push back against their superiors, but they can get back at the organization by theft, sabotage, or withholding production and performance.

One critique of research on property and production deviance is that it concentrates on a potentially narrow slice of the domain of misbehavior in organizations. Research in the last 25–30 years has focused on a potentially broader conception of misbehavior in organizations, in particular, counterproductive behavior. Counterproductive workplace behavior (CWB) is defined broadly as behavior that harms organizations and/or people in organizations (Sackett & DeVore, 2002; Martinko, Gundlach, & Douglas, 2002; Spector & Fox, 2005, 2010). CWBs are characterized by the disregard for both organizational and societal norms, standards, and values (Griffin, O'Leary-Kelly, & Collins, 1998), and they have been shown to harm both the profitability of firms and the quality of life of employees (Camara & Schneider, 1994; Dunlop & Lee, 2004; Robinson, Wang, & Kiewitz, 2014).

Research on CWBs has evolved considerably from the early focus on property-related misbehaviors (e.g., property and production deviance). First, it has become clear CWBs are related to but not solely determined by organization-level policies, practices, and behaviors. There is, for example, growing recognition that there can be significant variation in the type and level of CWB in different parts of an organization (e.g., Cole, Walter, & Bruch, 2008; Detert, Trevino, Burris, & Andiappan, 2007; Dunlop & Lee, 2004; Mayer, Kuenzi, Greenbaum, Bardes, & Salvador, 2009; Wright, Gardner, & Moynihan, 2003). This research suggests that CWBs might be common in some parts of organizations and rare in others, and they may occur in response to local conditions (e.g., a particularly bad supervisor) rather than organization-wide policies and practices. Second, efforts to classify CWB have provided important insights into the nature and determinants of misbehavior in organizations. Several typologies of CWB have emerged (e.g., Mangione & Quinn, 1975) that help us understand the many types of behavior that harm organizations and/or people in organizations. The most widely cited, and, in many ways, the most useful of these was proposed by Robinson and Bennett (1995). This taxonomy is shown in Figure 8.1.

Robinson and Bennett (1995) classified CWBs along two dimensions: (1) their target—organizations vs. individuals, and (2) their seriousness or harmfulness. They cite production deviance as a CWB that is aimed at organizations and that, in many of its manifestations (they cite examples such as leaving early, intentionally working slowly, taking excessive breaks), is not highly serious.[7] Property deviance is also aimed at the organization, but is often more serious. Robinson and Bennett (1995) cite examples such as stealing from the company, accepting bribes or kickbacks, and sabotage.

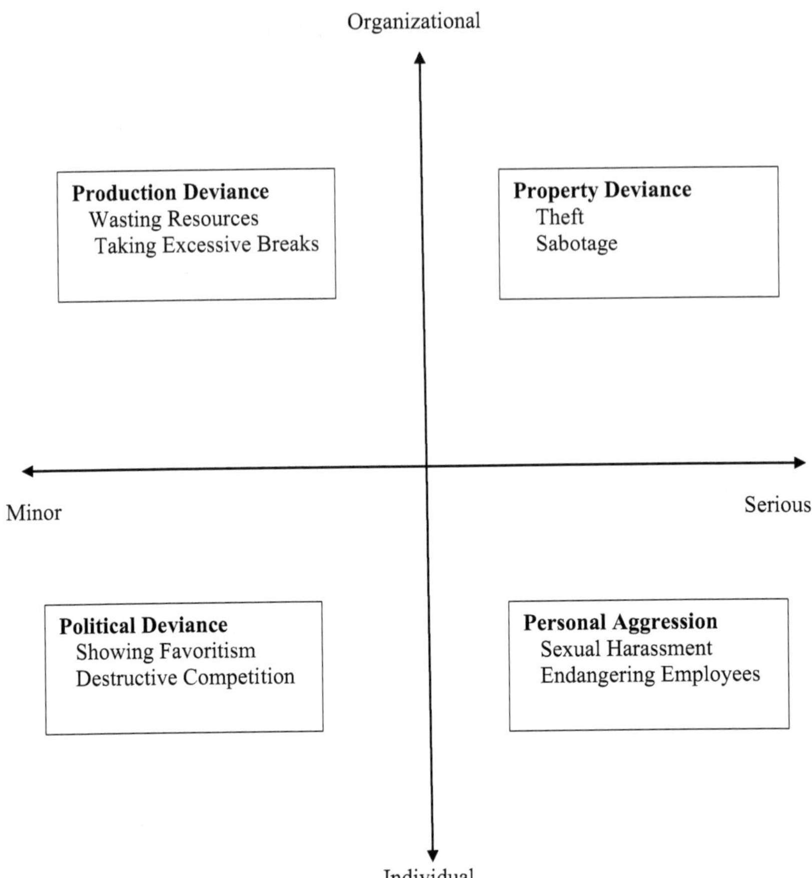

FIGURE 8.1 Taxonomy of Counterproductive Work Behaviors.

Adapted from Bennet and Robinson (1995), p. 565. Reprinted with Permission.

Other CWBs are aimed primarily at individuals rather than organizations. Robinson and Bennett (1995) describe the set of behaviors that are focused on individuals and are less serious in their outcomes (e.g., gossiping, showing favoritism) as political deviance. These behaviors are deviant in the sense that they depart from widely accepted norms that encourage us to treat others fairly and with consideration. Finally, they note that some CWBs are directed toward individuals and have greater potential to do more substantial harm. They use the label "Personal Aggression" to describe behaviors such as sexual harassment, bullying and verbal abuse, and stealing from or endangering coworkers.

Figure 8.1 is very useful for categorizing and making sense of the varieties of misbehavior in organizations, but it is important to keep in mind that any two-dimensional figure is likely to oversimplify some aspects of the relationships among types of misbehavior. For example, it is tempting to conclude from Figure 8.1 that interpersonal and organizational deviance are distinct, and perhaps even unrelated phenomena. This is not the case. Mackey, McAllister, Ellen and Carson's (in press) review suggests that the relationship between interpersonal and organizational deviance is relatively strong (ρ =.67).[8] That is, the same people who engage in acts of organizational deviance are more likely to engage in acts of interpersonal deviance, and the people who avoid organizational deviance are also less likely to engage in acts of interpersonal deviance.

Why engage in CWB?

There has been considerable interest in *why* individuals engage in CWBs, and here the distinction between interpersonal and organizational deviance seems highly relevant. A consistent theme in research on production and property deviance is that these acts can best be understood as a form of protest or as a way of getting back at the organization for perceived mistreatment (Altheide, Adler, Alder & Altheide, 1978; Henry & Mars, 1978; Hollinger & Clark, 1982). Research on organizationally directed CWBs has suggested similar conclusions. For example, employees' perceptions of the fairness of their supervisor's decisions and actions are strongly linked to CWB (Colquitt et al., 2013; Tepper, Simon, & Park, 2017).

Social Exchange Theory (Blau, 1964 Colquitt et al., 2013; Greenberg & Scott, 1996) provides a useful framework for understanding the psychology of property and production deviance. This theory focuses on the norm of reciprocity and that suggests the acts of one party create obligations for others to respond with similar treatment (Gouldner, 1960). Summarizing more than 30 years of research, Kish-Gephart and colleagues (Kish-Gephart, Harrison, & Treviño, 2010) found that employees who perceive the policies and practices of their organization as fair and ethical are less likely to engage in CWB. Conversely, organizations that are seen as treating their employees badly or unfairly (e.g., low pay, poor working conditions, arbitrary rules, and unfair policies and procedures) are more likely to become targets for deviant behavior (Colquitt et al., 2013; Hollinger & Clark, 1982).

Several researchers have focused on the "psychological contract" and its role in shaping attitudes toward organizations and misbehaviors that target organizations (Bordia, Restubog, & Tang, 2008; Robinson, 1995; Robinson & Brown, 2004; Zhao, Wayne, Glibkowski, & Bravo, 2007). Many employees have contracts or job descriptions that specify their roles, duties, and responsibilities, but these formal documents cover only a part of the relationship between employees and organizations. For example, contracts rarely say that employers will treat employees fairly and with consideration or that employees will show some level of loyalty to their organization. Employers and employees often develop clear, but unwritten, mutual understandings about how organizations will treat their employees and about how employees will behave in the workplace (Rousseau, 1995). A simplified version of this psychological contract is captured by the saying "A fair day's work for a fair day's pay", but as the expectations of organizations have grown (e.g., employees are often expected to give more in terms of their time, effort, and flexibility), the nature of the psychological contract has expanded in similar ways (e.g., employees often expect to receive better opportunities for growth and development; Maslach, Schaufeli, & Leiter, 2001).

Because the psychological contract is unwritten and implicit, it is possible, and probably not unusual, for different parties in the implicit agreement to have different ideas about what obligations the contract places on employers and employees. One implication is that perceptions of violation of the psychological contract can come via one or both of two routes: (1) violations of mutually agreed-upon obligations, and (2) perceived violations that result in incompatible expectations of what obligations each side has undertaken. Unfortunately, violations of psychological contracts seem common (Robinson & Rousseau, 1994), and regardless of how a perceived violation comes about (e.g., by a genuine violation or a misperception of roles and obligations), violations of the psychological contract are associated with less favorable work attitudes (e.g., job satisfaction, commitment to organizations; Robinson, 1995; Robinson & Brown, 2004). One response to violations of the psychological contract is to engage in behaviors that get back at the organization—that is, CWBs. Thus, behaviors ranging from to production deviance to employee theft are often a response to perceived violations of the psychological contract (Greenberg & Scott, 1996; Murphy, 1993) or responses to injustice in the workplace (Braverman, 1974).

BOX 8.2 THE INVISIBLE WAGE

Employees usually receive a paycheck from their employers, but in many workplaces and occupations, part of the compensation employees receive is in the form of "invisible wages", including tips, fiddles, perks, and pilferage (Ditton, 1977b). In this context, the term "fiddles" refers to informal practices for bending work rules and restrictions to allow employees to boost their compensation. For example, in his ethnographic analysis of workers in a large bakery, Ditton (1977a) described how workers would occasionally take home or sell spare loaves of bread and discussed how some level of pilferage was both expected and tolerated. While pilferage is formally a type of misbehavior, there are many situations in which it is reasonably widespread and the opportunity to take a bit for yourself might represent an important part of the total compensation package for that job.

In contrast to pilferage, which might be overlooked or tolerated, perquisites (perks) represent special rights that are traditionally associated with a position, and a worker who exercises these perks is generally not thought to be misbehaving. In his series of novels describing life on British warships during the Napoleonic wars, Patrick O'Brien described the traditional perquisites of ships' doctors (Queen Anne's gift—a bounty also used to augment the salary of poor churchmen), hangmen (who were allowed to sell the rope used to hang their victims, as well as the victim's clothing), and bosuns (who had a right to spare sail material). Henry (1987) described how these perks and fiddles often represent continuations of old feudal rights, where tradition would dictate who had the right to various products and resources.

Tipping represents a uniquely American aspect of the invisible wage. In most of the world, waiters, bartenders, and people in other service jobs might receive a small tip for good service (such as rounding up the bill to the next Euro), but in the U.S., tips are such an important part of the total compensation package that the minimum wage for tipped jobs is substantially lower than for jobs in which tips are not expected.[9] Tips are arguably another holdover from feudalism, in the sense that the person providing service depends to some extent on the tipper's willingness to grant a cash reward. If customers do not tip, there may be little a waiter, bartender, or other servers can do about it.

Perks are rarely written into contracts or job descriptions but are often sufficiently supported by tradition to be implicitly accepted by employers and employees. Thus, workers who exercise perks are likely to believe that they are acting within their rights and are likely to take offense if they are denied a perk that is traditionally theirs. Pilferage is rarely accepted per se, but it is often tolerated within certain limits, and employees who stay within these limits are apt to think that they are not doing anything wrong.

Perks and even pilferage can represent a type of gray area in evaluating misbehavior by employees, especially because they are sometimes tolerated by employers. One of the complexities in this analysis is that expectations about perks and pilferage are more likely to be part of the psychological contract than the formal contract between employers and employees. As a result, employees might believe they have rights to some funds, products, or supplies or that a certain amount of pilferage is viewed as acceptable (e.g., taking home small amounts of office supplies), and therefore might not see these acts as misbehaviors. Employers might not always have the same views about what falls within employee rights or about what behaviors are acceptable, and the potential for friction in the relationship between employers and employees over perceived rights and about which behaviors are tolerated can be substantial.

The term CWB covers a wide range of behaviors, but many behaviors that harm organizations and their members do not fall handily in the Robinson and Bennett (1995) typology. For example, an important distinction has been drawn between misbehaviors that are intended to harm organizations and misbehaviors that are intended (at least at the time they occur) to help the organization. Murphy (1993) describes this distinction in terms of stealing *from* the organization vs. stealing *for* the organization. In a similar vein, Vardi and Wiener (1996) distinguish among three types of organizational misbehavior: (1) Type S misbehavior that intends to benefit the self, (2) Type O misbehavior that intends to benefit the organization, and (3) Type D misbehavior that intends to inflict damage. Analyses of white-collar crime and corporate corruption (e.g., Ashforth & Anand, 2003; Ashforth, Gioia, Robinson & Treviño, 2008; Benson, 1985; Clarke, 1990; Simpson & Weisbund, 2009; Sutherland, 1949; Tyler, 2009; Vikas, Ashford, & Joshi, 2004; Zyglidopoulos & Fleming, 2009) make it clear that many of the people who participate in the types of schemes described at the beginning of this chapter (e.g., scandals at Enron, WorldCom, Volkswagen, etc.) believe that they are acting for the organization's benefit, and often for the organization's survival. In Vardi and Wiener's (1996) terms, many white-collar criminals and other participants in corporate frauds are likely to believe that they are engaging in type O behavior.

The motivation of members of formal organizations who steal, lie, and cheat *for* the organization are often quite different from those who steal *from* the organization. For example, there is evidence that individuals with strong attachments to and identification with their employer may also be the most likely to engage in unethical pro-organizational behaviors (Umphress & Bingham, 2011; Umphress, Bingham, & Mitchell, 2010). I will examine the factors that motivate members of organizations to engage in misbehaviors that are intended to benefit the organization in more detail in Chapters 11–12.

Abusive Behaviors in Organization

Robinson and Bennett's (1995) typology includes behaviors that are directed against individuals as opposed to organizations. Some of these could reasonably be described as CWBs. Abusive behaviors such as sexual harassment and bullying harm organizations and their members, but likely both the motivations that drive behaviors directed against individuals and their effects on organizations are different from behaviors directed against organizations. Earlier in this chapter, I noted the frequency and severity of abusive behaviors such as sexual harassment. In this section, I examine abusive behaviors in organizations in more detail.

As Hackney and Perrewé (2018) note, abusive acts in organizations encompass several categories of behavior, including workplace aggression, workplace harassment, interpersonal deviance, workplace violence, bullying, and incivility. Two categories of abusive behavior in organizations, aggression and harassment and abusive supervision, have been the focus of a substantial body of research in the last 25 years.

Aggression and Harassment

Organizations are too often a hostile and even a dangerous place for their members. Earlier in this chapter, I noted that between 25 and 75% of female employees are targets of or witnesses to sexual harassment in organizations. Men are not immune to this form of harassment. Over the last ten years, men have consistently accounted for approximately 15% of sexual harassment claims filed with the Equal Employment Opportunity Commission.[10] Like harassment, bullying is unfortunately common in organizations. For example, approximately 20% of employees report systematic bullying in the workplace. In many cases, workplace aggression is not limited to insults or verbal assaults (Baron & Neuman, 1998; Neuman & Baron, 1998). The U.S. Occupational Safety and Health Administration reports that there are approximately 1.7 million non-fatal assaults in the workplace each year,[11] and many of these are committed by coworkers (Bulatao & VandenBos, 1996). Three forms of aggression and harassment in organizations have been the particular focus of research: (1) incivility, (2) bullying, and (3) harassment.

Andersson and Pearson (1999) define incivility in organizations as acting rudely or discourteously without regard for others and in violation of organizational norms for respect in interactions. They classify incivility as low-intensity behaviors with frequently ambiguous intent to cause harm to others. For example, some workers may use language (e.g., swearing) that others find offensive (Baruch & Jenkins, 2007), perhaps without even knowing that their behavior is offensive. Members of organizations might undermine other members by expressing negative emotions, criticizing them, or giving them negative evaluations (Duffy, Ganster, & Pagon, 2002), without necessarily engaging in any conscious attempt to harm them.

It might seem that rudeness, negativity, and other forms of incivility are not a big deal, and it is likely that isolated instances of incivility are unpleasant but hardly unbearable. However, chronic or repeated incivility is a significant stressor that can have substantial negative effects on physical and mental health (Lim, Cortina, & Magley, 2008; Lim & Lee, 2011). Even witnessing incivility, as opposed to directly experiencing it, can be a significant stressor (Schilpzand, De Pater, & Erez, 2016).

Chronic incivility is a significant source of stress, but even relatively isolated incidents of incivility can be stressful for individuals who are not in a position to complain about or respond to incivility (Kern & Grandey, 2009). There are individual, demographic, and cultural differences in the way people respond to incivility in organizations (e.g., Welbourne, Gangadharan, & Sariol, 2015). One of the cruel ironies of this class of behaviors is that the people who are most strongly affected by and most likely to complain about incivility in organizations are also most likely to be criticized if they react negatively (e.g., they may be told you are overly sensitive, cannot take a joke, etc.; Andersson & Pearson, 1999).

Incivility is sometimes selective. Cortina and colleagues (e.g., Cortina, 2008; Cortina, Kabat-Farr, Leskinen, Huerta, & Magley, 2013) have argued that incivility is sometimes a thinly veiled manifestation of racism and sexism, particularly when it is directed toward members of underrepresented groups. There is evidence, for example, that women are more likely to be targets of incivility than men, and that the experience of incivility can disproportionally influence women's perceptions of organizations (Settles & O'Connor, 2014).

Incivility is not always intended to be harmful. You might work with one or more louts who do not even know that their behavior is upsetting to others. Bullying, in contrast, is usually thought to be intentionally harmful. There are many definitions of bullying, but they usually share a few common threads, including (1) hostility—bullying is usually a conscious behavioral choice that involves some level of hostility to the victim, either individually or as an exemplar of a group, (2) repeated acts—acts of bullying are rarely isolated, and they are often repeated, (3) aggression—bullying might represent different combinations of verbal and physical aggression, and (4) victimization—the persons and groups who are targets of bullying are often unable to defend themselves effectively from bullying. Bullying might be carried out by individuals or groups; the term "mobbing" is often used to refer to bullying by groups. Like incivility, bullying can have serious consequences for the physical and mental health of its targets and witnesses (Aquino & Thau, 2009).

Bullying in organizations has many parallels with bullying in the schoolyard. Adolescent bullying has many motives, but it is probably best understood in terms of a strategy for achieving social dominance (Juvonen & Graham, 2014). Bullies are rarely challenged, and they often receive support from their peer groups (Salmivalli, 2010). Furthermore, bullies often have a good understanding of how their behavior affects the targets of bullying (Sutton, Smith, & Swettenham, 1999).

Both perceptions of and the experience of bullying vary along gender lines (Salin & Hoel, 2013), but it is clear that both men and women bully and are bullied. Organizations are often slow to respond effectively to bullying (Beale & Hoel, 2011), and in many cases organizations have cultures that encourage and perpetuate bullying (Pheko, Monteiro, & Segopolo, 2017).

Finally, harassment on the basis of gender (e.g., Fitzgerald et al., 1997), race,[12] LGBT status (Ragins & Cornwell, 2001), obesity (King, Shapiro, Hebl, Singletary, & Turner, 2006), etc. is distressingly common in organizations. Sexual harassment, in particular, has been extensively studied. This type of harassment is common (roughly a quarter of women experience sexual harassment at work; Ilies, Hauserman, Schwochau, & Stibal, 2003; National Academies of Sciences, Engineering, and Medicine, 2018), and it has substantial effects on the health and welfare of its targets and witnesses (e.g., Cortina & Berdahl, 2008; Holland &

Cortina, 2016). Sexual harassment is sometimes an isolated phenomenon (i.e., one person harassing another), but it is often pervasive and is sometimes tolerated and even encouraged by the cultures of organizations (Glomb, Richman, Hulin, Drasgow, Schneider, & Fitzgerald, 1997). Similar to bullying, sexual harassment appears to have more to do with power and dominance than with sex (Berdahl, 2007; Cleveland & Kerst, 1993). Harassment can take many forms, including unwarranted sexualization of the work environment, unwelcome sexual advances, requests for sexual favors, and sexual assault.

Two common themes run through research on incivility, bullying, and harassment in organizations. First, these behaviors are both widespread and harmful. Second, organizations often do little to control or reduce these behaviors. In many cases, organizations openly tolerate and sometimes encourage incivility, bullying, and harassment. Several of the remaining chapters will examine why this is the case and what might be done about misbehaviors in organizations that target their members.

Abusive Supervision

Abusive supervision has much in common with the forms of abuse and aggression described previously, but it adds a crucial component—that is, power and authority. Many of the behaviors described earlier are carried out by superiors and are targeted at subordinates who are not in a position to complain or respond. What makes abusive supervision different is that it is carried out by individuals acting in their role as supervisors.

Like bullying, abusive supervision is usually defined in terms of a sustained pattern of behavior that involves unduly hostile verbal and nonverbal behavior. A supervisor who gives you a negative evaluation when you perform poorly at an important task is not being abusive. A supervisor who repeatedly insults you or yells at you or who takes actions intended to undermine you *is* being abusive. Abusive supervision is common (Martinko, Harvey, Brees, & Mackey, 2013; Tepper, 2007) and it has serious negative consequences for both its targets and its witnesses (Tepper, 2000, 2007).

The motives and explanations for abusive supervision are potentially more elusive than for some other types of workplace aggression. It is possible, for example, that some abusive supervision is the result of supervisors' inability to or lack of understanding of how to lead. Some people confuse leadership with barking out orders and chewing out their subordinates, and there are almost certainly supervisors who follow this strategy because this is how they think they should behave as a leader. On the other hand, abusive supervision might be a reflection of the culture of the organization and the supervisor's experience with his or her supervisor (Mawritz, Mayer, Hoobler, Wayne, & Marinova, 2012; Thau, Bennett, Mitchell, & Marrs, 2009). Supervisors who see others in the organization act that way may be more included to follow their lead. Finally, abusive supervision might be a reflection of the supervisor's psychological state (e.g., depression, difficulty in self-regulation; Tepper, Duffy, Henle, & Lambert, 2006; Thau et al., 2009; Thau & Mitchell, 2010). People who have difficulty regulating their behavior may be more inclined to be abusive.

Perhaps because it is part of the authority structure of the organization, abusive supervision can have particularly harmful effects for the organization. One common response to abusive supervision is an increase in workplace deviance on the part of the targets and witnesses of that abuse (Mawritz, Mayer, Hoobler, Wayne, & Marinova, 2012). Workers may not have effective means of dealing directly with an abusive supervisor, especially in organizations where little is done about complaints, but they can and often do find ways to get back at organizations through acts of production and property deviance, and as I noted at the beginning of this chapter, these can be very costly to organizations. This leads to the question of why organizations allow and sometimes encourage abusive supervision; I take this question up in Chapters 9–12.

Summary

Several of the defining characteristics of formal organizations have the potential to contribute to misbehavior. Roles and authority structures define and limit people's actions in ways that can dramatically increase the likelihood of harmful behaviors because they support rationalizations like "I was just doing my job" or "I was following orders". Organizations often develop elaborate procedures to monitor and evaluate the behavior of their members, using rewards and sanctions to channel behavior in directions that can be highly destructive. For example, large-scale corporate scandals (e.g., Enron, WorldCom, Volkswagen) require the cooperation of many individuals. As a result, the systems organizations have in place to monitor, reward, and sanction their members are a significant part of the process that guarantees this cooperation.

Misbehavior in organizations is widespread and the consequences of this misbehavior can be substantial. Work organizations lose billions per year to theft, fraud, and production deviance. Investors have lost hundreds of billions, and tens of thousands have lost jobs because of corporate fraud and white-collar crimes. Workers are exposed to high levels of chronic incivility, bullying, and harassment, all of which have significant costs and all of which have negative effects on the physical and mental health of the targets of and witnesses to these behaviors.

Misbehavior in organizations can be sorted into behaviors directed at the organization (e.g., production and property deviance) and behaviors directed at individuals (e.g., bullying and harassment). Organizationally directed misbehaviors are often the result of the perceived failure of organizations to live up to the terms of its psychological contract with its members (e.g., a fair day's work for a fair day's pay). Misbehaviors directed at individuals, on the other hand, often involve efforts to assert power and achieve social dominance. The processes that contribute to both categories of misbehavior and the ways organizations respond to them are explored in detail in several of the remaining chapters.

Notes

1. www.jobmonkey.com/uniquejobs4/phone-psychic/
2. Parkour is the sport of moving rapidly through a set of urban obstacles
3. www.vice.com/en_us/article/avyebp/i-was-a-phone-psychic-without-psychic-abilities-629
4. A Ponzi scheme is a form of fraud that pays profits to early investors with funds from subsequent investments
5. During an emissions test, your engine is running, and your wheels are turning, but your steering wheel is locked in place, a set of conditions rarely encountered while driving. This makes it easy to detect when you are in an emissions test vs. when you are on the road
6. A report from the International Labor Organization in 2020 (www.washingtonpost.com/world/2020/04/29/coronavirus-latest-news/#link-HJIQBOCAIJFPXKSDSVB2IXP7SY) suggests that nearly half the global workforce participates in the informal economy
7. Its cumulative costs could, however, mount if the behavior is widespread and frequent
8. ρ represents an estimate of the correlation between two variables in the population
9. Under the Fair Labor Standards Act, the minimum cash wage in tipped jobs is less than one-third the minimum wage in non-tipped jobs
10. www.eeoc.gov/eeoc/statistics/enforcement/sexual_harassment_new.cfm
11. www.osha.gov/archive/oshinfo/priorities/violence.html
12. www.eeoc.gov/laws/types/race_color.cfm

References

Ackroyd, S. & Thompson, P. (1999). *Organizational Misbehaviour*. London: Sage.

Aguinis, H. (2013). *Performance Management* (3rd Ed.). Upper Saddle River, NJ: Pearson/Prentice Hall.

Altheide, D.L., Adler, P.A., Alder, P. & Altheide, D.A. (1978). The social meanings of employee theft. In J.M. Johnson & J.D. Douglas (Eds.), *Crime at the Top: Deviance in Business and the Professions*. Philadelphia: J.B. Lippincott.

Anand, V., Ashforth, B.E. & Joshi, M. (2004). Business as usual: The acceptance and perpetuation of corruption in organizations. *Academy of Management Executive, 18*, 39–53.

Andersson, L.M. & Pearson, C.M. (1999). Effect of tit for tat? The spiraling in the workplace incivility. *Academy of Management Review, 24*, 452–471.

Andreoli, N. & Lefkowitz, J. (2009). Individual and organizational antecedents of misconduct in organizations. *Journal of Business Ethics, 85*, 309–332.

Aquino, K. & Thau, S. (2009). Workplace victimisation: Aggression from the target's perspective. *Annual Review of Psychology, 60*, 717–741.

Ashforth, B.E. & Anand, V. (2003). The normalization of corruption in organizations. In R.M. Kramer & B.M. Staw (Eds.), *Research in Organizational Behavior: An Annual Series of Analytical Essays and Critical Reviews* (Vol. 25, pp. 1–52). Oxford, England: Elsevier Science.

Ashforth, B.E., Gioia, D.A., Robinson, S.L. & Treviño, L.K. (2008). Re-viewing organizational corruption. *Academy of Management Review, 33*, 670–684.

Association of Certified Fraud Examiners. (2008). 2008 *Report to the Nations on Occupational Fraud and Abuse*. www.acfe.com/documents/2008-rttn.pdf

Baron, R.A. & Neuman, J.H. (1998). Workplace aggression—The iceberg beneath the tip of workplace violence: Evidence on its forms, frequency, and targets. *Public Administration Quarterly, 21*, 446–464.

Baruch, Y. & Jenkins, S. (2007). Swearing at work and permissive leadership culture: When anti-social becomes social and incivility is acceptable. *Leadership and Organization Development Journal, 28*, 492–507.

Beale, D. & Hoel, H. (2011). Workplace bullying and the employment relationship: Exploring questions of prevention, control and context. *Work, Employment and Society, 25*, 5–18.

Bennett, R.J. & Robinson, S.L. (2000). Development of a measure of workplace deviance. *Journal of Applied Psychology, 85*, 349–360.

Benson, M.L. (1985). Denying the guilty mind: Accounting for involvement in a white-collar crime. *Criminology, 23*, 583–607.

Berdahl, J.L. (2007). The sexual harassment of uppity women. *Journal of Applied Psychology, 92*, 425–437.

Blau, P. (1964). *Exchange and Power in Social Life*. New York: John Wiley.

Bordia, P., Restubog, S.L.D. & Tang, R.L. (2008). When employees strike back: Investigating mediating mechanisms between psychological contract breach and workplace deviance. *Journal of Applied Psychology, 93*, 1104–1117.

Braverman, H. (1974). *Labor and Monopoly Capital: The Degradation of Work in the Twentieth Century*. New York: Monthly Review Press.

Buckingham, M. & Goodall, A. (2015). Reinventing performance management. *Harvard Business Review, April, 93*, 40–50.

Bulatao, E.Q. & VandenBos, G.R. (1996). Workplace violence: Its scope and the issues. In G.R. VandenBos & E.Q. Bulatao (Eds.), *Violence on the Job: Identifying Risks and Developing Solutions* (pp. 1–23). Washington, DC: American Psychological Association.

Camara, W.J. & Schneider, D.L. (1994). Integrity tests: Facts and unresolved issues. *American Psychologist, 49*, 112.

Chang, I. (1997). *The Rape of Nanking*. New York: Basic Books.

Clarke, M. (1990). *Business Crime: Its Nature and Control*. Cambridge: Polity Press.

Cleveland, J.N. & Kerst, M.E. (1993). Sexual harassment and perceptions of power: An under-articulated relationship. *Journal of Vocational Behavior, 42*(1), 49–67.

Cohn, A., Fehr, E. & Marechal, M.A. (2014). Business culture and dishonesty in the banking industry. *Nature, 516*, 86–89.

Cole, M.S., Walter, F. & Bruch, H. (2008). Affective mechanisms linking dysfunctional behavior to performance in work teams: A moderated mediation study. *Journal of Applied Psychology, 93*, 945–958.

Colquitt, J.A., Scott, B.A., Rodell, J.B., Long, D.M., Zapata, C.P., Conlon, D.E. & Wesson, M.J. (2013). Justice at the millennium, a decade later: A meta-analytic test of social exchange and affect-based perspectives. *Journal of Applied Psychology, 98*, 199–236.

Cortina, L.M. (2008). Unseen injustice: Incivility as modern discrimination in organizations. *Academy of Management Review, 33*, 55–75.

Cortina, L.M. & Berdahl, J.L. (2008). Sexual harassment in organizations: A decade of research in review. In J. Barling & C.L. Cooper (Eds.), *The Sage Handbook of Organizational Behavior: Volume 1 Micro Approaches* (pp. 469–497). London: Sage.

Cortina, L.M., Kabat-Farr, D., Leskinen, E.A., Huerta, M. & Magley, V.J. (2013). Selective incivility as modern discrimination in organizations: Evidence and impact. *Journal of Management, 39*, 1579–1605.

Detert, J.R., Treviño, L.K., Burris, E.R. & Andiappan, M. (2007). Managerial modes of influence and counter productivity in organizations: A longitudinal business-unit-level investigation. *Journal of Applied Psychology, 92*, 993–1005.

Ditton, J. (1977a). *Part-Time Crime: An Ethnography of Fiddling and Pilferage*. London: Macmillan.

Ditton, J. (1977b). Perks, pilferage, and the fiddle: The historical structure of invisible wages. *Theory and Society, 4*, 1–38.

Duffy, M.K., Ganster, D.C. & Pagon, M. (2002). Social undermining in the workplace. *Academy of Management Journal, 45*, 331–351.

Dunlop, P.D. & Lee, K. (2004). Workplace deviance, organizational citizenship behavior, and business unit performance: The bad apples do spoil the whole barrel. *Journal of Organizational Behavior, 25*, 67–80.

Ehrbar, A. (2006). *Fallen Giant: The Amazing Story of Hank Greenberg and the History of AIG*. New York: Wiley.

Ewing, J. (2017, March 16). Engineering a deception: What led to Volkswagen's diesel scandal. *New York Times*, www.nytimes.com/interactive/2017/business/volkswagen-diesel-emissions-timeline.html

Feldman, D.C. (1984). The development and enforcement of group norms. *Academy of Management Review, 9*, 47–53.

Fitzgerald, L.F., Drasgow, F., Hulin, C.L., Gelfand, M.J. & Magley, V.J. (1997). Antecedents and consequences of sexual harassment in organizations: A test of an integrated model. *Journal of Applied Psychology, 82*, 578–589.

French, J. & Raven, B.H. (1959). The bases of social power. In D. Cartwright (Ed.), *Studies in Social Power* (pp. 251–260). Ann Arbor: Institute for Social Research, University of Michigan.

Freudenheim, M. (2004, January 1). Health South audit finds as much as $4.6 billion in fraud. *New York Times*, www.nytimes.com/2004/01/21/business/healthsouth-audit-finds-as-much-as-4.6-billion-in-fraud.html

Gabor, T. (1994). *Everybody Does It: Crime by the Public*. Toronto, Ontario, Canada: University of Toronto Press.

Gino, F., Ayal, S. & Ariely, D. (2009). Contagion and differentiation in unethical behavior: The effect of one bad apple on the barrel. *Psychological Science, 20*, 393–398.

Glomb, T.M. & Liao, H. (2003). Interpersonal aggression in work groups: Social influence, reciprocal, and individual effects. *Academy of Management Journal, 46*, 486–496.

Glomb, T.M., Richman, W.L., Hulin, C.L., Drasgow, F., Schneider, K.T. & Fitzgerald, L.F. (1997). Ambient sexual harassment: An integrated model of antecedents and consequences. *Organizational Behavior and Human Decision. Processes, 71*, 309–328.

Gouldner, A.W. (1960). The norm of reciprocity: A preliminary statement. *American Sociological Review, 25*, 161–178.

Greenberg, J. (2010). *Insidious Workplace Behavior*. New York: Routledge.

Greenberg, J. & Scott, K.S. (1996). Why do workers bite the hands that feed them? Employee theft as a Social Exchange Process. In B.M. Staw & L.L. Cummings (Eds.), *Research in Organizational Behavior* (Vol. 18, pp. 111–156). Greenwich, CT, and London: JAI Press.

Griffin, R.W. & O'Leary-Kelly, A. (2004). *The Dark Side of Organizational Behavior*. San Francisco: Jossey-Bass.

Griffin, R.W., O'Leary-Kelly, A.E. & Collins, J.M. (1998). *Dysfunctional Behavior in Organizations: Violent and Deviant Behavior*. Oxford, U.K.: Elsevier Science/JAI Press.

Hackney, K.J. & Perrewé, P.L. (2018). A review of abusive behaviors at work: The development of a process model for studying abuse. *Organizational Psychology Review, 8*, 70–92.

Hauge, L.J., Skogstad, A. & Einarsen, S. (2010). The relative impact of workplace bullying as a social stressor at work. *Scandinavian Journal of Psychology, 51*, 426–433.

Henle, C.A., Giacalone, R.A. & Jurkiewicz, C.L. (2005). The role of ethical ideology in workplace deviance. *Journal of Business Ethics, 56*, 219–230.

Henry, S. (1987). The political economy of informal economies. *The Annals of the American Academy of Political and Social Science, 493*(September), 137–153.

Henry, S. & Mars, G. (1978). Crime at work: The social construction of amateur property theft. *Sociology, 12*, 245–263.

Herzog, L. (2018). *Reclaiming the System: Moral Responsibility, Divided Labour, and the Role of Organizations in Society*. Oxford: Oxford University Press.

Hockenos, P. (2018, April 2). End of the road. Are diesel cars on the way out in Europe? *Yale Environment 360*, https://e360.yale.edu/features/end-of-the-road-are-diesel-cars-on-the-way-out-in-europe

Holland, K.J. & Cortina, L.M. (2016). Sexual harassment: Undermining the wellbeing of working women. In M.L. Connerley & J. Wu (Eds.), *Handbook on Well-Being of Working Women* (pp. 83–101). New York: Springer.

Hollinger, R.C. (1986). Acts against the workplace: Social bonding and employee deviance. *Deviant Behavior, 7*, 53–75.

Hollinger, R.C. & Clark, J.P. (1982). Employee deviance: A response to the perceived quality of the work experience. *Work and Occupations, 9*, 97–114.

Hollinger, R.C. & Clark, J.P. (1983). *Theft by Employees*. Lexington, MA: Heath.

Hollinger, R.C., Slora, K.B. & Terris, W. (1992). Deviance in the fast-food restaurant: Correlates of employee theft, altruism, and counter productivity. *Deviant Behavior, 13*, 155–184.

Ilies, R., Hauserman, N., Schwochau, S. & Stibal, J. (2003). Reported incidence rates of work-related sexual harassment in the United States: Using meta-analysis to explain reported rate disparities. *Personnel Psychology, 56*, 607–631.

Juvonen, J. & Graham, S. (2014). Bullying in schools: The power of bullies and the plight of victims. *Annual Review of Psychology, 65*, 159–185.

Kern, J.H. & Grandey, A.A. (2009). Customer incivility as a social stressor: The role of race and racial identity for service employees. *Journal of Occupational Health Psychology, 14*, 46–57.

King, E.B., Shapiro, J.R., Hebl, M.R., Singletary, S.L. & Turner, S. (2006). The stigma of obesity in customer service: A mechanism for remediation and bottom-line consequences of interpersonal discrimination. *Journal of Applied Psychology, 91*, 579–593.

Kish-Gephart, J.J., Harrison, D.A. & Treviño, L.K. (2010). Bad apples, bad cases, and bad barrels: Meta-analytic evidence about sources of unethical decisions at work. *Journal of Applied Psychology, 95*, 1–31.

Lefkowitz, J. (2017). *Ethics and Values in Industrial-Organizational Psychology*. New York: Routledge.

Lim, S., Cortina, L.M. & Magley, V.J. (2008). Personal and workgroup incivility: Impact on work and health outcomes. *Journal of Applied Psychology, 93*, 95–107.

Lim, S. & Lee, A. (2011). Work and nonwork outcomes of workplace incivility: Does family support help? *Journal of Occupational Health Psychology*, 16, 95–111.

Lim, V.K.G. (2002). The IT way of loafing on the job: Cyber loafing, neutralizing and organizational justice. *Journal of Organizational Behavior, 23*, 675–694.

Mackey, J.D., McAllister, C.P., Ellen, B.P. & Carson, J.E. (in press). A meta-analysis of individual and organizational workplace deviance research. *Journal of Management.*

Mangione, T.W. & Quinn, R.P. (1975). Job satisfaction, counterproductive behavior, and drug use at work. *Journal of Applied Psychology, 60*, 114–116.

Mars, G. (1973). Chance, punters and the fiddle: Institutionalized pilferage in a hotel dining room. In M. Warner (Ed.), *The Sociology of the Workplace: An Interdisciplinary Approach* (pp. 200–210). London: Allen & Urwin.

Martin, L.E., Brock, M.E., Buckley, M.R. & Ketchen, D.J. (2010). Time banditry: Examining the purloining of time in organizations. *Human Resource Management Review, 20*, 26–34.

Martinko, M.J., Gundlach, M.J. & Douglas, S.C. (2002). Toward an integrative theory of counterproductive workplace behavior: A causal reasoning perspective. *International Journal of Selection and Assessment, 10*, 36–50.

Martinko, M.J., Harvey, P., Brees, J.R. & Mackey, J. (2013). A review of abusive supervision research. *Journal of Organizational Behavior, 34*, 120–137.

Maslach, C., Schaufeli, W. & Leiter, M. (2001). Job burnout. *Annual Review of Psychology, 52*, 397–422.

Mawritz, M.B., Mayer, D.M., Hoobler, J.M., Wayne, S.J. & Marinova, S.V. (2012). A trickle-down model of abusive supervision. *Pers Psychol, 65*(2), 325–357.

Mayer, D.M., Kuenzi, M., Greenbaum, R., Bardes, M. & Salvador, R. (2009). How low does ethical leadership flow? Test of a trickle-down model. *Organizational Behavior and Human Decision Processes, 108*, 1–13.

Mazar, N., Amir, O. & Ariely, D. (2008). The dishonesty of honest people: A theory of self-concept maintenance. *Journal of Marketing Research, 45*, 633–644.

McClean, B. & Elkind, P. (2003). *The Smartest Guys in the Room: The Amazing Rise and Scandalous Fall of Enron*. New York: Penguin.

McCue, F. (2019, January 31). Inventory shrink cost the US retail industry $46.8 billion. *Forbes*, www.forbes.com/sites/tjmccue/2019/01/31/inventory-shrink-cost-the-us-retail-industry-46-8-billion/#75dfff2a6b70

Mitchell, M.S., Baer, M.D., Ambrose, M.L., Folger, R. & Palmer, N.F. (2018). Cheating under pressure: A self-protection model of workplace cheating behavior. *Journal of Applied Psychology, 103*, 54–73.

Moraca, B. & Hollinger, R. (2017). 2017 *National retail security survey*. https://nrf.com/system/tdf/Documents/NRSS-Industry-Research-Survey-2017.pdf?file=1&title=National%20Retail%20Security%20Survey%202017

Murphy, K.R. (1993). *Honesty in the Workplace*. Monterey, CA: Brooks/Cole.

Murphy, K.R., Cleveland, J.N. & Hanscom, M.E. (2018). *Performance Appraisal and Management*. Thousand Oaks, CA: Sage.

National Academies of Sciences, Engineering, and Medicine. (2018). *Sexual Harassment of Women: Climate, Culture, and Consequences in Academic Sciences, Engineering, and Medicine*. Washington, DC: The National Academies Press.

Neuman, J.H. & Baron, R.A. (1998). Workplace violence and workplace aggression: Evidence concerning specific forms, potential causes, and preferred targets. *Journal of Management, 24*, 391–419.

Noll, E. (2010, May 9). Psychic hot line secrets: Clairvoyance or hoax? *ABC News*, https://abcnews.go.com/GMA/Weekend/psychic-reveals-tricks-trade/story?id=10590096

O'Leary-Kelly, A.M., Griffin, R.W. & Glew, D.J. (1996). Organization-motivated aggression: A research framework. *Academy of Management Review, 21*, 235–253.

O'Regan, S.V. (2020, January 9). When a psychic reading costs you $74,000. *Gentleman's Quarterly*, www.gq.com/story/the-curse-of-psychic-zoe.

Pheko, M.M., Monteiro, N.M. & Segopolo, M.T. (2017). When work hurts: A conceptual framework explaining how organizational culture may perpetuate workplace bullying. *Journal of Human Behavior in the Social Environment, 27*, 571–588.

Puffer, S.M. (1987). Prosocial behavior, noncompliant behavior, and work performance among commission salespeople. *Journal of Applied Psychology, 72*, 615–621.

Ragins, B.R. & Cornwell, J.M. (2001). Pink triangles: Antecedents and consequences of Perceived workplace discrimination against gay and lesbian employees. *Journal of Applied Psychology, 86*, 1244–1261.

Robinson, S.L. (1995). Violation of psychological contracts: Impact on employee attitudes. In L.E. Tetrick & J. Barling (Eds.), *Changing Employment Relations: Behavioral and Social Perspectives* (pp. 91–108). Washington, DC: American Psychological Association.

Robinson, S.L. & Bennett, R.J. (1995). A typology of deviant workplace behaviors: A multidimensional scaling study. *Academy of Management Journal, 38*, 555–572.

Robinson, S.L. & Brown, G. (2004). Psychological contract breach and violation in organizations. In R.W. Griffin & A. O'Leary-Kelly (Eds.), *The Dark Side of Organizational Behavior* (pp. 309–337). San Francisco, CA: Wiley.

Robinson, S.L. & O'Leary-Kelly, A.M. (1998). Monkey see, monkey do: The influence of workgroups on the antisocial behavior of employees. *Academy of Management Journal, 41*, 658–672.

Robinson, S.L. & Rousseau, D.M. (1994). Violating the psychological contract: Not the exception but the norm. *Journal of Organizational Behavior, 15*, 245–259.

Robinson, S.L., Wang, W. & Kiewitz, C. (2014). Coworkers behaving badly: The impact of coworker deviant behavior upon individual employees. *Annual Review of Organizational Psychology and Organizational Behavior, 1*, 123–143.

Romero, S. & Atlas, R.D. (2002, July 22). WorldCom's collapse: The overview; WorldCom files for bankruptcy; largest U.S. case. *New York Times*, www.nytimes.com/2002/07/22/us/worldcom-s-collapse-the-overview-worldcom-files-for-bankruptcy-largest-us-case.html

Rousseau, D.M. (1995). *Psychological Contracts in Organizations: Understanding Written and Unwritten Agreements*. Newbery Park, CA: Sage.

Sackett, P.R. & DeVore, C.J. (2002). *Counterproductive Behaviors at Work*. Thousand Oaks, CA: Sage Publications.

Sagie, A., Stashevsky, S. & Koslowsky, M. (2003). *Misbehaviour and Dysfunctional Attitudes in Organizations*. New York: Palgrave Macmillan.

Salin, D. & Hoel, H. (2013). Workplace bullying as a gendered phenomenon. *Journal of Managerial Psychology, 28*, 235–251.

Salmivalli, C. (2010). Bullying and the peer group: A review. *Aggression and Violent Behavior, 15*, 112–120.

Schilpzand, P., De Pater, I.E. & Erez, A. (2016). Workplace incivility: A review of the literature and agenda for future research. *Journal of Organizational Behavior, 37*, S57-S88.

Scott, C.R. (2013). *Anonymous Agencies, Backstreet Businesses and Covert Collectives: Rethinking Organizations in the 21st Century*. Stanford, CA: Stanford University Press.

Select Task Force on the Study of Harassment in the Workplace. (2016). *Report of the Co-Chairs*. Washington, DC: Equal Employment Opportunity Commission.

Settles, I.H. & O'Connor, R.C. (2014). Incivility at academic conferences: Gender differences and the mediating role of climate. *Sex Roles, 71*, 71–82.

Sherif, M. (1958). Superordinate goals in the reduction of intergroup conflict. *American Journal of Sociology, 63*, 349–356.

Shirer, W.L. (1960). *The Rise and Fall of the Third Reich: A History of Nazi Germany*. New York: Simon & Schuster.

Simpson, S.S. & Weisbund, D. (2009). *The Criminology of White-Collar Crime*. New York: Springer.

Sims, R.L. (2009). A study of deviance as a retaliatory response to organizational power. *Journal of Business Ethics, 92*, 553–563.

Spector, P.E. & Fox, S. (2005). A model of counter-productive work behavior. In S. Fox & P.E. Spector (Eds.), *Counterproductive Workplace Behavior: Investigations of Actors and Targets* (pp. 151–174). Washington, DC: American Psychological Association.

Spector, P.E. & Fox, S. (2010). Counterproductive work behavior and organizational citizenship behavior: Are they opposite forms of active behavior? *Applied Psychology: An International Review, 59*, 21–39.

Spector, P.E., Fox, S., Penney, L.M., Bruursema, K., Goh, A. & Kessler, S. (2006). The dimensionality of counter-productivity: Are counterproductive behaviors created equal? *Journal of Vocational Behavior, 68*, 446–460.

Speights, D. & Hilinski, M. (2005). Return fraud and abuse: How to protect profits. *Retailing Issues Letter, 17*(1), 1–5.

Sutton J., Smith, P.K. & Swettenham, J. (1999). Bullying and "theory of mind": A critique of the "social skills deficit" view of anti-social behaviour. *Social Development, 8*, 117–127.

Sutherland, E.H. (1949). *White Collar Crime*. New York: Dryden Press.

Tabuchi, H. & Ewing, J. (2016, June 27). Volkswagen to pay $14.7 billion to settle diesel claims in U.S. *New York Times*, www.nytimes.com/2016/06/28/business/volkswagen-settlement-diesel-scandal.html?module=inline

Tepper, B.J. (2000). Consequences of abusive supervision. *Academy of Management Journal, 43*, 178–190.

Tepper, B.J. (2007). Abusive supervision in work organizations: Review, synthesis, and research agenda. *Journal of Management, 33*, 261–289.

Tepper, B.J., Duffy, M.K., Henle, C.A. & Lambert, L.S. (2006). Procedural injustice, victim precipitation, and abusive supervision. *Personnel Psychology, 59*, 101–123.

Tepper, B.J., Simon, L. & Park, H.M. (2017). Abusive supervision. *Annual Review of Organizational Psychology and Organizational Behavior, 4*, 123–152.

Thau, S., Bennett, R.J., Mitchell, M.S. & Marrs, M.B. (2009). How management style moderates the relationship between abusive supervision and workplace deviance: An uncertainty management theory perspective. *Organizational Behavior and Human Decision Processes, 108*, 79–92.

Thau, S. & Mitchell, M.S. (2010). Self-gain or self-regulation impairment? Tests of competing explanations of the supervisor abuse and employee deviance relationship through perceptions of distributive justice. *Journal of Applied Psychology, 95*, 1009–1031.

Treviño, L.K., Butterfield, K.D. & McCabe, D.L. (1998). The ethical context in organizations: Influences on employee attitudes and behaviors. *Business Ethics Quarterly, 8*, 447–476.

Tyler, T.R. (2009). Self-regulatory approaches to white-collar crime: The importance of legitimacy and procedural justice. In S. Simpson & D. Weisburd (Eds.), *The Criminology of White-Collar Crime* (pp. 195–216). New York: Springer.

Umphress, E.E. & Bingham, J.B. (2011). When employees do bad things for good reasons: Examining unethical pro-organizational behaviors. *Organization Science, 22*, 621–640.

Umphress, E.E., Bingham, J.B. & Mitchell, M.S. (2010). Unethical behavior in the name of the company: The moderating effect of organizational identification and positive reciprocity beliefs on unethical pro-organizational behavior. *Journal of Applied Psychology, 95*, 769–780.

Vardi, Y. & Weitz, E. (2016). *Misbehavior in Organizations: A Dynamic Approach*. New York: Routledge.

Vardi, Y. & Wiener, Y. (1996). Misbehavior in organizations: A motivational framework. *Organization Science*, 7, 151–165.

Vikas, A., Ashford, B.E. & Joshi, M. (2004). Business as usual: The acceptance and perpetuation of corruption in organizations. *Academy of Management Executive, 18*, 39–53.

Wang, H.J., Demerouti, E. & Bakker, A.B. (2017). A review of job crafting research: The role of leader behaviors in cultivating successful job crafters. In S.K. Parker & U.K. Bindl (Eds.), *Proactivity at Work* (pp. 77–104). New York: Routledge.

WBI Workplace Bullying Survey, June 2017 www.workplacebullying.org/wbiresearch/wbi-2017-survey

Welbourne, J.L., Gangadharan, A. & Sariol, A.M. (2015). Ethnicity and cultural values as predictors of the occurrence and impact of experienced workplace incivility. *Journal of Occupational Health Psychology, 20*, 205–217.

Wimbush, J.C. & Dalton, D.R. (1997). Base rates for employee theft: Convergence of multiple methods. *Journal of Applied Psychology, 82*, 756–763.

Wright, P.M., Gardner, T.M. & Moynihan, L.M. (2003). The impact of HR practices on the performance of business units. *Human Resource Management Journal, 13*, 21–36.

Zhao, H.A.O., Wayne, S.J., Glibkowski, B.C. & Bravo, J. (2007). The impact of psychological contract breach on work-related outcomes: A meta-analysis. *Personnel Psychology, 60*, 647–680.

Zyglidopoulos, S.C. & Fleming, O. (2009). The escalation of corruption in organizations. In C. Cooper & R. Burke (Eds.), *Research Companion to Crime and Corruption in Organizations* (pp. 104–122). Cheltenham, UK. Northampton, MA: Edward Elgar.

9

CONTEXTUAL, SOCIAL, AND ORGANIZATIONAL PROCESSES THAT ENCOURAGE MISBEHAVIOR

Chapter 8 described some features of organizations (particularly work organizations) that can, often inadvertently, lead to misbehavior. These include well-defined roles, authority structures, systems for monitoring behavior, and the use of rewards and sanctions to enforce compliance with organizational rules and norms. These structures and systems are usually designed and used to encourage behaviors that are constructive and for socially appropriate purposes (e.g., production, managing a political campaign, creating volunteer organizations), but when the norms or goals of an organization turn in particular directions, these same systems can become engines of destruction. For example, organizational systems that monitor the behavior of their members and reward behavior that conforms to organizational norms can become a serious source of misbehavior if the norms of the organization are racist or sexist or if the goals of the organization have become corrupted. As noted earlier, organizations ranging from Enron to Volkswagen have been found guilty of engaging in systematic efforts to cheat customers, mislead regulators, etc. and the reward and control systems of these organizations were likely to be a significant factor in employees' willingness to participate in these frauds.

This chapter continues my examination of the processes in organizations that can inadvertently encourage misbehavior. In Chapter 8, I examined systems and processes in organizations explicitly designed to channel and regulate behavior, such as role definitions, authority structures, systems for monitoring and evaluating the behavior or members of the organization, and systems for distributing rewards and sanctions to members of the organization. In this chapter, I consider several structural features of organizations and the contexts within which they operate, as well as social and psychological processes in organizations that can encourage specific types of misbehavior. As Figure 9.1 illustrates, several

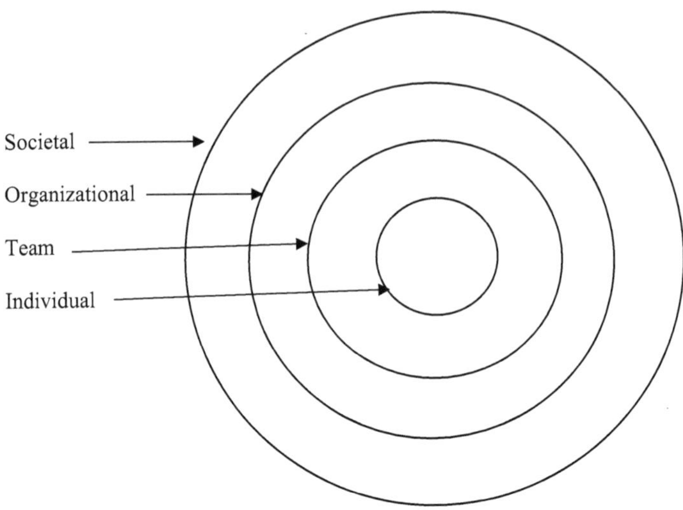

FIGURE 9.1 Multiple Levels of Context

levels of analysis must be considered when evaluating the factors that influence misbehavior.

Contextual Factors That Influence Misbehavior

Organizations exist as part of a broader society, and there are several features of the context in which organizations operate that have the potential to encourage misbehavior. For example, national cultures often promote specific values such as individualism or respect for authority (Hofstede, 1980; 2001; Hofstede, Hofstede, & Minkov, 2010; Hofstede, Neuijen, Ohayv, & Sanders, 1990), and these can sometimes be a source of misbehavior. There is a substantial body of research examining the effects of national cultures and socio-political systems on the way organizations operate (Cheng, 1994; Johns, 2017, 2018). Much of this work focuses on work organizations, but it has clear relevance for all types of organizations.

Cultural Values

Hofstede and his colleagues have argued that national differences in organizationally relevant values and preferences can be understood in terms of a small number of dimensions: (1) power distance—social inequality, or the degree of separation between people at different levels in organizations or groups, (2) individualism-collectivism—an orientation toward individuals vs. groups, (3) masculinity-femininity—preference for achievement and assertiveness vs. cooperation and caring, (4) uncertainty avoidance—tolerance for vs. avoidance of ambiguity and lack of control, (5) long-term vs. short-term normative orientation—focus on immediate vs. more distant outcomes, and (6) indulgence vs. restraint—an orientation toward free expression and satisfaction of desires vs. suppression of these desires (Hofstede, 1980; 2001; Hofstede et al., 2010; Hofstede, Neuijen, Ohayv, & Sanders, 1990). Three of these cultural values have clear implications for misbehavior, at least for determining which types of misbehavior might be especially prevalent in different societies.

Power Distance

Societies that are high on power distance encourage high levels of deference to and respect for leaders. This deference can increase the likelihood of two types of misbehavior. First, if a leader proposes a course of action that appears to be unethical or dishonest, the likelihood that subordinates will go along with this suggestion is likely to be higher in cultures where power distance is especially high (e.g., Latin America, East Asia, the Arab world) than in countries where power distance is lower (e.g., North American, Germanic countries). To be sure, lower levels of power distance do not shield organizations from following leaders who advocate dishonest behavior. Germany is a country with low power distance, but this did not prevent employees at Volkswagen from participating in a large-scale, worldwide program designed to cheat on emissions tests (Ewing, 2017). Nevertheless, it is reasonable to expect that high levels of power distance would make people more likely to follow orders and directives that violate general social norms.

The second way high levels of power distance might contribute to misbehavior is a bit more indirect. In cultures where power distance is high, subordinates are less willing to challenge or even to give honest feedback to their superiors (Sweetman, 2012). This not only increases the likelihood that leaders of organizations will make bad decisions, it also increases the likelihood that subordinates will do their best to implement those decisions. Of course, not all bad decisions in organizations involve misbehavior. A leader of a political campaign might choose an ineffective message and believe he or she has made a good choice because subordinates support this choice. However, some bad decisions can have serious negative consequences for members of organizations or their stakeholders (e.g., an investment firm might choose risky strategies that cost employees and shareholders a great deal of money), and the process of implementing bad decisions made by superiors might require subordinates to act in ways that they know will harm others (e.g., foreclose on mortgages, lay off employees).

Individualism-Collectivism

Extreme levels at either end of the individualism-collectivism continuum might lead to particular types of misbehavior. Members of highly collective societies tend to value group harmony, which implies a greater willingness to go along with group norms, even when these norms tolerate or support behavior that harms others, such as bullying or sexual harassment. Members of highly individualistic societies may be more inclined to behaviors that break rules or defy norms (e.g., production deviance).

Masculinity-Femininity

Finally, some cultures are higher on masculinity than others, and this cultural value might encourage higher levels of competition and assertiveness. Competition and assertiveness are not themselves types of misbehavior, but a strong emphasis on these behaviors might lead to increased levels of destructive competition and social undermining (Duffy, Ganster, & Pagon, 2002), and even to bullying and harassment.

How Cultural Values Affect Behavior

The effects of cultural values on the behavior of organizations and their members are far from uniform. Gelfand et al. (2011) note that some cultures are tighter than others, in the sense that some cultures have stronger norms and less tolerance for deviations from those norms. Pakistan, Malaysia, and India are examples of tight cultures, and in these nations, it is likely that behavior is more tightly linked to cultural norms and values than in culturally loose nations (e.g., Ukraine, Estonia, Hungary).

Cultural values represent an important feature of the societies in which organizations are embedded, but they are not the only important dimensions of society that influence the way organizations function. Different societies adopt different political and legal systems, and these systems also have a strong effect on organizations (Thompson & Martin, 2010). Legal systems, in particular, are concerned with defining and suppressing misbehavior, and these systems convey strong messages about what types of misbehavior are taken seriously in a society and what types are not. Laws differ substantially from country to country, and behaviors that are ignored or treated as trivial offenses in some counties (e.g., spitting chewing gum on the sidewalk) are treated as serious offenses in others (e.g., Singapore). There are also important differences in the way laws are enforced, and these differences convey clear messages about what behaviors are tolerated and what behaviors are treated as serious offenses. Consider, for example, the reactions of different countries to the financial collapse of 2008, which was driven in large part by overinvestment in shaky financial vehicles and subprime mortgages. Most Western countries have strict laws regulating banks and investment firms, and in several countries, bankers and investment managers were sent to jail for their role in this crisis. In the United States, only one banker (who was affiliated with a foreign bank) was jailed for his role in inflating the prices of subprime mortgages

(Noonan, Tilford, Milne, Mount, & Wise, 2018). This record of inaction in the U.S. conveyed a strong set of messages about the relative importance of banking laws vs. bankers in this country.

There are two distinct ways cultures and legal and political systems influence behavior: (1) by establishing and communicating norms that describe behaviors and actions that are or are not viewed favorably (Griffin, 2007; Hofstede et al., 2010; Johns, 2006, 2017, 2018; Meyer & Dalal, 2009) and (2) by providing constraints on or opportunities for the pursuit of particular courses of action (Forehand & Von Haller, 1964; Johns, 2006, 2017). For example, both the United States and the European Union have strong laws and regulations dealing with discrimination in employment, but the enforcement of these laws differs substantially. In the U.S., anti-discrimination laws are monitored and enforced by numerous state and federal agencies, and a parallel system of private enforcement through class-action lawsuits means that American employers tend to be careful to avoid even inadvertent discrimination. In contrast, enforcement of similar laws and regulations in many European countries is weak and sporadic, which means that employers in those countries sometimes pay less attention to the possibility that employment decisions will be discriminatory.

Political and legal systems create constraints, but they also create opportunities for different types of organizations to form and operate. I noted in Chapter 6, there are over 9,000 trade and professional associations that operate in the United States, and this is partly a reflection of the American political system, which is relatively decentralized (meaning that associations may need to deal with and attempt to influence both federal and state governments) and relatively open to lobbying and input from organizations or stakeholders. Some of this lobbying may lead to acts that help a favored few but harm the rest of society.

Ideology and Misbehavior

In Chapter 8, I noted that bullying is a widespread and serious problem in many organizations (particularly in the workplace). Beale and Hoel (2011) note that a substantial proportion of bullying in organizations is carried out by managers and that managers are often themselves bullied by their superiors. They suggest that bullying is consistent with Marxist theory regarding the exploitation of labor and that it can be interpreted as a form of managerial control. Marxist theory argues that control of labor is necessarily an exercise of power, and bullying is a method of establishing and asserting that control. Most discussions of bullying treat it as an aberration, but Beale and Hoel (2011) note that systematic bullying may be a conscious or unconscious tactic to establish and maintain control over the workforce.

Henry (1987) argued that many employment practices create an "invisible wage". He cites, for example, traditions that lead workers to believe that they have rights to certain forms of non-cash income (e.g., pilferage, tips, perquisites of the job) and argues that these are holdovers from feudalism. Shlapentokh and Woods (2011) make a broader argument—that is, that *many* of the structures of modern society are holdovers from feudalism. In particular, they note that organizations preserve many of the key features of the feudal model of organization, including increasing decentralization (Kolb & Putnam, 1992) and reliance on informal alliances and power centers rather than bureaucratic procedures to get things gone, the use of personal loyalty and fealty as a tool for managing decisions, and a class system that separates executives, management, and labor into their separate spheres, with distinct sets of rights and responsibilities. They show how many types of misbehavior, especially those that involve production deviance, can be understood in terms of commitment to and reliance on systems that are throwbacks to the organization of feudal society. In particular, conflicts between management and labor are often difficult to fully resolve, and many of the tactics of production and property deviance have roots in feudal understandings of the rights, responsibilities, and limitations of the different classes that constitute labor, management, and executives.

Dynamic Cultural Theory

Dynamic Cultural Theory (DCT; 6 Perri & Mars, 2007)[1] uses two dimensions, Grid and Group, to describe groups and organizations, and combinations of these two dimensions can be used to make predictions about misbehavior. The first dimension, Grid, assesses the relative strength of constraints operating in a situation. For example, when DCT is applied to jobs, the Grid dimension is reflected by whether there is an emphasis on classifying members by differences in rank or the requirement to wear uniforms, for instance, with controls over an incumbent's occupancy of space and whether there are restrictions over time. Grid is a measure of autonomy.

The second dimension, Group, assesses the degree of interaction (especially face-to-face interaction) that is typical in a group. An army platoon, for instance, is strong on the Group dimension since it is the basis not just of its members' work but of their leisure (i.e., members of platoons often play sports or engage in other recreational activities together). As a result, the platoon is a potent source of group identity and group controls. In contrast, the job of Independent Management Consultant would rate weakly on the Group dimension. The two dimensions of constraint/regulation and personal interaction are often reflected in differences in the cultures and legal/political systems in different societies, and they can be important drivers of misbehavior. For example, in work organizations where employees lack a meaningful voice in decisions (e.g., high Grid organizations), they may engage in higher levels of production deviance as a way of informally gaining some level of control.

Mars (2006) presents evidence of occupational deviance derived in large part from the way work is organized in terms of these two broad dimensions. Both

Ackroyd (2012) and Dundon and van den Broek (2012) argue that a strong commitment to the capitalist system leads organizations to assert higher levels of control over workers and that by removing opportunities for employees to gain and express power, they may create conditions that lead to higher levels of misbehavior. More generally, some organizations or groups within organizations place strong constraints on their members and give their members relatively few opportunities to work together to improve their lot (in the terminology of DCT, low Grid, low Group organizations). Consider, for example, countries in the Warsaw Pact (i.e., the U.S.S.R. and much of Eastern Europe) during the period 1945–1990, or China today. These countries were characterized by strong authoritarian rule with minimal opportunities for dissent or for group action. One characteristic form of social rebellion in these countries became production deviance (Somin, 2017). The old joke in the Soviet Union, "they pretend to pay us, and we pretend to work", encapsulated a widespread response to social and political constraints that led to the same forms of resistance Mars (2006) observed in his analysis of low-paying, low-responsibility jobs.

Means, Motive, and Opportunity for Misbehavior

A staple of many police procedurals on television is an attempt to build evidence that a particular suspect has the means, motive, and opportunity to commit a particular crime. There are often aspects of organizations that create the means and opportunity for particular types of misbehavior. For example, employee theft is particularly problematic in some types of stores (e.g., clothing, electronics, drugs), in part because there are things that are easily stolen and sold. It is likely to be less of a problem if your products are bulky and not particularly valuable in small quantities. Sabotage is more likely in manufacturing than in some other industries because there are more opportunities to commit acts that will damage or ruin products. In industries that rely extensively on computerization, opportunities for hacking and misdirection of resources are likely to increase.

A reporter once asked the bank robber Willie Sutton why he robbed banks. His alleged reply, "because that's where the money is",[2] has been adapted to medical training in the form of Sutton's Law. Sutton's Law states that when making a diagnosis, you should first run tests that will allow you to confirm or rule out the most obvious diagnosis. If you apply Sutton's Law to make predictions about misbehavior, it suggests that you should always think carefully about the opportunities that different situations present. For example, organizations that require people to interact frequently probably create more opportunities for bullying and harassment than organizations where people do not interact. Executives who have multiple opportunities to doctor their books or move money quickly and easily are more likely to engage in white-collar crime than executives who do not have these opportunities.

There is a legal doctrine of "attractive nuisance" which states that the owners of properties that are highly attractive to children but dangerous to them (e.g., swimming pools, construction sites) have a responsibility to put up barriers and fences and that the failure to fence these attractive nuisances properly can make them liable if children enter their property and get hurt. This idea has been extended more broadly in the field of security with the argument that organizations that create substantial temptations for employees or executives to steal but do nothing to effectively monitor or prevent theft are placing an unfair burden on those employees and executives, and that they share some of the liability for thefts that might occur (Murphy, 1993). To repeat an example from Chapter 1, suppose that a jeweler told his assistant "here is a big bag of rubies. I don't have a good sense of how many are in the bag. I am going to lunch and would like you to count them while I am gone". That jeweler would be placing a significant temptation in front of his or her employee to pocket a few rubies, and it can reasonably be argued that this is not only unwise, but it is also unethical. Organizations that take substantial and visible efforts to control misbehavior are not only doing themselves a favor (organizations lose billions through theft and fraud and may be liable for charges if they allow bullying or harassment to go unchecked) but are also helping their employees to avoid behaviors that are destructive and harmful.

Societal and Organizational Factors

This book is concerned with misbehavior in organizations. The preceding section considered factors outside of the organization, such as national cultures and legal systems, that influence the incidence and nature of misbehavior. In this section and the one that follows, I consider factors within organizations that are likely to influence misbehavior.

Organizational Socialization

When new members enter an organization, they often have only a general idea of what they are supposed to do and how they are supposed to act. The process by which employees learn the duties, responsibilities, and expectations associated with their role, as well as the informal rules and norms of the organization is referred to as socialization (Chao, O'Leary-Kelly, Wolf, Klein, & Gardner, 1994; Fisher, 1986). Socialization provides new entrants with information regarding their roles in the organization and about the norms, values, and goals of other parts of the organization and the organization itself (Anderson & Ostroff, 1997). Perhaps most important, socialization processes communicate informal norms, and these sometimes define behaviors that are usually thought to be unacceptable (e.g., bullying) but accepted as "the way things work around here"—that is, ethical and acceptable behaviors (Ditton, 1977).

Chao et al. (1994) note that socialization involves learning things that go well beyond your role, duties, and responsibilities and even beyond learning the informal norms of your workgroup. They note that new entrants need to learn about: (1) history—traditions, customs of the group and the organization, the background of the group, etc., (2) language—the terminology, slang, acronyms, and jargon of the group and the organization, (3) politics—understanding how things get done, who has control over information and resources, the motives different individuals and groups are likely to pursue, (5) people—relationships within and between groups, who can be trusted, who likes or dislikes who, (6) organizational goals and values—the goals, values, and strategy the organization is pursuing and your group's role in that pursuit, and (7) performance proficiency—information needed to perform your role effectively.

Organizational socialization typically involves several formal and informal activities, often starting with briefings and formal documents describing your role and responsibilities (e.g., a job description), but also including informal learning through observation and imitation of others in similar roles (Bandura, 1977). There may be formal or informal mentors or others in the organization who have some responsibility for making sure you learn and progress in your role. There may be formal or informal initiation activities and even hazing rituals, particularly when joining a close-knit, high-status group, such as a sports team or a fraternity (Keating, Pomerantz, Pommer, Ritt, Miller, & McCormick, 2005).

There are often multiple (sometimes competing) socialization sources within the organization (Chao et al., 1994), including divisions or departments, workgroups, and peers. Each of these socialization sources educates employees about normative expectations, monitors behavior, and reinforces adherence to normative standards. For example, in the workplace, formal socialization instructs the employee on becoming a productive, savvy, knowledgeable contributor to organizational success (Anderson & Ostroff, 1997), while at the same time informal socialization helps new entrants understand the way things are *really* done in this role and in this organization. Socialization into the informal norms of an organization can become a gateway to deviant behavior if these norms encourage behaviors that are generally discouraged by general societal norms (Allen, Eby, Chao, & Bauer, 2017; Bauer, Bodner, Erdogan, Truxillo, & Tucker, 2007; Hawkins, 1984; Hollinger & Clark, 1982a; Murphy, 1993). The socialization process (both formal and informal) "defines what range of behavior is acceptable and what is unacceptable . . . (and provides) rewards for acceptable behaviors and sanctions for unacceptable ones" (Murphy, 1993, p. 42).

Socialization Into Deviance

Peers, workgroups, and the like appear to have an especially strong influence on the likelihood that new entrants will become socialized to and adhere to norms that tolerate or encourage misbehavior. Peer groups regulate behavior by doling out rewards and punishments for adherence to or defiance of group norms (Hackman, 1992). For example, workgroups often punish non-conformers by ostracism and withholding information (Hackman, 1976; Roy, 1952, 1954). Compared to the informal rewards and sanctions of the workgroup, the formal recognition and punishments wielded by the organization are distal indeed, and they often carry less weight in shaping behavior (Hollinger & Clark, 1982b; Kamp & Brooks, 1991). Whereas the organization may set the general tone for deviant behavior, "employee deviance is regulated by the informally established normative consensus of the work group" (Hollinger & Clark, 1982b; p. 334).

While most workgroups follow societal and organizational conventions regarding honest behavior, it is not unusual for them to condone or encourage particular deviant behaviors including theft, sabotage, absenteeism, and production slowdowns (Greenberg, 1997; Roy, 1952, 1954). Research within workgroups has uncovered surprisingly comprehensive normative structures that define what deviant behaviors are or are not encouraged and how these behaviors are rationalized (Cressey, 1970; Ditton, 1977; Greenberg, 1998; Henry & Mars, 1978; Hollinger, 1991; Mars, 1994). If the norms of a group or an organization tolerate or encourage specific types of misbehavior, the likelihood that members of that organization will engage in those behaviors increases. Thus, one of the critical issues in understanding misbehavior in the workplace is to understand the conditions under which groups or organizations are likely to develop norms and expectations that encourage misbehavior. I will consider different theories of how dysfunctional norms develop and emerge in Chapter 10.

When dysfunctional norms develop within organizations, this creates conflicts between what is accepted within organizations and what is accepted outside of the organization. One way these conflicts are handled is to create psychological barriers between the two conflicting sets of norms and to focus the members of the organization on internal rather than external norms and standards. If sufficiently isolated from larger, external social concerns, organizations can constitute a kind of "moral microcosm" (Brief, Buttram, & Dukerich, 2001) into which new members are incorporated. This can produce an isolated style of moral thinking and acting, in which organization members uncritically equate organizational interests with public interests and ethical behavior (Brief et al., 2001).

Finally, it is important to keep in mind that the processes described here are usually designed, intended, and used to foster norms and expectations that are positive and productive. While many of the social and psychological processes described in this book *can* go off the rails and lead to misbehavior, this is not the norm, and you should not assume that all organizations, or even that the majority of organizations encourage and support misbehavior. The processes described here have the potential to support misbehavior, but they do not have to lead individuals in negative directions.

Attraction-Selection-Attrition Processes

Socialization helps to ensure a good fit between individuals and organizations, and it is an important part of the two-way processes of attraction, selection, and attrition (ASA, Anderson & Ostroff, 1997; Schneider, 1983, 1987, 2008; Schneider, Goldstein, & Smith, 1995). Potential members are attracted to organizations with goals, values, and beliefs similar to their own (attraction). Similarly, organizations generally prefer to attract and recruit members whose values, norms, and expectations are consistent with prevailing practices in the organization (selection). Members whose norms, values, and expectations do not fit with important aspects of the organization tend to leave (or to be forced out of) the organization (attrition), and this three-part process of attracting new members, selecting members from a potential pool of new entrants, and attrition of individuals who do not fit the role or the organization has a substantial effect on the way organizations develop and function.

This attraction-selection-attrition process ensures that the normative climate of most organizations is stable and self-perpetuating (Murphy, 1993; Schneider, 1983, 1987) and this process suggests that organizations are likely to become relatively homogeneous in terms of their members' values, norms, and personality characteristics over time (Schneider, Goldstein, & Smith, 1995). There is empirical evidence that the ASA process does create more homogeneity in organizations; individuals in the same organization, for example, often have more similarities in terms of shared personality than members of different organizations (Ployhart, Weekley, Baughman, 2006).

Another implication of the ASA model is that deviant organizations or workgroups will likely attract, select, and retain deviant members, thus perpetuating the deviant normative climate. In particular, deviant individuals are likely to seek out, select, and remain in situations that accommodate their predilections. According to Mars, "Those workers who cannot adjust (to the deviant atmosphere), leave; those who can adjust find that the working environment satisfies them and they stay on" (1994; p. 193). The ASA process is likely to filter throughout all levels of the organization, creating similar socialization pressures at many levels (Hackman, 1992; Treviño & Youngblood, 1990). In this process, deviance (or honesty) can become institutionalized as part of organizational culture.

Working Together: Teams and Workgroups

Members of organizations typically work together in carrying out the tasks and duties that are part of their roles. In work organizations, you might interact with the same workgroup every day for extended periods. In other formal organizations, you might interact with others less frequently, but you still are likely to be part of a group or team rather than an individual working alone. Your interactions might be virtual; during the coronavirus pandemic of 2020–2021, many people shifted from in-person to virtual interactions. Regardless of how you interact, the fact that performing your duties as a member of an organization by working with others has several important implications for misbehavior in organizations.

Sustained and ongoing reactions with a particular set of people create opportunities for conflict, bullying, and harassment. Conflict is not necessarily a component of or a precursor to misbehavior, and if it is managed appropriately, conflict is not necessarily a source of bad feelings of bad behavior. Conflict about task-related decisions and actions can even contribute to creativity (Yong, Sauer, & Mannix, 2014). Bullying is distinct from conflict in three important ways. First, it usually involves a difference in formal or informal power that makes it difficult for the target of bullying to respond (Juvonen & Graham, 2014). Second, bullying usually involves intentionally harming another person, often to establish or reinforce social dominance (Hawley, 1999). Third, and most critical, bullying involves repeated interactions, and this is where the requirement to interact with particular people over a potentially long period opens up opportunities for bullying.

Frequent and prolonged interactions probably also create enhanced opportunities for harassment. For example, sexual harassment is often a chronic experience in which the target is exposed to repeated instances of inappropriate sexualization of their work environment or the context within which they carry out their organizational roles (McGinley, Richmond, & Rospenda, 2011). By putting their members in positions in which particular sets of individuals are expected and required to interact repeatedly over time, organizations might sometimes inadvertently be creating conditions that make harassment more likely and more damaging.

Deviant Teams

Some tasks within organizations are accomplished by individuals working alone or groups of individuals working together, but important tasks are often accomplished by teams. Teams have several distinguishing characteristics, many of which are directly relevant to misbehavior. Teams are made up of people who occupy interdependent roles, who are focused on a common goal, and who share a sense of social identity. Team members share accountability for the success or failure of their team and they often show significantly higher levels of commitment to their team than to a comparable working group in which there is not a sense of interdependence and shared goals (Katzenbach & Smith, 1993).

The interdependence, identification, and commitment of team members is often highly beneficial to the team and the organization in which the team functions. However, these same characteristics of teams can serve to magnify misbehavior when team norms or expectations are dysfunctional. Schabram, Robinson, and Cruz (2018) note that deviance in organizations frequently involves teams acting badly (see also, Cialdini, Petrova, & Goldstein, 2004; Dunlop & Lee, 2004). The interdependence and commitment of the team make it more likely that members will go along with questionable behavior on the part of the team (Anand, Ashforth, & Joshi, 2004; Erickson & Jensen, 1977; Robinson & O'Leary-Kelly, 1998).

The very act of cooperating in dishonest or unethical activities can help build and reinforce solidarity and commitment to the team, at least among members who embrace the deviant norms of the team (Schabram et al., 2018). One of the themes of the 1973 movie *Serpico* was that members of a corrupt police squad distrusted Frank Serpico because he was honest and would not accept bribes, something that endangered his colleagues who were on the take.

Destructive Leadership

As we have noted in earlier chapters, leaders in organizations sometimes engage in behaviors such as bullying, harassment, or dishonesty that can best be described using the term "destructive leadership". Einarsen, Aasland, and Skogstad (2007) define destructive leadership as a systematic and repeated behavior on the part of individuals in positions of responsibility that violates the legitimate interests of the organization and its members and that undermines the success of the organization and the experience of its members. Thoroughgood and Padilla (2013) make the important point that destructive leadership does not occur in a vacuum, but rather requires an environment that will at least tolerate it and often support it. Padilla, Hogan, and Kaiser (2007) take this idea further in their discussion of the "toxic triangle" of leaders, followers, and environments. They note that destructive leadership starts with individuals in leadership positions who are characterized by high levels of charisma, a need for power, narcissism, and negative experiences and views.

Potentially destructive leaders are unlikely to exert a truly dangerous behavior pattern unless they are paired with susceptible followers. Padilla et al. (2007) describe two groups of followers who can contribute to destructive leadership—that is, conformers (who follow a destructive leader out of fear) and colluders (who actively collaborate with the leader) and detail the conditions that might lead followers to conform or collude. Finally, the toxic triangle only functions well in environments that support or at least tolerate destructive behavior. They describe how instability, perceived threats, cultural values, and/or the absence of effective checks and balances can contribute to the incidence and severity of destructive leadership.

This list of organizational factors that contribute to destructive leadership suggests that organizations may find it difficult to fully control leaders who bully, harass, or otherwise harm their subordinates. To be sure, some organization-level responses that can make a difference (e.g., establishing and enforcing checks and balances), but there are forces outside of the organization (e.g., external threats, cultural values that support or tolerate misbehavior) that are also important factors in destructive leadership, and if these external forces are sufficiently strong, organizations might find the control of destructive leadership a significant challenge.

Individual Differences: Perceptions of and Beliefs About Organizations

Members of organizations have perceptions of and beliefs about their organizations that have a significant effect on their behavior. First, perceptions of organizational climates and cultures provide important normative information that can either support and encourage or prevent particular types of misbehavior. Second, members of organizations have opinions, often strong opinions, about the fairness of decisions and procedures in their organizations, and these beliefs can motivate both prosocial and antisocial behaviors in organizations.

Organizational Climate and Culture

Two related concepts, organizational climate and organizational culture, have been used to describe a range of perceptions and beliefs members share about their organizations (Ehrhart & Schneider, 2016; Ehrhart, Schneider, & Macey, 2014). Culture refers to a system of shared values and norms that define appropriate attitudes and behaviors for organizational members (Deal & Kennedy, 1982; O'Reilly & Chatman, 1996), and it is reflected in the history, stories, and rituals of organizations. Organizational cultures are important for understanding misbehavior because they tell members what behaviors are valued and promoted by organizations. Climate is more tightly linked to the experience of individuals in organizations and the "shared meaning organizational members attach to the events, policies, practices, and procedures they experience and the behaviors they see being rewarded, supported, and expected" (Ehrhart et al., 2014, p. 69). Climates reflect reactions and are focused on the present, whereas cultures represent a more enduring understanding of what is valued and preferred by organizations. While distinctions can be made between these two constructs, they are often used almost interchangeably in the literature, and research on these two constructs often finds more similarities than differences (Ehrhart & Schneider, 2016). The interchangeability of these terms is particularly striking in the literature I reviewed in preparing to write this book; numerous articles refer to "ethical climates", "climate of honesty", "substance abuse climate" and the like, but they described cultures rather than or in addition to climates. Climates are important, but to the extent that there is a meaningful difference between climates and cultures, it is probably more useful to concentrate on culture, given its close link to norms and values.

Cultures vary from organization to organization, and differences in culture are linked to several measures of the effectiveness of organizations (Hartnell, Ou,

Kinicki, Choi, & Karam, 2019). Differences in organizational cultures have been associated with both positive or negative outcomes for organizations and their members (Deal & Kennedy, 1982). Positive outcomes for individual members of organizations potentially include motivation and satisfaction (O'Reilly, 1989), while negative outcomes might include job insecurity and stress (Kahn, Wolfe, Quinn, Snoek, & Rosenthal, 1964; Katz & Kahn, 1966). The business press often argues that a strong and consistent culture is essential to the success of organizations, but the effects of an organization's culture might depend substantially on the content of that organization's culture. For example, Matos, O'Neill, and Lei (2018) describe how a "masculinity contest culture", a "win-or-die" culture that emphasizes competition, social dominance, physical strength, and avoidance of weakness can lead to higher levels of abusive supervision and toxic leadership.

Culture Content

Given the importance of organizational culture as a construct, the literature describing what organizational cultures are like is still somewhat fragmented, with different researchers using very different taxonomies to describe and classify cultures. As I just noted, Matos et al. (2018) describe one specific type of culture that focuses on competition and dominance. Westrum (2004) described three types of cultures encountered in medical settings: (1) pathological—concerned with personal power, needs, and glory, (2) bureaucratic—concerned with roles, positions, and turf battles, and (3) generative—concerned with the mission itself. These different cultures handle information, responsibilities, and success and failure differently. For example, pathological cultures seek scapegoats when failure is encountered, whereas in generative cultures, failure leads to inquiry (e.g., how can we do better next time). In bureaucratic cultures, novelty is discouraged and seen as a source of problems, but in pathological cultures, it is actively suppressed.

Cameron and Freeman (1991) developed an influential taxonomy that sorts organizational cultures into four types: (1) clan—cohesive and participative, with a focus on building loyalty and cohesiveness, (2) adhocracy—creative, dynamic, and adaptive, with an emphasis on risk-taking, innovation, and growth, (3) hierarchy—an emphasis on order, rules, and regulations, with the goal of achieving stability and predictability and (4) market—competitive and achievement-striving, with an emphasis on productivity and market dominance. This taxonomy is built around Quinn and Rohrbaugh's (1981) competing values framework that uses two value dimensions (predictability and orientation) to describe different types of organizations. Figure 9.2 portrays the Cameron and Freeman (1991) model in the context of these competing values.

Rather than classifying organizational cultures into discrete types, Trompanaar and Hambden-Turner (1997) describe organizational cultures in terms of the dimensions shown in Table 9.1. They suggest that there is often a strong link between aspects of national culture and the corresponding organizational culture.

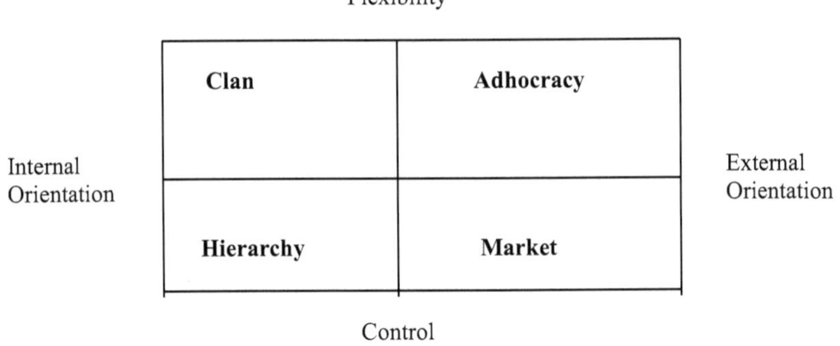

FIGURE 9.2 Cameron and Freeman's (1991) Taxonomy of Cultures

TABLE 9.1 Dimensions of Organizational Culture

1. Universal vs. particular—rules and standards are fixed vs. dependent on unique relationships and circumstances
2. Groups vs. individuals—emphasis on the collective (the group, the organization) vs. on individuals
3. Affective vs. neutral—interactions are emotion-laden vs. detached
4. Specific vs. diffuse—relationships are discrete and transactional vs. personal
5. Achievement vs. ascription—status is based on accomplishments and achievements vs. based on birth, gender, age, connection
6. Time orientation—relative focus on the past, present, or future
7. Orientation to the environment—emphasis on the context vs. on the individual

Source: Trompanaa and Hambden-Turner (1997)

For example, Japanese culture tends to be relatively collectivist; it tends to ascribe status to individuals based on their social class, the university they attended, etc.; and it is sensitive to the effects of individuals on their surrounding environment. In contrast, American culture tends to be more individualistic, focused on personal achievements rather than ascribed status, and focused on the needs and interests of individual customers and clients. They suggest that these broad cultural values filter down to organizations and can sometimes make it difficult for organizations that differ strongly on these dimensions to work together effectively.

To understand misbehavior in organizations, several aspects of organizational culture are likely to be important. First, the types of relationships among individuals that are expected and promoted within an organization are likely to make a difference in the types of misbehavior that might be expected. For example, a strong emphasis on internal competition in an organization can lead to social undercutting. A strong emphasis on dominance can contribute to bullying and harassment. Second, the way power is distributed and used in an organization is likely to influence misbehavior. For example, a strong emphasis on the power and authority of management vs. rights of employees can create greater risks of property and production deviance. A strong emphasis on top-down management may increase the risk that organization members will cooperate in illicit schemes and large-scale frauds. A reluctance to seek or act on upward feedback or information flowing from lower to higher levels of authority is likely to create greater risks of abusive supervision and destructive leadership. Third, the nature of the relationship between an organization and its customers and clients is likely to influence misbehavior. Sometimes, interactions with clients represent a one-off relationship (e.g., vendors selling items to tourists), but sometimes there are long-established relationships with particular customers and clients, and these different relationships might create different opportunities for and barriers to cheating and misrepresentation. If you are selling trinkets to tourists you will never see again, the temptation to cheat or pawn off substandard wares might be very different than if you are dealing with a customer you know and rely upon.

Culture Strength

Nations differ in terms of tightness-looseness of their cultures (Gelfand et al., 2011), and the same is almost certainly true of organizations (González-Romá & Peiró, 2014). A strong culture features a high level of consensus about and internalization of the norms, values, and beliefs that characterize an organization, whereas a weak culture might be characterized by little consistency or little strong feeling about these same norms, values, and beliefs. Nations with relatively tight cultures expect and usually receive a high level of normative regulation and conformity (Gelfand et al., 2011), and organizations with strong cultures are likely to see similar levels of acceptance and conformity with their norms and values.

The construct "situation strength" provides a useful framework for understanding how strong vs. weak organizational cultures are likely to influence the behavior or members of an organization (Hattrup & Jackson, 1996; Meyer, Dalal, & Hermida, 2010; Snyder & Ickes, 1985). Situations are described as strong when they provide clear and consistent cues of behaviors that are desired or preferred (Meyer & Dalal, 2009; Meyer et al., 2010). In strong situations, individual differences (e.g., in personality, values, beliefs) have relatively weaker effects on behavior; most people behave in ways that are consistent with cues about which behaviors are expected (Hough & Oswald, 2008). In weak situations, situational cues have relatively little effect on behavior, and individual differences of the type noted previously are likely to play a relatively stronger role. A strong organizational climate is one with consistent and clear messages about what the organization values, what behaviors are expected, and what behaviors meet with approval or disapproval.

Strong cultures are probably beneficial in many ways, but once again, this probably depends on the content of the culture. Aquino and Lamertz (2004) identified two types of cultural norms that support a link between organizational culture and workplace abuse. They proposed that when organizations have strong cultural norms supporting "the belief that punishments, aggression, and the exercise of coercive power are functional for motivating people" (2004, p. 1030), the likelihood of workplace abuse increases. Secondly, when organizations have strong norms supporting incivility and rude interpersonal behaviors, the likelihood of workplace abuse also increases. An organization that combines a strong climate with dysfunctional norms is likely to become a breeding ground for misbehavior.

Ethical Climates and Cultures

Climates and cultures can be broadly defined (e.g., clan vs. adhocracy structures) or they can be focused on more narrow domains. For example, climates for theft (Cherrington & Cherrington, 1985), substance abuse (Frone, 2009, 2012), and whistleblowing (Miceli & Near, 1992) have been discussed by organizational researchers. Ethical climates and cultures are particularly relevant for understanding misbehavior in organizations.

BOX 9.1 THE PENN STATE SCANDAL

In June 2012, Jerry Sandusky, a former Penn State assistant football coach, was found guilty of 45 counts of child sexual abuse against ten boys. Some of these incidents took place on the Penn State campus, and in 2001, an incident involving alleged sex acts between Sandusky and a boy in a shower on campus was reported to university authorities. High-level administrators, including the university president, debated how to respond to this report, and eventually decided not to go to the police or child protective services, but rather took some informal actions designed to limit future incidents.

In July of 2012, former director of the FBI Louis Freeh released the 267-page report after an eight-month independent investigation commissioned by the university's board, criticizing the disregard for the safety and welfare of Sandusky's child victims by the most senior leaders at Penn State (Freeh, Sporkin, & Sullivan, 2012). Freeh said at a news conference, "The most powerful men at Penn State failed to take any steps for 14 years to protect the children who Sandusky victimized". The report found that key university leaders—including former President Graham Spanier, football coach Joe Paterno, Athletic Director Tim Curley and Senior Vice President Gary Schultz—failed to report suspicions of child abuse and concealed Sandusky's actions from the Board of Trustees, the university community, and authorities.

Graham Spanier was a widely respected university president and Joe Paterno was a beloved football coach who had given generously to the university (when out-of-town visitors asked to see Joe Paterno's mansion, they were usually directed to the Patee-Paterno Library, the main library on the university's flagship campus) and who had helped to positively mold the lives of generations of players. How could such men and others involved turn a blind eye to the unfolding tragedy?[3]

Babcock (2012) argued that the climate, culture, and flawed leadership of the university contributed to the scandal. The relatively decentralized structure of the university (each college had its own vice president of human resources or some comparable officer) contributed to the problem because there was nobody who felt they were sufficiently powerful to intervene, especially given the great level of respect for and deference to Coach Paterno at the university. Joe Paterno, who served as head coach of the Penn State football team from 1966–2011 was the most victorious coach in NCAA history and in many ways was the public face of the university. The Freeh report argued that the university covered up reports of Sandusky's abuse out of fear that it would damage the sterling (and lucrative) reputation of Penn State football.

Alderfer (2013) argued that it is not possible to understand this scandal by looking at the university alone. He called attention to the numerous organizations that were involved in the Sandusky affair, ranging from the Second Mile (a foundation established by Sandusky) to the NCAA. Many of the participants were influenced by identification with and loyalty to the particular group they were a member of (football team, the athletic department, Penn State students), and this loyalty made it difficult for them to take corrective actions that would appear to harm their organization. As is usual for cover-ups of this sort, the eventual scandal was considerably worse than what would have emerged if the university and the other organizations involved had acted immediately and transparently when the 2002 incident was first reported.

One of the recurring themes in many corporate scandals is the way individuals are faced with a choice between doing what society would label as the right thing (e.g., blowing the whistle on corruption, reporting abuses to the authorities) and doing what appears to be good for the organization. Football holds a uniquely important place in many American universities, and its centrality to the image and the culture of Penn State was particularly strong at that time. Joe Paterno was almost universally respected on a national level as a person who put character first and who had contributed immensely to his players and his university. It is probably naïve to expect that many other University administrators would have acted differently than President Spanier and others at Penn State did.

Victor and Cullen (1988, p. 101) defined ethical climate as "the prevailing perceptions of typical organizational practices and procedures that have ethical content" and "those aspects of work climate that determine what constitutes ethical behavior at work". Treviño (1990) suggests that ethical culture is a subset of organizational culture and represents the interplay among the ethics-related formal (e.g., rules and policies, performance management systems) and informal (e.g., norms, language, rituals) organizational systems that influence employee ethical and unethical behavior.

There is evidence linking perceptions of the ethical climate and culture of organizations and misbehavior in those organizations. Kish-Gephart, Harrison, and Treviño's (2010) meta-analysis studied the influences of three types of ethical climate (egoistic, benevolent, and principled) on unethical choice (intentions and behaviors) in organizations and found that egoistic climates were positively associated with unethical choice, whereas benevolent and principled climates were negatively associated with unethical choice. Ethical climate and ethical culture are important predictors of the frequency of unethical acts within groups and organizational settings (Ford & Richardson, 1994; Loe, Ferrell, & Mansfield, 2000).

Perceived Organizational Support

The nature of the relationships between organizations and their members can have a significant bearing on misbehavior. In particular, supportive organizational cultures can help to minimize many types of misbehavior, particularly misbehavior directed at the organization (e.g., production and property deviance). Organizational Support Theory suggests that employees develop general beliefs concerning the extent to which their organization values their contributions and cares about their well-being (Eisenberger, Huntington, Hutchison, & Sowa, 1986; Rhoades & Eisenberger, 2002), and they act on those beliefs. First, a highly supportive organizational culture conveys the idea that the organization strongly values the employees' contributions, and this can lead members of an organization to feel there is a reciprocal obligation to care about the welfare of the organization (Caesens, Marique, Hanin, & Stinglhamber, 2016). Second, high levels of perceived organizational support (POS) can increase the likelihood that employees will identify with and be loyal to their organization (Rhoades & Eisenberger, 2002).

There have been many changes in organizations in recent years that have direct implications for POS. For example, as the occupational landscape has shifted in the direction of lower job security and more use of limited (as opposed to long-term) contracts, perceptions of organizational support have dropped (Baran, Shanock, & Miller, 2012). Similarly, organizations may find it more difficult to be supportive of their employees during periods of economic uncertainty. During the pandemic of 2020–2021, many organizations pledged to keep as many of their employees on their payrolls as possible, but as the pandemic dragged on, they often found it impossible to keep paying employees. This experience likely had a significant effect on perceptions that organizations were supportive of and truly cared about their employees.

Fairness and Justice

Organizational cultures, particularly strong ones, tell members of the organization *what* the organization wants them to do and not do. Beliefs and attitudes related to *how* organizations do things are also critically important for understanding misbehavior. In particular, beliefs about whether organizations treat their members fairly are an important determinant of counterproductive work behaviors (e.g., property and production deviance; Scott, 2003) and they are also important in determining how people react to bullying, harassment, and abusive leadership (Greenberg 1993; Lewicki, Poland, Minton, & Sheppard, 1997; Litzky, Eddleston, & Kidder, 2006).

Organizational researchers suggest that there are important distinctions among three different aspects of justice in organizations: (1) distributive justice—whether people get what they believe they deserve, (2) procedural justice—whether fair processes are followed when making decisions, and (3) interactional justice—whether people are treated with consideration and respect (Colquitt, Conlon, Wesson, Porter, & Yee, 2001; Folger & Cropanzano, 1998; Lind & Tyler, 1988; Skarlicki & Folger, 1997; Tyler, 2006a, 2006b; Tyler, Boeckmann, Smith, & Huo, 1997). Judgments about distributive justice typically focus on rewards (e.g., pay raises, praise), and the concern here is largely with whether they have been distributed in a way that seems fair and rational. Judgments about distributive justice have clear implications for understanding behavior in organizations. For example, one of the recurring problems with performance evaluation in organizations is that most employees appear to overestimate their performance level, and they are likely to believe that they deserve higher ratings and larger pay raises than their objective performance levels would justify (Murphy, Cleveland, & Hanscom, 2018).

Judgments about interactional justice reflect both interpersonal treatment (e.g., are members of an organization treated with dignity and respect by authorities and third parties) and whether or not people are provided with information and explanations about why particular decisions are made. Mistreatment in organizations, such as bullying, harassment, or abusive leadership are likely to trigger several reactions, one of which is a judgment that the targets of this behavior are not being treated with the dignity and respect they deserve.

Judgments about procedural justice involve assessments of the processes and procedures used to make important decisions in organizations, and these judgments are a particularly important determinant of misbehavior. Concern for proper processes and procedures has, for example, long been a hallmark of legal theory in the United States; both the Fifth and Fourteenth Amendments to the

U.S. Constitution contain important due process clauses. Organization members who believe that decisions are based on biased, inconsistent, or arbitrary procedures (e.g., favoritism, self-interest, rigged bids) are unlikely to accept the legitimacy of those decisions. In contrast, decisions that are made by neutral parties following objective and consistent rules are more likely to be accepted as fair, even if the outcomes of decisions are not completely favorable (Lind & Tyler, 1988).

Judgments about procedural justice are an important predictor of several outcomes, including commitment to organizations (Korsgaard, Schweiger, & Sapienza, 1995) and the likelihood that employees will stay with their organizations (Taylor, Tracy, Renard, Harrison, & Carroll, 1995). Most important, judgments about procedural justice are related to compliance with organizational rules. People are generally less willing to follow rules if they believe they are being applied unfairly (Tyler, 2006a, 2006b). More important, unfair application of rules or laws tends to lead to rule deactivation—that is, it robs formal rules of their force and legitimacy (Zoghbi-Manrique-de-Lara, 2010). Rules that are seen as illegitimate are very difficult to enforce.

Tyler (2009) makes the distinction between command-and-control models (in which external forces enforce rules) and self-regulatory models, in which people are motivated to comply. Many of the features of the modern workplace are the result of the use of the command and control model (e.g., the use of cameras, the monitoring of telephone calls and computer usage, random drug testing, the use of time clocks and other performance tracking devices), but there is considerable evidence that self-regulation is more effective (Kelman, 1958, Kelman & Hamilton, 1989; Tyler, 2006a, 2009). Organizations that fail to follow fair procedures risk sacrificing the legitimacy of their rules and regulations.

BOX 9.2 MUTINY!

On April 28, 1789, the crew of *HMS Bounty*, led by Fletcher Christian, mutinied. They cast their captain, William Bligh, adrift in the ship's launch with 18 of his followers. In one of the most remarkable displays of seamanship in the 18th century, Bligh sailed this open boat over 3,500 miles to Timor, where he reported the mutiny.

There have been many accounts of the mutiny, and controversy still rages over the roles of Bligh, Christian, and others. It is clear that Bligh was a strict disciplinarian, but at the time in the British Navy, discipline was often strict and punishments were harsh. Most accounts of the mutiny emphasize the inconsistency in the relationships between Bligh and Christian; Bligh alternated between viciously insulting his acting second in command and offering him help and friendship. They also suggest that Bligh may have overstepped traditional bounds in dealing with his officers and crew. For example, the best literary treatment of the mutiny, Nordoff and Hall's *Bounty Trilogy* (*Mutiny on the Bounty, Men Against the Sea, Pitcairn's Island*) argues that the mutiny occurred in part because Bligh's mistreatment of his officers and crew exceed traditional norms, which allowed for a certain amount of harsh treatment but set limits on what was acceptable.

Coye, Murphy, and Spencer (2010) reviewed historic descriptions of 30 mutinies, conceptualizing them as bottom-up upheavals that represent extreme attempts to respond to what was perceived as unfair treatment. They describe a mutiny "as an organized movement by members in an organization; based on perceived injustice, marked by coordinated extra-role behavior directed upward despite barriers, and intended to subvert the existing order by usurping or overriding legitimate authority" (p. 271), and note that they always involve some sort of collective action that occurs when there is a high level of perceived injustice coupled with barriers to upward communication. They note that mutinies are more likely when there are large gaps between upper and lower echelons of the organization, and that command and control systems that make it difficult for the lower levels of the organization to air their grievances make the organization more susceptible to outbreaks of this sort. Their larger point here is that the failure to give members of an organization fair and efficient processes to look out for their own interests does not prevent those members from asserting their rights; it merely channels this behavior into particularly disruptive forms of counterproductive behavior, including insurrection and mutiny.

The perceived legitimacy of organizational rules and regulations substantially influences the reasons why they are obeyed or disobeyed. Tyler and Blader's (2000, 2003) group engagement model suggests that the ethical values of members of organizations are shaped in part by their perceptions of how fairly they are treated by the organization. For example, there is evidence that employees' willingness to use deceit against the organization (and to believe that they are justified in using deceit) is affected by their perception that others in the organization use deceit (Shapiro, Lewicki, & Devine, 1995).

Unfair or unjust treatment (or treatment that is viewed by the recipient as unfair or unjust) is likely to lead to resentment and even revenge. Failures in procedural justice are particularly dangerous and damaging because of their collateral effects. You might feel disappointed not to get a raise you think you deserve, or to be treated disrespectfully, but if you believe that the organizational processes and policies are themselves unfair, that belief can undermine respect for the rules, regulations, and norms of the organization. Individuals who no longer accept these rules and regulations as legitimate are more likely to disobey them whenever the opportunity arises.

Summary

Organizations exist and function within a broader context, and aspects of the broader culture and the legal and political systems of the nations that are home to organizations can have a substantial impact on both the likelihood and the types of misbehavior you are likely to encounter. Broad dimensions of national culture, such as individualism vs. collectivism or deference to vs. disrespect for authority and status can push individuals in the directions of misbehaviors that fit the culture. For example, in organizations located in nations where there is a strong tradition of deference to authority, you might expect to see more incidents of collective misbehavior (e.g., cooperating in large-scale frauds) and few lone-wolf escapades. Some political and ideological systems might be more compatible with abusive leadership and the mistreatment of subordinates than others.

Organizations have their own cultures, and these cultures can have a decisive effect on the behavior of members of the organization, particularly when the culture sends strong and consistent messages about the types of behavior that are approved of and expected by the organization. The cultures of some organizations tolerate or encourage specific types of misbehavior (e.g., masculinity contest cultures are likely to view bullying and harassment more favorably than other cultures), and people who are socialized to internalize the norms and values of these cultures may be perfectly willing to engage in misbehaviors that are consistent with these norms without feeling they are doing anything wrong. Chapter 10 considers some of the processes that lead organizations to adopt cultures that are deviant or dysfunctional.

Perceptions of the way organizations treat their members, particularly the fairness of the procedures they use to make important decisions, appear to be a strong factor in misbehavior. Unfair procedures, or procedures that are perceived as unfair by members of the organization, are particularly damaging because they have the potential to undermine the legitimacy of the laws, rules, and regulations that help to govern most people's behavior. Perceptions of unfairness will often lead people to strike back at their organization (e.g., through production and property deviance), and in extreme cases, through insurrection and mutiny.

Notes

1. In 1983, the British social scientist David Ashworth changed his name to Perri 6. The usual convention in citing literature is to list the author's last name first, but the name "6, P." can be a source of confusion in citation to his work, and I cite his work here as 6 Perri & Mars, 2007
2. In his 1976 book, Sutton denies saying this

3. I joined the Penn State Faculty in 2000, and by that time, allegations about Sandusky's inappropriate behavior toward children were already common knowledge, but unproven

References

Ackroyd, S. (2012). Even more misbehavior: What has happened in the last twenty years? *Advances in Industrial and Labor Relations, 19*, 1–27.

Alderfer, C.P. (2013). Not just football: An intergroup perspective on the Sandusky scandal at Penn State. *Industrial and Organizational Psychology, 6*, 117–133.

Allen, T.D., Eby, L.T., Chao, G.T. & Bauer, T.N. (2017). Taking stock of two relational aspects of organizational life: Tracing the history and shaping the future of socialization and mentoring research. *Journal of Applied Psychology, 102*, 324.

Anand, V., Ashforth, B.E. & Joshi, M. (2004). Business as usual: The acceptance and perpetuation of corruption in organizations. *Academy of Management Executive, 18*, 39–53.

Anderson, N. & Ostroff, C. (1997). Selection as socialization. In N. Anderson & P. Herriot (Eds.), *International Handbook of Selection and Assessment* (pp. 413–440). Chichester, England: Wiley & Sons.

Aquino, K. & Lamertz, K. (2004). A relational model of workplace victimization: Social roles and patterns of victimization in dyadic relationships. *Journal of Applied Psychology, 89*, 1023–1034.

Babcock, P. (2012). Penn State's organizational flaws make for perfect storm. SHRM, www.shrm.org/resourcesandtools/hr-topics/behavioral-competencies/leadership-and-navigation/pages/pennstateorganizationalflaws.aspx

Bandura, A. (1977). *Social Learning Theory*. Englewood Cliffs, NJ: Prentice-Hall.

Baran, B., Shanock, L. & Miller, L. (2012). Advancing organizational support theory into the twenty-first century world of work. *Journal of Business and Psychology, 27*, 123–147.

Bauer, T.N., Bodner, T., Erdogan, B., Truxillo, D.M. & Tucker, J.S. (2007). Newcomer adjustment during organizational socialization: A meta-analytic review of antecedents, outcomes, and methods. *Journal of Applied Psychology, 92*, 707.

Beale, D. & Hoel, H. (2011). Workplace bullying and the employment relationship: Exploring questions of prevention, control and context. *Work, Employment and Society, 25*, 5–18.

Brief, A.P., Buttram, R.T. & Dukerich, J.M. (2001). Collective corruption in the corporate world: Toward a process model. In M.E. Turner (Ed.), *Groups at Work: Theory and Research* (pp. 471–499). Mahwah, NJ: Lawrence Erlbaum Associates.

Caesens, G. Marique, G., Hanin, D. & Stinglhamber, F. (2016). The relationship between perceived organizational support and proactive behaviour directed towards the organization. *European Journal of Work and Organizational Psychology, 25*, 398–411.

Cameron, K.S. & Freeman, S.J. (1991). Cultural congruence, strength and type: Relationships to Effectiveness. *Research in Organizational Change and Development, 5*, 23–58.

Cialdini, R.B., Petrova, P.K. & Goldstein, N.J. (2004, April 15). The hidden costs of organizational dishonesty. *MIT Sloan Management Review*. http://sloanreview.mit.edu/article/the-hidden-costs-of-organizational-dishonesty/

Chao, G.T., O'Leary-Kelly, A.M., Wolf, S., Klein, H.J. & Gardner, P.D. (1994). Organizational socialization: Its contents and consequences. *Journal of Applied Psychology, 79*, 730–743.

Cheng, J.L.C. (1994). On the concept of universal knowledge in organization science: Implications for cross-national research. *Management Science, 40*, 162–16.

Cherrington, D.J. & Cherrington, J.O. (1985). The climate of honesty in retail stores. In W. Terris (Ed.), *Employee Theft: Research, Theory, and Applications* (pp. 3–16). Park Ridge, IL: London House Press.

Colquitt, J.A., Conlon, D.E., Wesson, M.J., Porter, C.O. & Yee Ng, K. (2001). Justice at the millennium. *Journal of Applied Psychology, 86*, 425–445.

Coye, R.W., Murphy, P.J. & Spencer, P.E. (2010). Using historic mutinies to understand defiance in modern organizations. *Journal of Management History, 16*, 270–287.

Cressey, D.R. (1970). The violators' vocabularies of adjustment. In E.O. Smigel & H.L. Ross (Eds.), *Crimes Against Bureaucracy* (pp. 65–85). New York: Van Nostrand Reinhold.

Deal, T.E. & Kennedy, A.A. (1982). *Corporate Cultures: The Rites and Rituals of Corporate Life*. Reading, MA: Irwin.

Ditton, J. (1977). Perks, pilferage, and the fiddle: The historical structure of invisible wages. *Theory and Society, 4*, 1–38.

Duffy, M.K., Ganster, D.C. & Pagon, M. (2002). Social undermining in the workplace. *Academy of Management Journal, 45*, 331–351.

Dundon, T. & van den Broek, D. (2012). Incorporating institutionalism: Reconceptualizing the resistance and misbehavior binaries. *Advances in Industrial and Labor Relations, 19*, 141–160.

Dunlop, P.D. & Lee, K. (2004). Workplace deviance, organizational citizenship behavior, and business unit performance: The bad apples do spoil the whole barrel. *Journal of Organizational Behavior, 25*, 67–80.

Einarsen, S., Aasland, M.S. & Skogstad, A. (2007). Destructive leadership behaviour: A definition and conceptual model. *The Leadership Quarterly, 18*, 207–216.

Eisenberger, R., Huntington, R., Hutchison, S. & Sowa, D. (1986). Perceived organizational support. *Journal of Applied Psychology, 71*, 500–507.

Ehrhart, M.G. & Schneider, B. (2016). Organizational climate and culture. *Oxford Research Encyclopedia of Psychology*. doi:10.1093/acrefore/9780190236557.013.3

Ehrhart, M.G., Schneider, B. & Macey, W.H. (2014). *Organizational Climate and Culture: An Introduction to Theory, Research, and Practice*. New York: Routledge.

Erickson, M.L. & Jensen, G.F. (1977). Delinquency is still group behavior! Toward revitalizing the group premise in the sociology of deviance. *Journal of Criminal Law and Criminology, 68*, 262–273.

Ewing, J. (2017, March 16). Engineering a deception: What led to Volkswagen's diesel scandal. *New York Times*, www.nytimes.com/interactive/2017/business/volkswagen-diesel-emissions-timeline.html

Fisher, C.D. (1986). Organizational socialization: An integrative review. In K.M. Rowland & G.R. Ferris (Eds.), *Research in Personnel and Human Resource management* (Vol. 4, pp. 211–242). Greenwich, CT: JAI Press.

Folger, R. & Cropanzano, R. (1998). *Organizational Justice and Human Resource Management*. Thousand Oaks, CA: Sage.

Ford, R.C. & Richardson, W.D. (1994). Ethical decision making: An overview of the empirical literature. *Journal of Business Ethics, 13*, 205–221.

Forehand, G.A. & Von Haller, G. (1964). Environmental variation in studies of organizational behavior. *Psychological Bulletin, 62*, 361–382.

Freeh, Sporkin & Sullivan, LLP. (2012). Report of the special investigative counsel regarding the actions of Pennsylvania State University related to the child sexual abuse committed by Gerald A. Sandusky. https://archive.nytimes.com/www.nytimes.com/interactive/2012/07/12/sports/ncaafootball/13pennstate-document.html?module=inline

Frone, M.R. (2009). Does a permissive workplace substance use climate affect employees who do not use alcohol and drugs at work? A U.S. national study. *Psychology of Addictive Behaviors, 23*, 386–390.

Frone, M.R. (2012). Workplace substance use climate: Prevalence and distribution in the U.S. workforce. *Journal of Substance Use, 17*, 72–83.

Gelfand, M.J. et al. (2011). Differences between tight and loose cultures: A 33 nation study. *Science, 32*, 1100–1104.

González-Romá, V. & Peiró, J.M. (2014). Climate and culture strength. In B. Schneider & K.M. Barbera (Eds.), *The Oxford Handbook of Organizational Climate and Culture* (pp. 496–531). Oxford University Press.

Greenberg, J. (1993). Stealing in the name of justice: Informational and interpersonal moderators of theft reactions to underpayment inequity. *Organizational Behavior & Human Decision Processes, 54*, 81–103.

Greenberg, J. (1997). A social influence model of employee theft: Beyond the fraud triangle. In R.J. Lewicki, R.J. Bies, & B.H. Sheppard (Eds.), *Research on Negotiation in Organizations* (Vol. 6, pp. 29–51). Greenwich: Jai Press Inc.

Greenberg, J. (1998). The cognitive geometry of employee theft: Negotiating "the line" between taking and stealing. In R.W. Griffin, A. O'Leary-Kelly, & J.M. Collins (Eds.), *Dysfunctional Behavior in Organizations: Violent and Deviant Behavior* (pp. 147–193). Stamford, CT: JAI Press.

Griffin, M.A. (2007). Specifying organizational context: Systematic links between context and processes in organizational behavior. *Journal of Organizational Behavior, 28*, 859–863.

Hackman, J.R. (1976). Group influences on individuals. In M.D. Dunnette (Ed.), *Handbook of Industrial and Organizational Psychology* (1st Ed., pp. 1455–1525). Chicago: Rand McNally.

Hackman, J.R. (1992). Group influences on individuals in organizations. In M.D. Dunnette & L.M. Hough (Eds.), *Handbook of Industrial and Organizational Psychology* (2nd Ed., Vol. 3, pp. 199–267). Palo Alto, CA: Consulting Psychologists Press.

Hartnell, C.A., Ou, A.Y., Kinicki, A.J., Choi, D. & Karam, E.P. (2019). A meta-analytic test of organizational culture's association with elements of an organization's system and its relative predictive validity on organizational outcomes. *Journal of Applied Psychology, 104*, 832–850.

Hattrup, K. & Jackson, S.E. (1996). Learning about individual differences by taking situations seriously. In K.R. Murphy (Ed.), *Individual Differences and Behavior in Organizations* (pp. 507–547). San Francisco: Jossey-Bass.

Hawkins, R. (1984). Employee theft in the restaurant trade: Forms of ripping off waiters at work. *Deviant Behavior, 5*, 47–69.

Hawley, P. (1999). The ontogenesis of social dominance: A strategy-based evolutionary perspective. *Developmental Review, 19*, 97–132.

Henry, S. (1987). The political economy of informal economies. *The Annals of the American Academy of Political and Social Science, 493*(September), 137–153.

Henry, S. & Mars, G. (1978). Crime at work: The social construction of amateur property theft. *Sociology, 12*, 245–263.

Hofstede, G. (1980). *Culture's Consequences: International Differences in Work-Related Values*. Beverly Hills, CA: Sage.

Hofstede, G. (2001). *Culture's Consequences: Comparing Values, Behaviors, Institutions and Organizations Across Nations*. Thousand Oaks, CA: Sage.

Hofstede, G., Hofstede, G.J. & Minkov, M. (2010). *Cultures and Organizations: Software of the Mind*. Revised and Expanded 3rd Ed. New York: McGraw-Hill.

Hofstede, G., Neuijen, B., Ohayv, D.D. & Sanders, G. (1990). Measuring organizational cultures. *Administrative Science Quarterly*, *35*, 286–316.

Hollinger, R.C. (1991). Neutralizing in the workplace: An empirical analysis of property theft and production deviance. *Deviant Behavior*, *12*, 169–202.

Hollinger, R.C. & Clark, J.P. (1982a). Employee deviance: A response to the perceived quality of the work experience. *Work and Occupations*, *9*, 97–114.

Hollinger, R.C. & Clark, J.P. (1982b). Formal and informal social controls of employee deviance. *The Sociological Quarterly*, *23*, 333–343.

Hough, L.M. & Oswald, F.O. (2008). Personality testing and I-O psychology: Asking questions, offering answers, discussing unknowns, and providing direction. *Industrial and Organizational Psychology: Perspectives on Science and Practice*, *1*, 272–290.

Juvonen, J. & Graham, S. (2014). Bullying in schools: The power of bullies and the plight of victims. *Annual Review of Psychology*, *65*, 159–185.

Johns, G. (2006). The essential impact of context on organizational behavior. *Academy of Management Review*, *31*, 386–408.

Johns, G. (2017). Reflections of the 2016 Decade Award: Incorporating context in organizational research. *Academy of Management Review*, *42*, 577–595.

Johns, G. (2018). Advanced in the treatment of context in organizational research. *Annual Review of Organizational Psychology and Organizational Behavior*, *5*, 21–46.

Kahn, R.L., Wolfe, D.M., Quinn, R.P., Snoek, J.D. & Rosenthal, R.A. (1964). *Organizational Stress: Studies in Role Conflict and Ambiguity*. New York: Wiley.

Kamp, J. & Brooks, P. (1991). Perceived organizational climate and employee counterproductivity. *Journal of Business and Psychology*, *5*, 447–458.

Katz, D. & Kahn, R.L. (1966). *The Social Psychology of Organizations*. New York: Wiley.

Katzenbach, J.R. & Smith, D.K. (1993). *The Wisdom of Teams*. Boston: Harvard Business School Publishing.

Keating, C.F., Pomerantz, J., Pommer, S.D., Ritt, S.J.H., Miller, L.M. & McCormick, J. (2005). Going to college and unpacking hazing: A functional approach to decrypting initiation practices among undergraduates. *Group Dynamics: Theory, Research, and Practice*, *9*, 104–126.

Kelman, H.C. (1958). Compliance, identification, and internalization. *Journal of Conflict Resolution*, *2*, 51–60.

Kelman, H.C. & Hamilton, V.L. (1989). *Crimes of Obedience*. New Haven, CT: Yale University Press.

Kish-Gephart, J.J., Harrison, D.A. & Treviño, L.K. (2010). Bad apples, bad cases, and bad barrels: Meta-analytic evidence about sources of unethical decisions at work. *Journal of Applied Psychology*, *95*, 1–31.

Kolb, D.M. & Putnam, L.L. (1992). The multiple faces of conflict in organizations. *Journal of Organizational Behavior*, *13*, 311.

Korsgaard, M.A., Schweiger, D.M. & Sapienza, H.J. (1995). Building commitment, attachment, and trust in strategic decision-making teams: The role of procedural justice. *Academy of Management Journal*, *38*, 60–84.

Lewicki, R.J., Poland, T., Minton, J.W. & Sheppard, B.H. (1997). Dishonesty as deviance: A typology of workplace dishonesty and contributing factors, *Research on Negotiation in Organizations*, *6*, 53–86.

Lind, E.A. & Tyler, T.R. (1988). *The Social Psychology of Procedural Justice*. New York: Plenum.

Litzky, B.E., Eddleston, K.A. & Kidder, D.L. (2006). The good, the bad, and the misguided: How managers inadvertently encourage deviant behaviors. *Academy of Management Perspectives, 20*, 91–103.

Loe, T.W., Ferrell, L. & Mansfield, P. (2000). A review of empirical studies assessing ethical decision making in business. *Journal of Business Ethics, 25*, 185–204.

Mars, G. (1994). Cheats at Work: An Anthropology of Workplace Crime (Vol. 4). Brookfield, VT: Dartmouth.

Mars, G. (2006). Changes in occupational deviance: Scams, fiddles and sabotage in the twenty-first century. *Crime, Law and Social Change, 45*, 285–296.

Matos, K., O'Neill, O. & Lei, X. (2018). Toxic leadership and the masculinity contest culture: How "win or die" cultures breed abusive leadership. *Journal of Social Issues, 74*, 500–528.

McGinley, M., Richmond, J.A. & Rospenda, K.M. (2011). Duration of sexual harassment and generalized harassment in the workplace over ten years: Effects on deleterious drinking outcomes. *Journal of Addiction Disorders, 30*, 229–242.

Meyer, R.D. & Dalal, R.S. (2009). Situational strength as a means of conceptualizing context. *Industrial and Organizational Psychology: Perspectives on Science and Context, 2*, 99–102.

Meyer, R.D., Dalal, R.S. & Hermida, R. (2010). A review and synthesis of situational strength in the organizational sciences. *Journal of Management, 36*, 121–140.

Miceli, M.P. & Near, J.P. (1992). *Blowing the Whistle*. Riverside, NJ: Macmillan Publishing Company.

Murphy, K.R. (1993). *Honesty in the Workplace*. Monterey, CA: Brooks/Cole.

Murphy, K., Cleveland, J. & Hanscom, M. (2018). *Performance Appraisal and Management*. Thousand Oaks, CA: Sage.

Noonan, L., Tilford, C., Milne, R., Mount, I. & Wise, P. (2018, September 19). Who went to jail for their role in the financial crisis? *Financial Times*, https://ig.ft.com/jailed-bankers/

O'Reilly, C.A. (1989). Corporations, culture, and commitment: motivation and social control in organizations, *California Management Review, 31*, 9–25.

O'Reilly, C.A. & Chatman, J.A. (1996). Culture as social control: Corporations, cults, and commitment. *Research in Organizational Behavior, 18*, 157–200.

Padilla, A., Hogan, R. & Kaiser, R.B. (2007). The toxic triangle: Destructive leaders, Susceptible followers, and conducive environments. *The Leadership Quarterly, 18*, 176–194.

Perri, 6. & Mars, G. (2007). *Dynamic Cultural Theory*. Aldershot, UK: International Library of Anthropology, Ashgate.

Ployhart, R.E., Weekley, J.A. & Baughman, K. (2006). The structure and function of human capital emergence: A multilevel examination of the Attraction-Selection-Attrition Model. *Academy of Management Journal, 49*, 661–677.

Quinn, R.E. & Rohrbaugh, J. (1981) A competing values approach to organisational effectiveness. *Public Productivity Review, 5*, 122–140.

Rhoades, L. & Eisenberger, R. (2002). Perceived organizational support: A review of the literature. *Journal of Applied Psychology, 87*, 698–714.

Robinson, S.L. & O'Leary-Kelly, A.M. (1998). Monkey see, monkey do: The influence of workgroups on the antisocial behavior of employees. *Academy of Management Journal, 41*, 658–672.

Roy, D. (1952). Quota restrictions and goldbricking in a machine shop. *American Journal of Sociology, 57*, 427–442.

Roy, D. (1954). Efficiency and "the fix": Informal intergroup relations in a piecework machine shop. *American Journal of Sociology, 60*, 255–266.

Schabram, K., Robinson, S.L. & Cruz, K.S. (2018). Honor among thieves: The interaction of team and member deviance on trust in the team. *Journal of Applied Psychology, 103*, 1057–1066.

Schneider, B. (1983). Interactional psychology and organizational behavior. In B.M. Staw & L.L. Cummings (Eds.), *Research in Organizational Behavior* (Vol. 5, pp. 1–31). Greenwich, CT: JAI Press.

Schneider, B. (1987). The people make the place. *Personnel Psychology, 40*, 437–453.

Schneider, B. (2008). The people still make the place. In D.B. Smith (Ed.), *The People Make the Place: Dynamic Linkages Between Individuals and Organizations* (pp. 267–289). New York, NY: Taylor & Francis Group/Lawrence Erlbaum Associates.

Schneider, B., Goldstein, H.W. & Smith, D.B. (1995). The ASA framework: An update. *Personnel Psychology, 48*, 747–773.

Scott, E.D. (2003). Plane truth: A qualitative study of employee dishonesty in the airline industry. *Journal of Business Ethics, 42*, 321–337.

Shapiro, D.L., Lewicki, R.J. & Devine, P. (1995). When do employees choose deceptive tactics to stop unwanted organizational change? A relational perspective. In R.J. Bies, R.J. Lewicki, & B.H. Sheppard (Eds.), *Research on Negotiation in Organizations* (pp. 155–184). Greenwich, CT: JAI Press.

Shlapentokh, V. & Woods, J. (2011). *Feudal America: Elements of the Middle Ages in Modern Society*. University Park, PA: The Pennsylvania State University Press.

Skarlicki, D.P. & Folger, R. (1997). Retaliation in the workplace: The roles of distributive, procedural, and interactional justice. *Journal of Applied Psychology, 82*, 434–443.

Snyder, M. & Ickes, W. (1985). Personality and social behavior. In G. Lindzey & E. Aronson (Eds.), *Handbook of Social Psychology* (3rd Ed., pp. 883–948). New York: Random House.

Somin, I. (2017, November 7). Lessons from a century of communism. *New York Times*, www.washingtonpost.com/news/volokhconspiracy/wp/2017/11/07/lessons-from-a-century-of-communism/

Sweetman, K. (2012, April 10). In Asia, power gets in the way. *Harvard Business Review*, https://hbr.org/2012/04/in-asia-power-gets-in-the-way

Taylor, M.S., Tracy, K.B., Renard, M.K., Harrison, J.K. & Carroll, S.J. (1995). Due process in performance appraisal: A quasi-experiment in procedural justice. *Administrative Science Quarterly, 40*, 495–523.

Thompson, J. & Martin, F. (2010). *Strategic Management: Awareness and Change*. Andover, UK: Cengage Learning EMEA.

Thoroughgood, C.N. & Padilla, A. (2013). Destructive leadership and the Penn State scandal: A toxic triangle perspective. *Industrial and Organizational Psychology, 6*, 144–149.

Treviño, L.K. (1990). A cultural perspective on changing and developing organizational ethics. In R. Woodman & W. Passmore (Eds.), *Research in Organizational Change and Development* (Vol. 4, pp. 195–230). Greenwich, CT: JAI.

Treviño, L.K. & Youngblood, S.A. (1990). Bad apples in bad barrels: A causal analysis of ethical decision-making behavior. *Journal of Applied Psychology, 75*, 378–385.

Trompanaar, F. & Hambden-Turner, C. (1997). *Riding the Waves of Culture*. London: Nicholas Brealey Publishing.

Tyler, T.R. (2006a). *Why People Obey the Law: Procedural Justice, Legitimacy, and Compliance*. Princeton, NJ: Princeton University Press.

Tyler, T.R. (2006b). Psychological perspectives on legitimacy and legitimation. *Annual Review of Psychology*, *57*, 375–400.

Tyler, T.R. (2009). Self-regulatory approaches to white-collar crime: The importance of legitimacy and procedural justice. In S. Simpson & D. Weisburd (Eds.), *The Criminology of White-Collar Crime* (pp. 195–216). New York: Springer.

Tyler, T.R. & Blader, S.L. (2000). *Cooperation in Groups: Procedural Justice, Social Identity, and Behavioral Engagement*. Philadelphia, PA: Psychology Press.

Tyler, T.R. & Blader, S.L. (2003). The group engagement model: Procedural justice, social identity, and cooperative behavior. *Personality and Social Psychology Review*, *7*, 349–361.

Tyler, T.R., Boeckmann, R.J., Smith, H.J. & Huo, Y.J. (1997). *Social Justice in a Diverse Society*. Boulder, CO: Westview.

Victor, B. & Cullen, J.B. (1988). The organizational bases of ethical work climates. *Administrative Sciences Quarterly*, *33*, 101–125.

Westrum, R. (2004). A typology of organisational cultures. *BMJ Quality and Safety*, *13*, ii22–ii27.

Yong, K., Sauer, S.J. & Mannix, E.A. (2014). Conflict and creativity in interdisciplinary teams. *Small Group Research*, *45*, 266–289.

Zoghbi-Manrique-de-Lara, P. (2010). Do unfair procedures predict employees' ethical behavior by deactivating formal regulations? *Journal of Business Ethics*, *94*, 411–425.

10

HOW ORGANIZATIONS GO WRONG

Bad Apples or Bad Barrels?

Misbehavior in organizations is all too common. As I noted in previous chapters, a large percentage of employees have been the target of or have observed sexual harassment, bullying, or abusive leadership in their organizations. A 2005 survey found more than half of U.S. employees observed at least one example of workplace ethical misconduct (e.g., fraud, white-collar crime) in the previous year, and 36% observed two or more (Ethics Resource Center, 2005). In another survey of 725 executives and managers, 65% of the respondents had personally observed or obtained direct evidence of one or more types of fraud, waste, and overstatement of cost or mismanagement within their organizations (Keenan, 2000). The question of how to best explain the persistence of misbehavior in organizations has therefore been the focus of a substantial body of research.

There are two competing explanations for misbehavior in the organizations, bad apples or bad barrels (Ashkanasy, Windsor, & Treviño, 2006; Kish-Gephart, Harrison, & Treviño, 2010; Treviño & Youngblood, 1990). The "bad apples" approach ties misbehavior to the individuals who engage in harassment, bullying, or dishonesty, looking for character flaws or distorted attitudes and beliefs as explanations for this behavior. The "bad barrels" approach looks to the organization to explain misbehavior in the workplace. For example, many Silicon Valley startups are criticized for a "bro culture" that combines the worst aspects of fraternity life with the arrogance of sudden wealth. This type of culture is characterized by immature, misogynistic, male-oriented behavior in which the only rule is "boys will be boys", and in which misbehavior is not only tolerated but often encouraged.

There is a good dela of evidence that is consistent with the individual-oriented, bad-apples approach. Misbehavior in organizations has been explained in terms of individual predispositions including a lack of integrity (Frost & Rafilson, 1989), moral identity (Aquino & Reed, 2002; Reed & Aquino, 2003), low levels of self-control (Marcus & Schuler, 2004), lack of empathy (Eisenberg, 2000), or low levels of cognitive moral development (Treviño, 1986; Treviño & Youngblood, 1990; Weber & Wasieleski, 2001). Cognitive tendencies to disengage moral standards (Bandura, 1986), reframe behavior via rationalizing ideologies (Ashforth & Anand, 2003; Robinson & Kraatz, 1998), and use cognitive scripts that tend to exclude ethical dimensions (Gioia, 1992) are also cited as explanations for misbehavior. Some misbehavior is explained in terms of diagnosable psychopathologies, including psychopathic tendencies (Babiak & Hare, 2007). The recurring theme in these studies is that some people are more prone to misbehavior than others and that screening these people out of organizations is an important part of any strategy for reducing misbehavior.

Furnham and Taylor (2011) note that many different patterns of individual differences may lead to similar behavioral outcomes. For example, they suggest that individuals who obey authority figures' unethical directives or act merely to avoid punishment and individuals who manipulate others to orchestrate in pursuit of gain (i.e., are Machiavellian), individuals who fail to see the connection between their actions and outcomes (i.e., have an external locus of control), or individuals who believe that ethical choices are driven by circumstances (i.e., hold a relativistic moral philosophy) are all more likely to make unethical choices at work.

Other studies point to organizational causes of misbehavior—that is, bad barrels. Here, the assumption is that placing people into contexts where misbehavior is tolerated or encouraged increases the likelihood that they will behave badly. Suppose, for example, that many of the people you work with bully or harass their subordinates or lie, cheat, and steal. Social Learning Theory (Bandura, 1986) suggests that leaders and other members of an organization can influence individual antisocial and unethical behavior by modeling such behavior themselves (Ashforth & Anand, 2003; Brown, Treviño, & Harrison, 2005; Robinson & O'Leary-Kelly, 1998; Weaver, Treviño, & Agle, 2005). Organizational norms are also a potentially powerful source of misbehavior. Unethical organizational climates (Victor & Cullen, 1988) and cultures (Treviño, Butterfield, & McCabe, 1998) not only encourage but "legitimate" corrupt behavior. Sometimes, jobs and roles in organizations require, or at least encourage, people to make bad ethical choices (Brief, Buttram, & Dukerich, 2001; Gellerman, 1986). For example, suppose your job is to sell a product that you know does not work as advertised. Many individuals, when faced with the choice between trying to persuade customers to buy a shoddy product or losing their jobs will do what the job requires. Many organizational roles often encourage a narrow focus on goal achievement and provide incentives for unethical behavior (Ashkanasy, Windsor, & Treviño, 2006; Hegarty & Sims, 1978). Indeed, role and organizational identities can emerge that define unethical behavior not only as acceptable but normative (Ashforth & Anand, 2003; Giacalone, Riordan, & Rosenfeld, 1997; Greenberg, 1998; Weaver, 2006).

Research on "bad barrels" has attempted to identify characteristics of organizations that make them particularly vulnerable to tolerating or even encouraging destructive behavior. For example, many organizations have cultures or pursue strategies that make them particularly toxic. There have been several descriptions of a culture of arrogance, disdain for rules, and a tolerance of abuse in companies ranging from Uber to Fox News. Volkswagen's emissions cheating scandal can be traced in part to a corporate strategy in which top management set goals and targets without any clear sense of how these could be achieved, and then held their engineering and manufacturing departments responsible for meeting them. In the end, the only way to meet some goals was to cheat, and for over a decade, this is exactly what occurred (Ewing, 2017; Tabuchi & Ewing, 2017). This problem is by no means unique to Volkswagen; it is often assumed that that senior leaders are responsible for corrupt actions by setting unrealistic financial goals and modeling, condoning, or simply turning a blind eye to the means underlings use to achieve them (Ashforth & Anand, 2003; Brief et al., 2001; Clinard, 1990).

Sometimes, organizations put direct pressure on their members to act unethically (Robertson & Rymon, 2001), but this pressure is more often indirect. When important organizational goals are not met, this can increase the temptation to engage in unethical behavior, even in the case of goals that involve no tangible economic benefits. This temptation can be especially acute in situations when individuals are very close to achieving that goal (Schweitzer, Ordoñez, & Douma, 2004); cutting corners might have an especially strong appeal in this situation. Role conflict can also contribute to unethical behavior. For example, a banker has responsibilities to his or her clients (to safeguard their interests), but also to the organization (to maximize profits), and these conflicts are often a source of stress. One common method for reducing this conflict is to distort information or lie to customers or superiors (Grover, 1993a, 1993b, 1997).

Zyglidopoulos and Fleming (2009) suggest that the bad apples vs. bad barrels debate is essentially a contrast between free will and determinism. They suggest that both personal and situational factors are likely to be in play and that misbehavior in organizations might be better thought of as a process that escalates over time as a result of feedback between persons and organizations.

Bad Apples, Bad Barrels, and Bad Contexts

There is strong evidence supporting both individual and situational explanations of misbehavior in organizations. The most likely resolution of the bad apples vs. bad barrels debate is that both points of view have merit, but that neither explanation is sufficient to account for misbehavior (Andreoli & Lefkowitz, 2009; Kidder, 2005; Kish-Gephart, Harrison, & Treviño, 2010). One implication is that organizations must consider individual attributes, attributes of the organization, *and* their interaction when addressing misbehavior. There is evidence, for example, that the effectiveness of situational interventions targeting deviant behavior may be moderated by personal characteristics (Skarlicki, Folger, & Tesluk, 1999; Ryan, Schmit, Daum, Brutus, McCormick, & Brodke, 1997). For example, Ryan and colleagues compared high- and low-integrity groups on their perceptions of behaviors and situations regarding honesty in the workplace. They found that social controls (e.g., organizational policies, deterrents to misbehavior) were more effective for individuals who were relatively high on integrity (i.e., honest, responsible) than for individuals who were less honest and responsible. First, low-integrity groups perceived dishonest behaviors as less dishonest than their high-honesty counterparts. Second, low-integrity groups viewed social control factors (e.g., deterrents, policies, and facilitation of dishonesty) as less influential in controlling deviance than did the high-honesty group. The results suggest that dishonest workers may view workplace deviance as normal behavior in a dishonest world, making them less susceptible to the social controls organizations might use to deter misbehavior. In dealing with low-integrity groups, it might be critical to directly attack this belief that workplace deviance is nothing more than normal behavior in a dishonest world.

The incidence and nature of misbehavior in the workplace also depends on the type of work people do and the setting within which they work. As I note later in this chapter, corruption in police forces is a problem worldwide. There are several reasons for this, but one that cannot be overlooked is that police officers and others involved in law enforcement interact with individuals who are very willing to offer gifts and bribes to convince officers to look the other way. There is often pressure to go along with these schemes from fellow officers who are on the take. Similarly, employee theft is more of a problem in stores that sell high-end consumer electronic devices (e.g., phones, cameras) than in cement plants because it is easier and more profitable to steal the latest iPhone than to steal concrete.

Gonin, Palazzo, and Hoffrige (2012) note that the bad apple vs. bad barrel discussion overlooks the influence of the broader societal context on organizational behavior. They suggest that we should also consider "bad larder" as an explanation for misbehavior—that is, the context in which organizations are embedded might be a source of misbehavior. They note that several trends, but especially globalization, have tended to disrupt the links between general social norms and behavior in organizations. They argue that as corporations have become global, they exist in an environment with weak and contradictory legal and moral standards and institutions. O'Higgins (2006) analyzed corruption in the developing world and noted the importance of the broader context within which organizations operate in determining whether or not they will succumb to corruption. He proposed a "vicious cycle" model of corruption in the developing world in which multiple stakeholders, from companies to governments to NGOs (nongovernmental organizations) and beyond all play their part in an interdependent, self-sustaining web of corruption.

Zimbardo (2007) analyzed several cases of misbehavior in organizations, including his own Stanford Prison Experiment and the mistreatment of prisoners at Abu Gharib. He suggested that bad behavior is often a reflection of a triad of causes—personal dispositions, situational pressures, and the broader power structure. This third element, the system within which this behavior occurs, is critical to many instances of systematic abuse (e.g., war crimes). That is, the people who commit these crimes are often acting under authority structures that explicitly call for or implicitly condone these acts.

Figure 10.1 displays the relationship between contextual, organizational, and individual causes of misbehavior in organizations. First, the broader culture, economic, and legal systems within which organizations operate, tolerate, and even sanction some types of misbehavior. As I noted in an earlier chapter, despite laws forbidding the types of dishonest banking and trading practices that contributed to the 2008 financial collapse, and despite many public statements

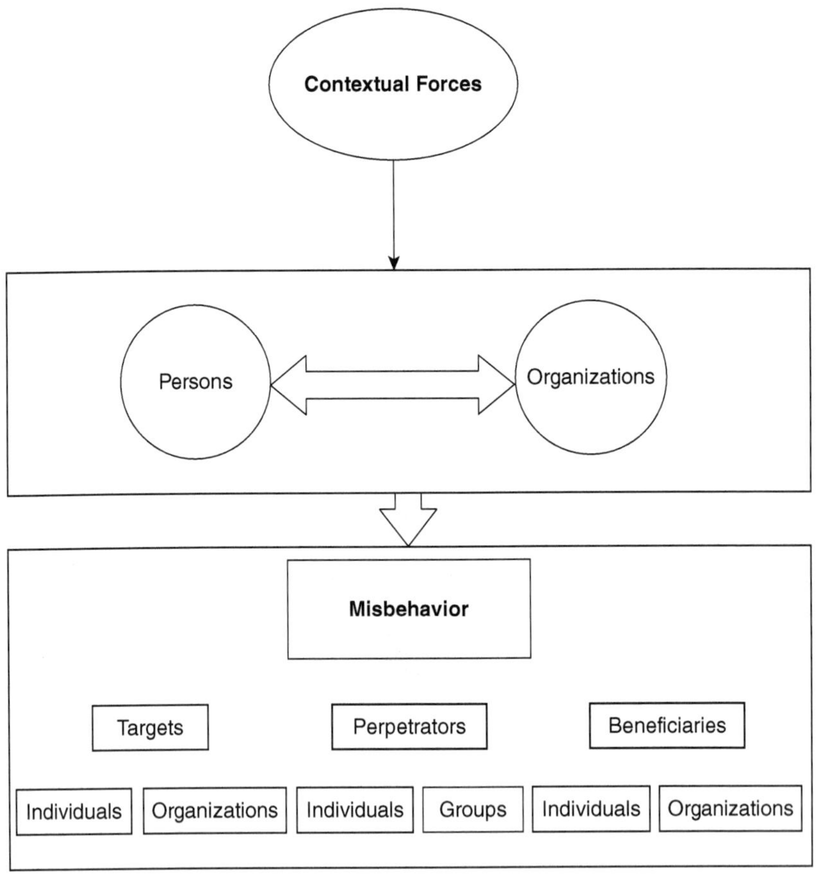

FIGURE 10.1 The Relationship Between Contextual, Organizational, and Individual Causes of Misbehavior in Organizations

of disapproval by government figures, the U.S. did little to prosecute the bankers and traders who contributed so substantially to the financial collapse. This sent a strong and clear message about the tolerance for white-collar crimes in this country.

Hofstede and his colleagues (Hofstede, 1980; 2001; Hofstede, Hofstede, & Minkov, 2010) have developed an influential model for studying and describing national cultures, and several dimensions of this model are useful for understanding misbehavior. As I have noted in earlier chapters, cultures that promote collectivism vs. individualism probably also differ in the types of misbehaviors they encourage or tolerate and the motivations for these behaviors (e.g., going along with others is probably a stronger factor in collectivist cultures). Similarly, in some cultures, there are strong norms that support respect for and deference to authority. For example, in cultures that encourage extensive power distance, organization members may be more willing to cooperate with corrupt schemes that are pushed by the leaders of the organization or to go along with illegal or immoral orders and directives. Other researchers have noted that factors such as strong attachment to conventional religion can be an important factor in misbehavior because this attachment often leads to strong pressures to conform (Klassen, 2007). In many cases, conventional religion will encourage people to conform with prosocial norms, but if the norms of a particular religion encourage particular antisocial behaviors (e.g., shunning disbelievers, religious strife), this same pressure to conform can lead to misbehavior.

Second, people and organizations mutually influence one another. As I will explain in sections that follow, the people who enter organizations, especially early in the organization's history, help to establish norms and expectations. Organizations attract, select, and retain individuals who fit the culture and norms of the organization. Over time, attraction-selection-attrition processes and social learning processes lead to the strengthening and diffusion of these norms and expectations, and if these norms support or encourage particular types of misbehavior, the likelihood of those behaviors occurring is likely to go up substantially.

Third, there are many different types of misbehavior, and these are likely to have different causes and determinants. For example, we can classify misbehaviors in terms of whether they target individuals (e.g., bullying, sexual harassment) or organizations (e.g., production deviance). Misbehaviors directed at individuals almost certainly have different antecedents than misbehaviors directed at the organization. Behaviors such as bullying, sexual harassment, or abusive leadership are likely to reflect some combination of individual predispositions (e.g., aggressive personality, sexist beliefs) and a climate that supports or at least tolerates this behavior (Einarsen, 1999). Misbehaviors directed at organizations (e.g., property and production deviance), on the other hand, often occur in reaction to some perceived mistreatment or injustice on the part of the organization (Murphy, 1993).

Classifying misbehavior in terms of its targets is useful for understanding both the antecedents and the consequences of that behavior. Pinto, Leanna, and Pil (2008) suggest two additional dimensions of misbehavior—that is, whether this behavior is: (1) carried out in groups vs. carried out individually and (2) designed to benefit the organization vs. designed to benefit the individuals who misbehave. Different attributes of individuals, organizations, and the broader context within which organizations are situated, as well as the interactions among these attributes, are likely to contribute to different classes of misbehavior. For example, Pinto et al. (2008) distinguish between organizations of corrupt individuals, in which personally corrupt individuals initiate corrupt action, and corrupt organizations, in which corruption is an organization-wide phenomenon. They point out that there are often structural features of organizations that make individually initiated vs. organization-wide corruption more likely. Thus, if the tasks an organization are structured into a series of jobs or roles that are autonomous and difficult to supervise or monitor, this creates more opportunities for individuals to initiate corrupt or dishonest behavior. If these same tasks are structured into a set of highly interdependent jobs or roles, with clear lines of authority and influence, this structure creates more opportunities for organization-wide corruption.

Finally, when individuals or groups misbehave, it is often useful to ask the question "Cui bono?"—that is, who benefits? For example, Murphy (1993) contrasts two very different types of organizational crime—that is, stealing *from* the organization vs. stealing *for* the organization. The motivations and social factors that lead individuals to steal from their employer are almost certainly different from those that lead individuals to cooperate in organizational corruption. In thinking about individuals who steal from the organization they work for or are part of, we might draw different inferences about motives depending on what they steal. In some industries (e.g., consumer electronics), there are opportunities to steal objects that are often small and valuable (e.g., mobile phones), and some individuals may steal for financial gain. Individuals who steal products from a factory that makes concrete castings probably have a different agenda (e.g., retaliation for perceived injustices). Even in cases of individual theft, there might be strong social factors at work. As Ditton (1977) notes, there are often norms regulating pilferage and the use of organizational resources, and employees who take products, supplies, or other organizational resources for their personal use may believe they are acting within their traditional rights, or at least that what they are doing is widely recognized as acceptable.

I have noted in several previous chapters that serious misbehaviors often occur for the apparent benefit of the organization. The individuals who colluded in large-scale frauds at Enron, WorldCom, Volkswagen, and the like may have stood to benefit themselves (e.g., they might receive bigger bonuses if the organization appears to be doing well), but interviews with participants highlight a recurring theme—that is, the individuals who participated in these frauds and crimes often believed that they were doing what was necessary for the organization to survive and succeed. Later in this chapter, I will expand on an idea that has been raised in several earlier chapters, that loyalty and commitment to organizations, even organizations whose main functions are to help and protect society (e.g., police forces, churches) can be a source of serious misbehavior.

The two-headed arrow in Figure 10.1 connecting individuals and organizations indicates a reciprocal influence, in which: (1) individuals affect organizations, changing their norms, bringing in new ideas, new information, and new skills, and (2) organizations affect individuals, changing their ideas about the behaviors that are or are not expected and approved of, opening new opportunities for both prosocial behavior and misbehavior, etc. Few organizations are likely to start out as corrupt entities in which misbehavior is tolerated and even encouraged, and it is useful to look in detail at the way the processes that lead to corruption unfold over time.

The Evolution of Corruption

Think back to the first day at work on your very first job. I am willing to bet that few of you started your first job intending to bully and harass coworkers, to steal from your employer, or to become part of a large-scale conspiracy to fleece your organization's customers. Similarly, it is fair to assume that most organizations were not founded with the idea that they would become a viper's nest of abusive supervision or that their executives would end up in prison. Unfortunately, many people end up misbehaving and many organizations end up corrupt, and it is useful to examine how they get that way and how they stay on this destructive path.

It is useful to be specific here about the meaning of the term "corruption" in this chapter. Traditional definitions of corruption in organizations focus on the misuse or abuse of a position of trust of power for personal gain, and many discussions of corruption focus on bribery and similar crimes committed by high-level managers and executives. I use the term corruption here more broadly, for two reasons. First, as I noted in Chapters 3 and 6, there are many bases for power and influence in organizations, and power is not limited to the formal leaders of organizations. Thus, many members of organizations have types and levels of power that have little to do with their formal title or duties, and they often use their informal power to bully and harass their colleagues. Organizational newcomers often learn norms that support misbehavior from their more senior colleagues, and a case can be made that the processes that turn new entrants into cynical miscreants who happily go along with norms that accept employee theft, misrepresentation, defrauding customers, and the like is best described as corruption. Second, a substantial portion of the literature reviewed next is framed explicitly in terms of organizational corruption, without always defining clearly precisely what constitutes corruption. In this chapter, I will use corruption to refer to both a process (i.e., the change from organizations or organization members who accept broad social norms to the point of accepting misbehavior as normal) and the result of this process. Thus, a person who has come to believe that particular misbehaviors are acceptable, normal, or even desirable can be referred to as corrupted or corrupt. Similarly, an organization in which misbehaviors have become part of the standard way the organization operates can be referred to as corrupted. In Chapters 11 and 12, I will describe sick organizations, in which some level of misbehavior is accepted and incorporated into the norms of the organization and corrupt organizations, in which dishonest behavior has become part of the business model by which the organization as a unit operates.

Evolution of Individuals Toward Corruption: Slippery Slope or Steep Cliff?

The evolution of members of organizations from a starting point of being well-intentioned and possibly naïve newcomers to the point where they engage in (and possibly persist in) behaviors that are not approved by general society and that have the potential to harm individuals and/or organizations is often described in terms of the metaphor of a slippery slope. The idea is that people start with some small misbehavior, which over time escalates to become more frequent and more severe. Escalation from small misbehaviors to more serious ones are thought to be especially likely if there are few negative consequences for the perpetrators. Among other things, the lack of consequences may change perceptions of the riskiness of the behavior.

People are very strongly motivated to maintain a positive self-concept, and the need to maintain a positive self-concept even when your behavior does not warrant it can have a powerful effect in misbehavior. The assumption in slippery slope models is that none of the small steps toward persistent and serious misbehavior is itself a big enough deal to force people to think seriously about their behavior and its consequences and that people go bad by small stages. That is, small transgressions do not require people to fundamentally reshape their self-concept, and people can often continue to think positively of themselves as they gradually move in the direction of corruption (Ariely, 2012; Gino & Bazerman. 2009). Corruption in organizations is often explained in similar terms, and it is often assumed that, like individuals, organizations become corrupt gradually, and that each step is sufficiently small that organizations do not have to grapple with the fact that they are becoming corrupt, but rather will come to accept corrupt practices as normal.

There are arguments in philosophy, law, and research methodology about whether the slippery slope argument is a logical fallacy (Murphy & Myors, 1995; Walton, 1992; Volokh, 2003), but the psychology of slippery slope arguments for dealing with changes in behavior is sound. In Chapter 4, I described psychological processes that can lead to misbehavior, such as rationalization and moral disengagement. These strategies can be used to reconcile positive self-images with negative behavior, but they require people to seriously distort their perceptions. If changes in behavior are small and gradual, people might have a much easier time reconciling their behavior with their self-image.

Köbis, van Prooijen, Righetti, and Van Lange (2017) note that while slippery slope models are very popular, they are rarely tested rigorously. In a series of experiments, they showed that there was a higher likelihood of severe corruption when participants are directly allowed to engage in it abruptly, compared with experimental conditions in which they had previously engaged in minor forms of corruption. They suggest that the corruption of individuals should be thought of as a steep cliff rather than a slippery slope.

The Köbis et al. (2017) paper reports converging results from several experiments, some done with students as subjects and some done sampling broader populations (e.g., via Amazon Turk). Experiments have many strengths. Through careful design, they allow researchers to make strong statements about causation, and the fact that experiments that differ in the specifics of their procedures (the tasks subjects were asked to complete varied across experiments) but still showed consistent results adds considerably to the confidence we can have in these findings. Nevertheless, serious concerns can be raised about the external validity of these findings. In most of Köbis et al.'s (2017) studies, subjects are completing a simulated bidding task in exchange for course credits or trivial sums of money. They can pretend to offer bribes or decline to pretend to offer a bribe, but they are doing just that—that is, pretending. There are no real-world consequences for their decisions, and they do not have any real interactions with others outside of the limited and short-term confines of their experiment. Thus, while their results are suggestive, it is not clear whether we can abandon the slippery slope metaphor in talking about the evolution of corruption in individuals.

The slippery slope and steep cliff models are not mutually exclusive. Rather, they might suggest different processes that might occur in the process of evolving from a naïve newcomer to a seasoned member of an organization who is set in a pattern of recurring misbehavior. The first point in thinking through the implication of small changes in the direction of misbehavior (slippery slopes) versus large and sudden shifts (steep cliff) is to keep the border context in mind. As I have noted earlier, people are very strongly motivated to maintain a positive self-image (Hales, 1985; Tajfel, 1982; Tajfel & Turner, 1979). How does a person maintain a positive self-image if his or her behavior violates broad social norms in a way that has the potential to harm others?

Slippery-slope theory suggests that small changes in behavior require correspondingly small changes in the way people think about their behavior (Ariely, 2012; Gino & Bazerman, 2009). Steep-cliff changes in behavior are likely to require larger changes in the way people think about what they have done. In Chapter 4, I reviewed cognitive mechanisms that people use to reconcile bad behavior with a positive self-image, including rationalization (e.g., denial of responsibility—"it is not my fault"; denial or harm—"nobody was really hurt") and moral justification (the misbehavior was in support of the greater good of the organization). There is not sufficient research to draw firm conclusions about this, but it is reasonable to believe that steep-cliff changes in misbehavior are easier to reconcile when there is normative support. For example, if the norm in your organization is that everyone pads their expense account (perhaps because members of the organization believe their compensation is unfairly low), it is likely to be easier for you to rationalize this same behavior. Similarly, if you see others in your organization sexually harass or bully others without sanctions or negative consequences, you might conclude that this sort of behavior is what your organization expects of you.

Small changes in misbehavior might not draw much attention, but steep-cliff changes are more likely to be noticed by others in your organization, opening the possibility that you will receive feedback from your environment. If the feedback about your behavior change is negative (e.g., coworkers or colleagues disapprove), you might discontinue those behaviors, but if the feedback is positive, or even if your behavior is ignored, you might conclude that you are behaving appropriately. All of this suggests that possibility that steep-cliff changes in misbehavior might require more external normative support. Without this support, people might find it difficult to reconcile their sudden shift in the direction of misbehavior with a positive self-image. By this logic, slippery-slope changes might be more likely in the absence of direct normative support. I want to emphasize that is a deduction and a prediction, and that we do not yet have sufficient data to determine whether it is true.

The Normalization of Corruption in Organizations

Understanding the process by which organizations become corrupt and by which members of the organization are drawn into corrupt acts is important for several reasons. First, large-scale corporate scandals involving losses in the billions have become almost routine. Thus, there is a strong practical case for investigating the processes by which these organizations become corrupted. Second, these corrupt acts often require knowing cooperation among numerous employees and often persist over time (Vikas, Ashford, & Joshi, 2004). That is, the corruption of corporations or other large-scale organizations inevitably also involved the corruption of many individuals. Understanding how and why organizations and their members become corrupt might give us insights into how to prevent or mitigate this corruption.

Ashforth and Anand (2003) suggest that corruption becomes accepted and normalized in organizations in a three-phase process. During *institutionalization*, a corrupt decision or act becomes embedded in corporate structures and processes. During *rationalization*, self-serving ideologies develop that enable individuals to justify corruption. And finally, during *socialization*, embedded systems and norms induce new employees to tolerate corruption and view it as permissible. The first phase, institutionalization, is probably most critical. Suppose a senior leader in an organization commits some offense, such as taking advantage of insider knowledge or helping to defraud clients and customers. In my discussion of the evolution of corruption in individuals, I noted that steep-slope changes in behavior might be likely to draw attention and feedback from others in the organization. If influential others disapprove, this dishonest act might be a one-off misbehavior, but if they tolerate or support this behavior, this behavior might become part of the standard operating practice. Feedback not only affects the individual who initiated this misbehavior, it also affects observers. If one leader gets away with or even is rewarded for something like taking advantage of insider knowledge, this is likely to encourage others to engage in this same behavior, institutionalizing this pattern of behavior as part of the way your organization does business.

The rationalization phase helps members of an organization reconcile themselves to behavior that violates broad social norms. In Chapter 4, I discussed several rationalization strategies, such as the denial of responsibility, denial of injury, selective social comparisons (others are even worse), or an appeal to higher loyalties (it is for the good of the organization). These rationalizing tactics allow members of the organization to think about their actions in such a way that they do not appear to be unethical at all.

The final phase of organizational corruption, socialization, is critical to the spread of the belief that corrupt acts are appropriate and approved of. Many discussions of the slippery slope hypothesis start with the assumption that a key to getting new members of an organization, or members who were not involved in the original corrupt acts to accept them involves getting them to first make small deviations from social norms or rules, and as they become comfortable with these changes, to make additional small deviation until they reach the point where they accept and even embrace corrupt acts (Köbis et al., 2017). The socialization phase of Ashforth and Anand's (2003) model might also include the use of rewards or incentives to induce positive attitude change toward these behaviors.

Factors That Facilitate Corruption

Several factors can facilitate the normalization of corruption. For example, if the job or organization is highly attractive, members of the organization will be motivated to adjust themselves to the organization's norms, including norms that support corruption. Isolation from others outside of the organization can create an "us vs. them" mentality, and this also facilitates the normalization of corruption.

BOX 10.1 ETHICAL CHEATING?

There is an old saying in NASCAR racing: "It's only cheating if you get caught". It embodies an attitude that drivers and their teams should do everything possible to get more performance out of their cars, including bending the rules. In this mindset, bending the rules enough to increase your car's performance, but not enough to attract the attention of race organizers is considered ethical, and failure to stretch the rules is likely to be considered letting your team down.

Are there times when it is ethical to cheat? Eabrasu (2020) suggests a value-free definition of cheating, to wit, "breaking the rules while deliberately leading or allowing others to think they have been respected" (p. 519) and suggests that this type of cheating is morally wrong only in environments where people broadly accept a moral requirement to follow rules. In the NASCAR example, where many participants are comfortable bending the rules, cheating might be normative and therefore not morally wrong. This argument implies that there are rules which do not entail moral obligations (e.g., you should wait for a green light to cross the street, but if the street is deserted, many people believe that it is fine to cross regardless of the light), and there are special circumstances where other more important obligations override the obligation to comply with the rules (e.g., a bank employee might give a family a few days beyond what their mortgage allows to make a payment to avoid evicting them from their home).

As Carr (1968) famously put it regarding bluffing, "falsehood ceases to be falsehood when it is understood on all sides that the truth is not expected to be spoken" (p. 143). The same principle might apply to cheating and it is one of the reasons for cross-cultural differences in attitudes toward cheating (Moore, 2013). In many cultures, there is some version of the belief "rules are made to be broken", and the more widespread and generalized this belief (e.g., does this apply to all rules or only some categories of rules?) the more likely it is that individuals will cheat without thinking they have done something wrong. Eabrasu (2020) even cites cases of *benevolent cheating*, for example, the case of Chuck Feeney, an entrepreneur who for more than a decade hid his profits using a secret off-shore foundation based in Bermuda, which allowed him to contribute more than $8 billion to philanthropic causes.

One of the factors common to many reports of corporate corruption is intense pressure for performance and growth. This is perhaps most vividly demonstrated by considering the Volkswagen diesel cheating scandal. They determined that their best path to growth was to develop a diesel engine with great economy, great performance, and low emmisions (Ewing, 2017; Hakim, 2015). As has been detailed elsewhere, it is not possible with current technology to do all three and Volkswagen "solved" the problem cheating—that is, by installing software that enabled the car to detect when it was in an emissions test and turn on pollution controls, which allowed the car to show very good emissions numbers. Emission controls tend to degrade both performance and mileage, and the cheat device turned these controls back off when the car was on the road (Ewing, 2017; Tabuchi & Ewing, 2016). Eventually, this scheme, which spanned many years and several continents (and by implication, a very large number of Volkswagen employees), was uncovered, and Volkswagen was eventually fined several billion dollars (Tabuchi & Ewing, 2016).

Taylor (2016) suggests that a strong emphasis on performance and growth has the potential to foster a culture in which the ends justify the means and in which leaders demand results that are difficult to achieve by ethical means. High levels of performance pressure can be particularly damaging when organizations have complex structures that allow leaders to shelter themselves from the corrupt practices their organization is engaged in.

Spread of Corruption

There are at least three ways the misbehavior of one member of an organization can influence other organizational members: (1) direct impact—where a member of the organization is the target of misbehavior, such as bullying, (2) vicarious impact—where an organization member witnesses or is informed of that misbehavior, or (3) ambient impact—where misbehavior is sufficiently widespread that others are encouraged to adopt the misbehavior (Robinson & O'Leary-Kelly 1998). Organization members who have direct or vicarious experience with misbehavior are not necessarily drawn to misbehave themselves; direct or vicarious experience with misbehavior tends to be a stressful (Ferguson & Barry, 2011) and unwelcome experience, and these experiences are unlikely to tempt individuals to initiate a program of similar misbehavior. However, when organizations reach a point where particular misbehaviors are sufficiently widespread that they are accepted as normal and as part of the culture of the organization, this can greatly increase the likelihood of new members of the organization or members who had previously not been involved in this misbehavior coming to act in ways that violate broad social norms. Understanding how misbehavior spreads in organizations is therefore important (Robinson, Wang, & Kiewitz, 2014).

Misbehavior is more likely to spread if the group or organization is cohesive (Ferguson & Barry, 2011), and if the behavior seems to produce relatively little harm (Wilermuth, Vincent, & Gino, 2017). Misbehavior on the part of high-status members is more likely to spread throughout the organization than misbehaviors by low-status members. Organizational leaders are particularly influential in setting the parameters for what types of behaviors are or are not accepted in organizations, and their example and the tolerance, support of, or disfavor they show for particular misbehaviors is likely to have a strong effect on the judgments of members of that organization about those misbehaviors.

Pinto et al. (2008) suggest that organizations of corrupt individuals start with "bad apples", but that corruption can become an organization-level phenomenon through diffusion and normalization. For example, Andersson and Pearson (1999) note an organization may become "uncivil" once the number of incivility spirals reaches a critical threshold in which corruption has become so widespread that it characterizes the organization as a whole. The entry of "bad apples" into otherwise good organizations represents a failure of personal selection; there are several assessment methods that can be used to screen for an increased likelihood of counterproductive behaviors, notably integrity tests and measures of conscientiousness (Murphy, 1993; Murphy & Lee, 1994; Ones, Viswesvaran, & Schmidt, 1993). However, once a sufficient number of corrupt individuals join an organization, they may corrupt the whole enterprise.

BOX 10.2 WHAT CONSTITUTES A CRITICAL THRESHOLD?

Andersson and Pearson (1999) suggest that an organization becomes corrupt when the number of instances of particular corrupt behavior reaches a critical threshold. Threshold models have been proposed for studying attitude change in groups (Galam & Moscovici, 1991) and choices made by groups (Granovetter, 1978). The idea behind this class of models is that there is some point at which the collective changes from one state to another (e.g., not corrupt to corrupt) and that this change is discontinuous. That is, an organization in which the number of corrupt individuals is below the threshold can suddenly become a corrupt organization if the number of corrupt individuals increases slightly.

Granovetter (1978) developed formal mathematical models of threshold effects in behavior change and noted that individual proclivities toward the behavior in question were an important component of understanding threshold changes. For example, riots often start with the actions of a single individual who breaks social norms (and possibly windows as well) by acting out against an unacceptable situation. Granovetter's (1978) model assumes that this individual is more predisposed to taking violent action than others in the crowd and that this person's behavior will push others who are slightly less predisposed toward this reaction to joining the riot. This model also assumes that social relationships might make people more amenable to antisocial influences, describing, for example, how social pressure might make youths in a gang more prone to steal than they would be acting alone.

One of the difficulties involved with using threshold models to explain behavior is that they are more likely to involve after-the-fact explanations rather than a priori predictions, in part because thresholds can be difficult to establish a priori. For example, what proportion of an organization has to participate in a corrupt pattern of action before the organization becomes collectively corrupt?

Two factors likely define this threshold. First, the threshold is likely to be higher for behaviors that most members of the organization strongly disapprove of. That is, the decision to accept and approve of an act they would have otherwise strongly rejected will require a larger critical mass if the behavior in question is serious than if it is one that they only mildly disapprove of. Second, the power, status, and attractiveness of actors involved in this behavior may matter more than the sheer numbers of people involved. That is, if misbehaviors are initiated or approved of by high-status members of the organization, the threshold for an attitude change on the part of other members is probably considerably lower than if misbehaviors are initiated or approved by members who have no special status. Many cases of organizational corruption involve decisions made by top executives and leaders, and likely, the threshold for an organization to normalize particular types of corruption is substantially higher when corruption is a bottom-up phenomenon than when it is initiated from the top of an organization.

The Rationalization of Corruption

The rationalization phase of organization corruption is critical to its spread through the organization. One of the hallmarks of rationalization is the reframing of misbehavior in sanitized terms that minimize the gravity of the offense (e.g., bending the rules, shortcuts) and emphasize that the behavior is normal and acceptable. Chinball and Saunders (1977) recount the trial of a businessman accused of using corrupt means to influence public officials. The businessman said,

> I will never believe I have done anything criminally wrong. I did what is business. If I bent any rules, who doesn't? If you are going to punish me, sweep away the system. If I am guilty, there are many others who should be by my side in the dock. What big company doesn't spend that much and more on entertaining and getting contracts?
>
> *(p. 142)*

The reframing of misbehaviors as normal and acceptable enables organization members to accept behaviors that would usually be seen negatively as a legitimate part of their role. Thus, employees at Volkswagen, Enron, WorldCom, and the like who would normally view deception and cheating negatively came to view their participation in large-scale, long-lasting frauds as just doing their job. Indeed, a recurring theme in investigations into organizational frauds is the perception that "that's the way we do things around here" makes it considerably easier for members of an organization to accept misbehavior as normal and acceptable.

Similarly, reframing unacceptable behaviors in more positive terms makes it more likely that those behaviors will be incorporated into the norms of the organizations. Organizations rarely endorse bullying, sexual harassment, or ethical violations, but they might proudly point to their competitive culture, their low tolerance for mediocrity, or their lofty performance standards, all of which might contribute substantially to misbehavior. As Victor and Cullen (1988) note, shared perceptions of what constitutes ethically correct behavior in an organization have a strong impact on choices members of the organization will make. There is strong empirical evidence that if norms in a workgroup or organization support unethical behavior, organization members will be more likely to act in deviant ways (Bamberger & Biron, 2007; Pierce & Snyder, 2008).

How Organizations Stay Corrupt—ASA Processes in Action

Once organizations become corrupt, it might be hard for them to change, in part because of the attraction-selection-attrition (ASA) process (Schneider, 1987, 2008; Schneider, Goldstein & Smith, 1995). Organizations often work hard to attract and select individuals whose values, norms, and expectations are consistent with those in the organization, and they often work equally hard to weed out people who do not fit.

Attraction and Selection

Corrupt organizations not only recruit members into engaging in corrupt behaviors for the organization's benefit, they also send messages that sanction (Brief, Buttram, & Dukerich, 2001) and therefore normalize and perpetuate the corruption in the organization (Anand, Ashforth, & Joshi, 2004; Ashforth & Anand, 2003.

Brief et al. (2001) describe implicit sanctioning as a message (sometimes clearly stated and sometimes only implied) received from the top that much more weight is attached to job completion, task success, closing the sale, etc. than to legal or ethical means of accomplishment. For example, most organizational mission statements include lofty phrases describing the organization's commitment to high ethical standards, but many lower-level managers and officials report strong pressures and inducements to get the numbers no matter what (Sonnenfeld & Lawrence, 1978).

The messages organizations send to their members about the relative importance of performance and accomplishment vs. how these performance goals are met are likely to filter into the recruitment and selection process. It is unlikely organizations will post help wanted ads that seek out potentially corrupt applicants (Crooks Wanted), or that they will design selection procedures that weed out honest applicants and advantage dishonest ones, but the core values and preferences of the firm likely influence both attraction and selection. Organizations work hard to attract and select individuals who fit into their culture (Maza, 2018), and both the materials that promote the organization to potential applicants and the sorts of questions that are asked in employment interviews are likely to prominently feature the culture of the organization, particularly if the organization has a strong and well-defined culture. Organizations with cultures that promote or tolerate particular misbehaviors (e.g., bullying and abusive leadership under the guise of "only the best will do", sexual harassment in a "bro" culture, disregard for rules and even laws in organizations that describe themselves as disruptive innovators) are likely to attract and select members who share these beliefs, values, and assumptions.

Attrition

The messages members receive from their organization help them make decisions about whether they fit the organization. Cialdini, Li, Samper, and Wellman (2019) suggest that organizations create selective attrition effects, where unethical leader behavior results in the retention of group members who are more comfortable with dishonesty. They present evidence that members who chose to remain in a group with an unethical leader were more likely than those who chose to leave to cheat their group in subsequent tasks.

Attrition can be initiated by the individual or by the organization. Individuals who are uncomfortable with a climate that encourages harassment and abuse or with organizational practices that require them to participate in ethically dubious work are likely to be motivated to seek other organizations to join. Corrupt organizations often find honest members to be threatening and may pressure them to leave; in Chapter 9, I noted that this forms an important part of the plot of the 1973 movie *Serpico*, where one police officer's refusal to take bribes was seen as threatening to his colleagues. Attrition pressure is often especially heavy on individuals who actively try to expose and remove corruption. In Chapter 12, I will look in some detail at the experiences of whistleblowers and at the social and psychological factors in organizations that lead them to shun and punish whistleblowers, but it is sufficient to say here that organizations often put a great deal of pressure on potential whistleblowers to keep their complaints to themselves.

The attraction-selection-attrition process tends to strengthen organizational cultures by seeking out individuals who share key beliefs and values and weeding out those who do not. Organizations with cultures that tolerate or encourage particular types of misbehavior may become increasingly entrenched through this ASA process, and the implications for misbehavior are stark. There is considerable evidence that organizations with sick or corrupt cultures will have employees who are more likely to engage in acts consistent with those cultures[1] (Lewicki, Poland, Minton, & Sheppard, 1997; Murphy, 1993; Ross & Robertson, 2000).

Cooperating in Bad Behavior: The Loyalty Trap

Misbehavior in organizations is not always, or even often, the product of malice or of a conscious decision by members of the organization to do things they believe are wrong. People who engage in abusive supervision, sexual harassment, and bullying are often acting in ways they think are consistent with the norms, culture, and values of their organization. People who steal from their organization often believe that they are justified because of the way their organization treats them. People who lie, cheat, and steal *for* their organization often do so for seemingly benign motives, in particular, a sense of loyalty.

People's loyalty to and identification with organizations can have important and substantial benefits, including increases in job satisfaction, lower turnover, and increased levels of job performance (Ashforth & Mael, 1989; Conroy, Becker, & Menges, 2017; Lee, Park, & Koo, 2015; Mathieu & Zajac, 1990; Meyer & Allen, 1997), but there are sometimes serious downsides to loyalty to and identification with organizations. In particular, loyalty to organizations can also be a significant factor in driving misbehavior (Hildreth, Gino, & Bazerman, 2016; Murphy, 1993; Naseer et al., 2020; Smith-Crowe & Warren, 2014). Research on social identification and commitment to organizations provides a useful starting point for understanding how loyalty to organizations can lead individuals to willingly join in and support corrupt acts and policies.

Organizational Identification

Ashforth and Mael (1989) define organizational identification as a perception of oneness with an organization. Identification goes beyond mere membership; when a person identifies strongly with an organization, that organization becomes a core part of his or her self-concept. Identification with organizations can have many positive outcomes, including job satisfaction, satisfaction with the organization, and organizational commitment (Ashforth & Mael, 1989), but there are potential downsides to identifying with your organization.

Dukerich, Kramer, and Parks (1998) noted that high levels of organizational identification can lead to "over-identification" in which an individual's needs become almost entirely based on organizational membership. A strong linkage of the image of the organization to one's self-image has potentially important consequences (Martin, Kish-Gephart, &Detert, 2014), particularly if the organization is engaged in or if it tolerates misbehavior. Individuals who identify strongly with an organization that encourages or tolerates misbehaviors will be strongly motivated to use rationalizations, moral disengagement, or appeals to higher loyalties to recast unethical behavior as justifiable (Ashforth & Anand, 2003).

Individuals who identify strongly with an organizations are prone toward unwavering support, in-group bias, favoritism of the organization and its members, and discrimination against groups outside of the organization (Reicher, Spears, & Haslam, 2010; Tajfel & Turner, 1986). Strong group affiliations increase willingness to forgive bad behavior and social-norm violations (Bernhard, Fehr, & Fischbacher, 2006). Thus, people judge an unethical action less harshly when an in-group member, as compared to an out-group member, is responsible. Group identification can also result in prejudice, biased behavior (e.g., Tajfel, 1982), and out-group hostility (Turner & Oakes, 1986). Furthermore, the more people identify with their groups, the more they condone and engage in out-group (vs. in-group) violence (Cohen, Montoya, & Insko, 2006).

One important consequence of strong identification with an organization is that it can motivate people to engage in unethical pro-organizational behavior (UPB), behavior intended to benefit the organization (e.g., cooking the books, destroying incriminating documents) even though it may ultimately hurt it by leading to criminal investigations, a tarnished reputation, and stakeholders losing faith (Umphress, Bingham, & Mitchell, 2010). Strongly identified employees are likely to also indirectly facilitate unethical behavior by failing to challenge or report it, covering it up, or making excuses to justify it. A strong sense of identification with the organization is often the glue that holds conspiracies to cheat customers, violate laws and regulations, and carry out wide-ranging and long-term acts of fraud and misrepresentation together, and it is often loyalty to the organization that explains the willingness of employees to cooperate in behavior that is both dishonest and destructive (Conroy, Henle, Shore, & Stelman, 2017).

Smith-Crowe and Warren (2014) proposed that organizational identification facilitates the spread of collective corruption. When corruption is ongoing in organizations, most will feel normative pressure to participate while employees who hinder corrupt behaviors are likely to be discredited and ostracized. Employees who strongly identify with their organization will feel more than normative pressure to misbehave; they are likely to internalize the belief that misbehavior is both justified and necessary, and will experience shame, guilt, or embarrassment if they do not act consistently with organizational norms. These feelings will align their thoughts and emotions with these corrupt practices, which will make it more likely that they will participate in future corruption.

Large-scale corruption in organizations is often viewed by its perpetrators as a response to competitive threats. That is the belief that "everyone does it" and that organizations who don't engage in corrupt practices put themselves in an untenable position is often used to justify fraud and corruption. Zuber (2015) suggests that employees with high levels of organizational identification are likely to perceive threats to their organization as threats to their identity and view not only the organization as a victim but themselves as well. This tendency to perceive personal victimization, even when not directly harmed, motivates employees to respond in kind with unethical behavior. Thus, the emotional power of identification may lead to unethical outcomes spreading through social networks. In particular, strong identification with an organization can lead people to act unethically for the benefit of the organization (Gino & Pierce, 2009, 2010; Wiltermuth, 2011). Individuals who act badly for the good of their organization are unlikely to view themselves or their actions as immoral (Ashforth & Anand, 2003; Benson, 1985) and are likely to tend to discount, rationalize, or justify the unethical actions of other members of their groups (Valdesolo & DeSteno, 2007).

High-Identity Organizations

People identify with all sorts of organizations, ranging from their bowling league to multinational organizations. There is a subset of organizations that can be described as "high-identity" organizations in which members view their profession or membership in the organization as an essential part of their identity and in which strong efforts are made to bond organization members together and to separate them from nonmembers. Examples include several branches of the military, paramilitary organizations (e.g., police and fire departments), and religious orders. All of these organizations use uniforms, distinctive dress, badges, and the like to identify their members, something that not only creates a strong sense of "us" among members but also creates a strong distinction between "us" and "them". Members of these organizations often show very high levels of dedication to their organization, and this dedication can be a strong force for good. Members of military and paramilitary organizations face dangers that most others shrink from, and members of religious orders deprive themselves of comforts many of us could not give up, and these behaviors are a vivid illustration of their commitment and devotion to their organization. This high level of involvement can also be a serious source of misbehavior. In particular, members of these organizations might be highly motivated to cover up wrongdoing in their organizations. Even though these organizations are devoted, in the large part, to prosocial activities, if members of these organizations believe that exposure or wrongdoing in their ranks will harm the organization, they may be willing to go to great lengths to hide this wrongdoing. Their unwillingness to allow the organization to be tainted by the bad behavior or some of its members may even make it possible for the wrongdoing to continue and even grow. Next, I describe two types of organizations that are prone to what I label the "loyalty trap"—that is, allowing their loyalty to their organization to outweigh harms their organization may perpetuate—police forces and the Catholic Church.

Police Corruption

There is evidence corruption occurs in police forces around the world; police forces in sub-Saharan Africa score highest on indices of police corruption, but there has been growing evidence of corruption on a global scale, with bribe payments being an especially common form of corruption (World Index Security and Police Index, 2016). In many respects, police corruption is almost inevitable. Because of their role in enforcing laws and regulations and the nature of the groups they interact with (e.g., accused criminals, organizations seeking to escape scrutiny or fines), law enforcement officers are more likely than most others to: (1) be in a position to abuse their authority, and (2) be offered bribes and incentives to look the other way.

BOX 10.3 NAVIGATING THE LANDSCAPE OF POLICE CORRUPTION

Corruption and misbehavior by members of law enforcement organizations can take many forms. Punch (1985, 2000) described several distinct forms of corruption and misbehavior, including

- Kickbacks—when an officer receives things for referring business to others
- Opportunistic Theft—stealing from arrestees
- Shakedowns—when an officer accepts a bribe in return for not following through with a criminal violation
- Protection of Illegal Activity—police protection of illegal activity which allows it to continue
- The Fix—undermining criminal investigations
- Flaking or Padding—planting or adding to evidence
- Extreme Violence—when markedly excessive force is used in dealing with suspects
- Sexual Harassment and Racism—disparate treatment of coworkers, suspects, members of the public on the basis of sex or race
- Drug Dealing—direct involvement in the selling or distribution of drugs

A few common threads run through this litany of offenses. First, because police have front-line responsibility for enforcing criminal law, they also have considerable opportunities to influence who gets arrested and who doesn't, what evidence is used to prosecute offenders and what evidence is ignored or covered up. Second, members of law enforcement organizations often have unique opportunities to commit crimes themselves (e.g., drug dealing, opportunistic theft). To be sure, there are often units within law enforcement agencies whose job it is to "police the police", but these groups often lack the resources, and most critically, the cooperation necessary to enforce laws that are broken by members of the law enforcement community.

As with many other topics investigated in this book, it is important to keep some perspective about police corruption. At various times, corruption can be found in many, if not most, large law enforcement agencies, but that does not mean that most police are corrupt. The "blue wall of silence" may make many police officers complicit in allowing corruption to survive in their departments, and this is almost certainly evidence of the high degree of loyalty to and identification with the organization—that is, the loyalty trap. Police officers are often under intense scrutiny; in the U.S.A., protests over the killing of Black men by police officers led to demands on the part of many politicians to defund or reform police departments. This scrutiny and criticism is likely to lead police officers to show even higher levels of identification with and loyalty to their organization ("circling the wagons" in the face of external attacks), and reform efforts may prove very difficult to carry out.

Porter's (2005) review suggested that both organizational and social factors play a significant role in police corruption. Organizational factors include organizational culture, leadership, opportunities for corruption (e.g., undercover work), and informant handling. Social factors include socialization and social culture, for social customs among officers that encourage solidarity and discourage reporting fellow officers. This last facet of police corruption, the reluctance to report crimes of fellow officers' misbehaviors, is directly relevant to the theme of this section; there is compelling evidence that this reluctance is linked to officers' loyalty to their department and their calling as law enforcement officers.

This reluctance to expose the corruption of fellow officers is sometimes referred to as the "blue wall of silence" (Albrecht, 2017; Skolnick, 2002). More than two-thirds of the police officers surveyed by Weisburd, Greenspan, Hamilton, Williams, and Bryant (2000) agreed that officers who report their colleagues' misdoings will be given the "cold shoulder" by other police officers and more than half agreed that it is not unusual for police officers to turn a blind eye to other officers' misconduct. Officers who report their colleagues' misdeeds may even have reasons to fear for their safety. The strong degree of loyalty many police officers show to their organization and to law enforcement can foster cultures of crime by demanding members' silence to others' transgressions (Graham & Keeley, 1992; Rothwell & Baldwin, 2007; Skolnick, 2002).

Two factors appear to be especially important in maintaining this blue wall of silence. First, being a law enforcement officer is an important part of many officers' identity and self-concept, and anything that tends to bring the department or the agency into disrespect is therefore an attack on this self-concept. Second, members of military and paramilitary organizations often report a strong feeling of "us vs. them". Many factors (e.g., their uniforms, the tasks they are asked to perform) separate those involved in law enforcement from the rest of society, and this separation is likely to be an important factor in maintaining this wall of silence. Reporting fellow officers' misbehavior runs the risk that the solution to these problems will fall outside of the "family", and members of these closed communities often show a preference for dealing with problems internally.

Scandal in the Catholic Church

In the last 30 years, allegations of the sexual abuse of minors by clergy in the Catholic Church have received worldwide attention (Berry, 1992: France, 2004). The scope of this crisis has been shocking to many. For example, a recent report by a grand jury in Pennsylvania details allegations and supporting evidence that implicates over 30 priests in the abuse of over 1,000 children.[2] There have been reports of sexual abuse of minors by priests and other clergy in many countries, with tens of thousands of reports of abuse, if not more, worldwide.

It is important to keep in mind that while tales of sexual abuse by clergy members get a great deal of attention in the press, sexual abuse is not a problem that is unique to the Catholic clergy. Sexual abuse rates by Catholic clergy are not higher than clergy from other religions, and if anything, are lower than comparable abuse rates for teachers or for the population in general.[3] An exhaustive review of 60 years of data conducted by the John Jay College of Criminal Justice, City University of New York (Terry, Smith, Schuth, Kelly, Vollman, & Massey, 2011) suggests that approximately 4% of Catholic priests sexually violated a minor child during the last half of the 20th century. To put this in context, during the same period, approximately 5–7% of public-school teachers engaged in similar sexually abusive behavior with their students (U.S. Department of Education, Office of the Under Secretary, 2004).

The reports of abuse have been truly horrific, but one of the most shocking aspects of this scandal has been the apparent response of the Church to this scandal. A common response of the Church, which is noted in the Pennsylvania report, is to engage in a variety of activities designed to minimize and cover up the abuse. These include transferring predator priests from parish to parish, or even country to country[4] and paying "hush money" to victims, ensuring their silence with restrictive nondisclosure agreements.[5] As an organization, the Catholic Church has been highly aggressive and relatively successful in covering up numerous instances of sexual abuse, sometimes with the assistance of public officials who receive political support from the Church, and it is only the dogged actions of grand juries, newspapers (e.g., the movie *Spotlight* tells the story of the efforts of the *Boston Globe* to investigate and publicize abuse), and commissions (e.g., the Catholic Church Commission on Child Sexual Abuse, also known as the Hussey Commission, in Ireland) that have bought forth detailed and credible information about sexual abuse by the clergy. Will (2019) notes that the scandal and the subsequent cover-up is so widespread and wide-ranging that it could constitute the greatest crime in American history.

The perpetrators of child sexual abuse are sometimes deeply troubled individuals, many of whom are themselves victims of childhood sexual abuse and/or suffer from a variety of serious mental problems.[6] This is not a way of excusing their actions, but it is notable to contrast the clergy who commit these acts of abuse with the Bishops, Cardinals and even, perhaps, Popes, who have for so many years worked to minimize and cover up these horrible offenses. There is little evidence that these senior officials of the Church are mentally deficient or victims of some sort. Rather, they are generally smart and talented individuals who engage in a variety of truly noble acts, but who have also been a willing part of a machinery of corruption and deceit that gravely undermines the moral authority of the Church. The question is why such good people consistently engage in such bad behavior.

First, it is important to keep in mind how common and widespread the instinct to cover up abuses appears to be. Efforts by the Church as an institution to minimize and cover up sexual abuse have occurred across the globe and these efforts often extend for many years. This suggests that the causes of this behavior are systemic and are not merely the result of the moral shortcomings of a few flawed individuals. In studies of misbehavior in organizations, a distinction is often made between bad apples (flawed individuals) and bad barrels (flawed organizations), and here, the problem appears to be a shortcoming of the organization rather than shortcomings of the individual Bishops, Cardinals, and the like.

In many ways, scandals in the Church resemble scandals in many police forces and departments. That is, they involve two key patterns of thinking—that is, an "us vs. them" orientation and a strong level of commitment to the organization. Being a member of the clergy is different from being an employee of some company or corporation. Clergy members are set apart from the rest of society in many ways (e.g., distinctive titles and dress) and they think of the Church as a critical part of their identity, not simply as the place where they happen to work. This level of distinctiveness, identity, and even devotion is a tremendous asset in many ways, but it can also be a genuine problem when there is a threat to the organization. When an institution of this sort is threatened, there is a strong tendency for members of this institution to "circle the wagons" and protect the institution at all costs. It is precisely because the Church is so much a part of the identity of so many of the clergy that they will be willing to do things that seem so counter to the morality that the Church preaches, such as shuffling priests from parish to parish so that their misdeeds do not catch up with them (one of the priests accused of sexual abuse in Pennsylvania was allegedly moved out of the priesthood into a job at Walt Disney World at the recommendation of the diocese[7]).

It is often said that the "cover-up is worse than the crime" (cf. Liebreich, 2019). It is unlikely in this case that this is entirely true because the crime itself is so horrible. It is important, however, to understand that the cover-up is quite *different* from the crime. Sexual abuse is often the act of an individual who may feel compelled to behave in this way and who may be influenced by his or her own experiences of abuse. This is not always the case; there are almost certainly many abusers who are cold, rational, and calculating in their abuse of children under their supervision and care. The cover-up, however, is very often the act of people in authority who mistakenly believe they are acting for the best to protect an institution that is at the core of their identity. Loyalty and identification are usually thought to be important and valuable traits, but loyalty to the institution can pull people in the direction of misbehavior that is ultimately quite destructive of the institution they so cherish.

Summary

There is a long-standing debate over the causes and explanations for misbehavior in organizations, and a significant body of research has examined two competing theories—that is, bad apples vs. bad barrels. Both explanations are partially true and misbehavior in organizations is a function of individual tendencies to misbehave *and* organizational norms, expectations, and pressures. Furthermore, organizations function within broader social contexts, and contextual factors such as national culture may be just as much to blame for some forms of misbehavior as individual or organizational factors.

The corruption of organizations or individuals within organizations is a process that unfolds over time, and that involves many of the social and psychological processes described in Chapters 3 and 4. One of the significant challenges in dealing with corruption in organizations is that the individuals who harass or bully members of their organizations, who steal from or steal for the organization, or who organize and participate in large-scale frauds and even more serious crimes (e.g., war crimes) very often believe that they have not done anything wrong. People who misbehave have strong motivations to rationalize or explain their behavior in socially acceptable ways, and organizations often facilitate this process, especially when the misbehaviors are consistent with the organization's norms and culture or when the misbehaviors are seen as necessary for the success or survival of the organization.

Loyalty to and identification with organizations can have positive outcomes for both individuals and organizations, but it can also create pressures to engage in or to cover up corruption. In law enforcement agencies, the "blue wall of silence" often frustrates attempts to expose or prosecute corruption. Members of police forces and other similar agencies often have a strong level of identification with and loyalty to their organization, and their unwillingness to expose their organization to external criticism often makes it difficult for them to oppose or expose corruption. Similarly, the scandal over sexual abuse of minors on the part of clergy has been magnified by the frequent response of church hierarchies to cover up rather than confront abuse. The loyalty of Bishops and senior clergy to their organization has often had tragic consequences for the targets of abuse, the community, and the Church itself.

Notes

1. Chapters 11 and 12 explore these two types of organizational cultures
2. www.cnn.com/2018/08/14/us/pennsylvania-catholic-church-grand-jury/index.html
3. www.psychologytoday.com/us/blog/do-the-right-thing/201003/six-myths-about-clergy-sexual-abuse-in-the-catholic-church
4. www.cbsnews.com/news/predator-priests-shuffled-around-globe/
5. www.thetimes.co.uk/article/church-pays-hush-money-to-sex-abuse-victims-bfrjkj6ccb9
6. http://victimsofcrime.org/media/reporting-on-child-sexual-abuse/statistics-on-perpetrators-of-csa; www.childabuseroyalcommission.gov.au/sites/default/files/file-list/Research%20Report%20-%20Evidence%20and%20frameworks%20for%20understanding%20perpetrators%20of%20institutional%20child%20sexual%20abuse%20-%20Causes.pdf
7. www.nydailynews.com/news/national/ny-news-catholic-priest-sex-abuse-disney-world-20180814-story.html

References

Albrecht J.F. (2017). *Police Brutality, Misconduct, and Corruption*. Springer Briefs in Criminology. Springer, Cham

Anand, V., Ashforth, B.E. & Joshi, M. (2004). Business as usual: The acceptance and perpetuation of corruption in organizations. *Academy of Management Executive, 18*, 39–53.

Andersson, L.M. & Pearson, C.M. (1999). Tit for tat? The spiraling effect of incivility in the workplace. *Academy of Management Review, 24*, 452–471.

Andreoli, N. & Lefkowitz, J. (2009). Individual and organizational antecedents of misconduct in organizations. *Journal of Business Ethics, 85*, 309–332.

Aquino, K. & Reed, A., II. (2002). The self-importance of moral identity. *Journal of Personality and Social Psychology, 83*, 1423–1440.

Ariely, D. (2012). *The (Honest) Truth about Dishonesty: How We Lie to Everyone—Especially Ourselves*. London: HarperCollins.

Ashforth, B.E. & Anand, V. (2003). The normalization of corruption in organizations. In R.M. Kramer & B.M. Staw (Eds.), *Research in Organizational Behavior: An Annual Series of Analytical Essays and Critical Reviews* (Vol. 25, pp. 1–52). Oxford, England: Elsevier Science.

Ashforth, B.E. & Mael, F. (1989). Social identity theory and the organization. *Academy of Management Review, 14*, 20–39.

Ashkanasy, N.M., Windsor, C.A. & Treviño, L.K. (2006). Bad apples in bad barrels revisited: Cognitive moral development, just world beliefs, rewards, and ethical decision-making. *Business Ethics Quarterly, 16*, 449–473.

Babiak, P. & Hare, R.D. (2007). *Snakes in Suits: When Psychopaths Go to Work*. New York: Harper Business.

Bamberger, P. & Biron, M. (2007). Group norms and excessive absenteeism: The role of peer referent others. *Organizational Behavior and Human Decision Processes, 103*, 179–196.

Bandura, A. (1986). *Social Foundations of Thought and Action: A Social Cognitive Theory*. Englewood Cliffs, NJ: Prentice-Hall.

Benson, M.L. (1985). Denying the guilty mind: Accounting for involvement in a white-collar crime. *Criminology, 23*, 583–607.

Bernhard, H., Fehr, E. & Fischbacher, U. (2006). Group affiliation and altruistic norm enforcement. *The American Economic Review, 96*, 217–221.

Berry, J. (1992). *Lead Us Not Into Temptation: Catholic Priests and the Sexual Abuse of Children*. New York: Doubleday.

Brief, A.P., Buttram, R.T. & Dukerich, J.M. (2001). Collective corruption in the corporate world: Toward a process model. In M.E. Turner (Ed.), *Groups at Work: Theory and Research* (p. 471–499). Mahwah, NJ: Lawrence Erlbaum Associates.

Brown, M.E., Treviño, L.K. & Harrison, D.A. (2005). Ethical leadership: A social learning perspective for construct development and testing. *Organizational Behavior and Human Decision Processes, 97*, 117–134.

Carr, A.Z. (1968). Is business bluffing ethical? *Harvard Business Review* (January-February), 143–153.

Cialdini, R., Li, Y.J., Samper, A. & Wellman, N. (2019). How bad apples promote bad barrels: Unethical leader behavior and the selective attrition effect. *Journal of Business Ethics*, https://doi.org/10.1007/s10551-019-04252-2

Chinball, S. & Saunders, P. (1977). Worlds apart: Notes on the social reality of corruption. *The British Journal of Sociology, 28*, 138–154.

Clinard, M.B. (1990). *Corporate Corruption: The Abuse of Power*. New York: Praeger.

Cohen, T.R., Montoya, R.M. & Insko, C.A. (2006). Group morality and intergroup relations: Cross-cultural and experimental evidence. *Personality and Social Psychology Bulletin, 32*, 1559–1572.

Conroy, S., Becker, W. & Menges, J. (2017). The meaning of my feelings depends on who I am: Work-related identifications shape emotion effects in organizations. *Academy of Management Journal, 60*, 1071–1093.

Conroy, S., Henle, C., Shore, L. & Stelman, S. (2017). Where there is light, there is dark: A review of the detrimental outcomes of organizational identification. *Journal of Organizational Behavior, 38*, 184–203.

Ditton, J. (1977). Perks, pilferage, and the fiddle: The historical structure of invisible wages. *Theory and Society, 4*, 1–38.

Dukerich, J.M., Kramer, R. & Parks, J.M. (1998). The dark side of organizational identification. In D.A. Whetten & P. Godfrey (Eds.), *Identity in Organizations: Building Theory through Conversations* (pp. 245–256). Newbury Park, CA: Sage.

Eabrasu, M. (2020). Cheating in business: A metaethical perspective. *Journal of Business Ethics, 162*, 519–532.

Einarsen, S. (1999). The nature and causes of bullying at work. *International Journal of Manpower, 20*, 16–27.

Eisenberg, N. (2000). Emotion, regulation, and moral development. *Annual Review of Psychology, 51*, 665–697.

Ethics Resource Center. (2005). *National Business Ethics Survey: How Employees Perceive Ethics at Work*. Washington, DC: Ethics Resource Center.

Ewing, J. (2017, March 16). Engineering a deception: What led to Volkswagen's diesel scandal. *New York Times*, www.nytimes.com/interactive/2017/business/volkswagen-diesel-emissions-timeline.html

France, D. (2004). *Our Fathers: The Secret Life of the Catholic Church in the Age of Scandal*. New York: Broadway Books.

Frost, A.G. & Rafilson, F.M. (1989). Overt integrity tests versus personality-based measures of delinquency: An empirical comparison. *Journal of Business and Psychology, 3*, 269–277.

Ferguson, M. & Barry, B. (2011). I know what you did: The effects of interpersonal deviance on bystanders. *Journal of Occupational Health Psychology, 16*, 80–94.

Furnham, A.J. & Taylor, J. (2011). *Bad Apples: Identify, Prevent and Manage Bad Behavior at Work*. New York: Palgrave MacMillan.

Galam, S. & Moscovici, S. (1991). Towards a theory of collective phenomena: Consensus and attitude changes in groups. *European Journal of Social Psychology, 21*, 49–74.

Gellerman, S.W. (1986). Why "good" managers make bad ethical choices. *Harvard Business Review, 64*(4), 85–90.

Giacalone, R.A., Riordan, C.A. & Rosenfeld, P. (1997). Employee sabotage: Toward a practitioner-scholar understanding. In R.A. Giacalone & J. Greenberg (Eds.), *Antisocial Behavior in Organizations* (pp. 109–129). Thousand Oaks, CA: Sage.

Gino, F. & Bazerman, M. (2009). When misconduct goes unnoticed: The acceptability of gradual erosion in others' unethical behavior. *Journal of Experimental Social Psychology, 45*, 708–719.

Gino, F. & Pierce, L. (2009). The abundance effect: Unethical behavior in the presence of wealth. *Organizational Behavior and Human Decision Processes, 109*, 142–155.

Gino, F. & Pierce, L. (2010). Lying to level the playing field: Why people may dishonestly help or hurt others to create equity. *Journal of Business Ethics, 95*, 89–103.

Gioia, D.A. (1992). Pinto fires and personal ethics: A script analysis of missed opportunities. *Journal of Business Ethics, 11*, 379–389.

Gonin, M., Palazzo, G. & Hoffrige, U. (2012). Neither bad apple nor bad barrel: How the societal context impacts unethical behavior in organizations. *Business Ethics: A European Review, 21*, 31–46.

Graham, J.W. & Keeley, M. (1992). Hirschman's loyalty construct. *Employee Responsibilities and Rights Journal, 5*, 191–200.

Granovetter, M. (1978). Threshold models of collective behavior. *The American Journal of Sociology, 83*, 1420–1443.

Greenberg, J. (1998). The cognitive geometry of employee theft: Negotiating "the line" between taking and stealing. In R.W. Griffin, A. O'Leary-Kelly, & J.M. Collins (Eds.), *Dysfunctional Behavior in Organizations: Violent and Deviant Behavior* (pp. 147–193). Stamford, CT: JAI Press.

Grover, S.L. (1993a). Lying, deceit, and subterfuge: A model of dishonesty in the workplace. *Organization Science, 4*, 478–495.

Grover, S. (1993b). Why professionals lie: The impact of professional role conflict on reporting activity. *Organizational Behavior and Human Decision Processes, 55*, 251–272.

Grover, S. (1997). Lying in organizations: Theory, research and future directions. In R.A. Giacolone & J. Greenberg (Eds.), *Antisocial Behavior in Organizations* (pp. 68–84). Thousand Oaks, CA: Sage.

Hakim, D. (2015, September 26). As Volkswagen pushed to be number one, ambitions fueled a scandal. *New York Times*, www.nytimes.com/2015/09/27/business/as-vw-pushed-to-be-no-1-ambitions-fueled-a-scandal.html?_r=0

Hales, S. (1985). The inadvertent rediscovery of self in social psychology. *Journal for the Theory of Social Behavior, 15*, 237–282.

Hegarty, W.H. & Sims, H.P. (1978). Some determinants of unethical decision behavior: An experiment. *Journal of Applied Psychology, 63*, 451–457.

Hildreth, J.A.D., Gino, F. & Bazerman M. (2016). Blind loyalty? When group loyalty makes us see evil or engage in it. *Organizational Behavior and Human Decision Processes, 132*, 16–36.

Hofstede, G. (1980). *Culture's Consequences: International Differences in Work-Related values.* Beverly Hills, CA: Sage.

Hofstede, G. (2001). *Culture's Consequences: Comparing Values, Behaviors, Institutions and Organizations Across Nations.* Thousand Oaks, CA: Sage.

Hofstede, G., Hofstede, G.J. & Minkov, M. (2010). *Cultures and Organizations: Software of the Mind.* Revised and Expanded 3rd Ed. New York: McGraw-Hill.

Keenan, J.P. (2000). Blowing the whistle on less serious forms of fraud: A study of executives and managers. *Employee Responsibilities and Rights Journal, 12*, 199–217.

Kidder, D.L. (2005). Is it 'who I am', 'what I can get away with', or 'what you've done to me'?: A multi-theory examination of employee misconduct. *Journal of Business Ethics, 57*, 389–398.

Kish-Gephart, J.J., Harrison, D.A. & Treviño, L.K. (2010). Bad apples, bad cases, and bad barrels: Meta-analytic evidence about sources of unethical decisions at work. *Journal of Applied Psychology, 95*, 1–31.

Klassen, M.L. (2007). *Bad Religion: The Psychology of Religious Misbehavior.* Lanham, MD: University Press America.

Köbis, N.C., van Prooijen, J.W., Righetti, F. & Van Lange, P.A.M. (2017). The road to bribery and corruption: Slippery slope or steep cliff? *Psychological Science, 28*, 297–306.

Lee, E.S., Park, T.Y. & Koo, B. (2015). Identifying organizational identification as a basis for attitudes and behaviors: A meta-analytic review. *Psychological Bulletin, 141*, 1049–1080.

Lewicki, R.J., Poland, T., Minton, J.W. & Sheppard, B.H. (1997). Dishonesty as deviance: A typology of workplace dishonesty and contributing factors. *Research on Negotiation in Organizations, 6*, 53–86.

Liebreich, K. (2019). *The Catholic Church has a long history of child sexual abuse and coverups.* www.washingtonpost.com/opinions/the-catholic-church-has-a-long-history-of-child-sexual-abuse-and-coverups/2019/02/18/53c1f284–3396–11e9-af5b-b51b7ff322e9_story.html?utm_term=.4c2c0c23864d

Marcus, B. & Schuler, H. (2004). Antecedents of counterproductive behavior at work: A general perspective. *Journal of Applied Psychology, 89*, 647–660.

Martin, S.R., Kish-Gephart, J.J. & Detert, J.R. (2014). Blind forces: Ethical infrastructures and moral disengagement in organizations. *Organizational Psychology Review, 4*, 295–325.

Mathieu, J.E. & Zajac, D.M. (1990). A review and meta-analysis of the antecedents, correlates, and consequences of organizational commitment. *Psychological Bulletin, 108*, 171–194.

Maza, V. (2018, September 28). What is means to hire for 'culture fit' and how to do it right. *Forbes,* www.forbes.com/sites/forbeshumanresourcescouncil/2018/09/28/what-it-means-to-hire-for-culture-fit-and-how-to-do-it-right/#5969c9aa7986

Meyer, J.P. & Allen, N.J. (1997). *Commitment in the Workplace: Theory, Research, and Application.* Thousand Oaks, CA: Sage.

Moore, M. (2013, June 20). *Riot after Chinese teachers try to stop pupils cheating.* www.telegraph.co.uk/news/worldnews/asia/china/10132391/Riot-after-Chinese-teachers-try-to-stop-pupils-cheating.html

Murphy, K.R. (1993). *Honesty in the Workplace.* Monterey, CA: Brooks/Cole.

Murphy, K.R. & Lee, S.L (1994). Does conscientiousness explain the relationship between integrity and performance? *International Journal of Selection and Assessment, 2*, 226–233.

Murphy, K.R. & Myors, B.M. (1995). Evaluating the logical critique of banding. *Human Performance, 8*, 191–201.

Naseer, S. et al. (2020). The malevolent side of organizational identification: Unraveling the impact of psychological entitlement and manipulative personality on unethical work behaviors. *Journal of Business and Psychology, 35*, 333–346.

O'Higgins, E.R.E. (2006). Corruption, underdevelopment, and extractive resource industries: Addressing the vicious cycle. *Business Ethics Quarterly, 16*, 235–254.

Ones, D.S., Viswesvaran, C. & Schmidt, F.L. (1993). Comprehensive meta-analysis of integrity test validities: Findings and implications for personnel selection and theories of job performance. *Journal of Applied Psychology, 78*, 679–703.

Pierce, L. & Snyder, J. (2008). Ethical spillovers in firms: Evidence from vehicle emissions testing. *Management Science, 54*, 1891–1903.

Pinto, J., Leanna, C.R. & Pil, F.K. (2008). Corrupt organizations or organizations of corrupt individuals? Two types of organization-level corruption. *Academy of Management Review, 33*, 685–709.

Porter, L.E. (2005). Policing the police service: Theoretical and practical contributions of psychologists to understanding and preventing corruption. In L.J. Alison (Ed.), *A Forensic Psychologist's Casebook: Psychological Profiling and Criminal Investigation* (pp. 143–169). Cullompton, Devon: Willan.

Punch, M. (1985). *Conduct Unbecoming: The social construction of police deviance and control.* London: Tavistock.

Punch, M. (2000). Police corruption and its prevention. *European Journal on Criminal Policy and Research, 8*, 301–324.

Reed, A. & Aquino, K.F. (2003). Moral identity and the expanding circle of moral regard toward out-groups. *Journal of Personality and Social Psychology, 84*, 1270–1286.

Reicher, S., Spears, R. & Haslam, S.A. (2010). The social identity approach in social psychology. In M. Wetherell & C. Mohanthy (Eds.), *The Sage Handbook of Identities* (pp. 45–62). Thousand Oaks, CA: Sage.

Robertson, D.C. & Rymon, T. (2001). Purchasing agents' deceptive behavior: A randomized response technique study. *Business Ethics Quarterly, 11*, 455–479.

Robinson, S.L. & Kraatz, M.S. (1998). Constructing the reality of normative behavior: The use of neutralization strategies by organizational deviants. In R.W. Griffin, A. O'Leary-Kelly, & J.M. Collins (Eds.), *Dysfunctional Behavior in Organizations: Non-violent Dysfunctional Behavior* (pp. 203–220). Stamford, CT: JAI Press.

Robinson, S.L. & O'Leary-Kelly, A.M. (1998). Monkey see, monkey do: The influence of workgroups on the antisocial behavior of employees. *Academy of Management Journal, 41*, 658–672.

Robinson, S.L., Wang, W. & Kiewitz, C. (2014). Coworkers behaving badly: The impact of coworker deviant behavior upon individual employees. *Annual Review of Organizational Psychology and Organizational Behavior, 1*, 123–143.

Ross, W.T. & Robertson, D.C. (2000). Lying: The impact of decision context. *Business Ethics Quarterly, 10*, 409–440.

Rothwell, G.R. & Baldwin, J.N. (2007). Ethical climate theory, whistle-blowing, and the code of silence in police agencies in the state of Georgia. *Journal of Business Ethics, 70*, 341–361.

Ryan, A.M., Schmit, M.J., Daum, D.L., Brutus, S., McCormick, S.A. & Brodke, M.H. (1997). Workplace integrity: Differences in perceptions of behaviors and situational factors. *Journal of Business and Psychology, 12*, 67–83.

Schneider, B. (1987). The people make the place. *Personnel Psychology, 40*, 437–453.

Schneider, B. (2008). The people still make the place. In D.B. Smith (Ed.), *The People Make the Place: Dynamic Linkages Between Individuals and Organizations* (pp. 267–289). New York, NY: Taylor & Francis Group/Lawrence Erlbaum Associates.

Schneider, B., Goldstein, H.W. & Smith, D.B. (1995). The ASA framework: An update. *Personnel Psychology, 48*, 747–773.

Schweitzer, M.E., Ordóñez, L. & Douma, B. (2004). Goal setting as a motivator of unethi cal behavior. *Academy of Management Journal, 47*, 422–432.

Skarlicki, D.P., Folger, R. & Tesluk, P. (1999). Personality as a moderator in the relationship between fairness and retaliation. *Academy of Management Journal, 42*, 100–108.

Skolnick, J. (2002). Corruption and the blue code of silence. *Police Practice and Research, 3*, 7–19.

Smith-Crowe, K. & Warren, D.E. (2014). The emotion-evoked collective corruption model: The role of emotion in the spread of corruption within organizations. *Organization Science, 25*, 1154–1171.

Sonnenfeld, J. & Lawrence, P.R. (1978). Why do companies succumb to price fixing? *Harvard Business Review, 56*, 145–157.

Tabuchi, H. & Ewing, J. (2017, July 27). Volkswagen to pay $14.7 billion to settle diesel claims in U.S. *New York Times*, www.nytimes.com/2016/06/28/business/volkswagen-settlement-diesel-scandal.html?module=inline

Tajfel, H. (1982). *Social Identity and Intergroup Relations*. Cambridge, UK: Cambridge University Press.

Tajfel, H. & Turner, J.C. (1979). An integrative theory of intergroup conflict. In S. Worchel & W.G. Austin (Eds.), *The Social Psychology of Intergroup Relations* (pp. 33–37). Chicago: Nelson Hall.

Tajfel, H. & Turner, J. (1986). The social identity theory of intergroup behavior. In S. Worchel & W.G. Austin (Eds.), *The Psychology of Intergroup Relations* (pp. 7–24). Chicago, IL: Nelson-Hall.

Taylor, A. (2016, April). *What Do Corrupt Firms Have in Common? Red Flags of Corruption in Organizational Culture*. Center for the Advancement of Public Integrity, Columbia Law School, www.law.columbia.edu/CAPI

Terry, K.J., Smith, M.L., Schuth, K., Kelly, J.R., Vollman, B. & Massey, C. (2011). *The Causes and Context of Sexual Abuse of Minors by Catholic Priests in the United States, 1950–2010*. Washington, DC: United States Conference of Bishops.

Treviño, L.K. (1986). Ethical decision making in organizations: A person-situation interactionist model. *Academy of Management Review, 11*, 601–617.

Treviño, L.K., Butterfield, K.D. & McCabe, D.L. (1998). The ethical context in organizations: Influences on employee attitudes and behaviors. *Business Ethics Quarterly, 8*, 447–476.

Treviño, L.K. & Youngblood, S.A. (1990). Bad apples in bad barrels: A causal analysis of ethical decision-making behavior. *Journal of Applied Psychology, 75*, 378–385.

Turner, J.C. & Oakes, P.J. (1986). The significance of the social identity concept for social psychology with reference to individualism, interactionism, and social influence. *British Journal of Social Psychology, 25*, 237–252.

Umphress, E.E., Bingham, J.B. & Mitchell, M.S. (2010). Unethical behavior in the name of the company: The moderating effect of organizational identification and positive reciprocity beliefs on unethical pro-organizational behavior. *Journal of Applied Psychology, 95*, 769–780.

U.S. Department of Education, Office of the Under Secretary. (2004). *Educator Sexual Misconduct: A Synthesis of Existing Literature*. Washington, DC.

Valdesolo, P. & DeSteno, D. (2007). Moral hypocrisy social groups and the flexibility of virtue. *Psychological Science, 18*, 689–690.

Victor, B. & Cullen, J.B. (1988). The organizational bases of ethical work climates. *Administrative Sciences Quarterly, 33*, 101–125.

Vikas, A., Ashford, B.E. & Joshi, M. (2004). Business as usual: The acceptance and perpetuation of corruption in organizations. *Academy of Management Executive, 18*, 39–53.

Volokh, E. (February 2003). The mechanisms of the slippery slope. *Harvard Law Review, 116*, 1026–1137.

Walton, D. (1992). *Slippery Slope Arguments*. New York: Oxford University Press.

Weaver, G.R. (2006). Virtue in organizations: Moral identity as a foundation for moral agency. *Organization Studies, 27*, 341–368.

Weaver, G.R., Treviño, L.K. & Agle, B.R. (2005). "Somebody I look up to": Ethical role modeling in organizations. *Organizational Dynamics, 34*, 313–330.

Weber, J. & Wasieleski, D. (2001). Investigating influences on managers' moral reasoning: The impact of context and personal and organizational factors. *Business & Society, 40*, 79–110.

Weisburd, D., Greenspan, R., Hamilton, E.E., Williams, H. & Bryant, K.A. (2000, May). *Police Attitudes Toward Abuse of Authority: Findings From a National Study*. Washington, DC: National Institute of Justice.

Will, G. (2019). *Has Catholic Church Committed Worst Crime in American History*? https://triblive.com/opinion/george-will-has-catholic-church-committed-worst-crime-in-american-history/

Wiltermuth, S.S. (2011). Cheating more when the spoils are split. *Organizational Behavior and Human Decision Processes, 115*, 157–168.

Wilermuth, S.S., Vincent, L.C. & Gino, F. (2017). Creativity in unethical behavior attenuates condemnation and breeds social contagion when transgressions seem to create little harm. *Organizational Behavior and Human Decision Processes, 139*, 106–126.

World Index Security and Police Index. (2016). *International Police Association*, Land O' Lakes, FL.

Zimbardo, P. (2007). *The Lucifer Effect: Understanding How Good People Turn Evil*. New York: Random House.

Zuber, F. (2015). Spread of unethical behavior in organizations: A dynamic social network perspective. *Journal of Business Ethics, 131*, 151–172.

Zyglidopoulos, S.C. & Fleming, O. (2009). The escalation of corruption in organizations. In C. Cooper & R. Burke (Eds.), *Research Companion to Crime and Corruption in Organizations* (pp. 104–122). Cheltenham, UK; Northampton, MA: Edward Elgar.

11

SICK ORGANIZATIONS

Organizations are often difficult and sometimes even dangerous places for many of their members. A substantial portion of the members of some organizations will witness, participate in, or be subject to bullying, harassment, abusive leadership, theft and fraud, and/or violence. Some organizations might even be life-threatening for their members; approximately 10% of deaths in the workplace are thought to be homicides (Van Fleet & Griffin, 2006). However, some organizations are almost certainly worse than others in terms of the frequency and intensity of misbehaviors. This chapter deals with organizations in which misbehavior is especially likely—what I label "sick organizations".

A sick organization is an organization in which some types of misbehaviors are widely tolerated and even encouraged. In these organizations, misbehavior is sufficiently pervasive as to represent a feature or a by-product of the organization's culture. For example, organizations whose cultures emphasize toughness or perfectionism might create a breeding ground for bullying and harassment. Organizations whose cultures emphasize winning at any cost might become hot-spots for theft or fraud. Misbehavior might not pervade the entire organization, but if deviant sub-cultures emerge and are tolerated in the organization, they may become a significant source of systematic misbehavior, even if formal organizational norms and values do not encourage those behaviors (Litzky, Eddletson, & Kidder, 2006; Parilla, Hollinger, & Clark, 1988).

This chapter deals with sick organizations; the chapter that follows will deal with corrupt organizations, in which behaviors that violate broadly accepted social norms and that have the potential to harm others not only occur but form a core part of the organization's business model. In both chapters, it is useful to keep the broader context in mind; sick organizations might be a symptom of a sick society, and corrupt organizations might similarly flourish in societies where there is a higher tolerance for corruption. For example, there is evidence linking national levels of corruption with dishonest behavior on the part of individuals (Makin, 2017); sick or corrupt societies are likely to breed sick and corrupt organizations. Thus, factors beyond the organization might influence an organization's tolerance for or involvement in particular types of misbehavior.

Sick Cultures

The central premise of this chapter is that systematic misbehavior in an organization is usually a sign that the culture of that organization tolerates, and perhaps encourages that behavior. The critical term here is "systematic". Any organization may have some members who behave badly, but many organizations make good-faith efforts to reduce or eliminate misbehaviors. Misbehavior becomes an organizational problem when it is sufficiently widespread to harm the organization, its members, or the community. Sick organizations ignore, tolerate, or encourage this misbehavior.

Robinson and O'Leary-Kelly (1998) note that two different processes can lead to the development and maintenance of an organizational culture that tolerates or encourages misbehavior. First, Social Learning Theory (Bandura, 1977, 1986) suggests that the presence of role models who exhibit antisocial behavior increases the likelihood of that behavior spreading. Members of organizations get information about what is acceptable from social groups and role models, and if they see powerful or high-status individuals misbehave, they are likely to conclude that the organization approves of this behavior. Second, the attraction-selection-attrition (ASA) process described by Schneider, Goldstein, and Smith (1995) suggests that once a sick culture is established in an organization, people with antisocial tendencies will be more likely to be attracted to that organization and members of that organization will tend to adapt to the norms that have developed in their organization. Both processes become self-sustaining as the dysfunctional culture of the organization develops and strengthens (MacLean, 2001). Strong levels of attachment to the group or organization are thought to strengthen both social learning and ASA processes, and this attachment can contribute to misbehavior.

The Role of Leaders

The senior leaders of organizations are thought to be the most powerful determinant of that organization's culture (Appelbaum & Roy-Girard, 2007). Toxic leaders can have a significant negative effect on organizational values and norms (Lipman-Blumen, 2004; Seeger, Ulmer, Novak, & Sellnow, 2005). In particular, when these leaders endorse or accept deviant behavior, their values and norms set an example for their subordinates, which ultimately helps to shape and rationalize deviant behavior in their organization (Greenberg, 1997a; Litzky, Eddleston, & Kidder, 2006; Thau, Bennett, Mitchell, & Marrs, 2009; Van Fleet & Griffin, 2006).

Burton (2002) notes that leaders often do more to create a dysfunctional culture than simply set a bad example. She cites a variety of more direct ways toxic leaders create dysfunctional cultures, for example by exhibiting threatening behaviors toward subordinates; through displays of negative emotion, verbal abuse, and bullying; by harassing subordinates; and even by physically assaulting subordinates.

Leaders often have a substantial effect on organizational cultures, but they are not necessarily the only source of sick organizational cultures. Earlier, I noted that there are important differences in national cultures that can influence misbehavior and the tolerance for misbehavior. It is also possible that misbehavior starts at the bottom without the active support of explicit approval of leaders. However, it is unlikely that misbehavior will be incorporated into the culture of an organization without the tacit approval of leaders, or at least their tacit agreement to look the other way. In Chapter 10, I described the role of the leaders of the Catholic Church in the decades-long scandal over the sexual abuse of minors by priests and other members of the clergy and noted that their loyalty to and identification with the Church was likely a significant factor in their decision to move abusive priests from one location to another and to cover up abuse. The same process is likely to occur in other organizations. Top leaders, who are often strongly identified with their organizations, may be more inclined to ignore or paper over misbehavior by organization members precisely because of their desire to maintain the organization's positive image.

A Taxonomy of Sick Cultures

There are several ways of describing organizational cultures. Balthazard, Cooke, and Potter (2006) developed a model of culture that focuses on three styles of behaviors: aggressive/defensive (e.g., competition, perfectionism), constructive (e.g., affiliation, achievement), and passive/defensive (e.g., avoidance, dependence). Two of these three behavioral styles are potentially dysfunctional, especially if the defensive aspects of these styles are dominant. For example, they describe a passive/defensive avoidance culture as one in which organizations fail to reward success but punish failure. Cultures that focus on controlling behavior, avoiding mistakes, assigning blame, or rigidly following all rules and policies have the potential to lead to poor performance, low levels of satisfaction, and low levels of commitment to organizations.

An alternative Balthazard et al. (2006) model is to develop a taxonomy that focuses on particular types of misbehavior and the organizational cultures that are most consistent with those behaviors. The range of behaviors that fall under the heading of "misbehavior in organizations" is substantial, and different types of organizational cultures encourage or lead to a tolerance for different types of misbehavior. Table 11.1 describes four types of sick cultures that might lead to particular types of misbehavior in organizations.

TABLE 11.1 Cultures of Sick Organizations

	Defining Trait	*Types of Misbehavior*
Culture of Mistreatment	Dominance	Incivility, Bullying, Sexual Harassment, Violence
Inauthentic Culture	Mendacity	Misrepresentation, Fraud
Revenge Culture	Perceived Mistreatment	Property and Production Deviance
Rigid Culture	Intolerance	Racism, Sexism, Disregard for Rules

Some organizations have cultures that tolerate or encourage the mistreatment of some of their members. Other organizations have cultures in which dishonesty is common. Other organizations have cultures in which their members believe (often correctly) that they are being systematically mistreated (e.g., low pay, poor working conditions, bad supervision) and that they are entitled to get back at the company for this mistreatment. Finally, still other organizations have a rigid culture, in which deviations from norms, rules, and customs are not tolerated and in which these norms, rules, and customs tightly control the behavior of members of the organization. Some organizations might have cultures that combine features of each of these types; an organization might be characterized by both rampant dishonest and the frequent mistreatment of some of its members, and different combinations of cultures might foster particular patterns of misbehavior.

Culture of Mistreatment

In some organizations, it is not unusual for many members of that organization to treat other members badly. This treatment might range from microaggressions (brief but recurring interactions and subtle snubs that communicate hostility or derogatory attitudes) to assault and violence. It is important at the outset to distinguish mistreatment from other behaviors in organizations that might have negative consequences for some members of the organization. The common thread that links the various types of mistreatment together is that they involve or indicate some level of hostility and that they are unwarranted. The fact that a particular behavior might have negative consequences for individuals does not necessarily make that behavior mistreatment. Suppose, for example, that you receive a very negative performance evaluation. If that evaluation is based on a fair and accurate assessment process, this negative evaluation would not represent mistreatment. Similarly, you may lose your job as the result of an economic downturn or a reversal of the company's fortune but losing your job would not necessarily represent mistreatment. Mistreatment is, by definition, unwarranted or disproportionate. Thus, if you make a small mistake and your supervisor corrects you and shows you how to do better, this is not mistreatment. If a small mistake leads to being yelled at, attacked, or heavily sanctioned, this is more likely to constitute mistreatment.

Microaggressions

A culture of mistreatment might be manifest in terms of a range of behaviors. For example, widespread microaggressions could be a sign of a culture of mistreatment. Sue, Capodilup, Torino, Bucceri, Holder, Nadal, and Esquilin (2007) studied racial microaggressions and provided a clear and simple definition of this sometimes-misunderstood concept. They noted that "racial microaggressions are brief and commonplace daily verbal, behavioral, or environmental indignities, whether intentional or unintentional, that communicate hostile, derogatory, or negative racial slights and insults toward people of color" (p. 188). Microaggressions often consist of small slights, which may be completely unintentional, but which nevertheless convey some level of hostility and derogatory attitudes. Even though individual slights might be perceived as inconsequential, microaggressions can have substantial negative effects because they are chronic rather than isolated instances of hostility. Repeated microaggressions create a negative climate, which can have substantial effects on the attitudes, health, and welfare of their targets (Ong, Burrow, Fuller-Rowell, Ja, & Sue, 2013; Solorzano, Ceja, & Yosso, 2000). In an organization in which the culture tolerates or encourages the mistreatment of some members, microaggressions of this sort might be frequent and unchallenged.

Incivility

Microaggressions are usually thought to be targeted at particular groups, and the literature on microaggression often focuses on mistreatment based on race or gender. Another possibility is that patterns of behavior that create palpable distress for many members of an organization might not be directed at specific groups. Incivility provides a good example of this category of behaviors. Incivility has been defined as "low-intensity deviant behavior[s], with ambiguous intent to harm the target, in violation of workplace norms for mutual respect. Uncivil behaviors are characteristically rude and discourteous, displaying a lack of regard for others" (Andersson & Pearson 1999, p. 457). Several studies have documented the prevalence, costs, and correlates of incivility: this research shows that targets of and witnesses to workplace incivility suffer personally and professionally and that organizations face financial and productivity loses (for recent reviews see Cortina, Kabat-Farr, Magley, & Nelson, 2017; Schilpzand, De Pater, & Erez, 2016; Yang, Caughlin, Gazica, Truxillo, & Spector, 2014).

We usually think about incivility as an ambient, unpleasant and stressful aspect of the environment that is all around us and harmful, much like air pollution. However, we can also think of forms of incivility that are used as a tactic for asserting power and dominance—that is, selective incivility. That is, acts of rudeness might be a sign of bias against particular groups, particularly when it is disproportionally targeted at members of those groups. Selective incivility is often a tactic for asserting power and control (Cortina, 2008) and it can have substantial negative effects on its targets and witnesses. For example, there is evidence that disproportionate uncivil treatment helps to account for the underrepresentation of women and members of racial and ethnic minority groups in the upper echelons of organizations (Cortina, Kabat-Farr, Leskinen, Huerta, & Magley, 2013). There is also evidence that negative interpersonal experiences, such as greater experiences of incivility for women may shape how they view the larger organizational climate, including perceptions of a sexist climate (Settles & O'Connor, 2014). However, not all research finds increased risk of incivility for stigmatized groups (see, for example, Kern & Grandey, 2009; Welbourne, Gangadharan, & Sariol, 2015), leading to important questions regarding contextual and individual moderating factors.

Harassment

The cultures of some organizations encourage or tolerate the harassment of some organization members based on demographic characteristics such as race or gender. For example, racism is depressingly common in organizations; Glassdoor's 2019 Diversity & Inclusion Study reported that over 40% of the U.S. workers surveyed had witnessed racist acts in the workplace.[1] The Equal Employment Opportunity Commission (EEOC) describes a range of workplace behaviors that can represent violations of federal law, including racial discrimination in hiring, pay, promotions, and the like, as well as behaviors that create a hostile working environment, such as racial slurs, derogatory comments on the basis of race, and displays of racially offensive symbols.[2] In the period 1997–2012, the EEOC received over 450,000 complaints of racial discrimination in the workplace.[3]

Organizations can be racist without recognizing it. For example, many organizations encourage or require "professional" behavior from their members. Gray (2019) argues that "professionalism" is implicitly a set of norms that favors the dominant group by creating standards of dress, speech, interaction, etc. that conform to the dominant (White) culture. A standard that tells members of an organization that there is one best way to behave invariably channels behavior in directions that are most consistent with the dominant culture.

Isolated racists acts do not necessarily make an organization racist. What is more critical in determining whether the culture of an organization endorses or tolerates racism is the way the organization reacts to acts of racial discrimination or harassment, particularly when these acts are carried out by those in positions of authority. Organizations that fail to act when they learn of acts of racial discrimination or harassment are likely to face increasing legal liability; organizations in which acts of racial discrimination or harassment are ignored, tolerated, or even encouraged can be thought of as showing a culture of mistreatment.

The nature of racism and racial attitudes has changed significantly over time (Augoustinos & Reynolds, 2001; Bobo, Kluegel, & Smith, 1997; Dovidio & Gaertner, 1991; see, however, Leach, 2005), making it more difficult to identify racist environments. The type of open bigotry that was acceptable in many organizations decades ago is no longer socially acceptable in most organizations, but this does not mean that racism has disappeared. Modern racism revolves around a set of beliefs that discrimination is a thing of the past and that efforts to remediate discrimination go too far and are unfair to Whites (McConahay, 1983). Individuals who subscribe to these beliefs often think of themselves as unprejudiced (McConahay, 1986), and they are likely to resist efforts to label an organizational culture built around such beliefs as racist.

Like racism, sexual harassment is widespread in organizations (Dhanani, Beus, & Joseph, 2018; Dhanani & Palme, 2019; Hulin, Fitzgerald, & Drasgow, 1996). Between 2010 and 2019, the EEOC received approximately 125,000 sexual harassment complaints, with remarkably little variation from year to year.[4] As I noted in Chapter 8, between 25 and 75% of employed women report experiencing sexual harassment in the workplace. This harassment might take many forms, including sexual coercion (sexual advances, making the conditions of employment contingent upon sexual cooperation), unwanted sexual expression (e.g., expressions of romantic or sexual interest that are unwelcome, unreciprocated, and offensive to the target; Fitzgerald, Gelfand, & Drasgow, 1995; Fitzgerald, Swan, & Magley, 1997), or gender harassment (a broad range of verbal and nonverbal behaviors not aimed at sexual cooperation but that convey insulting, hostile, and degrading attitudes about members of one gender; Fitzgerald et al., 1995). All three of these behaviors appear to be motivated by a desire to exert power over women and devalue them (Berdahl, 2007b; Cortina & Berdahl, 2008). More generally, sexual harassment is often understood as a means of protecting social status (Berdahl, 2007a, 2007b); the perpetrators of sexual harassment are more likely to be higher in status than their targets (Sojo, Wood, & Genat, 2016).

The Report of the Co-Chairs of the EEOC Select Task Force on the Study of Harassment in the Workplace (2016) analyzed harassment complaints received by the EEOC and suggested that employees and members of other organizations are harassed on the basis of a range of demographic characteristics, including sex (45%), race (34%), disabilities (19%), age (15%), national origin (13%), and religion (5%).[5] They identified several risk factors for harassment, including (1) homogeneous workforces—lack of diversity increases harassment, (2) cultural and language divides, (3) societal trends—more coarsened social discourse outside of the workplace, (4) workplace with many young workers—more junior employees are more vulnerable to harassment, (5) workplaces with high-status, high-value employees, (6) workplaces with significant power disparities, (7) workplaces that rely on customer service/satisfaction, (8) workplaces with monotonous, low-intensity tasks, (9) isolated workplaces, (10) work cultures that tolerate alcohol consumption, and (11) decentralized workplaces. They also identified specific aspects of organizational cultures that can contribute to harassment, in particular: (1) the perceived risk to those who report sexually harassing behavior, (2) a lack of sanctions against offenders, and (3) the perception that one's report of sexually harassing behavior will not be taken seriously.

There is clear evidence that organizational cultures that tolerate or support sexual harassment increase the likelihood that members of the organization will be harassed (Holmes et al., 2020; Pryor, LaVie, & Stoller, 1993). Cultures that tolerate sexual harassment make it more difficult for the targets of harassment to report their experience because they believe their complaints will not be taken seriously or that they will be subject to retaliation (Hulin, Fitzgerald, & Drasgow 1996; Offermann & Malamut 2002; Rubino et al., 2018).

Bullying and Abusive Supervision

Bullying involves the use of threats, force, verbal or physical abuse to dominate or intimidate others. It often involves chronic, repeated negative interactions. Abusive supervision involves the sustained display of verbal or nonverbal hostility, excluding physical contact, by someone in a position of authority (Tepper, 2000). Both bullying and abusive supervision involve the use of hostile and aggressive tactics to assert power and dominance. Both have significant negative consequences for individuals and organizations. Abusive supervision is associated with negative work attitudes, lower levels of personal and family well-being and performance, and lower perceptions of fairness (Martinko, Harvey, Brees, & Mackey, 2013; Schyns & Schilling, 2013; Tepper, 2007). Bullying has similar effects on work attitudes and well-being (Vartia, 2001).

Both bullying and abusive supervision are common in the workplace and similar organizations. For example, Niedhammer, David, Degioanni, Drummond, and Philip (2009) found that up to 12% of employees were exposed to workplace bullying at any point in time. As I noted in Chapter 8, almost 20% of employees report being targets of bullying in the workplace, and an equal number reported witnessing bullying (WBI Workplace Bullying Survey, 2017). Sometimes, bullying involves individuals acting alone, but bullying by groups (i.e., mobbing) is also a frequent occurrence.

Permissive organizational cultures are thought to play an important role in both bullying and abusive supervision (O'Farrell & Nordstrom, 2013). As with the other forms of mistreatment noted here, the likelihood that bullying and/or abusive supervision will become part of the culture of an organization depends largely on the organization's response. If the organization systematically ignores or condones these behaviors, they will create a culture of mistreatment in which bullying and/or abusive supervision are not only tolerated but are likely to increase in their frequency and seriousness.

Violence

Almost 20% of all violent crime occurs in the workplace (Bureau of Justice Statistics, 2013), half of all workplaces with 1,000 or more employees report incidents of violence, and more than one-third of violent episodes in the workplace take place between coworkers (Dillon, 2012). These episodes range from minor altercations to murder; homicide is cited as one of the leading causes of workplace deaths.[6] In her assessment of the causes of violence in the workplace, Dillon (2012) cites the failure of organizations to respond to violence as one of the most important factors in determining whether violent episodes will recur.

The incidence of violence in other types of organizations has not been studied as extensively as in the workplace, but it is clear that violence is common in some other organizations. In particular, authoritarian political parties often rely on violence as a means of building electoral strength and controlling their members (Shirer, 1960). Political parties are particularly likely to resort to violence when their level of support in the population is low (Fjelde, 2020).

Professional sports are often the site of violent fan behavior; football hooliganism has been a long-standing problem throughout Europe. Sometimes, violence at sporting events represents an unplanned event, but there are numerous hooligan gangs or organizations whose purpose is to sponsor and organize violent confrontations with the fans of competitors (Lowles & Nicholls, 2005).

Finally, criminal organizations often rely on violence as a means of enforcing their will and protecting their organization. Like authoritarian political parties, they might also use violence as a method of controlling their members.

Consistent Themes Across Varieties of Mistreatment

A culture of mistreatment might condone or encourage a range of different behaviors, from microaggression to homicide, but there are consistent themes across the various studies cited in this section. First, mistreatment is usually used as a means of asserting power and dominance over others. Even in cases where mistreatment might have other motivations, dominance seems to be central to understanding the behavior. For example, sexual harassment might be used to obtain sexual gratification, but it is much more likely to involve power than sex (Cleveland & Kerst, 1993; Report of the Co-Chairs of the EEOC Select Task Force on the Study of Harassment in the Workplace, 2016). Similarly, bullying might be the result of particular conflicts or animosity between particular individuals, but in most cases, it follows and reinforces power hierarchies (Juvonen & Graham, 2001, 2014).

Second, organizations have choices in dealing with mistreatment, and in many organizations, the choice is to ignore it. This can be a fateful choice because organizations that fail to respond to mistreatment are sending their members a clear message about the sorts of behaviors that are and are not acceptable. By choosing to ignore mistreatment, organizations might inadvertently increase the likelihood of future mistreatment. Mistreatment might also be the result of prevailing beliefs and norms in the organization. Hackney and Perrewé (2018) note that some organizational cultures incorporate the belief that punishments, coercive power, and aggression are useful tools for motivating people. This type of culture is particularly likely to tolerate and even encourage mistreatment.

Third, all types of mistreatment have the potential to substantially harm the targets of mistreatment, witnesses to mistreatment, and the organization itself. Mistreatment can result in significant levels of stress and lower levels of mental and physical health (Duffy, Ganster, & Pagon, 2002; Lim, Cortina, & Magley, 2008; O'Reilly, Robinson, Berdahl, & Banki, 2014). Mistreatment can contribute to negative attitudes toward organizations and to perceptions of unfairness (Chang & Lyons 2012). Employees who are themselves targets of mistreatment may even be more likely to mistreat others in the organization (Glomb & Liao 2003; Twenge, Baumeister, Tice, & Stucke, 2001).

BOX 11.1 SEXIST SCIENTISTS

If you think about where you might expect to encounter sex discrimination and sexual harassment, you will probably cite some traditionally masculine occupations, such as a firefighter or mechanic. You might be surprised to find out that sexual harassment is rampant in the sciences, engineering, and medicine (National Academies of Sciences, Engineering, and Medicine, 2018). Ilies, Hauserman, Schwochau, and Stibal's (2003) meta-analysis revealed that 58% of female academic faculty and staff experienced sexual harassment, a figure that is roughly on par with the U.S. military.

Heilman's (1983) Lack of Fit model is useful for explaining the prevalence of sexual harassment in scientific fields. Jobs like a scientist or an engineer do not necessarily involve traditionally masculine traits (e.g., physical strength), but these are highly masculine fields. For example, if you think about your mental image of a scientist or an engineer, it is likely that a male comes most readily to mind. Women do not fit our stereotype of scientist or engineer quite so readily, and that this can lead to discrimination against women, including behavior that creates a hostile environment for women, such as sexual harassment.

Four aspects of the science, engineering, and academic medicine field tend to contribute to harassment and to make it difficult for victims of harassment to file complaints: (1) the fields are still largely male-dominated; (2) scientists, engineers, and new doctors rely on advisors and mentors for career advancement; (3) the "macho" culture is present in some fields; and

(4) rumors and accusations are spread within and across specialized programs and fields via an informal communications network. Efforts to reduce sexism and sexual harassment in these fields have taken many forms, with special attention to building a better pipeline for women to enter these fields. In particular, efforts to increase young girls' interest and confidence in STEM (science, technology, engineering, and mathematics) fields and the efforts of many high-tech firms to bring more women into the technical workforce have emerged as a potential long-term solution for the prevalence of sex discrimination and sexual harassment in these fields.

Inauthentic Culture

In some organizations, there is a persistent gap between appearances and claims about the organization and its members and reality. An inauthentic culture might refer to something as simple as a gap between a widely used slogan (e.g., "People are our #1 product") and the reality of how this organization treats people. At the extreme, lying and misrepresentation might be so endemic that nothing the organization or its members says can be taken as factual. If the culture of an organization is one in which lying or misrepresentation is common and widely accepted, this might open the floodgates for a wide range of offenses and misbehaviors that involve misrepresentation (e.g., fraud, mistreatment of customers and clients).

It is important to recognize that some jobs and roles in organizations require people to misrepresent their opinions and feelings. Customer service jobs, in particular, often require "service with a smile"—that is, presenting a positive and calm image when interacting with customers and clients, even angry or impatient ones. Grandey and her colleagues have examined the consequences of organizational requirements to present a positive face to customers and clients and have used the concept of emotional labor to analyze these requirements (Grandey & Melloy, 2017; Grandey & Sayre, 2019). These studies suggest that there is an important distinction between surface acting (appearing to be calm and pleasant) vs. deep acting (changing one's mood and emotions to become more calm and pleasant in a stressful situation) and note that both of these strategies require substantial effort on the part of employees. On the whole, surface acting, which requires suppression of emotions, is more likely to have negative consequences for employee well-being (Grandey & Sayre, 2019; Totterdell & Holman, 2003), but both types of emotional labor can be stressful for employees.

In Chapter 10, I described Carr's (1968) assertion that "falsehood ceases to be falsehood when it is understood on all sides that the truth is not expected to be spoken" (p. 143). In customer service occupations, the requirement to put on a happy face should probably not be treated as a requirement to lie or mislead, because calm and positive customer service interactions are expected and required regardless of how the service provider feels. There is even evidence that smiling, even when it is a forced smile, can reduce stress (Kraft & Pressman, 2012). The requirement that customer service workers maintain a positive demeanor is so nearly universal[7] that it should probably not be taken as evidence of an inauthentic culture in an organization; an organization with an inauthentic culture is one in which lies and misleading statements are common in situations where they would usually not be expected.

Unfortunately, there are more situations in organizations where lies and misleading statements are common than we might like to admit. For example, it is thought the 30–50% of all resumes include one or more false claims about job titles, degrees, experience, accomplishments, and the like.[8] These misrepresentations cannot be attributed to the organizations that receive fraudulent resumes, but rather are likely to reflect a widespread belief that resume fraud is so widespread as to be not only acceptable but necessary. That is, if you believe that most other job applicants are presenting inflated titles or fraudulent claims regarding degrees on their resumes, you will be more likely to do the same (Murphy, 1993).

Politicians are almost uniformly regarded as dishonest, and many political organizations create or contribute to inauthentic cultures. For example, it is rare to find a national politician without a cadre of "spin doctors" whose job it is to make the news look as favorable as possible. Again, it is possible to argue that because some shading of the facts is expected of politicians, political spin might not be interpreted by its practitioners or its audience in the same way that bald-faced lies might be interpreted. There are, however, some governments and political operations that have embraced an inauthentic culture, in which propaganda and misleading communication are standard methods of operation. For example, Russia under Vladimir Putin is thought to maintain an extensive and extremely active propaganda operation aimed at bolstering his regime abroad and at home and interfering with rival governments (Muller, 2019). However, the clearest example of a culture in which lies and misrepresentation are a routine part of daily operations is presented by the administration of President Donald Trump.

President Trump's administration was so notorious for mistruth (starting with claims by the president's press secretary in the earliest days of his administration that crowds for Trump's inauguration were larger than crowds for his predecessor's inauguration, despite unmistakable photographic evidence to the contrary) that many news organizations developed full-time fact-checking operations. Fact-checkers for the *Washington Post* claim that President Trump averages 15–16 lies or substantial misstatements in his public comments per day, with the rate of deception increasing as the end of his term approached.[9] This newspaper routinely checks the public statements of politicians and government officials, awarding 1–4 Pinocchios to statements, depending on how far from the truth they are. They felt compelled to create a new category, the Bottomless Pinocchio, for demonstrably false claims that are repeated over and over again, almost exclusively by the president or members of his administration.[10] Other news outlets that are more sympathetic to President Trump suggest lower counts for lies and misleading statements, but few credible sources argue that this administration is honest within the parameters usually expected for national politicians.

We often assume that people lie for sinister reasons (e.g., to achieve a financial gain), but lying in organizational settings can serve a very different purpose. For example, in many organizations, lying is a tool used to uphold a positive image of the organization when the organization seems to be under threat (Cooper & Thatcher, 2010). Lies and misleading statements can be part of a process of constructing and maintaining shared social reality in the face of uncertainty. A culture with ambiguous attitudes toward the truth can, however, have serious negative consequences. Lying, even about the seemingly mundane issues, has been identified as a critical antecedent of organizational corruption (Ashforth & Anand, 2003).

Inauthentic Leadership

In the last 15 years, there has been a steady stream of research on authentic leadership (Avolio & Gardner, 2005; Avolio, Gardner, Walumbwa, Luthans, & May, 2004; Cooper, Scandura, & Schriesheim, 2005; Luthans & Avolio, 2003). Authentic Leadership Theory is normative rather than descriptive (Cooper et al., 2005); it describes how leaders *should* act rather than describing how they necessarily *will* act. Authentic leaders are described as: (1) being deeply aware of how they think and behave, (2) aware of the context in which they operate, (3) perceived as acting from well-developed values and moral frameworks, and (4) confident, optimistic, resilient, and of a high moral character. George (2003) describes authentic leadership in terms of a set of attributes, such as purpose, values, and self-discipline. Ibarra (2015) notes that the definition of authentic leadership is complex and different ideas of what it means to be authentic may lead to different behaviors or predictions about behavior.

Although there are different definitions of authentic leadership in the literature, two themes consistently emerge from discussions of this construct: (1) that authentic leaders are aware of their values and moral responsibilities, and (2) that they act accordingly. This suggests a way of defining the obverse of an authentic leader—that is, an inauthentic leader. Inauthentic leaders act in opposition to values or norms they purport to abide by. They may not be aware of their values or their actions; as Crandal (2007) noted, authentic leadership requires both self-knowledge (e.g., am I acting consistent with organizational values?) and self-regulation (e.g., can I control my behavior in the face of environmental pressures to act unethically?). Similarly, inauthentic organizations are run in ways that contradict proclaimed values and norms. For example, an organization's mission statement might include lofty phrases about the importance of developing its members, but it might budget only nominal amounts of time and resources to developmental activities. Similarly, almost every work organization will describe itself as an equal opportunity employer, yet many continue to use methods for selecting, promoting, and compensating employees that discriminate against women, older workers, members of ethnic and racial minority groups, etc.

Inauthentic leaders can inspire cynicism, especially if the gap between espoused values and behavior is large and obvious. They also fail to inspire trust, especially when leaders are seen as acting from self-interest rather than acting in the interest of the organization (Bass & Bass, 2008). Cynicism and distrust can have corrosive effects in organizations; both breed disrespect for organizational norms and espoused values, rules, and regulations, which can in turn increase the likelihood of misbehavior.

Impression Management

There are many settings, such as job interviews and performance evaluations, where people make a concerted effort to make a good impression (Peck & Levashina, 2017). In some organizations, the task of creating a positive impression is not limited to interviews and the like, but rather is a frequent activity, with many members working hard to convey a particular image, regardless of whether this image is an authentic one (Tedeschi & Melburg, 1984). Organization members might use a range of tactics, including strategic self-presentation, ingratiation, attraction, and liking to manage the impression they make on others.

There are many reasons people manage impressions, including (1) to take credit and avoid blame, (2) to maintain a positive self-image, (3) to gain power and influence, and (4) to accomplish important goals (Tedeschi & Reiss, 1981). Impression management (IM) can take several different forms and can be tactical (short term), strategic (long term), assertive (initiated by the actor), or defensive (used by the actor to respond to an undesired image; Tedeschi & Melburg, 1984). IM can even be used to minimize threats; Gove, Hughes, and Geerken (1980) discuss the strategy of "playing dumb" to avoid presenting a threat or to avoid blame.

Impression management (IM) is not always deceptive (Bolino, Long, & Turnley, 2016); something as simple as making sure other members of your organization know about your contributions to important projects might be thought of as IM. However, IM often has a slightly distasteful connotation because it often represents a combination of boasting (self-presentation) and sucking up (ingratiation). IM can even undermine otherwise positive behaviors. It is likely, for example, that many prosocial behaviors in organizations (e.g., helping others) represent efforts to manage impressions rather than sincere efforts to help. One hallmark of an inauthentic culture is the widespread use of impression management (Bolino, Long, & Turnley, 2016; Klotz, He, Yam, Bolino, Wei, & Houston, 2018; Leary & Kowalski, 1990).

Klotz et al. (2018) argue that constantly managing impressions can have several negative effects. IM requires constant effort (much like emotional labor) and it can be draining. The stress and effort required to constantly manage impressions can deplete people's cognitive resources, making them more prone to mistakes and even to misbehavior.

Consequences of an Inauthentic Culture

A culture in which lies and misrepresentation are tolerated and even expected is likely to have two detrimental effects on organizations. First, it will encourage cynicism and mistrust. Statements the organization makes about its goals and values are likely to be ignored if the behavior of the organization is inconsistent with those goals. Communications among members of the organization are likely to be difficult and guarded because the possibility of ulterior motives cannot be easily dismissed.

There are specific forms of misbehavior that are likely to be associated with inauthentic cultures. For example, a culture in which it is common for people to strategically misrepresent facts or events is likely to promote similar behaviors when members of the organization interact with customers, clients, or other organizations. That is, if the bar for honesty is set low within an organization, it is reasonable to believe that this will affect interactions with people outside of the organization.

Earlier, I noted that resume fraud is quite common. People routinely claim credit for degrees they never completed and inflate their job titles and descriptions of job responsibilities. One explanation for this finding is that many job applicants expect *other* applicants to inflate their resumes and believe that they cannot compete with a bit of embellishment. The same phenomenon is likely to occur at an organization level. If organization members believe that many others in their organization shade the truth, present a false image of competence and accomplishment, and ignore the stated values of the organization when making key decisions, they are more likely to engage in similar behaviors. This, like a culture of mistreatment, an inauthentic culture can create a self-reinforcing cycle in which one misrepresentation begets many others.

Revenge Culture

Organizations in which: (1) people believe they are being treated badly or unfairly and (2) they believe they have no effective means for protesting or changing that unfair treatment, can develop a culture in which members feel justified in getting back at the organization—that is, a revenge culture. In a revenge culture, members of an organization are likely to feel justified in doing things that harm or embarrass the organization and will often see revenge as the only effective way to restore a feeling of equity.

There is clear evidence that organizations that create difficult or stressful environments for their members are likely to see an uptick in misbehavior (Fox, Spector, & Miles, 2001), particularly misbehavior directed toward the organization (e.g., theft, sabotage, badmouthing the organization; O'Leary-Kelly, Griffin, & Glew, 1996). This effect is magnified when people believe they are being treated unfairly (Cohen-Charash & Mueller, 2007; Folger & Cropanzano, 1998). While stress and injustice are important factors in misbehavior in organizations, these factors alone might not be sufficient to create a revenge culture. The second critical factor is the lack of an effective means of correcting the injustice. Members of an organization who feel they have been mistreated, but who also believe have some effective means of correcting that injustice may not feel a need to resort to revenge, but if there is no effective means of protesting and reversing injustices, they may be motivated to take things into their own hands.

A revenge culture is different from many other organizational cultures in the sense that it is usually a bottom-up rather than a top-down phenomenon. That is, a revenge culture is one in which members of an organization who lack the power to respond directly to unfair treatment develop a norm that supports or at least tolerates an indirect response, such as theft or sabotage (Homans, 1961). That is, in a situation where members of an organization cannot respond effectively through regular channels to unfair treatment, they may develop the norm that the appropriate response to this treatment is to get back at the organization by harming it in some way.

A recurring finding in studies of employee theft and sabotage is that employees who believe they are being treated unfairly often resort to tactics such as sabotage (e.g., destruction of property of machinery, slowing down or interfering with production) or theft to get back at the organization (Giacalone & Rosenfeld, 1987; Greenberg, 1997b, 1998; Henry & Mars, 1978; Skarlicki & Folger, 1997). Revenge is not the only motive for these behaviors (Giacalone & Rosenfeld, 1987), but if revenge is incorporated into the culture of an organization, it can be an important explanation for theft, sabotage, and other acts of organizational revenge.

BOX 11.2 WANT TO PREVENT THEFT? MAKE IT BORING

Latham (2001) described a study of employee theft in a sawmill. Employees described many reasons for stealing, including the thrill of the theft and the prestige they were accorded for successfully getting something out of the sawmill, even if it was something they could not possibly use or sell. When asked how they would respond if security cameras were installed, they replied that the cameras would only make the theft that much more thrilling and that in the end they would steal the cameras as well.

Latham (2001) proposed an intervention that would take the thrill out of employee theft. The company created a "library" system where employees could check out parts or supplies, along with an "amnesty day", when employees could return anything they had taken, no questions asked. Latham (2001) reported that "theft dropped to zero immediately and has remained inconsequential . . . for three years subsequent to the intervention" (p. 714).

Many years ago, I had the opportunity to collaborate with one of the leading experts on counterterrorism, Dr. John Horgan. One of the proposals we developed to reduce terrorism was to use the *realistic job preview* (Phillips, 1998). John Horgan devoted a significant portion of his career interviewing former terrorists, and one of the recurring themes is that terrorism is not a thrilling enterprise. Most terrorists spend most of their time hanging around in dingy locations waiting for orders or information, and few are ever involved in operational activities. We proposed developing a series of media presentations aimed at prospective recruits to terrorist groups showing them just how uneventful and boring the work was. Many agencies expressed interest, but we were never able to put this program to the test.

Taking the thrill out of misbehavior is an under-appreciated strategy for prevention. Many grocery stores have placed a display or a box near the part of the store where they sell fresh fruit that provides samples or pieces of fruit for anyone to take. There are many reasons for creating a "fruit for all" box, but one is that it reduces the temptation to steal, and this box might result in less unpaid-for fruit going out of the store.

In the last 50 years, there has been a steady stream of research on the social construction of employee theft and sabotage (Altheide, Adler, Alder, & Altheide, 1978; Henry & Mars, 1978; Hollinger & Clark, 1983; Mars, 1973, 1994; Greenberg, 1990, 1993, 1997a, 1997b, 1998, 2002). This research suggests that there are many possible explanations for theft and other acts that are intended to harm organizations. For example, Kemper (1966) suggested a "reciprocal deviance" hypothesis, arguing that if an organization does not follow its own rules and does not uphold its obligations, members of the organization are likely to feel that they do not need to follow rules or uphold obligations either. Mars (1973; see also Henry & Mars, 1978) suggests that elaborate and well-defined norms often develop in organizations that specify what types of misbehaviors will be tolerated by the organization. Thus, in a bakery, taking an occasional loaf of bread home at the end of the shift might be thought of as normal and right, whereas grabbing a dozen loaves on the way out might be regarded by the bakery and its employees as unjustifiable theft.

Greenberg (1997b) developed a STEAL framework to capture a complex set of potential motives for employee theft, depending on whether the actor's motive is prosocial or antisocial and on whether the target is the organization or coworkers. Thus, we might have prosocial motives that involve *support* (stealing is consistent with workgroup norms) or *approval* (it is consistent with supervisor norms or supervisor behavior) for theft. Antisocial norms might involve *evening* the score (getting back at the organization) or *thwarting* other members of the organization (e.g., stealing to harm other organization members, purposefully violating group norms to demonstrate that they do not control your behavior).

The notion of finding a way to even the score is central to a revenge culture. Adams' (1965) Equity Theory is often cited to explain the notion of revenge as a response to injustice. Imagine, for example, that you are (or you believe you are) underpaid. Equity Theory suggests that there are two ways a person might respond to being underpaid: (1) by increasing outcomes—negotiating for better pay, or (2) reducing inputs—working less. Applying this theory to organizational injustice, suppose an organization hurts you in some way. If you do not have an effective way of correcting this injustice, you might be able to restore some feeling of equity by hurting the organization back.

In Chapter 8, I discussed the psychological contract between organizations and their members—that is, the mutually understood set of duties and obligations that define the relationship between organizations and their members. The simplest version of such a contract is "A fair day's work for a fair day's pay", but these contracts often evolve to include a complex set of norms and expectations. Violation of the psychological contract occurs when one party defaults on their obligations to the other, which results in "a specific form of distributive justice that may have unique and intense attitudinal, behavioral, and emotional reactions for the parties involved" (Robinson, 1995; pp. 94–95). In addition to creating feelings of distributive injustice, violations of the psychological contract also produce feelings of procedural injustice (Robinson & Morrison, 1995).

The feelings of injustice following violations of the psychological contract are central to a revenge culture because this sense of violation is precisely what leads members to want to "even the score" with the organization (Greenberg, 1990, 1997b; Robinson & Bennett, 1997; Sieh, 1987, Szwajkowski, 1989; Tucker, 1989). There is strong empirical evidence that the failure of organizations to live up to obligations or the unfair treatment of employees has been linked to deviance targeting the organization (Bies, Tripp, & Kramer, 1997; Kemper, 1966; Lewicki, Poland, Minton, & Sheppard, 1997; O'Leary-Kelly, et al., 1996; Szwajkowski, 1989). Similarly, there is a robust relationship between distributive and procedural justice perceptions and a wide range of deviant work behaviors, including property deviance (e.g., theft and sabotage, Giacalone & Rosenfeld, 1987; Greenberg,

1990, 1997b; O'Bannon, Goldinger, & Appleby, 1989; Mars, 1994; Taylor & Walton, 1971) and production deviance (e.g., absenteeism and production slowdowns; Adams, 1965; Dailey & Kirk, 1992; Dittrich & Carrell, 1979; Hollinger, Slora, & Terris, 1992).

Revenge serves many purposes in organizations. For example, dissatisfied employees may behave in ways that harm organizations to counteract negative feelings associated with dissatisfaction (Lehman & Simpson, 1992; Locke, 1976). Thus, dissatisfied employees are more liable to steal from their employers (Cherrington & Cherrington, 1985; Hollinger & Clark, 1983), use drugs and alcohol at work (Hollinger, 1988; Mangione & Quinn, 1975), engage in higher levels of counterproductive behavior (Gottfredson & Holland, 1990; Guinn, 1983; Mangione & Quinn, 1975; Moretti, 1986), and exhibit increased absenteeism and turnover intentions (Locke, 1976).

Finally, it is important to distinguish between individual acts of retribution and a broad culture that supports and encourages revenge. The hallmark of a revenge culture is broad social approval for, and even admiration for people who get back at their organization. Latham (2001) described a set of interventions used to reduce employee theft at a sawmill. One of his observations was that particularly daring thefts won respect and admiration from one's coworkers. If the norms of coworkers or fellow members of the organization support and justify theft, sabotage or other acts that harm the organization, it may be very difficult to suppress misbehaviors directed at the organization.

Rigid Culture

A rigid culture is one that places extensive and strict limitations on the range of behaviors that are tolerated; the watchword of a rigid culture is "my way or the highway". This culture might take several forms, some of which might not, on the surface, appear to be dysfunctional. For example, an organization might have a culture that places a strong emphasis on high standards, perfectionism, and the like. An organizational culture that insists on "one best way" can have surprisingly negative consequences.

Suppose the culture of your organization revolves around a fairly rigid and narrow set of behavioral expectations and shows a low tolerance for deviations from those expectations. Earlier, I described how a culture with a strong focus on "professionalism" could inadvertently foster both racism and sexism because the norms of dress, speech, interaction, time management, etc. that define "professionalism" are essentially White, upper-class male norms (Gray, 2019). In an organization with strong norms of "professionalism", people who do not follow these norms precisely are labeled as deviant and strongly criticized. More generally, a rigid culture sets very narrow and sometimes arbitrary rules about the behaviors that will or will not be tolerated and deals harshly with deviations from these rigid specifications. Consider, for example, the "tan suit" controversy during the second term of Barrack Obama's presidency, which was mentioned in Chapter 3.

On August 28, 2014, Barrack Obama held a White House news conference that discussed military responses to the Islamic State of Syria, a Jihadist group in the Middle East. In contrast to the dark suits he and other Presidents usually wore at events of this sort, he showed up wearing a well-tailored tan suit to that briefing. Cable news and Republican politicians were up in arms, accusing the president of showing a lack of seriousness (Farzan, 2019). The fury of his political opponents over this seeming breach of decorum, even though several previous presidents had worn similar suits, is hard to interpret in terms that do not at least partially involve race. That is, a Black president arguably has a narrower range of acceptable behaviors than his White counterparts were likely to be afforded. At a minimum, the harsh reaction to this seemingly trivial departure from expectations was certainly a reflection of the strong political polarization in the country; Obama's political opponents were poised to jump on the most trivial misbehavior.

It is useful to contrast a rigid culture, with its emphasis on perfection, one best way, and a low tolerance for even trivial deviations from norms (e.g., tan vs. dark suits) with cosmopolitan and multicultural responses to differences in norms, customs, and traditions. Organizations face a range of choices when determining how to deal with diversity in cultures and traditions. They might suppress diversity, insisting that all members of the organization conform to a strict and well-defined set of possible behaviors. They might be indifferent to diversity of this sort. They might search for ways to accommodate these differences. If a rigid organizational culture defines one end of this continuum of responses, the opposite end can probably be best defined in terms of multiculturalism.

Multiculturalism is a term that has a range of possible interpretations, from the simply descriptive (e.g., multiple cultural groups live within a particular state) to prescriptive (e.g., all cultures and ways of life are equally valuable), and it is not always clear precisely which version of multiculturalism people have in mind when they use this term (Bachvarova, 2014; Kymlicka, 1995; Song, 2005). If posed as a contrast to a rigid culture that insists that there is only one acceptable way of acting, interacting, etc., a multicultural culture is one that accepts and potentially values diversity in beliefs, traditions, and identities. An organization with a cosmopolitan or multicultural orientation would embrace the notion that there are multiple patterns of behavior that might be appropriate in a particular situation, and no one pattern is always superior.

There are both advantages and disadvantages to the contrasting strategies for dealing with diversity—that is, suppressing diversity vs. celebrating diversity (Bachvarova, 2014; Barry, 2001), and a case can be made that an extremely loose culture, where there are no core norms, beliefs, or traditions could be just as problematic as an extremely tight culture. Gelfand (2018; see also Gelfand et al. 2011) has explored the implications of tight vs. loose national cultures and has argued that tight cultures (characterized by more restrictive norms and lower tolerance for violation of those norms) can help nations cope with threats, such as natural disasters. Morley, Murphy, Cleveland, Heraty, and McCarthy (2021) have applied the concept of cultural tightness to studying human resource practices in multinational organizations, and have argued that organizations operating in tight cultures have less freedom in choosing among human resource practices if some of those practices conflict with broad cultural norms (e.g., using peer assessments to evaluate employees in a country with a culture that emphasizes hierarchy and authority).

While tight cultures might help nations cope with external threats, an overly tight organizational culture can increase the probability of certain types of misbehavior. Earlier, I mentioned the potential link between a strict "professional" culture and the emergence of racism and sexism. The norms and standards that define "professionalism" are very likely to mirror those of the dominant group (often, White males), and a culture that labels even small (e.g., tan suit) violations of these norms and standards as unprofessional is setting up a situation in which women and members of racial and ethnic minority groups are likely to be dismissed as failing to abide by professional standards, even when their behavior involves what appear to be trivial deviations from the narrow norms of permissible behavior. For example, I once had a colleague who failed in a job interview with a Fortune 500 organization. One piece of feedback he received was that he was rejected because he wore brown shoes to the interview in what was a decidedly black-shoe firm.

In addition to creating conditions that are amenable to sexist and racist behavior, rigid cultures might lead to an erosion in perceptions of legitimate power, particularly if the restrictions of behavior that are imposed are seen as arbitrary. One of the foundations of legitimate power is that it is not absolute but rather exists within a system of bounds and constraints that make it acceptable to society and therefore legitimate (Bressman, 2003).

If a rigid culture extends beyond the bounds of what would normally be considered the prerogatives of managers or leaders (e.g., by attempting to control behaviors that are not linked to the legitimate goals of the organization), leadership can devolve into dominance, and while members of an organization might be coerced into going along with arbitrary standards and expectations, their respect for the *right* of leaders to impose these standards, as opposed to their ability to coerce organization members into obedience, is likely to erode.

Rigid cultures can lead to increased levels of racism and sexism, especially if narrowly male, White, and upper-class standards are held up as the only acceptable sets of behavior. This is not, however, the only risk associated with a rigid culture. A culture that is so rigid that it creates and enforces arbitrary rules and regulations that are not relevant to the purpose of the organization undermines legitimate authority. Once some rules are viewed as arbitrary and therefore not worthy of respect, all rules might come under similar scrutiny. This delegitimization of rules and norms has the potential to create conditions that support virtually any type of rule-breaking, especially in situations where coercive enforcement of rules is difficult. Cultures that try to tightly control members of an organization tend to engender resistance and rebellion, and if an organization's culture attempts to over-regulate the behaviors, the viability of the organization can be fatally undermined.

Summary

This chapter deals with organizations in which particular types of misbehavior are tolerated, and sometimes even encouraged. Four particular types of organizational cultures are described, each of which is likely to lead to an increase in a characteristic set of misbehaviors. Cultures of mistreatment encourage incivility, bullying, harassment, and aggression, all of which can be thought of as tactics for asserting dominance. Organizations with a culture of mistreatment tend to respond to these misbehaviors by ignoring, minimizing, or condoning them.

Inauthentic cultures tolerate or encourage lying and misrepresentation. One of the hallmarks of this culture is that it can become difficult to accept anything a person says or does at its face value. In an inauthentic organization, members might devote considerable time and effort to managing impressions and to presenting false fronts, and as a result, these cultures can breed fraud, misrepresentation, and mistrust.

Organizations in which members believe that have been treated unfairly and that they lack any effective means of addressing or reversing this mistreatment are likely to develop a revenge culture, in which there is broad social support for behaviors that harm the organization (e.g., property and production deviance, badmouthing the organization). The central theme of revenge cultures is the need to restore equity. Thus, if an organization harms you, you might feel compelled to return harm for harm.

Finally, rigid cultures create wide-ranging sets of expectations, rules, regulations, and norms that tightly control the behavior of their members. Tight control, especially in areas that appear to have little to do with the mission of the organization, is likely to be resented and likely to motivate resistance. The characteristic misbehaviors associated with tight cultures include racism and sexism. The rules and norms of these organizations almost invariably reflect the preferences and experiences of a narrow group of leaders, in most case, upper-class White males, and if the only pattern of behavior that is accepted in one that is comfortable and familiar for this group, other groups in the organization (e.g., women, members of minority groups) are likely to be marginalized. If taken too far, cultural rigidity has the potential to undermine the legitimacy of the organization and its rules.

These four cultures are not necessarily the only ones that might encourage or tolerate misbehavior, and some organizations might show a mix of several of these cultures or a different pattern of norms and expectations that leads to tolerance for specific types of misbehavior. This taxonomy described four variations of organizational culture that are frequently discussed in studies of misbehavior in organizations and should be thought of as a starting point for understanding how organizations might become hotbeds for misbehavior rather than as a definitive taxonomy.

Notes

1. Glassdoor is a leading recruitment firm. This survey can be accessed at https://about-content.glassdoor.com//app/uploads/sites/2/2019/10/Glassdoor-Diversity-Survey-Supplement-1.pdf
2. www.eeoc.gov/racecolor-discrimination
3. www.eeoc.gov/enforcement/race-based-charges-charges-filed-eeoc-fy-1997-fy-2019
4. www.eeoc.gov/enforcement/charges-alleging-sex-based-harassment-charges-filed-eeoc-fy-2010-fy-2019
5. These figures sum to more than 100% because many complaints include charges of multiple types of harassment
6. www.osha.gov/SLTC/workplaceviolence/
7. The bar and restaurant chain Dick's Last Resort turns this requirement on its head. The wait staff are trained to playfully insult their guests and project an air of surly indifference
8. www.lawcrossing.com/article/1599/Honesty-is-the-best-policy-for-resumes-too/
9. www.washingtonpost.com/politics/2020/06/01/president-trump-made-19127-false-or-misleading-claims-1226-days/
10. www.washingtonpost.com/politics/2018/12/10/meet-bottomless-pinocchio-new-rating-false-claim-repeated-over-over-again/

References

Altheide, D.L., Adler, P.A., Alder, P. & Altheide, D.A. (1978). The social meanings of employee theft. In J.M. Johnson & J.D. Douglas (Eds.), *Crime at the Top: Deviance in Business and the Professions*. Philadelphia: J.B. Lippincott.

Andersson, L.M. & Pearson, C.M. (1999). Effect of tit for tat? The spiraling in the workplace incivility. *Academy of Management Review*, *24*, 452–471.

Appelbaum, S.H. & Roy-Girard, D. (2007). Toxins in the workplace: Affect on organizations and employees. *Corporate Governance*, 7, 17–28.

Adams, J.S. (1965). Inequity in social exchange. *Advances in Experimental Social Psychology*, *2*, 267–299.

Ashforth, B.E. & Anand, V. (2003). The normalization of corruption in organizations. In R.M. Kramer & B.M. Staw (Eds.), *Research in Organizational Behavior: An Annual Series of Analytical Essays and Critical Reviews* (Vol. 25, pp. 1–52). Oxford, England: Elsevier Science.

Augoustinos, M. & Reynolds, K.J. (2001). *The Changing Nature of Racism: From Old to New*. London: Sage.

Avolio, B.J. & Gardner, W.L. (2005). Authentic leadership development: Getting to the root of positive forms of leadership. *The Leadership Quarterly*, *16*(3).

Avolio, B.J., Gardner, W.L., Walumbwa, F.O., Luthans, F. & May, D.R. (2004). Unlocking the mask: A look at the process by which authentic leaders impact follower attitudes and behavior. *The Leadership Quarterly*, *15*, 801–823.

Bachvarova, M. (2014). Multicultural accommodation and the ideal of non-domination. *Critical Review of International Social and Political Philosophy, 17*, 652–673.

Balthazard, P.A., Cooke, R.A. & Potter, R.E. (2006). Dysfunctional culture, dysfunctional organization: Capturing the behavioral norms that form organizational culture and drive performance. *Journal of Managerial Psychology, 21*, 709–732.

Bandura, A. (1977). *Social Learning Theory*. Englewood Cliffs, NJ: Prentice-Hall.

Bandura, A. (1986). *Social Foundations of Thought and Action: A Social Cognitive Theory*. Englewood Cliffs, NJ: Prentice-Hall.

Barry, B. (2001). *Culture and Equality: An Egalitarian Critique of Multiculturalism*. Cambridge, MA: Harvard.

Bass, B.M. & Bass, R. (2008). *The Bass Handbook of Leadership* (4th Ed.). New York: Free Press.

Berdahl, J.L. (2007a). Harassment based on sex: Protecting social status in the context of gender hierarchy. *Academy of Management Review, 32*, 641–658.

Berdahl, J.L. (2007b). The sexual harassment of uppity women. *Journal of Applied Psychology, 92*, 425–437.

Bies, R.J., Tripp, T.M. & Kramer, R.M. (1997). At the breaking point: Cognitive and social dynamics of revenge in organizations. In R. Giacalone & J. Greenberg (Eds.), *Antisocial behavior in organizations* (pp. 18–36). Thousand Oaks, CA: Sage.

Bobo, L., Kluegel, J.R. & Smith, R.A. (1997). Laissez-faire racism: The crystallization of a kinder, gentler, antiblack ideology. In S.A. Tuch & J.K. Martin (Eds.), *Racial Attitudes in the 1990s: Continuity and Change* (pp. 15–41). Westport, CT: Praeger.

Bolino, M., Long, D. & Turnley, W.H. (2016). Impression management in organizations: Critical questions, answers, and areas for future research. *Annual Review of Organizational Psychology and Organizational Behavior, 3*, 377–406.

Bressman, J. (2003). Beyond accountability: Arbitrariness and legitimacy in the administrative state. *New York Law Review, 78*, 461–556.

Bureau of Justice Statistics. (2013). Workplace Violence Against Government Employees, 1994–2011, NCJ 241349. Washington, DC: United States Department of Justice. Office of Justice Programs. Bureau of Justice Statistics.

Burton, J. (2002). The leadership factor: Management practices can make employees sick. *Accident Prevention* (January–February), 22–26.

Carr, A.Z. (1968). Is business bluffing ethical? *Harvard Business Review* (January–February), 143–153.

Chang, C.H. & Lyons, B.J. (2012). Not all aggressions are created equal: A multi-foci approach to workplace aggression. *Journal of Occupational Health Psychology, 17*, 79–92.

Cherrington, D.J. & Cherrington, J.O. (1985). The climate of honesty in retail stores. In W. Terris (Ed.) *Employee Theft: Research, Theory, and Applications* (pp. 3–16). Park Ridge, IL: London House Press.

Cleveland, J.N. & Kerst, M.E. (1993). Sexual harassment and perceptions of power: An under-articulated relationship. *Journal of Vocational Behavior, 42*(1), 49–67.

Cohen-Charash, Y. & Mueller, J.S. (2007). Does perceived unfairness exacerbate or mitigate interpersonal counterproductive work behaviors related to envy? *Journal of Applied Psychology, 92*, 666–680.

Cooper, C., Scandura, T.A. & Schriesheim, C.A. (2005). Looking forward but learning from our past: Potential challenges to developing authentic leadership theory and authentic leaders. *Leadership Quarterly, 16*, 475–493.

Cooper, D. & Thatcher, S.M. (2010). Identification in organizations: The role of self-concept orientations and identification motives. *Academy of Management Review, 35*, 516–538.

Cortina, L.M. (2008). Unseen injustice: Incivility as modern discrimination in organizations. *Academy of Management Review, 33*, 55–75.

Cortina, L.M. & Berdahl, J.L. (2008). Sexual harassment in organizations: A decade of research in review. In J. Barling & C.L. Cooper (Eds.), *The Sage Handbook of Organizational Behavior: Volume 1 Micro Approaches* (pp. 469–497). London: Sage.

Cortina, L.M., Kabat-Farr, D., Leskinen, E.A., Huerta, M. & Magley, V.J. (2013). Selective incivility as modern discrimination in organizations: Evidence and impact. *Journal of Management, 39*, 1579–1605.

Cortina, L.M., Kabat-Farr, D., Magley, V.J. & Nelson, K. (2017). Researching rudeness: The past, present, and future of the science of incivility. *Journal of Occupational Health Psychology, 22*, 299–313.

Crandall, D. (2007). *Leadership Lessons from West Point.* San Francisco: Jossey Bass.

Dailey, R.C. & Kirk, D.J. (1992). Distributive and procedural justice as antecedents of job dissatisfaction and intent to turnover. *Human Relations, 45*, 305–317.

Dhanani, L.Y., Beus, J.M. & Joseph, D.L. (2018). Workplace discrimination: A meta-analytic extension, critique, and future research agenda. *Personnel Psychology, 71*(2), 147–179.

Dhanani, L.Y. & LaPalme, M.L. (2019). It's not personal: A review and theoretical integration of research on vicarious workplace mistreatment. *Journal of Management, 45*(6), 2322–2351.

Dillon, B.L. (2012). Workplace violence: Impact, causes, and prevention. *Work: Journal of Prevention, Assessment & Rehabilitation, 42*, 15–20.

Dittrich, J.E. & Carrell, M.R. (1979). Organizational equity perceptions, employee job satisfaction, and departmental absence and turnover rates. *Organizational Behavior and Human Performance, 24*, 29–40.

Dovidio. J.F. & Gaertner, S.L. (1991). Changes in the expression and assessment of racial prejudice. In H.J. Knopke, R.J. Norrell, & R.W. Rogers (Eds.), *Opening Doors: Perspectives on Race Relations in Contemporary America* (pp. 119–148). Tuscaloosa, AL: The University of Alabama Press.

Duffy, M.K., Ganster, D.C. & Pagon, M. (2002). Social undermining in the workplace. *Academy of Management Journal, 45*, 331–351.

Farzan, A.N. (2019, August 28). Five years ago, Obama was blasted for wearing a tan suit. Now, it's used to contrast him with Trump. *Washington Post*, www.washingtonpost.com/nation/2019/08/28/tan-suit-scandal-obama-trump/

Fitzgerald, L.F., Gelfand, M.J. & Drasgow, F. (1995). Measuring sexual harassment: Theoretical and psychometric advances. *Basic and Applied Social Psychology, 17*, 425–445.

Fitzgerald, L.F., Swan, S. & Magley, V. (1997). But was it really sexual harassment?: Legal, behavioral, and psychological definitions of the workplace victimization of women. In W.T. O'Donohue (Ed.), *Sexual Harassment: Theory, Research, and Treatment.* New York: Pearson.

Fjelde, H. (2020). Political party strength and electoral violence. *Journal of Peace Research, 57*, 140–155.

Folger, R. & Cropanzano, R. (1998). *Organizational Justice and Human Resource Management.* Thousand Oaks, CA: Sage.

Fox, S., Spector, P.E. & Miles, D. (2001). Counterproductive work behavior (CWB) in response to job stressors and organizational justice: Some mediator and moderator tests for autonomy and emotions. *Journal of Vocational Behavior, 59*, 291–309.

Gelfand, M.J. (2018). *Rule Makers, Rule Breakers: How Tight and Loose Cultures Wire Our World*. New York: Scribner.

Gelfand, M.J. et al. (2011). Differences between tight and loose cultures: A 33 nation study. *Science, 32*, 1100–1104.

George, B. (2003). *Authentic Leadership: Rediscovering the Secrets to Creating Lasting Value*. San Francisco: Jossey-Bass.

Giacalone, R.A. & Rosenfeld, P. (1987). Reasons for employee sabotage in the workplace. *Journal of Business and Psychology, 1*, 367–378.

Glomb, T.M. & Liao, H. (2003). Interpersonal aggression in work groups: Social influence, reciprocal, and individual effects. *Academy of Management Journal, 46*, 486–496.

Gottfredson, G.D. & Holland, J.L. (1990). A longitudinal test of the influence of congruence: Job satisfaction, competency utilization, and counterproductive behavior. *Journal of Counseling Psychology, 37*, 389–398.

Gove, W.R., Hughes, M. & Geerken, M.R. (1980). Playing dumb: A form of impression management with undesirable side effects. *Social Psychology Quarterly, 43*, 89–102.

Grandey, A.A. & Melloy, R.C. (2017). The state of the heart: Emotional labor as emotion regulation reviewed and revised. *Journal of Occupational Health Psychology, 22*, 407–422.

Grandey, A.A. & Sayre, G.M. (2019). Emotional labor: Regulating emotions for a wage. *Current Directions in Psychological Science, 28*, 131–137.

Gray, A. (2019, June 4). The bias of "professionalism" standards. *Stanford Social Innovation Review*, https://ssir.org/articles/entry/the_bias_of_professionalism_standards

Greenberg, J. (1990). Employee theft as a reaction to underpayment inequity: The hidden cost of pay cuts. *Journal of Applied Psychology, 75*, 561–568.

Greenberg, J. (1993). Stealing in the name of justice: Informational and interpersonal moderators of theft reactions to underpayment inequity. *Organizational Behavior & Human Decision Processes, 54*, 81–103.

Greenberg, J. (1997a). A social influence model of employee theft: Beyond the fraud triangle. In R.J. Lewicki, R.J. Bies, & B.H. Sheppard (Eds.), *Research on Negotiation in Organizations* (Vol. 6, pp. 29–51). Greenwich: Jai Press Inc.

Greenberg, J. (1997b). The STEAL motive: Managing the social determinants of employee theft. In R. Giacalone & J. Greenberg (Eds.), *Antisocial Behavior in Organizations* (pp. 85–108). Thousand Oaks, CA: Sage.

Greenberg, J. (1998). The cognitive geometry of employee theft: Negotiating "the line" between taking and stealing. In R.W. Griffin, A. O'Leary-Kelly, & J.M. Collins (Eds.), *Dysfunctional Behavior in Organizations: Violent and Deviant Behavior* (pp. 147–193). Stamford, CT: JAI Press.

Greenberg, J. (2002). Who stole the money, and when? Individual and situational determinants of employee theft. *Organizational Behavior and Human Decision Processes, 89*, 985–1003

Guinn, B. (1983). Job satisfaction, counterproductive behavior and circumstantial drug use among long-distance truckers. *Journal of Psychoactive Drugs, 15*, 185–188.

Hackney, K.J. & Perrewé, P.L. (2018). A review of abusive behaviors at work: The development of a process model for studying abuse. *Organizational Psychology Review, 8*, 70–92.

Heilman, M.E. (1983). Sex bias in work settings: The lack of fit model. *Research in Organizational Behavior, 5*, 269–298.

Henry, S. & Mars, G. (1978). Crime at work: The social construction of amateur property theft. *Sociology, 12*, 245–263.

Hollinger, R.C. (1988). Working under the influence (WUI): Correlates of employees' use of alcohol and other drugs. *Journal of Applied Behavioral Science, 24*, 439–454.

Hollinger, R.C. & Clark, J.P. (1983). *Theft by Employees*. Lexington, MA: Heath.

Hollinger, R.C., Slora, K.B. & Terris, W. (1992). Deviance in the fast-food restaurant: Correlates of employee theft, altruism, and counterproductivity. *Deviant Behavior, 13*, 155–184.

Holmes IV, O., Jiang, K., Avery, D.R., McKay, P.F., Oh, I.S. & Tillman, C.J. (2020). A Meta-Analysis Integrating 25 Years of Diversity Climate Research. *Journal of Management*, https://doi.org/10.1177/0149206320934547

Homans, G.C. (1961). *Social Behavior: Its Elementary Forms*. New York: Harcourt, Brace & World.

Hulin, C.L., Fitzgerald, L.F. & Drasgow, F. (1996). Organizational influences on sexual harassment. In M. Stockdale (Ed.), *Sexual Harassment in the Workplace: Perspectives, Frontiers, and Response Strategies* (pp. 127–150). Thousand Oaks, CA: Sage.

Ibarra, H. (2015, January-February). The authenticity paradox. *Harvard Business Review*, https://hbr.org/2015/01/the-authenticity-paradox

Ilies, R., Hauserman, N., Schwochau, S. & Stibal, J. (2003). Reported incidence rates of work-related sexual harassment in the United States: Using meta-analysis to explain reported rate disparities. *Personnel Psychology, 56*, 607–631.

Juvonen J. & Graham S. (2001). *Peer Harassment in School: The Plight of the Vulnerable and Victimized*. New York: Guilford.

Juvonen, J. & Graham, S. (2014). Bullying in schools: The power of bullies and the plight of victims. *Annual Review of Psychology, 65*, 159–85

Kemper, T.D. (1966). Representative roles and the legitimation of deviance. *Social Problems, 13*, 288–298.

Kern, J.H. & Grandey, A.A. (2009). Customer incivility as a social stressor: The role of race and racial identity for service employees. *Journal of Occupational Health Psychology, 14*, 46–57.

Klotz, A.C., He, W., Yam, K., Bolino, M.C., Wei, W. & Houston, L. (2018). Good actors but bad apples: Deviant consequences of daily impression management at work. *Journal of Applied Psychology, 103*, 1145–1154.

Kymlicka, W. (1995). *Multicultural Citizenship: A Liberal Theory of Minority Rights*. Oxford: Oxford University Press.

Kraft T.L. & Pressman, S.D. (2012). Grin and bear it: The influence of manipulated facial expression on the stress response. *Psychological Science, 23*, 1372–1378.

Latham, G.P. (2001). The importance of understanding and changing employee outcome expectancies for gaining commitment to an organizational goal. *Personnel Psychology, 54*, 2001, 707–771

Leach, C.W. (2005). Against the notion of a 'new racism'. *Journal of Community and Applied Social Psychology, 15*, 432–445.

Leary, M.R. & Kowalski, R.M. (1990). Impression management: A literature review and two-component model. *Psychological Bulletin, 107*, 34–47.

Lehman, W.E.K. & Simpson, D.D. (1992). Employee substance use and on-the-job behaviors. *Journal of Applied Psychology, 77*, 309–321.

Lewicki, R.J., Poland, T., Minton, J.W. & Sheppard, B.H. (1997). Dishonesty as deviance: A typology of workplace dishonesty and contributing factors, *Research on Negotiation in Organizations*, *6*, 53–86.

Lim, S., Cortina, L.M. & Magley, V.J. (2008). Personal and workgroup incivility: Impact on work and health outcomes. *Journal of Applied Psychology*, *93*, 95–107.

Lipman-Blumen, J. (2004). *The Allure of Toxic Leaders: Why We follow Destructive Bosses and Corrupt Politicians and How We Can Survive Them*. New York: Oxford University Press.

Litzky, B.E., Eddleston, K.A. & Kidder, D.L. (2006). The good, the bad, and the misguided: How managers inadvertently encourage deviant behaviors. *Academy of Management Perspectives*, *20*, 91–103.

Locke, E.A. (1976). The nature and causes of job satisfaction. In M.D. Dunnette (Ed.), *Handbook of Industrial and Organizational Psychology* (pp. 1297–1349). Chicago: Rand McNally.

Lowles, N. & Nicholls, A. (2005). *Hooligans: A–L of Britain's Football Gangs*. Wrea Green, UK: Milo Books.

Luthans, F. & Avolio, B. (2003). Authentic leadership: A positive development approach. In K.S. Cameron, J.E. Dutton, & R.E. Quinn (Eds.), *Positive Organizational Scholarship: Foundations of a New Discipline* (pp. 241–261). San Francisco, CA: Berrett-Kochler.

MacLean, T.L. (2001). Thick as thieves: A social embeddedness model of rule breaking in organizations. *Business and Society*, *40*, 167–196.

Makin, S. (2017, March 1). A shady government influences the moral behavior of its citizens. *Scientific American Mind*, *28*, 15.

Mangione, T.W. & Quinn, R.P. (1975). Job satisfaction, counterproductive behavior, and drug use at work. *Journal of Applied Psychology*, *60*, 114–116.

Mars, G. (1973). Chance, punters and the fiddle: Institutionalized pilferage in a hotel dining room. In M. Warner (Ed.). *The Sociology of the Workplace: An Interdisciplinary Approach* (pp. 200–210). London: Allen & Urwin.

Mars, G. (1994). *Cheats at Work: An Anthropology of Workplace Crime* (Vol. 4). Brookfield, VT: Dartmouth.

Martinko, M.J., Harvey, P., Brees, J.R. & Mackey, J. (2013). A review of abusive supervision research. *Journal of Organizational Behavior*, *34*, 120–137.

McConahay, J.B. (1983). Modern racism and modern discrimination: The effects of race, racial attitudes, and context on simulated hiring decisions. *Personality and Social Psychology Bulletin*, *9*, 551–558.

McConahay, J.B. (1986). Modem racism, ambivalence, and the modem racism scale. In J.F. Dovidio & S.L. Gaertner (Eds.) *Prejudice, Discrimination, and Racism* (pp. 35–60). New York: Academic Press.

Moretti, D.M. (1986). The prediction of employee counterproductivity through attitude assessment. *Journal of Business & Psychology*, *1*, 134–147.

Morley, M., Murphy, K.R., Cleveland, J.N., Heraty, N. & McCarthy, J. (2021). Testing the effects of the big three distal home and host contextual factors on performance appraisal processes and purposes in multinational enterprises: A 22 country study. *Human Resource Management*.

Muller, R. (2019). *Report on the Investigation into Russian Interference in the 2016 Presidential Election*. Washington, DC: U.S. Department of Justice.

Murphy, K.R. (1993). *Honesty in the workplace*. Monterey, CA: Brooks/Cole.

National Academies of Sciences, Engineering, and Medicine. (2018). *Sexual Harassment of Women: Climate, Culture, and Consequences in Academic Sciences, Engineering, and Medicine*. Washington, DC: The National Academies Press.

Niedhammer, I., David, S., Degioanni, S., Drummond, A. & Philip, P. (2009). Workplace Bullying and sleep disturbances: Findings from a large scale cross-sectional survey in the French working population. *Sleep, 32*, 1211–1219.

O'Bannon, R.M., Goldinger, L.A. & Appleby, J.D. (1989). *Honesty and integrity testing: A practical guide*. Atlanta: Applied Information Resources.

O'Farrell, C. & Nordstrom, C.R. (2013). Workplace bullying: Examining self-monitoring and organizational culture. *Journal of Psychological Issues in Organizational Culture, 3*, 6–17.

Offermann, L.R. & Malamut, A.B. (2002). When leaders harass: The impact of target perceptions of organizational leadership and climate on harassment reporting and outcomes. *Journal of Applied Psychology, 87*, 885.

Ong, A.D., Burrow, A.L., Fuller-Rowell, T.E., Ja, N.M. & Sue, D.W. (2013). Racial microaggressions and daily well-being among Asian Americans. *Journal of Counseling Psychology, 60*, 188–199.

O'Leary-Kelly, A.M., Griffin, R.W. & Glew, D.J. (1996). Organization-motivated aggression: A research framework. *Academy of Management Review, 21*, 225–253.

O'Reilly, J., Robinson, S.L., Berdahl, J.L. & Banki, S. (2014). Is negative attention better than no attention? The comparative effects of ostracism and harassment at work. *Organizational Science, 26*, 773–794.

Parilla, P.F., Hollinger, R.C. & Clark, J.P. (1988). Organizational control of deviant behavior: The case of employee theft. *Social Science Quarterly, 69*, 261–280.

Peck, J.A. & Levashina, J. (2017). Impression management and interview and job performance ratings: A meta-analysis of research design with tactics in mind. *Frontiers in Psychology, 8*(201), 1–10.

Phillips, J.M. (1998). Effects of realistic job previews on multiple organizational outcomes: A meta-analysis. *Academy of Management Journal, 41*, 673–690.

Pryor, J.B., Lavite, C.M. & Stoller, L.M. (1993). A social psychological analysis of sexual harassment: The person/situation interaction. *Journal of Vocational Behavior, 42*, 68–83.

Report of the Co-Chairs of the EEOC. (2016). *Select Task Force on the Study of Harassment in the Workplace*. Washington, DC: Equal Employment Opportunity Commission.

Robinson, S.L. (1995). Violation of psychological contracts: Impact on employee attitudes. In L.E. Tetrick & J. Barling (Eds.), *Changing Employment Relations: Behavioral and Social Perspectives* (pp. 91–108). Washington, DC: American Psychological Association.

Robinson, S.L. & Bennett, R.J. (1997). Workplace deviance: Its definitions, its manifestations, and its causes. In R.J. Lewicki, R.J. Bies, & B.H. Sheppard (Eds.), *Research on Negotiations in Organizations* (vol. 6, pp. 3–28). Greenwich, CT: JAI Press Inc.

Robinson, S.L. & Morrison, E.W. (1995). Psychological contracts and OCB: The effect of unfulfilled obligations on civic virtue behavior. *Journal of Organizational Behavior, 16*, 289–298.

Robinson, S.L. & O'Leary-Kelly, A.M. (1998). Monkey see, monkey do: The influence of workgroups on the antisocial behavior of employees. *Academy of Management Journal, 41*, 658–672.

Rubino, C., Avery, D.R., McKay, P.F., Moore, B.L., Wilson, D.C., Van Driel, M.S., . . . & McDonald, D.P. (2018). And justice for all: How organizational justice climate deters sexual harassment. *Personnel Psychology, 71*, 519–544.

Schilpzand, P., De Pater, I.E. & Erez, A. (2016). Workplace incivility: A review of the literature and agenda for future research. *Journal of Organizational Behavior, 37*, S57-S88.

Schneider, B., Goldstein, H.W. & Smith, D.B. (1995). The ASA framework: An update. *Personnel Psychology, 48*, 747–773.

Schyns, B. & Schilling, J. (2013). How bad are the effects of bad leaders? A meta-analysis of destructive leadership and its outcomes. *The Leadership Quarterly, 24*, 138–158.

Seeger, M.W., Ulmer, R.R., Novak, J.M. & Sellnow, T. (2005). Postcrisis discourse and organizational change, failure and renewal. *Journal of Organizational Change Management, 18*, 78–95.

Settles, I.H. & O'Connor, R.C. (2014). Incivility at academic conferences: Gender differences and the mediating role of climate. *Sex Roles, 71*, 71–82.

Shirer, W.L. (1960). *The Rise and Fall of the Third Reich: A History of Nazi Germany*. New York: Simon & Schuster.

Sieh, E.W. (1987). Garment workers: Perceptions of inequity and employee theft. *British Journal of Criminology, 27*, 174–190.

Skarlicki, D. & Folger, R. (1997). Retaliation in the workplace: The roles of distributive, procedural, and interactional justice. *Journal of Applied Psychology, 82*, 434–443.

Sojo, V.E., Wood, R.E. & Genat, A.E. (2016). Harmful workplace experiences and women's occupational well-being: A meta-analysis. *Psychology of Women Quarterly, 40*, 10–40.

Solorzano, D., Ceja, M. & Yosso, T. (2000, Winter). Critical race theory, racial microaggressions, and campus racial climate: The experiences of African American college students. *Journal of Negro Education, 69*, 60–73.

Song, S. (2005). Majority norms, multiculturalism, and gender equality, *American Political Science Review, 99*, 1473–1489.

Sue, D.W., Capodilup, C.M., Torino, G.C., Bucceri, J.M., Holder, A.M.B., Nadal, K.L. & Esquilin, M. (2007). Racial microaggressions in everyday life. *American Psychologist, 62*, 271–286.

Szwajkowski, E. (1989). Lessons for the consultant from research on employee misconduct. *Consultation, 8*, 181–189.

Taylor, L. & Walton, P. (1971). Industrial sabotage: Motives and meanings. In S. Cohen (Ed.), *Images of Deviance* (pp. 219–245). Baltimore, MD: Penguin Books.

Tedeschi, J.T. & Melburg, V. (1984). Impression management and influence in the organization. In S.B. Bacharach & E.J. Lawler (Eds.), *Research in the Sociology of Organizations* (pp. 31–58). Greenwich, CT: JA.

Tedeschi, J.T. & Reiss, M. (1981). Identities, the phenomenological self and laboratory research. In J.T. Tedeschi (Ed.), *Impression Management Theory and Social Psychological Research* (pp. 3–22). New York: Academic Press.

Tepper, B.J. (2000). Consequences of abusive supervision. *Academy of Management Journal, 43*, 178–190.

Tepper, B.J. (2007). Abusive supervision in work organizations: Review, synthesis, and research agenda. *Journal of Management, 33*, 261–289.

Thau, S., Bennett, R.J., Mitchell, M.S. & Marrs, M.B. (2009). How management style moderates the relationship between abusive supervision and workplace deviance: An uncertainty management theory perspective. *Organizational Behavior and Human Decision Processes, 108*, 79–92.

Totterdell, P. & Holman, D. (2003). Emotion regulation in customer service roles: Testing a model of emotional labor. *Journal of Occupational Health Psychology, 8*, 55–73.

Tucker, J.C. (1989). Employee theft as social control. *Deviant Behavior, 10*, 319–334.

Twenge, J.M., Baumeister, R.F., Tice, D.M. & Stucke, T.S. (2001). If you can't join them, beat them: Effects of social exclusion on aggressive behavior. *Journal of Personality and Social Psychology, 81*, 1058–1069.

Van Fleet, D.D. & Griffin, R.W. (2006). Dysfunctional organization culture: The role of leadership in motivating dysfunctional work behaviors. *Journal of Managerial Psychology, 21*, 698–708.

Vartia, M.L. (2001). Consequences of workplace bullying with respect to the well-being of its targets and the observers of bullying. *Scandinavian Journal of Work and Environmental Health, 27*, 63–69.

WBI Workplace Bullying Survey, June 2017 www.workplacebullying.org/wbiresearch/wbi-2017-survey.

Welbourne, J.L., Gangadharan, A. & Sariol, A.M. (2015). Ethnicity and cultural values as predictors of the occurrence and impact of experienced workplace incivility. *Journal of Occupational Health Psychology, 20*, 205–217.

Yang, L.Q., Caughlin, D.E., Gazica, M.W., Truxillo, D.M. & Spector, P.E. (2014). Workplace mistreatment climate and potential employee and organizational outcomes: A meta-analytic review from the target's perspective. *Journal of Occupational Health Psychology, 19*, 315.

12

THE CORRUPTION OF ORGANIZATIONS

In Chapter 11, I discussed the distinction between sick organizations, in which particular types of misbehavior (e.g., bullying, sexual harassment) are widespread and broadly tolerated and corrupt organizations, in which behavior that violates broadly accepted social norms, as well as relevant rules, regulations, and laws is an integral part of the business model of the organization. In some corrupt organizations, such as criminal gangs, the violation of rules, norms, and laws is virtually the defining feature of the organization—that is, these organization exist to carry out actions that are unlawful or that are generally considered to be wrong by society. Other corrupt organizations have, or once had, a legitimate purpose, but at some point, came to embrace corrupt means as an integral part of how they do business.

In this chapter, I start with a discussion of organizations (e.g., criminal gangs, organized crime, terrorist organizations) whose primary purpose is corrupt or unlawful. I then focus on organizations that mix corrupt practices with the provision of genuine lawful services (e.g., at the same time they were orchestrating a worldwide program of emissions cheating, Volkswagen, Audi, and others were also manufacturing many excellent cars and trucks), and on the processes by which these organizations become corrupted. Finally, I revisit the bad apples vs. bad barrels debate that was discussed in depth in Chapter 10.

Is Corruption Central or Peripheral to the Organization's Operations?

There is a useful distinction between organizations whose primary purposes are corrupt (e.g., organized crime) and organizations whose primary purposes are legitimate and even laudable but have embraced corrupt means as an integral part of their normal methods of operation. I refer to this latter group as "corrupted organizations".

It is sometimes easy to determine whether organizations have become corrupted; Volkswagen and Wells Fargo represent textbook examples of organizations in which corrupt means were normalized and were important to the success of the organization, but in which most of the day-to-day activity of the organization was neither illegal nor corrupt. By this standard, a case could be made for labeling the Catholic Church as a corrupted organization.

In Chapter 10, I described a worldwide scandal involving decades of the sexual abuse of minors by Catholic clergy and their associates. I noted that while horrific, the level of sexual abuse by Catholic clergy was *lower* than comparable levels for other professions who interact frequently with minors (e.g., educators). The bigger scandal has been the way the Church has handled reports of abuse. There is a well-documented pattern of cover-up and of transferring abusive clergy to new locations where they can escape prosecution for their previous crimes and start again with a new set of children. Will (2019) has labeled this the largest crime in American history, and a case can be made that despite its many good works and laudable programs, the Catholic Church at times functioned, and is arguably continuing to function, as a corrupted organization. As with Volkswagen and Wells Fargo, much if not most of the Church's activity is laudable rather than corrupt, but corrupt means appear to have been embraced by upper management (i.e., Bisops, Cardinals, and even Popes) for handling the scandal associated with the sexual abuse of children by members of the clergy.

Corrupt Organizations

In some organizations, corruption is central to the organization's mission and existence. The clearest examples are provided by criminal groups and organizations, but there are other groups such as terrorists whose central mission violates laws and widely held societal norms.

Organized Crime and Criminal Gangs

We "know" a great deal about organized crime from movies such as *The Godfather*, *Goodfellas* and *Casino* and television shows going back to *The Untouchables* (1959–1963, with unforgettable narration by the gossip columnist Walter Winchell). The problem, of course, is that it is likely that much of what we "know" is incorrect or exaggerated. We do, however, know a few useful things about criminal organizations *as organizations*.

Starting in the 1930s there was a substantial degree of organization to some types of criminal activity in America, starting with The Commission, founded by Lucky Luciano. The Commission functioned similarly to a standard board of directors and helped mediate conflicts between major mob families. The first major test of The Commission's power came when Dutch Schultz attempted to kill Special Prosecutor (and eventual presidential candidate) Tom Dewey. The Commission believed that this killing would lead to a crackdown on illegal activity, and it eventually ordered the murder of Dutch Shultz, who was gunned down in Newark before he could assassinate Dewey.

The Commission continued in one form or another for over 50 years and is said by some to still exist, but with dramatically reduced power. Lyman's (2015) review suggests that if we look beyond traditional Mafia families, organized crime resembles loosely organized work organizations, similar to small business partnerships. Crime organizations are typically not centralized, formalized, or divided into departments, and there are rarely written organizational charts or job descriptions. Criminal organization depend more on personal relationships and internalized norms than on formalized roles and job descriptions, and new members are often socialized into their roles in criminal organizations in ways that are not dissimilar to the socialization of new employees in an organization (i.e., they are introduced to other members, told who to go to for different sorts of information and resources, told about the informal chain of command, etc.). Ironically, the 2020–2021 COVID-19 pandemic has made the organization of legitimate businesses resemble the organization of criminal activity in important ways, with more decentralization, independence of action for organization members, and infrequent personal interactions. Like members of organized crime gangs, workers in many organizations do not come to the office to work and are not closely supervised daily, but they are expected to carry out assigned activities and to continue to produce for the organization.

Van Duyne (2000) notes that criminal organizations face unique problems of information and risk management in a hostile environment. Because their core activities are constantly being monitored or investigated by law enforcement agencies, criminal organizations cannot function with the predictability, structure, and accountability that is common in non-criminal enterprises. Their willful embrace of illegality creates a continuous challenge to their viability as an organization (Hobbs, 1995, 2013). Nevertheless, many of the concepts we use to analyze and understand other types of organizations (e.g., culture, norms, reward and control systems, commitment) are likely relevant for understanding the behavior of members of criminal organizations.

Lyman (2015) reviews several theories that attempt to explain organized crime. He notes, for example, that Rational Choice Theory suggests that the perceived benefits of participating in criminal activity exceed the perceived risks. Differential Association Theory suggests that criminal behavior is learned through association with others. Other researchers point to the role of shared values and norms (e.g., emphasis on masculinity and honor in traditional Italian Mafia organizations) in attracting members to organized crime (Travaglino, Abrams, de Moura, & Russo, 2014). Organized crime families and criminal gangs are not normless, they just embrace a set of norms and beliefs that justify, in their eyes, committing crimes and violating the norms of the broader society within which they are embedded.

Like other organizations, they have both formal and informal leadership structures, and they face the problem of recruiting, selecting, and retaining members, as well as the problem of distributing rewards and sanctions to control the behavior of their members. They probably have a wider array of rewards and sanctions available to them than other organizations (if you betray secrets at the office, you will probably not be shot), but they face many of the same problems as other organizations face, and their solutions to these problems are sometimes quite similar to the solutions chosen by legitimate organizations (e.g., promotion, succession planning).

Criminal gangs, especially those whose membership is relatively young, differ from more traditional organized crime families in two ways. First, they typically show even lower levels of organization than organized crime families. They are usually small or localized, although gangs that expand to national or even worldwide status exist (e.g., the U.S. Department of Justice and several European law enforcement agencies consider the motorcycle club Hells Angels to be an organized crime syndicate). Second, and more importantly, they perform an important social function for their members, and they are often explicitly built to foster a strong sense of social identity (Whyte, 1943). Gang norms, styles of dress, and other means they use to announce their identity (e.g., distinctive vehicles) help to shape the way members think about themselves and other members, and these forces are especially important to young gang members who have not had access to alternative socialization sources (Vigil, 1988). Gangs not only provide a sense of belonging; they also help to manage unpredictable and dangerous environments.

Group cohesion and group identification are positively related to criminal and violent behavior among gang members (Hennigan & Spanovic, 2012); the stronger one's identification with the gang, the stronger the individual's focus on the gang's normative expectations. Alleyne and Wood (2013) note that social status within a gang is also an important predictor of gang-related crime, especially when anti-authority attitudes are an important part of the gang's identity.

Terrorist Groups

There is a vast literature describing terrorism. In this chapter, I will focus on what we know about terrorist groups *as organizations*. In many ways, terrorist groups are similar to criminal gangs. First, there is a good deal of evidence that collective identity is one of the factors that most strongly motivates terrorist behavior (e.g., Post, 2010; Victoroff & Kruglanski, 2009).

In their studies of why individuals are attracted to terrorist groups, Webber and Kruglanski (2018) conclude that three factors are critical to radicalization: (1) the individual need that motivates one to engage in political violence, (2) the ideological narrative that justifies political violence, and (3) the social network that influences one's decisions along the pathway to extremism. Arena and Arrigo (2005) suggest that this social network is especially important to individuals who have not developed a strong sense of identity that links them to the society in which they live. They conclude that the lack of a well-formed identity motivates individuals to turn to the collective identity of the extremist organization to experience purpose and meaning in their lives. In particular, they argue that individuals are drawn to totalitarianism or totalitarian movements because they find comfort and meaning in an organization's authoritarian dogma. This dogma provides clarity and purpose to people whose lives are often missing both. Youth gangs and terrorist organizations are both similar in that they help to provide an answer to an aspiring member's question "Who am I?". They provide an anchor and an identity to members who are often otherwise only loosely connected to the broader society.

Second, terrorist groups are sometimes more loosely organized than popular media would suggest. There are terror groups with tight chains of command and semi-military structures, but many terrorists and terror groups are amateur and *ad hoc* (Hoffman, 1999). An analysis of contemporary terrorist threats in the U.S. carried out by the Center for Strategic and International Studies (Jones, Doxsee, & Harrison, 2020) suggests that the loosely organized groups and coalitions associated with the far-right and White supremacists represent the most significant terrorist threat in the foreseeable future. These groups often have fluid membership and vague chains of authority, and they often operate on the fringes of society. Not surprisingly, there are often links between terrorist organizations and organized crime (Dugan & Gibbs, 2009). Both operate outside of the law, and they can both be instrumental in providing each other information and material (e.g., intelligence, explosives, guns) needed to carry out their core activities.

Corrupted Organizations

The organizations described so far in this chapter exist primarily for corrupt purposes, and their *raison d'être* involves illegal acts and violations of social norms and rules (e.g., robbery, drug-running). In this section, I discuss *corrupted organizations*—that is, organizations that once existed or even currently exist for purposes that are above-board, well within the law and consistent with general social norms, but that have embraced corrupt means for performing significant parts of their otherwise legitimate functions. In earlier chapters (e.g., Chapters 8, 10), I described in some detail the Volkswagen diesel emissions scandal (Ewing, 2017, 2019; Tabuchi & Ewing, 2017). Even though corruption became an important part of their business model, Volkswagen continued throughout this period to produce many high-quality automobiles and to function as a legitimate business. Similar arguments can be made regarding the case of Wells Fargo.

BOX 12.1 PYRAMID SCHEME VS. LEGITIMATE BUSINESS: THE CASE OF AMWAY

Amway is a large multilevel marketing (MLM) company; in 2018 it sold over $8 billion in products. In 1999, the corporation was renamed Alticor and its sales divisions renamed Quixtar and Access Business Group. Sellers pay substantial fees to become "independent business owners" and they receive fees for recruiting new distributors, as well as additional fees when the distributors they recruit bring in new distributors working under them. Amway has long been criticized for running a pyramid scheme, and they have paid out tens of millions in lawsuits alleging unfair or deceptive business practices (Knape, 2010).

The question of whether companies like Amway represent illegal pyramid schemes is surprisingly complex. At one time, the legal test depended on the proportion of the company's products that was sold to customers outside its recruitment network, but more recent court decisions have focused on whether the company's primary purpose involved recruiting new members vs. selling its products (Nocera, 2015). Multilevel marketing companies often bring in a substantial amount of money from recruiting new members and from selling them materials (e.g., motivational books and tapes) that will, purportedly, help them sell the organization's products, and establishing the balance between income from products vs. income from recruiting new members can be a complex problem.

The more interesting question is whether multilevel marketing companies are essentially cults. MLM companies, including but not limited to Amway, often attract individuals who become strongly identified with their company, sometimes to the extent of losing constructive contact with their friends and families (Hong, 2020). One of the common characteristics of many MLM companies is the use of charismatic recruiters and large group meetings designed to emotionally arouse the crowd, with attempts to dominate the time and the thinking of members, and the resulting high level of identification of members, many of whom are highly loyal to the organization even though they make very little income (a recent lawsuit accuses Amway and its successors of creating an income model that fails to pay minimum wage; Eidelson 2020). In Chapter 10, I commented on the potential dangers of high levels of identification with organizations. MLM organizations often work hard to make the organization an integral part of a person's identity, and this can have beneficial effects for both individuals and organizations. It can also have detrimental effects, in the case of MLM organizations encouraging individuals to devote a great deal of time and effort for little reward, often less than they might reasonably expect from a minimum-wage job.

Wells Fargo was founded during the California Gold Rush to provide freight, stagecoach, and banking services. In the 1990s, Wells Fargo embarked on a series of bank acquisitions and in 1998 it merged with Norwest. The head of Norwest became president and CEO of Wells Fargo, and he initiated an aggressive program to sell bank customers on a wide array of financial products (e.g., credit cards, loans, additional accounts). He bought the "Going for Gr-eight" initiative, which had pressured Norwest employees to sell eight financial products to each customer, to Wells Fargo. The pressure to sell was intense, and bank employees eventually "solved" the problem of selling so many products to their customers by cheating. In particular, they created millions of new accounts for their customers, often without their knowledge or consent (Ewing, 2017). As with Volkswagen, when Wells Fargo employees were pressured to do something that was essentially impossible, they took the only feasible approach—they cheated. This cheating was eventually uncovered, leading to large fines and the firing of thousands of employees. Like Volkswagen, Wells Fargo continued to provide valuable banking and investment services to millions of its customers at the same time as its large-scale pattern of creating fraudulent accounts was going on.

This pattern of fraudulent activity going on at the same time as the organization is engaged in normal and honest activity is common; there are companies whose activities appear to be almost entirely fraudulent and corrupt. In the last few months (as of this writing), a leading German financial transfer firm, Wirecard, suffered a spectacular collapse. Wirecard provided technology that made quick and inexpensive transfers of funds (e.g., credit card purchases) possible. They claimed record profits, although exactly how they made money was never completely clear. In mid-2020, Wirecard's financial empire collapsed when the company was forced to admit that $2 billion that they listed on their balance sheets never existed (Alderman & Schuetze, 2020). Their CEO was arrested on accusations of inflating sales volume with fake income to lure investors and a former chief operating officer fled the country.

Criminogenic Organizations

What types of organizations are likely to become corrupted? Gross (1978, p. 56) argues that "all organizations are inherently criminogenic"—that is, prone to criminality or corruption. For example, business success often requires obtaining some sort of advantage over your competitors, and the temptation to cut corners (especially if you believe that others are already cutting those same corners) can be overwhelming. However, even if the system (e.g., competitive markets) can encourage criminal behavior or corruption, not all organizations are corrupt; there is only a subset of organizations that incorporate corruption into their normal business practices.

It is widely believed that organizational corruption is at least partly a function of the organization's culture (Anand, Ashforth, & Joshi, 2004; Ashforth, Gioia,

Robinson, & Treviño, 2008; Gault, 2017; Pinto, Leanna, & Pil, 2008). In the section that follows, I will describe three specific types of organizational cultures that can contribute to organizational corruption. However, culture is not the only factor involved in organizational corruption. There are also attraction and selection processes at work here. Apel and Paternoster (2009) note that certain types of persons may be attracted to certain industries or firms. For example, those who have a greater tolerance for risky behavior may be attracted to firms or industries that have a history or culture of taking risks or conducting their business activities right up to (or just over) the line of illegality.

In Chapter 10, I noted how corruption becomes accepted as part of the normal process of doing business. For example, Ashforth and Anad (2003) discuss the rationalization of corruption, a process by which members of an organization come to recognize corrupt and criminal behavior as an acceptable pattern of behavior. This psychological reframing of corrupt and criminal activities as normal business practices is critical to the process of organization corruption; organizational leaders and members are typically less willing to engage in behaviors that they think of as wrong. One of the recurring themes of research on white-collar crime is that individuals convicted of these crimes tend to acknowledge that they might have broken some rules, but often deny criminal intent and the label of criminal (Benson, 1985; Cressey, 1970). In a later section that describes the cultures of corrupted organizations, I will explore some of the rationales members of these organizations use to justify their behaviors.

Cui Bono (Who Benefits)?

Why do members of corrupted organizations go along with criminal or corrupt activities? One way to understand this behavior is to ask who benefits from organizational corruption, the organization or the individuals who engage in corrupt acts? As Pinto, Leanna, and Pil (2008) note, our understanding of organizational corruption might be quite different if members of a corrupted organization focus on benefiting themselves vs. benefiting the organization.

There are certainly some individuals who participate in organizational corruption primarily to line their own pockets (e.g., rogue traders, such as Nick Leeson of Barings Bank, whose fraudulent trades led to the 1995 downfall of that venerable institution) but the very nature of the phenomenon suggests that the individuals involved are more likely working for the benefit of the organization and its owners/shareholders than solely for themselves (Daboub, Rasheed, Priem, & Gray, 1995; Schrager & Short, 1978). Corruption on a scale large enough to influence the very business model of an organization necessarily involves the active involvement or at least the tacit acceptance of a large number of members of the organization. For example, when the Volkswagen diesel emissions cheating scandal first broke, there were efforts to blame this on a few "bad apples"—that is, lower-level engineers and staff members acting on their own (Drumm, 2015), but it quickly became clear that this scandal involved top executives and numerous managers, engineers, technicians, and sales personnel in multiple organizations (Ewing, 2017, 2019).

Two factors appear most critical in explaining why members of an organization are willing to engage in corrupt and criminal behavior that primarily benefits the organization. First, an organization's culture often leads members of the organization to reframe corrupt and criminal behavior as a normal business practice (Campbell & Göritz, 2014). Second, as I noted in Chapter 10, loyalty and commitment to organizations can lead people to violate norms, laws, and rules to help the organization survive and prosper. Pinto et al. (2008) suggest that cooperation with corrupt or criminal acts is often best understood as a case of organizational citizenship "gone bad". We often describe organizational citizenship using the analogy of the "good soldier" (Bateman & Organ, 1983; Organ, 1988), in the sense that members of an organization are often willing to go along with the norms and practices of their organization, even if they think that similar practices would be wrong if they happened elsewhere. Individuals caught in organizational corruption often defend their actions by claiming that they were just doing what was best for the organization.

In this section, I have discussed corruption that benefits the individual vs. corruption that benefits the organization, but this binary structure is probably an oversimplification. The individuals who cooperate in organizational corruption almost always benefit personally, at least in the short term. That is, people who engage in dishonest, corrupt, or criminal acts to help their organization often receive direct benefits, ranging from keeping their jobs to substantial bonuses directly tied to their corrupt acts. Going back again to Volkswagen, numerous executives, engineers, and employees benefited from the company's success during the period when Volkswagen had appeared to solve the problem of creating a clean diesel engine with good performance and economy. Thus, we cannot think of individuals who engage in corrupt acts designed to benefit the organization as acting in a completely altruistic manner. Nevertheless, large-scale corruption is virtually impossible unless many members of an organization are willing to cooperate in corrupt acts, and the motivating factors in these actions usually involve efforts to help and support the organization, even if these efforts will also benefit the individuals involved.

Cultures of Corrupted Organizations

In Chapter 11, I described several types of organizational cultures one might find in "sick" organizations. Next, I describe three cultures, cutthroat cultures, defensive cultures, and unethical cultures, along with characteristics types of misbehavior that one might encounter in corrupted organizations. Table 12.1 describes the defining traits and characteristics of this type of misbehavior associated with each of these three cultures.

TABLE 12.1 Cultures of Corrupted Organizations

	Defining Trait	*Types of Misbehavior*
Cutthroat Culture	Destructive competition	Fraud, undermining
Defensive Culture	External threats	Rationalization of misbehavior
Anethical Culture	Avoidance of moral judgments	Moral drift

Cutthroat Cultures

A cutthroat culture is characterized by a strong emphasis on ends over means, combined with high levels of internal competitiveness. These two factors can lead to substantial pressure on employees to cut corners, engage in unethical schemes and defraud customers and clients. The internal competitiveness that this culture encouraged can lead to unhealthy competition and social undermining. Both Wells Fargo (McLean, 2017) and Volkswagen (Ewing, 2017) have been described as exhibiting cutthroat cultures.

Cases like Wells Fargo and Volkswagen have something striking in common—systematic and widespread programs that defrauded customers and clients that can be traced back to a strong message that unrealistic goals must be accomplished without much apparent concern for *how* those goals are met. An executive who announces very difficult goals and says or leads subordinates to believe that it does not matter how those goals are accomplished is practically begging employees to cheat (Litzky, Eddleston, & Kidder, 2006). Top executives on these organizations sometimes mouth support for high ethical standards, but many of the lower officials see only strong pressures and inducements to "get the numbers no matter what" (Sonnenfeld & Lawrence, 1978, p. 149). The very fact that seemingly impossible goals are being achieved should probably be taken as an indication that someone is cheating, but as victims of numerous frauds and Ponzi schemes can attest, high returns and dazzling profits can turn even sophisticated clients and investors into easy marks and willing participants in corrupt schemes (Yang, 2014).

For example, Wells Fargo had what was described as a "pressure-cooker sales culture", characterized by the relentless pressure to boost sales and show larger profits, and this culture is cited as one of the key reasons for the widespread practice of opening accounts in customers' names without their permission and persuading customers to take on loans, debt, and unnecessary credit lines (McLean, 2017). Similar cultures have been reported at numerous other banks and financial companies and are thought to encourage unethical behavior among employees (Gino, 2014; Harris & Bromiley, 2007).

These cultures are not limited to banks and financial institutions. Ordóñez, Schweitzer, Galinsky, and Bazerman (2009) describe the way challenging performance goals contributed to many organizational failures and scandals—the Ford

Pinto, where the gas tank was positioned behind the rear axle with only 10 inches of crush space, making it more vulnerable to fires on rear-end collisions. The pressure to complete production on time and within the allotted budget caused Ford to omit small repairs and design changes that would have reduced this threat.

The second feature of cutthroat organizational cultures is internal competitiveness. In a "dog-eat-dog" or "pressure-cooker" environment, internal competition for advancement, resources, and the like will create temptation to cut corners. This temptation is especially dangerous when members of the organization believe that the norms of the organization tolerate or even encourage dishonest behavior. Individuals are often willing and able to resist many types of temptation, but if they believe that "the way things are done" in their business or their organization involves bending rules or other forms of dishonest behavior, they are much more likely to be willing to go along with behaviors that, if left to their own devices, they would not engage in (Murphy, 1993).

Internal competition can lead to social undermining, particularly if you believe that another person's success might come at your expense (Duffy, Ganster, & Pagon, 2002). Undermining behaviors might range from expressing negative evaluations of other members of the organization to active efforts to sabotage their work, and the incentive to undermine your peers can be especially strong in organizations with a strong "bottom line" mentality (Greenbaum, Mawritz, & Eissa, 2012).

As I have noted in several earlier chapters, strong levels of identification with and loyalty to an organization may increase the risk that a cutthroat culture will have corrosive effect on the members of the organization. Organizations usually work hard to build commitment and attachment among their employees, but perhaps they should be careful what they wish for. In some organizations, a high level of commitment is the final ingredient needed to perfect a recipe for short-term gain and long-term disaster—a criminogenic organizational culture.

BOX 12.2 PSYCHIC SCAMS

One of the biggest cons in history (Ellis & Hicken, 2018) involves letters sent by an apparent psychic, Maria Duvall, who appeared to seek payment to protect recipients against bad fortune. Millions of people are alleged to have sent over $200 million over 20 years to ward off the disasters that supposedly awaited them if they did not send money. The scam used a system of personalized letters (often drawing personal information from publicly available databases) targeting sick and elderly victims.

The scam originated from a purported psychic of Italian origin named Maria Carolina Gamba, who used "Maria Duval" as her trade name. Gamba gave psychic consultations in France and eventually sold the rights to the psychic services of "Maria Duval" to a group of people who used those to promote the sale of astrology charts. Through a complex and convoluted process, the group that purchased the Maria Duval copyrights and their later partners developed their scam into a worldwide phenomenon. They mailed personalized letters to potential victims, offering feats of divination by Maria Duval for a small fee. Victims would receive what appeared to be handwritten letters from Maria Duval giving them what appeared to be personally tailored psychic advice. This scam was permanently shut down in the U.S. by the Department of Justice in 2016.

In Chapter 8, I described the job of a telephone psychic (Noll, 2010: O'Regan, 2020). The people giving you psychic advice over the phone often know that they do not possess special psychic powers. There has been considerable controversy about what Maria Carolina Gamba knew about the Maria Duval scam and about her continuing role in the scam. There have even been questions about Gamba's true identity. What is not mysterious is why scams like this continue to flourish. Psychic scams almost always involve two elements, vulnerable targets and the desire to believe.

The Marie Duval scam deliberately targeted the elderly and the sick, who often needed help of one sort or another and who were not well-equipped to sort useful advice from flimflam. Second, and more important, psychics offer something many of us desperately want—that is, the ability to see into the future or to see things hidden from others. Psychics sell certainty in an uncertain world, and the lure of this outcome is often enough to overcome even the most skeptical client.

Defensive Cultures

In their examination of the dynamics of organizational corruption, Campbell and Göritz (2014) noted that one of the key recurring themes in their interviews with experts and with individuals who had worked with corrupt organizations is that "corrupt organizations perceive themselves to fight in a war, which leads to their taken-for-granted assumption that "the end justifies the means" (p. 291). As a result, members of these organizations regard "competing organizations as enemies that need to be defeated to secure the continuity of their own company" (p. 298). Seen in this way, corruption is viewed as necessary for survival, not as a crime or wrongdoing. This "end justifies the means" approach allows members of corrupt organizations to rationalize a wide range of corrupt and illegal behaviors as responses to existential threats (Beenen & Pinto, 2009).

This analogy to war is a very important one, because in war virtually anything can be rationalized. Consider the changing stance of the Allied powers toward the bombing of civilian targets in World War II. Early in the war, there were strict orders against the bombing of targets if the likelihood of civilian losses was deemed too high. In August of 1940, the Luftwaffe accidentally (and against Hitler's orders) dropped a few bombs on London. The British launched a retaliatory raid against Berlin, and what followed was a series of tit-for-tat attacks against cities by both Allied and Axis Powers. In part because of their inability to consistently hit military targets from the air, the Allies eventually adopted a tactic of area bombing—that is, the indiscriminate bombing of an entire area of a city or district, and by the end of the war, many German cities were in ruins (Keegan, 2005).

The purpose of the last paragraph is not to debate the morality or even the wisdom of the Allied bombing campaign. Rather, it should serve as a stark illustration of the point that in war, virtually anything goes, and all sorts of behaviors that would normally be viewed as unacceptable (e.g., purposely bombing civilian targets) can be rationalized. More to the point, war often leads to escalation, in the sense that once an organization believes it is at war (and especially if it is losing that war), acts that were once unacceptable might later be seen as necessary and even desirable. Organizations that adopt a defensive culture because they believe they are at war are making a potentially disastrous choice in framing their relationships with their competitors. Genuine warfare can create genuine existential risks, but the competition between companies is not war. Companies may go under, and their employees may suffer, but conflicts between competitors in a market do not pose the same risks as genuine war, and they typically do not justify the same "end justifies the means" response.

Companies often face external threats of one sort or another. A competitor might develop a better product or process. They might secure contracts your company was hoping to land. They might lure key employees away. The key to a defensive culture is the response to those threats. Organizations that convince themselves and their members that they are at war risk opening the floodgates for misbehavior. Once members of an organization accept the belief that they are at war, there is little they might be unwilling to do to win that war.

Anethical Culture

An unethical culture is one that actively embraces unethical means; both cutthroat and defensive cultures are likely to become unethical. An *anethical* culture is one in which ethics are not given serious weight when important decisions are made. Victor and Cullen (1988) define the ethical climate of an organization in terms of shared perceptions of what is ethically correct behavior and how ethical issues should be handled in the organization. Several studies have demonstrated that the ethical climate of an organization significantly influences the ethical behavior of the employees (Andreoli & Lefkowitz, 2009; Deshpande, George, & Joseph, 2000; Fritzsche, 2000).

Organizations often have multiple systems that communicate what is important and valued by the organization. In the workplace, systems for goal setting, performance management, and reward allocation all communicate to members what behaviors and outcomes are valued by the organization (Treviño, Den Nieuwenboer, & Kish-Gaphart, 2014). Informal organizations use less structured methods (e.g., the socialization of new members), but they also communicate a great deal about what is important to the group. Organizations that fail to pay attention to the ethical dimensions of decision making, or that give it transparently dismissive lip service are communicating that ethics are not an important part of their decisions.

Organizational cultures that give little weight to ethical issues may be more prone than others to moral drift—that is, to slowly becoming corrupt without ever consciously choosing this path. A slow drift in the direction of unethical behavior is possible, especially if each new unethical behavior seems to produce relatively little harm Wilermuth, Vincent, and Gino (2017). Gino and Bazerman (2009) note that there can be a *slippery slope* effect, in which small deviations from societal ethical standards do not attract much notice. The cumulative effects of these small deviations can be substantial, but in an organization in which the ethical dimensions of decisions do not receive much attention, constant small moves in the direction of corruption may attract little attention or disapproval.

One reason why a lack of concern about ethics poses a particular problem in organizations is that ethical concerns often act as constraints on behavior. When these constraints are lifted, ignored, or simply not strongly felt, members of organizations are free to make a wider range of choices. This by itself does not automatically mean that they will choose misbehavior, but in many settings (e.g., organizations competing in the same market), behaviors that would normally be constrained by ethical considerations may offer at least a short-term advantage (e.g., spying on your competitor, rigging bids), and this advantage might be sufficient to motivate a drift toward dishonest or unethical organizational practices.

Cutthroat and defensive cultures are defined by the presence of specific beliefs and behaviors (e.g., strong performance pressure, internal competition, perception of external threats). Anethical cultures are harder to pin down because they are defined by the *absence* of a particular attribute—that is, attention to the ethical consequences of one's decisions and actions. There are, however, some concrete indications that an organization embraces a culture in which ethical considerations are not given much weight. First, almost every modern corporation claims to support ethical values; organizational mission statements are often littered with platitudes (e.g., people are our most important product) and mealy-mouthed expressions of support for ethical choices. These corporations often have senior managers or executives charged with investigating complaints and ensuring compliance (ombudspersons or compliance officers). The key to understanding anethical organizations is that they may issue lofty statements about the importance of ethics, but their behavior often suggests otherwise.

In an anethical organization, the mission statement might be filled with platitudes and there might be ombudspersons scattered throughout the organization, but these words and these people may not have much effective power. Thus, the question is often not whether there is someone to complain to about ethical violations but what happens when these complaints are made. In Chapter 9, I described the Penn State scandal. An assistant coach of the football team, Jerry Sandusky, had been abusing boys, on and off campus, for many years. Over the years, numerous reports and complaints were made to various offices in the university, but no meaningful actions were taken until the scandal finally broke into public view. This scandal has particular personal relevance; I have my Ph.D. from Penn State (1979) and was on the Penn State faculty from 2000–2011, leaving shortly before the scandal broke. Allegations about Sandusky's behavior had been public knowledge even before I came back to join the faculty and were still swirling when I left. Despite the many fine things this university and its members did during the time I was there, it is hard to avoid the conclusion that in a conflict between ethics and football, football consistently won.

BOX 12.3 THE GREAT OIL SNIFFER HOAX

In 1979, the French oil company Elf Aquitaine lost $150 million in a hoax that involved "Avions Renifleurs" (Sniffer Aircraft). A Belgian Count, Alain de Villegas, became interested in a desalinization device developed by Aldo Bonassoli, and when this device failed to perform as advertised, they created a team that claimed to develop devices that could remotely detect underground water deposits and oil fields. These devices were allegedly based on the well-known scientific principle that sensitive gravity meters can detect underground objects, but de Villegas and Bonassoli were very secretive and refused to allow independent scientific evaluations of their devices. Nevertheless, given the rising price of oil following the Yom Kippur War, they were able to interest Elf Aquitaine in their work. They fitted their devices in a transport aircraft, flew the aircraft over a known oil field (making sure that there were no independent scientists on the flight) and were able to convince Elf Aquitaine officials that their machine could accurately map that underground oil field.

After several flights failed to detect new oil fields, skepticism mounted, but Bonassoli was able to hold critics at bay by staging apparent demonstrations of his machine's ability to detect hidden objects. Eventually, it was revealed that his machine housed a photocopier that would simply copy and spit out Bonassoli's hand-drawn renderings of whatever object the device was designed to detect. Despite this clear evidence of fraud, important champions of the project, including an ex-president of France (Valéry Giscard d'Estaing), continued to defend the idea. Eventually, Elf Aquitaine withdrew from this project and several political careers were damaged in the ensuing scandal.

Why do scandals of this sort succeed? Often, they succeed because they promise something that the people being scammed desperately need. At the time, Elf Aquitaine has few productive oil fields and poor prospects for developing new ones. Laroche, Steyer, and Théron (2019) document the extensive steps the scammers used to develop trust and overcome the suspicions of Elf Aquitaine personnel. However, their narrative makes it clear that this scam could not have worked without Elf Aquitaine's strong need for it to succeed.

Who Corrupts Whom?

Do bad people corrupt organizations, or do bad organizations corrupt people? This is the essence of the bad apples vs. bad barrels debate that was discussed in detail in Chapter 10 (Ashkanasy, Windsor, & Treviño, 2006; Kish-Gephart, Harrison, & Treviño, 2010; Treviño & Youngblood, 1990). The answer to this question might change over time. In this chapter, I distinguished between organizations that exist primarily for corrupt purposes and organizations that exist for non-corrupt purposes and that come to embrace some form of corruption as a core component of their business model (i.e., corrupted organizations). It is reasonable to believe that most corrupted organizations start off embracing norms, values, laws, and rules that are generally accepted in society, and that they become corrupted as a result of choices made by formal and informal leaders.[1] At the point where these choices are made, we might explain organizational corruption in terms of bad apples. However, once organizational corruption becomes normalized (Ashforth & Anand, 2003)—that is, accepted as the way this organization operates and with behavior that is both accepted and expected, a bad barrel explanation seems more compelling.

The bad apples vs. bad barrels debate is an oversimplification because in most cases there are likely both individual (bad apples) and organizational (bad barrels) factors at work in the process of organizational corruption. For example, attraction-selection-attrition (ASA) processes (Schneider, 1987, 2008) are likely to lead organizations to attract and select individuals who are more open to corruption, while those who are less open to corruption may not last in the organization. Thus, individuals' likelihood of being corrupted by their organizations may depend in part on their interest in and tolerance for behaviors that would be labeled as unethical in most organizations.

Two of the organizational processes discussed in depth in Chapter 10 are also likely to factor into the corruption of individuals—that is, rationalization and socialization. In several previous chapters (e.g., Chapters 1, 6, 10, 11), I have noted the high value most people assign to maintaining a positive self-image. If your organization expects or requires you to engage in behavior that is unethical or illegal, the rationalization of these behaviors is essential to maintaining this positive self-image. Thus, individuals who engage in corrupt or criminal behaviors in organizations may come to believe that what they are doing is not *really* wrong, or that it is necessary to serve some higher purpose (e.g., the viability of the organization). Socialization is important as a tool for convincing new members of an organization that the corrupt practices they will be asked to participate in are acceptable to and valued by the organization. A combination of rationalization and socialization processes may lead people who think of themselves as honest, upright, and moral to go along with corrupt processes in their organization (Smith-Crowe & Warren, 2014).

There is a striking contrast between the developmental trajectory of most types of crime and the development of crime and corruption in organizations. Crimes such as theft, selling drugs, assault, and the like are largely a young person's (usually a young man) game. Some people remain involved in crime well into late adulthood, but most criminal activity peaks relatively early in life and tails off as individuals get older (Hirschi & Gottfredson, 1983; Sampson & Laub, 2003). White-collar crime shows a distinctly different pattern. White-collar criminals tend to be older, in part because of the strong association between age and organizational level. Serious and sustained organizational corruption usually requires the active involvement and assent of high-level managers and executives, and these individuals do not usually reach these jobs in their 20s and 30s. Theories of criminal behavior in youth often emphasize factors such as lack of self-control (Hirschi & Gottfredson, 1983) or disruptive interactions early in life (Thornberry, 1987). These explanations seem less compelling when applied to criminal and corrupt behavior in organizations.

Organizations are most likely to corrupt their members or to provide an outlet for pre-existing willingness to engage in corrupt behaviors when corruption becomes normalized in their organization. This provides a potent combination of ASA, rationalization, and socialization processes that make it increasingly likely that organizations will attract and select individuals who are open to corruption and convince new members of the organization that what appears to be corrupt behavior is normal, acceptable, and even necessary.

Summary

Corrupt organizations are ones in which dishonest, criminal, or unethical behavior is not only accepted but is an important component of the day-to-day workings of the organizations. Some organizations exist for fundamentally corrupt purposes (e.g., organized crime, youth gangs, terrorist organizations) while others are primarily devoted to legitimate pursuits but have embraced corrupt means as an essential part of their business model. Like other organizations, organized crime, criminal gangs, and terrorist organizations perform important social functions for their members. They form an important part of the social identities of their members, and because the activities of these organizations tend to isolate their members, to some extent, from the rest of society, they may have a critical role in shaping their members' self-perceptions.

It is easy to understand why members of an organized crime family or criminal gang go along with activities that violate laws and general social norms. If you object to committing crimes, you are unlikely to join or to remain in an organization whose main purpose is to commit crimes. It is harder to understand why individuals who have joined organizations whose main purpose is entirely legitimate (e.g., manufacturing cars) might be willing to participate in criminal or corrupt activities. Organizational commitment and loyalty appear to be the key here. Some people participate in organizational corruption solely to line their own pockets, but most of the participants in white-collar crimes or organizational frauds and corruption appear to break laws and social norms to help and protect their organization.

I discussed three types of cultures of organizations that succumb to criminality and corruption: (1) cutthroat cultures, (2) defensive cultures, and (3) anethical cultures. Strong pressure to perform, internal competition, and external threats can all lead members of otherwise legitimate organizations to embrace and to rationalize corrupt practices. Organizations that do not put undue pressures on their members to perform and that are not strongly threatened by their competitors can nevertheless become corrupt if they do not include ethical considerations as an important part of their decision making. Almost all organizations claim to support ethical values, but many give these values little more than lip service, and this makes them vulnerable to drifting in the direction of corruption.

Finally, I revisited the bad apples vs. bad barrels debate that was discussed in depth in Chapter 10. This debate is concerned with whether people corrupt organizations or organizations corrupt people. The most likely resolution of this debate is that both occur, perhaps at different times. Few legitimate organizations start as thoroughly corrupt, and there is probably some point where the decisions of a few formal or informal leaders (bad apples) push the organization in the direction of corruption. Once an organization becomes corrupted, a combination of ASA processes (they attract, select, and retain individuals who are more prone to accept corrupt behavior) and rationalization and socialization processes (i.e., redefining corruption behaviors as necessary, acceptable, and even laudable, shaping the norms of new members to accept and participate in corrupt actions) is likely to help maintain this level of corruption.

Note

1. In his widely acclaimed biography of U.S. Grant, Chernow (2017) makes the case the companies that were formed to create the transcontinental railroad were likely corrupt from their start, reflecting a broad pattern of political and business corruption in what would later be called the Gilded Age

References

Alderman, L. & Schuetze, C.F. (2020, June 26). *In a German tech giant's fall, charges of lies, spies and missing billions.* www.nytimes.com/2020/06/26/business/wirecard-collapse-markus-braun.html

Alleyne, E. & Wood, J.L. (2013). Gang-related crime: The social, psychological and behavioral correlates. *Psychology, Crime and Law, 19*, 611–627.

Anand, V., Ashforth, B.E. & Joshi, M. (2004). Business as usual: The acceptance and perpetuation of corruption in organizations. *Academy of Management Executive, 18*, 39–53.

Andreoli, N. & Lefkowitz, J. (2009). Individual and organizational antecedents of misconduct in organizations. *Journal of Business Ethics, 85*, 309–332.

Apel, R. & Paternoster, R. (2009). Understanding "criminogenic" corporate culture: What white-collar crime researchers can learn from studies of the adolescent employment–crime relationship. In S. Simpson & D. Weisburd (Eds.), *The Criminology of White-Collar Crime* (pp. 15–34). New York: Springer.

Arena, M.P. & Arrigo, B.A. (2005). Social psychology, terrorism, and identity: A preliminary re-examination of theory, culture, self, and society. *Behavioral Sciences and the Law, 23*, 485–506.

Ashforth, B.E. & Anand, V. (2003). The normalization of corruption in organizations. In R.M. Kramer & B.M. Staw (Eds.), *Research in Organizational Behavior: An Annual Series of Analytical Essays and Critical Reviews* (Vol. 25, pp. 1–52). Oxford, England: Elsevier Science.

Ashforth, B.E., Gioia, D.A., Robinson, S.L. & Treviño, L.K. (2008). Re-viewing organizational corruption. *Academy of Management Review, 33*, 670–684.

Ashkanasy, N.M., Windsor, C.A. & Treviño, L.K. (2006). Bad apples in bad barrels revisited: Cognitive moral development, just world beliefs, rewards, and ethical decision-making. *Business Ethics Quarterly, 16*, 449–473.

Bateman, T.S. & Organ, D.W. (1983). Job satisfaction and the good soldier: The relationship between affect and employee "citizenship". *Academy of Management Journal, 26*, 587–595.

Beenen, G. & Pinto, J. (2009). Resisting organizational-level corruption: An interview with Enron whistle-blower Sherron Watkins. *Academy of Management Learning and Education, 8*, 275–289.

Benson, M.L. (1985). Denying the guilty mind: Accounting for involvement in a white-collar crime. *Criminology, 23*, 583–607.

Campbell, J.L. & Göritz, A. (2014). Culture corrupts! A qualitative study of organizational culture in corrupt organizations. *Journal of Business Ethics, 120*, 291–311.

Chernow, R. (2017). *Grant.* New York: Penguin.

Cressey, D.R. (1970). The violators' vocabularies of adjustment. In E.O. Smigel & H.L. Ross (Eds.), *Crimes Against Bureaucracy* (pp. 65–85). New York: Van Nostrand Reinhold.

Daboub, A.J., Rasheed, A.M.A., Priem, R.L. & Gray, D.A. (1995). Top management team characteristics and corporate illegal activity. *Academy of Management Review,*

Deshpande, S.P., George, E. & Joseph, J. (2000), Ethical climates and managerial success in Russian organizations. *Journal of Business Ethics*, *23*, 211–217.

Drumm, K. (2015, September 26). VW tries to blame engine emissions fraud on low-level "engineers and technicians". *Mother Jones*, www.motherjones.com/kevin-drum/2015/09/vw-tries-blame-engine-emissions-fraud-low-level-engineers-and-technicians/

Duffy, M.K., Ganster, D.C. & Pagon, M. (2002). Social undermining in the workplace. *Academy of Management Journal*, *45*, 331–351.

Dugan, L. & Gibbs, C. (2009). The role of organizational structure in the control of corporate crime and terrorism. In S. Simpson & D. Weisburd (Eds.), *The Criminology of White-Collar Crime* (pp. 111–128). New York: Springer.

Eidelson, J. (2020, January 10). Amway, welcome to the gig economy: You're being sued over pay. *Bloomberg*, www.bloomberg.com/news/articles/2020-01-10/amway-welcome-to-the-gig-economy-you-re-being-sued-over-pay

Ellis, B. & Hicken, B. (2018). *A Deal with the Devil: The Dark and Twisted True Story of One of the Biggest Cons in History*. New York: Atria.

Ewing, J. (2017, March 16). Engineering a deception: What led to Volkswagen's diesel scandal. *New York Times*, www.nytimes.com/interactive/2017/business/volkswagen-diesel-emissions-timeline.html

Ewing, J. (2019, July 26). 'A few dirty tricks': Documents show Audi's role in the Volkswagen emissions scandal. *New York Times*, www.nytimes.com/2019/07/26/business/audi-vw-emissions-scandal.

Fritzsche, D.J. (2000). Ethical climates and the ethical dimension of decision-making. *Journal of Business Ethics*, *24*, 125–140.

Gault, D.A. (2017). Corruption as an organizational process: Understanding the logic of the denormalization of corruption. Contaduría y Administración, *62*, 847–862.

Gino, F. (2014, December 30). Banking culture encouraged dishonesty. *Scientific American*, www.scientificamerican.com/article/banking-culture-encourages-dishonesty

Gino, F. & Bazerman, M (2009). When misconduct goes unnoticed: The acceptability of gradual erosion in others' unethical behavior. *Journal of Experimental Social Psychology*, *45*, 708–719.

Greenbaum, R.L., Mawritz, M. & Eissa, G. (2012). Bottom-line mentality as an antecedent of social undermining and the moderating roles of core self-evaluations and conscientiousness. *Journal of Applied Psychology*, *97*, 343–359.

Gross, E. (1978). Organizational crime: A theoretical perspective. In N.K. Denzin (Ed.), *Studies in Symbolic Interaction* (Vol. 1, pp. 55–85). Greenwich, CT: JAI Press.

Harris, J. & Bromiley, P. (2007). Incentives to cheat: The influence of executive compensation and firm performance on financial misrepresentation. *Organization Science*, *18*, 350–367.

Hennigan, K. & Spanovic, M. (2012). Gang dynamics through the lens of social identity theory. *Youth Gangs: An International Perspective* (pp. 127–149). New York: Springer.

Hirschi, T. & Gottfredson, M. (1983). Age and the explanation of crime. *American Journal of Sociology*, *90*, 1330–1333.

Hobbs, D. (1995). *Bad Business: Professional Crime in Modern Britain*. Oxford: Oxford University Press.

Hobbs, D. (2013). *Lush Life: Constructing Organised Crime in the UK*. Oxford: Clarendon.

Hoffman, B. (1999). *Terrorism and Weapons of Mass Destruction: An Analysis of Trends and Motivation*. Santa Monica, CA: RAND Corporation.

Hong, N. (2020, January 29). Nxivm 'Sex Cult' was also a huge pyramid scheme, lawsuit says. *New York Times*. www.nytimes.com/2020/01/29/nyregion/nxivm-lawsuit-keith-raniere.html

Jones, S.G., Doxsee, C. & Harrison, N. (2020). The escalating terrorism problem in the United States. CSIS Briefs. Center for Strategic and International Studies, https://csis-website-prod.s3.amazonaws.com/s3fs-public/publication/200612_Jones_Domestic Terrorism_v6.pdf

Keegan, J. (2005) *The Second World War*. New York: Penguin.

Kish-Gephart, J.J., Harrison, D.A. & Treviño, L.K. (2010). Bad apples, bad cases, and bad barrels: Meta-analytic evidence about sources of unethical decisions at work. *Journal of Applied Psychology*, *95*, 1–31.

Knape, C. (2010, November 3). *Amway agrees to pay $56 million, settle case alleging it operates a 'pyramid scheme'*, www.mlive.com/business/west-michigan/2010/11/amway_agrees_to_pay_56_million.html

Laroche, H., Steyer, V. & Théron, C. (2019). How could you be so gullible? Scams and Over-trust in organizations. *Journal of Business Ethics*, *160*, 641–656.

Litzky, B.E., Eddleston, K.A. & Kidder, D.L. (2006). The good, the bad, and the misguided: How managers inadvertently encourage deviant behaviors. *Academy of Management Perspectives*, *20*, 91–103.

Lyman, M.D. (2015). *Organized Crime* (6th Ed.). New York: Pearson.

McLean, B. (2017, May 31). How Wells Fargo's cutthroat corporate culture allegedly drove bankers to fraud. *Vanity Fair*, www.vanityfair.com/news/2017/05/wells-fargo-corporate-culture-fraud

Murphy, K.R. (1993). *Honesty in the Workplace*. Monterey, CA: Brooks/Cole.

Nocera, J. (2015, September 15). The pyramid scheme problem. *New York Times*, www.nytimes.com/2015/09/15/opinion/joe-nocera-the-pyramid-scheme-problem.html

Noll, E. (2010, May 9). Psychic hot line secrets: Clairvoyance or hoax? *ABC News*, https://abcnews.go.com/GMA/Weekend/psychic-reveals-tricks-trade/story?id=10590096

Ordóñez, L., Schweitzer, M., Galinsky, S. & Bazerman, M. (2009). Goals gone wild: The systematic side effects of overprescribing goal-setting. *Academy of Management Perspectives*, *22*, 6–16.

O'Regan, S.V. (2020, January 9). When a psychic reading costs you $74,000. *Gentleman's Quarterly*, www.gq.com/story/the-curse-of-psychic-zoe

Organ, D.W. (1988). *Organizational Citizenship Behavior: The Good Soldier Syndrome*. Lexington, MA: Lexington Books.

Pinto, J., Leanna, C.R. & Pil, F.K. (2008). Corrupt organizations or organizations of corrupt individuals? Two types of organization-level corruption. *Academy of Management Review*, *33*, 685–709.

Post, J.M. (2010). When hatred is bred in the bone: The social psychology of terrorism. *Annals of the New York Academy of Sciences*, *1208*, 15–23.

Sampson, R.J. & Laub, J.H. (2003). Life-course desisters? Trajectories of crime among delinquent boys followed to age 70. *Criminology*, *41*, 555–592.

Schneider, B. (1987). The people make the place. *Personnel Psychology*, *40*, 437–453.

Schneider, B. (2008). The people still make the place. In D.B. Smith (Ed.), *The People Make the Place: Dynamic Linkages Between Individuals and Organizations* (pp. 267–289). New York, NY: Taylor & Francis Group/Lawrence Erlbaum Associates.

Schrager, L.S. & Short, J.F. (1978). Toward a sociology of organizational crime. *Social Problems, 25*, 407–491.

Smith-Crowe, K. & Warren, D.E. (2014). The emotion-evoked collective corruption model: The role of emotion in the spread of corruption within organizations. *Organization Science*, *25*, 1154–1171.

Sonnenfeld, J. & Lawrence, P.R. (1978). Why do companies succumb to price fixing? *Harvard Business Review, 56*, 145–157.

Tabuchi, H. & Ewing, J. (2017, July 27). Volkswagen to pay $14.7 billion to settle diesel claims in U.S. *New York Times*, www.nytimes.com/2016/06/28/business/volkswagen-settlement-diesel-scandal.html?module=inline

Thornberry. (1987). *Toward an interaction theory of delinquency. Criminology, 25*, 863–892.

Travaglino, G.A., Abrams, D., de Moura, G.R. & Russo, G. (2014). Organized crime and group-based ideology: The association between masculine honor and collective opposition against criminal organizations. *Group Processes and Intergroup Relations, 17*, 799–812.

Treviño, L.K., Den Nieuwenboer, N.A. & Kish-Gaphart, J.J. (2014). (Un)ethical behavior in organizations, *Annual Review of Psychology, 65*, 635–660.

Treviño, L.K. & Youngblood, S.A. (1990). Bad apples in bad barrels: A causal analysis of ethical decision-making behavior. *Journal of Applied Psychology, 75*, 378–385.

Van Duyne, P.C. (2000). Mobsters are human too: Behavioral science and organized crime Investigation. *Crime, Law and Social Change, 34*, 369–390.

Victor, B. & Cullen, J.B. (1988). The organizational bases of ethical work climates. *Administrative Sciences Quarterly, 33*, 101–125.

Victoroff, J. & Kruglanski, A.W. (2009). *Key readings in social psychology. Psychology of terrorism: Classic and contemporary insights*. New York: Psychology Press.

Vigil. J.D. (1988). Group processes and street identity: Adolescent Chicano gang members. *Ethos, 16*, 421–445.

Webber, D. & Kruglanski, A.W. (2018). The social psychological makings of a terrorist. *Current Opinion in Psychology, 19*, 131–134.

Whyte, W.F. (1943). *Street Corner Society: The Social Structure of an Italian Slum*. Chicago: University of Chicago Press.

Wilermuth, S.S., Vincent, L.C. & Gino, F. (2017). Creativity in unethical behavior attenuates condemnation and breeds social contagion when transgressions seem to create little harm. *Organizational Behavior and Human Decision Processes, 139*, 106–126.

Will, G. (2019). *Has Catholic Church Committed Worst Crime in American History*? https://triblive.com/opinion/george-will-has-catholic-church-committed-worst-crime-in-american-history/

Yang, S. (2014, July 1). 5 Years Ago Bernie Madoff was sentenced to 150 years in prison—Here's how his scheme worked. *Business Insider*, www.businessinsider.com/how-bernie-madoffs-ponzi-scheme-worked-2014-7

PART III

Positive Behavior in Organizations

13

PROSOCIAL BEHAVIOR IN ORGANIZATIONS

Chapters 1–12 were concerned with understanding misbehavior in organizations. The final two chapters in this book look at the positive side. This chapter deals with prosocial behavior in organizations and Chapter 14 takes up the way organizations recover from sick or corrupt cultures and patterns of behaviors.

Prosocial organizational behavior has been defined as behavior that is: (1) performed by a member of an organization, (2) directed toward an individual, group, or organization with whom he or she interacts while carrying out his or her organizational role, and (3) performed to promote the welfare of the individual, group, or organization toward which it is directed (Brief & Motowidlo, 1986, p. 711). Thus, broadly defined, prosocial organizational behavior can be thought of as behavior that is carried out to help individuals and organizations.

Prosocial behaviors are usually consistent with and supported by general social norms. Indeed, this alignment with the norms of society is an important part of the definition of prosocial behavior. As I noted in Chapter 11, many forms of organizational corruption involve behaviors that are intended to help the organization in the short term but helping your organization defraud its customers, cheat its suppliers, or evade lawfully owed taxes and fees is not helpful in the long term and would typically not be thought of as prosocial behavior.

In-Role Prosocial Behaviors

Prosocial organizational behaviors include both behaviors that are required or expected as a function of your role in the organization (i.e., in-role behavior) and behaviors that are discretionary (i.e., extra-role behavior)—that is, are not normally required or expected. Organizations often take pains to encourage and enforce behaviors that are required as part of a person's role in that organization (Organ, 1997). For example, in a work organization, your job description lays out a set of behaviors, duties, and responsibilities that define your role in the organization, and faithfully carrying these out can be thought of as prosocial behavior. Work organizations are careful to create a series of rewards and sanctions that are tied to performing these in-role behaviors (e.g., salary increases, promotions, terminations), and at first, it might appear that these are sufficient to explain why people engage in in-role prosocial behavior. Research on rewards and sanctions in organizations suggests that the explanation for why most people do the things their jobs require them to do is not so simple.

What Motivates In-Role Prosocial Behavior?

In theory, people who do not perform their key job responsibilities should worry about being fired, particularly in American companies. Several U.S. states have highly permissive "at will" employment laws that, on paper, give employers the right to terminate employees for a broad range of reasons. However, even when employment is at will, terminating employees can be legally perilous and companies can be held liable if dismissal appears to be discriminatory, retaliatory (e.g., firing an employee who has made a legal claim regarding compensation) or done in bad faith (Feffer, 2017). As a result, terminations of individual employees are relatively rare in either the public or private sector.

One way to explain in-role behavior is the desire to avoid sanctions. Another way to explain why people are willing to perform in-role behaviors is the desire to gain rewards. For example, many organizations have some sort of merit pay system, in which better performers receive larger raises. There has been a great deal of research on merit pay systems; there is surprisingly little evidence that merit pay is effective (Heneman, 1992; Milkovich & Wigdor, 1991). In particular, there is little evidence that linking pay to performance leads to better performance.

Part of the problem with merit pay systems is that organizations are often unwilling to commit to meaningful resources to providing performance-contingent rewards. Murphy, Cleveland, and Hanscom (2018) note that merit-based salary increases are typically in the range of 2–3% of annual salary. There is evidence that pay increases are not seen by recipients as meaningful unless they are at least 7% of one's annual salary (Mitra, Gupta, & Jenkins, 1997; Mitra, Tenihälä, & Shaw, 2016). Murphy et al. (2018) suggest that organizations that give merit-based pay raises in the 2–3% range are more likely to breed cynicism than to motivate their employees. In a typical merit-based pay system, truly superior performers receive salary increases that are hardly different from those received by average or poor performers, and the raises they do receive are usually far short of what they would regard as a meaningful raise.

Informal organizations are less likely to have in place systematic programs of sanctions and rewards to encourage or enforce expectations regarding in-role behaviors. For example, I have been a member of several professional associations (e.g., American Psychological Association, Society for Industrial and Organizational Psychology, European Association of Work and Organizational Psychologists). All of these organizations have provisions for sanctioning members for gross abuses of professional standards (e.g., the American Psychological Association publishes annual lists of members who have been expelled for particular violations of professional ethics) and some limited provisions for giving rewards to members whose contributions are noteworthy (e.g., annual awards, promotion to Fellow status), but these pale in comparison to the systems work organizations use to attempt to enforce role expectations in the workforce. Given the limited evidence that sanctions such as dismissal or rewards such as a pay raise have a meaningful effect on workers' behavior, it is unlikely that the formalized rewards or sanctions deployed by informal organizations have much bite.

Norms and In-Role Prosocial Behavior

In both formal and informal organizations, norms play a critical role in understanding in-role prosocial behavior. Most jobs include several tasks and activities that most people would rather avoid (e.g., going to meetings), and one of the best explanations for why people show up every day, go to meetings that they dread, stay till the end of the day even if their work is done, etc. is that this is what is expected of them. Both formal groups (e.g., your workgroup) and informal ones (e.g., your bowling league) have well-established norms that describe what people in different roles are expected and required to do, and they work hard to enforce these norms (Feldman, 1984). Group members who violate social norms are likely to be met with disapproval and even sanctions, especially members who are lower in the power and status hierarchy of the group. Virtually everyone is a member of one or more small groups where interactions are fairly frequent and where group membership is important (e.g., families, friendship groups), and the norms of these groups can have an especially strong effect on the behavior of individuals.

Group norms are an important part of the equation for understanding why people faithfully carry out behaviors their role requires, even if those behaviors are unpleasant (e.g., sitting through a meeting), disagreeable (e.g., dealing with a dissatisfied customer), or dangerous (e.g., going into a burning building to rescue trapped inhabitants). These norms are especially powerful as they become internalized (Axelrod, 1986; Kelman, 1958; Scott, 1971). Once a group member accepts a norm, moving from being told what to do to accepting and believing that he or she *should* do particular things, the process of norm enforcement moves from an external one, in which praise or sanctions from group members control behavior to an internal self-policing process, in which a person becomes less willing to deviate from group norms.

The internalization of norms is especially critical in regulating the behavior of members of loosely organized groups. In some groups (e.g., a professional association), your interaction with other group members might be infrequent and minimal, which implies very little normative regulation from other group members. Why, then, do so many people devote time and energy to carrying out their duties and obligations as members of these loosely organized groups? Perhaps the most compelling answer is that group membership is an important part of a person's social identity, and this identification with groups motivates people to take on roles, responsibilities, and duties and to internalize the norm that they should devote time and effort to them (Hogg & Abrams, 1988).

Rewards, sanctions, and norms are likely the most important factors in influencing in-role behavior, but they are not the only factors. Many people are motivated to engage in prosocial behavior even if there are no rewards, sanctions, or norms supporting those behaviors. Bolino and Grant (2016) suggest that prosocial behavior in organizations is a complex phenomenon that involves prosocial motivation (desire to benefit others or expend effort out of concern for others; Grant, 2008), prosocial action (acts that benefit individuals, groups, or organizations; Brief & Motowidlo, 1986), and prosocial impact (making a positive difference in the lives of others through one's work; Grant, 2007; Grant & Sonnentag, 2010). The links between prosocial motivation, action, and impact are not always strong or simple.

There is controversy over the nature and the causes of prosocial motivation; prosocial behaviors can be both self-serving and other serving (e.g., helping others may contribute to a positive self-image), and the line between prosocial motivation and pure altruism (interest in the good of others, even if this harms your interests) is not always clear (Batson & Shaw, 1991; Grant & Berry, 2011). Prosocial motivation is linked to broader personality traits, notably agreeableness (Penner, Fritzsche, Craiger, & Freifeld, 1995). There is also evidence that prosocial motivation is linked with empathy (Batson & Shaw, 1991), which suggests some possible limits to prosocial motivation. There is, for example, considerable evidence that we are more likely to show empathy toward people and groups who are similar to us than to people and groups who are different (Fourie, Subramoney, & Gobodo-Madikizela, 2017), and the same might be true for prosocial behavior. We might be more willing to follow social rules and norms when interacting with people or groups who are similar to us, and less likely to do so when dealing with people or groups who are not so similar to us.

Extra-Role Prosocial Behavior: Organizational Citizenship

Prosocial behavior includes both in-role behaviors (i.e., doing the things that are expected and required as a result of your role in a group or organization) and extra-role behaviors (i.e., behaviors that go beyond role expectations); a substantial body of research on extra-role behavior has focused on organizational citizenship (Bateman & Organ, 1983; Motowidlo & Van Scotter, 1994; Organ, Podsakoff, & MacKenzie, 2006; Smith, Organ, & Near, 1983). Organ (1988) described organizational citizenship in terms of a "good soldier" syndrome—that is, someone who goes above and beyond the requirements of his or her role for the good of the organization. Organ (1997) defined this type of organizational citizenship as behavior that "supports the social and psychological environment in which task performance takes place" (p. 95).

In the workplace, organizational citizenship behavior (OCB) is often defined in terms of behaviors that are not necessary to accomplish the specific tasks that are laid out in an individual's job description and not part of the formal reward structure of most organizations, but are necessary for the smooth functioning of teams and organizations (Borman & Motowidlo, 1993; Borman & Penner, 2001; Brief & Motowidlo, 1986; Edwards & Morrison, 1994; Hoffman, Blair, Meriac, & Woehr, 2007; Organ, 1988; Smith, Organ, & Near, 1983). For example, Organ (1988, 1990) describes organizational citizenship in terms of behaviors such as altruism, courtesy, conscientiousness, civic virtue, sportsmanship, peacekeeping, and cheerleading. Van Scotter and Motowidlo (1996) suggest there are two major dimensions to organizational citizenship—interpersonal facilitation behaviors (e.g., helping coworkers) and job dedication (e.g., taking initiative, working hard).

Borman and his colleagues developed what is probably the most complete description of organizational citizenship, which they suggest can be summarized in terms of three broad dimensions: (1) personal support, (2) organizational support, and (3) conscientious initiative (Borman et al., 2001). Personal support includes behaviors such as helping, cooperating, and showing courtesy. Organizational support includes behaviors such as loyalty to the organization and compliance with its rules and policies. Conscientious initiative includes behaviors such as self-development and showing initiative and persistence (Dorsey, Cortina, & Luchman, 2010). Table 13.1 describes these three general dimensions of OCB in more detail.

The common thread running through all of these OCB models is that organizational citizenship represents a set of behaviors that help to build and maintain the social structure of the group or organization. One of the assumptions of research on organizational citizenship in work organizations is that if everyone does the tasks required by his or her job, but nobody is willing to go beyond their job description to help others when help is needed, to develop new skills, to make sure that each member of the organization is treated with courtesy and consideration, and to encourage others, it will be very difficult to maintain a viable organization. Take, for example, sportsmanship—a willingness to put up with minor inconveniences at work without complaining. Very few job descriptions will include a phrase like "don't whine", but if most members of an organization

TABLE 13.1 Model of Organizational Citizenship Behavior

Dimension	*Examples*
Personal Support	Helping others, performing tasks for them Teaching and mentoring others Providing emotional support Cooperating with others Keeping others informed Showing consideration and tact when dealing with others
Organizational Support	Representing the organization well Promoting the organization Expressing satisfaction with the organization Expressing loyalty and commitment to the organization Supporting the organization's mission Complying with organizational rules and policies
Conscientious Initiative	Showing extra effort and persistence Developing knowledge and skills that are valuable to the organization Finding additional productive work when your duties are done Taking initiative to make sure important goals are met

Source: Borman et al. (2001)

complain and appeal to higher authority whenever they don't get what they want or whenever they experience some minor annoyance, the workplace will become an impossibly toxic place. Similarly, an organization where nobody helps anyone else, nobody takes responsibility for their behavior, everyone talks disparagingly about their organization, and nobody puts the good of the group or the good of the organization above their own will soon become a very difficult and unattractive place to work.

Most models of organizational citizenship focus on content—that is, they describe the behaviors that constitute OCB. Another way of classifying and describing OCBs is in terms of their targets. Williams and Anderson (1991) distinguish between organizational citizenship behaviors directed toward the other individuals (OCB-I) and organizational citizenship behaviors directed toward the organization (OCB-O). For example, they suggest that Organ's (1988, 1990) altruism dimension is an excellent exemplar of OCB-I, in that it is intended to help other individuals. Other OCBs, such as courtesy, peacekeeping, and cheerleading behaviors are aimed at helping the organization and are examples of OCB-O. As I will note later in this chapter, one reason this distinction is important is that there is evidence that OCB-I and OCB-O behaviors often have different antecedents.

Van Dyne and LePine (1998) suggested yet another way of classifying OCBs in terms of what these behaviors are intended to produce. They suggest that it is useful to distinguish between affiliative OCBs, which aim to maintain and protect the status quo, and challenging or change-oriented OCBs, which aim to change (and presumably improve) the organization in which they occur (Chiaburu, Lorinkova, & Van Dyne, 2013; Van Dyne & LePine, 1998).

While the distinctions between different groups or types of OCB make good conceptual sense, there is clear evidence that different types of OCBs tend to be correlated. This implies that it is reasonable to talk about OCB as a single entity—that is, that people show higher levels of OCB than others, much in the same way that it is possible to talk sensibly about overall job performance, even though this construct is known to be multidimensional (Viswesvaran, Schmidt, & Ones, 2005). That is, people who engage in high levels of some OCBs (e.g., courtesy and sportsmanship) are likely to exhibit other OCBs as well.

In Chapter 8, I discussed counterproductive workplace behaviors (CWB), such as property and production deviance, bullying and harassment, theft and white-collar crime. There are some similarities in the conceptualization of OCB and CWB. Like OCB, CWB can be described in terms of destructive behaviors that are aimed at individuals (CWB-I) vs. those aimed at organizations (CWB-O). Early research suggested that while OBC and CWB were not absolute mirror images, they were negatively correlated, which suggests that individuals who engage in OCB would not be likely to also engage in CWB (Dalal, 2005). Subsequent research has painted a more complicated picture. The correlations between OCB and CWB are generally positive, sometimes modest (Berry, Ones, & Sackett, 2007), and sometimes more substantial (Mackey, McAllister, Ellen, & Carson, in press); the relationship between these constructs may depend on how OCB is measured (Henderson, Foster, Matthews, & Zickar, 2019). Thus, the same individual who is courteous and a good sport at work might also be stealing from the organization or cooperating in an organization-wide fraud.

BOX 13.1 IS PROFESSIONALISM ANOTHER NAME FOR ORGANIZATIONAL CITIZENSHIP?

The U.S. Department of Labor describes professionalism as one of the important "Skills to Pay the Bills".[1] They describe professionalism in terms of:

- Conducting oneself with responsibility, integrity, accountability, and excellence
- Looking clean and neat and dressing appropriately for the job
- Communicating effectively and appropriately and always finding a way to be productive
- Arriving on time for work and managing time effectively

- Taking responsibility for one's own and working effectively with others
- Demonstrating high-quality work standards, honesty, and integrity

This description of professionalism has a great deal in common with organizational citizenship, which suggests that if we just encouraged people to take a more professional approach to their work, organizational citizenship would take care of itself. One problem with this approach is that professionalism may serve as a barrier to diversity.

Gray (2019) argues that "Professionalism" is just another term for a set of norms that favors the dominant group by creating standards of dress, speech, interaction, etc. that conform to the dominant White, upper-class culture in organizations. It is easier to be "professional" if you have the sort of support system many members of the upper class have—for example, someone to take care of your home and your children (often a wife) so that you can devote extra time and effort to work. Many citizenship behaviors have at least a suggestion of *noblesse oblige* (e.g., we help others at work, presumably those not so fortunate or talented to take care of themselves), and the idea that you should go beyond the requirements and duties associated with your role for the good of the organization may not get as much support among members of the working class as it gets among members of the upper class.

Explaining Organizational Citizenship

As was the case for misbehavior, explanations for prosocial behaviors, including organizational citizenship, rely on both personal and situational factors. First, there are several attributes of individuals (e.g., personality traits, stable attitudes) that influence the likelihood that an individual will engage in OCB. Second, features of the organizational context within which OCBs occur that can either enhance or suppress OCB, including leadership, perceptions of organizations, and organizational climates and cultures.

Individual Determinants of OCB

Organizational citizenship has been tied to individual differences in other-orientation and concern for others (Korsgaard, Meglino, & Lester, 1997; McNeely & Meglino, 1994; Meglino & Korsgaard, 2007), prosocial values (Rioux & Penner, 2001), and prosocial personality (Penner et al., 1995). More general personality traits such as conscientiousness, agreeableness, and positive affectivity have been used to predict prosocial behavior (Borman & Motowidlo, 1993; Murphy & Shiarella, 1997; Podsakoff, MacKenzie, Paine, & Bachrach,

2000; Thomas, Whitman, & Viswesvaran, 2010; Tornau & Frese, 2013). There are also consistent correlations between OCB and other types of ethical behavior in organizations. Individuals who exhibit higher levels of ethical behavior in organizations also tend to exhibit more OCBs (Turnipseed, 2002).

Prosocial organizational behavior, including OCB, is relatively stable over time (Caesens, Marique, Hanin, & Stinglhamber, 2016), which would be expected if OCBs were largely driven by stable individual differences. On the other hand, the situational factors that influence OCB are also often relatively stable, meaning that we cannot necessarily use temporal stability in OCB to argue for the primacy of individual differences. The clearest tests of personal vs. situational explanations would come from a study that includes many people who frequently change organizations *and* in which they change into organizations with very different climates, cultures, leadership, etc. Unfortunately, data of this sort is very hard to come by.

Different types of OCB may have different antecedents (Williams & Anderson, 1991). For example, Uymaz (2014) notes that prosocial behaviors toward organizations are positively related to perceptions of organizational support, whereas prosocial behaviors oriented toward individuals appear to depend more heavily on personality traits. Likely, attitudes toward organizations are more closely linked with OCB aimed at organizations than OCB aimed at individuals (Podsakoff et al., 2000).

Organizational citizenship behaviors might even be affected by one's mood; people are more likely to reach out to help others (both individuals and organizations) when they are in a positive mood. Organ and Konovsky (1989) presented evidence for consistent links between moods and OCB, but they also conclude that the influence of relatively stable attitudes toward the job and the organization are stronger drivers of OCB than more transient moods.

Finally, OCB is not the same thing as altruism, and some people engage in OCB to further their interests.[2] Bolino (1999) suggests that while employees often engage in OCBs because they are "good soldiers" who care about the organization or their colleagues, some employees may also perform OCBs to appear to be "good actors". These OCBs can enhance their image at work, and as I will note in a section to follow, they can often lead directly to valued rewards, such as pay raises and promotions.

Situational Determinants of OCB

There is clear evidence that situational factors influence OCB (e.g., Podsakoff et al., 2000), and that their influence might be at least as important as the influence of individual differences.[3] For example, the willingness of employees to demonstrate OCB is linked to the behavior of their leaders, especially the extent to which leaders appear to behave fairly (Farh, Podsakoff, & Organ, 1990; Moorman, 1991). Employees are more likely to demonstrate citizenship behaviors when they work in enriched jobs characterized by task significance, task identity, skill variety (i.e., are you doing something meaningful, able to perform the whole task as opposed to some small part, and do you use a variety of skills in doing your job?), autonomy, and feedback (Piccolo & Colquitt, 2006). OCBs are less common when tasks are routinized and when employees face role conflict and ambiguity (Podsakoff et al., 2000). Job attitudes, such as satisfaction and organizational commitment, are thought to represent cognitive and affective reactions to one's job and one's organization, and measures of these attitudes are positively related to measures of OCBs such as helping, courtesy, initiative, sportsmanship, civic virtue, and compliance (Podsakoff et al., 2000).

Perceived organizational support (POS) is an important construct for understanding OCB. Perceived organizational support refers to the degree to which members of an organization believe that the organization values their contributions, cares for their welfare, and provides them with psychological and emotional support (Eisenberger, Huntington, Hutchison, & Sowa, 1986; Rhoades. & Eisenberger, 2002). POS is positively related to OCB; individuals who believe their organization values and supports them are more likely to exhibit organizational citizenship behaviors (Caesens et al., 2016). One likely explanation for this link is a reciprocity norm—that is, the belief that if the organization goes out of its way to treat you well, you have some obligation to reciprocate and go beyond the most basic requirements of your job or role to help the organization and its members.

Organizational climates and cultures are often cited as important determinants of OCB. Quinn and Rohrbaugh's (1983) Competing Values Framework (CVF) provides a taxonomy of organizational cultures based on the goals that an organization pursues (Cameron & Quinn, 1999), and it is useful for understanding the types of organizational cultures that might elicit or suppress OCB (Marinova, Cao, & Park, 2019). This framework classifies organizational cultures based on: (1) whether the organization focuses on stability and control vs. adaptability and flexibility and (2) the extent to which the organization is internally vs. externally focused. The 2 x 2 CVF model, shown in Figure 13.1, describes four fundamentally different types of organizational culture.

Organizations whose culture is flexible and internally focused exhibit what this model describes as a *Clan* culture, in which the underlying assumption is that people will behave appropriately if they have trust in and loyalty to the organization, and in which the primary values reflect attachment and support. This Clan structure, because of its focus on trust and support, is likely to foster OCB, particularly OCB-O.

Organizations whose culture is stable and internally focused exhibit a Hierarchy culture, in which the underlying assumption is that people will behave appropriately if they have clear, well-defined roles and formally defined policies and procedures to follow, and in which the primary values reflect communication and formalization. This culture, with its strong emphasis on formal rules and policies,

	Internal Focus	External Focus
Flexibility	Focus on attachment, trust, support—*Clan Structure*	Focus on rapid and flexible responses to the environment—*Adhocracy Structure*
Stability	Focus on achievement and goal setting—*Hierarchy Structure*	Focus on risk taking, creativity, adaptability —*Market Structure*

FIGURE 13.1 The Competing Values Framework of Organizational Cultures

provides a good deal of support for prosocial in-role behavior (i.e., doing what you are supposed to do) but is much less likely to support OCB.

Organizations whose culture is flexible and externally focused exhibit an Adhocracy culture, in which the underlying assumption is that people will behave appropriately if they understand the importance and the impact of the tasks they are asked to perform, and in which the primary values reflect growth and autonomy. This culture will support some types of OCB, especially those that involve taking responsibility for the success of the group or the organization.

Organizations whose culture is stable and externally focused exhibit a Market culture, in which the underlying assumption is that people will behave appropriately if they have clear objectives and are rewarded for their accomplishments, and in which the primary values reflect achievement and competence. Like the Hierarchy culture, this organizational culture is likely to support behaviors that are consistent with role requirements but is less likely to support extra-role behaviors, especially those designed to help others.

There is clear evidence that healthy cultures foster OCBs (Härtel & Ashkanasy, 2011). Marinova et al. (2019) suggest that rather than seeing the CVF as a set of four mutually exclusive climates, we think of it as a taxonomy of beliefs and behaviors, many of which might be present in the same organization. They define a constructive organizational values climate as one that shows relatively high levels of market, human relations, and innovation climate and medium levels of the bureaucratic climate and propose that a constructive organizational values climate can help foster both a healthy bond between individuals and organizations and a willingness to perform OCBs.

Suppose your goal was to build and foster an organizational culture that encourages members of your organization to act ethically. There are several ways organizational cultures might be used to increase the likelihood of ethical behavior and decrease the likelihood of behaviors that might harm individuals or organizations. Bandura (1999) suggests that since most people are guided by personal standards of ethical behavior, organizations should take steps to activate and support these standards. For example, if members of an organization are asked to consider the ethical implications of their actions or recommendations when making important decisions, this is likely to make their ethical standards more salient. When these standards are activated, they help in playing a self-regulatory role by guiding good behavior (consistent with the standards) and deterring misconduct (that would violate the standards). Thus, ethical conduct is regulated largely through "anticipatory self-sanctions" that keep behavior in line with personal standards and help the individual avoid unethical behavior that would lead to self-censure (Bandura, 1999).

Vidaver-Cohen (1998) suggests that emphasizing an employee focus and concern within an organization's mission statement may help facilitate a more moral climate. However, mission statements are often little more than platitudes, and changing the mission statement without changing the behavior of members of the organization is unlikely to do much to enhance ethical behavior. Vidaver-Cohen (1998) suggests that an organization is most likely to be successful in creating an ethical climate if it focuses on the behavior of senior leaders. For example, if senior leaders in an organization are visibly engaging in ethical and prosocial behavior, this may increase the salience and perceived value of ethical and prosocial behavior. There is indeed evidence that when leaders behave ethically, subordinates are less likely to engage in antisocial behavior such as workplace deviance (Litzky, Eddleston, & Kidder, 2006). Vidaver-Cohen (1998) also suggests that ethical issues should be an integral part of socialization practices in an organization. For instance, organizations could emphasize their commitment to ethical behavior in new employee orientations and training.

There is evidence that ethical organizational cultures can reduce unethical behaviors in organizations (Loe, Ferrell, & Mansfield, 2000). It is reasonable to expect that these cultures can increase the likelihood of both in-role and extra-role prosocial behaviors. First, ethical cultures encourage you to go beyond narrow consideration when making decisions, thinking about what you *should* do rather than thinking solely in terms of what you are obligated by your role or your job description to do. Second, these cultures ask the members of an organization to think critically about their behaviors rather than simply do what they are told.

OCBs Are Valued

Citizenship behaviors such as altruism, courtesy, conscientiousness, sportsmanship, and peacekeeping are rarely included in job descriptions and are rarely articulated in defining people's roles in less formal groups or organizations, but these are recognized as valuable and important to the organization. For example in work organizations, where citizenship is not part of most job descriptions, supervisors nevertheless pay attention to both task performance and organizational citizenship when evaluating the performance of their subordinates (Allen & Rush, 1998; Conway, 1996; Johnson, 2001; Motowidlo & Van Scotter, 1994; Posthuma, 2000; Werner, 1994; Whiting, Podsakoff, & Pierce, 2008) and organizational citizenship is taken into account when making decisions about rewards and promotions (Van Scotter, Motowidlo, & Cross, 2000). Podsakoff et al. (2009) summarize evidence from multiple studies showing the citizenship behavior is related to important individual and organizational outcomes, and that these behaviors do indeed contribute to the successful functioning of organizations. In many cases, citizenship behaviors seem as important as task performance to organizations (Podsakoff, Whiting, Podsakoff, & Blume, 2009). Supervisors are especially likely to give credit for citizenship behaviors that they believe are performed because of concern for others (Halbesleben, Bowler, Bolino, & Turnley, 2010).

There is evidence that supervisors and their subordinates believe that it is appropriate and fair to consider citizenship behaviors in evaluating job performance (Johnson, Holladay, & Quinones, 2009). Contextual performance is probably more important in jobs where workers interact and depend on one another. For example, Bachrach, Powell, Bendoly, and Richey (2006) present evidence that OCBs are seen as more important when there is extensive task interdependence than when workers perform their tasks independently.

There is also evidence that groups with higher average levels of OCB tend to perform better, both in terms of getting their tasks done and in terms of maintaining healthy relationships within and between groups (Nielsen, Hrivnak, & Shaw, 2009). Organizational citizenship behaviors are critical to maintaining the social networks that constitute organizations, and organizations of all sorts depend heavily on the proposition that members will go beyond the minimal requirements of their roles and will devote substantial and sustained efforts to building and maintaining the social networks that underlie all organizations.

The Dark Side of Organizational Citizenship

Organizational citizenship behaviors benefit organizations and their members, but there are potential downsides to these behaviors. First, there are often tradeoffs between engaging in OCB vs. carrying out the tasks that are central to your role. In the workplace, task performance and OCB can place competing demands on workers, and workers who devote an extensive amount of their time and energy to citizenship behaviors might not be able to accomplish their tasks. I have argued earlier in this chapter that a worker who focuses exclusively on the tasks and duties listed in his or her job description and never takes steps to help out colleagues who require assistance or to represent their company well to customers might not be an effective employee. On the other hand, an employee who is always volunteering to help but who never gets his or her main tasks done might be similarly ineffective.

Ellington, Dierdorff, and Rubin (2014) studied potential tradeoffs between task performance and citizenship behaviors. Their results suggest that this tradeoff depends on the social context in which work is performed and that when work is highly interdependent, there may not always be any such thing as too much organizational citizenship. On the whole, OCB has more payoff (in terms of the overall evaluations and rewards ratees receive) for employees who also have strong task performance. When task performance is weaker, high levels of OCB might not be enough to compensate for the inability to get one's core job tasks done (Kiker & Motowidlo, 1999).

The OCB-task performance tradeoff may be different for men vs. women. Bergeron, Shipp, Rosen, and Furst (2013) note that women are often expected to engage in more organizational citizenship behaviors than men. This can make it more difficult for women than men to accomplish their key tasks and to advance their careers.

Second, OCBs can lead to higher levels of role overload, and work-family conflict (Bolino & Turnley, 2005; Halbesleben, Harvey, & Bolino, 2009). Bolino, Turnley, Gilstrap, and Suazo (2010) note that although OCB is usually thought of as voluntary and discretionary, employees often feel pressured to demonstrate OCB if citizenship behavior is informally encouraged and rewarded. Prosocial behaviors can be a significant source of stress and burnout, especially if employees feel pressured to help (Bolino, Turnley, Gilstrap, & Suazo, 2010; Grant, 2008; Weinstein & Ryan, 2010). If OCB is sufficiently common and frequent to become the norm in a workgroup, individuals may feel compelled to demonstrate OCB, even if they would prefer to stick with the duties and responsibilities laid out in their job description. Bolino and Turnley (2003) warn of *escalating citizenship*, in which the desire to go the extra mile becomes so widespread that individuals find themselves competing to demonstrate increasingly high levels of OCB. Job descriptions usually lay out what is required of a worker, but there is no limit to the types of citizenship behaviors they might engage in, and some workers are likely to overdo things. This can contribute to citizenship fatigue (Bolino, Hsiung, Harvey, & LePine, 2015), in which energy devoted to organizational citizenship behaviors exhausts employees.

Finally, and most important, organization members who are "good soldiers" may be more willing to break rules, violate laws, and cooperate in corrupt schemes if these behaviors are seen as necessary or as helpful to the organization (Bolino & Grant, 2016). In Chapter 10, I described how a strong level of attachment and commitment to one's organization can be a causal factor in white-collar crime and other large-scale organizational patterns of misbehavior (e.g., the cover-up of child abuse by members of the Roman Catholic clergy). Commitment and loyalty to the organization are an important part of organizational citizenship; in the Borman et al. (2001) model, commitment and loyalty are important parts of the broader dimension of organizational support. Likely, many of the participants in the frauds perpetrated by Volkswagen, Wells Fargo, Enron, WorldCom, etc. were willing to go along with corrupt practices because they sincerely believed that such practices were helpful to their organization, and perhaps even necessary for its survival. In Chapter 2, I described two horrific cases of mass violence, the Rape of Nanjing and the Holocaust. In both cases, soldiers and other functionaries of the Japanese and German regimes were willing to kill, maim, and rape civilians, often without direct orders. Indeed, violence was often the direct result of soldiers, guards, policemen, and the like anticipating the orders and preferences of their superiors and acting as "good soldiers" who carried out horrific acts that went beyond the formal requirements of their roles (Chang, 1997; Goldhagen, 1996).

Loyalty and commitment are not the only aspects of OCB that could contribute to misbehavior in organizations. Once corruption becomes normalized in an organization, almost all of the citizenship behaviors shown in Table 13.1 might contribute to further that corruption. For example, in a corrupted organization, an employee who takes initiative, shows extra effort, and develops knowledge and skills useful to the organization might put all of the work into furthering corrupt schemes (e.g., development and deployment of the Volkswagen cheat device). Similarly, an employee who helps, mentors, and trains a new employee or who provides that employee with emotional support might do so to keep the flow of phony bank accounts growing (as was allegedly done at Wells Fargo). Efforts to support the organization's mission and promote the organization might be a tremendous help to an organization that is pursuing corrupt goals (e.g., IG Farben, which used slave labor in its synthetic rubber plant next to Auschwitz during the Second World War).

A case can be made that corrupt practices in organizations would not be possible, or at least would be much harder to pull off, without a cadre of good organizational citizens willing to go along with the scheme and to work hard to pull it off. The very commitment of these good organizational citizens, together with their willingness to do whatever is needed for the organization to succeed is a necessary ingredient to many white-collar crimes and organizational frauds, and it represents the darkest side of OCB.

Unwelcome Citizenship: Whistleblowing

Near and Miceli (1985) define whistleblowing as "the disclosure by organization members . . . of illegal, immoral, or illegitimate practices under the control of their employers, to persons or organizations that may be able to effect action" (p. 9). Whistleblowing can be thought of as the outcome of a conflict between one's obligation as a citizen (who should report illegal or corrupt activities) and one's obligation as an organizational citizen (who is supposed to be loyal to the organization). The decision to blow the whistle involves a conflict between two sets of responsibilities (i.e., to society and the organization), and there is a substantial body of research on the decision to blow the whistle when you see apparent wrongdoing in your organization (Dungan, Waytz, & Young, 2014, 2015).

Anvari, Wenzel, Woodyatt, and Halsam (2019) suggest that the decision to blow the whistle involves considerations of social identity and perceived power. For example, it is harder to blow the whistle if you identify with the offending group and easier if you identify with some superordinate group (e.g., a professional society) that does not approve of the activity in question. Similarly, it is easier to blow the whistle if you believe you have the power to influence changes than if you do not. Mesmer-Magnus and Viswesvaran's (2005) meta-analysis found that females, more tenured employees, higher performers, and those at higher job levels are more likely to blow the whistle. They also found that ethical judgment was significantly correlated with whistleblowing intentions, but not actual whistleblowing behavior. They reported meaningful relationships between whistleblowing intentions and contextual variables such as climate, the threat of retaliation, supervisor support, the severity of the transgression, and closeness to the wrongdoer.

Anvari et al. (2019) suggest that Social Identity Theory (Tajfel, 1982; Tajfel & Turner, 1986) provides a useful framework for understanding whistleblowing. Whistleblowing involves reporting perceived wrongdoing to some external agency, and Anvari et al. (2019) suggest that this external reporting is unlikely if individuals identify strongly with their organization. As I have noted in several previous chapters, most individuals identify with multiple groups (e.g., friends, family, workgroup), and the decision to blow the whistle often depends on the relative strength of the organization vs. other groups as a source of social identity. The stronger the links to superordinate groups (e.g., society in general) relative to the organization, the higher the likelihood of whistleblowing.

Whistleblowers are likely to view their actions as prosocial behavior (Dozier & Miceli, 1985) but their organizational colleagues often think otherwise (Alford, 2016). Whistleblowers are likely to face disapproval and retaliation from their organization. First, whistleblowers are seen as disloyal; whistleblowers themselves are likely to believe that their loyalties to the broader society transcend loyalties to the organization. Second, whistleblowing represents an implicit moral reproach to other organization members who fail to blow the whistle and rejecting whistleblowers makes it easier to maintain a positive self-image while going along with or failing to report offenses and corrupt behavior (Monin, Sawyer, & Marquez, 2008). Whistleblowers represent a threat to organizations in part because whistleblowing usually implies reporting suspected wrongdoing to an external agency (reporting suspected wrongdoing to your boss is not typically thought of as whistleblowing). This almost by definition creates a divide between team players and whistleblowers, and it is one of the many factors that motivate retaliation against whistleblowers.

Retaliation can come from the organization (e.g., a whistleblower might be demoted or fired), but peers and coworkers are also often a significant source of retaliatory behavior (Park, Bjørkelo, & Blenkinsopp, 2020). For example, surveys of military personnel who report sexual harassment include numerous reports of mistreatment of whistleblowers by other members of their units.[4] Even in cases where leaders or managers are careful to safeguard the rights of whistleblowers, it can be very difficult to shelter them from retaliation by their peers, especially if the whistleblower is seen as betraying his or her unit.

Whistleblowers have some legal protection. The Whistleblower Protection Act of 1989 is designed to protect whistleblowers in federal agencies from retaliation if they report violations of the law, rules, or regulations or gross misuse of funds; numerous specific laws and regulations have also been put into place to protect whistleblowers. Many organizations, particularly governmental organizations, have whistleblower protection programs and hotlines in place. There is even a U.S. National Whistleblower Appreciation Day (June 30) and a World Whistleblowing Day (June 23). The effectiveness of these protections, however, is often in doubt. For example, in a phone call with the Ukraine's president, President Trump asked the Ukraine to investigate one of his political rivals, Joseph Biden. Lt. Col. Alexander S. Vindman, a Ukraine expert who was on this call considered such a request as damaging to U.S. interests and reported the call to national security officials. This call was an important factor in President Trump's impeachment. Despite whistleblower protection laws, Lt. Col. Vindman was denied a promotion and hounded out of the army by the President and his allies.

BOX 13.2 WHISTLEBLOWERS: HEROES OR MALCONTENTS?

How should we think about whistleblowers? The answer might depend on the incident that led to whistleblowing (e.g., was the organization involved in a serious offense vs. a technical violation of a minor rule), the consequences of the offense (e.g., Ford's decision to ignore problems with the fuel tanks of the Pinto exploding in rear-end collisions led to the loss of many lives, which seems disproportionate given the small costs required the fix the defect), and your relationship with the target of the whistleblower (Democrats were much more sympathetic to the plight of Lt. Col. Vindman, who blew the whistle on President Trump's Ukraine phone call, than Republicans). It might depend on whether the whistle is blown on some other organization or *your* organization. It might also depend on the apparent motives for whistleblowing. Individuals who blow the whistle out of concern for morality are sometimes seen as the "saints of secular culture" (Grant, 2002). Individuals who blow the whistle to gain financial rewards may be seen in a very different light (Weinberg, 2005).

Whistleblowers are likely to suffer for their actions. Whistleblowers show higher levels of distress, drug and alcohol problems, paranoid behavior at work, acute anxiety, nightmares, flashbacks and intrusive thoughts (Peters, Luck, Hutchinson, Wilkes, Andrew, & Jackson, 2011). They face ostracism and retaliation, despite the legal protections afforded whistleblowers, and they are usually well aware of the risks they face when they blow the whistle. Nevertheless, they cannot automatically be thought of as heroes. As with much else in this book, context matters. For example, Anvari et al. (2019) note that most whistleblowers first report their concerns to their supervisors or some other person in authority within the organization and decide to take their concerns outside of the organization only when it is clear that their internal reports will not lead to action or change. Whistleblowers who immediately take their concerns to outside agencies, without first trying to report their concerns through the normal chain of command, are more likely to be seen as malcontents, whereas whistleblowers who make good-faith efforts within their organization and only resort to external whistleblowing when it is clear the organization is unwilling to respond are more likely to be seen in a favorable light.

Prosocial Behaviors and Misbehavior—Similarities and Differences

Chapters 1–12 were devoted to understanding and explaining misbehavior. As this chapter shows, many of the concepts used to explain misbehavior also apply when explaining prosocial behaviors in organizations. First, both have personal and situation explanations. There are stable attitudes and personality traits that affect the likelihood of both antisocial and prosocial behaviors. Second, both prosocial and antisocial behaviors flourish where there is clear normative support. If the norms of your organization or the groups within that organization you identify with suggest that you should engage in prosocial behavior, the likelihood you will show prosocial behavior increases, perhaps substantially. In much the same way, when the norms of your organization treat misbehavior as normal, broadly accepted and even laudable, the likelihood that you will misbehave goes up. Indeed, the counterpart to the belief often associated with misbehaviors that "everyone does it" is the belief among people who engage in prosocial behaviors that they are not notable or unusual, but rather that "everyone does it". Third, many types of misbehavior are perceived by their perpetrators as prosocial behavior. White-collar criminals, for example, rarely think they have done anything wrong. Rather, they often believe that their crimes were necessary for the survival and success of their organization.

Finally, misbehaviors will usually be met with disapproval if exposed, but the same can be said for at least some types of prosocial behavior. Consider a new employee who joins a workgroup and shows high levels of effort, persistence, and initiative. We have known for decades that rate-busters (individuals who work harder than or produce more than their peers) are often disliked and resented by their peers (Dalton 1948). Rate-busters not only make their peers look bad, but their behavior can have adverse effects on peers, who might be required to match the rates these individuals achieve.

Despite the similarities, there are important differences in the causes of prosocial vs. antisocial behaviors. First, prosocial behavior is often viewed in a positive light by society, whereas the definition of misbehavior includes the idea that these behaviors violate broad social norms, rules, regulations, and laws. Prosocial behaviors might be contrary to (or irrelevant to) the norms of your organization or your workgroup, but there is rarely conflict between the broad norms of society and prosocial behavior. This means that less cognitive effort is likely to be needed to rationalize or justify prosocial behaviors; people are likely to believe, at least at some level, that prosocial behaviors represent things they ought to do or are expected to do.

Finally, both types of behavior flourish when there is strong normative support, but the processes by which norms supporting prosocial behavior vs. misbehavior are likely to differ. Prosocial behaviors are generally consistent with broad social norms that define what is right vs. wrong, and what behaviors are desirable. Norms that support misbehavior are necessarily more complex because they must include or incorporate reasons why behaviors that are viewed as wrong by society, in general, are viewed as acceptable and even laudable in your organization. Thus, someone who has been taught since childhood that stealing is wrong will have to internalize whatever evasions his or her organization uses to convince its members that what they are doing is not *really* stealing. Some corrupt organizations maintain "two sets of books", one set showing the trades, purchases, expenditures, etc. they carry out and another showing fictitious trades, purchases, etc. that conform to legal standards. If you subscribe to a set of norms that supports or tolerates misbehavior in organizations, you have to keep two sets of moral standards operating simultaneously, one that describes how society, in general, wants you to behave and another that describes "the way we do things around here". There are plenty of examples of people who are otherwise good and generous, but who are ruthless, dishonest, and cruel when they take on their organizational role, but a life of misbehavior requires a different and more complex moral calculus than one in which you uphold similar moral standard when serving in your organizational role than when you go home.

Summary

This chapter deals with prosocial behavior. Like misbehavior, both personal and situational factors explain why people do what their roles require and why they sometimes go beyond the requirements of their roles to help their organization and its members. The standard explanation for in-role prosocial behavior is that organizations use a combination of rewards and sanctions to enforce role requirements. This explanation is helpful but incomplete. In work organizations, for example, rewards are often trivial (a great performer might get a 3% raise, while others get 2.25%) and sanctions are often toothless (even in "employment at will" states, there are often substantial disincentives to firing or demoting employees). Norms appear to be an important factor in explaining prosocial behavior, much in the same way they explain misbehavior.

People often go well beyond the minimal requirements of their jobs or roles to help others and to benefit the organization. This set of behaviors is often referred to as organizational citizenship behavior (OCB). OCB is often critical to building and maintaining the social structure of organizations and can be critical to an organization's survival and success. OCBs are rarely included in the formal descriptions of roles in organizations; few job descriptions include statements like "help others when they need it", "don't complain too much", "stay after closing time if the work is not done". Nevertheless, these behaviors are often critical; an organization in which everyone does exactly what his or her contract or job description calls for and nothing else can be a very difficult place.

OCBs benefit individuals and organizations, but there are potential downsides to OCB. First, people who devote the majority of their time and effort to OCBs might not get their main tasks done. Second, people who engage in OCBs on top of their main tasks may experience stress, role overload, work-family conflict, and burnout. Third, and most important, "good soldiers" (i.e., organization members who regularly exhibit OCB) are more likely than other members of organizations to go along with illegal or corrupt schemes. Their very level of commitment and loyalty to the organization, together with the persistence and initiative that is characteristic of OCB make them the ideal candidates to do what the organization seems to require. For example, the development and worldwide deployment of cheat devices that allowed Volkswagen's diesel cars to pass emissions tests required skill, hard work, and dedication, and it is a reasonable bet that many of the people involved in this scheme were very good organizational citizens.

Prosocial behaviors and misbehaviors show many similarities. They both have personal and situational causes. Both types of behavior carry a mix of costs and benefits for individuals and organizations. Norms are critical to support both types of behavior. The big difference is that misbehavior requires a set of norms that run counter to general societal norms, and thus require more moral gymnastics to reconcile the belief that "X is wrong" with "but in this organization, or these circumstances, X is fine".

Notes

1. www.dol.gov/sites/dolgov/files/odep/topics/youth/softskills/professionalism.pdf
2. Even though OCBs are sometimes rewarded in organizations, there is evidence that devoting time and effort to OCB can lead to less favorable career outcomes (e.g., lower pay raises; Bergeron, Shipp, Rosen & Furst, 2013), and individuals may need to consider the benefits of appearing to be a "good soldier" vs. the costs of this pattern of behavior

3. Situational factors are also an important determinant of CWBs (Martinko, Gundlach, & Douglas, 2002; Ostroff, 1993).
4. www.stripes.com/news/retaliation-still-a-major-issue-for-troops-who-report-sexual-assault-study-finds-1.317544

References

Alford, C.F. (2016). What makes whistleblowers so threatening? *International Journal of Health Policy Management, 5*, 71–73.

Allen, T.D. & Rush, M.C. (1998). The effects of organizational citizenship behavior on performance judgments: A field study and a laboratory experiment. *Journal of Applied Psychology, 83*, 247–260.

Anvari, F., Wenzel, M., Woodyatt, L. & Halsam, S.A. (2019). The social psychology of whistleblowing: An integrated model. *Organizational Psychology Review, 9*, 41–67.

Axelrod, R. (1986). An evolutionary approach to norms. *American Political Science Review, 80*, 1095–1111.

Bachrach, D.G., Powell, B.C., Bendoly, E. & Richey, R.G. (2006). Organizational citizenship behavior and performance evaluations: Exploring the impact of task interdependence. *Journal of Applied Psychology, 91,* 193–201.

Bandura, A. (1999). Moral disengagement in the perpetration of inhumanities. *Personality and Social Psychology Review, 3*, 193–209.

Bateman, T.S. & Organ, D.W. (1983). Job satisfaction and the good soldier: The relationship between affect and employee "citizenship". *Academy of Management Journal, 26*, 587–595.

Batson, C.D. & Shaw, L.L. (1991). Evidence for altruism: Toward a pluralism of prosocial motives. *Psychological Inquiry, 2*, 1–7–122.

Bergeron, D.M., Shipp, A.J., Rosen, B. & Furst, S.A. (2013). Organizational citizenship behavior and career outcomes: The cost of being a good citizen. *Journal of Management, 39*, 958–984.

Berry, C.M., Ones, D.S. & Sackett, P.R. (2007). Interpersonal deviance, organizational deviance, and their common correlates: A review and meta-analysis. *Journal of Applied Psychology, 92*, 410–442.

Bolino, M.C. (1999). Citizenship and impression management: Good soldiers or good actors? *Academy of Management Review, 24*, 82–98.

Bolino, M.C. & Grant, A.M. (2016). The bright side of being prosocial at work, and the dark side, too: A review and agenda for research on other-oriented motives, behavior, and impact in organizations. *Annals of Academy of Management, 10*, 599–670.

Bolino, M.C., Hsiung, H.H., Harvey, J. & LePine, J.A. (2015). "Well, I'm tired of tryin'!" Organizational citizenship behavior and citizenship fatigue. *Journal of Applied Psychology, 100*, 56–74.

Bolino, M.C. & Turnley, W.H. (2003). Going the extra mile: Cultivating and managing employee citizenship behavior. *The Academy of Management Executive, 17*, 60–71.

Bolino, M.C. & Turnley, W.H. (2005). The personal costs of citizenship behavior: The relationship between individual initiative and role overload, job stress, and work-family conflict. *Journal of Applied Psychology, 90*, 740–748.

Bolino, M.C., Turnley, W.H., Gilstrap, J.B. & Suazo, M.M. (2010). Citizenship under pressure: What's a "good soldier" to do? *Journal of Organizational Behavior, 31*, 835–855.

Borman, W.C., Buck, D.E., Hanson, M.A., Motowidlo, S.J., Stark, S. & Drasgow, F. (2001). An examination of the comparative reliability, validity, and accuracy of performance ratings made using computerized adaptive rating scales. *Journal of Applied Psychology, 86*, 965–973.

Borman, W.C. & Motowidlo, S.J. (1993). Expanding the criterion domain to include elements of contextual performance. In N. Schmitt & W.C. Borman (Eds.), *Personnel Selection in Organizations* (pp. 71–98). San Francisco: Jossey-Bass.

Borman, W.C. & Penner, L.A. (2001). Personality predictors of citizenship performance. In B.W. Roberts & R. Hogan (Eds.), *Personality Psychology in the Workplace* (pp. 45–61). American Psychological Association.

Brief, A.P. & Motowidlo, S.J. (1986). Prosocial organizational behaviors. *Academy of Management Review, 11*, 710–725.

Caesens, G. Marique, G., Hanin, D. & Stinglhamber, F. (2016). The relationship between perceived organizational support and proactive behaviour directed towards the organization. *European Journal of Work and Organizational Psychology, 25*, 398–411.

Cameron, K.S. & Quinn, R.E. (1999). *Diagnosing and Changing Organizational Culture: Based on the Competing Values Framework*. Reading, MA: Addison-Wesley.

Chang, I. (1997). *The Rape of Nanking*. New York: Basic Books.

Chiaburu, D., Lorinkova, N. & Van Dyne, L. (2013). Employees' social context and change-oriented citizenship: A meta-analysis of leader, coworker, and organizational influences. *Group and Organization Management, 38*, 291–333.

Conway, J.M. (1996). Additional construct validity evidence for the task/contextual performance distinction. *Human Performance, 9*, 309–331.

Dalal, R.S. (2005). A meta-analysis of the relationship between organizational citizenship behavior and counterproductive work behavior. *Journal of Applied Psychology, 90*, 1241–1255.

Dalton, M. (1948). The industrial "Rate Buster": A characterization. *Human Organization*, 7(1), 5–18.

Dorsey, D.W., Cortina, J.M. & Luchman, J. (2010). Adaptive and citizenship-related behaviors at work. In J. Farr & N. Tippins (Eds.), *Handbook of Employee Selection* (pp. 463–488). New York: Routledge.

Dozier, J.B. & Miceli, M.P. (1985). Potential predictors of whistleblowing: A prosocial behavior perspective. *Academy of Management Review, 10*, 823–836.

Dungan, J., Waytz, A. & Young, L. (2014). Corruption in the context of moral trade-offs. *Journal of Interdisciplinary Economics, 26*, 97–118.

Dugan, J., Waytz, A. & Young, L. (2015). The psychology of whistleblowing. *Science Direct, 6*, 129–133.

Edwards, J.E. & Morrison, R.F. (1994). Selecting and classifying future naval officers: The paradox of greater specialization in broader arenas. In M. Rumsey, C. Walker, & J. Harris (Eds.), *Personnel Selection and Classification* (pp. 69–84). Hillsdale, NJ: Sage.

Eisenberger, R., Huntington, R., Hutchison, S. & Sowa, D. (1986). Perceived organizational support. *Journal of Applied Psychology, 71*, 500–507.

Ellington, J.K., Dierdorff, E.C. & Rubin, R.S. (2014). Decelerating the diminishing returns of citizenship on task performance: The role of social context and interpersonal skill. *Journal of Applied Psychology, 99*, 748–758.

Farh, J., Podsakoff, P.M. & Organ, D.W. (1990). Accounting for organizational citizenship behavior: Leader fairness and task scope versus satisfaction. *Journal of Management, 16*, 705–721.

Feffer, M. (2017, November 17). 'Employment at will' isn't a blank check to terminate employees you don't like. *Society for Human Resource Management*, www.shrm.org/resourcesandtools/hr-topics/employee-relations/pages/employment-at-will-isnt-a-blank-check-to-terminate-employees-you-dont-like.aspx

Feldman, D.C. (1984). The development and enforcement of group norms. *Academy of Management Review, 9*, 47–53.

Fourie, M.M., Subramoney, S. & Gobodo-Madikizela, P. (2017). A less attractive feature of empathy: Intergroup empathy bias. In M. Kondo (Ed.), *Empathy: An Evidence-Based Interdisciplinary Perspective* (pp. 45–62). Rijeka, Croatia: InTech.

Goldhagen, D. (1996). *Hitler's Willing Executioners: Ordinary Germans and the Holocaust*. New York: Knauf.

Grant, A.M. (2007). Relational job design and the motivation to make a prosocial difference. *Academy of Management Review, 32*, 393–417.

Grant, A.M. (2008). Does intrinsic motivation fuel the prosocial fire? Motivational synergy in predicting persistence, performance, and productivity. *Journal of Applied Psychology, 93*, 48–58.

Grant, A.M. & Berry, J.W. (2011). The necessity of others is the mother of invention: Intrinsic and prosocial motivations, perspective taking, and creativity. *Academy of Management Journal, 54*, 73–96.

Grant, A.M. & Sonnentag, S. (2010). Doing good buffers against feeling bad: Prosocial impact compensates for negative task and self-evaluations. *Organizational Behavior and Human Decision Processes, 111*, 13–22.

Grant, C. (2002). Whistle blowers: Saints of secular culture. *Journal of Business Ethics, 39*, 391–399.

Gray, A. (2019, June 4). The bias of "professionalism" standards. *Stanford Social Innovation Review*, https://ssir.org/articles/entry/the_bias_of_professionalism_standards

Halbesleben, J.R., Bowler, W.M., Bolino, M.C. & Turnley, W.H. (2010). Organizational concern, prosocial values, or impression management? How supervisors attribute motives to organizational citizenship behavior. *Journal of Applied Social Psychology, 40*, 1450–1489.

Halbesleben, J.R.B., Harvey, J. & Bolino, M.C. (2009). Too engaged? A conservation of resources view of the relationship between work engagement and work interference with family. *Journal of Applied Psychology, 94*, 1452–1465.

Härtel, C.E.J. & Ashkanasy, N.M. (2011). Healthy human cultures as positive work environments. In N.M. Ashkanasy, C.P M. Wilderom, & M.F. Peterson (Eds.), *The Handbook of Organizational Culture and Climate* (2nd Ed., pp. 85–100). Thousand Oaks, CA: Sage.

Henderson, A., Foster, G., Matthews, R. & Zickar, M. (2019). A psychometric assessment of OCB: Clarifying the distinction between OCB and CWB and developing a revised OCB measure. *Journal of Business and Psychology, 35*, 697–712.

Heneman, R.L. (1992). *Merit Pay*. Reading, MA: Addison-Wesley.

Hoffman, B.J., Blair, C.A., Meriac, J.P. & Woehr, D.J. (2007). Expanding the criterion domain? A quantitative review of the OCB literature. *Journal of Applied Psychology, 92*, 555–566.

Hogg, M.A. & Abrams, D. (1988). *Social Identifications: A Social Psychology of Intergroup Relations and Group Processes*. London: Routledge.

Johnson, J.W. (2001). The relative importance of task and contextual performance dimensions to supervisor judgments of overall performance. *Journal of Applied Psychology, 86*, 984–996.

Johnson, S., Holladay, C. & Quinones, M. (2009). Organizational citizenship behavior in performance evaluations: Distributive justice or injustice? *Journal of Business and Psychology, 24*, 409–418.

Kelman, H.C. (1958). Compliance, identification, and internalization. *Journal of Conflict Resolution, 2*, 51–60.

Kiker, D.S. & Motowidlo, S.J. (1999). Main and interaction effects of task and contextual performance on supervisory reward decisions. *Journal of Applied Psychology, 84*, 602–609.

Korsgaard, M.A., Meglino, B. & Lester, S.W. (1997). Beyond helping: Do other-oriented values have broader implications in organizations? *Journal of Applied Psychology, 82*, 160–177.

Litzky, B.E., Eddleston, K.A. & Kidder, D.L. (2006). The good, the bad, and the misguided: How managers inadvertently encourage deviant behaviors. *Academy of Management Perspectives, 20*, 91–103.

Loe, T.W., Ferrell, L. & Mansfield, P. (2000). A review of empirical studies assessing ethical decision making in business. *Journal of Business Ethics, 25*, 185–204.

Mackey, J.D., McAllister, C.P., Ellen, B.P. & Carson, J.E. (In press). A meta-analysis of individual and organizational workplace deviance research. *Journal of Management.*

Marinova, S.V., Cao, X. & Park, H. (2019). Constructive organizational values climate and organizational citizenship behaviors: A configurational view. *Journal of Management, 45*, 2045–2071.

Martinko, M.J., Gundlach, M.J. & Douglas, S.C. (2002). Toward an integrative theory of counterproductive workplace behavior: A causal reasoning perspective. *International Journal of Selection and Assessment, 10*, 36–50.

McNeely, B.L. & Meglino, B.M. (1994). The role of dispositional and situational antecedents in prosocial organizational behavior: An examination of the intended beneficiaries of prosocial behavior. *Journal of Applied Psychology, 79*, 836–844.

Meglino, B.M. & Korsgaard, M.A. (2007). The role of other orientation in reactions to job characteristics. *Journal of Management, 33*, 57–83.

Mesmer-Magnus, J. & Viswesvaran, C. (2005). Whistleblowing in organizations: An examination of correlates of whistleblowing intentions, actions, and retaliation. *Journal of Business Ethics, 62*, 277–297.

Milkovich, G.T. & Wigdor, A.K. (1991). *Pay for Performance.* Washington, DC: National Academies Press.

Mitra, A., Gupta, N. & Jenkins, C.D. (1997). A drop in the bucket: When is a pay raise a pay raise? *Journal of Organizational Behavior, 18*, 117–137.

Mitra, A., Tenihälä, A. & Shaw, J.D. (2016). Smallest meaningful pay increases: Field test, constructive replication, and extension. *Human Resource Management, 55*, 69–81.

Monin, B. Sawyer, P.J. & Marquez, M.J. (2008). The rejection of moral rebels: Resenting those who do the right thing. *Journal of Personality and Social Psychology, 95*, 76–93.

Moorman, R.H. (1991). Relationship between organizational justice and organizational citizenship behaviors: Do fairness perceptions influence employee citizenship? *Journal of Applied Psychology, 76*, 845–855.

Motowidlo, S.J. & Van Scotter, J.R. (1994). Evidence that task performance should be distinguished from contextual performance. *Journal of Applied Psychology, 79*, 475–480.

Murphy, K.R., Cleveland, J.N. & Hanscom, M. (2018). *Performance Appraisal and Management.* Thousand Oaks, CA: Sage.

Murphy, K.R. & Shiarella, A. (1997). Implications of the multidimensional nature of job performance for the validity of selection tests: Multivariate frameworks for studying test validity. *Personnel Psychology, 50*, 823–854.

Near, J.P. & Miceli, M.P. (1985). Organizational dissidence: The case of whistle blowing. *Journal of Business Ethics, 4*, 1–16.

Nielsen, T., Hrivnak, G.A. & Shaw, M. (2009). Organizational citizenship behavior and performance: A meta-analysis of group-level research. *Small Group Research, 40*, 555–577.

Organ, D.W. (1988). *Organizational Citizenship Behavior: The Good Soldier Syndrome*. Lexington, MA: Lexington Books.

Organ, D.W. (1990). The motivational basis of organizational citizenship behavior. In B.M. Staw & L.L. Cummings (Eds.), *Research in Organizational Behavior* (Vol. 12, pp. 43–72). Greenwich, CT: JAI Press.

Organ, D.W. (1997). Organizational citizenship behavior: It's construct clean-up time. *Human Performance, 10*, 85–97.

Organ, D.W. & Konovsky, M.A. (1989). Cognitive versus affective determinants of organizational citizenship behavior. *Journal of Applied Psychology, 74*, 157–164.

Organ, D.W., Podsakoff, P.M. & MacKenzie, S.B. (2006). *Organizational Citizenship Behavior: Its Nature, Antecedents, and Consequences*. Thousand Oaks, CA: Sage.

Ostroff, C. (1993). The effects of climate and personal influences on individual behavior and attitudes in organizations. *Organizational Behavior and Human Decision Processes, 56*, 56–90.

Park, H., Bjørkelo, B. & Blenkinsopp, J. (2020). External whistleblowers' experiences of workplace bullying by superiors and colleagues. *Journal of Business Ethics, 161*, 591–601.

Penner, L.A., Fritzsche, B.A., Craiger, J.P. & Freifeld, T.R. (1995). Measuring the prosocial personality. *Advances in Personality Assessment, 10*, 147–163.

Peters, K., Luck, L., Hutchinson, M., Wilkes, L., Andrew, S. & Jackson, D. (2011). The emotional sequelae of whistleblowing: Findings from a qualitative study. *Journal of Clinical Nursing, 20*, 2907–2914.

Piccolo, R.F. & Colquitt, J.A. (2006). Transformational leadership and job behaviors: The mediating role of core job characteristics. *Academy of Management Journal, 49*, 327–340.

Podsakoff, N.P., Whiting, S.W., Podsakoff, P.M. & Blume, B.D. (2009). Individual and organizational-level consequences of organizational citizenship behaviors: A meta-analysis. *Journal of Applied Psychology, 94*, 122–141.

Podsakoff, P.M., MacKenzie, S.B., Paine, J.B. & Bachrach, D.G. (2000). Organizational citizenship behaviors: A critical review of the literature and suggestions for future research. *Journal of Management, 3*, 513–563.

Posthuma, R.A. (2000). The dimensionality of supervisor evaluations of job performance. *Journal of Business and Psychology, 14*, 481–487.

Quinn, R.E. & Rohrbaugh, J. (1983). A spatial model of effectiveness criteria: Towards a competing values approach to organizational analysis. *Management Science, 3*, 363–377.

Rhoades, L. & Eisenberger, R. (2002). Perceived organizational support: A review of the literature. *Journal of Applied Psychology, 87*, 698–714.

Rioux, S.M. & Penner, L.A. (2001). The causes of organizational citizenship behavior: A motivational analysis. *Journal of Applied Psychology, 86*, 1306–1314.

Scott, J.F. (1971). *Internalization of Norms: A Sociological Theory of Moral Commitment*. Englewood Cliffs, NJ: Prentice Hall.

Smith, C.A., Organ, D.W. & Near, J.P. (1983). Organizational citizenship behavior: Its nature and antecedents. *Journal of Applied Psychology, 68*, 453–463.

Tajfel, H. (1982). *Social Identity and Intergroup Relations*. Cambridge, UK: Cambridge University Press.

Tajfel, H. & Turner, J. (1986). The social identity theory of intergroup behavior. In S. Worchel & W.G. Austin (Eds.), *The psychology of intergroup relations* (pp. 7–24). Chicago, IL: Nelson-Hall.

Thomas, J.P., Whitman, D.S. & Viswesvaran, C. (2010). Employee proactivity in organizations: A comparative meta-analysis of emergent proactive constructs. *Journal of Occupational and Organizational Psychology, 83*, 275–300.

Tornau, K. & Frese, M. (2013). Construct clean-up in proactivity research: A meta-analysis on the nomological net of work-related proactivity concepts and their incremental validities. *Applied Psychology: An International Review*, *62*, 44–96.

Turnipseed, D.L (2002). Are good soldiers good?: Exploring the link between organization citizenship behavior and personal ethics, *Journal of Business Research*, *55*, 1–15.

Uymaz, A. (2014). Prosocial organizational behavior: Is it a personal trait or an organizational one? *European Journal of Business and Management*, *6*, 124–129.

Van Dyne, L. & LePine, J.A. (1998). Helping and voice extra-role behaviors: Evidence of construct and predictive validity. *Academy of Management Journal*, *41*, 108–119.

Van Scotter, J.R. & Motowidlo, S.J. (1996). Interpersonal facilitation and job dedication as separate facets of contextual performance. *Journal of Applied Psychology*, *25*, 577–600.

Van Scotter, J.R., Motowidlo, S.J. & Cross, T.C. (2000). Effects of task performance and contextual performance on systemic rewards. *Journal of Applied Psychology*, *85*, 526–536.

Vidaver-Cohen, D. (1998). Moral climate in business firms: A conceptual framework for analysis and change. *Journal of Business Ethics*, *17*, 1211–1226.

Viswesvaran, C., Schmidt, F.L. & Ones, D.S. (2005). Is there a general factor in ratings of job performance? A meta-analytic framework for disentangling substantive and error influences. *Journal of Applied Psychology, 90*, 108–131.

Weinberg, N. (2005, March 14). The dark side of whistleblowing. *Forbes*. www.forbes.com/forbes/2005/0314/090.html

Weinstein, N. & Ryan, R.M. (2010). When helping helps: Autonomous motivation for prosocial behavior and its influence on well-being for the helper and recipient. *Journal of Personality and Social Psychology*, *98*, 222–244.

Werner, J.M. (1994). Dimensions that make a difference: Examining the impact of in-role and extrarole behaviors on supervisory ratings. *Journal of Applied Psychology*, *79*, 98–107.

Whiting, S.W., Podsakoff, P.M. & Pierce, J.R. (2008). Effects of task performance, helping, voice, and organizational loyalty on performance appraisal ratings. *Journal of Applied Psychology*, *93*, 125–139.

Williams, L.K. & Anderson, S.E. (1991). Job satisfaction and organizational commitment a predictors of organizational citizenship and in-role behaviors. *Journal of Management*, *17*, 601–617.

14

BUILDING BETTER ORGANIZATIONS

In this chapter, I examine ways groups and organizations can recover from ingrained patterns of misbehavior and can become more effective forces for good. I will focus on formal organizations, but many of the principles articulated in this chapter apply equally to the types of informal groups and hybrid organizations discussed in Chapters 5 and 6. For example, one key to understanding and reversing misbehavior in organizations is to understand the norms of that organization and to change the parts of those norms that support misbehavior. This same principle applies to informal groups and hybrid organizations such as professional associations.

Reforming and Improving Organizations

Suppose an organization is sick (i.e., it tolerates misbehavior) or corrupted (i.e., misbehavior is incorporated into its day-to-day operations). What might be done to reform the organization? Organizations often pursue one of two strategies: (1) structural reforms—changing the policies of organizations, instituting oversight, or (2) behavioral changes—changing the behavior of people in organizations or changing the people. On the whole, structural reforms do not have a strong track record of success. Behavior reforms are difficult, but there are a few concrete steps that have been shown to be useful in reforming and improving organizations.

Structural Changes

The typical response of organizations that seek to reduce misbehavior is to make some changes in their policies, practices, or standards. For example, virtually all corporations have written mission statements and codes of conduct, and one strategy organizations use to deal with the threat of misbehavior is to change or strengthen written documents that describe how the organization *should* act. A more aggressive response might be a change in policies, structures, and operational procedures designed to discourage misbehavior. Finally, organizations might create and strengthen external oversight of their operations.

Mission Statements and Codes of Conduct

Almost every corporation has some form of a written mission statement. Perhaps the most famous is the Johnson & Johnson Credo, drafted in 1943 by the company's third president, Robert Wood Johnson. This Credo is still on prominent display in Johnson & Johnson's corporate offices and serves as the basis for the company's code of business conduct (this code is subtitled "Live our Credo, Know Our Code"). It describes the company's responsibilities to the people who use its products, its employees, and the communities within which it operates.

Some mission statements talk about the strategies the organization follows, the market it seeks to influence, or the type of product it specializes in, but virtually all mission statements include statements bordering on platitudes describing how "people are our most important product" or how much they care for the environment and communities. In many cases, these mission statements are little more than boilerplate that have little bearing on the day-to-day operations of the organizations.

Codes of conduct have a more specific purpose. For example, the Johnson & Johnson Code of Business Conduct[1] describes how the organization conducts business (e.g., how they deal with anti-corruption and antitrust laws, human rights, public procurement, privacy, etc.), how it manages the fair treatment of employees (e.g., nondiscrimination, preventing harassment, worker safety, etc.), how it manages financial integrity (e.g., treatment of intellectual property, company secrets, company and public records, insider trading, etc.) and how conflicts of interest are defined and managed.

Codes of conduct and mission statements can be helpful, but they are rarely enough to guarantee good behavior, in part because they describe values and norms that may be upheld by only a portion of the members of an organization. As Wolfgast (1992) notes, corporations are *artificial persons*. As entities, they do not have values, norms, or moral intentions and they cannot be held criminally responsible for their actions. As a result, statements about what a corporation *should* do might not tell us a great deal about their actions. To be sure, policies, practices, and norms can reflect different moral stances of corporations' owners and leaders, and they might even reflect norms that are widely shared within an organization. Bradley, Brief, and Smith-Crowe (2008) suggest that it is possible to define good organizations and that a good corporation is more than a corporation that is not bad—avoiding abuse and misbehavior is necessary but not sufficient to identify a good corporation. They suggest that good corporations "walk the talk" by establishing a strong correspondence between proclaimed policies and actual organizational behavior.

Virtually every organization has written documents describing their supposed values; the defining feature of a good corporation is that these values are put into practice. The most important factor in promoting this linkage appears to be organizational culture. Mission statements, codes of conduct, and other compliance procedures can be useful, but they are unlikely to be effective unless paired with an organizational climate to support and insist on following laws and norms (Andreoli & Lefkowitz, 2009).

BOX 14.1 THE JOHNSON & JOHNSON CREDO

The Johnson & Johnson Credo is a famous and noteworthy attempt to articulate values that this company tries to encourage and live by. It starts by stating that their first responsibility is to the patients, doctors, and nurses, to mothers and fathers, etc. who use their products rather than to their shareholders. It describes a commitment to keeping prices reasonable while recognizing that their business partners must have an opportunity to make a fair profit.

It articulates responsibilities to employees, with an emphasis on recognizing their worth and dignity and a commitment to provide jobs that pay well, provide clean and safe working conditions, and provide employees opportunities for fulfillment and meaningful work. It articulates commitments to providing for the career development, health, well-being, and work-life balance of their employees. It also articulates responsibilities to the communities within which Johnson & Johnson operates and to the environment.

Finally, this Credo articulates responsibilities to their shareholders, with a commitment to a fair return on investment and ongoing efforts to innovate and grow.[2] Taken together, this is an impressive and wide-ranging set of commitments, which Johnson & Johnson continues to strive to honor.

Krawiec (2005) notes that organizations often appear to adopt a "cosmetic approach to organizational compliance" (p. 577) in which policies that exist on paper are not taken seriously by employees because they do not believe that they can be or will be enforced. He also notes that organizations are less likely to effectively control violations of rules and codes if the organization benefits from those violations. Research suggests that codes and similar sets of formal rules have produced mixed results (Misangy & Weaver, 2008). Kish-Gephart, Harrison, and Treviño's (2010) meta-analytic review, the most comprehensive to date, found no significant effect of having or not having a code on unethical choice. The available evidence suggests that codes of conduct by themselves do not have a consistent effect on the behavior of organization members (Kaptein & Schwartz, 2007; White & Montgomery, 1980).

Some authors have suggested that codes of conduct and policy statements are often little more than statements made to comply with legal mandates (Anand, Ashforth, & Joshi, 2004). Indeed, codes of conduct may be more effective for reducing organizational liability than for controlling misbehavior. That is, when members of an organization are accused of misbehavior, the organization might be able to avoid blame by pointing to codes of conduct that condemn these behaviors, regardless of whether the codes have any demonstrable effect on behavior.

Changing Organizational Policies and Practices

Codes of conduct represent one possible response to the possibility of misbehavior. A more targeted response might be to change the specific policies or practices that appear to contribute to misbehavior. For example, there is evidence that weak corporate governance (examples of governance mechanisms include legal systems, boards of directors, and executive compensation systems pegged to specific outcomes or metrics) is an important factor in organizational corruption and misbehavior, especially in less advanced economies (Yiu, Wan, & Xu, 2019). Yiu et al. (2019) suggest that formal systems of governance can be supplanted by informal alternatives, such as alliances among organizations, pressure from business groups, or state ownership of a stake in the business. These additions to organizations' formal systems of governance can help provide more stable and honest operations in organizations operating in countries with weak legal and regulatory systems.

Organizations can use existing practices and procedures to signal to their members what behaviors are desired or preferred. For example, performance appraisal and compensation systems can be used by organizations to formally communicate which behaviors and activities are valued by the organization (Martocchio, 2011). These systems can also send powerful messages (unfortunately, often negative ones) about the importance of compliance with organizational policies. For example, suppose your organization has strict policies on its books forbidding sexual harassment in the workplace. If employees or other members of an organization continue to receive positive reviews, raises, and promotions even though they are in clear violation of those policies, both the individuals involved and other members of the organization who observe these outcomes are likely to swiftly conclude that organizational sexual harassment policies are not taken seriously. On the other hand, organizations can create policies designed to reduce or eliminate discrimination and harassment (Boehm, Kunze, & Bruch, 2014), and these can convey a powerful message about the values of the organization.

Sometimes, the policies that are enacted in organizations and designed to reduce the likelihood of misbehavior can have unintended consequences. In 2017, controversy arose over Vice President Mike Pence's policy of refusing to have a meal alone or to meet after work hours with any female other than his wife (Tolentino, 2017). Pence describes himself as a conservative Christian, and this policy of separation of the sexes is consistent with conservative religious practice across many faiths (conservative Jews and Muslims observe similar restrictions). A strict policy of separation of the sexes can arguably reduce the likelihood of some forms of sexual harassment and misbehavior. However, as Tolentino (2017) points out, this policy also significantly restricts the career prospects of women. Female reporters who are denied the possibility of one-on-one interviews and female staff who are not included in activities that might involve after-hours one-on-one meetings arguably lose valuable opportunities to perform their jobs and demonstrate their skills.

Even when policies are carefully designed to avoid the sort of unintended consequences noted previously, organizational policies by themselves are generally insufficient mechanisms for ensuring compliance (Anand et al., 2004; Kaptein & Schwartz, 2007; Krawiec, 2005). In addition to policies that forbid or restrict specific types of misbehavior (e.g., fraud, sexual harassment), organizations must carefully monitor organization members' compliance with those policies. More importantly, there must be visible and proportional consequences for non-compliance (Krawiec, 2005). If members of an organization are convinced that they will not be challenged if they violate organizational policies, or that the consequences of violating those policies will be a slap on the wrist, they will not feel constrained by those policies.

Institutional Oversight

Many organizations rely on independent boards of directors (e.g., a board that does not include members of the organization) or some other form of external oversight to provide scrutiny and an external review of their decisions. In theory, an independent board should discourage widespread misbehavior, in part because the board members are assumed to identify with their own organizations and should not feel compelled by loyalty or commitment to the organization the board oversees to overlook misbehavior. In practice, however, the independence of boards of directors is only weakly related to ethical behavior (Neville, Byron, Post, & Ward, 2019).

There is a growing literature dealing with the failure of boards of directors to provide effective oversight to organizations. Kress (2018) noted that the members of these boards often face competing demands on their time and attention. They are typically full-time executives in their home organization, and many serve on multiple boards. There are also implicit conflicts of interest in the way board members are selected and paid. As Nguyen, Hagendorff, and Eshraghi (2016) note, board members are often selected by the same CEOs they are charged with overseeing, and their compensation and reappointment often depend on decisions made by that CEO. More important, boards often depend on the CEOs and executives they oversee for information about the company and its activities.

Boards of directors are not the only mechanism for institutional oversight. Governmental agencies often take a strong role in overseeing particular activities to prevent misbehavior. For example, in response to several instances of research misconduct in the 1980s and 1990s, the U.S. Office of Science and Technology Policy, along with Offices of Research Integrity in several U.S. agencies, have adopted strict guidelines for defining and reducing research misconduct. Universities typically have boards and offices set up to review various types of research (e.g., research with human subjects), and detailed reviews are often needed to assure that proposed studies meet legal and ethical guidelines. The effectiveness of these guidelines and this oversight is not always clear (National Academies of Sciences, Engineering, and Medicine, 2017), but it is likely that enhanced oversight, together with vigorous efforts of non-governmental actors to expose research misconduct (blogs and websites such as Retraction Watch help to publicize cases of apparent research misconduct) help to discourage unethical research practices.

As with codes of conduct or organizational policies, the effectiveness of external oversight mechanisms probably depends on a combination of structural and contextual factors. First, oversight must have some teeth; there must be effective mechanisms for detecting violations of rules, norms, laws or regulations and there must be some mechanism for visible and meaningful sanctions. This is one way in which a legal system that depends heavily on individual and class action litigation often fails society, even when it provides a fair settlement of the particular issues that are litigated. Many cases involving misbehavior (e.g., sexual harassment, race discrimination, research misconduct) are settled before they reach trial, and these settlements often include strict confidentiality requirements. In a similar vein, many organizations require their members to sign nondisclosure agreements which make it possible for the details of misbehavior and the organization's response to misbehavior to remain secret. These confidentiality and nondisclosure agreements violate one of the key conditions for codes, policies, oversight, etc. to work effectively—that is, that the consequences of violating these policies or rules must be made visible and clear.

Even when strict rules, policies, and oversight are in place, they are unlikely to be effective if they come into conflict with the norms and the culture of the organization. Organizations encourage, support, and normalize misbehavior by conveying the belief that these behaviors are necessary, justified, and/or common. In an organization whose culture encourages these norms and beliefs, strict rules, careful monitoring, and stiff public penalties may not be enough to convince members to abide by written policies, rules, or regulations. The closer the alignment between the culture and norms of an organization and the policies and rules that are used to control misbehavior, the more likely it is that members of the organization will follow them. When these norms and policies and rules are misaligned with the values and norms of key members of the organization, they are less likely to be effective in changing the behavior of members of an organization.

Changing Behavior in Organizations

There are many ways to change behavior in organizations. The most obvious, especially when the behavior you are hoping to change is the direct result of decisions of top leadership, is to change leaders. In other cases, leaders might not be the source of misbehavior, but rather the impetus for change. That is, leaders might recognize that some of the behaviors in their organization are dysfunctional and may attempt to institute a top-down program of change. Finally, an organization might undertake a systematic program to change its norms and its typical patterns of behavior. This type of organizational development has been the focus of research and practice in organizations since the 1970s, and this sort of change in norms, values, and behaviors can occur in organizations, although the process of organizational development is often strenuous and uncertain.

Change at the Top

In some organizations, misbehavior is the direct result of the behavior and the demands of top leadership and changing leaders can be an effective method of reducing misbehavior. The case of the Belgian Congo illustrates this process.

If I asked you to think about a European country whose overseas empire was the watchword for ruthless cruelty and exploitation, you might cite the empires of Spain and Portugal, who dominated Central and South America in the 16th and 17th centuries. One country that would probably not come immediately to mind is Belgium. You might think about Belgium in terms of its intricate lace, excellent beer, or fine chocolates, but from 1885–1909, King Leopold II of Belgium held one of the most brutal colonial empires in modern history. Leopold's 19th- and 20th-century empire rivaled its 16th- and 17th-century cousins in terms of its scope, its atrocities, and its dehumanizing cruelty (Hochschild, 1998).

Starting in 1885, the Congo Free State was essentially a personal possession of Leopold's, who ruled this large section of Africa in the style of an absolute monarch, or, more properly, an absentee landlord. His avarice and indifference to the methods used to extract wealth from the Congo led to a ruthless and murderous colonial regime that became the setting of Conrad's memorable novel *Heart of Darkness*. Between 8–10 million Congolese died as a result of their treatment as disposable slave labor (Stanley, 2012, cites figures as high as 15 million). Villages in the Congo Free State were given a quota of rubber sap to collect, that if that quota was not met, hostages were taken and shot. Each victim's hand was severed to verify the killing, and a brisk trade in severed hands developed among villagers and police who could not meet their quotas.

Remarkably, Leopold was successful in portraying himself as a philanthropist and a Christian benefactor to his subjects in the Congo. Even after the atrocities of his rule in the Congo were exposed, Leopold was honored in his country, and it is only recently that there has been a reckoning with the racist past of Belgium (Casert, 2020). In 2020, on the 60th anniversary of the independence of the Belgian Congo, the current King of Belgium (Phillipe) made the first Royal statement on the bloody history of Leopold's reign, offering statements of regret.[3]

As a result of the courageous and relentless work of several journalists, Leopold was forced by international pressure to hand this territory over to Belgium, which continued to hold the Belgian Congo (founded in 1908) as a colony until 1960. Once Leopold's rule ended, the level of violence and exploitation diminished rapidly. Forced labor was in theory outlawed, but it did not fully end for decades. As Hochschild (1998) notes, despite the improvements in the administration of the Congo subsequent to Leopold's bloody regime, the death rate among Congolese natives remained abnormally high for at least a decade after the end of Leopold's direct rule. Nevertheless, the Congo Free State is a prime example of misbehavior directed from the top of an organization and of how removing the person at the top can lead to a substantial and lasting reduction in misbehavior.

The Congo Free State illustrates the potential for a single leader to corrupt an entire enterprise, but it is probably an extreme example of how removing a corrupt leader reduces corruption in an organization. Frequently, the same processes that remove corrupt leaders from organizations can also lead to the destruction of the organization; organizations such as Enron and WorldCom simply collapsed when the corruption of their leaders was revealed. There are examples in politics (e.g., Nixon's resignation as president ended a corrupt administration and led to a notably more honest one under his successor, Gerald Ford) and business (e.g., Wells Fargo has shaken up its board of directors and has done away with the high-pressure sales targets that led to the opening of fraudulent accounts), where the removal of a corrupt leader did *not* lead the organization to collapse, but it is also often that case that corruption goes beyond a single leader, and that more systematic changes in the organization are needed to root corruption out.

BOX 14.2 THE HEART OF DARKNESS EXPOSED

George Washington Williams, a Black Civil War veteran, built a distinguished career as a journalist and historian. In 1890, after meeting King Leopold II of Belgium, Williams traveled to the Congo, where he was surprised and horrified to find widespread abuse and slavery. His open letter to King Leopold II asking for an end to these abuses helped to spark an international outcry over Leopold's regime in the Congo. Up to that time, Leopold had successfully convinced the world that his reign in Congo was benign. To silence criticism of his treatment of the Congo, Leopold had created a Commission for the Protection of the Natives, which conducted sham investigations into stories of atrocities Leopold's African holdings, giving Leopold a temporary respite from international pressure.

Starting in 1900, the journalist E.D. Morel helped to re-ignite scrutiny of the abuses in the Congo, writing numerous articles and pamphlets exposing the mistreatment of natives. Enlisting the support of notables and celebrities (e.g., Roger Casement, Arthur Conan Doyle, Mark Twain, and Anatole France) to his Congo Reform Association, he conducted a relentless campaign to force Leopold to sell the Belgian Congo to the Belgian government. In reaction to this pressure, Leopold created a new Commission of Enquiry, which to his surprise conducted a genuine investigation. This commission helped to expose the horrors of his regime in the Congo.

Conrad's *Heart of Darkness*, first published in 1899, helped raise worldwide awareness of the cruelty of Leopold's regime, but the process of fully coming to terms with this shameful legacy was a long and difficult one. In the 1970s, Jules Marchal, a Belgian diplomat and historian first became aware of his country's shameful legacy in the Congo. The fact that a man in this position did not know about the conduct of his own monarch in the Congo is a vivid illustration of the success of Leopold's propaganda and his government's subsequent willingness to sweep history under a rug. Marchal obtained access to long-suppressed files in his country's archives and writing under the pseudonym A.M. Delathuy, finally bought much of the shameful history of the Belgian Congo to light.

Change From the Top

There are two ways the leaders of an organization can work to reduce misbehavior and increase ethical behavior in organizations: (1) by setting an example, and (2) by driving top-down change. First, leaders who exhibit and model honesty and moral behavior can have a substantial impact on the behavior of organization members (Moore et al., 2019). They not only serve as role models, they also influence the way their subordinates think about and understand moral choices, and more critically, the likelihood of ethical and moral disengagement on the part of employees.

If leaders can build in ethicality into their roles, this increases the likelihood that followers will also see ethical behavior as a genuine job requirement rather than an add-on (Paterson & Huang, 2019).[4] Perceptions of top management's commitment to a bottom-line orientation can also have a substantial impact on misbehavior. If leaders are seen as committed to the bottom line, regardless of what it takes to produce more favorable numbers, misbehavior is likely to increase, in part because the behaviors of these leaders activate a transactional, self-interest perspective on the part of employees (Babalola et al., 2020). On the other hand, if top management can make it clear that factors other than the bottom line are important (e.g., safety and the well-being of the workforce; Zohar & Luria, 2005), this might reduce perceived pressures to use unscrupulous means to drive profits.

Second, leaders can work to influence the climate and cultures of their organizations. They may attempt to instill a compliance culture that focuses on abiding by, and perhaps even internalizing, laws, rules, and regulations (Burdon & Sourer, 2020). Leaders who can successfully convince their subordinates that these laws, rules, and regulations are legitimate (e.g., laws that are fair and are based on widely accepted rights) will be more likely to inspire compliance than leaders who attempt to use rewards and punishments to convince their subordinates to comply (Tyler, 2006). Some leaders may attempt to go beyond simple compliance to influence the ethical standards their subordinates use to evaluate their own actions, by modifying the organization's ethical climate.

An ethical climate is defined as a shared perception among organization members regarding the criteria (e.g., egoism, benevolence, and principle) and focus (e.g., individual, group, society) of ethical reasoning within an organization (Schminke, Ambrose, & Neubaum, 2005; Victor & Cullen, 1988). There is evidence that ethical leader behavior influences the ethical climates in organizations (Kuenzi, Mayer, & Greenbaum, 2020), in part by increasing the salience and perceived value of ethical and prosocial behavior (Vidaver-Cohen, 1998). A leader who can build norms that encourage followers to consider ethical questions when making decisions in organizations can help to substantially reduce the likelihood of misbehavior and increase the likelihood of the types of prosocial behaviors discussed in Chapter 13.

Leaders often attempt to directly influence the beliefs, attitudes, and norms of their subordinates rather than simply setting a good example and hoping that this will influence the ethical climate of their organization; one way to influence beliefs, attitudes, and norms is to change the way you communicate about ethical issues in your organization. Treviño, Weaver, Gibson, and Toffler (1999) showed that the degree to which individuals openly talk about ethics in an organization is a good predictor of ethical conduct in that organization. Similarly, organizational situations characterized by "moral muteness" appear to support ethically problematic behavior (Bird, 2015).

There is a large literature dealing with the ways, the feelings, attitudes, and perspectives of leaders trickle down to their followers (Wo, Schminke, & Ambrose, 2019). Wo et al. (2019) note that social influence does not always proceed from the top down; patterns of trickle-up (subordinates influencing leaders), trickle-in (influence coming from outside the organization), and trickle-around (peer-to-peer) influence are often exhibited in organizations. Wo et al. (2019) suggest that the effectiveness of influence, almost regardless of its direction, is a function of the transmitter's and the receiver's motivation and ability to process information. Thus, rather than thinking only about what leaders do, we might need to consider influences from others in an organization before we can predict whether or not leaders will be successful in changing the behavior of members of an organization. For example, there is evidence that leader influence interacts with peer influence in determining whether members of an organization will report misconduct they observe (Mayer, Nurmohamed, Treviño, Shapiro, & Schminke, 2013); employees are more likely to feel safe reporting misconduct if they believe they have the support of both peers and leaders. Ethical leaders are more likely to influence organization members if the norms, beliefs, and attitudes they hope to instill are at least reasonably consistent with existing norms, beliefs, and attitudes. If there are sharp differences between existing norms and beliefs and the norms and beliefs a leader hopes to instill, that leader may experience considerable resistance.

Research on peer influences on ethical behavior demonstrates the importance of considering contextual factors that can limit the effectiveness of top-down efforts to change ethical norms and standards in an organization. Leaders might proclaim that particular values or beliefs *should be* the norm, but it is often peers who set the norms that govern behavior in an organization. For example, when group members (especially high-status members of a group) cheat, others in the group are also likely to cheat (Gino, Ayal, & Ariely, 2009). Pierce and Snyder (2008) found that when working across different facilities (i.e., switching job locations), inspectors adjusted their level of unethical behavior not gradually but almost immediately to conform to the local organizational norms of unethical behavior. In this case, if local norms for inspecting vehicles were lax, they allowed vehicles to pass the inspection which would have failed in other locations. One of the significant barriers encountered by leaders who attempt to instill prosocial norms is the existence of antisocial norms in groups. On the whole, research on the strong role peers play in determining unethical behavior suggests that top-down change efforts will often fail. Efforts to make organization-wide changes in norms, standards, and modes of action often involve the process of organizational development, which is described next.

Organizational Development

Organizational development (OD) involves using behavioral science to implement planned organizational change targeted at the cultures, values, strategies, and structures of an organization, to create healthier and more effective organizations. OD often involves articulating a vision of what the organization should become and working with individuals and teams to build the skills, knowledge, and understanding to achieve that vision. Successful OD usually requires a long-term, collaborative process that pays particular attention to the human side of organizations (Burke, 1994; Cameron & Quinn, 2011; French & Bell, 1999).

Most definitions of organizational development (OD) highlight its scientific basis, but the practice of OD is more of an art than a science. The underlying model of OD is often referred to as "action research", a term coined by Kurt Lewin to refer to a process of organizational change that involves simultaneously doing research and taking actions to change organizations. It starts with a process of interactive inquiry, in which both the OD practitioner leading the development process and the organization which is the target of change cooperate to frame analyses of the problems the organization faces and the organization's responses to efforts to change its norms, standards, and practices. The key assumption of action research is that the development process and the inquiry that is part of this process is not fixed in advance, but rather evolves as changes unfold. The distinctive feature of this type of interactive inquiry is that members of the organization are partners in rather than subjects of inquiry. The OD process often starts with a preliminary diagnosis of the issues facing an organization, action to address these issues, and assessment of the results of these actions. The results of this assessment will then lead to further inquiry, action, and feedback in a looping process that continues until the organization reaches the desired state defined in its vision of where the organization needs to go.

Organization development is often described in terms of a three-part model of change. Development starts with *unfreezing*, in which members of an organization become aware of and committed to the need for change, then proceed to *change* behaviors and norms in an organization using the iterative process described earlier. The third step is *refreezing*, in which new behaviors are put into place, practiced, and reinforced. Successful organizational change leads to changes in both behavior and norms.

McPhearson (2017) notes that meaningful change in organizations is hard; the great majority of organizational change efforts fail. He suggests that successful organizational change requires several prerequisites, including

- A change-ready culture
- A change catalyst (an OD professional or a manager) who drives the process of development
- A unified and committed leadership team
- A clear sense of what the organization hopes to achieve
- Clear understanding of the implications of the desired change
- A high level of commitment and engagement at all levels of the organization
- Planning and opportunities to examine and evaluate ongoing changes (a "pause for reflection")

This list of requirements suggests a paradox—that is, that organizational change is unlikely to succeed unless there is a strong commitment from a substantial portion of the organization to make that change. That is, the first prerequisite for success is "buy in". Organizations will not change unless they are ready and willing to do so, and it does little good for leaders to announce or to call for changes in norms, values, beliefs, and behaviors unless a significant portion of the organization's members are on board with the proposed change. The OD literature does not provide many examples of successful change when significant groups in the organizations are unwilling to change their norms and behaviors.

Recovery From Corruption

Suppose an organization has become corrupt. What are the prospects for recovery? In earlier chapters, I have noted that organizations rarely start off as corrupt enterprises, but once an organization becomes corrupt, is it possible to shake off corrupt norms and practices? We know that individuals can resist corruption. Several scholars have discussed the concept of positive deviance—that is, intentional behavior that deviates from the norms of the reference group in honorable ways (Quinn, 1996; Spreitzer & Sonenshein, 2004). It is less clear whether organizations can change once they have become thoroughly corrupted (Mehta, 2003).

Changing from a corrupt organization to an honest one is almost certainly more difficult than changing from honest to corrupt (DiFanzo, Alongi, & Wiele, 2020). Mehta (2003) suggests that recovery from corruption is most likely when organizations "clean house"—by getting rid of bad employees, and perhaps even changing the name and identity of a company. However, there may be steps short of wholesale changes in personnel and identity that can assist in recovering from corruption.

First, organizations must acknowledge and face up to their transgressions. Unfortunately, the first instinct of many organizations is to deny or minimize their misdeeds. For example, the pharmaceutical giant Merck consistently denied knowing the dangers of Vioxx, despite evidence dated as early as 2001 that it distributed internal memos headed with "Dodge Vioxx" to its sales force (Angell, 2004; Martinez, 2004). In contrast, when Texaco was accused of racial discrimination, its executives acted quickly and decisively to make details of this scandal public (Brinson & Benoit, 1999; Singer, 2004). Instead of denying the allegations or hoping the charges would disappear, CEO Peter Bijur publicly announced his intent to investigate the allegations (Brinson & Benoit, 1999). In the wake of this discrimination scandal, Texaco fired one executive, suspended another, and revoked the retirement benefits of two other high-ranking officials (Singer, 2004). In comparison to organizations like Merck, which attempted to deny and hide its misdeeds, Texaco's reputation recovered quite quickly from what could have been a debilitating scandal.

After a serious transgression, organizations can take concrete steps to restore legitimacy. This might involve working to discover the facts of the transgression, providing an appropriate explanation of their wrongdoing, accepting and serving an equitable punishment, and/or making consistent internal and external rehabilitative changes (Pfaffer, Decelles, Smith, & Taylor, 2008). DiFanzo et al.

(2020) present evidence that apologies and restitution (especially in combination) can help an organization recover its legitimacy.

One strategy that organizations sometimes use to deal with misbehavior is "naming and shaming"—that is, making information about misbehavior public. While acknowledging misdeeds is an important part of the recovery process, the strategy of naming and shaming can be risky and even counterproductive. In their review of research on shame in organizations, Daniels and Robinson (2019) point out that shame implies a discrepancy between an individual's behavior and the norms or standards that individual subscribes to. As a result, individuals who feel they have done nothing wrong are likely to feel angry rather than feeling remorse or shame when their misdeeds are made public. Even if they do feel shame when their misdeeds are revealed, individuals' reactions to shame can be difficult to predict. Daniels and Robinson (2019) note that shame can lead to prosocial behavior and attempts to make amends, but that it can also lead to withdrawal behaviors, such as absenteeism, reduced engagement, and even alcohol and drug abuse. Shame can even lead to aggressive behavior, and it can cause more harm rather than reducing the harm caused by the original misbehaviors.

The most effective strategies for dealing with an organization's misdeeds focus more strongly on the organization than on individuals within the organization who can be conveniently blamed for misdeeds. The first reaction of many organizations when misdeeds are revealed is to blame them on a few "bad apples", in an attempt to deflect blame from the organization. A much more productive strategy is to accept blame for misbehavior and attempt to make some sort of amends.

South Africa's Truth and Reconciliation Commission is an example of the restorative power of exposing misdeeds of an organization, or in this case, a political regime, rather than framing them in terms of the fault of specific individuals who might be named and shamed. This commission held a series of public hearings, lasting for seven years (1996–2003), into human rights abuses of the South African apartheid regime. The commission's mandate was to bear witness to, record, and in some cases grant amnesty to the perpetrators of crimes relating to human rights violations, as well as offering reparation and rehabilitation to the victims. The commission established a register of reconciliation, where individual South Africans could express regret and remorse for their involvement in human rights abuses under South Africa's apartheid regime.

The Truth and Reconciliation Commission has been described as the "gold standard for how a divided society with a violent past might work through that past and move forward".[5] This commission did not resolve all of the problems of a racially divided society, but there is some consensus that the restorative justice model of this commission has been more successful than the retributive justice model pursued after the Second World War (e.g., the Nuremberg Trials).[6] More than 40 nations (e.g., Canada, Chile, Rwanda) have established similar Truth and Reconciliation commissions.

Admitting misdeeds, offering apologies and restitution are all important parts of the recovery from corruption, but they by themselves do not guarantee that the organization will recover. Corruption must also become de-institutionalized (Misangy & Weaver, 2008). If corrupt practices are encouraged, rewarded, or tolerated by organizational leaders, they can become habitual and routinized, defining "the way we do things around here" (Ashforth & Anand, 2003; Brief, Buttram, & Dukerich, 2001). It can be challenging to change these organizational habits, especially if they become part of the socialization process, in which new members of the organization learn what behaviors are expected and valued in this organization.

Corruption is most insidious if it becomes incorporated into the ways people define their normal roles in organizations. One of the recurring themes in explorations of corruption in organizations is that well-meaning people often end up doing deeply unethical things in the belief that they are just doing what their job or their role requires (Ashforth, 2001; Aquino & Reed, 2002; Reed, Aquino, & Levy, 2007). Earlier, I noted the importance of building ethicality into organizational roles (Paterson & Huang, 2019). This might be accomplished using a three-part process that mirrors the processes often used in organizational development. First, as part of *unfreezing*, an organization might conduct a careful analysis of roles as they are currently defined, looking for ways in which role definitions leave people blind to the ethical implications of their actions (e.g., making people responsible for decisions without providing them information about the likely consequences of the choices they might make). This diagnostic process can be followed by a process of creating new role definitions (*change*), followed by a *refreezing* process in which members of the organization try out and practice their redefined roles.

Mehta (2003) strikes a pessimistic note, observing that efforts to recover from corruption have a dismal track record. Corrupt organizations are more likely to implode than to improve if their corruption is exposed (e.g., Enron, Bernard L. Madoff Investment Securities). On the other hand, a review of the historical record suggests that recovery is indeed possible. During America's Gilded Age (approximately 1870–1900), corruption in politics and in organizations was endemic. This was the age of "robber barons" (business tycoons who profited from corrupt methods) and political machines (e.g., New York's Tammany Hall). Railroads were notoriously corrupt; the Crédit Mobilier scandal (Crédit Mobilier was a sham construction company that submitted vastly inflated bills for work on the transcontinental railroad) was the beginning of a series of scandals that tainted the presidency of Ulysses Grant (Chernow, 2017). Corruption in politics and business is still with us, but the gross abuses of the Gilded Age are a thing of the past, at least in most industrialized nations. Recovery from corruption is a long, hard, and uncertain process, but it is far from a hopeless one.

Corporate Social Responsibility

In an influential *New York Times* article, the economist Milton Friedman (1970) argued that the sole purpose and responsibility of a business was to generate profit for its stockholders, as long as they operated within the law and the commonly understood "rules of the game". Thus, any activity that detracts from or distracts an organization from the goal of maximizing shareholder profit is in his view unethical. In some ways, Friedman's article can be seen as a reaction to a movement to promote corporate social responsibility, a movement he did not approve of.

In 1971, the Committee on Economic Development of the Conference Board (a nonpartisan, nonprofit business-led committee that was instrumental in the development of the Marshall Plan and the Bretton Woods Agreement of 1946 that created the modern international system of finance and trade) advanced the concept of a social contract between businesses and society. This implicit contract created an obligation for businesses to constructively serve the needs of the societies within which they operate (e.g., by providing jobs and economic growth, by working to improve conditions in those communities and the environment), and it can be thought of as a precursor to the current movement for corporate social responsibility (CSR).[7]

One key concept in defining corporate social responsibility is that organizations have multiple stakeholders—that is, groups or individuals who can influence or who are affected by decisions organizations make. These include owners and shareholders but also staff and employees, their families, suppliers, customers, and the communities within which the organization operates. One assumption of CSR is that all of these groups have a legitimate stake in the decisions an organization might make and that organizations have a responsibility to consider their welfare and interests when making decisions. Bazerman (2020) noted that the interests of different stakeholders sometimes come into conflict and that many CSR choices involve tradeoffs among competing values (e.g., maximizing profit vs. maximizing the quality of the environment).

Laws and regulations often define particular responsibilities that are placed on organizations. For example, numerous laws define the obligations of work organizations to provide for the health and safety of their employees, and agencies such as the U.S. Occupational Safety and Health Administration are charged with enforcing these laws. Advocates of CSR note the importance of these laws, but they often call for organizations to adopt an approach to their responsibilities that involves doing the right thing beyond the legal minima (Aguinis, 2011).

Perhaps the most comprehensive statement of organizational responsibilities is laid out in the United Nations Global Compact (United Nations Global Compact, 2008). The Global Compact describes ten principles in the areas of human rights, labor standards, the environment, and anti-corruption that contracting organizations are committed to upholding. These principles are summarized in Table 14.1.

The principles articulated in Table 14.1 are noble, but they are not universally accepted. For example, Principle 3 states that businesses should uphold "the

TABLE 14.1 Principles of the United Nations Global Compact

Human Rights
Principle 1: Businesses should support and respect the protection of internationally proclaimed human rights
Principle 2: make sure that they are not complicit in human rights abuses
Labour Standards
Principle 3: Businesses should uphold the freedom of association and the effective recognition of the right to collective bargaining
Principle 4: the elimination of all forms of forced and compulsory labour
Principle 5: the effective abolition of child labour
Principle 6: the elimination of discrimination in respect of employment and occupation
Environment
Principle 7: Businesses should support a precautionary approach to environmental challenges
Principle 8: undertake initiatives to promote greater environmental responsibility
Principle 9: encourage the development and diffusion of environmentally friendly technologies
Anti-Corruption
Principle 10: Businesses should work against corruption in all its forms, including extortion and bribery

Source: From The Ten Principles, by the United Nations Global Compact (www.unglobalcompact.org/AbouttheGC/TheTenPrinciples/).

effective recognition of the right to collective bargaining". These rights have been under sustained assault in many American states (Hogler, 2011), where there are often concerted efforts to discourage and defund unions. Most definitions of CSR focus on a somewhat narrower set of criteria than those outlined in Table 14.1.

The Holy Grail of CSR is the notion of "doing well by doing good". This is often defined in terms of the concept of a *triple bottom line*. The triple bottom line refers to the three key criteria that define CSR, a corporation's profits, its impact on people, and its impact on the environment (Aguinis, 2011; Cross & Miller, 2015). Many definitions of CSR emphasize being a good corporate citizen, making ethical decisions, paying attention to the environment, and improving society.

Goedeke and Fogliasso (2020) note CSR is quickly becoming a corporate requirement. For example, large corporations in India are required by law to spend 2% of their net profit on social development and the environment. In other countries, the participation rate of organizations in some form of CSR is so high that it has become a norm. Goedeke and Fogliasso (2020) claim that all Fortune 500 companies practice CSR at varying levels of engagement. Some organizations embed CSR in their daily operations, but many engage in peripheral CSR activities, such as philanthropy, that are not directly linked to their strategic goals or their regular business activities (Aguinis & Glavas, 2013).

There have been some excellent reviews of research on CSR (e.g., Aguinis, 2011; Aguinis & Glavas, 2013; Peloza & Shang, 2011), but research on CSR has been hampered by the lack of a clear universal definition for CSR (Aldag, 2013; Aldag & Jackson, 1977; Goedeke & Fogliasso, 2020). Questions about the effects and the effectiveness of CSR have been difficult to definitively answer because the specific activities that constitute CSR interventions vary so much across organizations. Perhaps for this reason, studies of the impact of CSR on firm performance have yielded inconsistent results; positive, negative, and neutral effects have been reported in the literature (Orlitzky, Schmidt, & Rynes, 2003; Sun, Yao, & Govind, 2019). Sun et al. (2019), which suggests a nonlinear relationship between CSR and firm performance, specifically an inverted U form. They argue that CSR can be beneficial up to a point, but that "an increase in CSR can raise problems such as resource depletion and skeptical attitudes from key stakeholders" (p. 1002). Ng, Yam, and Aguinis (2019) argue that CSR can have indirect benefits to an organization, independent of any effects of CSR on the bottom line. In particular, CSR activities can be a source of employee pride, commitment to, and identification with the organization, and perhaps lower turnover.

How should we evaluate CSR activities? In one respect, it is an outgrowth and a realization of ideas first laid out by Andrew Carnegie is his "Gospel of Wealth".[8] Carnegie's article is regarded as the foundation of modern philanthropy. It argues that the wealthy have an affirmative obligation to put their surplus wealth to use to benefit society. The CSR movement has tried to go beyond this somewhat paternalistic approach to argue that organizations function within a broader society, without which they would be unable to function. They depend on all sorts of public goods (e.g., roads, bridges, postal services) and their decisions have sometimes profound effects on stakeholders. As a result, they are obligated to take these stakeholders into account when they act.

The underlying philosophy of CSR is attractive in many ways, and it serves as a useful counterpoint to Friedman's (1970) argument that the sole purpose of business organizations is to generate profit for its stockholders. On the other hand, translating CSR into effective action has been challenging. Virtually all large organizations have CSR activities on their books, but the effectiveness of these activities is often hard to determine and is rarely systematically assessed.

A cynic might see CSR pronouncements as meaningless boilerplate and as a cover-up for the more sinister activities of the organization. It is worth remembering that Carnegie's Gospel of Wealth was written several years after Carnegie's organization used armed Pinkerton guards to break the Homestead Strike, killing and wounding many striking steelworkers in the process. The Gospel of Wealth helped to rehabilitate Carnegie's image, although to be fair to Carnegie, his actions (using his wealth to build public works, libraries, concert halls, etc.)

probably had more impact on his reputation than his writings. Nevertheless, it is fair to ask whether the universal embrace of CSR by large organizations reflects their commitment to the ideals such as those laid out in the United Nations Global Compact or whether they are simply window dressing designed to make organizations look good. The likeliest answer is that both explanations are partly true. Corporations probably do meaningful good with their CSR activities (and they may benefit from them as well); corporations that fail to at least symbolically embrace CSR are likely to be the targets of criticism, boycotts, and ostracism. Organizations are unlikely to fully realize the principles expressed by the United Nations Global Compact, but CSR activities are nevertheless likely to benefit organizations and their stakeholders.

Summary

The process of counteracting corruption and reducing misbehavior sometimes requires systematic efforts to reform and improve organizations. Organizations typically pursue one of two broad strategies. The most common response, to make structural changes (e.g., new codes of conduct, changes in policies and practices, external oversight), rarely succeeds, especially when the norms of the organization support or tolerate misbehavior. The other option is to change the behavior of members of the organization. If the problem is limited to top leadership, a change of leaders can be effective. In most cases, however, it is necessary to try and change the norms, standards, values, and beliefs of organization members. Top-down changes can be effective, particularly when top leaders actively model the desired norms and behaviors, but resistance to top-down change can be significant, especially if deviant norms are well established in an organization. Some organizations undertake broad-based organizational development (OD) efforts, but again, the success of this approach depends substantially on the willingness of members across the organization to change.

Recovery from corruption is challenging, but there are definite sets of actions organizations can take to increase the likelihood of success. These include disclosure, apology, and restitution. Careful efforts to redefine roles in organizations to include systematic consideration of the ethical dimensions involved when making decisions in organizations also have the potential to pay off. The OD process of unfreezing, changing and refreezing might be especially useful in making these changes.

Finally, this chapter considers the question of defining the purpose and responsibilities of organizations in the modern world. Avoiding corruption and misbehavior are good, but they are probably not sufficient. The corporate social responsibility (CSR) movement suggests that organizations have affirmative responsibilities to many stakeholders. At a minimum, corporations have responsibilities to their owners and stockholders, to the people who work for the organization, to their families, and to the communities and the environment within which they operate. Virtually all large organizations engage in some activities that go beyond the bottom line to focus on improving communities and the environment. The effects of these activities are sometimes hard to evaluate, but on the whole it seems reasonable to believe that both organizations and their many stakeholders have at least a reasonable chance to benefit from organizations' commitment to CSR.

Notes

1. www.jnj.com/sites/default/files/pdf/code-of-business-conduct-english-us.pdf
2. www.jnj.com/sites/default/files/pdf/code-of-business-conduct-english-us.pdf
3. www.thetimes.co.uk/edition/world/king-philippe-of-belgium-apologises-to-congo-for-colonial-atrocities-c3m823b78
4. On the other hand, subordinates who observe their superiors acting unethically may follow suit, particularly subordinates who show a tendency to morally disengage (Fehr, Fulmer & Keng, 2020).
5. www.pri.org/stories/2017-04-06/south-africas-imperfect-progress-20-years-after-truth-reconciliation-commission
6. https://theconversation.com/do-truth-and-reconciliation-commissions-heal-divided-nations-109925
7. Aguinis (2011) prefers the term "organizational responsibility", noting that nonprofit firms, governmental agencies, startups, and other non-corporate forms of organization also have responsibilities to their communities
8. https://books.google.com/books?id=q5ALvRp61wgC&printsec=titlepage&dq=Carnegie+onCuba&lr=&sou . . .#v=onepage&q&f=false

References

Aguinis, H. (2011). Organizational responsibility: Doing good and doing well. In S. Zedeck (Ed.), *APA Handbooks in Psychology. APA Handbook of Industrial and Organizational Psychology, Vol. 3. Maintaining, Expanding, and Contracting the organization* (pp. 855–879). Washington, DC: American Psychological Association.

Aguinis, H. & Glavas, A. (2013). Embedded versus peripheral corporate social responsibility: Psychological foundations. *Industrial and Organizational Psychology, 6*, 314–332.

Aldag, R.J. (2013). No CPR for CSR: A call to abandon search for the 'Holy Grail'. *Industrial and Organizational Psychology, 6*, 314–332.

Aldag, R.J. & Jackson, D. (1977). Assessment of attitudes toward social responsibilities. *Journal of Business Administration, 8*, 65–80.

Anand, V., Ashforth, B.E. & Joshi, M. (2004). Business as usual: The acceptance and perpetuation of corruption in organizations. *Academy of Management Executive, 18*, 39–53.

Andreoli, N. & Lefkowitz, J. (2009). Individual and organizational antecedents of misconduct in organizations. *Journal of Business Ethics, 85*, 309–332.

Angell, M. (2004). Merck downplayed risk. *Wall Street Journal*, October 7: A13.

Aquino, K. & Reed II, A. (2002). The self-importance of moral identity. *Journal of Personality and Social Psychology, 83*, 1423–1440.

Ashforth, B.E. (2001). *Role Transitions in Organizational Life: An Identity-Based Perspective.* Mahwah, NJ: Lawrence Erlbaum Associates.

Ashforth, B.E. & Anand, V. (2003). The normalization of corruption in organizations. In R.M. Kramer & B.M. Staw (Eds.), *Research in Organizational Behavior: An Annual Series of Analytical Essays and Critical Reviews* (Vol. 25, pp. 1–52). Oxford, England: Elsevier Science.

Babalola, M.T., Greenbaum, R.L., Amarnani, R.K., Shoss, M.K., Deng, Y., Garba, O.A. & Guo, L. (2020). A business frame perspective on why perceptions of top management's bottom-line mentality result in employees' good and bad behaviors. *Personnel Psychology, 73*, 19–41.

Bazerman, M.H. (2020). A new model for ethical leadership: Creating value for society. *Harvard Business Review*, September-October, 91–97.

Bird, F. (2015). Moral muteness. In C.L. Cooper et al. (Eds.). *Wiley Encyclopedia of Management* (Vol. 2). doi:10.1002/9781118785317.weom020151

Boehm, S.A., Kunze, F. & Bruch, H. (2014). Spotlight on age-diversity climate: The impact of age-inclusive HR practices on firm-level outcomes. *Personnel Psychology, 67*, 667–704.

Bradley, J.C., Brief, A.P. & Smith-Crowe, K. (2008). The good corporation. In D.B. Smith (Ed.), *The People Make the Place: Exploring Dynamic Linkages Between Individuals and Organizations* (pp. 175–223). Mahwah, NJ: Lawrence Erlbaum Associates.

Brief, A.P., Buttram, R.T. & Dukerich, J.M. (2001). Collective corruption in the corporate world: Toward a process model. In M.E. Turner (Ed.), *Groups at Work: Theory and Research* (pp. 471–499). Mahwah, NJ: Lawrence Erlbaum Associates.

Brinson, S.L. & Benoit, W.L. (1999). The tarnished star: Restoring Texaco's damaged public image. *Management Communication Quarterly, 12*, 483–510.

Burdon, W.M. & Sourer, M.K. (2020). Institutional theory and evolution of 'a legitimate' compliance culture: The case of the UK financial service sector. *Journal of Business Ethics, 162*, 47–80.

Burke, W.W. (1994). *Organization Development: A Process of Learning and Changing*. Boston: Addison-Wesley.

Cameron, K.S. & Quinn, R.E. (2011). *Diagnosing and Changing Organizational Culture: Based on the Competing Values Framework* (3rd Ed.). San Francisco: Jossey-Bass.

Casert, R. (2020, June 11). As protests grow, Belgium faces its racist colonial past. *AP News*, https://apnews.com/b405027b7232c42b8d9dab407ff87aa1

Chernow, R. (2017). *Grant*. New York: Penguin Press.

Cross, F.B. & Miller, R.L. (2015). *The Legal Environment of Business*. Stamford, CT: Cengage Learning.

Daniels, M.A. & Robinson, S.L. (2019). The shame of it all: A review of shame in organizational life. *Journal of Management, 45*, 2448–2473.

DiFanzo, N., Alongi, A. & Wiele, P. (2020). Apology, restitution, and forgiveness after psychological contract breach. *Journal of Business Ethics, 161*, 53–69.

Fehr, R., Fulmer, A. & Keng, H.F.T. (2020). How do employees react to leaders' unethical behavior? The role of moral disengagement. *Personnel Psychology, 73*, 73–93.

French, W.L. & Bell, C.H. (1999). *Organization Development: Behavioral Science Interventions for Organization Improvement*. Upper Saddle River, NJ: Prentice-Hall.

Friedman, M. (1970). The social responsibility of business is to enhance its profits. *New York Times, 32*(13), 122–126.

Gino, F., Ayal, S. & Ariely, D. (2009). Contagion and differentiation in unethical behavior: The effect of one bad apple on the barrel. *Psychological Science, 20*, 393–398.

Goedeke, M. & Fogliasso, C. (2020). Is CSR becoming a corporate requirement? *Journal of Managerial Issues, 32*, 162–175.

Hochschild, A. (1998). *King Leopold's Ghost: A Story of Greed, Terror and Heroism in Colonial Africa*. New York: Houghton-Mifflin.

Hogler, R. (2011). How Right to Work is destroying the American labor movement: From the Ku Klux Klan to the Tea Party. *Employee Responsibilities and Rights Journal, 23*, 105–119.

Kaptein, M. & Schwartz, M. (2007). The effectiveness of business codes: A critical examination of existing studies and development of an integrated research model. *Erasmus Institute of Management Report*, ERS-2007-030-ORG.

Kish-Gephart, J.J., Harrison, D.A. & Treviño, L.K. (2010). Bad apples, bad cases, and bad barrels: Meta-analytic evidence about sources of unethical decisions at work. *Journal of Applied Psychology, 95*, 1–31.

Krawiec, K.D. (2005). Organizational misconduct: Beyond the principal-agent model. *Florida State University Law Review, 32*, 571–615.

Kress, J.C. (2018, March 26). Board to death: How busy directors could cause the next financial. *Boston College Law Review*, 58, 877–929.

Kuenzi, M., Mayer, D.M. & Greenbaum, R.L. (2020). Creating an ethical organizational environment: The relationship between ethical leadership, ethical organizational climate, and unethical behavior. *Personnel Psychology, 73*, 43–71.

Martinez, B. (2004). Merck & Co. offers rationale, context for Vioxx memos. *Wall Street Journal*, November 15: A5.

Martocchio, J.J. (2011). *Strategic Compensation: A Human Resource Management Approach.* Upper Saddle River, NJ: Prentice Hall.

Mayer, D.M., Nurmohamed, S., Treviño, L.K., Shapiro, D.L. & Schminke, M. (2013). Encouraging employees to report unethical conduct internally: It takes a village. *Organizational Behavior and Human Decision Processes, 121*, 89–103.

McPhearson, C. (2017). *The Change Catalyst: Secrets to Success and Sustainable Business Change.* Chichester, UK: Wiley.

Mehta, S.N. (2003). MCI: Is being good good enough? *Fortune* (October 27), 117–124.

Misangy, V.F. & Weaver, G.R. (2008). Ending corruption: The interplay among institutional logics, resources, and institutional entrepreneurs. *Academy of Management Review, 33*, 73–770.

Moore, C., Meyer, D.M., Chiang, F.F.T., Crossley, C., Karlesky, M.J. & Birtch, T.A. (2019). Leaders matter morally: The role of ethical leadership in shaping employee moral cognition and misconduct. *Journal of Applied Psychology, 104*, 123–145.

National Academies of Sciences, Engineering, and Medicine. (2017). *Fostering Integrity in Research.* Washington, DC: The National Academies Press.

Neville, F., Byron, K., Post, C. & Ward, A. (2019). Board independence and corporate misconduct: A cross-national meta-analysis. *Journal of Management, 45*, 2538–2569.

Ng, T.W.H., Yam, K.C. & Aguinis, H. (2019). Employee perceptions of corporate social responsibility: Effects on pride, embeddedness, and turnover. *Personnel Psychology, 72*, 107–137.

Nguyen, D., Hagendorff, J. & Eshraghi, A. (2016). Can bank boards prevent misconduct? *Review of Finance, 20*(1), 1–36.

Orlitzky, M., Schmidt, F.L. & Rynes, S.L. (2003). Corporate social and financial performance: A meta-analysis. *Organization Studies, 24*, 403–441.

Paterson, T.A. & Huang, L. (2019). Am I expected to be ethical? A role-definition perspective of ethical leadership and unethical behavior. *Journal of Management, 45*, 2837–2860.

Peloza, J. & Shang, J. (2011). How can corporate social responsibility activities create value for stakeholders? A systematic review. *Journal of the Academy of Marketing Science, 39*, 117–135.

Pfaffer, M.D., Decelles, K.E., Smith, K.G. & Taylor, M.S. (2008). After the fall: Reintegrating the corrupt organization. *Academy of Management Review, 33,* 730–749.

Pierce, L. & Snyder, J. (2008). Ethical spillovers in firms: Evidence from vehicle emissions testing. *Management Science, 54,* 1891–1903.

Quinn, R.E. (1996). *Deep change: Discovering the leader within.* San Francisco: Jossey-Bass.

Reed, A., Aquino K. & Levy, E. (2007). Moral identity and judgements of charitable behaviors. *Journal of Marketing, 171,* 178–193.

Schminke, M., Ambrose, M.L. & Neubaum, D.O. (2005). The effect of leader moral development on ethical climate and employee attitudes. *Organizational Behavior and Human Decision Processes, 97,* 135–151.

Singer, A.W. (2004). Your good name after you've lost it. *Across the Board, 41*(6), 33–38.

Spreitzer, G.M. & Sonenshein, S. (2004). Toward the construct definition of positive deviance. *American Behavioral Scientist, 47,* 828–847.

Stanley, T. (2012). Belgium's heart of darkness. *History Today, 62*(10), www.historytoday.com/archive/contrarian/belgiums-heart-darkness

Sun, W., Yao, S. & Govind, R. (2019). Reexamining corporate social responsibility and shareholder value: The inverted-u-shaped relationship and the moderation of marketing capability. *Journal of Business Ethics, 160,* 1001–1017.

Tolentino, J. (2017, March 31). Mike Pence's marriage and the beliefs that keep women from power. *New Yorker.* www.newyorker.com/culture/jia-tolentino/mike-pences-marriage-and-the-beliefs-that-keep-women-from-power

Treviño, L.K., Weaver, G.R., Gibson, D. & Toffler, B. (1999). Managing ethics and legal compliance: What works and what hurts. *California Management Review, 41,* 131–151.

Tyler, T.R. (2006). *Why People Obey the Law: Procedural Justice, Legitimacy, and Compliance.* Princeton, NJ: Princeton University Press.

United Nations Global Compact. (2008). www.unglobalcompact.org/AbouttheGC/TheTenPrinciples/

Victor, B. & Cullen, J.B. (1988). The organizational bases of ethical work climates. *Administrative Sciences Quarterly, 33,* 101–125.

Vidaver-Cohen, D. (1998). Moral climate in business firms: A conceptual framework for analysis and change. *Journal of Business Ethics, 17,* 1211–1226.

White, B. & Montgomery, B. (1980). Corporate codes of conduct. *California Management Review, 23,* 80–87.

Wo, D.X.H, Schminke, M. & Ambrose, M.L. (2019). Trickle-down, trickle-out, trickle-up, trickle-in, and trickle-around effects: An integrative perspective on indirect social influence phenomena. *Journal of Management, 45,* 2263–2292.

Wolfgast, E. (1992). *The Ethics of an Artificial Person: Lost Responsibility in the Professions and Organizations.* Stanford, CA: Stanford University Press.

Yiu, D.W., Wan, W.P. & Xu, Y. (2019). Alternative governance and corporate financial fraud in transition economies: Evidence from China. *Journal of Management, 45,* 2685–2720.

Zohar, D. & Luria, G. (2005). A multilevel model of safety climate: Cross-level relationships between organization and group-level climates. *Journal of Applied Psychology, 90,* 616.

EPILOGUE

I have long-standing interests in both history and psychology, and this book is in many ways a result of thinking like a psychologist when reading history. Many histories include interviews or descriptions of soldiers charged with committing war crimes, members of lynch mobs, corporate executives who organize and carry out fraudulent schemes, and politicians who sell their votes, and the like. A recurring theme in these is that the people involved often do not think they have done anything wrong. Several years ago, I started to think seriously about why this happens, and I realized that many of the concepts we study in social and organizational psychology were very useful for understanding why people sometimes feel no remorse about behaving badly.

Most of us are taught from an early age to obey social norms, rules, and laws. Why, then, is misbehavior so common? For example, as I documented in this book, bullying, harassment, and aggressive behavior are endemic in many organizations. Individual differences are probably important in explaining some of this behavior, but the most compelling explanation for the persistence of misbehavior is that important groups support and encourage this behavior.

We live and work in groups (e.g., workgroups, families, friendship groups), and these groups play an important part in defining our sense of what we should or should not do. In this book, I have tried to lay out how the norms of various groups develop and how they influence behavior. One of the major themes of this book is that the norms of groups that are important to individuals often develop in ways that encourage, or at least tolerate misbehavior, and once these norms are set and communicated, it is difficult for people to ignore them.

One of the most insidious messages groups often convey to their members is that there are two sets of rules, one for society and one for members of their group. For example, executives in an organization that is defrauding its investors may understand that cheating and telling lies is wrong in the abstract but believe that because of the competitive position of their organization it is acceptable for *them* to lie and cheat. These beliefs are often the product of norms that are widely shared in their organizations.

As an organizational psychologist, I have long thought and taught that commitment and loyalty to organizations is a good thing, but these attitudes and beliefs can also create serious risks in organizations in some organizations. Large-scale misbehavior, ranging from fraud to war crimes, often requires large-scale organization, and commitment and loyalty to a sick or corrupt organization can have tragic consequences. In a similar way, devotion to a cause or a movement can motivate noble behaviors and laudable outcomes, but this same devotion can lead people to tolerate and engage in serious crimes and misbehaviors. One of the challenges facing organizational psychologists is to help organizations, movements, and causes that have gone wrong to rebuild and reform, and this has turned out to be a significant challenge. I think we know a great deal about how informal groups, associations, movements, and formal groups influence our behavior, and how this influence can become malevolent. We know much less about how to solve this problem; changing the norms of groups, organizations, and movements has turned out to be a good deal more difficult than it once seemed.

I spend a lot of time detailing the way groups and organizations can lead individuals down the wrong path, but it is important to keep in mind that the influence of groups and organizations is more often beneficial than malevolent. Informal groups (e.g., friends, families) and organizations are an important part of the glue that holds society together, and they play an important role in developing and supporting prosocial as well as antisocial behaviors. Indeed, the same processes that can lead members of groups to misbehave can also lead them to go above and beyond what is normally expected or required. Thus, the challenge is not to decide whether groups and organizations are good or bad, but rather to recognize the ways that they can encourage and support both positive and negative behaviors and to use the tools psychology and other social sciences provide to help maximize the positive and minimize the negative. Without groups and organizations, there would be few war crimes, but there would also be no cathedrals, hospitals, and museums. Groups and organizations *can* encourage bad behavior, but they don't have to, and they often don't. I hope that this book will give you a better understanding of the way other people influence our behavior and the ways that influence can push us in the direction of both prosocial and antisocial behaviors.

INDEX

Page numbers in **bold** indicate a table on the corresponding page.